Butler's Lives of
PATRON SAINTS

Butler's Lives of PATRON SAINTS

Edited and with additional material by
Michael Walsh

Foreword by Cardinal Basil Hume, O.S.B.,
Archbishop of Westminster

1817

HARPER & ROW, PUBLISHERS, SAN FRANCISCO
Cambridge, Hagerstown, New York, Philadelphia, Washington,
London, Mexico City, São Paulo, Singapore, Sydney

Nihil obstat: Father Anton Cowan, Censor.
Imprimatur: Rt. Rev. John Crowley, V. G.
          Bishop in Central London
Westminster: 14th June 1987

First published 1987
Copyright © 1956, 1985, 1987 Burns & Oates

Foreword copyright © Burns & Oates 1981, 1985, 1987

Butler's Lives of the Saints was originally published in
1756–9. The revised edition in four volumes edited by
Herbert J. Thurston, S.J., was published in 1926–38.
Copyright Burns & Oates. The second edition of that
revision, edited by Herbert J. Thurston, S.J., and Donald
Attwater, on which this volume is based, was published
in 1956 and a further printing with additions and
corrections was published in 1966. That edition was
reprinted in 1981 and 1982. Copyright © Burns & Oates
1956.

Library of Congress Catalog Card Number: 87–45198

ISBN 0–06–069262–6

87·88 89 90 91 SP 10 9 8 7 6 5 4 3 2 1

Typeset by Phoenix Photosetting, Chatham
Printed in Great Britain by
Robert Hartnoll (1985) Limited, Bodmin, Cornwall

Foreword

Most people have an interest in the patron saints of their countries. The Irish wear shamrock on St Patrick's Day, the Welsh have daffodils for St David, the Scots their thistle for St Andrew and even the English have been known to wear the rose for St George. How many people, who profess little religion, wear a St Christopher or believe that St Jude can help them in desperate situations?

Various almanacs give lists of patron saints but not the reasons why these particular saints have been chosen. While it is easy to understand why St. Thérèse of Lisieux, the Little Flower, is the patron of florists, we might need an explanation for her also being one of the patron saints of missions.

The heroic men and women described and speculated upon in this book have bequeathed to us both particular patronages and a general inspiration that transcends ordinary history. It is not surprising then, that there should be a demand today for information about saints' lives but also for some description of how certain saints have become associated traditionally, or over the years, with particular areas of human activity or aspects of the human condition.

Butler's Lives of Patron Saints, then, is welcome, not least because of the curiously attractive echoes of its original eighteenth-century style. The modern re-editing, moreover, tends to belie the modest comment of Father Herbert Thurston, who edited the first edition of *Butler's Lives* in this century, that 'This book is not intended for scholars'. I hope that many people will find inspiration in reading it.

Basil Hume

Archbishop of Westminster

Contents

NOTES ON THE ILLUSTRATIONS

The decorations in the text are principally taken from the representations of saints in *Legenda Aurea*, by Jacobus de Voragine (Wynkyn de Worde, Westminster, 1498), from a copy in the Heythrop College Library; and from *La Sainte Bible* (J. de Tournes, Lyon, 1557).

Editor's Introduction

Two years ago I edited *Butler's Lives of the Saints* from its four-volume edition into a one-volume, concise edition. At the back of the concise edition there was printed a two-page list of patron saints. Shortly after the book appeared I was telephoned by a diarist from a well-known newspaper. He had noticed the list, and thought there might be some stories in the more unlikely patronages I had included.

This journalist's interest is indicative of a general curiosity about patron saints, even among those who would never for a moment consider praying to them, or lighting a candle before a statue. Any librarian who works in a theological library will, I think, bear out my experience. For most who enquire, the level of concern is little higher than sheer curiosity or the need to solve a crossword puzzle, but for a number it is a matter of some importance. The flight between Lima and Cuzco in Peru is always a bumpy one, travelling as it does across the peaks of the Andes. Making that journey on one occasion an air-hostess, or flight attendant, produced for me a whole wallet-full of holy pictures. They were images of the saints to whom she prayed for the safety of the flight. Being unsure of the precise patron of flying, she carried pictures of several possible candidates.

There is plenty of choice. As I remarked in my introduction to the earlier volume, the 1926 edition of the January volume of *Butler's Lives of the Saints* has 258 entries for those saints whose feast day falls in that month, while the equivalent French volume for the same month, produced by the Paris Benedictines, has more than 500 entries. The *Bibliotheca Sanctorum*, however, which, despite its Latin name is in Italian, has almost 1,000 names. Again, as I pointed out in the earlier volume, the difficulty lies in deciding who is, or who is not, a saint.

For the names of those holy men and women who lived in the earliest centuries of the Christian era, scholars have to rely upon 'martyrologies', or lists of saints and especially martyrs, which record little more than a name and place and date of death and burial. In the first instance they were specific to one particular church. The earliest identifiable martyrology was begun in Rome in 336 and kept up until 354. Perhaps the best known of these first martyrologies is that (wrongly) attributed to St Jerome, to which much reference is made in the full edition of *Butler*, but there were many others.

These organized the saints who were mentioned in them in order of the date of commemoration of their feasts – usually the day of their deaths or occasionally their reburial in some new location. This meant, of course, that there were some days without names attached to them. In the eighth century began the practice of adding names to fill in the gaps. Bede, who is thought to have been the first to do this, was an historian of considerable skill. Others were not so careful. The desire for greater knowledge of the saints frequently led to quite fanciful additions to the bare details of the earlier martyrologies. It also led to the multiplication of saints. According to Dr David Farmer's *Oxford Dictionary of Saints*, the Irish martyrologies mention no less than 300 individuals with the name Colman.

There were of course some very early 'lives of saints' built around the apostles and immediate followers of Jesus. These 'pious novels' constitute what is now referred to as the 'apocryphal' literature of early Christianity: the *Acts of Paul and Thecla*, for example, or the various versions of the gospels attributed to apostles. But there were also the *passiones* of some of the martyrs, accounts of their trial before Roman judges, and their subsequent execution. Unlike the apocryphal literature, some at least of the *passiones* appear to be very accurate accounts – so much so that they may even have depended for their information upon official transcripts of the trials. And from the fourth century onwards there were lives of saints, such as Athanasius' life of Antony the Abbot or Gregory of Nyssa's life of his sister Macrina (not to mention Augustine's account of his own early life in the *Confessions*) which, though possibly more informative about the ways saints were regarded than about the biographical detail, nonetheless contain much useful information.

That there were 'saints' in early Christianity is not a matter of dispute. There is clear evidence of special devotion being given to certain 'heroes' from the very first centuries of the Christian era. The date of Polycarp's martyrdom is disputed, but it was somewhere about the middle of the second century A.D. The contemporary account of his death indicates that his bones were gathered together after the cremation of his body, that they were then put in an appropriate place and his 'birthday' (i.e., his birthday into heaven, meaning the day of death) was celebrated from then on.

This does not in itself imply that the saints were thought to have any special intercessory powers. But that they were so regarded becomes clear a century later during the persecution of Decius (A.D. 250–1). Unlike previous persecutions, this one was systematic. It began in Rome, but many suffered imprisonment or death throughout the Roman Empire. And many, who could not face the suffering that being a Christian entailed, renounced their faith. They were the *lapsi*. Some of the *lapsi*, however, promptly repented their fall from grace. The Church was unwilling to receive them back without the imposition of a severe penance. On the other hand if a martyr (which means 'witness', one in prison for the faith) should provide a certificate, then the person for whom it was provided might be received back into the Christian fold without more ado.

This was a very practical example of a 'saint's' intercession, but it had much wider significance. As Peter Brown points out in his study *The Cult of the Saints*, though other religions may have shown considerable reverence for the dead, they nevertheless made a sharp distinction between the dead and the living. And it was not only a mental distinction, it was also physical: cemeteries were placed outside the towns, both for Jews and for Romans. Even if Christians did likewise, at least at first, the cemetery became a place of pilgrimage. People set off there from the towns, spent time, perhaps whole nights, in vigil at the tombs of saints, established in the process new sets of relationships in which rich and poor, men and women, townspeople and country-folk rubbed shoulders. If the Church emerged in late antiquity as an alternative society, it had much to do, in Brown's view, with the cult of the saints.

As he sums it up, 'The need for intimacy with a protector with whom one could identify as a fellow human being, relations with whom could be conceived of in terms open to the nuances of known human relations between patron and client, is a hallmark of late fourth-century Christian piety. It insensibly tended to oust reverence for beings, who, as gods or angels, had owed their position to their role as intermediaries between men and beings other than men in the soaring hierarchy of the late antique universe' (*op. cit.* p. 61).

It had been common to think of the evolution of the cult of the saints as something on a par with the pagan belief in 'daemons', spirits in a two-tier universe of gods and human beings. In this interpretation saints were a carry-over from the lesser gods of paganism. Peter Brown's *Cult of the Saints* has successfully dispelled that notion. But there was a carry-over of considerable importance. It was in the notion of patron and client.

Patronage at Rome had a distinguished history, reaching back to the earliest days of the city as an identifiable entity. Rich Romans attached poorer ones to themselves, offering assistance of various kinds in return for services, frequently political. The patron-client relationship did not have the force of law, but it was sanctified by tradition. Later on municipalities found it advisable to have patrons at Rome to represent their interests. By the time the cult of the saints began, wealthy Roman citizens were offering their protection, especially against tax-gatherers, to peasant farmers and to the poor in general in return for services, or for the surrender of land.

This concept of patronage is quite secular, but there is evidence, at least from the apocryphal literature, that it was transferred across to a religious context. Monsignor Domenico Cortesini in his series of articles for the Roman periodical *Monitor Ecclesiasticus* cites two examples, though it must be admitted that both of them come from an era (the fifth-sixth century) which is rather later than the rise of the cult of the saints.

Though the evidence may be late, or at best indirect, the value of the line of argument adopted explicitly by Brown and implicitly by Cortesini, linking the concept of saint to the Roman structure of patronage, is a valuable one. It has the great advantage that it seems to work. It appears to make sense of the information we have. As Peter Brown writes, 'Faced by the ambiguities of the patronage system in which they were caught, those with no other defense, often the women, opted dramatically for dependence on an ideal *dominus* at his distant shrine, rather than for dependence on the all too palpable wielders of power in their locality' (*op. cit.* p. 123).

It is the task of another book to chronicle the development of the cult of the saints from the earliest times through the Middle Ages and down to our own day. The point of this modest excursus into the origins of the devotion is simply to suggest that, in its beginnings, the cult of the saints was the cult of *patron* saints: all saints were patrons.

At first, as has been suggested, these patrons were 'martyrs'. They had borne witness to their faith either by dying, or by imprisonment. What was celebrated was the day of their death or burial. Pagan feasts at gravesides were held on the birthdays of those who had died: the birthdays of the Christian martyrs were the feasts of their deaths, and therefore rebirth into heaven. Later the notion of saint was extended to those – such as Antony the Abbot (*c.* 251–356) – who were renowned simply for the holiness of their lives. That holiness was recognized by those they lived among. It may have been sanctioned by the authority of the local bishop, but it did not require the solemn pronouncement of a canonization.

Canonization, now the customary way to create saints, was a comparatively late development in the history of the Church. Veneration of an individual was usually local in the first instance, though it may then have been spread by the fame of a shrine for its miracles, by the devotion of travellers, by communities of monks or nuns establishing new houses in another district, and so on. The 'cult', or formal, liturgical veneration, needed only the approval of the bishop of the region, once a devotion to the saint's memory was well-established.

From the eleventh century onwards, however, formal approval of a cult became increasingly the prerogative of the pope. It began simply enough with papal ratification of an episcopal canonization, probably with the intention of giving the event greater prestige. The first evidence that remains of papal intervention of this sort is in the canonization, in 973, of St Udalricus. From then on it became increasingly common until the process which led up to canonization, the investigations into a potential saint's life and the miracles performed during life or after death, had to be done under papal supervision. From 1234, when papal enquiries were declared to be the only proper sort, papal control over canonizations was complete – though of course preliminary preparations for them were, and remain, at the level of the diocese or religious order.

When the papal court, the Roman Curia, was reorganized towards the end of the sixteenth century, canonization procedures were handed over to the newly-established Sacred Congregation of Rites, a committee of cardinals and other officials, some full-time, others employed as consultants, which was chiefly concerned with matters of worship. Mention of decrees of this Congregation will be found frequently in this book, because it was by decrees, or by papal (usually called 'Apostolic') letters prepared by the Congregation but formally sent by the pope of the day, that patronages were officially authorized. In 1969 the Congregation of Rites was divided. Canonizations and patronages are now the concern of the Congregation for the Causes of Saints.

A great many of the patronages exercised by saints have, of course, not formally been ratified; or, if ratified, have only been so recently, though the devotion may have roots far in the past. Some of the patronages are not difficult to explain. The legends of St Giles, for example, present him as a cripple – so he is the patron of cripples. But in the Middle Ages cripples were also very frequently beggars, so he is the patron of beggars as well as of cripples. Others are not so obvious, especially when a single saint is cited as the patron of a whole variety of quite disparate occupations or situations. In this case it would seem that there was a strong, widespread devotion to the particular saint who was therefore chosen to be their patron by a whole host of local guilds or pious associations. Another common occurrence is to choose as patron of a trade someone who either carried on, or is believed to have carried on, that occupation. Martin de Porres, who was apprenticed to a hairdresser, is the patron of that profession.

It was remarked earlier that the cult of a saint was usually, in its beginnings, quite local. In a sense the same is true of patronages. In the first instance they were, and are, quite precise, at least in so far as they are normally recognized by the Church.

Maria Goretti, for example, has been officially acknowledged as patron of the association known as the Children of Mary, but because of her age and the manner of her death she is frequently presented, non-officially, as patron of all teenagers, and especially of young girls. Similarly Dominic Savio is formally patron of choirboys – but is by extension thought of in some places as the patron of boys in general and even, by further extension, of juvenile delinquents. John Bosco is another example. As properly recognized by the Church, he is patron of the young people of Mexico, but in the United States he is equally honoured as a guide of youth.

Locally based devotions tend to spread. The same is true of narrowly defined patronage: the archangel Gabriel was appropriately chosen as the patron of telecommunications – but it is only a few logical steps from that to recognizing him as patron of Argentinian ambassadors and, no doubt, eventually of all ambassadors. That is one of the reasons why some seemingly rather restricted patronages have been included in the book which follows, if they have been officially approved. They tend to grow wider.

One exception to all this, and a very important one in the calendar of patronage, is the Blessed Virgin Mary. Devotion to her is at least as old as that to saints in general, and the notion of her as a protector is expressed in the prayer *Sub tuum praesidium* ('We fly to thy protection . . .') which goes back at least to the beginning of the fourth century. But Mary was not a local saint. She was, and is, celebrated by a series of feasts which commemorate incidents in her life – the Annunciation, for example, or her birthday – or recall some theological attribute, such as her Immaculate Conception. Other feasts, however, isolate particular forms of devotion to Mary, and these, more commonly than the general celebrations, have come to be taken as patronal feasts.

Possibly the best known of these is the feast of Our Lady of Guadalupe, which has become for Mexico a very potent national symbol as well as an occasion in the liturgical calendar. This devotion has helped to mould Mexican unity, and to create a nation out of very disparate elements. Local shrines to the Virgin Mary have commonly arisen because of an alleged vision, or as a result of the supposedly miraculous discovery of an image, or simply because of veneration paid to a well-loved painting or statue in a particular church. Although devotion to the Virgin under a title such as Our Lady of Guadalupe, or Our Lady of Lujan, to take two Latin American examples, may have begun locally, they, too, tended to spread in the manner of devotion to the saints.

The text which follows attempts to explain why it is that some saint, or the Virgin Mary under a particular title, has been chosen as patron of a country, trade or situation. In most cases this has been possible, though in a few instances not even inspired guesswork has been able to suggest an explanation. Where a patronage has been formally recognized by the Holy See, a reason is usually given, but not always. Where the only source of information at my disposal has been a reference to a decree of the Congregation of Rites it has only rarely been possible to consult the decree itself. Apostolic Letters are more readily available.

There are any number of lists of patron saints, not all of them wholly reliable. The most useful, and authoritative, one is without doubt that published by Domenico Cortesini in a series of articles. Mgr Cortesini worked for the Congregation of Rites at the time when it was bringing up-to-date the formal list of patronages, and he has included all for which there was documentary evidence of approval by the Holy See as well as some others recognized 'from time immemorial'. Cortesini's list was produced in 1962–3. For more recent grants of patrons one has to look in the official journal of the Holy See, the *Acta Apostolicae Sedis*, or in *Notitiae*, the journal of the Congregation for Divine Worship.

There is an enormous list of patron saints in the *Bibliotheca Sanctorum*, the thirteen-volume series of saints' lives produced by Rome's Lateran University between 1961 and 1970. Most of the patronages mentioned are of towns or dioceses, and no 'geographical' patronage of an area less than a country has been included in this book, with the exception of a handful of major cities. Those apart, there remains a very large number of patrons given for trades or life situations, for example. Unfortunately it proved very difficult to discover what justification this admirable work had for a good many of its attributions. The same is true of the list brought out by Michael Gibson in his *Saints of Patronage and Invocation*. Indeed, in the latter case I found it impossible even to identify some of the saints who were mentioned. What both books brought home to me was the need for more research into medieval popular religion than has been practicable in the preparation of this collection of saints' lives.

Such research would involve in many cases the writing of wholly new biographies. The idea behind this volume, however, was to use the lives as given by Alban Butler in his *The Lives of the Fathers, Martyrs and other Principal Saints*, first published between 1756 and 1759, but regularly up-dated, most notably by Fr Herbert Thurston and Donald Attwater between 1926 and 1938. In some cases, of course, the saints are too recent to have been included, even in the revised version produced by Attwater in 1956. I have added these lives myself, as also the information about shrines and other particular devotions to the Virgin Mary. The majority of the text is, nonetheless, based upon *Butler's Lives*. I am wholly in agreement with those who believe this work should not simply be up-dated but entirely re-worked: the need for an English *Bibliotheca Sanctorum* is urgent. Unhappily, without the appearance on the scene of an ecclesiastical Maecenas the chance of such a task being undertaken is slim indeed.

This present enterprise was originally conceived in a dictionary format, each saint being listed under his or her particular patronage. So complex did the cross-referencing become, however, that this approach proved impracticable. The presentation eventually adopted owes much to the editorial imagination of John Bright-Holmes, and for that I thank him. My own labour in producing the book would have been far greater had it not been for the assistance given me by my colleague in the Heythrop College Library, Madeleine Jeffery. She was an indefatigable digger-out of obscure references and curious details. Her ability to spot the word 'patron' in a variety of languages must be second to none. Her suggestions have frequently been incorporated into the text. Her interest in the book has been a great source of encouragement.

Just about the time the manuscript was reaching completion, my mother died. On her bedside cabinet I found a copy of the concise edition of *Butler's Lives of the Saints* which I published in 1985. The bookmark indicated that she had been reading in it the brief life of the saint of the day a few hours before her death. This volume is in memory of her.

Heythrop College　　　　　　　　　　　　　　　　MICHAEL J. WALSH
Feast of St Hermenegild
13 April 1986

SELECT BIBLIOGRAPHY TO INTRODUCTION

Acta Apostolicae Sedis, Rome, 1909–

Attwater, Donald (ed.), *A Dictionary of Mary*, London, 1957

Bibliotheca Sanctorum, Rome, 1961–70

Brown, Peter, *The Cult of the Saints*, London, 1981

Cabrol, J.B. (ed.) *Mariology*, Milwaukee, 1955–61

Cortesini, Domenico, 'De Caelestium Patronorum Titulariumque Electione et Confirmatione' in *Monitor Ecclesiasticus*, vol. 87 (1962) pp. 141–166, 295–334, 572–606 and vol. 88 (1963) pp. 81–115

Cross, F.L. and Livingstone, E. (comps.), *The Oxford Dictionary of the Christian Church*, Oxford, 1974

Dictionaire d'Histoire et de Geographie Ecclesiastique, Paris, 1912–

Dizionario degli Istituti di Perfezione, Rome, 1974–

Du Manoir, H. (ed.), *Maria*, Paris, 1949–71

Farmer, D.H. (comp.), *The Oxford Dictionary of the Saints*, Oxford, 2nd Ed., 1987

Gibson, Michael (comp.) *Saints of Patronage and Invocation*, Bristol, 1982

Holweck, F.G. (comp.), *A Biographical Dictionary of the Saints*, London, 1924

New Catholic Encyclopaedia, New York, 1967–78

'Normae circa Patronos Constituendos et Imagines B.M. Virginis Coronandas' in *Acta Apostolicae Sedis* vol. 65 (1973), pp. 276–279

Thurston, H. and Attwater, D. (eds.), *Butler's Lives of the Saints*, London, 1956.

THE PATRON SAINTS
An Index of Devotions

The Patron Saints
An Index of Devotions

The index that follows gives an alphabetical list of subjects – countries, places, professions, occupations, conditions medical and social, etc. – and of the patron saints, often more than one, usually attached to them. The biographies of the saints, and a note on the background and occasion of their election, is given on the page numbers indicated.

The Lives and
Devotions of the
PATRON SAINTS

ABDON AND SENNEN (A.D. 303?)

PATRON SAINTS OF BARREL MAKERS OR COOPERS

30 JULY

Although the choice of Abdon and Sennen as patrons of barrel makers, or coopers, is traditional and does not appear to be built upon any particular event in their lives, it is interesting to note that in 1948 a chest of cypress wood was discovered under the altar of the church of Pope San Marco in Rome. It contained a parchment dated 1474, and numerous relics claiming to be those of Pope St Mark, of Abdon and Sennen, and others.

Abdon and Sennen were Persians who courageously confessed the faith of Christ in the persecution of Decius, ministering to their fellows and burying the bodies of the martyrs. They were brought to Rome as prisoners, refused to sacrifice, and spat upon the images of the gods, wherefore they were exposed to the beasts; as neither lions nor bears would touch them they were hewn into pieces by gladiators. But the more their bodies were mangled and covered with wounds the more were their souls adorned and beautified with divine grace, and rendered glorious in the sight of Heaven. The Christians at Rome did not treat them as strangers, but as brethren united to them in the hope of the same blessed country; and their bodies were buried by night at the house of a subdeacon called Quirinus. In the reign of Constantine their relics were removed to the burying-place of Pontian (called also, from some sign, the 'Bear and Cap', *Ad Ursum Pileatum*), situated near the Tiber on the road to Port; this translation took place in consequence of a vision wherein the martyrs revealed their place of burial. These particulars are derived from their late and unreliable 'acts', but the veneration of SS. Abdon and Sennen in Rome can be traced back to the fourth century.

The acts state that they gave burial in Persia to SS. Olympias (Olympiades) and Maximus, and these two victims of persecution are mentioned in the Roman Martyrology on 15 April.

ADALBERT, BISHOP OF PRAGUE, MARTYR (A.D. 997)

PATRON SAINT OF BOHEMIA, CZECHOSLOVAKIA, POLAND, AND PRUSSIA

23 APRIL

Adalbert is traditionally the patron of that part of modern Czechoslovakia which was once Bohemia, for reasons which are clear from the saint's own life. His links with Poland and Prussia are equally clear for the area of Prussia which he evangelized is now part of Poland. He is regarded therefore both as the apostle, and the patron, of

Prussia; and is venerated as a secondary patron of Poland, a devotion confirmed by a decree of the Sacred Congregation of Rites dated 31 August 1962.

St Adalbert was born of a noble family in Bohemia in 956 and received in baptism the name of Voytiekh. He was sent to be educated under St Adalbert at Magdeburg, who gave him his own name at confirmation. On the death of the archbishop the young man returned to Bohemia with a library of books he had collected, and two years later he was ordained subdeacon by Bishop Thietmar of Prague, who died in 982. Adalbert, though so young, was elected to the vacant bishopric. He had been much impressed by the death-bed scruples of Thietmar as to whether he had neglected his episcopal duties. Barefoot he entered Prague, where he was received with enthusiasm by Boleslaus II of Bohemia and the people. His first care was to divide the revenues of his see into four parts, of which one was devoted to the upkeep of the fabric and ornaments of the church, a second to the maintenance of his canons, a third to the relief of the poor, whilst the fourth portion was reserved for his own use and for that of his household and guests.

After his consecration at Mainz Adalbert had met St Majolus, abbot of Cluny, at Pavia, and had been fired with Cluniac ideals; but though he preached assiduously and visited the poor in their homes and the prisoners in their dungeons, he seemed unable to make any impression upon his flock, some of whom were still heathen, while many of the rest were Christian only in name. Thoroughly discouraged, he left his diocese in 990 and went to Rome. A good bishop, of course, does not abandon his charge in the face of pastoral difficulties, and there is evidence that there were serious political complications behind Adalbert's action.

In Italy he came under the influence of the Greek abbot St Nilus at Vallelucio and, together with his step-brother Gaudentius, the bishop became a monk of the abbey of SS. Boniface and Alexis in Rome. But soon Duke Boleslaus asked for his return, and at the bidding of Pope John XV Adalbert returned to Prague, on the understanding, it is said, that he should receive proper support from the civil power. He was well received, and at once proceeded to establish the famous Benedictine abbey of Brevnov, whose church he consecrated in 993. But difficulties again arose, culminating when a noblewoman, convicted of adultery, took refuge with the bishop to escape the sentence of death that was the penalty in those barbarous times. Adalbert sheltered her in the church of some nuns, and defied her accusers in the name of penitence and sanctuary. But the unhappy woman was dragged from the altar and slain on the spot. Adalbert thereupon excommunicated the principals in the affair; and this so aggravated the malice of his political opponents that he had to leave Prague a second time.

St Adalbert went back to his monastery in Rome, and there he remained as prior until a synod under Pope Gregory V, on the insistence of his metropolitan, St Willigis of Mainz, ordered him back again. He was prepared to obey;

but it was agreed that he should be free to go and preach the gospel to the heathen if he found it impossible to return to Bohemia, for a powerful section of the citizens of Prague had massacred a number of his kinsmen and burnt their castles. To go amongst them against their will was only to provoke further bloodshed, and therefore the saint turned aside to visit his friend Duke Boleslaus of Poland, by whose advice he sent to Prague to inquire if the people would admit him and obey him as their bishop. They replied with threats, callously adding that they were too bad to mend their ways. Under the patronage of Duke Boleslaus, St Adalbert then directed his efforts to the conversion of pagan Prussians in Pomerania. With his two companions, Benedict and Gaudentius, he made some converts in Danzig, but also met with opposition, for they were regarded with suspicion as Polish spies and told to leave the country. But they refused to abandon their Christian mission, and very soon, on 23 April 997, St Adalbert and his brethren were done to death. Traditionally this happened not far from Königsberg, at a spot between Fischausen and Pillau, but is more likely to have been somewhere between the Elbing canal and the Nogat river. Adalbert's body was thrown into the water and, being washed up on the Polish coast, it was eventually enshrined at Gniezno; in 1039 the relics were translated (by force) to Prague.

ADAM

PATRON OF GARDENERS AND HORTICULTURALISTS

The story of Adam in Eden, cultivating the earth by the sweat of his brow, is enough to account for the choice of this Old Testament figure as a patron of gardeners and horticulturalists.

According to the Bible, Adam was the first man, the father of the human race. The Book of Genesis relates how God created him, then created Eve as his companion, giving them charge over all the animals, and setting them to care for the garden of Eden. He forbade them only to eat the fruit of one tree. But tempted by the devil in the guise of a serpent they ate of the forbidden fruit, and they were expelled from Eden, God placing an angel with a flaming sword at its entrance to prevent their return. Thenceforth they had to labour to cultivate the earth, and were subject to suffering and death even though both Adam and Eve repented of their act of disobedience. Despite this repentance, the Church in the West has never regarded Adam as a saint, but his feast has been celebrated on various dates by the Church of the East.

ADJUTOR, or AYOUTRE (A.D. 1131)

PATRON SAINT OF SWIMMERS; AND AGAINST DEATH BY DROWNING

30 APRIL

The cult of St Adjutor spread rapidly out from Rouen, and a number of legends became attached to his name. According to one he heard of a whirlpool in the River Seine which was claiming the lives of many boatmen. He asked to be taken there, blessed the whirlpool, sprinkled it with holy water, and it disappeared. For this reason he has been regarded as the patron of swimmers, and is invoked against danger of death from drowning.

Saint Adjutor was born into a noble Norman family at Vernon-sur-Seine in the last quarter of the eleventh century. Even his childhood, as it was later recounted by Hugues III, Archbishop of Rouen and a personal friend, was remarkable for piety and austerity. In 1095 he was old enough to join the first Crusade, and set off for the Holy Land. There he fought with distinction for sixteen years, before being captured and, for some considerable time, imprisoned within Jerusalem. His constancy in the faith during this period of his life he ascribed to his devotion to Mary Magdalen, to Bernard of Tiron – who had died only in 1116 – and to his own devout mother. St Mary Magdalen and Bernard one night appeared to him in a vision, struck off his chains, and transported him back to Vernon. There he carried out a pledge he had made while on the crusade, and built a chapel to Mary Magdalen. After this he went to Tiron and, handing over all his possessions to the monastery, entered the community. Some years later, however, he was permitted to leave the monastery and to spend his last years in a specially built cell behind the altar in the chapel he had erected to Mary Magdalen. It was there that he died, most probably on 30 April 1131.

ADRIAN OF NICOMEDIA, MARTYR (C. 304)

PATRON SAINT OF ARMS DEALERS; BUTCHERS; AND PRISON GUARDS

4 MARCH

Because he was a soldier, Adrian was often depicted with a sword in his hand. Because he was executed by being pulled apart while stretched over an anvil, he is also portrayed with an anvil beside him. The sword and anvil together, it is suggested, is the reason why he was taken by the makers of arms as their patron. But he is also taken as patron by prison guards, because he was one himself, and by butchers – presumably because of the manner of his death.

The accounts of the sufferings and death of St Adrian say that he was a soldier in the service of the Emperor and was married to a Christian wife,

Natalia. He was put in charge of twenty-three Christian prisoners, and he was so impressed by their fortitude that he became a Christian himself, and was promptly thrown into prison. There he was visited and comforted by Natalia before being put to death in a particularly cruel fashion, his body being torn apart by the executioner. His remains were ordered to be burnt, the story goes on, but a violent storm extinguished the flames and, instead, his body was taken to a place near Constantinople for burial. Natalia followed, lived close by, and was eventually buried beside her husband.

AGATHA (DATE UNKNOWN)

PATRON SAINT OF BELL FOUNDERS; FOR PROTECTION FROM VOLCANIC ERUPTIONS, AND FIRE

5 FEBRUARY

Because Agatha was particularly popular in Sicily, and from a very early date, it is not surprising that she should have come to be invoked by those who felt themselves in danger from Mount Etna – and, by extension, in danger from fire in general.

Her association with bell-founders is certain, and is of long-standing; but the reason is less clear. It may derive, however, from the ringing of church bells to warn people of danger from volcanic eruptions or from any outbreak of fire – so much so that bells and fire became linked in people's mind, and Agatha became patron of both.

The cities of Palermo and Catania in Sicily dispute the honour of St Agatha's birth, but it is agreed that she received the crown of martyrdom at Catania. Her 'acts', which with many variations exist in both Latin and Greek, but which are of no historical value, state that she belonged to a rich and illustrious family and, having been consecrated to God from her earliest years, she triumphed over many assaults upon her purity. Quintian, a man of consular dignity, thought he could carry out his evil designs upon Agatha by means of the emperor's edict against Christians. He therefore had her brought before him. Seeing herself in the hands of her persecutors, she prayed, 'Jesus Christ, Lord of all, thou seest my heart, thou knowest my desires. Do thou alone possess all that I am. I am thy sheep: make me worthy to overcome the Devil.'

Quintian ordered her to be handed over to Aphrodisia, a most wicked woman who with her six daughters kept a house of ill-fame. In this dreadful place Agatha suffered assaults and stratagems upon her honour more terrible to her than torture or death, but she stood firm. After a month Quintian tried to frighten her with threats, but she remained undaunted and declared that to be a servant of Jesus Christ was to be truly at liberty. The judge, offended at her resolute answers, commanded her to be beaten and taken to prison. The next day she underwent another examination, and she asserted that Jesus Christ was her light and salvation. Quintian then ordered her to be stretched on the rack – a torment generally accompanied by stripes, the tearing of the sides with iron hooks, and by burning with blazing torches. The governor, enraged at seeing her suffer all this with cheerfulness, ordered her breasts to be cruelly crushed and then cut off. Afterwards he remanded her to prison, enjoining that neither food nor medical care should be supplied to her. But God gave her comfort: she had a vision of St Peter who filled her dungeon with a heavenly light, and who consoled and healed her. Four days later Quintian caused her to be rolled naked over live coals mixed with broken potsherds. As she was carried back to prison, she prayed, 'Lord, my Creator, thou hast always protected me from the cradle; thou hast taken me from the love of the world and given me patience to suffer. Receive now my soul.' After saying these words, she breathed out her life.

ALBERT THE GREAT, DOCTOR OF THE CHURCH (A.D. 1280)

PATRON SAINT OF SCIENTISTS

15 NOVEMBER

Pius XII declared St Albert to be the patron of scientists, pointing out in his Apostolic Letter of 16 December 1941 that, because of the Saint's reputation for learning, there were already a large number of Catholic universities and colleges world-wide which were dedicated to him. Pius XII's declaration was dated ten years to the day after his predecessor, Pius XI, had proclaimed Saint Albert a Doctor of the Church.

He was a Swabian by descent, born of the family of Bollstädt at the castle of Lauingen on the Danube in 1206. Little is known of his youth or the age at which he went to the University of Padua, but in 1222 Bd Jordan of Saxony, second master general of the Friars Preachers, wrote from that city that he had received ten postulants for the order. One of them was Albert, whose uncle in Padua had tried to keep him away from the Dominican church, but had failed before the influence of Bd Jordan. When he heard that his son was clothed as a mendicant the Count of Bollstädt was most indignant, and there was talk of retrieving him by force, but nothing came of it for Albert was discreetly removed to another friary. This was probably Cologne, where he was teaching in 1228; afterwards he supervised the studies and taught at Hildesheim, Freiburg-im-Breisgau, Regensburg, Strasburg and back again at Cologne. He was instructed to go to Paris and he was there some years, lecturing under a master until he himself took his master's degree. At the end of this time the Dominicans decided to open four new *studia generalia*, and in 1248 St Albert was sent to be regent of that at Cologne, where until 1252 he had among his students a young friar called Thomas Aquinas.

The writings of St Albert fill thirty-eight quarto volumes in print. He was an authority on physics, geography, astronomy, minerology, alchemy (*i.e.* chemistry) and biology, so that it is not surprising that legends grew up that he had and used magical powers. He wrote a treatise on botany and another on human and animal physiology. But his principal fame as a doctor resides not in these achievements, but in the fact that, realizing the autonomy of philosophy and seeing the use that could be made of philosophy of Aristotle in ordering the science of theology, he re-wrote the works of the philosopher so as to make them acceptable to Christian critics, and by the application of Aristotelean methods and principles to the study of theology inaugurated (with the Englishman Alexander of Hales) the scholastic system which was to be brought to perfection by his pupil St Thomas Aquinas. In 1254 he was made prior provincial of his order in Germany. Two years later he attended in that capacity the chapter general in Paris which forbade Friars Preachers at the universities to be called 'master' or 'doctor', or anything but their right name.

Albert went to Italy to defend the mendicant orders against the attacks being made on them at Paris and elsewhere, especially as voiced by William of Saint-Amour in a tract 'On the Dangers of these Present Times'. While he was in Rome, St Albert filled the office of master of the sacred place (*i.e.* the pope's personal theologian and canonist, always a Dominican friar) and preached in the churches of the City. In 1260 he received an order from the Holy See to undertake the government of the diocese of Regensburg.

He was bishop for under two years, Pope Urban IV then accepting his resignation. St Albert return to the *studium* at Cologne. But the next year he was called away again, this time to help the Franciscan Berthold of Ratisbon to preach the crusade in Germany. This over, he went back again to Cologne and taught and wrote there in peace till 1274, when he was bidden to attend the fourteenth general council at Lyons.

St Albert probably made his last public appearance three years later, when some of the writings of St Thomas were seriously attacked by Stephen Tempier, Bishop of Paris, and other theologians. He hurried to Paris to defend the teaching of his dead disciple, teaching that was in great measure his own as well; he challenged the university to examine himself personally upon it, but he could not avert the local condemnation of certain points. In 1278, during a lecture, his memory suddenly failed. The loss of memory became acute, the strength of his mind failed, and after two years St Albert died, peacefully and without illness, sitting in his chair among his brethren at Cologne, on 15 November, 1280.

ALEXANDER THE CHARCOAL-BURNER, BISHOP OF COMANA, MARTYR (A.D. 275?)

PATRON SAINT OF CHARCOAL-BURNERS

11 AUGUST

The traditional devotion of charcoal-burners to St Alexander is explained by his original profession.

The Christian community of Comana in Pontus having grown to be suffi-ciently large to require a bishop, St Gregory the Wonderworker, Bishop of Neocaesarea, went thither to preside at the election. He rejected all the candidates put forward by the clergy and people, especially one who was favoured because of his high birth and wealth, reminding them that the Apostles were poor and common men. Someone exclaimed, 'Very well then. Why not appoint Alexander the charcoal-burner?' St Gregory, know-ing that the Holy Spirit was as likely to make Himself heard by means of this sarcastic suggestion as any other way, was moved to send for the said Alexander, who presented himself all dirty and blackened from his trade. Gregory looked at him and saw through the grime and the rags; he took him aside and questioned him, and soon discovered that Alexander was a man of good birth and education, who had given away his goods and taken up this trade the more literally to follow Christ; the Roman Martyrology says that he was 'a most learned philosopher', though there is no reason to think that anything more is meant by this than that he was a man of wisdom. St Gregory accordingly put Alexander forward, he having signified his willing-ness, as his own choice for the vacant see; it was ratified by the people, and the new bishop was consecrated. St Gregory of Nyssa, who relates this happening, speaks highly of St Alexander as a bishop and teacher. He eventually gave his life for the faith, being martyred by fire.

ALOYSIUS (A.D. 1591)

PATRON SAINT OF YOUNG CHRISTIAN PEOPLE AND STUDENTS IN JESUIT COLLEGES

21 JUNE

Citing St Aloysius' work for young people, as well as the young age, twenty-three, at which he died and by which he had achieved sanctity, Pius XI proclaimed him patron of all Christian youth in an Apostolic Letter of 13 June 1926. Three centuries earlier, on 31 December 1726, very soon after he was canonized, Benedict XIII had declared him the patron of all those who studied in the colleges of the Society of Jesus.

St Aloysius, or Luigi Gonzaga, was born on 9 March, 1568, in the castle of Castiglione delle Stivieri in Lombardy. He was the eldest son of Ferrante,

Marquis of Castiglione, and of Marta Tana Santena, lady of honour to the wife of Philip II of Spain, in whose court the marquis also held a high position. His father's one ambition was that his first-born son should become a great soldier. He was about seven when he experienced what may perhaps best be described as a spiritual quickening or sudden development of his religious faculties. He had said his morning and evening prayers from babyhood; now he began every day to recite the Office of our Lady, the seven penitential psalms, and other devotions.

In 1577 his father took him and his brother, Ridolfo, to Florence, and left them there under the charge of tutors to improve their Latin and to learn to speak the pure Italian of Tuscany. Whatever may have been his progress in those secular subjects, Aloysius made such rapid strides in the science of the saints that he used to call Florence the mother of piety. The boys had been living in Florence a little more than two years when their father removed them and placed them at the court of the Duke of Mantua, who had lately made him governor of Montserrat. This was in November 1579, when Aloysius was eleven and eight months. Even then he had it in his mind to resign to his brother his right to succession to the marquisate of Castiglione, although he had already received investiture from the emperor. A painful kidney disease furnished him with an adequate excuse for appearing little in public, and he spent most of his time in prayer and in reading the collection of the Lives of the Saints made by Surius.

Another book he read about this time, describing the experiences of the Jesuit missionaries in India, seems to have suggested the idea of entering the Society of Jesus in order to labour for the conversion of the heathen. As a first step to a future missionary career he set about instructing the poor boys of Castiglione in the catechism, during the summer holidays. At Casale-Monferrato, where the winter was spent, he haunted the churches of the Capuchins and the Barnabites: he also began to practise the austerities of a monk, fasting three days a week on bread and water, scourging himself with his dog-whip and rising at midnight to pray on the stone floor of a room in which he would suffer no fire to be lighted however bitter the weather.

In 1581 Don Ferrante was summoned to attend the Empress Mary of Austria on her journey from Bohemia to Spain. His family accompanied him, and on their arrival in Spain, Aloysius and Ridolfo were appointed pages to Don Diego, Prince of the Asturias. Although, as in duty bound, Aloysius waited on the young *infante* and shared his studies, yet he never omitted or curtailed his devotions.

He was not quite resolved to become a Jesuit. His mother, whom he first approached, approved, but when she communicated their son's decision to his father, Don Ferrante was furious. However, through the mediation of friends, he so far relented as to give a grudging and provisional consent. The death of the *infante* released the young Gonzagas from their court duties, and after a two-years' stay in Spain they returned to Italy in July, 1584. Upon their arrival at Castiglione the contest broke out again, and Aloysius found his vocation opposed not only by his father but by most of his relations, including the Duke of Mantua. Eminent churchmen and laymen were sent to argue with him, and promises and threats employed by turns as dissuasives. Don Ferrante insisted on sending him to visit all the rulers of Northern Italy and then engaged him in a number of secular commissions in the hope of awakening some new interest, or at least of putting off the evil hour. But nothing could move Aloysius. After giving his consent and retracting it several times. Don Ferrante finally capitulated when the imperial commission arrived transferring the succession to Ridolfo. Shortly afterwards Aloysius set out for Rome, and, on 25 November, 1585, he entered the Jesuit novitiate house of Sant' Andrea.

There is little to be said about St Aloysius during the next two years except that he proved in all respects an ideal novice. Being under regular discipline he was obliged to take recreation, to eat more, and to distract his mind. Moreover, because of his weak health, he was forbidden to pray or meditate except at stated times. He was at Milan when one day, during his morning prayers, he had a revelation that he had not long to live. This filled him with joy and weaned his heart still more from the things of the world. Out of consideration for his precarious health he was recalled from Milan to Rome to complete his theological course in the City.

In 1591 an epidemic of plague caused great ravages in Rome. The Jesuits opened a hospital of their own, in which the father general himself and many members of the order rendered personal service. Aloysius, at his own entreaty, was one of the number. He instructed and exhorted the patients, washed them, made their beds, and performed with zeal the lowliest offices of the hospital. Several of the fathers fell victims to the disease and Aloysius caught it. He believed that he was dying, and, with a joy which he afterwards feared might have been impatience, he received viaticum and was anointed. Contrary to all expectations he recovered from the plague, but only to fall into a low fever which in three months reduced him to great weakness. As long as he possibly could, he would rise from his bed at night to worship before his crucifix and would kiss his sacred pictures, going from one to another; then he would kneel in prayer, propped up between the bed and the wall. Very humbly and anxiously he asked his confessor, St Robert Bellarmine, if he thought that anyone could go straight into the presence of God without passing through Purgatory. St Robert replied in the affirmative and, from his knowledge of Aloysius, encouraged him to hope that this grace might be his. Aloysius immediately fell into an ecstasy which lasted throughout the night, and during which he learnt that he would die on the octave of Corpus Christi.

On the octave-day he seemed so much better that the rector spoke of sending him to Frascati. Aloysius, however, maintained that he would die before the morrow and again received viaticum. In the evening, as he was thought to be in no immediate danger, all but two or three watchers were told to retire to rest. Nevertheless, at the request of Aloysius, Father Bellarmine recited the prayers for the departing. Afterwards the patient lay very still, occasionally murmuring, 'Into thy hands'. Between ten and eleven a change came over him and it was evident that he was sinking. With his eyes fixed on the crucifix and with the name of Jesus upon his lips he died about midnight between 20 and 21 June, 1591. He had attained the age of twenty-three years and eight months. The relics of St Aloysius now lie under the altar in the Lancellotti chapel of the church of St Ignatius in Rome; he was canonized in 1726.

ALPHONSUS DE' LIGUORI, DOCTOR OF THE CHURCH (A.D. 1787)

PATRON SAINT OF CONFESSORS AND OF MORAL THEOLOGIANS

1 AUGUST

As his life indicates, the choice of St Alphonsus as patron of priests who hear confessions (confessors), and also of those who teach and practise moral theology, is a natural one. He was proclaimed their patron, with due solemnity, in an Apostolic Letter of Pope Pius XII, dated 26 April 1950.

St Alphonsus was born near Naples in 1696; his parents were Don Joseph de' Liguori, captain of the royal galleys, and Donna Anna Cavalieri, both people of virtuous and distinguished life. The boy was baptized Alphonsus Mary Antony John Francis Cosmas Damian Michael Caspar, but preferred to call himself simply Alfonso Maria; the use of the Latin form of his name has become usual in English. Don Joseph was determined that his first-born should have every advantage that formal education could give him, and he was early put under tutors. At thirteen he began the study of jurisprudence, and when sixteen he was allowed, by dispensation of four years, to present himself before the university of Naples for examination for the doctor's degree in both laws (civil and canon); it was granted him with acclamation. His reputation as a barrister is testified by the tradition (not certainly true) that in eight years of practice he never lost a case. In 1717 Don Joseph arranged a marriage for his son, but it came to nothing; for a year or two some slackness in religious care was observable, coupled with and perhaps due to an affection for 'society life' and fashionable amusements, but a retreat with the Lazarists during the Lent of 1722 and reception of the sacrament of Confirmation in the following autumn steadied him and revived his fervour. At the next Lent he made a private resolution not to marry and to continue in his profession only until it should appear that God wished him to abandon it. What he took to be a clear indication of the divine will was shown him only a few months later.

35

A certain Neapolitan nobleman was suing the grand-duke of Tuscany. Alphonsus was briefed in the case, and made a great speech on his client's behalf which much impressed the court. When he sat down opposing counsel coolly remarked, 'You have wasted your breath. You have disregarded the evidence on which the whole case depends.' 'How?' asked Alphonsus. He was handed a document which he had read through several times, but with a passage marked that had entirely escaped his notice. The point at issue was whether the estate was held under Lombard law or under the Angevin capitularies: this clause made the point clear, and decided against the client of Alphonsus. For a moment he was silent. Then he said, 'I have made a mistake. The case is yours,' and left the court. Braving the fiery indignation of his father, Alphonsus refused either to go on with his profession or to entertain a second project for his marriage. While visiting the sick in the hospital for incurables he twice heard, as it were an interior voice, saying, 'Leave the world, and give yourself to me'; he went to the church of our Lady of Ransom, laid his sword on her altar, and then offered himself to the priests of the Oratory. Don Joseph tried every way to dissuade his son, but was at last constrained to agree to his being a priest, provided that, instead of joining the Oratory, he should stay at home. On the advice of his director, Father Pagano, himself an Oratorian, Alphonsus accepted this condition.

He began his theological studies at home, and in 1726 was advanced to the priesthood. For the two following years he was engaged in missionary work throughout the kingdom of Naples, and at once made his mark. He preached simply and without affectation: 'It is a pleasure to listen to your sermons; you forget yourself and preach Jesus Christ', somebody said to him, and he afterwards instructed his missioners: 'Your style must be simple, but the sermon must be well constructed. If skill be lacking, it is unconnected and tasteless; if it be bombastic, the simple cannot understand it. I have never preached a sermon which the poorest old woman in the congregation could not understand.' He treated his penitents as souls to be saved rather than as criminals to be punished or frightened into better ways; he is said never to have refused absolution to a penitent. This was not pleasing to everybody, and some looked with suspicion on Don Alphonsus. He organized the *lazzaroni* of Naples into groups which met for instruction in Christian doctrine and virtue; one of the members was reproved by Don Alphonsus for his imprudent fasting, and another priest added, 'It is God's will that we should eat in order to live. If you are given cutlets, eat them and be thankful. They will do good,' The remark was taken up and twisted into a matter of offence: the clubs were secret societies of Epicureans, of Quietists, of some other heresy, there was a new sect, 'of Cutlets'. The solemn wiseacres of church and state took the matter up, arrests were made, and Don Alphonsus had to make explanations. The archbishop counselled him to be more careful, the 'Cutlet clubs' continued undisturbed, and developed into the great Association of the Chapels which numbers thousands of working-men who meet daily for prayer and instruction in the confraternity chapels.

In 1729, being then thirty-three years old, Alphonsus left his father's house to become chaplain to a college for the training of missionaries to China. Here he met Thomas Falcoia and became friendly with him; he was a priest twice his own age, whose life had been devoted to trying to establish a new religious institute in accordance with a vision he claimed to have had in Rome. All he had succeeded in doing was to establish a convent of nuns of Scala, near Amalfi, to whom he had given a version of the rule of the Visitandines. One of the nuns, however, Sister Mary Celeste, alleged that she had received a revelation of the rule which the nuns were to follow, and when Father Falcoia discovered that its provisions tallied with those intimated to him twenty years before he was naturally impressed. In 1730 he got St Alphonsus interested in the matter. About the same time an unexpected turn was given to events by Falcoia's appointment to the see of Castellamare; this left him free to associate himself with the convent of Scala again, and one of his first episcopal acts was to invite Alphonsus to give a retreat to the nuns, a step that had far-reaching consequences for everybody concerned.

St Alphonsus went to Scala, and in addition to giving the retreat he investigated, with a lawyer's precision, the matter of Sister Mary Celeste's revelation, and came to the conclusion that it was from God and not an hallucination. He therefore recommended, and the nuns agreed, that the convent should be re-organized in accordance with the vision, and the bishop of Scala gave his consent; on the feast of the Transfiguration 1731 the nuns put on their new habit, of red and blue, and entered upon their strictly enclosed and penitential life. Thus began the Redemptoristines, who flourish in several lands. The new rule had been expanded and made more explicit by St Alphonsus himself, and Mgr Falcoia proposed that he should now undertake the establishment of a new congregation of missionaries to work especially among the peasants of the country districts. St Alphonsus agreed, but had to face a storm of opposition. At last, after a long and painful leave-taking with his father, he left Naples in November 1732 and went to Scala. There the Congregation of the Most Holy Redeemer was born on the 9th of that month, and its first home was in a small house belonging to the convent of nuns. There were seven postulants under Alphonsus, with Mgr Falcoia as informal superior general, and dissensions began at once, centring chiefly in this very matter of who was in supreme authority; a party opposed the bishop, and consequently Alphonsus, and a schism was formed in both houses. Sister Mary Celeste went off to found a convent at Foggia, and at the end of five months St Alphonsus was alone but for one lay-brother. But other subjects came, a larger house became necessary, and in the autumn of 1733 successful missions were given in the diocese of

Amalfi. In the following January a second foundation was made at Villa degli Schiavi, and here Alphonsus went to reside, and conducted missions.

But the troubles of the young Redemptorists were not over: indeed they had hardly begun. In the same year as the foundation at Villa degli Schiavi, Spain re-asserted its authority over Naples, the absolutist Charles III was in power, and he had as his prime minister the Marquis Bernard Tanucci, who was to be the life-long opponent of the new congregation. In 1737 a priest of bad character spread evil reports about the establishment at Villa, the comminity was attacked by armed men, and it was deemed wise to close the house; in the following year troubles caused Scala too to be abandoned. On the other hand Cardinal Spinelli, Archbishop of Naples, put St Alphonsus at the head of a general mission throughout his diocese, and for two years the saint organized and conducted this, until the death of Mgr Falcoia recalled him to the work of the congregation. A general chapter was held, at which St Alphonsus was elected rector major (*i.e.* superior general), vows were taken, and rules and constitutions were drawn up. They were now constituted as a religious institute and proceeded in the following years to make several new foundations, all under great difficulties of local and official opposition; 'regalism' was in the ascendant and the implacable anti-clericalism of Tanucci was a sword at all times threatening the existence of the congregation.

The first edition of the *Moral Theology* of St Alphonsus, in the form of annotations to the work of Busembaum, a Jesuit theologian, was published at Naples in 1748, and the second edition, which is properly the first of his own complete work, in 1753–55. It was approved by Pope Benedict XIV and had an immediate success, for with consummate wisdom it steered a middle course between the rigorism of Jansenism and an improper laxity; seven more editions were called for in the author's lifetime.

Attempts have been made to impugn the morality of the teaching of St Alphonsus about lying: his was the ordinary teaching of the Church, namely, that all lies are intrinsically wrong and illicit. Among the consequences of the teachings of the Jansensits was that holy communion can be received worthily only very rarely and that devotion to our Lady is a useless superstition; St Alphonsus vigorously attacked both these errors, the last-named particularly by the publication in 1750 of *The Glories of Mary*.

From the time of the death of Mgr Falcoia in 1743 St Alphonsus led a life of extraordinary industry: guiding and fostering his new congregation through troubles both external and internal, trying to get it authorized by the king, ministering to individual souls, conducting missions all over Naples and Sicily, even finding time to write hymns, compose music, and paint pictures. After 1752 his health was failing, his missionary vigour decreased, and he devoted much more time to writing. He was strict, but tender and compassionate, and, often suffering acutely from scrupulosity himself, was particularly kind to others afflicted in the same way.

When he was sixty-six years old St Alphonsus was made by Pope Clement XIII bishop of Sant' Agata dei Goti, between Benevento and Capua. When the messenger of the nuncio apostolic presented himself at Nocera, greeted him as 'Most Illustrious Lord', and handed over the letter announcing the appointment, Alphonsus read it through and handed it back, saying, 'Please do not come back again with any more of your "Most Illustrious"; it would be the death of me'. But the pope would take no refusal, and he was consecrated in the church of the Minerva at Rome. Sant' Agata was only a small diocese, but that was about all that could be said in its favour; it numbered 30,000 souls with 17 religious houses and 400 secular priests, of whom some did no pastoral work at all, living on the proceeds of an easy benefice, and others were not only slack but positively evil-living. The laity were to match, and rapidly getting worse; the results of nearly thirty years of neglect were apparent on all sides. After having established his own modest household, the new bishop sent out a band of priests to conduct a general mission throughout the diocese: they were recruited from all orders and institutes in Naples except, for reasons of tact and prudence, his own congregation of Redemptorists.

Alphonsus recommended two things only to these missioners, simplicity in the pulpit, charity in the confessional. At the same time he set about a reform of the seminary, and of the careless way that benefices were granted. Some priests were in the habit of saying Mass in fifteen minutes or less; these were suspended *ipso facto* until they amended their ways, and the bishop wrote a moving treatise on the subject.

After he had been at Sant' Agata a short time famine broke out, with its usual accompaniment of plague. Alphonsus had foreseen this calamity several times in the previous two years, but nothing had been done to avert it. Thousands were starving, and he sold everything to buy food for the sufferers, down to his carriage and mules and his uncle's episcopal ring; the Holy See authorized him to make use of the endowment of the see for the same purpose, and he contracted debts right and left in his efforts at relief. When the mob clamoured for the life of the mayor of Sant' Agata, who was wrongfully accused of withholding food, Alphonsus braved their fury, offered his own life for that of the mayor, and finally distracted them by distributing the rations of the next two days. The bishop was most vigorous in his concern for public morality; he always began with kindness, but when amendment was not promised or relapse occurred he took strong measures, invoking the help of the civil authorities. This made him many enemies, and several times his life was in danger from people of rank and others against whom he instituted proceedings.

In June 1767 St Alphonsus was attacked by terrible rheumatic pains which developed into an illness from which he was not expected to recover: not only did he receive the last sacraments but preparations were begun for his funeral. After twelve months his life was saved, but he was left with a permanent and incurable bending of the neck, familiar from the portraits of him; until the surgeons had succeeded in straightening it a little the pressure of the chin caused a raw wound in his chest and he was unable to celebrate Mass, which afterwards he could do with the aid of a chair at the communion. In addition to attacks on his moral theology, he had to face an accusation against the Redemptorists of carrying on the Society of Jesus under another name (the Jesuits had been suppressed in the Spanish dominions in 1767), and an action against them, begun but adjourned some time before, was revived in 1770. The case dragged on for another thirteen years before it was decided in favour of Alphonsus on all counts. Pope Clement XIV died on 22 September, 1774, and St Alphonsus in the following year petitioned his successor, Pius VI, for permission to resign his see. Similar petitions had been refused by Clement XIII and XIV, but the effects of his rheumatic fever were now taken into consideration; permission was granted, and the aged bishop retired to his Redemptorist's cell at Nocera, hoping to end his days in peace.

But it was not to be. The Redemptorists having in 1777 been subjected to another attack, Alphonsus determined to make another effort to get the royal sanction for his rule (it was as religious rather than as priests that the congregation was objected to); in addition to four houses in Naples and one in Sicily, it had now four others in the Papal States. What followed was nothing less than tragic. Alphonsus agreed with the royal almoner, Mgr Testa, to waive any request to be allowed to hold property in common, but otherwise to submit the rule unchanged, and the almoner would put it before the king. Then Testa betrayed him. He altered the rule in several vital respects, even to the extent of abolishing the vows of religion; he won over to his plot one of the consultors of the congregation, Father Majone, and this altered rule (*regolamento*) was presented to Alponsus, written in a small hand and with many erasures. He was old, crippled, deaf, his sight was bad: he read over the familiar opening lines of the document – and signed it. Even his vicar general, Father Andrew Villani, seems to have connived at the cruel deception, probably through fear of the others. The king approved the *regolamento*, it became legally binding, and its provisions were made known to the Redemptorists – and to their founder. The storm broke on him: 'You have founded the congregation and you have destroyed it', he was told. To refuse to accept the *regolamento* now would mean suppression of the Redemptorists by the king; to accept it would mean suppression by the pope, for the Holy See had already approved the original rule. Alphonsus cast about in every direction to save a *débâcle*, but in vain; he would consult the pope, but the Redemptorists in the Papal States had forestalled him, for they had at once denounced the new rule and put themselves under the protection of the Holy See. Pius VI forbade them to accept the *regolamento*, and withdrew them from the jurisdiction of St Alphonsus; he provisionally recognized those of the Papal States as the only true Redemptorists, and named Father Francis de Paula their superior general. In 1781 the fathers of Naples accepted the *regolamento*, with a slight modification which the king had agreed; but this was not acceptable at Rome and the provisional decree was made final. Thus was St Alphonsus excluded from the order which he had founded.

He bore the humiliation, inflicted by the authority he so loved and respected, with the utmost patience, and without murmuring accepted the apparent end of all his hopes as the will of God. But there was still one more bitter trial for him: during the years 1784–85 he went through a terrible 'dark night of the soul'. He was assailed by temptations against every article of faith and against every virtue, prostrated by scruples and vain fears, and visited by diabolical illusions. For eighteen months this torment lasted, with intervals of light and relief, and was followed by a period when ecstasies were frequent, and prophecy and miracles took the place of interior trials. The end came peacefully on the night of 31 July–1 August 1787, when he was within two months of his ninety-first birthday. Pius VI, the pope who had condemned him under a misapprehension, in 1796 decreed the introduction of the cause of Alphonsus Liguori, in 1816 he was beatified, in 1839 canonized, and in 1871 declared a doctor of the Church. St Alphonsus predicted that the separated houses in the Papal States would prosper and spread the Redemptorist congregation, but that reunion would not come about till after his death. These predictions were verified; St Clement Hofbauer in 1785 first established the congregation beyond the Alps, and in 1793 the Neapolitan government recognized the original rule and the Redemptorists were again united. Today they are established as missioners throughout Europe and America, and in several other parts of the world.

AMAND, BISHOP (*c.* A.D. 679)

PATRON SAINT OF BREWERS, WINE-MERCHANTS, MEMBERS OF THE WINE AND DRINKS TRADE

6 FEBRUARY

The cult of Amand spread swiftly throughout Northern France and what is now Belgium – strong beer-drinking areas. He has been adopted by brewers, by wine-merchants, and also by others, such as those who work in bars, who are associated with the production and sale of alcoholic drink.

This great missionary was born in Lower Poitou about the year 584. At the age of twenty he retired to a small monastery in the island of Yeu, near that of Ré. He had not been there more than a year when his father discovered him and tried to persuade him to return home. When he threatened to disinherit him, the saint cheerfully replied, 'Christ is my only inheritance'.

Amand afterwards went to Tours, where he was ordained, and then to Bourges, where he lived fifteen years under the direction of St Austregisilus the bishop, in a cell near the cathedral. After a pilgrimage to Rome, he returned to France and was consecrated bishop in 629 without any fixed see, receiving a general commission to teach the faith to the heathen. He preached the gospel in Flanders and northern France, with a brief excursion to the Slavs in Carinthia and perhaps to Gascony. He reproved King Dagobert I for his crimes and accordingly was banished. But Dagobert soon recalled him, and asked him to baptize his new-born son Sigebert, afterwards king and saint. The people about Ghent were so ferociously hostile that no preacher dared to venture amongst them. This moved Amand to attempt that mission, in the course of which he was sometimes beaten and thrown into the river. He persevered, however, although for a long time he saw no fruit, and in the end people came in crowds to be baptized.

As well as being a great missionary St Amand was a father of monasticism in ancient Belgium, and a score of monasteries claimed him as founder. He did in fact found houses at Elnone (Saint-Amand-les-Eaux), near Tournai, which became his headquarters; St Peter's on Mont-Blandin at Ghent, but probably not St Bavo's there as well; Nivelles, for nuns, with Bd Ida and St Gertrude; Barisis-au-Bois, and probably three more, including Marchiennes. It is said, though the fact is not certain, that in 646 he was chosen bishop of Maestricht, but that three years later he resigned that see to St Remaclus and returned to his missions, which he always had most at heart. He continued his labours among the heathen until a great age, when, broken with infirmities, he retired to Elnone. There he governed as abbot for four years, spending his time in preparing for the death which came to him at last soon after 676.

AMBROSE, BISHOP OF MILAN, DOCTOR OF THE CHURCH (A.D. 397)

PATRON SAINT OF THE FRENCH ARMY COMMISSARIAT

7 DECEMBER

In an Apostolic Letter of 18 February 1981 John Paul II declared Ambrose to be patron of those in the French army who were responsible for procurement and administration. This was at the request of the Military Vicar, and the choice of patron was apparently made on the grounds that Ambrose ran his diocese efficiently.

At the time of Ambrose's birth at Trier, probably in 340, his father, whose name also was Ambrose, was prefect of Gaul. Ambrose senior died while his youngest child was still young, and his widow returned with her family to Rome. She took great care in the upbringing of her children, and Ambrose owed much both to her and to his sister, St Marcellina. He learned Greek, became a good poet and orator, went to the bar, and was soon taken notice of, particularly by Anicius Probus and Symmachus, the last-named being prefect of Rome and still a pagan. The other was praetorian prefect of Italy, and in his court St Ambrose pleaded causes with so much success that Probus made choice of him to be his assessor. Then the emperor Valentinian made him governor of Liguria and Aemilia, with his residence at Milan.

Auxentius, an Arian, who had held the see of Milan for almost twenty years, died in 374. The city was distracted by party strife about the election of a new bishop, some demanding an Arian, others a Catholic. To prevent, if possible, too outrageous a disorder St Ambrose went to the church in which the assembly was held. There he made a speech to the people, exhorting them to proceed in their choice in the spirit of peace and without tumult. While he was speaking a voice cried out: 'Ambrose, bishop!' and the whole assembly took up the cry with enthusiasm. This unexpected choice astounded Ambrose, for though professedly a Christian, he was still unbaptized.

A relation of all that had passed was sent to the emperor, and Ambrose wrote also on his own behalf, asking that he might be excused. Valentinian answered that it gave him the greatest pleasure that he had chosen governors who were fit for the episcopal office; and at the same time sent an order to the *vicarius* of the province to see that the election took place. In the meantime Ambrose tried to escape, and hid himself in the house of the senator Leontius, who, when he heard the imperial decision, gave him up, and Ambrose received episcopal consecration a week later, on 7 December, 374. He was about thirty-five years old.

St Ambrose was acutely conscious of his ignorance of theological science, and at once applied himself to study the Holy Scriptures and the works of religious writers, particularly Origen and St Basil. His personal life was one of simplicity and hard work; he dined only on Sundays, the feasts of certain famous martyrs, and all Saturdays, on which it was the custom at Milan never to fast (but when he was at Rome he fasted on Saturdays); he excused himself from going to banquets, and entertained others with decent frugality. Every day he offered the Holy Sacrifice for his people, and devoted himself entirely to the service of his flock, any member of which could see and speak with him at any time, so that his people loved and admired him. It was his rule never to have any hand in making matches, never to persuade anyone to serve in the army, and never recommend to places at court. Ambrose in his discourses frequently spoke in praise of the state and virtue of virginity undertaken for God's sake, and he had many consecrated virgins under this direction. At the request of his sister, St Marcellina, he collected his sermons on this subject, making hereby a famous treatise. Mothers tried to keep their daughters away from his sermons, and he was charged with trying to depopulate the empire. Wars, he said, and not maidens, are the destroyers of the human race.

The Goths having invaded Roman territories in the East, the Emperor

Gratian determined to lead an army to the succour of his uncle, Valens. But in order to guard himself against Arianism, of which Valens was the protector, he asked St Ambrose for instruction against that heresy. He accordingly wrote in 377 the work entitled *To Gratian, concerning the Faith*, which he afterwards expanded. After the murder of Gratian in 383 the Empress Justina implored St Ambrose to treat with the usurper Maximus lest he attack her son, Valentinian II. He went and induced Maximus at Trier to confine himself to Gaul, Spain and Britain. This is said to have been the first occasion on which a minister of the gospel was called on to interfere in matters of high politics.

At this time certain senators at Rome attempted to restore the cult of the goddess of Victory. At their head was Quintus Aurelius Symmachus, son and successor of that prefect of the city who had patronized the young Ambrose, and an admirable scholar, statesmen and orator. This man presented a request to Valentinian begging that the altar of Victory might be re-established in the senate-house; to it he ascribed the victories and prosperity of ancient Rome. It was a skilfully drawn and in some respects moving document. 'What does it matter', he asked, 'the way in which each seeks for truth? There must be more than one road to the great mystery.' The petition was particularly a covert attack on St Ambrose and he remonstrated with the emperor for not having at once consulted him, since it was a matter of religion. He then drew up a reply whose eloquence surpassed that of Symmachus. Both documents, that of Symmachus and that of Ambrose, were read before Valentinian in council. There was no discussion. Then the emperor spoke: 'My father did not take away the altar. Nor was he asked to put it back. I therefore follow him in changing nothing that was done before my time.'

The Empress Justina dared not openly espouse the interests of the Arians during the lives of her husband and of Gratian, but when the peace which St Ambrose arranged between Maximus and her son gave her an opportunity to oppose the Catholic bishop, she forgot the obligations which she had to him. When Easter was near, in 385, she induced Valentinian to demand the Portian basilica, now called St Victor's, outside Milan, for the use of the Arians, herself and many officers of the court. The saint replied that he could never give up the temple of God. By messengers Valentinian then demanded the new basilica of the Apostles; but the bishop was inflexible. Officers of the court were sent to take possession of the basilica.

Throughout these troubles, when St Ambrose had the bulk of the excited people and even of the army on his side, he was studiously careful to say or do nothing that would precipitate violence or endanger the position of the emperor and his mother. He was resolute in his refusal to give up the churches, but would not himself officiate in either for fear of creating disturbance. While he was expounding a passage of Job to the people in a chapel a party of soldiers, who had been sent to take charge of the larger basilica, came in. They had refused to obey orders and wished to pray with the Catholics. At once the people surged into the adjoining basilica, and tore down the decorations put up for the emperor's visit, giving them to the children to play with. But Ambrose did not enter the church himself until Easter day, when Valentinian had ordered the guards to be removed, upon which all joined in joy and thanksgiving.

In January of the following year Justina persuaded her son to make a law authorizing the religious assemblies of the Arians and, in effect, proscribing those of the Catholics. It forbade anyone, under pain of death, to oppose Arian assemblies, and no one could so much as present a petition against a church being yielded up to them without danger of being proscribed. St Ambrose disregarded the law, would not give up a single church, and no one dare touch him.

On Palm Sunday he preached on not giving up churches, and then, fears being entertained for his life, the people barricaded themselves in the basilica with their pastor. The imperial troops surrounded the place to starve them out, but on Easter Sunday they were still there. To occupy their time Ambrose taught the people psalms and hymns composed by himself, which they sang at his direction divided into two choirs singing alternate stanzas. Then Dalmatius, a tribune, came to St Ambrose from the emperor, with an order that he should choose judges, as the Arian bishop, Auxentius, had done on his side, that his and Auxentius's cause might be tried before them; if he refused, he was forthwith to retire and yield his see to Auxentius. Ambrose wrote asking to be excused and forcibly reminding Valentinian that laymen (lay-judges had been stipulated) could not judge bishops or make ecclesiastical laws. Then he occupied his episcopal *cathedra* and related to the people all that had passed between him and Valentinian during the previous year. And in a memorable sentence he summed up the principle at stake: 'The emperor is in the Church, not over it.'

Meanwhile it became known that Maximus was preparing to invade Italy. Valentinian and Justina asked St Ambrose to venture on a second embassy to stop the march of a usurper. At Trier Maximus refused to admit him to audience except in public consistory, though he was both bishop and imperial ambassador. When, therefore, he was introduced into the consistory and Maximus rose to give him a kiss, Ambrose stood still and refused to approach to receive it. On his arrival St Ambrose had refused to hold communion with the court prelates who had connived at the execution of the heretic Priscillian, which meant with Maximus himself, and the next day he was ordered to leave Trier. He therefore returned to Milan, writing to Valentinian an account of events and advising him to be cautious how he treated with Maximus. Then Maximus suddenly marched into Italy. Leaving St Ambrose alone to meet the storm at Milan, Justina and Valentinian fled to Greece and threw themselves on the mercy of the Eastern emperor, Theodosius. He declared war on Maximus, defeated and executed him in

Pannonia, and restored Valentinian to his own territories and to those of the dead usurper. But henceforward Theodosius was the real ruler of the whole empire.

As was almost inevitable, conflicts arose between Theodosius himself and Ambrose, in the first of which right does not seem to have been wholly on the side of the bishop. At Kallinikum, in Mesopotamia, Christians pulled down the synagogue. Theodosius, when informed of the affair, ordered the bishop to rebuild it. St Ambrose was appealed to, and he wrote a letter to Theodosius in which he based his protest, not on the uncertainty of the actual circumstances, but on the statement that no Christian bishop could pay for the erection of a building to be used for false worship. Theodosius disregarded the protest, and Ambrose preached against him to his face; whereupon a discussion took place between them in the church, and he would not go up to the altar to sing Mass till he had procured a promise of the revocation of the order.

In the year 390 news of a dreadful massacre committed at Thessalonica was brought to Milan. Butheric, the governor, had a charioteer put in prison for having seduced a servant in his family, and refused to release him when his appearance in the circus was demanded by the public. The people were so enraged that some officers were stoned to death and Butheric himself was slain. Theodosius ordered reprisals. While the people were assembled in the circus, soldiers surrounded it and rushed in on them. The slaughter continued for hours and seven thousand were massacred, without distinguishing age or sex or the innocent from the guilty. Ambrose took counsel with his fellow bishops. Then he wrote to Theodosius exhorting him to penance, and declaring that he neither could nor would receive his offering at the altar or celebrate the Divine Mysteries before him till that obligation was satisfied.

In the funeral oration over Theodosius, St Ambrose himself says simply that: 'He stripped himself of every sign of royalty and bewailed his sin openly in church. He, an emperor, was not ashamed to do the public penance which lesser individuals shrink from, and to the end of his life he never ceased to grieve for his error.' By this triumph of grace in Theodosius and of pastoral duty in Ambrose, Christianity was vindicated as being no respecter of persons. And the emperor himself testified to the personal influence of St Ambrose. He was, he said, the only bishop he knew who was worthy of the name.

In 393 occurred the death of the young Valentinian, murdered by Arbogastes while alone among his enemies in Gaul. Arbogastes manoeuvred for the support of Ambrose for his ambitions but Ambrose left Milan before the arrival of Eugenius, the imperial nominee of Arbogastes, who now openly boasted the approaching overthrow of Christianity. St Ambrose went from city to city, strengthening the people against the invaders. Then he returned to his see and there received the letter of Theodosius announcing his victory over Arbogastes at Aquileia, the final blow to the old paganism within the empire. A few months later Theodosius himself died, in the arms of St Ambrose.

St Ambrose survived him only two years, and one of his last treatises was on the 'Goodness of Death'. His written works, mostly homiletical in origin, exegetical, theological, ascetical and poetical, were numerous; as the Roman empire declined in the West he inaugurated a new lease of life for its language, and in the service of Christianity. When he fell sick he foretold his death, but said he should live till Easter. On the day of his death he lay with his hands extended in the form of a cross for several hours, moving his lips in constant prayer. St Honoratus of Vercelli was there, resting in another room, when he seemed to hear a voice crying three times to him, 'Arise! Make haste! He is going'. He went down and gave him the Body of the Lord, and soon after St Ambrose was dead. It was Good Friday, 4 April 397, and he was about fifty-seven years old. He was buried on Easter day, and his relics rest under the high altar of his basilica, where they were buried in 835.

ANDREW, APOSTLE (FIRST CENTURY)

PATRON SAINT OF SCOTLAND; OF RUSSIA; AND OF FISHERMEN

30 NOVEMBER

The reasons for Scotland's choice of St Andrew as the national patron are lost in legend. According to one account a St Regulus (or Rule) brought the relics of the Apostle directly to Scotland from Constantinople, and passed them over to the Scottish King Angus. There was indeed a King Angus, reigning c.730, who dethroned Nechthan. King Nechthan had put his kingdom under the patronage of St Peter, so it may be that Angus chose Peter's brother as the patron of his kingdom. There is a much more authentic story, however, that some relics, believed to be those of the Apostle Andrew, were brought to Hexham in Northumbria, whence some of them – or simply devotion to the saint which was strong in and around Hexham – might have strayed into Scotland in the wake of regular invasions.

St Andrew is the patron saint of Russia, on account of a valueless tradition that he preached in that country so far as Kiev, as well as of Scotland. It is not claimed that he preached in Scotland, but there is a legend, preserved by John of Fordun and in the Aberdeen Breviary, that is retold in Butler's Lives of the Saints. According to this when St Regulus had charge of the relics of St Andrew, he was warned by an angel in a dream to take a part of those relics and convey them to a place that would be indicated. He did as he was told, going forth in a north-westerly direction 'towards the ends of the earth', until by a sign the angel stopped him at the place we call Saint Andrews, where he built a church to shelter them, was made its first bishop and evangelized the people for thirty years. This story may have originated in the eighth century. A feast of the translation is observed in the archdiocese of Saint Andrews on 9 May.

The name of St Andrew appears in the canon of the Mass with those of the other apostles, and he is also named with our Lady and SS. Peter and Paul in the embolism after the Lord's Prayer. This is generally attributed to the personal devotion of Pope St Gregory the Great for the saint, but the usage may antedate his time.

St Andrew was a native of Bethsaida, a town in Galilee upon the banks of the lake of Genesareth. He was the son of Jona, a fisherman of that town, and brother to Simon Peter, but whether older or younger the Holy Scriptures do not say. They had a house at Capharnaum, where Jesus lodged when he preached in that city. When St John Baptist began to preach penance, Andrew became his disciple, and he was with his master when St John, seeing Jesus pass by the way after He had been baptized by him, said, 'Behold the Lamb of God!' Andrew was so far enlightened as to comprehend this mysterious saying, and without delay he and another disciple of the Baptist went after Jesus, who saw them with the eyes of His spirit before He beheld them with His corporal eyes. Turning back as he walked, he said, 'What seek ye?' They said they wanted to know where He dwelt, and He bade them come and see. There remained but two hours of that day, which they spent with him, and Andrew clearly learned that Jesus was the Messias and resolved from that moment to follow Him; he was thus the first of His disciples, and therefore is styled by the Greeks the 'Protoclete' or First-called. He then fetched his brother, that he might also know Him, and Simon was no sooner come to Jesus than the Saviour admitted him also as a disciple, and gave him the name of Peter. From this time they were His followers, not constantly attending Him as they afterwards did, but hearing Him as frequently as their business would permit and returning to their trade and family affairs again. When Jesus, going up to Jerusalem to celebrate the Passover, stayed some days in Judaea and baptized in the Jordan, Peter and Andrew were baptized by His authority and in His name. Our Saviour, being come back into Galilee and meeting Peter and Andrew fishing in the lake, He called them permanently to the ministry of the gospel, saying that He would make them fishers of men. Whereupon they immediately left their nets to follow Him, and never went from Him again. The year following our Lord chose twelve to be His apostles, and St Andrew is named among the first four in all the biblical lists. He is also mentioned in connection with the feeding of the five thousand (John vi 8, 9) and the Gentiles who would see Jesus (John xii 2–22).

Apart from a few words in Eusebius, who informs us that St Andrew preached in Scythia and that certain spurious 'acts' bearing his name were made use of by heretics, we have practically nothing but apocryphal writings which profess to tell us anything of the later history of St Andrew. There is, however, one curious mention in the ancient document known as the Muratorian Fragment. This dates from the very beginning of the third century and therein it is stated: 'The fourth gospel [was written by] John one of the disciples [*i.e.* apostles]. When his fellow disciples and bishops urgently pressed him, he said, "Fast with me from today, for three days, and let us tell one another what revelation may be made to us, either for or against [the plan of writing]." On the same night it was revealed to Andrew, one of the apostles, that John should relate all in his own name, and that all should review his writing.' Theodoret tells us that Andrew passed into Greece; St Gregory Nazianzen mentions particularly Epirus, and St Jerome Achaia. St Philastrius says that he came out of Pontus into Greece, and that in his time (fourth century) people at Sinope believed that they had his true picture and the *ambo* from which he preached in that city. Though there is agreement among these as to the direction of St Andrew's apostolate there is no certainty about it. The favourite view of the middle ages was that he eventually came to Byzantium and there left his disciple Stachys (Romans xvi 9) as bishop. This tradition is due to a document forged at a time when it was a great help to the ecclesiastical position of Constantinople apparently to have an apostolic origin for their church, like Rome, Alexandria and Antioch. (The first historically certain bishop of Byzantium was St Metrophanes, early in the fourth century.) The place and manner of the death of St Andrew are equally in doubt. His apocryphal *passio* says that he was crucified at Patras in Achaia, being not nailed but bound to a cross, on which he suffered and preached to the people for two days before he died. The idea that his cross was of the kind called saltire or decussate (X-shaped) was apparently not known before the fourteenth century. Under the Emperor Constantius II (d. 361) what purported to be the relics of St Andrew were translated from Patras to the church of the Apostles at Constantinople; after the seizure of that city by the Crusaders in 1204 they were stolen and given to the cathedral of Amalfi in Italy.

ANDREW AVELLINO (A.D. 1608)

PATRON SAINT OF SUDDEN DEATH; OF APOPLEXY; ALSO OF NAPLES AND SICILY

10 NOVEMBER

The invocation of Andrew Avellino against sudden death is traditional, and apparently stems from the manner of his own death when he was struck down by apoplexy just as he was about to celebrate mass. He lived until the afternoon of that same day, consoled, it is said, by a heavenly vision.

The devotion to St Andrew Avellino of Naples, and of Sicily, which for long was part of the same jurisdiction, is traditional. The saint came from the Kingdom of Naples, and spent a great deal of his life there.

St Andrew Avellino was a native of Castronuovo, a small town in the kingdom of Naples, and born in 1521. His parents gave him the name of Lancelot at baptism. He determined to enter the clerical state, and was sent to Naples to study civil and canon law. Being there promoted to the degree of doctor and to the priesthood, he began to practise in the ecclesiastical courts. This employment, however, too much engrossed his thoughts and dissipated his mind; and, having while pleading a cause caught himself in a lie, and reading that same evening the words of Holy Scripture, 'The mouth that belieth killeth the soul,' he resolved to give himself up entirely to the spiritual care of souls. This he did, and with such prudence and ability that in 1556 Cardinal Scipio Ribiba entrusted to him the task of trying to reform the nuns of Sant' Arcangelo at Baiano. This convent had an evil reputation, and the efforts of the young priest were ill received both by some of the nuns and certain men who used to visit them. These did not stop short of physical violence, but Don Lancelot's strivings and willingness to give his life for the good of souls met with little success, for eventually the convent had to be suppressed.

Don Lancelot in the meantime determined to put himself under a rule, and joined the congregation of clerks regular called Theatines, which had been founded at Naples by St Cajetan thirty years before; his novice-master was Bd John Marinoni. Lancelot himself was now thirty-five, and on changing his way of life he also changed his name, to Andrew. He remained in the Theatine house at Naples for fourteen years, his goodness, spiritual fervour and exactness in discipline causing him to be employed as master of novices, and then elected superior. Among those whom he trained was Father Lorenzo Scupoli, author of the *Spiritual Combat*, who became a clerk regular when he was forty. The fine qualities of St Andrew Avellino and his zeal for a better priesthood were recognized by many reforming prelates in Italy, particularly Cardinal Paul Aresio and St Charles Borromeo. The last-named in 1570 asked the provost general of the Theatines to send St Andrew into Lombardy, where he founded a house of his congregation at Milan and became a close friend and counsellor of St Charles. He then founded another house, at Piacenza, where his preaching converted several noble ladies, induced others to enter the religious life, and generally 'turned the city upside down', so that complaints were made to the Duke of Parma, who sent for him. St Andrew was able to satisfy the duke, and so impressed his wife that she asked him to be her spiritual director. In 1582 St Andrew returned to Naples, and preached with great fruit in the conversion of sinners and the disabusing of the minds of the people of the beginnings of Protestant error which had penetrated even into southern Italy. A number of miraculous happenings are recorded in his life, including the case of a man who denied the real presence of our Lord in the Blessed Sacrament. This man is said to have gone to holy communion out of human respect and fear, but removed the Host from his mouth and wrapped It up in a handkerchief, which he subsequently found stained with blood. In remorse and terror he went to St Andrew, who published the story but refused to divulge the penitent man's name lest he should be proceeded against for sacrilege.

On November 10, 1608, being in his eighty-eighth year, St Andrew Avellino had an attack of apoplexy just as he was beginning to celebrate Mass, and died that same afternoon. His body was laid out in the crypt of the church of St Paul, where it was visited by large crowds of the faithful, many of whom snipped off locks of his hair to be carried away as relics. In so doing they seem to have made cuts in the skin of his face. The next morning, thirty-six hours after death, these cuts were seen to have exuded blood, and as the body of the saint was still warm it is natural to suppose that he was not really dead. Further incisions were made by physicians, and for another thirty-six hours blood continued to trickle from them. This blood was, of course, carefully kept, and four days later it was seen to be bubbling; in subsequent years it is recorded that, on the anniversary of St Andrew's death, the solidified blood liquefied, after the manner of that St Januarius in the same city of Naples. St Andrew was canonized in 1712.

ANDRONICUS (WITH ST ATHANASIA) (FIFTH CENTURY)

PATRON SAINT OF SILVERSMITHS

9 OCTOBER

St Andronicus is traditionally the patron of silversmiths because of his own first profession. Devotion to the saint – or rather saints, for his wife was linked to him in all popular cults – was not common except among Copts and Ethiopians. It is said to have been especially strong in Cyprus.

Andronicus was a native of Alexandria who settled in Antioch to carry on the business of silversmith. He was happily married to a young woman named Athanasia, they had two children, John and Mary, and their trade flourished; but when they had been married twelve years both their children suddenly died on the same day, and Athanasia thereafter spent much of her time weeping at their grave and praying in a neighbouring church. She was here one day when suddenly a stranger stood before her, who assured her that John and Mary were happy in Heaven. Then he disappeared, and Athanasia knew that she had seen a vision of St Julian, the martyr in whose memory the church was dedicated. She went home rejoicing to her husband, and suggested to him that the time had come for them to renounce the world. Andronicus agreed; and as they left their home, leaving the door standing open, St Athanasia called down the blessing of the God of Abraham and Sara upon herself and her husband, beseeching Him that, 'as we leave this house door open for love of thee, so open to us the gates of thy kingdom'. They made their way into their native Egypt, where they sought out St Daniel, known as 'of Many Miracles', among the solitaries of Skete. He sent St Andronicus to the monastery of Tabenna, and St Athanasia to be an anchoress in the wilderness, dressed in the habit of a man. And so they lived for twelve years.

At the end of that time St Andronicus fell in with a beardless old monk, who said that his name was Athanasius and that he was going to Jerusalem. They travelled together, made their religious exercises together, and returned once more to the place where they had met. Then they realized that they had a great regard and affection for one another and were unwilling to be parted; so they both went to the monastery called Eighteen, because it was so many miles from Alexandria, and a cell was found there for Father Athanasius near to that of Andronicus. When the time came for Athanasius to die it was seen that he was weeping, and a monk asked him why he wept when he was about to go to God. 'I am grieved for my father Andronicus,' was the reply, 'for he will miss me. But when I am gone, give him the writing that you will find under my pillow.' After he was dead the writing was found, and when he read it St Andronicus knew – what the other had known since they met on the way to Jerusalem – that Athanasius was his wife Athanasia. Then the monks came, dressed in white and carrying branches of palm and tamarisk, and bore the body of St Athanasia to burial. A monk stopped with St Andronicus until they had celebrated the seventh day of Athanasia, and then tried to persuade the old man to come away with him; and he would not. So the monk departed alone, but he had not gone a day's journey when a messenger overtook him, saying that Father Andronicus was at the point of death. He hurried back, summoning the other monks, and St Andronicus died peacefully amid the prayers of his brethren. They buried him beside his wife.

BD (FRA) ANGELICO (A.D. 1455)

PATRON SAINT OF PAINTERS AND ARTISTS

18 MARCH

It is uncertain how Fra Angelico came by that name – and he has never been beatified. Nonetheless, said John Paul II in his Apostolic Letter of 21 February 1984, because of the excellence of his pictures Fra Angelico deserves to be the patron of artists and especially of painters. Both by his own natural gifts and by his 'ministry of painting' he had continued to be spiritually useful, and of pastoral help, down the ages, the Pope added, even down to the present day. The letter could be regarded as a form of unofficial beatification.

Fra Angelico has never been beatified, nor his cult officially recognized by the Church, but despite that in Italy he is commonly known as Beato Angelico. He was born in 1387, as Guido di Pietro, in the mountainous region to the North of Florence. In 1407 he entered the Dominican order at Fiesole, at a convent much under the reformist influence of Raymond of Capua and Catherine of Siena – St Antoninus was a contemporary of the young friar who there became known as Friar John of Fiesole. From 1409 to 1418 he was at Foligno and Cortona, and then he returned to Fiesole until 1436 when he moved to the convent of St Mark at Florence, where he came into contact with the finest artists and humanists of the age. Fra Angelico's skill as an artist reached Rome, and he was called thither in 1445 to decorate the Vatican for successive popes. He died on 18 March 1455.

ANNE, MOTHER OF OUR LADY (FIRST CENTURY B.C.)

PATRON SAINT OF CHILDLESS WOMEN; AND OF MINERS

26 JULY

Devotion to St Anne as patroness of childless women goes back to the Middle ages, and clearly has its origin in the legend that Anne gave birth to Mary only after many years of marriage.

The devotion to St Anne as patron of miners appears to arise from the medieval comparison between the Virgin Mary and Christ and precious metals – silver and gold respectively. Anne's womb, therefore, was the source form which these metals were mined.

Of the mother of our Lady nothing is known; even for her name and that of her husband Joachim we have to depend on the testimony of the apocryphal *Protevangelium of James* which, though its earliest form is very ancient, is not a trustworthy document. The story told there is that his childlessness was made a public reproach to Joachim, who retired to the desert for forty days to fast and pray to God. At the same time Anne (*Hannah*, which signifies 'grace') 'mourned in two mournings, and lamented in two lamentations', and as she sat praying beneath a laurel bush an angel appeared and said to her, 'Anne, the Lord hath heard thy prayer, and thou shalt conceive and bring forth, and thy seed shall be spoken of in all the world'. And Anne replied, 'As the Lord my God liveth, if I beget either male or female I will bring it as a gift to the Lord my God; and it shall minister to Him in holy things all the days of its life'. Likewise an angel appeared to her husband, and in due time was born of them Mary, who was to be the mother of God.

It will be noticed that this story bears a startling resemblance to that of the conception and birth of Samuel, whose mother was called Anne (I Kings i); the early Eastern fathers saw in this only a parallel, but it is one which suggests confusion or imitation in a way that the obvious parallel between the parents of Samuel and those of St John the Baptist does not.

The early *cultus* of St Anne in Constantinople is attested by the fact that in the middle of the sixth century the Emperor Justinian I dedicated a shrine to her. The devotion was probably introduced into Rome by Pope Constantine (708–715). There are two eighth-century representations of St Anne in the frescoes of S. Maria Antiqua; she is mentioned conspicuously in a list of relics belonging to S. Angelo in Pescheria, and we know that Pope St Leo III (795–816) presented a vestment to St Mary Major which was embroidered with the Annunciation and St Joachim and St Anne. There is very little to suggest any widespread *cultus* of the saint before the middle of the fourteenth century, but this devotion a hundred years afterwards became enormously popular, and was later on acrimoniously derided by Luther. The first papal pronouncement on the subject, enjoining the observance of an annual feast, was addressed by Urban VI in 1382, at the request, as the pope said, of certain English petitioners, to the bishops of England alone. It is quite possible that it was occasioned by the marriage of King Richard II to Anne of Bohemia in that year. The feast was extended to the whole Western church in 1584.

ANSKAR, ARCHBISHOP OF HAMBURG AND BREMEN (A.D. 865)

PATRON SAINT OF DENMARK; GERMANY; ICELAND

3 FEBRUARY

The choice of Anskar as patron of Denmark and of Germany follows naturally from his life. Both were confirmed by a decree of the Sacred Congregation of Rites of 22 June 1914. So does his patronship of Iceland, confirmed by the same decree, for Iceland was linked to Denmark for over 500 years, achieving independence only in 1918.

Anskar was born about 801 of a noble family not far from Amiens, and was sent to acquire learning at the neighbouring monastery of Old Corbie in Picardy, where a near relation of the Emperor Charlemagne loved him greatly and Pischasius Radbertus is said to have been his tutor. A vision he had of the Blessed Virgin and of the death of the Emperor Charlemagne so impressed him that he lost all youthful gaiety and thought only of preaching to the heathen as the nearest road to martyrdom. He became a monk, first at Old Corbie and afterwards at New Corbie (Corvey) in Westphalia, where he first engaged in pastoral work. Harold, King of Denmark, as a fugitive from his country, had been baptized at the court of Louis the Debonair. When he was about to return to his kingdom he took Anskar with him, as well as the monk Autbert, to convert the Danes. They were very successful, winning many to the faith and starting a school, probably at Hedeby. At the invitation of Björn, King of Sweden, Anskar then went with several others to spread the gospel there. In 831 King Louis named him abbot of New Corbie and first archbishop of Hamburg, to which Pope Gregory IV added the dignity of legate of the Holy See to the northern peoples. There he worked for thirteen years, organizing the missions in Denmark, Norway and Sweden as well as in North Germany, building churches and founding a library.

A great incursion of heathen Northmen in 845 destroyed Hamburg, whereupon Sweden and Denmark relapsed into idolatry. Anskar still supported his desolate churches in Germany until the see of Bremen becoming vacant, Pope St Nicholas I eventually united it with Hamburg and appointed Anskar over both. He returned to Denmark and his presence soon made the faith revive. In Sweden the superstitious King Olaf cast lots as to whether the Christian missionaries should be admitted or not. The saint grieved to see the cause of religion treated with such levity, and recommended the issue to the care of God. The lot proved favourable, and the bishop established many churches, which he left under zealous pastors before his return to Bremen.

St Anskar had an extraordinary talent for preaching, and his charity to the poor knew no bounds; he washed their feet and waited upon them at table. When one of his disciples was loudly vaunting the miracles which the saint had wrought, Anskar rebuked him by saying, 'Were I worthy of such a favour from my God, I would ask that He would grant to me this one miracle, that by His grace He would make of me a good man'. He wore a rough hair shirt and, whilst his health permitted it, lived on bread and water. As a stimulus to devotion he made a collection of short prayers, one or other of which he placed at the end of each psalm. Insertions of this kind may be found in many old manuscript psalters. He died at Bremen in the sixty-seventh year of his life and the thirty-fourth of his prelacy, and the whole North bewailed him. But although St Anskar was the first to preach the gospel in Sweden, it relapsed entirely into paganism after his death. The conversion of the country was due to St Sigfrid and other missionaries in the eleventh century.

ANTONY THE ABBOT (A.D. 356)

PATRON SAINT OF SKIN DISEASES; OF DOMESTIC ANIMALS AND PETS; OF BASKET MAKERS; AND OF ST ANTONY'S FIRE

17 JANUARY

The precise connection between Antony and skin diseases – in particular ergotism or 'St Antony's Fire' – is difficult to determine. He had a reputation as a healer in general, and for that reason was the object of much devotion in the Middle Ages. When all other remedies had failed, sufferers from St Antony's Fire would take themselves to the relics of the saint in the church of St Antony at La Motte. There grew up an order of Hospitallers of St Antony to look after the pilgrims to the shrine, and it may be one of the practices of the Order of Hospitallers which accounts for Antony also being the patron of domestic animals. Possibly to provide for the support of their hospitals, it seems the members of the Order owned pigs, which used to wander about freely except that they were identified by a bell hung around their necks. Even when animals were forbidden to roam at will, the Hospitallers' pigs, with their bells, were still permitted to do so, and the bells which identified them were sometimes given to the people as a kind of lucky charm to be attached to their own beasts. To combat the dangers of idleness, St Antony also took up the weaving of rush mats and baskets.

St Antony was born at a village south of Memphis in Upper Egypt in 251. His parents, who were Christians, kept him always at home, so that he grew up in ignorance of what was then regarded as polite literature, and could read no language but his own. At their death he found himself possessed of a considerable estate and charged with the care of a younger sister, before he was twenty years of age. Some six months afterwards he heard read in the church those words of Christ to the rich young man: 'Go, sell what thou hast, and give it to the poor, and thou shalt have treasure in Heaven'. Considering these words as addressed to himself, he went home and made over to his neighbours his best land, and the rest of his estate he sold and gave the price to the poor, except what he thought necessary for himself and his sister. Soon after, hearing in the church those other words of Christ, 'Be not solicitous for tomorrow', he also distributed in alms the moveables which he had reserved, and placed his sister in a house of maidens, which is commonly assumed to be the first recorded mention of a nunnery. Antony himself retired into solitude, in imitation of a certain old man who led the life of a hermit in the neighbourhood.

He soon became a model of humility, charity, prayerfulness and many more virtues. The saint's food was only bread, with a little salt, and he drank nothing but water; he never ate before sunset, and sometimes only once in three or four days. When he took his rest he lay on a rush mat or the bare floor. In quest of a more remote solitude he withdrew to an old burial-place, where a friend brought him bread from time to time. Satan was permitted to assault him in a visible manner, and to terrify him with gruesome noises; indeed, on one occasion he so grieviously beat him that he lay almost dead, and in this condition was found by his friend.

Hitherto Antony, ever since he turned his back on the world in 272, had lived in solitary places not very far from his village of Koman. About the year 285, however, at the age of thirty-five, he crossed the eastern branch of the Nile and took up his abode in some ruins on the top of a mountain, in which solitude he lived almost twenty years, rarely seeing any man except one who brought him bread every six months.

To satisfy the importunities of others, about the year 305, the fifty-fourth of his age, he came down from his mountain and founded his first monastery, in the Fayum. This originally consisted of scattered cells, but we cannot be sure that the various colonies of ascetics which he planted out in this way were all arranged upon the same plan. He did not stay permanently with any such community, but he visited them occasionally.

In the year 311, when the persecution was renewed under Maximinus, St Antony went to Alexandria in order to give courage to the martyrs. He publicly wore his white tunic of sheep-skin and appreared in the sight of the governor, yet took care never presumptuously to provoke the judges or impeach himself, as some rashly did. The persecution having abated, he returned to his monastery, and some time after organized another, called Pispir, near the Nile; but he chose for the most part to shut himself up in a cell upon a mountain difficult of access with Marcarius, a disciple whose duty it was to interview visitors. St Antony cultivated a little garden on his desert mountain, but this tillage was not the only manual labour in which he employed himself. St Athanasius speaks of his making mats and baskets as an ordinary occupation.

At the request of the bishops, about the year 355, he took a journey to Alexandria to confute the Arians, preaching that God the Son is not a creature, but of the same substance with the Father; and that the Arians, who called him a creature, did not differ from the heathen themselves, 'who worshipped and served the creature rather than the Creator'. All the people ran to see him, and rejoiced to hear him; even the pagans, struck with the dignity of his character, flocked around him. He converted many, and even worked miracles. St Athanasius conducted him back as far as the gates of the city, where he cured a girl possessed by an evil spirit.

St Jerome relates that at Alexandria Antony met the famous Didymus, the blind head of the catechetical school there, and exhorted him not to regret overmuch the loss of eyes, which were common even to insects, but to rejoice in the treasure of that inner light which the apostles enjoyed, by which we see God and kindle the fire of His love in our souls. Heathen philosophers and others often went to discuss with him, and returned astonished at his meekness and wisdom. About the year 337 Constantine the Great and his two sons, Constantius and Constans, wrote a letter to the saint, recommending themselves to his prayers. St Antony, seeing his monks surprised, said, 'Do not wonder that the emperor writes to us, a man even as I am; rather be astounded that God should have written to us, and that He has spoken to us by His Son'. He said he knew not how to answer it; but at last, through the importunity of his disciples, he penned a letter to the emperor and his sons, which St Athanasius has preserved, in which he exhorts them to constant remembrance of the judgement to come. St Jerome mentions seven other letters of St Antony to divers monasteries. A maxim which he frequently repeats is, that the knowledge of ourselves is the necessary and only step by which we can ascend to the knowledge and love of God.

St Antony made a visitation of his monks a little before his death, which he foretold, but no tears could move him to die among them. He gave orders that he should be buried in the earth beside his mountain cells by his two disciples, Macarius and Amathas. Hastening back to his solitude on Mount Kolzim near the Red Sea, he some time after fell ill; whereupon he repeated to these disciples his orders that they should bury his body secretly in that place. He ordered them to give one of his sheep-skins, with the cloak upon which he lay, to the bishop Athanasius, as a public testimony of his being united in faith and communion with that holy prelate; to give his other sheep-skin to the bishop Serapion; and to keep for themselves his sackcloth. 'Farewell, my children. Antony is departing, and will no longer be with you.' At these words they embraced him, and he, stretching out his feet without any other sign, calmly ceased to breathe. His death occurred in the year 356, probably on 17 January, on which day the most ancient martyrologies commemorate him. He was one hundred and five years old.

ANTONY CLARET, ARCHBISHOP OF SANTIAGO DE CUBA (A.D. 1870)

FOUNDER OF THE MISSIONARY SONS OF THE IMMACULATE HEART OF MARY
PATRON SAINT OF WEAVERS; AND OF SAVINGS BANKS

24 OCTOBER

There has been no formal acknowledgement of the many types of patronage which are attributed to St Antony Claret, but because he began life as a weaver, this particular role is readily explained. In February 1854, however, in order to help the poor of his diocese of Santiago, Antony set up a savings bank with branches in every one of the diocese's parishes. He has therefore come to be regarded as patron of savings and savings banks.

Born in 1807 at Sallent in the north of Spain, Antony practised his father's trade of cloth-weaving, and in his spare time learned Latin and printing. When he was twenty-two he entered the seminary at Vich, where he was ordained priest in 1835. After a few years he again began to entertain the idea of a Carthusian vocation, but as that seemed to be beyond his physical strength, he proceeded to Rome and eventually entered the Jesuit noviciate with the idea of consecrating his life to the foreign missions. Here, however, his health broke down, and he was advised by the Jesuit father general to return to Spain and busy himself with the evangelization of his countrymen. This course he adopted and for ten years he was engaged in giving missions and retreats throughout Catalonia; he was associated with Bd Joachima de Mas in the establishment of the Carmelites of Charity. His zeal inspired other priests to join in the same work, and in 1849 he was mainly instrumental in founding the congregation of Missionary Sons of the Immaculate

Heart of Mary. The institute, commonly known by his name as 'The Chare-tians', has spread and flourished, not only in Spain, but in the Americas and beyond.

Almost immediately after this great work had been inaugurated, Father Claret was appointed archbishop of Santiago de Cuba. The task was one of exceptional difficulty, in which his efforts to bring about much-needed reforms were resisted. Several attempts were made upon his life, and in one instance a serious wound was inflicted by an assassin infuriated by the loss of his mistress who had been won back to an honest life. In 1857 St Antony returned to Spain to become confessor to Queen Isabella II. He resigned his Cuban archbishopric, but avoided residence at the court for any longer than his official duties required, devoting himself to missionary work and the diffusion of good literature, especially in his native Catalan.

In the course of his life St Antony is said to have preached 10,000 sermons and to have published 200 books or pamphlets for the instruction and edification of clergy and people. While rector of the Escorial he established a science laboratory, a museum of natural history, schools of music and languages, and other foundations. His continual union with God was rewarded by many supernatural graces not only in the way of ecstasies and the gift of prophecy, but also by the miraculous cure of bodily diseases.

Political conditions in Spain and the queen's attitude towards the Holy See made St Antony's position very difficult, and in the revolution of 1868 he was exiled together with the queen. He then went to Rome, where he made his influence felt in promoting the definition of papal infallibility. An attempt was made to bring him back to Spain, but it failed; a fatal illness came upon him in France, and he went to his reward in the Cistercian monastery of Fontfroide, near Narbonne, on 24 October 1870. He was canonized in 1950.

ANTONY OF PADUA, DOCTOR OF THE CHURCH (A.D. 1231)

PATRON SAINT OF LOST ARTICLES; OF PORTUGAL; OF THE POOR; AND OF HARVESTS

13 JUNE

There seems to be no particular reason why Antony should be so well known as the saint to whom prayers are directed in order to find articles which are lost. His life, and the legends which have grown up around him, however, are so full of miraculous happenings that he became one of the most popular saints of the late medieval and early modern periods, and recourse was had to him in all manner of situations.

Despite the title by which he has become known, Antony was born in Lisbon and spent much of his early life in Portugal, where there remains considerable devotion to him. For that reason Pius XI, in an Apostolic Letter of 13 June 1934, declared him patron of Portugal alongside Francis Borgia.

Antony, like the early Franciscans in general, was renowned for his service of the poor. In his case, however, a special devotion developed in which loaves of bread – known as St Antony's bread – were baked to be distributed to the poor on his feast day. The saint is frequently portrayed carrying a sheaf of corn, and at least two miracles attributed to Antony may account for the traditional devotion to him as patron of harvests. On one occasion he miraculously preserved a field of grain from attack by a flock of birds, and on another a field miraculously produced abundant harvest after it had been trampled down by a crowd of people coming to listen to a sermon by the saint.

A Portuguese by nationality and a native of Lisbon, St Antony nevertheless derives his surname from the Italian city of Padua where he made his last home and where his relics are still venerated. He was born in 1195 and was baptized Ferdinand, a name which he was to change to that of Antony when he entered the Order of Friars Minor, out of devotion to the great patriarch of monks who was titular saint of the chapel in which he received the Franciscan habit.

His parents, young members of the Portuguese nobility, confided his early education to the clergy of the cathedral of Lisbon, but at the age of fifteen he joined the regular canons of St Augustine who were settled near the city. Two years later he obtained leave to be transferred to the priory at Coîmbra – then the capital of Portugal – in order to avoid the distractions caused by the numerous visits of friends. There he devoted himself to prayer and study, acquiring, with the help of an unusually retentive memory, an extraordinary knowledge of the Bible. He had been living at Coîmbra for eight years when Don Pedro of Portugal brought from Morocco in 1220 the relics of the Franciscans who had there lately suffered a glorious martyrdom. Ferdinand was profoundly moved, and conceived an ardent desire to lay down his life for Christ – an aspiration he had little prospect of realizing as a canon regular. To some Franciscans who came to his monastery of Holy Cross to beg, he laid open his heart, and eventually he was admitted to their order in 1221.

Within a very short time he was permitted to embark for Morocco with the intention of preaching the Gospel there. But he was prostrated by a severe illness which eventually necessitated his return to Europe. The vessel in which he sailed was driven off its course and he found himself at Messina in Sicily. He made his way to Assisi where, as he had learnt from his Sicilian brethren, a general chapter was about to be held. It was the great gathering of 1221 – the last chapter open to all members of the order – and was presided over by Brother Elias as vicar general, with St Francis seated at his feet. It cannot fail to have deeply impressed the young Portuguese friar. At the close the brethren returned to the posts allocated to them, and Antony was appointed to the lonely hermitage of San Paolo near Forli. It happened that an ordination was held at Forli, on which occasion the Dominican and Franciscan candidates were entertained at the Minorite convent there.

Through some misunderstanding none of the Dominicans had come prepared to deliver the customary address at the ceremony, and as no one among the Franciscans seemed capable of filling the breach St Antony, who was present, was told to come forward and speak whatever the Holy Spirit should put into his mouth. Very diffidently he obeyed; but once he had begun he delivered an address which amazed all who heard it by its eloquence, its fervour, and the learning it displayed. The minister provincial, informed of the talent possessed by the young friar he had brought from Assisi, promptly recalled him from his retreat and sent him to preach in various parts of Romagna, which then comprised the whole of Lombardy.

In addition to his commission as a preacher, he was appointed lector in theology to his brethen – the first member of his order to fill such a post. But it became more and more evident that his true mission lay in the pulpit. He had indeed all the qualifications – learning, eloquence, great power of persuasion, a burning zeal for souls and a sonorous voice which carried far. Though undersized and inclined to corpulence, he had an attractive, almost magnetic, personality. Sometimes the mere sight of him brought sinners to their knees: he appeared to radiate holiness. Wherever he went crowds flocked to hear him and hardened criminals, careless folk, and heretics alike were converted and brought to confession.

Shortly after the death of St Francis he was recalled to Italy, apparently to be minister provincial of Emilia or Romagna. He seems to have acted as envoy from the chapter general in 1226 to Pope Gregory IX, charged to lay before him for his decision the questions that had arisen. Antony on that occasion obtained from the pope his release from office that he might devote himself to preaching.

From that time St Antony resided at Padua – a city where he had previously laboured, in which he was greatly beloved, and where, more than anywhere else, he was privileged to see the great fruit which resulted from his ministry.

After preaching a course of sermons in the spring of 1231, St Antony's strength gave out and he retired with two other friars to a woodland retreat at Camposanpiero. It was soon clear that his days were numbered, and he asked to be taken back to Padua. He never reached the city, but only its outskirts. On 13 June 1231, in the apartment reserved for the chaplain of the Poor Clares of Arcella, he received the last rites and passed to his eternal reward. He was only thirty-six.

Within a year of his death Antony was canonized; on that occasion Pope Gregory IX intoned the anthem 'O doctor optime' in his honour, thus anticipating the year 1946 when Pope Pius XII declared him a doctor of the Church.

APOLLONIA, MARTYR (A.D. 249)

PATRON SAINT OF DENTISTS; AND OF SUFFERERS FROM TOOTHACHE

7 FEBRUARY

Because of the manner of her death, Apollonia is invoked as patron not only by dentists, but by all who are suffering from toothache. She is frequently depicted holding a pair of pincers which holds a tooth, or with a tooth suspended on a necklace.

St Dionysius of Alexandria wrote to Fabius, Bishop of Antioch, an account of the persecution of the Christians by the heathen populace of Alexandria in the last year of the reign of the Emperor Philip. The first victim of their rage was a venerable old man named Metras or Metrius, whom they tried to compel to utter blasphemies against God. When he refused, they beat him, thrust splinters of reeds into his eyes, and stoned him to death. The next person they seized was a Christian woman, called Quinta, whom they carried to one of their temples to force her to worship the idol. She addressed their false god with words of scorn which so exasperated the people that they dragged her by the heels over the cobbles, scourged and then stoned her. By this time the rioters were at the height of their fury. The Christians offered no resistance but betook themselves to flight, abandoning their goods without complaint because their hearts had no ties upon earth. Their constancy was so general that St Dionysius knew of none who had renounced Christ. Apollonia, an aged deaconess, was seized. With blows in the face they knocked out all her teeth, and then, kindling a great fire outside the city, they threatened to cast her into it unless she uttered certain impious words. She begged for a moment's delay, as if to consider the proposal; then, to convince her persecutors that her sacrifice was perfectly voluntary, she no sooner found herself free than she leaped into the flames of her own accord. They next wreaked their fury on a holy man named Serapion and tortured him in his own house, then they threw him headlong from the roof.

We meet with churches and altars dedicated in honour of St Apollonia in most parts of the Western church, but she is not venerated in any Oriental church, though she suffered in Alexandria. To account for her action in thus anticipating her death St Augustine supposes that she acted by a particular direction of the Holy Ghost, since it would not otherwise be lawful for anyone to hasten his own end.

BARBARA, VIRGIN AND MARTYR (FOURTH CENTURY)

PATRON SAINT OF GUNNERS AND ARTILLERY; OF ITALIAN MARINES, MILITARY
ENGINEERS AND FIREMEN; AND OF MINERS

4 DECEMBER (NO LONGER IN THE ROMAN CALENDAR)

*In his Letter of 4 December 1951 confirming St Barbara as the patron of Italian
marines, military engineers and firemen, Pope Pius XII commented that she had been
regarded as the patron of gunners at least from the early years of the sixteenth
century. This tradition seems to stem from the story of her father being struck down
by fire descending from heaven; but it was the suddenness of this event that caused
Barbara to be invoked in the Middle Ages against disasters and calamities, and
particularly against sudden disasters in mining.*

'In the time that Maximian reigned there was a rich man, a paynim, which
adored and worshipped idols, which man was named Dioscorus. This
Dioscorus had a young daughter which was named Barbara, for whom he
did make a high and strong tower in which he did keep and close this
Barbara to the end that no man should see her because of her great beauty.
Then came many princes unto the same Dioscorus for to treat with him for
the marriage of his daughter, which went anon unto her and said: "My
daughter, certain princes be come to me which require me for to have thee in
marriage, wherefore tell to me thine intent and what will ye have to do."
Then St Barbara returned all angry towards her father and said: "My father, I
pray you that ye will not constrain me to marry, for thereto I have no will nor
thought." . . . After this he departed thence and went into a far country
where he long sojourned.
    'The St Barbara, the handmaid of our Lord Jesu Christ, descended from
the tower for to come to see [a bath-house which her father was having built]
and anon she perceived that there were but two windows only, that one
against the south, and that other against the north, whereof she was much
abashed and amarvelled, and demanded of the workmen why they had not
made no more windows, and they answered that her father had so commanded and ordained. Then St Barbara said to them: "Make me here
another window." . . . In this same bath-house was this holy maid baptized
of a holy man, and lived there a cerain space of time, taking only for her
refection honeysuckles and locusts, following the holy precursor of our
Lord, St John Baptist. This bath-house is like to the fountain of Siloe, in
which he that was born blind recovered there his sight. . . . On a time this
blessed maid went upon the tower and there she beheld the idols to which
her father sacrificed and worshipped, and suddenly she received the Holy
Ghost and became marvellously subtle and clear in the love of Jesu Christ,
for she was environed with the grace of God Almighty, of sovereign glory
and pure chastity. This holy maid Barbara, adorned with faith, surmounted

63

the Devil, for when she beheld the idols she scratched them in their visages, despising them all and saying: "All they be made like unto you which have made you to err, and all them that have faith in you"; and then she went into the tower and worshipped our Lord.

'And when the work was full performed her father returned from his voyage, and when he saw there three windows he demanded of the workmen: "Wherefore have ye made three windows?" And they answered: "Your daughter hath commanded so." Then he made his daughter to come afore him and demanded her why she had to make three windows, and she answered to him and said: "I have done them to be made because three windows lighten all the world and all creatures, but two make darkness." Then her father took her and went down into the bath-house, demanding her how three windows give more light than two. And St Barbara answered: "These three windows betoken clearly the Father, the Son and the Holy Ghost, the which be three persons and one very God, on whom we ought to believe and worship." Then he, being replenished with fury, incontinent drew his sword to have slain her, but the holy virgin made her prayer and then marvellously she was taken in a stone and borne into a mountain on which two shepherds kept their sheep, the which saw her fly. . . . And then her father took her by the hair and drew her down from the mountain and shut her fast in prison. . . . Then sat the judge in judgement, and when he saw the great beauty of Barbara he said to her: "Now choose whether ye will spare yourself and offer to the gods, or else die by cruel torments." St Barbara answered to him: "I offer myself to my god, Jesu Christ, the which hath created Heaven and earth and all other things. . . ."'

When she had been beaten, and comforted by a vision of our Lord in her prison, and again scourged and tortured, 'the judge commanded to slay her with the sword. And then her father, all enraged, took her out of the hands of the judge and led her up on a mountain, and St Barbara rejoiced in hastening to receive the salary of her victory. And then when she was drawn thither she made her orison, saying: "Lord Jesu Christ, which hast formed Heaven and earth, I beseech thee to grant me thy grace and hear my prayer for all they that have memory of thy name and thy passion; I pray thee, that thou wilt not remember their sins, for thou knowest our fragility." Then came there a voice down from Heaven saying unto her: "Come, my spouse Barbara, and rest in the chamber of God my Father which is in Heaven, and I grant to thee that thou hast required of me." And when this was said, she came to her father and received the end of her martyrdom, with St Juliana. But when her father descended from the mountain, a fire from Heaven descended on him, and consumed him in such wise that there could not be found only ashes of all his body. This blessed virgin, St Barbara, received martyrdom with St Juliana the second nones of December. A noble man called Valentine buried the bodies of these two martyrs, and laid them in a little town in which many miracles were showed in praise and glory of God Almighty.'

So is told in Caxton's version of the *Golden Legend* the story of one of the most popular saints of the Middle Ages. There is, however, considerable doubt of the existence of a virgin martyr called Barbara and it is quite certain that her legend is spurious. There is no mention of her in the earlier martyrologies, her legend is not older than the seventh century, and her *cultus* did not spread till the ninth. Various verions differ both as to the time and place of her martyrdom: it is located in Tuscany, Rome, Antioch, Heliopolis and Nicomedia.

BARNABAS, APOSTLE (*c*. A.D. 61?)

PATRON SAINT OF CYPRUS

11 JUNE

Barnabas came from Cyprus; and in The Acts of the Apostles he is last heard of there. Thus he makes a natural patron of Cyprus, as the Sacred Congregation of Rites has recognized.

Although St Barnabas was not one of the twelve chosen by our Lord, yet he is styled an apostle by the early fathers and by St Luke himself on account of the special commission he received from the Holy Ghost and the great part he took in apostolic work. He was a Jew of the tribe of Levi, but was born in Cyprus; his name was originally Joseph, but the apostles changed it to Barnabas – which word St Luke interprets as meaning 'man of encouragement'. The first mention we find of him in the Holy Scriptures is in the fourth chapter of the Acts of the Apostles, where it is stated that the first converts at Jerusalem lived in common and that as many as were owners of lands or houses sold them and laid the proceeds at the feet of the apostles for distribution. St Barnabas's sale of his estate is singled out for mention on this occasion. When St Paul came to Jerusalem three years after his conversion the faithful were suspicious of the genuineness of this conversion, and avoided him. Barnabas it was who then 'took him by the hand' and vouched for him among the other apostles.

Some time later, certain disciples having preached the Gospel with success at Antioch, it was thought desirable that someone should be sent by the Church in Jerusalem to guide and confirm the neophytes. The man selected was St Barnabas – 'a good man, full of the Holy Ghost and of faith,' as we read in the Acts of the Apostles. Upon his arrival he rejoiced exceedingly at the progress the Gospel had made and by his preaching added greatly to the number of converts. Finding himself in need of an able assistant he went to Tarsus to enlist the co-operation of St Paul, who accompanied him back and spent a whole year at Antioch. Their labours were crowned with success, and it was in that same city and at this period

65

that the name 'Christians' was first given to the followers of our Lord.

A little later the flourishing church of Antioch raised money for the relief of the poor brethren in Judaea during a famine. This they sent to the heads of the church of Jerusalem by the hands of Paul and Barnabas, who returned accompanied by John Mark. Antioch was by this time well supplied with teachers and prophets, amongst whom were Simeon called Niger, Lucius of Cyrene, and Herod's foster-brother Manahen. As they were worshipping God, the Holy Ghost said to them by some of these prophets, 'Separate me Paul and Barnabas for the work whereunto I have taken them'. Accordingly, after all had fasted and prayed, Paul and Barnabas received their commission by the laying on of hands and set forth on their first missionary journey. Taking with them John Mark, they went first to Seleucia and then to Salamis in Cyprus. After they had preached Christ there in the synagogues they proceeded to Paphos, where they converted Sergius Paulus, the Roman proconsul. Embarking again at Paphos, they sailed to Perga in Pamphylia. At this stage John Mark left them to return by himself to Jerusalem. Paul and Barnabas then travelled north of Antioch in Pisidia; they addressed themselves first to the Jews, but finding them bitterly hostile they now openly declared that henceforth they would preach the Gospel to the Gentiles.

At Iconium, the capital of Lycaonia, they narrowly escaped stoning at the hands of the mob whom the rulers had stirred up against them. A miraculous cure wrought by St Paul upon a cripple at Lystra led the pagan inhabitants to conclude that the gods were come amongst them. They hailed St Paul as Hermes or Mercury because he was the chief speaker, and St Barnabas as Zeus or Jupiter and were with difficulty restrained from offering sacrifices to them. But, with the proverbial fickleness of the mob, they soon rushed to the other extreme and stoned St Paul, severely wounding him. After a stay at Derbe, where they made many converts, the two apostles retraced their steps, passing through the cities they had previously visited in order to confirm the converts and to ordain presbyters. Their first missionary journey thus completed, they returned to Antioch in Syria.

Shortly afterwards a dispute arose in the church of Antioch with regard to the observance of Jewish rites, some maintaining in opposition to the opinion of St Paul and St Barnabas that pagans entering the Church must be circumcized as well as baptized. This led to the calling of a council at Jerusalem, and in the presence of this assembly St Paul and St Barnabas gave a full account of their labours among the Gentiles and received approbation of their mission. The council, moreover, emphatically declared that Gentile converts were exempt from the obligation to be circumcized. Nevertheless, there continued to be such a marked division between Jewish and Gentile converts that St Peter, when on a visit to Antioch, refrained from eating with the Gentiles out of deference for the susceptibilities of the Jews – an example which St Barnabas followed. St Paul upbraided them both, and his expostulations carried the day. Another difference, however, arose between him and St Barnabas on the eve of their departure on a visitation to the churches they had founded, for St Barnabas wished to take John Mark, and St Paul demurred in view of the young man's previous defection. The contention between them became so sharp that they separated, St Paul proceeding on his projected tour with Silas, whilst St Barnabas sailed to Cyprus with John Mark. Here the Acts leave him without further mention. It seems clear, from the allusion to Barnabas in I Corinthians ix, 5 and 6 that he was living and working in A.D. 56 or 57, but St Paul's subsequent invitation to John Mark to join him when he was a prisoner in Rome leads us to infer that by A.D. 60 or 61 St Barnabas must have been dead: he is said to have been stoned to death at Salamis.

BASIL THE GREAT, DOCTOR OF THE CHURCH (A.D. 379)

PATRIARCH OF EASTERN MONKS
A PATRON SAINT OF RUSSIA

2 JANUARY

As patriarch of Eastern monks, Basil has always enjoyed great fame in Russia, and was one of the special protectors of Russia, mentioned by Pius XI in his letter of 2 February 1930 alongside St Joseph, Husband of Our Lady.

St Basil was born at Caesarea, the capital of Cappadocia in Asia Minor, in the year 329. One of a family of ten, which included St Gregory of Nyssa, St Macrina the Younger, and St Peter of Sebaste, he was descended on both sides from Christians who had suffered persecution. His father, St Basil the Elder, and his mother, St Emmelia, were possessed of considerable landed property, and Basil's early years were spent at the country house of his grandmother, St Macrina, whose example and teaching he never forgot. He studied at Constantinople and completed his education at Athens. He had there as fellow students St Gregory of Nazianzus who became his inseparable friend, and Julian, the future emperor and apostate. The two young Cappadocians associated with the most serious-minded of their contemporaries and, according to St Gregory, knew only two streets, those leading to the church and to the schools. As soon as Basil had learnt all that his masters could teach him, he returned to Caesarea. For some years he taught rhetoric in the city, but on the very threshold of a brilliant career he was led to abandon the world through the influence of his eldest sister, Macrina, who, after helping to educate and settle her sisters and youngest brother, had retired with her widowed mother and other women to live a community life on one of the family estates at Annesi on the river Iris.

About the same time Basil appears to have been baptized; and determined from thenceforth to serve God in evangelical poverty, he visited the principal monasteries of Egypt, Palestine, Syria and Mesopotamia to study the religious life. Upon his return he withdrew to a wild and beautiful spot in Pontus, separated by the river Iris from Annesi, and devoted himself to prayer and study. With the disciples who soon gathered round him, including his brother Peter, he formed the first monastery in Asia Minor and for them he organized the life and enunciated the principles which have continued through the centuries down to the present day to regulate the lives of monks of the Eastern church. Basil lived the life of a monk in the strict sense for only five years; but in the history of Christian monachism he ranks in importance with St Benedict himself.

At this time the Arian heresy was at its height, and heretical emperors were persecuting the orthodox. In 363 Basil was persuaded to be ordained deacon and priest at Caesarea; but the archbishop, Eusebius, became jealous of his influence, and the saint quietly retired again to Pontus to aid in the foundation and direction of new monasteries. Caesarea, however, could not spare him for long. In 365, St Gregory of Nazianzus, on behalf of the orthodox, fetched Basil from his retreat to assist them in the defence of their faith, their clergy, and their churches. A reconciliation was effected between him and Eusebius, Basil remained on in Caesarea to become the bishop's right hand and actually to rule the church, whilst tactfully giving credit to Eusebius for all that he was really doing himself. During a season of drought followed by famine he not only distributed his maternal inheritance in charity, but he also organized a great system of relief with a soup kitchen in which he could be seen, girt with an apron, dealing out food to the hungry. Eusebius died in 370, and Basil, in spite of considerable opposition, was elected to fill the vacant see on June 14 – to the great joy of St Athanasius and the equally great mortification of the Arian emperor, Valens. It was indeed an important post and in Basil's case a difficult one, because as bishop of Caesarea he was exarch of Pontus and metropolitan over fifty suffragans, many of whom had opposed his election and continued to be hostile until by patience and charity he was able to win their confidence and support.

Within twelve months of Basil's accession, the Emperor Valens was in Caesarea, after having conducted in Bithynia and Galatia a ruthless campaign of persecution. He had sent on in advance the prefect Modestus, to induce Basil to submit or at any rate to agree to some compromise. Neither to Modestus, however, nor to the emperor would the holy bishop yield, either to keep silence about Arianism or to admit Arians to communion. Promises and threats were equally useless. 'Nothing short of violence can avail against such a man', was the report of Modestus to his master, and violence Valens was unwilling – perhaps afraid – to attempt. He decided in favour of banishment, but thrice in succession the reed pen with which he was signing the edict split in his hand. A weak man himself, he was overawed and moved to reluctant admiration by Basil's determination, and eventually took his departure, never again to interfere with the ecclesiastical affairs of

Caesarea. This contest ended, the saint soon found himself involved in another struggle, owing to the division of Cappadocia into two civil provinces and the consequent claim of Anthimus, Bishop of Tyana, to be metropolitan of New Cappadocia. The dispute was an unfortunate one for Basil, not so much because he was obliged to yield to the division of his archdiocese, as because it led to an estrangement from St Gregory of Nazianzus, whom he insisted on consecrating to the bishopric of Sasima, a miserable town on debatable ground between the two Cappadocias.

Whilst he was thus engaged in defending the church of Caesarea against attacks upon its faith and jurisdiction, St Basil was no less zealously fulfilling his strictly pastoral duties. Even on working days he preached morning and evening to congregations so vast that he himself compared them to the sea. His people were in the habit of making their communion every Sunday, Wednesday, Friday and Saturday. Amongst other practices which he had observed on his travels and had introduced among his flock, was that of assembling in church before sunrise to sing psalms. For the benefit of the sick poor he organized outside the gate of Caesarea a hospital which St Gregory of Nazianzus described as almost a new city and worthy to be reckoned one of the wonders of the world. It came to be called the Basiliad and continued to be famous long after its founder's death. Away from his own episcopal residence, in spite of chronic ill-health, he made frequent visitations into mountainous districts, and by his vigilant supervision of his clergy and his insistence on the ordination of none but suitable candidates he made of his archdiocese a model of ecclesiastical order and discipline.

He was less successful in his efforts on behalf of the Church outside his own province. Left by the death of St Athanasius the champion of orthodoxy in the East, he strove persistently to rally and unite his fellow Catholics who, crushed by Arian tyranny and rent by schisms and dissensions amongst themselves, seemed threatened with extinction. His advances, however, were ill-received and he found himself misunderstood, misrepresented, and accused of ambition and of heresy. Even appeals which he and his friends made to Pope St Damasus and the Western bishops to intervene in the affairs of the East and to heal the troubles met with little response – apparently because aspersions upon their good faith had been made in Rome itself. 'For my sins I seem to be unsuccessful in everything!' wrote St Basil in a mood of deep discouragement.

Nevertheless, relief was at hand, and that from an unexpected quarter. On 9 August 378, the Emperor Valens was mortally wounded at the battle of Adrianople, and with the accession of his nephew, Gratian, came the end of the Arian ascendancy in the East. When the news reached St Basil he was on his death-bed, but it brought him consolation in his last moments. He died on 1 January 379, at the age of forty-nine, worn out by his austerities, his hard work, and a painful disease. The whole of Caesarea mourned him as a father and protector – pagans, Jews, and strangers joining in the general lamentation. Seventy-two years after his death the Council of Chalcedon described him as 'The great Basil, the minister of grace who has expounded the truth to the whole earth'. He was undoubtedly one of the most eloquent orators the Church has ever produced and his writings have entitled him to a high place amongst her doctors.

BASILIDES, (c. A.D. 202)

PATRON SAINT OF PRISON OFFICERS (ITALIAN)

28 JUNE

The connection between Basilides and prison guards is an obvious one, though why a decree of the Sacred Congregation of Rites of 2 September 1948 should have appointed him to be the patron specifically of Italian prison officers is not clear, unless there was a confusion between this Alexandrian Basilides and a Roman martyr of the same name. The latter was sometimes said to be, but again for no very clear reason, a patron of children. He was buried at the twelfth milestone of the Via Aurelia, and his feast day is 12 June; but nothing certain is known about this second Basilides.

The catechetical school of Origen at Alexandria was a training ground in virtue: for the master, not content with lecturing on the sciences, made a great point of inculcating upon his pupils the loftiest principles of Christian perfection. The school furnished some illustrious martyrs in the persecution of Severus which raged with great fury from 202 – the year before Origen was appointed catechist – until the death of the emperor in 211.

The first to suffer was St Plutarch, brother of St Heraclas, afterwards bishop of Alexandria. The two brothers had been converted to the faith together, through listening to the lectures of Origen. Women as well as men attended the catechetical school, and three of them suffered martyrdom. Herais, a maiden who was still a catechumen, was baptized by fire – to quote Origen's own words.

The other two, Marcella and Potamiaena, were mother and daughter. Attempts were made to induce Potamiaena to purchase her freedom at the expense of her chastity, for she was young, accomplished and beautiful, but she rejected the proposals with scorn. She was then condemned to be stripped and cast into a cauldron of boiling pitch. Upon hearing her sentence, she said to the judge, 'I beg of you, by the life of the emperor whom you honour, not to oblige me to appear unclothed; rather suffer me to be slowly lowered into the cauldron fully dressed, that you may see the patience which Jesus Christ, whom you know not, bestows upon those who trust Him.' The magistrate granted her request and charged Basilides, one of the guards, to lead her to execution. The man treated her with respect, protecting her from the insults and pressure of the crowd. She thanked him for his courtesy and told him that after her death she would obtain his salvation from God. The cruel sentence was then carried out. Her mother suffered at the same time.

Shortly afterwards Basilides surprised his fellow soldiers by refusing to take an oath when called upon to do so: he was a Christian, he said, and could not swear by false gods. At first they thought he was joking, but when he persisted they took him to the prefect, who consigned him to prison. In reply to the inquiries of Christians who came to visit him in gaol, he told them that Potamiaena had appeared to him after her martyrdom and had placed on his head a crown which she said she had won for him by her prayers. He received baptism in prison and, having made a glorious confession of faith before the magistrate, was beheaded.

BASILISSA, MARTYR (c. A.D. 296?)

PATRON SAINT OF NURSING MOTHERS; AND OF SUFFERERS FROM CHILBLAINS

3 SEPTEMBER

Basilissa was invoked by women who found it difficult to breast-feed their babies, but nothing in her legends suggests why this should be – nor why she should also be invoked by people suffering from chilblains.

That as late as the fourteenth century the cult of St Basilissa was flourishing at Constantinople is in no doubt. Otherwise there is little else certain about her, for the records of her life are late and unreliable. According to these she was a girl of only nine years of age who, for her faith, was stripped naked and beaten, and then thrown to two lions who tore her to pieces.

BENEDICT, ABBOT, PATRIARCH OF WESTERN MONKS (c. A.D. 547)

PATRON SAINT OF EUROPE; OF THE ITALIAN KNIGHTS OF LABOUR; OF FARM WORKERS AND ITALIAN FARMERS; OF ITALIAN SPELEOLOGISTS (OR POTHOLERS AND SPELUNKERS), ENGINEERS AND ARCHITECTS; OF POISON; AND OF THE DYING.

11 JULY

Pope Paul VI proclaimed St Benedict patron of Europe not so much for the saint's own life, but because of that of the monks who followed his Rule. With book, plough and the cross, said the Pope, they had brought a spiritual unity from the Mediterranean to Scandinavia, from Ireland to Poland. The Apostolic Letter declaring this was issued on 24 October 1964 to commemorate the reconsecration of Monte Cassino after the abbey had been destroyed in the Second World War.

Pope John XXIII had appointed Benedict the patron saint of the Italian Knights of Labour on 21 March 1962 because the saint had wanted monastic life to contain both

prayer and work. The monks who drew their inspiration from Benedict were respon-
sible, as farm workers, for the cultivation of waste land – not only in Italy after the
barbarian invasions, but also, for example, in some of the less hospitable areas of
England. It was because the Benedictines had thus restored cultivation to Italy that
Pope John XXIII, in an Apostolic Letter of 12 July 1961, had proclaimed Benedict the
patron saint of farm workers in general and of Italian farmers, and a number of their
associations, in particular.

Pius XII had declared St Benedict patron of Italian speleologists, or potholers and
spelunkers, in an Apostolic Letter of 20 July 1954. He was chosen because, as the Pope
pointed out, he spent three years at Subiaco living in a 'high and almost impenetrable
cave'. On the other hand it was because of his role in having buildings constructed
that St Benedict was declared patron of both Italian engineers and architects by an
Apostolic Letter of Pope Pius XII dated 19 November 1957.

There is a story that an attempt was made on Benedict's life with a poisoned drink
but, after blessing the drink, Benedict consumed it without incurring harm.

The invocation of Benedict by those who are dying is traditional, although nothing
in his life appears to provide a specific reason for this devotion beyond the fact that he is
said to have been forewarned of his own death, and died at prayer, in the chapel of his
monastery.

The little we know about Benedict's earlier life comes from the *Dialogues* of St
Gregory, who does not furnish a connected history, but merely a series of
sketches to illustrate the miraculous incidents in his career.

Benedict was of good birth, and was born and brought up at the ancient
Sabine town of Nursia (Norcia). Of his twin sister Scholastica, we read that
from her infancy she had vowed herself to God, but we do not hear of her
again until towards the close of her brother's life. He was sent to Rome for
his 'liberal education', being accompanied by a 'nurse', probably to act as
housekeeper. He was then in his early teens, or perhaps a little more.
Overrun by pagan and Arian tribes, the civilized world seemed during the
closing years of the fifth century to be rapidly lapsing into barbarism: the
Church was rent by schisms, town and country were desolated by war and
pillage, shameful sins were rampant amongst Christians as well as
heathens, and it was noted that there was not a sovereign or a ruler who was
not an atheist, a pagan or a heretic. The youths in schools and colleges
imitated the vices of their elders, and Benedict, revolted by the licentious-
ness of his companions, yet fearing lest he might become contaminated by
their example, made up his mind to leave Rome. He made his escape
without telling anyone of his plans excepting his nurse, who accompanied
him. There has been considerable difference of opinion as to his age when he
left the paternal roof, but he may have been nearly twenty. They made their
way to the village of Enfide in the mountains thirty miles from Rome. What
was the length of his stay we do not know, but it was sufficient to enable him
to determine his next step. Absence from the temptations of Rome, he soon

realized, was not enough; God was calling him to be a solitary and to abandon the world, and the youth could no more live a hidden life in a village than in the city – especially after he had miraculously mended an earthenware sieve which his nurse had borrowed and had accidentally broken.

In search of complete solitude Benedict started forth once more, alone, and climbed further among the hills until he reached a place now known as Subiaco (Sublacum, from the artificial lake formed in the days of Claudius by the banking up of the waters of the Anio). In this wild and rocky country he came upon a monk called Romanus, to whom he opened his heart, explaining his intention of leading the life of a hermit. Romanus himself lived in a monastery at no great distance, but he eagerly assisted the young man, clothing him with a sheepskin habit and leading him to a cave in the mountain. It was roofed by a high rock over which there was no descent, and the ascent from below was rendered perilous by precipices as well as by thick woods and undergrowth. In this desolate cavern Benedict spent the next three years of his life, unknown to all except Romanus, who kept his secret and daily brought bread for the younger recluse, who drew it up in a basket let down by a rope over the rock. Gregory reports that the first outsider to find his way to the cave was a priest who, when preparing a dinner for himself on Easter Sunday, heard a voice which said to him, 'You are preparing yourself a savoury dish whilst my servant Benedict is afflicted with hunger'. The priest immediately set out in quest of the hermit, whom he found with great difficulty. After they had discoursed for some time on God and heavenly things the priest invited him to eat, saying that it was Easter day, on which it was not reasonable to fast. Benedict, who doubtless had lost all sense of time and certainly had no means of calculating lunar cycles, replied that he did not know it was the day of so great a solemnity. They ate their meal together, and the priest went home. Shortly afterwards the saint was discovered by some shepherds, who took him at first for a wild animal because he was clothed in the skin of beasts and because they did not think any human being could live among the rocks. When they discovered that he was a servant of God they were greatly impressed, and derived much good from his discourses. From that time he began to be known and many people visited him, bringing such sustenance as he would accept and receiving from him instruction and advice.

Although he lived thus sequestered from the world, St Benedict, like the fathers in the desert, had to meet the temptations of the flesh and of the Devil, one of which has been described by St Gregory. 'On a certain day when he was alone the tempter presented himself. For a small dark bird, commonly called a blackbird, began to fly round his face, and came so near to him that, if he had wished, he could have seized it with his hand. But on his making the sign of the cross, the bird flew away. Then such a violent temptation of the flesh followed as he had never before experienced. The

evil spirit brought before his imagination a certain woman whom he had
formerly seen, and inflamed his heart with such vehement desire at the
memory of her that he had very great difficulty in repressing it; and being
almost overcome he thought of leaving his solitude. Suddenly, however,
helped by divine grace, he found the strength he needed, and seeing close
by a thick growth of briars and nettles, he stripped off his garment and cast
himsel into the midst of them. There he rolled until his whole body was
lacerated. Thus, through those bodily wounds he cured the wound of his
soul', and was never again troubled in the same way.

Between Tivoli and Subiaco, at Vicovaro, on the summit of a cliff overlooking the Anio, there resided at that time a community of monks who, having
lost their abbot by death, resolved to ask St Benedict to take his place. He at
first refused, assuring the community, who had come to him in a body, that
their ways and his would not agree – perhaps he knew of them by reputation. Their importunity, however, induced him to consent, and he returned
with them to take up the government. It soon became evident that his strict
notions of monastic discipline did not suit them, for all that they lived in
rock-hewn cells; and in order to get rid of him they went so far as to mingle
poison in his wine. When as was his wont he made the sign of the cross over
the jug, it broke in pieces as if a stone had fallen upon it. 'God forgive you,
brothers', the abbot said without anger. 'Why have you plotted this wicked
thing against me? Did I not tell you that my customs would not accord with
yours? Go and find an abbot to your taste, for after this deed you can no
longer keep me among you.' With these words he returned to Subiaco – no
longer, however, to live a life of seclusion, but to begin the great work for
which God had been preparing him during those three hidden years.

Disciples began to gather about him, attracted by his sanctity and by his
miraculous powers, seculars fleeing from the world as well as solitaries who
lived dispersed among the mountains; and St Benedict found himself in a
position to initiate that great scheme, evolved perhaps or revealed to him in
the silent cave, of 'gathering together in this place as in one fold of the Lord
many and different families of holy monks, dispersed in various monasteries and regions, in order to make of them one flock after His own heart, to
strengthen them more, and bind them together by fraternal bonds in one
house of the Lord under one regular observance, and in the permanent
worship of the name of God'. He therefore settled all who would obey him in
twelve wood-built monasteries of twelve monks, each with its prior. He
himself exercised the supreme direction over all from where he lived with
certain chosen monks whom he wished to train with special care. So far they
had no written rule of their own: but according to a very ancient document
'the monks of the twelve monasteries were taught the religious life, not by
following any written rule, but only by following the example of St Benedict's deeds'. Romans and barbarians, rich and poor, placed themselves at
the disposal of the saint, who made no distinction of rank or nation, and

after a time parents came to entrust him with their sons to be educated and trained for the monastic life.

St Gregory tells of a rough untutored Goth who came to St Benedict and was received with joy and clothed in the monastic habit. Sent with a hedge-hook to clear the thick undergrowth from ground overlooking the lake, he worked so vigorously that the head flew off the haft and disappeared into the lake. The poor man was overwhelmed with distress, but as soon as St Benedict heard of the accident he led the culprit to the water's edge, and taking the haft from him, threw it into the lake. Immediately from the bottom rose up the iron head, which proceeded to fasten itself automatically to the haft, and the abbot returned the tool saying, 'There! Go on with your work and don't be miserable'. It was not the least of St Benedict's miracles that he broke down the deeply-rooted prejudice against manual work as being degrading and servile: he believed that labour was not only dignified but conducive to holiness, and therefore he made it compulsory for all who joined his community – nobles and plebeians alike.

We do not know how long the saint remained at Subiaco, but he stayed long enough to establish his monasteries on a firm and permanent basis. His departure was sudden and seems to have been unpremeditated. There lived in the neighbourhood an unworthy priest called Florentius, who, seeing the success which attended St Benedict and the great concourse of people who flocked to him, was moved to envy and tried to ruin him. Having failed in all attempts to take away his character by slander, and his life by sending him a poisoned loaf (which St Gregory says was removed miraculously by a raven), he tried to seduce his monks by introducing women of evil life. The abbot, who fully realized that the wicked schemes of Florentius were aimed at him personally, resolved to leave Subiaco, lest the souls of his spiritual children should continue to be assailed and endangered. Having set all things in order, he withdrew from Subiaco to the territory of Monte Cassino. It is a solitary elevation on the boundaries of Campania, commanding on three sides narrow valleys running up towards the mountains, and on the fourth, as far as the Mediterranean, an undulating plain which had once been rich and fertile but having fallen out of cultivation owing to repeated irruptions of the barbarians, it had become marshy and malarial. The town of Casinum, once an important place, had been destroyed by the Goths, and the remnant of its inhabitants had relapsed into – or perhaps had never lost – their paganism. They were wont to offer sacrifice in a temple dedicated to Apollo, which stood on the crest of Monte Cassino, and the saint made it his first work after a forty days' fast to preach to the people and to bring them to Christ. His teaching and miracles made many converts, with whose help he proceeded to overthrow the temple, its idol and its sacred grove. Upon the site of the temple he built two chapels, and round about these sanctuaries there rose little by little the great pile which was destined to become the most famous abbey the world has even known, the foundation of which is likely to have been laid by St Benedict in the year 530 or thereabouts. It was from here that went forth the influence that was to play so great a part in the christianization and civilization of post-Roman Europe: it was no mere ecclesiastical museum that was destroyed during the second World War.

It is probable that Benedict, who was now in middle age, again spent some time as a hermit; but disciples soon flocked to Monte Cassino too. Profiting no doubt by the experience gained at Subiaco, he no longer placed them in separate houses but gathered them together in one establishment, ruled over by a prior and deans under his general supervision. It almost immediately became necessary to add guest-chambers, for Monte Cassino, unlike Subiaco, was easily accessible from Rome and Capua. Not only laymen but dignitaries of the Church came to confer with the holy founder, whose reputation for sanctity, wisdom and miracles became widespread. It is almost certainly at this period that he composed his Rule, of which St Gregory says that in it may be understood 'all his manner of life and discipline, for the holy man could not possibly teach otherwise than he lived'. Though it was primarily intended for the monks at Monte Cassino, yet, as Abbot Chapman has pointed out, there is something in favour of the view that it was written at the desire of Pope St Hormisdas for all monks of the West. It is addressed to all those who, renouncing their own will, take upon them 'the strong and bright armour of obedience to fight under the Lord Christ, our true king', and it prescribes a life of liturgical prayer, study ('sacred reading') and work, lived socially in a community under one common father. Then and for long afterwards a monk was but rarely in holy orders, and there is no evidence that St Benedict himself was ever a priest. He sought to provide 'a school for the Lord's service', intended for beginners, and the asceticism of the rule is notably moderate. Self-chosen and abnormal austerities were not encouraged, and when a hermit, occupying a cave near Monte Cassino, chained his foot to the rock, Benedict sent him a message, saying, 'If you are truly a servant of God, chain not yourself with a chain of iron but with the chain of Christ'. The great vision, when Benedict saw as in one sunbeam the whole world in the light of God, sums up the inspiration of his life and rule.

The holy abbot, far from confining his ministrations to those who would follow his rule, extended his solicitude to the population of the surrounding country: he cured their sick, relieved the distressed, distributed alms and food to the poor, and is said to have raised the dead on more than one occasion. While Campania was suffering from a severe famine he gave away all the provisions in the abbey, with the exception of five loaves. 'You have not enough to-day,' he said to his monks, marking their dismay, 'but to-morrow you will have too much.' The following morning two hundred bushels of flour were laid by an unknown hand at the monastery gate. Other instances have been handed down in illustration of St Benedict's prophetic powers, to which was added ability to read men's thoughts. A nobleman he had converted once found him in tears and inquired the cause of his grief. The abbot replied, 'This monastery which I have built and all that I have prepared for my brethren has been delivered up to the heathen by a sentence of the Almighty. Scarcely have I been able to obtain mercy for their lives.' The prophecy was verified some forty years later, when the abbey of Monte Cassino was destroyed by the Lombards.

When Totila the Goth was making a triumphal progress through central Italy, he conceived a wish to visit St Benedict, of whom he had heard much. He therefore sent word of his coming to the abbot, who replied that he would see him. To discover whether the saint really possessed the powers attributed to him, Totila ordered Riggo, the captain of his guard, to don his own purple robes, and sent him, with the three counts who usually attended the king, to Monte Cassino. The impersonation did not deceive St Benedict, who greeted Riggo with the words, 'My son, take off what you are wearing; it is not yours'. His visitor withdrew in haste to tell his master that he had been detected. Then Totila came himself to the man of God and, we are told, was so much awed that he fell prostrate. But Benedict, raising him from the ground, rebuked him for his evil deeds, and foretold in a few words all that should befall him. Thereupon the king craved his prayers and departed, but from that time he was less cruel. This interview took place in 542, and St Benedict can hardly have lived long enough to see the complete fulfilment of his own prophecy.

The great saint who had foretold so many other things was also forewarned of his own approaching death. He notified it to his disciples and six days before the end bade them dig his grave. As soon as this had been done he was stricken with fever, and on the last day he received the Body and Blood of the Lord. Then, while the loving hands of the brethren were supporting his weak limbs, he uttered a few final words of prayer and died – standing on his feet in the chapel, with his hands uplifted towards heaven. He was buried beside St Scholastica his sister, on the site of the altar of Apollo which he had cast down.

BERNARD, ABBOT OF CLAIRVAUX, DOCTOR OF THE CHURCH (A.D. 1153)

PATRON SAINT OF GIBRALTAR

20 AUGUST

Bernard was declared patron of Gibraltar in a decree of the Sacred Congregation of Rites dated 21 January 1914. There is, however, no connection between that and his own life, and the reason remains mysterious.

St Bernard was the third son of Tescelin Sorrel, a Burgundian noble, and Aleth, who was daughter of Bernard, Lord of Montbard. He was born in

1090 at Fontaines, a castle near Dijon, a lordship belonging to his father. His parents had seven children, namely, Bd Guy, Bd Gerard, St Bernard, Bd Humbeline, Andrew, Bartholomew and Bd Nivard. They were all well educated, and learned Latin and verse-making before the sons were applied to military exercise and feats of arms; but Bernard was sent to Châtillon on the Seine, to pursue a complete course of studies in a college of secular canons.

Bernard made his appearance in the world with all the advantages and talents which can make it attractive to a young man, but he presently began to think of forsaking the world and the pursuit of letters and of going to Cîteaux, where only a few years before SS. Robert, Alberic and Stephen Harding had established a first monastery of that strict interpretation of the Benedictine rule, called after it 'Cistercian'. His friends endeavoured to dissuade him from it; but he not only remained firm – he enlisted four of his brothers as well, and an uncle. Hugh of Mâcon (who afterward founded the monastery of Pontigny,and died bishop of Auxerre), an intimate friend, wept bitterly at the thought of separation, but by two interviews was induced to become his companion. Nor were these the only ones who, with apparently no previous thought of the religious life, suddenly decided to leave the world for the austere life of Cîteaux. Bernard induced in all thirty-one men to follow him – he who himself had been uncertain of his call only a few weeks before.

They assembled at Châtillon, and the company arrived at Cîteaux about Easter in 1112. The abbot, the English St Stephen, who had not had a novice for several years, received them with open arms. St Bernard was then twenty-two years old. After three years the abbot, seeing the great progress which Bernard had made and his extraordinary abilities, ordered him to go with twelve monks to found a new house in the diocese of Langres in Champagne. They walked in procession, singing psalms, with their new abbot at their head, and settled in a place called the Valley of Wormwood, surrounded by a forest. These thirteen monks grubbed up a sufficient area and, with the assistance of the bishop and the people of the country, built themselves a house. This young colony lived through a period of extreme and grinding hardship. The land was poor and their bread was of coarse barley; boiled beech leaves were sometimes served up instead of vegetables. Bernard at first was so severe in his discipline, coming down upon the smallest distractions and least transgressions of his brethren, whether in confession or in chapter, that although his monks behaved with the utmost humility and obedience they began to be discouraged, which made the abbot sensible of his fault. He condemned himself for it to a long silence. At length he resumed his preaching, and provided that meals should be more regular, though the food was still of the coarsest. The reputation of the house and of the holiness of its abbot soon became so great that the number of monks had risen to a hundred and thirty; and the name of the valley was changed to Clairvaux, because it was situated right in the eye of the sun. Bernard's aged father Tescelin and the young Nivard followed him in 1117, and received the habit at his hands. The first four daughter-houses of Cîteaux became each a mother-house to others, and Clairvaux had the most numerous offspring, including Rievaulx and, in a sense, Fountains in England.

Notwithstanding St Bernard's love of retirement, obedience and the Church's needs frequently drew him from his cell. So great was the reputation of his character and powers that princes desired to have their differences determined by him and bishops regarded his decisions with the greatest respect, referring to him important affairs of their churches. The popes looked upon his advice as the greatest support of the Holy See.

After the disputed papal election of 1130 the cause of Pope Innocent II took St Bernard up and down France, Germany and Italy. On one of his returns to Clairvaux he took with him a new postulant, a canon of Pisa, Peter Bernard Paganelli, who was to become a beatified pope as Eugenius III; for the present he was put to stoke the fire in the monastery calefactory. After the general acknowledgement of Innocent II Bernard was present at the tenth general council in Rome, the second of the Lateran, and it was at this period that he first met St Malachy of Armagh; the ensuing friendship between the two lasted until Malachy's death in Bernard's arms nine years later. All this time Bernard had continued diligently to preach to his monks whenever he was able, notably those famous discourses on the Song of Songs. In 1140 he preached for the first time in a public pulpit, primarily to the students of Paris.

Probably about the beginning of the year 1142 the first Cistercian foundation was made in Ireland, from Clairvaux, where St Malachy had put some young Irishmen with St Bernard to be trained. The abbey was called Mellifont, in county Louth, and within ten years of its foundation six daughter-houses had been planted out. At the same time Bernard was busied in the affair of the disputed succession to the see of York, in the course of which Pope Innocent II died. His third successor, within eighteen months, was the Cistercian abbot of Tre Fontane, that Peter Bernard of Pisa to whom reference has been made, known to history as Bd Eugenius III.

In the meantime the Albigensian heresy and its social and moral implications had been making alarming progress in the south of France. St Bernard had already been called on to deal with a similar sect in Cologne, and in 1145 the papel legate Cardinal Alberic, asked him to go to Languedoc. Bernard was ill and weak and hardly able to make the journey, but he obeyed. He preached against the heresy throughout the Languedoc; its supporters were stubborn and violent, especially at Toulouse and Albi, but in a very short time he had restored the country to orthodoxy and returned to Clairvaux. But he left too soon, the restoration was more apparent than real, and twenty-five years later Albigensianism had a stronger hold than ever. Then came St Dominic.

On Christmas-day, 1144, the Seljuk Turks had captured Edessa, centre of one of the four principalities of the Latin kingdom of Jerusalem, and appeals for help were at once sent to Europe, for the whole position was in danger. Pope Eugenius commissioned St Bernard to preach a crusade. He began at Vézelay on Palm Sunday 1146, when Queen Eleanor and many nobles were the first to take the cross, and were followed by such large numbers of people moved by the monk's burning words, that the supply of badges was exhausted and he had to tear strips from his habit to make others. When he had roused France, he wrote letters to the rulers and peoples of western and central Europe, and then went in person into Germany. The Emperor Conrad III took the cross from him, and set out with an army in the May of 1147, followed by Louis of France. But this, the second, crusade was a miserable failure; Conrad's forces were cut to pieces in Asia Minor and Louis did not get beyond laying siege to Damascus.

Early in the year 1153 St Bernard entered on his last illness. For a time he mended a little in the spring, and was called on for the last time to leave Clairvaux.

The inhabitants of Metz having been attacked by the duke of Lorraine, they were vehemently bent on revenge. To prevent the shedding of more blood the archbishop of Trier went to Clairvaux, and implored Bernard to journey to Metz in order to reconcile the parties that were at variance. At this call of charity he forgot his infirmity and made his way into Lorraine, where he prevailed on both sides to lay aside their arms and accept a treaty which he drew up.

God took him to Himself, on 20 August, 1153; he was sixty-three years old, had been abbot for about thirty-eight, and sixty-eight monasteries had been founded from Clairvaux – Bernard may indeed be counted among the founders of the Cistercian Order, who brought it out of obscurity into the centre of western Christendom. He was canonized in 1174, and in 1830 formally declared a doctor of the Church: *Doctor mellifluus*, the Honey-sweet Doctor, as he is now universally called.

BERNARD OF MONTJOUX (A.D. 1081?)

PATRON SAINT OF MOUNTAINEERS AND MOUNTAIN CLIMBERS, AND OF THE INHABITANTS OF, AND TRAVELLERS IN, THE ALPS

28 MAY

St Bernard was declared the patron of all inhabitants in, and travellers through, the Alps, as well as of mountaineers, by Pope Pius XI in an Apostolic Letter of 20 August 1923. Before his elevation to the papacy, Pius had himself been a keen climber, and the Letter strongly recommends this form of exercise.

He is often referred to as Bernard of Methon because of his alleged birth in Savoy, son of Count Richard of Menthon and his wife of the Duyn family. He was in fact probably of Italian birth, and his parentage is unknown; and the story of his projected marriage and flight therefrom seems to be pure invention. We are told that after his ordination Bernard eventually was appointed vicar general in the diocese of Aosta; and that for forty-two years he travelled up and down the country, visiting the most remote Alpine valleys where the remnants of heathen superstition still lingered, extending his missionary labours even beyond his own jurisdiction into the neighbouring dioceses of Novara, Tarantaise and Geneva. In the territory under his immediate control he founded schools, restored clerical discipline, and insisted that the churches should be well kept. His solicitude went out to all those in need, but especially to the travellers – often French or German pilgrims on their way to Rome – who attempted the crossing of the Alps by the two mountain passes which led into the territory of Aosta. Some lost their way and were frozen to death, some wandered into snow-drifts, whilst others who could face the severity of the climate were plundered or held to ransom by brigands. With the help of the bishop and other generous donors, St Bernard built hospices on the summit of the two passes which were renamed after him the Great and the Little St Bernard.

Actually, his was not the first venture of the kind in those regions. Some sort of hospice under clerical auspices is known to have existed in the ninth century on the Mona Jovis (Montjoux), as it was then called, but the enterprise had lapsed long before the days of St Bernard. The rest-houses which he constructed were new foundations. Provision was made in them for the reception of all travellers indiscriminately, and the hospices were placed under the care of clerics and laymen, who eventually became Augustinian canons regular, for whom a monastery was built close at hand. The same order has continued to direct them to the present day. The boon thus conferred on travellers soon made St Bernard's name famous, and great men were eager to visit the hospices and contribute to their endowment. At some time St Bernard went to Rome, where he is said to have received from the then pope the formal approbation of the hospices together with the privilege of receiving novices to perpetuate his congregation. The saint lived to the age of eighty-five and died probably on 28 May, 1081, in the monastery of St Laurence at Novara.

BD BERNARDINO OF FELTRE (A.D. 1494)

PATRON SAINT OF PAWNBROKERS; AND OF BANKERS

28 SEPTEMBER

As an ardent promoter of the montes pietatis, *it is hardly surprising that Bernardino should have been invoked by pawnbrokers – and by bankers – as their patron from time immemorial.*

He was born in 1439, at Feltre in Venezia of the noble family of Tomitani (though some have claimed for him a more humble origin at Tome), the eldest of ten children, and received at baptism the name of Martin. Martin was the studious one of the family. When he was twelve he could write Latin verse, and his mother had to force him to play games for the good of his health; and he cut off his luxuriant hair, saying he would rather use a pen than a comb. In 1454 his father got him admitted into the local college of notaries, and after two years sent him to the University of Padua where he plunged ardently into the study of philosophy and law, and began that acquaintance with the fashionable thought of his time which was afterwards valuable to him as a preacher. The sudden death of two of his professors at Padua had a profound effect on the young student, and soon after he came under the influence of the Franciscan St James of the March, who preached the Lent at Padua in 1456. In May of the same year Martin was clothed as a novice among the Friars Minor of the Observance, and took the name of Bernardino, after him of Siena who had just been canonized. Friar Bernardino was ordained priest in 1463, and for six more years continued quietly in study and prayer.

Hitherto Friar Bernardino had done no public preaching, and when in 1469 a chapter at Venice appointed him a preacher he was much troubled. He was nervous, lacked confidence in himself, and seemed physically ill-equipped, for he was very short in stature. This was sufficiently noticeable to earn him the nickname of *Parvulus* from Pope Innocent VIII, and he used to sign himself 'piccolino e poverello'.

When he first went into the pulpit before a large congregation at Mantua on the feast of his patron, he was seized with panic; he forgot everything, what he wanted to say, how he wanted to say it, all his carefully prepared points and periods. But he remembered his love and admiration for the virtues of St Bernardino of Siena, and he spoke of those, spontaneously, easily and compellingly. He never again tried to preach a sermon prepared in detail, but trusted to his heart made virtuous by prayer. 'Prayer,' he said, 'is a better preparation than study: it is both more efficacious and quicker.' Bd Bernardino preached up and down Italy for twenty-five years. Crowds acclaimed him; the wise and holy, popes, bishops, other great preachers praised him; the wicked raged against him; all proclaimed his power.

Churches were too small to hold the crowds who wanted to hear him. At Florence and Pavia his congregations covered the main square, and all could hear; at Padua and Feltre people from afar booked up all the lodgings throughout his stay; three thousand people followed him through the night from Crema that they might hear him again the next day at Lodi. It has been estimated that Bd Bernardino preached over 3600 times, but only some 120 of his sermons are extant. From these it can be judged that he spoke simply, with liveliness, and without any oratorical flourishes.

Bernardino was sent to minister to a society that was in great part selfish, proud and depraved; he opposed to its vices charity, humility and austerity. He never forgot he was a Friar Minor: he washed the feet of visitors when he was at home, refused the hospitality of the rich, and lodged in lowly places when abroad. But a good example alone is not always enough; he had to inveigh plainly and often against the evils he saw around him. 'When he attacks vice,' wrote Jerome of Ravenna, 'he does not speak – he thunders and lightens.' Twice this slightly-built little man broke a blood-vessel in the fury of his denunciation of public scandals. 'He has a heavy hand and he does not know how to flatter,' said Cardinal d'Agria. Naturally he made enemies for himself, and several attempts were made on his life, but he pursued his way unperturbed. He got the disorders of carnival time controlled and public gambling establishments suppressed in several cities; the races at Brescia on the feast of the Assumption were abolished because of their abuses; in many places vicious images and books were destroyed by the public authorities; and, of course, he had continually to attack the extravagances of female dress. Like St Bernardino of Siena before him and Savonarola contemporaneously he finished each mission by having a public bonfire of cards, dice, obscene books and pictures, useless finery, false hair, superstitious philtres, badges of factions, and other vanities. This he called the 'burning of the Devil's stronghold', and it was designed not so much to be practical removal of occasions of sin as to be a gesture forcibly to strike the imagination of the public. At his appeal civil authorities enacted or repealed laws. Men and women were separated in the public gaols; the Married Women's Property Act was anticipated and husbands were prevented from wasting the goods of their wives; the senates of Venice and Vicenza ceased to grant immunity to transgressors who should bring the heads of outlawed relatives.

In 1462 the Franciscan Barnabas of Terni founded at Perugia a 'pawnshop' which should make small loans to the poor upon pledged objects at a low rate of interest. It was immediately successful, and in the following year another was established, at Orvieto, and the institution soon spread to the Marches, the Papal States, Tuscany and elsewhere. The scheme was taken up, organized, and perfected by Bd Bernardino. In 1484 he opened a *mons pietatis* at Mantua (it soon succumbed to the hostility of usurers), and was responsible for twenty more during the following eight years. The details of the organization varied, but they were generally administered by mixed committees of friars and laymen representative of different trades, and some were municipally controlled. The initial capital fund was obtained in part from voluntary subscriptions and in part by loans from the Jews themselves; all profits were added to capital and applied to the reduction of rates of interests. It was natural that Bernardino should be fiercely attacked by the Jews and Lombards, who succeeded in getting some of his *montes pietatis* closed; but a more serious and no less inevitable opposition came from some canonists and moral theologians who insisted that the interest charged was usurious within the meaning of canon law and therefore sinful. They wished the loans to be free. This would have meant that the *montes* could not be self-supporting, and Bd Bernardino stood firmly for the charging of small interest. The controversy was fierce and was never settled in his time. But the fifth General Council of the Lateran decreed in 1515 that *montes pietatis* were lawful and worthy of all encouragement, and thereafter they became common throughout western Europe, except in the British Isles.

Bd Bernardino worked up to the last. Early in 1494 he told the Florentines he would never see them again, and when he arrived in Siena he heard a report of his own death. 'I'm always dying, if one can believe all one hears,' he observed. 'But the day will come, and come soon, when it will be true.' He welcomed Cardinal Francis Piccolomini (afterwards Pope Pius III), who wished to be his penitent: 'We are both of us little men (*piccolomini*)', was his remark to his Eminence. At the end of August he dragged himself to Pavia to preach, and warned the city that he could 'hear the French shoeing their horses for the invasion of Italy' – which within a few months King Charles VIII did. But Bernardino did not live to see it, for he died at Pavia on 28 September following. His *cultus* was approved in 1728.

BERNARDINO OF SIENA (A.D. 1444)

PATRON SAINT OF ADVERTISERS AND ADVERTISING; AND OF HOARSENESS

20 MAY

Pope Pius XII proclaimed St Bernardino patron of advertisers in Italy in an Apostolic Letter dated 19 October 1956, and Pope John XXIII extended this to France in a further Apostolic Letter, of 20 May 1960. In his proclamation Pope Pius XII drew attention to the saint's suitability for this role by citing his ability to persuade people of the truths of the Catholic faith by the use of few words, and telling symbols – above all, the monogram IHS.

St Bernardino has traditionally been regarded also as the saint to invoke against hoarseness because, when he began his preaching career, he himself suffered from this complaint; and from an inability to make himself heard. He was cured, he believed, by prayer to the Blessed Virgin.

St Bernardino was born in the Tuscan town of Massa Marittima, in which his father, a member of the noble Sienese family of the Albizeschi, occupied the post of governor. The little boy lost both his parents before he was seven and was entrusted to the care of a maternal aunt and her daughter who gave him a religious training and loved him as though he had been their own child. Upon reaching the age of eleven or twelve he was placed by his uncles at school in Siena, where he passed with great credit through the course of studies.

In 1400 Siena was visited by the plague. Twelve to twenty persons died daily in the famous hospital of Santa Maria della Scala, which found itself bereft of almost all who tended the sick. Bernardino offered to take charge of the establishment, with the help of some other young men whom he had fired with the determination to sacrifice their lives if necessary to aid the sufferers. For four months they worked tirelessly, day and night, under the direction of Bernardino, who, besides nursing the patients and preparing them for death, saw to everything and brought order as well as cleanliness into the hospital. Though several of his companions died, Bernardino escaped the contagion and returned home after the epidemic was over. He was, however, so exhausted by his labours that he fell an easy prey to a fever which laid him low for several months.

Upon his recovery he found that his immediate duty lay close at hand. An aunt named Bartolomea, to whom he was much attached, had become blind as well as bedridden, and to her he devoted himself as he had done to the plague-stricken in the hospital. When, fourteen months later, God called the invalid to Himself, it was in the arms of her nephew that she breathed her last. Free now from all earthly ties, Bernardino set himself by prayer and fasting to learn God's will as to his future. He was led to enter the Franciscan Order, the habit of which he received shortly afterwards in Siena. The house, however, proved too accessible to the novice's many friends and relations, and with the consent of his superiors he retired to the convent of Colombaio outside the city, where the rule of St Francis was strictly observed. Here in 1403 he was professed and here he was ordained priest – exactly a year later, on the feast of the Birthday of our Lady which was his birthday.

During the next twelve years he preached occasionally, but his life was mainly spent in retirement. Gradually he was being prepared by God for the twofold mission of apostle and reformer. He opened his apostolic career at Milan to which he went as a complete stranger towards the end of 1417, but soon his eloquence and zeal began to attract enormous congregations. Before he was allowed to leave the city to preach elsewhere in Lombardy he was obliged to promise that he would return the following year.

It is impossible to follow him on his missionary journeys, for in them he covered nearly the whole of Italy with the exception of the kingdom of Naples. He travelled always on foot, preached sometimes for three or four consecutive hours and often delivered several sermons on the same day. All over Italy people spoke of the wonderful fruit of St Bernardino's missions. Nevertheless there were some who took exception to this teaching and accused him of encouraging superstitious practices. They went so far as to denounce him to Pope Martin V, who for a time commanded him to keep silence. However, an examination of his doctrine and conduct led to a complete vindication and he received permission to preach wherever he liked. The same pope, in 1427, urged him to accept the bishopric of Siena but he refused it, as he afterwards declined the sees of Ferrara and of Urbino.

In 1430, however, he was obliged to give up missionary work to become vicar general of the friars of the Strict Observance. He accomplished this task with so much wisdom and tact that many convents passed voluntarily and without friction from the Conventual to the Observant rule. The original Observants had shunned scholarship as they had shunned riches, but St Bernardino insisted upon instruction in theology and canon law as part of the regular curriculum.

The saint longed to return to his apostolic labours which he regarded as his only vocation, and in 1442 he obtained permission from the pope to resign his office as vicar general. He then resumed his missionary journeys, which led him through the Romagna, Ferrara and Lombardy. He was by this time in failing health, yet at Massa Marittima in 1444 he preached on fifty consecutive days. Though obviously dying, he still continued his apostolic work and set out for Naples, preaching as he went. He succeeded in reaching Aquila, but there his strength gave out and he died on the eve of the Ascension, 20 May 1444, in the monastery of the Conventuals. He had almost reached the age of sixty-four years, forty-two of which he had spent as a religious. His tomb at Aquila was honoured by many miracles and he was canonized within six years of his death.

BLAISE, BISHOP OF SEBASTEA, MARTYR (A.D. 316?)

PATRON SAINT OF THROAT COMPLAINTS

3 FEBRUARY

Legend has it that, while in prison, Blaise cured a boy who was bought to him with a fish bone stuck in his throat. As early as the sixth century in the East he therefore became patron of all manner of throat complaints and the cult had spread to the West by the ninth century. The practice of blessing throats with candles on his feast day seems to have begun in the sixteenth century.

There seems to be no evidence earlier than the eighth century for the cult of St Blaise, but the accounts furnished at a later date agree in stating that he was bishop of Sebastea in Armenia and that he was crowned with martyrdom in the persecution of Licinius by command of Agricolaus, governor of Cappadocia and Lesser Armenia. It is mentioned in the legendary acts of St Eustratius, who is said to have perished in the reign of Diocietian, that St Blaise honourably received his relics, deposited them with those of St Orestes, and punctually executed every article of the last will and testament of St Eustratius.

This is all which can be affirmed with any faint probability concerning St Blaise, but according to his 'legendary acts' he was born of rich and noble parents, receiving a Christian education and being made a bishop while still quite young. When persecution arose, he withdrew by divine direction to a cave in the mountains which was frequented only by wild beasts. These he healed when they were sick or wounded, and they used to come round him to receive his blessing. Hunters, who had been sent to secure animals for the amphitheatre, found the saint surrounded by the beasts, and, though greatly amazed, they seized him and took him to Argricolaus. On their way they met a poor woman whose pig had been carried off by a wolf; at the command of St Blaise, the wolf restored the pig unhurt.

The governor ordered Blaise to be scourged and deprived of food, but the woman whose pig had been restored brought provisions to him and also tapers to dispel the darkness of his gloomy prison. Then Licinius tortured him by tearing his flesh with iron combs, and afterwards had him beheaded.

BONA (A.D. 1207)

PATRON SAINT OF AIR HOSTESSES, AIR STEWARDESSES AND FLIGHT ATTENDANTS

29 MAY

John XXIII, in an Apostolic Letter of 2 March 1962, declared Bona to be patron of air hostesses and flight attendants because of her own frequent journeys on pilgrimage.

Bona was born in Pisa about the year 1156 and was brought up by her mother, for her father died when she was still quite young. Even in childhood it is recounted that she was blessed with visions, and as a result of one of them she determined to go on pilgrimage to Jerusalem. This she did, but on her way home she encountered a hermit who persuaded her to undertake a mission to the Saracens. Her efforts to convert them, however, ended in imprisonment for a time.

This unhappy experience did not dull her eagerness to visit sacred places, and she next took herself to Santiago de Compostela and, later, to the tomb of St Peter in Rome. To judge by the, admittedly somewhat late, accounts of her life she was blessed with extraordinary graces, including that of being able to read hearts and minds. She died on 29 Mary 1207 and was buried in the church of San Martino in Pisa, where her tomb rapidly became a place of pilgrimage.

BRIDGET, OR BIRGITTA, (A.D. 1373)

FOUNDER OF THE ORDER OF THE MOST HOLY SAVIOUR
PATRON SAINT OF SWEDEN

23 JULY

It was Pope Leo XIII who formally recognized Bridget, or Birgitta, as patron of her native country in an Apostolic Letter of 1 October 1891. This was confirmed by a decree of the Sacred Congregation of Rites dated 10 March 1926.

St Birgitta, more commonly called Bridget, was daughter of Birger, governor of Upland, the principal province of Sweden, and his second wife, Ingeborg, daughter to the governor of East Gothland. Ingeborg, who had several other children, died about the year 1315, some twelve years after the birth of Bridget, who thenceforward was brought up by an aunt at Aspenäs on Lake Sommen. Before she was fourteen, Bridget married Ulf Gudmarsson, who was himself only eighteen, and the marriage subsisted happily for twenty-eight years. They had eight children, four boys and four girls, of whom one is venerated as St Catherine of Sweden. For some years Bridget led the life of a feudal lady on her husband's estate at Ulfasa, with the difference that she cultivated the friendship of a number of learned and virtuous men.

About the year 1335 St Bridget was summoned to the court of the young king of Sweden, Magnus II, to be principal lady-in-waiting to his newly-wedded queen, Blanche of Namur. Magnus was weak and tended to be wicked; Blanche was good-willed but irresponsible and luxury-loving. The saint bent all her energies to developing the better side of the queen's character and to establishing an influence for good over both of them.

The personal revelations which later were to make St Bridget so famous were already supporting her, and concerned matters so far apart as the necessity of washing and terms for peace between England and France. However the court did not seem susceptible to these influences: 'What was the Lady Bridget dreaming about last night?' became a byword. And St Bridget had troubles of her own. Her eldest daughter had married a riotous noble whom his mother-in-law refers to as 'the Brigand'; and about 1340 the youngest son, Gudmar, died. St Bridget thereupon made a pilgrimage to the shrine of St Olaf of Norway at Trondhjem, and on her return made a further attempt to curb the excesses of Magnus and Blanche. Meeting with no more success than before, she got leave of absence from the court, and with Ulf went on pilgrimage to Compostela. On the way back Ulf was taken ill at Arras, where he received the last sacraments. Bridget spared neither pains nor prayers for his recovery, and he was in fact restored again to health, so husband and wife vowed henceforward to devote their lives to God in religious houses. But, apparently before this resolution could take effect, Ulf died in 1344, at the monastery of Alvastra of the Cistercian Order.

St Bridget continued to live at Alvastra for four years, having taken upon herself the state of a penitent. Her visions and revelations now became so insistent that she was alarmed, fearing to be deluded by the Devil or by her own imagination. But a thrice-repeated vision told her to submit them to Master Matthias, a canon of Linköping and a priest of experience and learning, and he pronounced them to be of God. From now to her death she communicated them as they occurred to Peter, prior at Alvastra, who wrote them down in Latin. Those of this period culminated in a command of our Lord to go to the royal court and warn King Magnus of the judgement of God on his sins. She did so, and included the queen, the nobles and the bishops in her denunciation. For a time Magnus mended his ways, and liberally endowed the monastery which St Bridget now, in consequences of a further vision, planned to found at Vadstena, on Lake Vättern.

In this house St Bridget provided for sixty nuns, and in a separate enclosure monks, to the number of thirteen priests, in honour of the twelve Apostles and St Paul, four deacons, representing the Doctors of the Church, and eight choir-brothers not in orders, making the number of our Lord's apostles and disciples, eighty-five, in all. She prescribed them certain particular constitutions which are said to have been dictated to her by our Saviour in a vision.

In this institute, as in the Order of Fontevrault, the men were subject to the abbess of the nuns in temporals, but in spirituals the women were subject to the superior of the monks, because the order was principally instituted for women and the men were admitted only to afford them spritual ministrations. The convents of the men and women were separated but had the same church, in which the nuns' choir was above in a gallery, so they could not even see one another. There are now no men in the Order of the Most Holy Saviour, or Bridgettines as they are commonly called, and where formerly there were seventy houses of nuns there are today but about a dozen. All surplus income had every year to be given to the poor, and ostentatious buildings were forbidden; but each religious could have as many books for study as he or she pleased.

In 1349, in spite of the Black Death that was ravaging Europe, she decided to go to popeless Rome for the year of jubilee in 1350. With her confessor, Peter of Skeninge and others, she embarked at Stralsund, amid the tears of the people who were never to see her again: for at Rome she settled down, to work among the people and for the return of the popes to their City. Among the places particularly associated with St Bridget in Rome are the churches of St Paul's-outside-the-Walls and San Francesco a Ripa. In the first is the most beautiful crucifix of Cavallini before which she prayed, which is said to have spoken to her, and in the second she had a vision of St Francis, who said to her, 'Come, eat and drink with me in my cell'. She took this to be an invitation to go to Assisi, which she accordingly did. Later she made a tour of shrines in Italy which lasted for two years.

The saint's prophecies and revelations had reference to most of the burning political and religious questions of her time, both of Sweden and Rome. She prophesied that pope and emperor would shortly meet amicably in Rome (which Bd Urban V and Charles IV did in 1368), and the using of her by factions did somewhat to abate her popularity among the Romans. Her prophecies that their iniquities would be visited with condign punishments had the same effect, and several times her ardour drew down persecution and slander upon her. On the other hand, she was not sparing of her cricitisms, and did not fear to denounce even a pope.

In 1371, in consequence of another vision, St Bridget embarked on the last of her journeys, a pilgrimage to the Holy Places, taking with her St Catherine, her daughter, her sons Charles and Birger, Alphonsus of Vadaterra and others. The expedition started inauspiciously, for at Naples Charles got himself entangled with Queen Joanna I, of unenviable reputation. Although his wife was still alive in Sweden, and her third husband in Spain, Joanna wanted to marry him, and he was far from unwilling. His mother was horror-stricken, and set herself to ceaseless prayer for the resolution of the difficulty. Charles was struck down by a fever, and after a fortnight's illness died in the arms of his mother. He was, with St Catherine, her favourite child, and Bridget after his funeral went on in deepest grief to Palestine. Here, after being nearly drowned in a wreck off Jaffa, her progress through the Holy Places was a succession of visions of the events that had happened there and other heavenly consolations. The party arrived back in Rome in March 1373. Bridget had been ailing for some months, and now she got weaker every day till, having received the last sacraments from her faithful friend, Peter of Alvastra, she died on 23 July in her seventy-first year.

St Bridget was canonized in 1391.

BRIGID, OR BRIDE, ABBESS OF KILDARE (c. A.D. 525)

A PATRON SAINT OF IRELAND

1 FEBRUARY

Brigid was confirmed as one of the formally recognised patrons of Ireland by a decree of the Sacred Congregation of Rites dated 3 December 1962.

What can be affirmed with certainty regarding the facts of St Brigid's history is remarkably little. We are probably safe in saying that she was born about the middle of the fifth century at Faughart, near Dundalk. She undoubtedly consecrated herself to God at an early age, but the statement that she was 'veiled' by St Maccaille at Mag Teloch and afterwards consecrated by St Mel at Ardagh sounds very questionable. The difficulty is increased by a gloss appended to St Broccan's hymn on St Brigid that St Mel 'conferred upon her the order of a bishop', and that from this Brigid's successor 'has always a right to have bishop's honour upon her'. Father John Ryan discusses the problem in his *Irish Monasticism*, and concludes that 'the story was occasioned by the exceptional honour paid, as a matter of traditional usage, to St Brigid's successor at Kildare, an honour that in some respects could be compared with the special honour shown to bishops in the hierarchy of the Church'. But, strangely enough, apart from the account of Cogitosus, St Brigid's foundation of the nunnery at Kildare is not much dwelt upon in the lives, though this seems to have been the great historic fact of her career and the achievement which made her in some sense the mother and exemplar of all the consecrated virgins of Ireland for many centuries to come.

Of the saint's great religious foundation at Kill-dara (the church of the oak) and of the rule which was there followed we know little or nothing that is reliable. It is generally supposed that it was a 'double monastery', *i.e.* that it included men as well as women, for such was the common practice in Celtic lands. It is also quite possible that St Brigid presided over both communities, for this arrangement would by no means have been without a parallel. But the text of her rule – there is mention of a 'regula Sanctae Brigidae' in the Life of St Kieran of Clonmacnois – appears not to have survived.

Despite the predominance of legendary material, the enthusiasm which the memory of St Brigid evoked among her countrymen is unmistakable. It would not be easy to find anything more fervent in expression than the rhapsodies of the *Book of Lismore:*

> Everything that Brigid would ask of the Lord was granted her at once. For this was her desire: to satisfy the poor, to expel every hardship, to spare every miserable man. Now there never hath been anyone more bashful or more modest or more gentle or more humble or more discerning or more harmonious than Brigid. In the sight of other people she never washed her hands or her feet or her head. She never looked at the face of man. She never spoke without blushing. She was abstemious, she was innocent, she was prayerful, she was patient: she was glad in God's commandments: she was firm, she was humble, she was forgiving, she was loving: she was a consecrated casket for keeping Christ's body and His blood; she was a temple of God. Her heart and her mind were a throne of rest for the Holy Ghost. She was single-hearted [towards God]: she was compassionate towards the wretched; she was splendid in miracles and marvels: wherefore her name among created things is Dove among birds, Vine among trees, Sun among stars. This is the father of that holy virgin, the Heavenly Father: this is her son, Jesus Christ: this is her fosterer, the Holy Ghost: wherefore this holy virgin performs such great marvels and innumerable miracles. It is she that helpeth every one who is in straits and in danger: it is she that abateth the pestilences: it is she that quelleth the rage and storm of the sea. She is the prophetess of Christ: she is the Queen of the South: she is the Mary of the Gael.

CAMILLUS DE LELLIS, (A.D. 1614)

FOUNDER OF THE MINISTERS OF THE SICK
PATRON OF NURSES AND OF NURSES' ASSOCIATIONS

14 JULY

Together with St John of God, St Camillus was declared to be patron of 'all nurses of either sex who are alive now, and all future nurses' and of nurses' associations, by Pope Pius XI on 28 August 1930.

Camillus de Lellis was born in 1550 at Bocchianico in the Abruzzi, when his mother was nearly sixty. He grew to be a very big man – 6 feet 6 inches tall and the rest in proportion – and when he was seventeen he went off with his father to fight with the Venetians against the Turks; but soon he had contracted that painful and repulsive disease in his leg that was to afflict him for the rest of his life. In 1571 he was admitted to the San Giacomo hospital for incurables at Rome, as a patient and servant; after nine months he was dismissed, for his quarrelsomeness among other things, and he returned to active service in the Turkish war. Though Camillus habitually referred to himself as a great sinner, his worst disorder was an addiction to gambling. In the autumn of 1574 he gambled away his savings, his arms, everything down to the proverbial shirt, which was stripped off his back in the streets of Naples.

The indigence to which he had reduced himself, and the memory of a vow he had made in a fit of remorse to join the Franciscans, caused him to accept work as a labourer on the new Capuchin buildings at Manfredonia, and there a moving exhortation which the guardian of the friars one day made him completed his conversion. Ruminating on it as he rode upon his business, he at length fell on his knees, and with tears deplored his past unthinking life, and cried to Heaven for mercy. This happened on Candlemas day in the year 1575, the twenty-fifth of his age. He entered the novitiate of the Capuchins, but could not be admitted to profession of account of the disease in his leg. He therefore returned to the hospital of San Giacomo and devoted himself to the service of the sick. The administrators, having been witnesses to his charity and ability, after some time appointed him superintendent of the hospital.

Camillus, grieving to see the unscrupulous and slackness of hired servants in attending the sick, formed a project of associating for that office some of the attendants who desired to devote themselves to it out of a motive of charity. He found several persons so disposed, but met with great obstacles in the execution of his design, particularly from that jealousy and suspicion that are so often provoked by disinterested reformers. To make himself more useful in spiritually assisting the sick, he resolved, with the approval of his confessor, St Philip Neri, to receive holy orders, and was ordained by the vicegerent of Rome, Thomas Goldwell, Bishop of St Asaph, the exiled last bishop of the old English hierarchy. A certain gentleman of Rome named Fermo Calvi gave him an annuity as his title of ordination. Camillus decided to sever connection with San Giacomo and start on his own, though to do so was contrary to the advice of St Philip; so with two companions he laid the foundations of his congregation: he prescribed certain short rules, and they went every day to the great hospital of the Holy Spirit where they served the sick with affection and diligence.

In 1585 he hired a larger house, and the success of his undertaking encouraged him to extend his activities: so he ordained that the members of his congregation should bind themselves to serve persons infected with the plague, prisoners, and those who lie dying in private houses; later, in 1595 and 1601, some of his religious were sent in the troops fighting in Hungary and Croatia, thus forming the first recorded 'military field ambulance'.

In 1588 Camillus was invited to Naples, and with twelve companions founded there a new house. Certain galleys having the plague on board were forbidden to enter the harbour, so the Ministers of the Sick (the name they took) went on board, and attended them: two of their number died of the pestilence, the first martyrs of charity in this institute. In 1591 Gregory XIV erected this congregation into a religious order, for perpetually serving the sick. The founder was, as has already been said, himself afflicted with many corporal sufferings: the disease in his leg for forty-six years; a rupture for thirty-eight years; two sores in the sole of one of his feet, which gave him great pain; and, for a long time before he died, a distaste for food and inability to retain it. Under this complication of infirmities he would not suffer anyone to wait on him, but sent all his brethen to serve others. St Camillus saw the foundation altogether of fifteen houses of his brothers and eight hospitals, and Almighty God acknowledged his zeal and selflessness by the spirit of prophecy and the gift of miracles, and by many heavenly communications and favours.

The saint laid down the canonical leadership of his order in 1607. But he assisted at the general chapter in Rome in 1613, and after it, with the new superior general, visited the houses, giving them his last exhortations. At Genoa he was extremely ill; he recovered so as to be able to finish the visitation of his hospitals, but soon relapsed, and his life was now despaired of. He received viaticum from the hands of Cardinal Ginnasi, and when he received the last anointing he made a moving exhortation to his brethren; he expired on 14 July 1614, being sixty-four years old. St Camillus de Lellis was canonized in 1746, by Pope Leo XIII.

CASIMIR OF POLAND (A.D. 1484)

A PATRON OF LITHUANIA; OF RUSSIA; AND OF THE YOUNG PEOPLE OF LITHUANIA

4 MARCH

The complex religious history of Eastern Europe, tying together Lithuania, Poland, Russia and other states, is exemplified in the life of Casimir. He died in Lithuania, and was officially recognized as patron of that country in a decree of the Sacred Congregation of Rites dated 16 July 1914. But a similar decree of 22 November 1922 numbered him among the chief patrons of Russia. In addition Casimir was declared patron of the young people of Lithuania by an Apostolic Letter of Pius XII dated 11 June 1948. The Pope cites the nobility of his life, his opposition to schism, and his chastity, as reasons for proposing him as a model, at the request, he remarks, of many of the citizens of Lithuania.

St Casimir, to whom the Poles gave the title of 'The Peace-maker', was born in 1458, the third of thirteen children of Casimir IV, King of Poland, and of Elizabeth of Austria, daughter of the Emperor Albert II. Casimir was the second son; he and his two brothers, Ladislaus and John, had as their tutor John Dlugosz, the historian, a canon of Cracow and a man of extraordinary learning and piety. All the princes were warmly attached to the holy man, but Casimir profited the most by his teaching and example. Devout from his infancy, the boy gave himself up to devotion and penance. His bed was often the ground, and he was wont to spend a great part of the night in prayer and meditation, chiefly on the passion of our Saviour. His clothes were plain, and under them he wore a hair-shirt. Living always in the presence of God he was invariably serene and cheerful, and pleasant to all.

The saint's love of God showed itself in his love of the poor, and for the relief of these the young prince gave all he possessed, using in their behalf the influence he had with his father and with his brother Ladislaus when he became king of Bohemia. In honour of the Blessed Virgin Mary Casimir frequently recited the long Latin hymn *'Omni die dic Mariae'*, a copy of which was by his desire buried with him. Though this hymn, part of which is familiar to us through Bittleston's version, 'Daily, daily sing to Mary', is not uncommonly called the Hymn of St Casimir, it was certainly not composed by him, but by Bernard of Cluny in the twelfth century.

The nobles of Hungary, dissatisfied with their king, Matthias Corvinus, in 1471 begged the King of Poland to allow them to place his son Casimir on the throne. The saint, at that time not fifteen years old, was very unwilling to consent, but in obedience to his father he went to the frontier at the head of an army. There, hearing that Matthias had himself assembled a large body of troops, and finding that his own soldiers were deserting in large numbers because they could not get their pay, he decided on the advice of his officers to return home. The knowledge that Pope Sixtus IV had sent an embassy to his father to deter him from the expedition made the young prince carry out his resolution with the firmer conviction that he was acting rightly. King Casimir, however, was greatly incensed at the failure of his ambitious projects and would not permit his son to return to Cracow, but relegated him to the castle of Dobzki. The young man obeyed and remained in confinement there for three months. Convinced of the injustice of the war upon which he had so nearly embarked, and determined to have no further part in these internecine conflicts which only facilitated the progress into Europe of the Turks, St Casimir could never again be persuaded to take up arms, though urged to do so by his father and invited once more by the disaffected Hungarian magnates. He returned to his studies and his prayers, though for a time he was viceroy in Poland during an absence of his father. An attempt was made to induce him to marry a daughter of the Emperor Frederick III, but he refused to relax the celibacy he had imposed on himself.

St Casimir's austerities did nothing to help the lung trouble from which he suffered, and he died at the age of twenty-three in 1484. He was buried at Vilna, where his relics still rest in the church of St Stanislaus. Miracles were reported at his tomb, and he was canonized in 1521.

CASSIAN OF IMOLA, MARTYR (DATE UNKNOWN)

PATRON SAINT OF SHORTHAND WRITERS AND STENOGRAPHERS

13 AUGUST

At the request of a congress of shorthand writers held in Naples in 1951, Pius XII proclaimed St Cassian the patron of their profession by an Apostolic Letter of 23 December 1952. The only connection between the saint and shorthand would seem to be the bizarre death which the legends recount.

Cassian was a Christian schoolmaster, and taught children to read and write at Imola, a city twenty-seven miles from Ravenna in Italy. A violent persecution being raised against the Church, he was taken up and interrogated by the governor of the province. As he refused to sacrifice to the gods, the barbarous judge, learning of what profession he was, commanded that his own scholars should stab him to death with their iron pens.* He was exposed naked in the midst of two hundred boys, 'by whom', says the Roman Martyrology, 'he had made himself disliked by teaching them'. Some threw their tablets, pens and knives at his face and head: others cut his

---

* At the time it was the custom in schools to write upon wax laid on a board of boxwood, in which the letters were formed with an iron *stylus* or pen, sharp at one end but blunt and smooth at the other, to erase what was to be effaced or corrected.

flesh, or stabbed him with their knives; and others pierced him with their pens, some only tearing the skin and some penetrating more deeply, or making it their barbarous sport to cut letters out of his skin. Covered with blood and wounded in every part of his body, he cheerfully bade the little fiends not to be afraid and to strike him with greater force: not meaning to encourage them in their sin, but to express the willingness he had to die for Christ. He was buried by the Christians at Imola. Prudentius tells us that in his journey to Rome he visited this martyr's tomb, and before it implored the divine mercy for the pardon of his sins. He describes a picture of the saint's martyrdom over the altar, representing his cruel death in the manner he has recorded it in verse.

CATHAL (OR CATALD), BISHOP OF TARANTO OR OF RACHAU (c. A.D. 685)

PATRON SAINT OF HERNIA SUFFERERS

10 MAY

From medieval times St Cathal has been invoked, for no obvious reason, by those who suffered from a hernia, the devotion apparently beginning in Malta where there is, near Medina, a 'catacomb of St Cathal' frequented by hernia sufferers.

The stories of St Cathal's life make him an Irish monk who taught at the great abbey of Lismore, probably in the early part of the seventh century. He then became bishop of 'Rachau', a see which can no longer be identified, and later went on pilgrimage to the Holy Land, performing miracles as he travelled. On the way home he was shipwrecked near the town of Taranto in Italy. When he arrived there he was appointed bishop of the town, the see being vacant at the time. He governed the diocese well for some fifteen years, and was buried in the cathedral upon his death in or about 685. Nothing was known of him, however, until his tomb was discovered in the cathedral towards the end of the eleventh century, at which time devotion to him spread rapidly especially in Italy, but also in neighbouring islands such as Sicily and Malta.

CATHERINE OF ALEXANDRIA, MARTYR (DATE UNKNOWN)

PATRON SAINT OF PHILOSOPHERS AND PHILOSOPHY; OF LEARNING AND
STUDENTS, PARTICULARLY WOMEN STUDENTS; OF CHRISTIAN APOLOGISTS;
OF LIBRARIANS AND LIBRARIES; OF YOUNG WOMEN; AND OF WHEELWRIGHTS

25 NOVEMBER

*Because, according to the legends about her, Catherine defeated fifty learned philoso-
phers in debate, she has been traditionally regarded as the patron of philosophers and
philosophy, of learning and students in general, and in particular of women students.
Because she won the debate about Christianity, she has also been taken by apologists
for the faith as their patron. Her association more specifically with libraries and
librarians may arise in part from her association with learning, but also from the
presence in antiquity of a famous library in her native city.*

*According to legend, when the Emperor Maxentius offered to marry her, she
refused, saying that she was already affianced to Christ. For this reason she has in
some places been regarded as the patron of young women, and especially of those about
to marry, or of marriageable age.*

*Because Catherine was martyred by being broken upon a wheel, she became the
patron of wheelwrights, and indeed of other crafts whose skill depended upon wheels
on something similar, including millers and spinners.*

Since about the tenth century or earlier, veneration for St Catherine of
Alexandria has been marked in the East; but from the time of the Crusades
until the eighteenth century her popularity was even greater in the West.
Numerous churches were dedicated in her honour and her feast was kept
with great solemnity – Adam of Saint-Victor wrote a poem in her honour;
hers was one of the heavenly voices claimed to have been heard by St Joan of
Arc; and to her Bossuet devoted one of his most celebrated panegyrics. But
not a single fact about the life or death of Catherine of Alexandria has been
established.

It is said in her completely worthless *acta* that she belonged to a patrician
family of Alexandria and devoted herself to learned studies, in the course of
which she learnt about Christianity. She was converted by a vision of our
Lady and the Holy Child. When Maxentius began persecuting, Catherine,
still only eighteen years old and of great beauty, went to him and rebuked
him for his tyranny. He could not answer her arguments against his gods, so
summoned fifty philosophers to oppose her. These confessed themselves
convinced by the learning of the Christian girl, and were therefore burned to
death by the infuriated emperor. Then he tried to seduce Catherine with an
offer of a consort's crown, and on her indignant refusal she was beaten and
imprisoned, and Maxentius went off to inspect a camp. On his return he
discovered that his wife and an officer had gone to see Catherine out of
curiosity and had both been converted, together with two hundred soldiers
of the guard. They accordingly were all slain and Catherine was sentenced

97

to be killed on a spiked wheel (whence our 'catherine-wheel'). When she was placed on it, her bonds were miraculously loosed and the wheel broke, its spikes flying off and killing many of the onlookers. Then she was beheaded, and there flowed from her severed veins a white milk-like liquid. There are variations of the story, including Catherine's conversion in Armenia, and the details introduced by the Cypriots when they claimed the saint for their island in the middle ages.

All the texts of the 'acts' of St Catherine state that her body was carried by angels to Mount Sinai, where a church and monastery were afterwards built, but the legend was not known to the earliest pilgrims to the mountains. In 527 the Emperor Justinian built a fortified monastery for the hermits of this place, and the supposed body of St Catherine was said to have been taken there in the eighth or ninth century, since when it has borne her name.

Alban Butler quotes Archbishop Falconio of Santa Severina as saying, 'As to what is said, that the body of this saint was conveyed by angels to Mount Sinai, the meaning is that it was carried by the monks of Sinai to their monastery, that they might devoutly enrich their dwelling with such a treasure. It is well known that the name of angelical habit was often used for a monastic habit, and that monks on account of their heavenly purity and functions were anciently called *angels*.' 'Angelical life' and 'angelical habit' are still current and usual expressions in Eastern monasticism.

CATHERINE OF GENOA (A.D. 1510)

PATRON SAINT OF NURSES (ITALIAN)

15 SEPTEMBER

The dedication of Catherine to the sick made her a most suitable patron of nurses, and she was declared such by Pius XII in an Apostolic Letter of 15 September 1943, alongside Catherine of Siena.

The Fieschi were a great Guelf family of Liguria, with a long and distinguished history. In 1234 it gave to the Church the vigorous Pope Innocent IV, and in 1276 his nephew, who ruled for a few weeks as Adrian V. By the middle of the fifteenth century it had reached the height of its power and splendour in Liguria, Piedmont and Lombardy; one member was a cardinal, and another, James, descended from the brother of Innocent IV, was viceroy of Naples for King René of Anjou. This James Fieschi was married to a Genoese lady, Francesca di Negro, and to them was born at Genoa in the year 1447 the fifth and last of the children, Caterinetta, now always called Catherine.

From the age of thirteen Catherine was undoubtedly strongly attracted to the religious life. Her sister was already a canoness regular and the chaplain of her convent was Catherine's confessor, so she asked him if she also could take the habit. In consultation with the nuns he put her off on account of her youth, and about the same time Catherine's father died. Then, at the age of sixteen, she was married.

The star of the Ghibelline family of the Adorni was in decline, and by an alliance with the powerful Fieschi they hoped to restore the fortunes of their house. The Fieschi were willing enough, and Catherine was their victim. Her bridegroom was Julian Adorno, a young man with too poor a character to bring any good out of his marriage as a marriage. Catherine was beautiful in person (as may be seen from her portraits), of great intelligence and sensibility, and deeply religious; of an intense temperament, without humour or wit. Julian was of very different fibre, incapable of appreciating his wife. He was, on his own admission, unfaithful to her; for the rest, he was pleasure-loving to an inordinate degree, undisciplined, hot-tempered and spendthrift. He was hardly ever at home, and for the first five years, of her married life Catherine lived in solitude and moped amid vain regrets. Then for another five she tried what consolations could be found in the gaieties and recreations of her world, and was little less sad and desperate than before.

She had, however, never lost trust in God, or at least so much of it as was implied in the continued practice of her religion, and on the eve of the feast of St Benedict in 1473 she asked that saint, 'St Benedict, pray to God that He make me stay three months sick in bed'. Two days later she was kneeling for a blessing before the chaplain at her sister's convent when she was suddenly overcome by a great love of God and realization of her own unworthiness. Within the next day or two she had a vision of our Lord carrying His cross which caused her to cry out, 'O Love, if it be necessary I am ready to confess my sins in public!' Then she made a general confession of her whole life with such sorrow 'as to pierce her soul'. On the feast of the Annunciation she received holy communion, the first time with fervour for ten years, and shortly after became a daily communicant, so remaining for the rest of her life.

At about this time his luxury and extravagance had brought Julian to the verge of ruin, and his wife's prayers, added to his misfortunes, brought about a reformation in his life. They moved from their *palazzo* into a small house, much more humble and in a poorer quarter than was necessary; agreed to live together in continence; and devoted themselves to the care of the sick in the hospital of Pammatone. Associated with them was a cousin of Catherine, Tommasina Fieschi, who after her widowhood became first a canoness and then a Dominican nun. This went on for six years until in 1479 the couple went to live in the hospital itself, of which eleven years later she was appointed matron. She proved as capable an administrator as she was a devoted nurse, especially during the plague of 1493, when four-fifths of those who remained in the city died. In 1496 Catherine's own health broke down and she had to resign the control of the hospital, though still living within the building, and in the following year her husband died after a painful illness.

From the year 1473 on St Catherine without intermission led a most intense spiritual life combined with unwearying activity on behalf of the sick and sad, not only in the hospital but throughout Genoa. The life of St Catherine has been taken as the text of a most searching work on the mystical element in religion yet she also kept the hospital accounts without ever being a farthing out and was so concerned for the right disposition of property that she made four wills with several codicils.

Catherine suffered from ill health for some years and had to give up not only her extraordinary fasts, but even to a certain extent those of the Church, and at length in 1507 her health gave way completely. She rapidly got worse, and for the last months of her life suffered great agony; among the physicians who attended her was John-Baptist Boerio, who had been the principal doctor of King Henry VII of England. On 13 September 1510, she was in a high fever and delirium, and died at dawn on 15 September.

She was beatified in 1737, and Benedict XIV added her name to the Roman Martyrology, with the title of saint.

CATHERINE OF SIENA (A.D. 1380)

A PRINCIPAL PATRON SAINT OF ITALY; AND OF ITALIAN NURSES

29 APRIL

Together with St Francis of Assisi, Catherine was declared a principal patron of Italy by Pope Pius XII on 18 June, 1939. He did so in response to a request from the Prefect of the Sacred Congregation of Rites and all the archbishops and bishops of Italy, speaking in the name of the people. She was made patron for her efforts to bring the papacy back to Rome after the long 'captivity' in Avignon. She had done so, said the Pope, for the honour of her country and the good of religion.

Pius XII, in a later Apostolic Letter of 15 September 1943, also declared St Catherine patron of women who administer to the sick in Italy, giving as his reasons for doing so her immense love for people, and her work for their temporal, as well as their spiritual, good.

St Catherine was born in Siena on the feast of the Annunciation 1347, she and a twin sister who did not long survive her birth being the youngest of twenty-five children. Their father, Giacomo Benincasa, a well-to-do dyer, lived with his wife Lapa, daughter of a now forgotten poet, in the spacious house which the piety of the Sienese has preserved almost intact to the present day. Catherine as a little girl is described as having been very merry, and sometimes on her way up or downstairs she used to kneel on every step to repeat a Hail Mary. She was only six years old when she had the remarkable mystical experience which may be said to have sealed her vocation.

When she had reached the age of twelve, her parents urged her to devote more care to her personal appearance. In order to please her mother and her sister Bonaventura she submitted for a time to have her hair dressed and to be decked out in the fashion, but she soon repented of her concession. Uncompromisingly she now declared that she would never marry, and as her parents still persisted in trying to find her a husband she cut off her golden-brown hair – her chief beauty. The family, roused to indignation, tried to overcome her resolution. She was harried and scolded from morning to night, set to do all the menial work of the house, and because she was known to love privacy she was never allowed to be alone, even her little bedroom being taken from her. All these trials she bore with patience which nothing could ever ruffle. At last her father realized that further opposition was useless, and Catherine was allowed to lead the life to which she felt called. She obtained what she had ardently desired – permission to receive the habit of a Dominican tertiary.

On Shrove Tuesday, 1366, while Siena was keeping carnival, she was praying in her room when the Saviour appeared to her, accompanied by His blessed Mother and a crowd of the heavenly host. Taking the girl's hand, our Lady held it up to her Son who placed a ring upon it and espoused Catherine to Himself, bidding her to be of good courage, for she was now armed with faith to overcome the assaults of the enemy. The ring remained visible to her though invisible to others. This spiritual betrothal marked the end of the years of solitude and preparation. Very shortly afterwards, it was revealed to Catherine that she must now go forth into the world to promote the salvation of her neighbour, and she began gradually to mix again with her fellow creatures. Gradually there gathered round her a band of friends and disciples – her Fellowship or Family, all of whom called her 'Mamma'.

As may be readily supposed, public opinion in Siena was sharply divided about Catherine, especially at this period. It may have been in consequence of accusations made against her that she was summoned to Florence, to appear before the chapter general of the Dominicans. If any charges were made, they were certainly disproved, and shortly afterwards the new lector to Siena, Bd Raymund of Capua, was appointed her confessor. Their association was a happy one for both. The learned Dominican became not only her director but in a great measure her disciple, whilst she obtained through him the support of the order. In later life he was to be the master general of the Dominicans and the biographer of his spiritual daughter.

Her reputation for holiness and wonders had by this time won for her a unique place in the estimation of her fellow citizens, many of whom proudly called her 'La Beata Popolana' and resorted to her in their various difficulties: three Dominicans were specially charged to hear the confessions of those who were induced by her to amend their lives. Moreover, because of her success in healing feuds, she was constantly being called upon to arbitrate. It was partly no doubt with a view to turning the belligerent energies of Christendom from fratricidal struggles that Catherine was moved to throw herself energetically into Pope Gregory XI's appeal for another crusade to wrest the Holy Sepulchre from the Turks. Her efforts in this direction brought her into direct correspondence with the pontiff himself.

In February 1375 she accepted an invitation to visit Pisa. She had only been in the city a few days when she had another of those great spiritual experiences which appear to have preluded new developments in her career. After making her communion in the little church of St Christina, she had been looking at the crucifix, rapt in meditation, when suddenly there seemed to come from it five blood-red rays which pierced her hands, feet and heart, causing such acute pain that she swooned. The wounds remained as stigmata, apparent to herself alone during her life, but clearly visible after her death.

She was still at Pisa when she received word that the people of Florence and Perugia had entered into a league against the Holy See and its French legates; and Bologna, Viterbo, Ancona, together with other cities, not without provocation from the mismanagement of papal officials, promptly rallied to the insurgents. That Lucca as well as Pisa and Siena held back for a time was largely due to the untiring efforts of Catherine, who paid a special visit to Lucca besides writing numerous letters of exhortation to all three towns. From Avignon, after an unsuccessful appeal to the Florentines, Pope Gregory despatched his legate Cardinal Robert of Geneva with an army, and laid Florence under a interdict. This ban soon entailed such serious effects upon the city that its rulers in alarm sent to Siena, to accept Catherine's offer to become their mediatrix with the Holy See.

Catherine arrived at Avignon on 18 June 1376, and soon had a conference with Pope Gregory. But the Florentine ambassadors disclaimed Catherine, and the pope's peace terms were so severe that nothing could be done.

Although the immediate purpose of her visit to Avignon had thus failed, Catherine's efforts in another direction were crowned with success. For seventy-four years the popes had been absent from Rome, living in Avignon, where the curia had become almost entirely French. It was a state of things deplored by all earnest Christians outside France, and the greatest men of the age had remonstrated against it in vain. Gregory XI had indeed himself proposed to transfer his residence to the Holy City, but had been deterred by the opposition of his French cardinals. Since Catherine in her letters had urged his return to Rome, it was only natural that the pope should talk with her on the subject when they came face to face. 'Fulfil what you have promised', was her reply – recalling to him, it is said, a vow which he had never disclosed to any human being. Gregory decided to act without loss of time. On 13 September 1376, he started from Avignon to travel by water to Rome, Catherine and her friends leaving the city on the same day to return overland to Siena. The two parties met again, almost accidentally, in Genoa, where Catherine was detained by the illness of two of her secretaries.

It was a month before she was back in Siena, from whence she continued to write to Pope Gregory, exhorting him to contribute by all means possible to the peace of Italy. By his special desire she went again to Florence, still rent by factions and obstinate in its disobedience. There she remained for some time, amidst daily murders and confiscations, in danger of her life but ever undaunted, even when swords were drawn against her. Finally she did indeed establish peace with the Holy See, although not during Gregory's reign. After this memorable reconciliation the saint returned to Siena where, as Raymund of Capua tell us, 'she occupied herself actively in the composition of a book which she dictated under the inspiration of the Holy Ghost'. This was the celebrated mystical work, written in four treatises, known as the 'Dialogue of St Catherine'.

But within two years of the ending of the papal 'captivity' at Avignon began the scandal of the great schism which followed the death of Gregory XI in 1378, when Urban VI was chosen in Rome and a rival pope was set up in Avignon by certain cardinals who declared Urban's election illegal. Christendom was divided into two camps, and Catherine wore herself out in her efforts to obtain for Urban the recognition which was his due. Letter after letter she addressed to the princes and leaders of the various European countries. To Urban himself she continued to write, sometimes to urge him to bear up under his trials, sometimes admonishing him to abate a harshness which was alienating even his supporters. Far from resenting her reproof, the pope told her to come to Rome that he might profit by her advice and assistance. In obedience to the call she took up her residence in the City, labouring indefatigably by her prayers, exhortations and letters to gain fresh adherents to the true pontiff. Her life, however, was almost ended. Early in 1380 she had a strange seizure, when a visible presentment of the ship of the Church seemed to crush her to the earth and she offered herself a victim for it. After this she never really recovered. On 21 April there supervened a paralytic stroke which disabled her from the waist downwards, and eight days later, at the age of thirty-three, St Catherine of Siena passed away in the arms of Alessia Saracini. She was canonized in 1461, and declared a doctor of the church in 1970.

CATHERINE OF SWEDEN (A.D. 1381)

PATRON SAINT FOR PROTECTION AGAINST ABORTION

24 MARCH

Pictures of Catherine frequently show her with a hind beside her. This hind, according to legend, preserved her from harm on numerous occasions, including from some attacks upon her chastity. It is perhaps because of the chastity of her life, even in marriage, that she came to be invoked against abortions.

Catherine, born about the year 1331, was one of the several children of St Bridget and her husband Ulf Gudmarsson. When still quite young she was sent to be educated to a convent. She was attracted to the life of a religious and wished to remain in the convent but, when she had reached the age of 13 or 14, she was married at her father's command. Both she and her husband, however, took a vow to live in continence. For the jubilee of 1350 she accompanied her mother to Rome, and while there learned of her husband's death. From then onwards she was able to live the life of devotion she had always desired. In 1372 she and her mother made a pilgrimage to the Holy Land, returning by way of Rome where St Bridget died. Catherine returned with her mother's body to Sweden, and there became abbess of the convent at Vadstena, founded by Bridget, which was the mother-house of the Bridgettine order. In 1375 she again returned to Rome, this time to win papal approval for the order, in which she succeeded, and to bring about the canonization of her mother, in which she was not successful. After a holy and eventful life she died on 24 March 1381, not long after her return from Rome.

CECILIA, OR CECILY, VIRGIN AND MARTYR (DATE UNKNOWN)

PATRON SAINT OF MUSIC

22 NOVEMBER

There is no very obvious reason why St Cecilia should be regarded as the patron of music. Until the middle ages St Gregory (q.v.) had played that role, but when the Roman Academy of Music was established in 1584 it was put under her protection, and devotion to her seems to have developed from there. In her 'acts' it is related that 'while the organs played', she, in her heart, 'sang only to God'. It appears that the Latin phrase 'cantantibus organis' was understood to mean that she was herself playing the organ at her own wedding: from the fourteenth or fifteenth century she has been represented in art as sitting at an organ.

Her 'acts' state that Cecilia was a patrician girl of Rome and that she was brought up a Christian. She wore a coarse garment beneath the clothes of her rank, fasted from food several days a week, and determined to remain a maiden for the love of God. But her father had other views, and gave her in marriage to a young patrician named Valerian. On the day of the marriage, when they retired to their room, she took her courage in both hands and said to her husband gently, 'I have a secret to tell you. You must know that I have an angel of God watching over me. If you touch me in the way of marriage he will be angry and you will suffer; but if you respect my maidenhood he will love you as he loves me.' 'Show me this angel,' Valerian replied.

Cecilia said, 'If you believe in the living and one true god and receive the water of baptism, then you shall see the angel'. Valerian agreed and was sent to find Bishop Urban. He was received with joy and baptized. Then he returned to Cecilia, and found standing by her side an angel, who put upon the head of each a chaplet of roses and lilies. Then appeared his brother, Tiburtius. He, too, was offered a deathless crown if he would renounce his false gods. Cecilia talked long to him, until he was convinced by what she told him of Jesus, and he, too, was baptized.

From that time forth the two young men gave themselves up to good works. Because of their zeal in burying the bodies of martyrs they were both arrested. Almachius, the prefect before whom they were brought, began to cross-examine them. Almachius told him to tell the court if he would sacrifice to the gods and go forth free. Tiburtius and Valerian both replied: 'No, not to the gods, but to the one God to whom we offer sacrifice daily.' The prefect asked whether Jupiter were the name of their god. 'No, indeed', said Valerian.

Valerian rejoiced when they were delivered over to be scourged. Even then the perfect was disposed to allow them a respite in which to reconsider their refusal, but his assessor assured him that they would only use the time to distribute their possessions, thus preventing the state from confiscating their property. They were accordingly condemned to death and were beheaded in a place called Pagus Triopius, four miles from Rome. With them perished one of the officials, a man called Maximus, who had declared himself a Christian after witnessing their fortitude.

Cecilia gave burial to the three bodies, and then she in turn was called upon to repudiate her faith. Instead she converted those who came to induce her to sacrifice; and when Pope Urban visited her at home he baptized over 400 persons there: one of them, Gordian, a man of rank, established a church in her house, which Urban later dedicated in her name. When she was eventually brought into court, Almachius argued with Cecilia at some length, and was not a little provoked by her attitude. At length she was sentenced to be suffocated to death in the bathroom of her own house. But though the furnace was fed with seven times its normal amount of fuel, Cecilia remained for a day and a night without receiving any harm, and a soldier was sent to behead her. He struck at her neck three times, and then left her lying. She was not dead and lingered three days, during which the

Christians flocked to her side and she formally made over her house to Urban and committed her household to his care. She was buried next to the papal crypt in the catacomb of St Callistus.

This well-known story, familiar to and loved by Christians for many ages, dates back to about the end of the fifth century, but unfortunately can by no means be regarded as trustworthy or even founded upon authentic materials. No mention is made of a Roman virgin martyr named Cecilia in the period immediately following the persecutions. There is no reference to her in the poems of Damasus or Prudentius, in the writings of Jerome or Ambrose, and her name does not occur in the *Depositio martyrum* (fourth century). Moreover, what was later called the *titulus Sanctae Caeciliae* was originally known simply as the *titulus Caeciliae, i.e.* the church founded by a lady named Cecilia.

CELESTINE V, POPE (A.D. 1296)

PATRON SAINT OF BOOKBINDERS

19 MAY

It is recorded that, from an early age, he was fond of books, and as a hermit he spent some of the time not devoted to prayer to copying books, and to binding them. For that reason he has been patron of bookbinders from medieval times.

Peter, who was the eleventh of twelve children, was born of peasant parents about the year 1210 at Isernia, in the Abruzzi. Because he showed unusual promise, his mother, though she was early left a widow, sent him to school – against the advice of her relations.

When he was twenty he left the world to live as a hermit on a solitary mountain where he made himself a cell so circumscribed that he could scarcely stand upright or lie down in it. In spite of his desire to remain hidden, he had occasional visitors, some of whom persuaded him to seek holy orders. He accordingly went to Rome and was ordained priest, but in 1246 he returned to the Abruzzi. On the way back he received the Benedictine habit from the Abbot of Faizola, by whom he was permitted to resume his solitary life. For five years he dwelt on Mount Morone, near Sulmona, but in 1251 the wood was cut on the mountain, and Peter, finding his privacy too much invaded, took refuge with two companions in the fastnesses of Monte Majella. His disciples, however, tracked him thither. So, after two further ineffectual attempts to live in solitude, he resigned himself to the inevitable and, returning to Monte Morone, became the head of a community of hermits who lived at first in scattered cells, but afterwards in a monastery. He gave his disciples a strict rule based on that of St Benedict and in 1274 he obtained from Pope Gregory X the approbation of his order, the members of which were afterwards known as Celestines.

After the death of Nicholas IV, the chair of St Peter remained vacant for over two years owing to the rivalry between two parties, neither of which would give way. To the cardinals assembled at Perugia came a message, it is said, from the hermit of Monte Morone threatening them with the wrath of God if they continued to delay. In any case, to bring the deadlock to an end, the conclave chose the hermit himself to become Christ's vicar upon earth. The five envoys who climbed the steeps of Morone to bear the official notification found the old man (he was eighty-four) red-eyed with weeping and appalled at the tiding of his election which had already reached him. Boundless enthusiasm prevailed at the choice of a pope so holy and so unworldly, while to many it seemed an inauguration of the new era foretold by Joachim del Fiore – the reign of the Holy Spirit when the religious orders would rule the world in peace and love. Two hundred thousand persons are said to have assembled in Aquila to acclaim the new pope as he rode to the cathedral on a donkey, its bridle held on the one side by the King of Hungary and on the other by Charles of Anjou, King of Naples.

Scarcely, however, were the consecration and coronation over than it became evident that Celestine V, as he was now called, was quite unequal to the task of ruling the Church. In his utter simplicity he became unwittingly a tool in the hands of King Charles, who used him for the furtherance of his schemes and induced him to live in Naples. He gave great offence to the Italian cardinals by refusing to go to Rome and by creating thirteen new cardinals, nearly all in the Franco-Neapolitan interest. Knowing little Latin and no canon law, his want of experience led him into mistakes of all kinds. To the rigorist *Spirituali* movement he was a pope sent direct from Heaven; to the place-hunters and the ruck he was a windfall: he gave to anybody anything they asked, and in his innocence would grant the same benefice several times over. Everything fell into hopeles confusion.

Miserable and frightened in these bewildering surroundings, he asked for himself only that a cell should be made in the palace, to which as Advent approached he proposed withdrawing into complete solitude and silence, leaving three cardinals to govern in his place; but he was warned that by so doing he was practically creating three rival popes. Conscious of failure, discouraged, and utterly weary, Celestine began to consider how he might lay down a burden he felt unable to bear. It was an unprecedented thing for a pope to abdicate; but Cardinal Gaëtani and other learned men whom he consulted decided that it was permissible, and even advisable in certain circumstances. Although the King of Naples and others strongly opposed, nevertheless on 13 December 1294, at a consistory of cardinals held in Naples, St Celestine read a solemn declaration of abdication, in which he pleaded his age, his ignorance, his incapacity, and his rough manners and speech. He then laid aside his pontifical robes and resumed a religious habit; and he cast himself at the feet of the assembly, begging pardon for his many errors and exhorting the cardinals to repair them as well as they chould by choosing a worthy successor to St Peter. The assembly, deeply moved, accepted his resignation, and the old man joyfully returned to the house of his monks at Sulmona.

He was not, however, destined to remain there in peace. Cardinal Gaëtani, who as Boniface VIII had been chosen pope in his place, found himself opposed by a bitterly hostile party and requested the King of Naples to send his too popular predecessor back to Rome, lest he should be used by his opponents. Celestine, duly warned, hoped to escape across the Adriatic; but after several months of wandering among the woods and mountains he was captured. Boniface shut him up in a small room in the castle of Fumone, near Anagni, and there after ten months of hardship he died, on 19 May 1296. 'I wanted nothing in the world but a cell,' he said, 'and a cell they have given me.' He was canonized in 1313.

The body of Pope St Celestine V rests in the church of Santa Maria del Colle at Aquila in the Abruzzi, the place where he was consecrated to the episcopate and the papacy.

CHARLES BORROMEO, ARCHBISHOP OF MILAN, AND CARDINAL (A.D. 1584)

PATRON SAINT OF CATECHISTS AND CATECHUMENS

4 NOVEMBER

Together with Robert Bellarmine, Charles Borromeo was declared patron of all those engaged in instructing others in the faith by an Apostolic Letter of Pius XI, dated 26 April 1932. The Pope made particular mention of the Saint's work on the Catechism of the Council of Trent, and his establishment of schools for Christian instruction. The Letter names him as patron both of the teachers of catechetics, and of their pupils.

He was an aristocrat by birth, his father being Count Gilbert Borromeo, himself a man of talent and sanctity. His mother, Margaret, was a Medici, whose younger brother became Pope Pius IV. Charles, the second of two sons in a family of six, was born in the castle of Arona on Lake Maggiore on 2 October 1538, and from his earliest years showed himself to be of a grave and devout disposition. At the age of twelve he received the clerical tonsure, and his uncle, Julius Caesar Borromeo, resigned to him the rich Benedictine abbey of SS. Gratian and Felinus, at Arona, which had been long enjoyed by members of his family *in commendam*.

Charles learned Latin at Milan and was afterwards sent to the university of Pavia, where he studied under Francis Alciati, who was later promoted cardinal by St Charles's interest. On account of an impediment in his speech and a lack of brilliance he was esteemed slow, yet he made good progress. Count Gilbert made his son a strictly limited allowance from the income of his abbey, and we learn from his letters that young Charles was continually short of cash, owing to the necessity in his position of keeping up a household. It was not till after the death of both his parents that he took his doctor's degree, in his twenty-second year. He then returned to Milan where he soon after received news that his uncle, Cardinal de Medici, was chosen pope, in 1559, at the conclave held after the death of Paul IV.

Early in 1560 the new pope created his nephew cardinal-deacon and on 8 February following nominated him administrator of the vacant see of Milan. Pius IV, however, detained him at Rome and entrusted him with many duties. In quick succession Charles was named legate of Bologna, Romagna and the March of Ancona, and protector of Portugal, the Low Countries, the Catholic cantons of Switzerland, and the orders of St Francis, the Carmelites, the Knights of Malta, and others. The recipient of all these honours and responsibilities was not yet twenty-three years old and only in minor orders. He still found time to look after his family affairs, and took recreation in music and physical exercise. He was a patron of learning, and promoted it among the clergy; and, among other establishments for this end, having also in view the amenities of the pope's court, he instituted in the Vatican a literary academy of clergy and laymen, some of whose conferences and studies appear among the saint's works as *Noctes Vaticanae*. He judged it so far necessary to conform to the custom of the renaissance papal court as to have a magnificent palace, to keep a large household and a table suitable to his secular rank, and to give entertainments. He had provided for the diocese of Milan, for its government and the remedying of its disorders, in the best manner he was able, but the command of the pope by which he was obliged to attend in Rome did not make him entirely easy on that head.

Pope Pius IV had announced soon after his election his intention of reassembling the council of Trent, which had been suspended in 1552. St Charles used all his influence and energy to bring this about, amid the most difficult and adverse ecclesiastical and political conditions. He was successful, and in January 1562 the council was reopened. But as much work, diplomacy and vigilance were required of Charles during the two years it sat as the negotiation for its assembly. Several times it nearly broke up with its work unfinished, but St Charles's never-failing attention and his support of the papal legates kept it together, and in nine sessions and numerous meetings for discussion many of the most important dogmatic and disciplinary decrees of the great reforming council were passed. To the efforts of St Charles more than of any other single man this result was due; he was the master-mind and the ruling spirit of the third and last period of the Council of Trent.

During its assembly Count Frederick Borromeo died, so that St Charles found himself the head of this noble family. Many took it for granted that he would leave the clerical state and marry. But Charles resigned his family position to his uncle Julius and received the priesthood in 1563. Two months later he was consecrated bishop.

He was not allowed to go to his diocese, and, in addition to his other duties, he had to supervise the drawing-up of the Catechism of the Council of Trent and the reform the liturgical books and church-music; to his commission we owe the composition of Palestrina's mass called 'Papae Marcelli'. Milan had been without a resident bishop for eighty years, and was in a deplorable state. St Charles's vicar there had done his best to carry out a programme of reform, assisted by a number of Jesuits specially sent, but he was far from successful and at length St Charles was given permission to go and hold a provincial council and make a visitation.

Ten suffragans attended the provincial council, and the excellence of its regulations for the observance of the decrees of the Council of Trent for the discipline and training of the clergy, the celebration of divine service, the administration of the sacraments, the giving of catechism on Sundays, and many other points, caused the pope to write to St Charles a letter of congratulation. But while discharging legatine duties in Tuscany he was summoned to Rome to assist Pius IV on his death-bed, where St Philip Neri was also present. The new pope, St Pius V, induced St Charles to stay on at Rome for a time in the same offices which he had discharged under his predecessor. But Charles saw the opportunity for which he had been waiting, and pressed his return to his people with such zeal that the pope presently dismissed him with his blessing.

St Charles arrived at Milan in April 1566 and went vigorously to work for the reformation of his diocese. He began by the regulation of his household then, he sold plate and other effects to the value of thirty thousand crowns, and applied the whole sum for the relief of distressed families. His almoner was ordered to give the poor two hundred crowns a month, besides whatever extra sums he could call upon the stewards for, which were very many. His liberality appears too in many monuments, and his help to the English College at Douai was such that Cardinal Allen called St Charles its founder. He arranged retreats for his clergy and himself went into retreat twice a year. It was his rule to confess himself every morning before celebrating Mass. His ordinary confessor was Dr Griffith Roberts, of the diocese of Bangor, author of a famous Welsh grammar. St Charles appointed another Welshman, Dr Owen Lewis (afterwards a bishop in Calabria), to be one of his vicars general, and he always had with him a little picture of St John Fisher. He had a great regard for the Church's liturgy, and never said any prayer or carried out any religious rite with haste.

St Charles, in provincial councils, diocesan synods and by many pastoral instructions, made regulations for the reform both of clergy and people which pastors have ever since regarded as a model and studied to emulate. He was one of the foremost of the great pastoral theologians who arose in the Church to remedy the disorders engendered by the decay of medieval life. Partly by tender entreaties and zealous remonstrances and partly by inflexible firmness in the execution of these decrees, without favour, distinction of persons or regard to rank or pretended privileges, the saint in time overcame the obstinate and broke down difficulties which would have daunted the most courageous. St Charles directed that children in particular should be properly instructed in Christian doctrine. Not content with enjoining parish-priests to give public catechism every Sunday and holy-day, he established the Confraternity of Christian Doctrine, whose schools are said to have numbered 740, with 3000 catechists and 40,000 pupils.

But the saint's reforms were far from being well received everywhere, and some were carried through only in the face of violent and unscrupulous opposition. The religious order called Humiliati having been reduced to a few members, but having many monasteries and great possessions, had submitted to reform at the hands of the archbishop. But the submission was unwilling and only apparent. They tried to annul the regulations which had been made. When they failed three priors of the order hatched a plot to assassinate St Charles. One of the Humiliati themselves, a priest called Jerome Donati Farina, agreed to do the deed for forty gold pieces, which sum was raised by selling the ornaments from a church. On 26 October 1569 Farina posted himself at the door of the chapel in the archbishop's house, whilst St Charles was at evening prayers with his household. An anthem by Orlando di Lasso was being sung, and at the words 'It is time therefore that I return to Him that sent me', Charles being on his knees before the altar, the assassin discharged a gun at him. Farina made good his escape during the ensuing confusion, and St Charles, imagining himself mortally wounded, commended himself to God. But it was found that the bullet had only struck his clothes in the back, raising a bruise, and fallen harmlessly to the floor. After a solemn thanksgiving and procession, he shut himself up for some days in a Carthusian monastery to consecrate his life anew to God.

St Charles then returned to the three valleys of his diocese in the Alps; and took that opportunity of visiting each of the Catholic cantons, wherein he converted a number of Zwinglians and restored discipline in the monasteries. The harvest having failed, Milan was afflicted the following year with a great famine. St Charles by his care and appeals procured supplies for the relief of the poor, and himself fed 3000 people daily for three months. He had been very unwell for some time and at doctors' orders he modified his way of life, but without getting any relief. After visiting Rome for the conclave which elected Pope Gregory XIII he returned to his normal habits, and soon recovered his health.

During his episcopate of eighteen years he held five provincial councils

111

and eleven diocesan synods. He was indefatigable in parochial visitations. The archdiocese of Milan owed three seminaries to the zeal of St Charles, for the requirements of three different classes of clerical student, and everywhere he urged that the Tridentine directions for sacerdotal training should be put into effect. In 1575 he went to Rome to gain the jubilee indulgence and in the following year published it at Milan. Huge crowds of penitents and others flocked to the city, and they brought with them the plague, which broke out with great virulence.

The governor fled and many of the rest of the nobility left the town. St Charles gave himself up completely to the care of the stricken. The number of priests of his own clergy to attend the sick not being sufficient, he assembled the superiors of the religious communities and begged their help. The effect of this appeal was that a number of religious at once volunteered, and were lodged by Charles in his own house. He then wrote to the governor, Don Antony de Guzman, upbraiding him for his cowardice, and induced him and other magistrates to return to their posts and try to cope with the disaster. The hospital of St Gregory was entirely inadequate, overflowing with dead, dying, sick and suspects, having nobody to care for them. The sight of their terrible state reduced St Charles to tears, but he had to send for priests and lay helpers to the Alpine valleys, for at first the Milanese clergy would not go near the place. With the coming of the plague commerce was at the end and want began. It is said that food had to be found daily for sixty or seventy thousand persons. St Charles literally exhausted all his resources in relief and incurred large debts on behalf of the sufferers. He even made use of the coloured fabrics that hung up from his house to the cathedral during processions, having it made up into clothes for the needy. Empty houses for the sick were taken outside the walls and temporary shelters built, lay helpers were organized for the clergy, and a score of altars set up in the streets so that the sick could assist at public worship from their windows. But the archbishop was not content with prayer and penance, organization and distribution; he personally ministered to the dying, waited on the sick and helped those in want. The pestilence lasted with varying degrees of intensity from the summer of 1576 until the beginning of 1578. Even during its continuance the magistrates of Milan tried to make mischief between St Charles and the pope. It is possible that some of their complaints were not altogether ill-founded, but the matters complained of were ultimately due to their own supineness and inefficiency. When it was over St Charles wanted to reorganize his cathedral chapter on a basis of common life, and it was the canons' refusal which finally decided him to organize his Oblates of St Ambrose.

In the spring of 1580 he entertained at Milan for a week a dozen young Englishmen, who were going on the English mission, and one of them preached before him. This was St Ralph Sherwin, who in some eighteen months' time was to give his life for the faith at Tyburn. In the same way he met his fellow martyr, St Edmund Campion, and talked with him. A little later in the same year St Charles met St Aloysius Gonzaga, then twelve years old, to whom he gave his first communion. At this time he was doing much travelling and the strain of work and worry was beginning to tell on him; moreover, he curtailed his sleep too much and Pope Gregory personally had to warn him not to overdo his Lenten fasting. At the end of 1583 he was sent as visitor apostolic to Switzerland, and in the Grisons he had to deal not only with Protestantism but with an outbreak of alleged witchcraft and sorcery.

During 1584 St Charles's health got worse and, after arranging for the establishment of a convalescent home in Milan, he went in October to Monte Varallo to make his annual retreat, having with him Father Adorno, s.j. He had clearly foretold to several persons that he should not remain long with them, and on 24 October he was taken ill. On 29 October he started off for Milan, where he arrived on All Souls', having celebrated Mass for the last time on the previous day at his birth-place, Arona. He went straight to bed and asked for the last sacraments, and after receiving them died quietly in the first part of the night between 3 and 4 November. He was only forty-six years old.

CHARLES LWANGA, MARTYR (A.D. 1886)

PATRON SAINT OF AFRICAN CATHOLIC YOUTH ACTION

3 JUNE

The reason for the choice of St Charles as patron of African youth, confirmed by Pope Pius XI in an Apostolic Letter of 22 June 1934, is a natural one, given the circumstances of his life and death. The Letter, to be precise, recognized him as patron of African Catholic Youth Action, and it did so – most unusually – before Charles had been canonized.

In the interior of central Africa the first Catholic missions were established by Cardinal Lavigerie's White Fathers in 1879. In Uganda some progress was made under the not unfriendly local ruler, Mtesa; but his successor, Mwanga, determined to root out Christianity among his people, especially after a Catholic subject, St Joseph Mkasa, reproached him for his debauchery and for his massacre of the Protestant missionary James Hannington and his caravan. Mwanga was addicted to unnatural vice and his anger against Christianity, already kindled by ambitious officers who played on his fears, was kept alight by the refusal of Christian boys in his service to minister to his wickedness.

Joseph Mkasa himself was the first victim: Mwanga seized on a trifling pretext and on 15 November 1885, had him beheaded. To the chieftain's astonishment the Christians were not cowed by this sudden outrage, and in May of the following year the storm burst. When he called for a young 'page' called Mwafu, Mwanga learned that he had been receiving religious instruction from another page, St Denis Sebuggwawo; Denis was sent for, and the king thrust a spear through his throat. That night guards were posted round the royal residence to prevent anyone from escaping.

St Charles Lwanga, who had succeeded Joseph Mkasa in charge of the 'pages', secretly baptized four of them who were catechumens; among them St Kizito, a boy of thirteen whom Lwanga had repeatedly saved from the designs of the king. Next morning the pages were all drawn up before Mwanga, and Christians were ordered to separate themselves from the rest: led by Lwanga and Kizito, the oldest and youngest, they did so – fifteen young men, all under twenty-five years of age. They were joined by two others already under arrest and by two soldiers. Mwanga asked them if they intended to remain Christians. 'Till death!' came the response. 'Then put them to death!'

The appointed place of execution, Namugongo, was thirty-seven miles away, and the convoy set out at once. Three of the youths were killed on the road; the others underwent a cruel imprisonment of seven days at Namugongo while a huge pyre was prepared. Then on Ascension day, 3 June 1886, they were brought out, stripped of their clothing, bound, and each wrapped in a mat of reed: the living faggots were laid on the pyre (one boy, St Mbaga, was first killed by a blow on the neck by order of his father who was the chief executioner), and it was set alight.

The persecution spread and Protestants as well as Catholics gave their lives rather than deny Christ. A leader among the confessors was St Matthias Murumba, who was put to death with revolting cruelty; he was a middle-aged man, assistant judge to the provincial chief, who first heard of Jesus Christ from Protestant missionaries and later was baptized by Father Livinhac, W.F. Another older victim, who was beheaded, was St Andrew Kagwa, chief of Kigowa, who had been the instrument of his wife's conversion and had gathered a large body of catechumens round him. This Andrew together with Charles Lwanga and Matthias Murumba and nineteen others (seventeen of the total being young royal servants) were solemnly beatified in 1920. They were canonized in 1964.

CHRISTOPHER, MARTYR (DATE UNKNOWN)

PATRON SAINT OF TRAVELLERS; SAFE JOURNEYS; MOTORISTS; PILGRIMS

25 JULY (NO LONGER IN THE ROMAN CALENDAR)

St Christopher is the traditional patron of travellers and journeys because of the legend that he spent part of his life carrying travellers over a river, and on one occasion carried Christ himself. He is further invoked by a number of different

professions involved in travel, or at risk from accidents during travel, such as motorists or pilgrims.

Christopher before his baptism was named Reprobus, but afterwards he was named Christopher, which is as much as to say as bearing Christ, for that he bare Christ in four manners: he bare Him on his shoulders by conveying and leading, in his body by making it lean, in mind by devotion, and in his mouth by confession and preaching. The following, with a few minor alterations, is his story from the Golden Legend as put into English by William Caxton, a story known all over Christendom, both East and West:

Christopher was of the lineage of the Canaanites, and he was of a right great stature and had a terrible and fearful face and appearance. And he was twelve cubits of length, and as it is read in some histories that, when he served and dwelled with the king of Canaan, it came in his mind that he would seek the greatest prince that was in the world, and him would he serve and obey. And so far he went that he came to a right great king, of whom the renown generally was that he was the greatest of the world. And when the king saw him, he received him into his service, and made him to dwell in his court. Upon a time a minstrel sang before him a song in which he named oft the Devil, and the king, who was a Christian man, when he heard him name the Devil, made anon the sign of the cross on his visage. And when Christopher saw that, he had a great marvel what sign it was and wherefore the king made it, and he demanded of him. And because the king would not say, he said: 'If thou tell me not, I shall no longer dwell with thee'; and then the king told him, saying: 'Alway when I hear the Devil named I fear that he should have power over me, and I garnish me with this sign that he grieve me not nor annoy me.' Then Christopher said to him: 'Doubtest thou the Devil that he hurt thee? Then is the Devil more mighty and greater than thou art. I am then deceived of my hope and purpose, for I had supposed I had found the most mighty and the most greatest lord in the world, but I commend thee to God, for I will go seek him for to be my lord, and I his servant.

And then he departed from this king and hasted him for to seek the Devil. And as he went by a great desert he saw a great company of knights, of which a knight cruel and horrible came to him and demanded whither he went, and Christopher answered him and said: 'I go seek the Devil, for to be my master.' And he said: 'I am he that thous seekest.' And then Christopher was glad, and bound him to be his servant perpetual and took him for his master and lord. And as they went together by a common way, they found there a cross erect and standing. And anon as the Devil saw the cross he was afeared and fled, and left the right way, and brought Christopher about by a sharp desert. And after, when they were past the cross, he brought him to the highway that they had left.

115

And when Christopher saw that, he marvelled, and demanded whereof he doubted and had left the high and fair way and had gone so far about by so rough a desert. And the Devil would not tell him in no wise. Then Christopher said to him: 'If thou wilt not tell me, I shall anon depart from thee and shall serve thee no more.' Wherefore the Devil was constrained to tell him, and said: 'There was a man called Christ which was hanged on the cross, and when I see His sign I am sore afraid and flee from it wheresoever I see it.' To whom Christopher said: 'Then He is greater and more mightier than thou, when thou art afraid of His sign, and I see well that I have laboured in vain when I have not founden the greatest lord of the world. And I will serve thee no longer; go thy way then, for I will go seek Christ.'

And when he had long sought and demanded where he should find Christ at last he came into a great desert, to an hermit that dwelt there, and this hermit preached to him of Jesu Christ and informed him in the faith diligently and said to him: 'This King whom thou desirest to serve requireth the service that thou must oft fast.' And Christopher said to him: 'Require of me some other thing and I shall do it, for that which thou requirest I may not do.' And the hermit said: 'Thou must then wake and make many prayers.' And Christopher said to him: 'I wot not what this is; I may do no such thing.' And then the hermit said to him: 'Knowest thou such-and-such a river, where many be perished and lost?' To whom Christopher said: 'I know it well.' Then said the hermit: 'Because thou art noble and high of stature and strong in thy members thou shalt be resident by that river, and thou shalt bear over all them that shall pass there, which shall be a thing right pleasing to our Lord Jesu Christ whom thou desirest to serve, and I hope He shall show Himself to thee.' Then said Christopher: 'Certainly this service may I well do, and I promise to Him for to do it.' Then went Christopher to this river and made there a dwelling-place for himself, and bare a great pole in his hand instead of a staff by which he sustained himself in the water, and bare over all manner of people without ceasing. And there he abode, thus doing, many days.

And in a time, as he slept in his lodge, he heard the voice of a child which called him and said: 'Christopher, come out and bear me over.' Then he awoke and went out, but found no man. And when he was again in his house he heard the same voice, and he ran out and found nobody. The third time he was called and came thither and found a child beside the edge of the river, which prayed him goodly to bear him over the water. And then Christopher lift up the child on his shoulders, and took up his staff, and entered into the river for to pass. And the water of the river arose and swelled more and more; and the child was heavy as lead, and alway as he went farther the water increased and grew more, and the child more and more waxed heavy, insomuch that Christopher had great anguish and was afeared to be drowned. And then he was escaped with great pain, and passed the water and set the child aground, he said to the child: 'Child, thou hast put me in great peril; thou weighest almost as I had all the world upon me: I might bear no greater burden.' And the child answered: 'Christopher, marvel thee nothing; for thou hast not only borne all the world upon thee, but thou hast borne Him that created and made all the world, upon thy shoulders. I am Jesu Christ, the King whom thou servest in this work. And because that thou know what I say to be the truth, set thy staff in the earth by thy house and thou shalt see to-morrow that it shall bear flowers and fruit,' and anon He vanished from his eyes. And then Christopher set his staff in the earth, and when he arose on the morn he found his staff like a palm tree, bearing flowers, leaves and dates.

And then Christopher went into the city of Lycia, and understood not their language. Then he prayed our Lord that he might understand them and so he did. And as he was in this prayer, the judges supposed that he had been a fool, and left him there. And then when Christopher understood the language, he covered his visage and went to the place where they martyred Christian men, and comforted them in our Lord. And then the judges smote him in the face, and Christopher said to them: 'If I were not a Christian, I should avenge mine injury.' And then Christopher pitched his rod in the earth and prayed to our Lord that for to convert the people it might bear flowers and fruit; and anon it did so. And then he converted eight thousand men. And then the king sent two knights for to fetch him, and they found him praying, and durst not tell him so. And anon after the king sent as many more, and anon they set them down for to pray with him. And when Christopher arose, he said to them: 'What seek ye?' And when they saw him in the visage, they said to him: 'The king hath sent us, that we should lead thee bound unto him.' And Christopher said to them: ''If I would, ye should not lead me to him, bound or unbound.' And they said to him: 'If thou wilt go thy way, go quit, where thou wilt. And we shall say to the king that we have not found thee.' 'It shall not be so,' said he, 'but I shall go with you.' And then he converted them in the Faith, and commanded them that they should bind his hands behind his back and lead him so bound to the king. And when the king saw him he was afeared and fell down off the seat; and his servants lifted him up again. And then the king enquired his name and his country; and Christopher said to him: 'Before I was baptized I was named Reprobus, and after I am Christopher; before Baptism, a Canaanite, now a Christian man.' To whom the king said: 'Thou hast a foolish name, that is, to wit, of Christ crucified, who could not help Himself and may not profit to thee. How therefore, thou cursed Canaanite, why wilt thou not do sacrifice to our gods?' To whom Christopher said: 'Thou art rightfully called Dagnus, for thou art the death of the world and fellow of the Devil, and thy gods be made with the heads of

117

men.' And the king said to him: 'Thou wert nourished among wild beasts and therefore thou mayst not say but wild language and words unknown to men. And if thou wilt now do sacrifice to the gods, I shall give to thee great gifts and great honours, and if not, I shall destroy thee and consume thee by great pains and torments.' But for all this he would in no wise do sacrifice, wherefore he was sent into prison, and the king did behead the other knights, that he had sent for him, whom he had converted.

And after this he sent into the prison to St Christopher two fair women, of whom the one was named Nicaea and the other Aquilina, and promised to them many great gifts if they could draw Christopher to sin with them. And when Christopher saw that, he set him down in prayer, and when he was constrained by them that embraced him to move, he arose and said: 'What seek ye? For what cause be ye come hither?' And they, which were afraid of his appearance and clearness of his visage, said: 'Holy saint of God, have pity on us so that we may believe in that God that thou preachest.' And when the king heard that, he commanded that they should be let out and brought before him. To whom he said: 'Ye be deceived. But I swear to you by my gods that, if ye do no sacrifice to my gods, ye shall anon perish by evil death.' And they said to him: 'If thou wilt that we shall do sacrifice, command that the places may be made clean and that all the people may assemble at the temple.' And when this was done they entered into the temple, and took their girdles and put them about the necks of the gods, and drew them to the earth and brake them all in pieces; and said to them that were there: 'Go and call physicians and leeches, for to heal your gods.' And then, by the commandment of the king, Aquilina was hanged, and a right great and heavy stone was hanged at her feet so that her members were most piteously broken. And when she was dead and passed to our Lord, her sister Nicaea was cast into a great fire, but she issued out without harm, all whole, and then they made to smite off her head, and so suffered death.

After this Christopher was brought before the king, and the king commanded that he should be beaten with rods of iron, and that there should be set upon his head a cross of iron red hot and burning, and then after he had made a seat of iron and had Christopher bound thereon, and after fire set under it, and cast therein pitch. But the seat melted like wax, and Christopher issued out without any harm or hurt. And when the king saw that, he commanded that he should be bound to a strong stake and that he should be through-shotten with arrows by forty knights archers. But none of the knights might attain him, for the arrows hung in the air about, nigh him, without touching. Then the king weened that he had been through-shotten by the arrows of the knights, and addressed him for to go to him. And one of the arrows returned suddenly from the air and smote him in the eye and blinded him. To whom Christopher said: 'Tyrant, I shall die to-morrow. Make a little clay, mixed with my blood, and anoint therewith thine eye, and thou shalt receive health.' Then by the commandment of the king he was led forth to be beheaded, and then there made he his orison, and his head was smitten off, and so suffered martyrdom. And the king then took a little of his blood and laid it on his eye, and said: 'In the name of God and of St Christopher!' and was anon healed. Then the king believed in God, and gave commendment that if any person blamed God or St Christopher, he should anon be slain with the sword.

This story did not take its final forms until the middle ages: Christopher's name, 'Christ-bearer', from having a spiritual meaning, was given a material one as well, and the story was embroidered by the liveliness of medieval fancy. Except that there was a martyr Christopher, nothing is certainly known about him: the Roman Martyrology says that he suffered in Lycia under Decius, shot with arrows and beheaded after he had been preserved from the flames.

CLARE, (A.D. 1253)

FOUNDRESS OF THE POOR CLARES OR MINORESSES
PATRON SAINT OF EMBROIDERERS; AND OF TELEVISION

11 AUGUST

Clare is the traditional patron of those who do embroidery because, during her years of illness, she is said to have spent her time embroidering cloths and vestments for use in the liturgy.

Aware of the potential value of television, but also aware of its dangers, Pope Pius XII proclaimed St Clare its patron in an Apostolic Letter of 14 February 1958. He chose St Clare, he said, because one Christmas Eve, when Clare was confined to her bed through sickness, she saw the crib, and heard the singing in the church just as if she had been present.

Clare was born about the year 1193. Her mother was Ortolana di Fiumi and her father Faverone Offreduccio, and she had a younger sister, Agnes, and another, Beatrice, but of her childhood, adolescence and home-life there are no certain facts. When she was eighteen St Francis came to preach the Lenten sermons at the church of San Giorgio in Assisi; his words fired her, she sought him out secretly, and he strengthened her nascent desire to leave all things for Christ. On Palm Sunday in the year 1212 Clare attended at the cathedral of Assisi for the blessing of palms; when all the rest went up to the altar-rails to receive their branch of olive a sudden shyness kept her in her place, which the bishop seeing, he went from the altar down to her and gave her the branch. In the evening she ran away from home and went a mile out of the town to the Portiuncula, where St Francis lived with his little community. He and his brethren met her at the door of the chapel of our Lady of the Angels with lighted tapers in their hands, and before the altar she put off her fine clothes, and St Francis cut off her hair, and gave her his penitential habit, which was a tunic of sackcloth tied about her with a cord. The holy father not having yet any nunnery of his own, placed her for the present in the Benedictine convent of St Paul near Bastia, where she was affectionately received.

No sooner was her action made public but her friends and relations came in a body to draw her out of her retreat. St Francis soon after removed her to another nunnery, that of Sant' Angelo di Panzo. There her sister Agnes joined her, which drew on them both a fresh persecution. Agnes's constancy proved at last victorious, and St Francis gave her also the habit, though she was only fifteen years of age. Eventually St Francis placed them in a poor house contiguous to the church of San Damiano, on the outskirts of Assisi, and appointed Clare the superior. She was later joined by her mother and others, among whom three were of the illustrious family of the Ubaldini in Florence.

St Clare saw founded within a few years monasteries of her nuns at several places in Italy, France and Germany. Bd Agnes, daughter to the King of Bohemia, founded a nunnery of the order in Prague, in which she took the habit. St Clare and her community had neither stockings, shoes, sandals nor any other covering on their feet; they slept on the ground, observed perpetual abstinence from meat, and never spoke but when they were obliged by necessity and charity. St Francis wished that his order should never possess any rents or other property even in common, subsisting on daily contributions, and St Clare possessed this spirit in perfection. Pope Gregory IX desired to mitigate this part of her rule, and offered to settle a yearly revenue on the Poor Ladies of San Damiano; but she persuaded him to leave her order in its first rigorous establishment. Gregory accordingly granted in 1228 the *Privilegium paupertatis*, that they might not be constrained by anyone to accept possessions. The convents of Perugia and Florence also received this privilege, but others thought it more prudent to accept a mitigation. After the death of Gregory IX (who as Cardinal Ugolino had drawn up the first written rule for the Poor Ladies of San Damiano), Innocent IV in 1247 published another recension of the rule which in some respects brought it nearer to Franciscan than to Benedictine observance, but which permitted the holding of property in common; he wrote that he did not wish to force this rule on any community unwilling to accept it. St Clare was unwilling, and she set to work to draw up a rule which should unequivocally provide that the sisters possess no property, either as individuals or as a community. It was not until two days before she died that this rule was approved for the convent of San Damiano by Pope Innocent IV.

From the time when she was appointed abbess, much against her will, by St Francis in 1215, St Clare governed the convent for forty years. Thomas of

Celano, who often heard St Francis warning his followers to avoid any injudicious association with the Poor Ladies, states categorically that St Clare never left the walls of San Damiano. Unhappily even during her life, and for long after her death at intervals, there was disagreement between the Poor Clares and the Friars Minor as to the relations of the two orders: the observant Clares maintaining that the friars were under obligation to serve them in things both spiritual and temporal.

St Clare bore years of sickness with sublime patience, and at last in 1253 the long-drawn-out agony began. Twice during its course she was visited by Pope Innocent IV, who gave her absolution. She died the day after the feast of St Laurence, the forty-second year after her religious profession, and the sixtieth of her age. She was buried on the day following, on which the Church keeps her festival. Pope Alexander IV canonized her at Anagni in 1255.

CLARUS, ABBOT (*c.* A.D. 660)

PATRON SAINT OF PERSONS AFFLICTED BY SHORT-SIGHTEDNESS

1 JANUARY

The invocation of Clarus by those who have problems with their sight seems to have arisen solely from his name – which means 'clear'.

St Clarus, whose name was given him in his youth from his 'brightness', not so much in human learning as in his perception of the things of God, is believed to have been made abbot of the monastery of St Marcellus, at Vienne in Dauphiné, early in the seventh century. A Latin life, which must be more than a hundred years later in date, relates many marvellous stories of the miracles he worked, but it is probably trustworthy when it tells us that Clarus was first a monk in the abbey of St Ferréol, that he was highly esteemed by Cadeoldus, Archbishop of Vienne, that he was made spiritual director of the convent of St Blandina, where his own mother and other widows took the veil, and that he ended his days (1 January *c.* 660) as abbot of St Marcellus. His *cultus* was confirmed in 1903.

COLOMAN, MARTYR (A.D. 1012)

A PATRON SAINT OF AUSTRIA

13 OCTOBER

As his brief life indicates, Coloman came to be regarded as one of the lesser patrons of Austria, a role confirmed, along with St Florian, by a decree of the Sacred Congregation of Rites dated 29 December 1913.

In the beginning of the eleventh century the neighbouring nations of Austria, Moravia and Bohemia were engaged against each other in dissensions and wars. Coloman, a Scot or Irishman who was going on a pilgrimage to Jerusalem, arrived by the Danube from the enemy's country at Stockerau, a town six miles above Vienna. The inhabitants, persuading themselves that he was a spy because, not knowing their language, he could not give a satisfactory account of himself, hanged him, on 13 July 1012. His patience under unjust sufferings was taken as a proof of the sanctity of Coloman, and it was esteemed to be confirmed by the incorruption of his body, which was said to be the occasion of many miracles. Three years after his death his body was translated to the abbey of Melk. After a time St Coloman came to be venerated as a minor patron of Austria, and a quite imaginary royal ancestry was invented for him. He is the titular of many churches in Austria, Hungary and Bavaria, and is invoked for the help and healing of horses and horned cattle. On his feast the blessing of these animals takes place at Hohenschwangau, near Füssen.

COLUMBA, OR COLMCILLE, ABBOT OF IONA (A.D. 597)

A PATRON SAINT OF IRELAND

9 JUNE

Together with SS. Patrick and Brigid, Columba was acknowledged as one of Ireland's patron saints by a decree of the Sacred Congregation of Rites on 2 December 1962.

The most famous of Scottish saints, Columba, was actually an Irishman of the Uí Néill of the North and was born, probably about the year 521, at Gartan in County Donegal. On both sides he was of royal lineage, for his father Fedhlimidh, or Phelim, was great-grandson to Niall of the Nine Hostages, overlord of Ireland, whilst his mother Eithne, besides being related to the princes of Scottish Dalriada, was herself descended from a king of Leinster. At his baptism, which was administered by his foster father the priest Cruithnechan, the little boy received the name of Colm, Colum or Columba. In later life he was commonly called Colmcille – a designation which Bede derives from *cella et Columba*, and which almost certainly refers to the many cells or religious foundations he established. As soon as he was considered old enough, he was removed from the care of his priest guardian at Temple Douglas to St Finnian's great school at Moville. There he must have spent a number of years, for he was a deacon when he left. From Moville he went to study in Leinster under an aged bard called Master Gemman. The bards preserved the records of Irish history and literature, and Columba himself was a poet of no mean order. He afterwards passed on to another famous monastic school, that of Clonard, presided over by another Finnian, who was called the tutor of Erin's saints. Columba was one of that distinguished band of his disciples who are reckoned as the Twelve Apostles of Erin. It was probably while he was at Clonard that he was ordained priest, but it may have been a little later when he was living at Glasnevin, with St Comgall, St Kieran and St Canice, under their former fellow student St Mobhi. In 543 an outbreak of plague compelled Mobhi to break up his flourishing school and Columba, now twenty-five years of age and fully trained, returned to his native Ulster.

A striking figure of great stature and of athletic build, with a voice 'so loud and melodious it could be heard a mile off', Columba spent the next fifteen years going about Ireland preaching and founding monasteries of which the chief were those of Derry, Durrow and Kells. Like the true scholar that he was, Columba dearly loved books and spared no pains to obtain them. Amongst the many precious manuscripts his former master, St Finnian, had obtained in Rome was the first copy of St Jerome's psalter to reach Ireland. St Columba borrowed the book of which he surreptitiously made a copy for his own use. St Finnian, however, on being told what he had done, laid claim to the transcript. Columba refused to give it up, and the case was laid before king Diarmaid, overlord of Ireland. The verdict went against Columba. 'To every cow her calf,' said the judge, 'and to every book its son-book. Therefore the copy which you have made, Colmcille, belongs to Finnian.'

This sentence Columba bitterly resented, but he was soon to have a much more serious grievance against the king. For when Curnan of Connaught, after fatally injuring an opponent in a hurling match, took refuge with Columba, he was dragged from his protector's arms and slain by Diarmaid's men in defiance of the rights of sanctuary. The war which broke out shortly afterwards between Columba's clan and Diarmaid's followers is stated in most of the Irish *Lives* to have been instigated by Columba, and after the battle of Cuil Dremne in which 3000 were slain he was accused of being morally responsible for their death. The synod of Telltown in Meath passed upon him a censure which would have been followed by an excommunication but for the intervention of St Brendan. Columba's own conscience was uneasy, and by the advice of St Molaise he determined to expiate his offence by exiling himself from his own country and by attempting to win for Christ as many souls as had perished in the battle of Cuil Dremne.

This is the traditional account of the events which led to Columba's departure from Ireland, and it is probably correct in the main. At the same time it must be admitted that missionary zeal and love of Christ are the only motives ascribed to him by his earliest biographers or by St Adamnan, who is our chief authority for his subsequent history. In the year 563 Columba embarked with twelve companions – all of them his blood relations – in a wicker coracle covered with leather, and on the eve of Pentecost he landed in the island of I, or Iona. He was in his forty-second year. His first work was the building of the monastery which was to be his home for the rest of his life and which was to be famous throughout western Christendom for centuries. The land was made over to him by his kinsman Conall, king of Scottish Dalriada, at whose invitation he may have come to Scotland. Situated opposite the border between the Picts of the north and the Scots of the south, Iona formed an ideal centre for missions to both peoples. At first Columba appears to have devoted his missionary effort to teaching the imperfectly instructed Christians of Dalriada – most of whom were of Irish descent – but after about two years he turned his attention to the evangelization of the Scotland Picts. Accompanied by St Comgall and St Canice he made his way to the castle of the redoubtable King Brude at Inverness.

That pagan monarch had given orders that they were not to be admitted, but when St Columba upraised his arm to make the sign of the cross, bolts were withdrawn, gates fell open, and the strangers entered unhindered. Impressed by their supernatural powers the king listened to their words and ever afterwards held Columba in high honour. He also, as overlord, confirmed him in the possession of Iona. We know from St Adamnan that two or three times the saint crossed the mountain range which divides the west of Scotland from the east and that his missionary zeal took him to Ardnamurchan, to Skye, to Kintyre, to Loch Ness and to Lochaber, and perhaps to Morven. He is commonly credited, furthermore, with having planted the Church in Aberdeenshire and with having evangelized practically the whole of Pictland, but this has been contested on various grounds. When the descendants of the Dalriada kings became the rulers of Scotland they were naturally eager to magnify St Columba and a tendency may well have arisen to bestow upon him the laurels won by other missionaries from Iona and elsewhere.

Columba never lost touch with Ireland. In 575 he attended the synod of Drumceat in Meath in company with Conall's successor Aidan, and there he was successful in defending the status and privileges of his Dalriada kinsfolk, in vetoing the proposed abolition of the order of bards, and in securing for women exemption from all military service. He was in Ireland again ten years later, and in 587 he seems to have been regarded as in some way responsible for another battle – this time at Cuil Feda, near Clonard. When not engaged on missionary or diplomatic expeditions his headquarters continued to be at Iona, where he was visited by persons of all conditions, some desiring spiritual or bodily help, some attracted by his reputation for sanctity, his miracles and his prophecies. His manner of life was most austere; and in his earlier life he was apt to be no less hard with others. Montalembert remarked that, 'Of all qualities, gentleness was precisely the one in which Columba failed the most'. But with the passage of time his character mellowed and the picture painted by St Adamnan of his serene old age shows him in a singularly attractive light, a lover of man and beast. Four years before his death he had an illness which threatened to prove fatal, but his life was prolonged in answer to the prayers of the community. As his strength began to fail he spent much time transcribing books. On the day before his death he was copying the Psalter, and had written, 'They that love the Lord shall lack no good thing', when he paused and said, 'Here I must stop: let Baithin do the rest'. Baithin was his cousin whom he had nominated as his successor.

That night when the monks came to the church for Matins, they found their beloved abbot outstretched helpless and dying before the altar. As his faithful attendant Diarmaid gently upraised him he made a feeble effort to bless his brethren and then immediately breathed his last. Columba was indeed dead, but his influence lasted on, extended until it came to dominate the churches of Scotland, Ireland and Northumbria. For three-quarters of a century and more, Celtic Christians in those lands upheld Columban traditions in certain matters of order and ritual in opposition to those of Rome itself, and the rule Columba had drawn up for his monks was followed in many of the monasteries of western Europe until it was superseded by the milder ordinances of St Benedict.

Adamnan, St Columba's biographer, had not personally known him, for he was born at least thirty years after his death, but as his kinsman by blood and a successor in the office of abbot at Iona itself, he must have been steeped in the traditions which such a personality could not fail to have created for those who followed in his footsteps. The portrait of Columba left by Adamnan in any case deserves to be quoted. 'He had the face of an angel; he was of an excellent nature, polished in speech, holy in deed, great in counsel. He never let a single hour pass without engaging in prayer or reading or writing or some other occupation. He endured the hardships of fasting and vigils without intermission by day and night, the burden of a single one of his labours would seem beyond the powers of man. And, in the midst of all his toils, he appeared loving unto all, serene and holy, rejoicing in the joy of the Holy Spirit in his inmost heart.'

And Columba's prophetical last blessing of the Isle of Iona came true: 'Unto this place, small and mean though it be, great homage shall yet be paid, not only by the kings and peoples of the Scots, but by the rules of barbarous and distant nations with their peoples. The saints, also, of other churches shall regard it with no common reverence.'

COSMAS AND DAMIAN, MARTYRS (DATE UNKNOWN)

PATRON SAINTS OF DOCTORS, PHYSICIANS AND SURGEONS; OF CHEMISTS,
PHARMACISTS, DRUGGISTS AND APOTHECARIES; OF BARBERS AND
HAIRDRESSERS; AND OF BLIND PEOPLE

26 SEPTEMBER

*The story that follows, a basic summary of the legends surrounding these twin saints,
is reason enough for their becoming, in the Middle Ages, the patrons of doctors, and,
indeed, of a variety of professions associated with medicine – such as, at one time,
barbers.*

Cosmas and Damian are the principal and best known of those saints
venerated in the East as ἀνάργυροι, 'moneyless ones', because they practised medicine without taking reward from their patients.

Saints Cosmas and Damian were twin brothers, born in Arabia, who
studied the sciences in Syria and became eminent for their skill in medicine. Being Christians, and full of the holy temper of charity, they practised
their profession with great application and success, but never took any fee
for their services. They lived at Aegeae on the bay of Alexandretta in
Cilicia, and were remarkable both for the love and respect which the
people bore them on account of the good offices which they received from
their charity, and for their zeal for the Christian faith, which they took
every opportunity their profession gave them to propagate. When persecution began to rage, it was impossible for persons of so distinguished a
character to lie concealed. They were therefore apprehended by the order
of Lysias, governor of Cilicia, and after various torments were beheaded
for the faith. Their bodies were carried into Syria, and buried at Cyrrhus,
which was the chief centre of their *cultus* and where the earliest references
locate their martyrdom.

The legends pad out this simple story with numerous marvels. For
example, before they were eventually beheaded they defied death by water,
fire and crucifixion. While they were hanging on the crosses the mob stoned
them, but the missiles recoiled on the heads of the throwers; in the same way
the arrows of archers who were brought up to shoot at them turned in the air
and scattered the bowmen (the same is recorded of St Christopher and
others). The three brothers of Cosmas and Damian – Anthimus, Leontius
and Euprepiu – are said to have suffered with them, and their names are
mentioned in the Roman Martyrology. Many miracles of healing were
ascribed to them after their death, the saints sometimes appearing to the
sufferers in sleep and prescribing for them or curing them there and then, as
was supposed to happen to pagan devotees in the temples of Aesculapius
and Serapis. Among the distinguished people who attributed recovery from
serious sickness to SS. Cosmas and Damian was the Emperor Justinian I
who, out of regard for their relics, honoured the city of Cyrrhus; and two

churches at Constantinople are said to have been built in honour of the martyrs in the early fifth century. Their basilica at Rome with its lovely mosaics was dedicated *c.* 530.

CRISPIN AND CRISPINIAN, MARTYRS (DATE UNKNOWN)

PATRON SAINTS OF SHOEMAKERS, COBBLERS, AND LEATHERWORKERS

25 OCTOBER

These two martyrs have been regarded since medieval times as the patrons of anyone who worked with leather, on the strength of the story of their lives.

The names of these two martyrs were famous throughout northern Europe in the Middle Ages, but are today known in England chiefly from the speech which Shakespeare puts into the mouth of King Henry V on the eve of Agincourt (*Henry V*, act iv, scene 3). Their very late *passio* unfortunately cannot be relied on. It says that they came from Rome to preach the faith in Gaul towards the middle of the third century, together with St Quintinus and others. Fixing their residence at Soissons, they instructed many in the faith of Christ, which they preached during the day; and, in imitation of St Paul, worked with their hands at night making shoes, though they are said to have been nobly born (and brothers). The infidels listened to their instructions and were astonished at the example of their lives, and the effect was the conversion of many to the Christian faith. They had continued this employment several years when, the Emperor Maximian coming into Gaul, a complaint was lodged against them. He, perhaps as much to gratify their accusers as to indulge his own superstition and cruelty, gave orders that they should be taken before Rictiovarus, an implacable enemy of Christians, who subjected them to various torments and in vain tried to kill them by drowning and boiling; this so infuriated him that he took his own life by jumping into the fire prepared for them. Thereupon Maximian commanded that they be beheaded, and this was done. Later a church was built over their tomb, and St Eligius the Smith embellished their shrine. SS. Crispin and Crispinian are supposed to have plied their trade without taking payment unless it was offered and thereby disposed men to listen to the gospel.

The Roman Martyrology says that the relics of these martyrs were translated from Soissons to the church of St Laurence *in Panisperna* at Rome. Nothing is certainly known about them, and it is possible – even more likely – that the reverse is the truth: that SS. Crispin and Crispinian were Roman martyrs whose relics were brought to Soissons and so started a local *cultus*.

There is a local tradition which associates these martyrs with the little port of Faversham in Kent. They are said to have fled thither to escape the persecution, and followed their trade of shoemaking at a house on the site of the Swan Inn, at the lower end of Preston Street, 'near the Cross Well'. A Mr Southouse, writing about the year 1670, says that in his time this house had 'considerable visits paid to it by the foreigners of that gentle calling', so it looks as if the tradition was also known abroad. There was an altar dedicated in honour of SS. Crispin and Crispinian in the parish church of St Mary of Charity.

CUNEGUND, EMPRESS (A.D. 1033)

A PATRON SAINT OF LUXEMBOURG; AND OF LITHUANIA

3 MARCH

Cunegund's association with Luxembourg is clear from the story of her life, and she was formally declared one of that country's patrons in a decree of the Sacred Congregation of Rites dated 19 May 1914. Long before, however, in a Letter dated 7 September 1715, she had been acknowledged by Clement XI as one of the patrons of Lithuania.

St Cunegund was piously trained from her earliest years by her parents, Siegfried of Luxembourg and his saintly wife Hedwig. She married St Henry, Duke of Bavaria, who gave her as a wedding present a crucifix of eastern workmanship which is said to be identical with one now existing in Munich. Later writers have asserted that they both took a vow of virginity on their wedding-day, but historians now seem to agree that there is no reliable evidence to corroborate the statement. Upon the death of the Emperor Otto III, Henry was elected king of the Romans, and his coronation by St Willigis at Mainz was followed, two months later, by that of his wife at Paderborn. In 1013 they went together to Rome to receive the imperial crown from Pope Benedict VIII.

It was partly at the instigation of St Cunegund that the emperor founded the monastery and cathedral of Bamberg, to the consecration of which Pope Benedict came in person, and she obtained for the city such privileges that by common report her silken threads were a better defence than walls. During a dangerous illness she had made a vow that if she recovered she would found a convent at Kaufungen, near Cassel, in Hesse. This she proceeded to do, and had nearly finished building a house for nuns of the Benedictine Order when St Henry died.

Her later biographers relate a quaint story about the first abbess. It appears that the empress had a young niece, called Judith or Jutta, to whom she was much attached, and whom she had educated with great care. When a superior had to be found for the new convent, St Cunegund appointed Judith and gave her many admonitions and much good advice. No sooner, however, did the young abbess find herself free, than she began to show symptoms of frivolity and lax observance: it was soon noticed that she was the first in the refectory and the last to come to chapel. The climax came when she failed to appear in the Sunday procession and was found feasting with some of the younger sisters. Filled with indignation St Cunegund sternly upbraided the culprit, and even struck her. The marks of her fingers remained impressed upon the abbess's cheek until her dying day, and the marvel not only converted her, but had a salutary effect upon the whole community.

On the anniversary of her husband's death in 1024 Cunegund invited a number of prelates to the dedication of her church at Kaufungen. When the gospel had been sung at Mass, she offered at the altar a piece of the true cross, and then, putting off her imperial robes, she was clothed in a nun's habit, and the bishop gave her the veil. Once she had been consecrated to God in religion, she seemed entirely to forget that she had ever been an empress and behaved as the lowest in the house, being convinced that she was so before God. She feared nothing more than anything that could recall her former dignity. She prayed and read much and especially made it her business to visit and comfort the sick. Thus she passed the last years of her life, dying on 3 March 1033 (or 1039). Her body was taken to Bamberg to be buried with her husband's.

CYPRIAN, BISHOP OF CARTHAGE (A.D. 258)

PATRON SAINT OF NORTH AFRICA; AND OF ALGERIA

16 SEPTEMBER

Given the region in which Cyprian spent his life, and of which he became such an ornament, it is hardly surprising that he should have been declared patron of North Africa by successive decrees of the Sacred Congregation of Rites dated 6 July 1914, 10 January 1958 and 27 July 1962. The first of those decrees declared him also to be the patron of Algeria in particular.

Caecilius Cyprianus, popularly known as Thascius, was born about the year 200, probably at Carthage; certainly he was, according to St Jerome, a native of Proconsular Africa. Very little is known of his pre-Christian life; he was a public orator, teacher of rhetoric, and pleader in the courts, and engaged to the full in the life of Carthage, both public and social. God's instrument of his conversion, somewhere about middle age, was an old priest, Caecilian, and Cyprian ever after reverenced him as his father and guardian angel. Caecilian, in turn, had the greatest confidence in his virtue and on his death-bed recommended his wife and children to Cyprian's care and protection. A complete change came over Cyprian's life. Before his baptism he made a vow of perfect chastity, which greatly astonished the

Carthaginians and drew even from his biographer St Pontius the exclamation, 'Who ever saw such a miracle!'

With the study of the Holy Scriptures St Cyprian joined that of their best expositors, and in a short time became acquainted with the works of the greatest religious writers: he particularly delighted in the writings of his countryman Tertullian. Cyprian was soon made priest, and in 248 he was designated for the bishopric of Carthage. At first he refused and sought to fly, but finding it in vain he yielded and was consecrated.

The Church continued to enjoy peace for about a year after St Cyprian's promotion to the see of Carthage, till the Emperor Decius began his reign by raising a persecution. Years of quietness and prosperity had had a weakening effect among the Christians, and when the edict reached Carthage there was a stampede to the capitol to register apostasies with the magistrates, amid cries of 'Cyprian to the lions!' from the pagan mob. The bishop was proscribed, and his goods ordered to be forfeited, but Cyprian had already retired to a hiding-place, a proceeding which brought upon him much adverse criticism both from Rome and in Africa. He felt put on his defence, and set out justifying reasons for his action in several letters to the clergy.

During the absence of St Cyprian a priest who had opposed his episcopal election, named Novatus, went into open schism. Some among the lapsed, and confessors who were displeased at St Cyprian's discipline towards the former, adhered to him, for Novatus received, without any canonical penance, all apostates who desired to return to the communion of the Church. St Cyprian denounced Novatus, and at a council convened at Carthage when the persecution slackened he read a treatise on the unity of the Church.

The leaders of the schismatics were excommunicated, and Novatus departed to Rome to help stir up trouble there, where Novatian had set himself up as antipope. Cyprian recognized Cornelius as the true pope and was active in his support both in Italy and Africa during the ensuing schism; with St Dionysius, Bishop of Alexandria, he rallied the bishops of the East to Cornelius, making it clear to them that to adhere to a false bishop of Rome was to be out of communion with the Church. In connexion with these disturbances he added to his treatise on Unity one on the question of the Lapsed.

St Cyprian complains in many parts of his works that the peace which the Church had enjoyed enervated in some Christians the watchfulness and spirit of their profession, and had opened a door to many converts who had no true spirit of faith, and many lacked courage to stand the trial. These, whether apostates who had sacrificed to idols or *libellaticii* who, without sacrificing, had purchased for money certificates that they *had* offered sacrifice, were the lapsed (*lapsi*), concerning the treatment of whom so great a controversy raged during and after the Decian persecution: on the side of excessive lenience Novatus went into schism, while Novatian's severity crystallized into the heresy that the Church cannot absolve an apostate at all. At this time those guilty of less heinous sins than apostasy were not admitted to assist at the holy Mysteries before they had gone through a rigorous course of public penance, consisting of four degrees and of several years' continuance. Relaxations of these penances were granted on certain extraordinary occasions, and it was also customary to grant 'indulgences' to penitents who received a recommendation from some martyr going to execution, or from some confessor in prison for the faith, containing a request on their behalf, which the bishop and his clergy examined and often ratified. In St Cyprian's time this custom degenerated in Africa into an abuse, by the number of such *libelli martyrum*, and their often being given in too vague or peremptory terms, and without examination or discernment.

Cyprian condemned these abuses severely, but though it would appear that he himself tended to severity he in fact pursued a middle way, and in practice was considerate and lenient. After he had consulted the Roman clergy he insisted that this episcopal ruling must be followed without question until the whole matter could be brought up for discussion by all the African bishops and priests. This was eventually done in 251, at the council at Carthage mentioned above, and it was decided that, whereas *libellaticii* might be restored after terms of penance varying in length according to the case, *sacrificati* could receive communion only at death. But in the following year the persecution of Gallus and Volusian began, and another African council decreed that 'all the penitents who professed themselves ready to enter the list afresh, there to abide the utmost heat of battle and manfully to fight for the name of the Lord and for their own salvation, should receive the peace of the Church'.

Between the years 252 and 254 Carthage was visited by a terrible plague, of the ravages of which St Pontius has left a vivid description. Cyprian organized the Christians of the city and spoke to them strongly on the duty of mercy and charity, teaching them that they ought to extend their care not only to their own people, but also to their enemies and persecutors. To comfort and fortify his flock during the plague, Cyprian wrote his teatise *De mortalitate*.

Whereas St Cyprian so strongly supported Pope St Cornelius in the closing years of his life he was moved to oppose Pope St Stephen I in the matter of baptism conferred by heretics and schismatics – he and the other African bishops refused to recognize its validity. Though Cyprian published a treatise on the goodness of patience, he displayed considerable warmth during this controversy, an excess for which, as St Augustine says, he atoned by his glorious martyrdom. For in August 257 was promulgated the first edict of Valerian's persecution, which forbade all assemblies of Christians and which required bishops, priests and deacons to take part in official worship under pain of exile, and on 30 August the bishop of Carthage was brought before the proconsul. Patternus ordered him into exile, but when Galerius replaced him as proconsul Cyprian was recalled from exile and again put on trial. Once more, however, he refused to offer sacrifice to the pagan gods, and on this occasion he was sentenced to death by beheading. The sentence was carried out immediately. It was 14 September, A.D. 258.

CYRIACUS (DATE UNKNOWN)

PATRON SAINT OF THOSE IN DANGER OF POSSESSION BY THE DEVIL

8 AUGUST

This saint was invoked in the Middle Ages against the danger of possession by the devil, especially at the moment of death, on the basis of his legendary life-story which Alban Butler describes as 'a romance devoid of historical value.'

Cyriacus was a deacon who, with Sissinius, Largus and Smaragdus, succoured the Christians who were being forced to work on the construction of the baths of Diocletian. Having been arrested, Cyriacus cured the emperor's daughter, Artemia, of demoniac possession, and was rewarded with the present of a house; herein he established a place of worship, the *titulus Cyriaci*. He was then sent to Persia at the request of its king, whose daughter suffered in the same way as Artemia, and her also he cured. After his return to Rome he was apprehended by order of Maximian, together with Largus and Smaragdus, and on March 16, in company with a score of others, he was tortured and beheaded at a spot on the Salarian Way. On 8 August Pope St Marcellus I translated the bodies to a burial-place, which received the name of Cyriacus, on the road to Ostia.

That Cyriacus was an authentic martyr, honoured on this day in Rome from an early date, is proved from the *Depositio Martyrum* of 354. Therein he is said to rest close beside the seventh milestone on the road to Ostia in company with Largus, 'Ixmaracdus', and three others, who are named. This Cyriacus has been confused with another Cyriacus, the founder of the *titulus Cyriaci*, and a fictitious story was later evolved which is best known to us as an episode in the spurious Acts of Pope St Marcellus.

CYRIL AND METHODIUS, ARCHBISHOP OF SIRMIUM
(A.D. 869 AND 884)

PATRON SAINTS OF YUGOSLAVIA; OF CZECHOSLOVAKIA, INCLUDING BOHEMIA
AND MORAVIA; AND OF EUROPE

14 FEBRUARY

As the biography relates, these two saints are regarded as the apostles of the Southern Slavs, and 'fathers' of Slavonic literary culture. It is therefore appropriate that they should be taken as patrons by Yugoslavia, formally recognized by the Sacred Congregation of Rites in a decree of 8 August 1917; and by Czechoslovakia, confirmed by a number of separate decrees for both Bohemia and Moravia, 4 May 1914, 11 December 1935 and 25 March 1936.

Pope John Paul II, himself a Slav, promoted Saints Cyril and Methodius joint patrons of Europe alongside St Benedict (q.v.) in an Apostolic Letter of 31 December 1980 for their work in bringing Christianity to the Slav peoples. By linking the two brother missionaries with St Benedict, Pope John Paul II wished to emphasize the unity of Europe, both East and West.

These brothers, natives of Thessalonika, are venerated as the apostles of the Southern Slavs and the fathers of Slavonic literary culture. Cyril, the younger of them, was baptized Constantine and assumed the name by which he is usually known only shortly before his death, when he received the habit of a monk. At an early age he was sent to Constantinople, where he studied at the imperial university under Leo the Grammarian and Photius. Here he learned all the profane sciences but no theology; however, he was ordained deacon (priest probably not till later) and in due course took over the chair of Photius, gaining for himself a great reputation, evidenced by the epithet 'the Philosopher'. For a time he retired to a religious house, but in 861 he was sent by the emperor, Michael III, on a religio-political mission to the ruler of the judaized Khazars between the Dnieper and the Volga. His elder brother, Methodius, who, after being governor of one of the Slav colonies in the Opsikion province, had become a monk, also took part in the mission to the Khazars, and on his return to Greece was elected abbot of an important monastery.

In 862 there arrived in Constantinople an ambassador charged by Rostislav, prince of Moravia, to ask that the emperor would send him missionaries capable of teaching his people in their own language. Photius, now patriarch of Constantinople, decided that Cyril and Methodius were most suitable for the work: they were learned men, who knew Slavonic, and the first requirement was the provision of characters in which the Slav tongue might be written. The characters now called 'cyrillic', from which are derived the present Russian, Serbian and Bulgarian letters, were invented from the Greek capitals, perhaps by the followers of St Cyril; the 'glagolithic'

133

alphabet, in which the Slav-Roman liturgical books of certain Yugoslav Catholics are printed, may be that prepared for this occasion by Cyril himself.

In 863 the two brothers set out with a number of assistants and came to the court of Rostislav. The new missionaries made free use of the vernacular in their preaching and ministrations, and this made immediate appeal to the local people. To the German clergy this was objectionable, and their opposition was strengthened when the Emperor Louis the German forced Rostislav to take an oath of fealty to him. The Byzantine missionaries, armed with their pericopes from the Scriptures and liturgical hymns in Slavonic, pursued their way with much success, but were soon handicapped by their lack of a bishop to ordain more priests. The German prelate, the bishop of Passau, would not do it, and Cyril therefore determined to seek help elsewhere, presumably from Constantinople whence he came.

On their way the brothers arrived in Venice. It was at a bad moment. Photius at Constantinople had incurred excommunication; the *protégés* of the Eastern emperor and their liturgical use of a new tongue were vehemently criticized. They came to Rome bringing with them alleged relics of Pope St Clement, which St Cyril had recovered when in the Crimea on his way back from the Khazars. Adrian II warmly welcomed the bearers of so great a gift. He examined their cause, and he gave judgement: Cyril and Methodius were to receive episcopal consecration, their neophytes were to be ordained, the use of the liturgy in Slavonic was approved.

While still in Rome Cyril died, on 14 February 869. He was buried with great pomp in the church of San Clemente on the Coelian, where the relics of St Clement had been enshrined. St Methodius now took up his brother's leadership. Having been consecrated bishop he returned, bearing a letter from the Holy See recommending him as a man of 'exact understanding and orthodoxy'. Kosel, prince of Pannonia, asked that the ancient archdiocese of Sirmium (now Mitrovitsa) be revived. Methodius was made metropolitan and the boundaries of his charge extended to the borders of Bulgaria. But the papal approval did not intimidate the Western clergy there, and the situation in Moravia had now changed. Rostislav's nephew, Svatopluk, had allied himself with Carloman of Bavaria and driven his uncle out. In 870 Methodius found himself haled before a synod of German bishops and interned in a leaking cell. Only after two years could the pope, now John VIII, get him released. John judged it prudent to withdraw the permission to use Slavonic ('a barbarous language', he called it), except for the purpose of preaching. At the same time he reminded the Germans that Pannonia and the disposition of sees throughout Illyricum belonged of old to the Holy See.

During the following years St Methodius continued his work of evangelization in Moravia, but he made an enemy of Svatopluk, whom he rebuked for the wickedness of his life. Accordingly in 878 the archbishop was delated to the Holy See both for continuing to conduct divine worship in Slavonic and for heresay, in that he omitted the words 'and the Son' from the creed (at that time these words had not been introduced everywhere in the West, and not in Rome). John VIII summoned him to Rome. Methodius was able to convince the pope both of his orthodoxy and of the desirability of the Slavonic liturgy, and John again conceded it, though with certain reservations. Unfortunately, in accordance with the wishes of Svatopluk, the pope also nominated to the see of Nitra, which was suffragan to Sirmium, a German priest called Wiching, an implacable opponent of Methodius. This unscrupulous prelate continued to persecute his metropolitan, even to the extent of forging pontifical documents. After his death, Wiching obtained the archiepiscopal see, banished the chief disciples of his predecessor, and undid much of his work in Moravia.

During the last four years of his life, according to the 'Pannonian legend', St Methodius completed the Slavonic translation of the Bible (except the books of Machabees) and also of the *Nomokanon*, a compliation of Byzantine ecclesiastical and civil law. This suggests that circumstances were preventing him from devoting all his time to missionary and episcopal concerns; in other words, he was fighting a losing battle with the German influence. He died, probably at Stare Mesto (Velehrad), worn out by his apostolic labours and the opposition of those who thought them misdirected, on 6 April 884.

DAMASUS, POPE (A.D. 384)

PATRON SAINT OF ARCHAEOLOGISTS

11 DECEMBER

It is for Damasus' work restoring the catacombs, providing inscriptions – epitaphs for his predecessors as Bishops of Rome in particular – and caring for relics, that he has been recognized as patron of archaeologists.

Pope Damasus is said in the *Liber Pontificalis* to have been a Spaniard, which may be true of his extraction, but he seems to have been born at Rome, where his father was a priest. Damasus himself was never married, and he became deacon in the church which his father served. When Pope Liberius died in 366, Damasus, who was then about sixty years old, was chosen bishop of Rome. His accession was far from unopposed, a minority electing another deacon, called Ursicinus or Ursinus, whom they supported with great violence. It appears that the civil power in its maintenance of Damasus used considerable cruelty. The adherents of the antipope were not easily quelled, and as late as 378 Damasus had to clear himself both before the Emperor Gratian and a Roman synod of a charge of incontinence maliciously laid against him by his enemies.

Pope St Damasus had to oppose several heresies, but in 380 Theodosius I in the East and Gratian in the West proclaimed Christianity, as professed by the bishops of Rome and Alexandria, to be the religion of the Roman state and Gratian, on the petition of the Christian senators, supported by St Damasus, removed the altar of Victory from the senate-house and laid aside the title of Pontifex Maximus. In the following year the second ecumenical council was held, the first of Constantinople, at which the pope was represented by legates. But the action of Damasus that was most far reaching was his patronage of St Jerome and encouragement of his biblical studies, which had their consummation in the Vulgate version of the Bible.

St Damasus is, too, specially remembered for his care for the relics and resting-places of the martyrs and for his work in the draining, opening out and adornment of the sacred catacombs and for the instructions which he set up therein.

St Damasus died on 11 December 384, at the age of about eighty. He had put up in the 'papal crypt' of the cemetery of St Callistus a general epitaph which ends:

> *I, Damasus, wished to be buried here, but I feared*
> *to offend the ashes of these holy ones.*

He was accordingly laid to rest with his mother and sister at a small church he had built on the Via Ardeatina; and among his epitaphs which have been preserved in writing is the one which he wrote for himself, an act of faith in Christ's resurrection and his own.

DAVID, OR DEWI, BISHOP OF MYNWYN (A.D. 589?)

PATRON SAINT OF WALES

1 MARCH

There is no lack of evidence to demonstrate the devotion in Wales to David – and especially in South Wales – from medieval times. So popular was he that in 1389 his feast was ordered to be kept throughout the province of Canterbury. Unhappily little is known for sure about the saint because all stories about him are based upon a biography written 500 years after his death, although possibly based on earlier materials, by the son of a bishop of St David's who was naturally concerned to uphold the primacy of his father's see.

According to the legend David was the son of Sant, of princely family in Ceredigion, and of St Non, grand-daughter of Brychan of Brecknock; and he was born perhaps about the year 520. Ordained priest in due course, he afterwards retired to study for several years under the Welsh St Paulinus, who lived on an island which has not been identified. He is said to have restored sight to his master, who had become blind through much weeping. Upon emerging from the monastery, David seems to have embarked upon a period of great activity, the details of which, however, are at least for the most part pure invention.

Finally, and here we are on surer ground, he settled in the extreme south-west corner of Wales, at Mynyw (Menevia), with a number of disciples and founded the principal of his many abbeys.

The community lived a life of extreme austerity. Hard manual labour was obligatory for all, and they were allowed no cattle to relieve them in tilling the ground. They might never speak without necessity, and they never ceased praying mentally, even when at work. Their food was bread, with vegetables and salt, and they drank only water, sometimes mingled with a little milk. For this reason St David was surnamed 'The Waterman', as being the head of those strictly teetotal ascetic Welsh monks whom St Gildas criticized as being sometimes more abstemious than Christian, and whose aim was to reproduce the lives of the hermits of the Thebaïd. When any outsider wished to join them, he had to wait at the gate for ten days and be subjected to harsh words ere he could be admitted. Always from Friday evening until dawn on Sunday a strict vigil was kept and prayer was maintained uninterruptedly, with only one hour's repose, on the Saturday after Matins.

We are told that a synod was held at Brefi in Cardigan to suppress the Pelagian heresy, which was springing up in Britain for the second time. There is, however, no trace of any preoccupation about Pelagianism in the decrees which were said to have been passed by the assembly. St David was invited to attend, but was unwilling to go until St Deiniol and St Dubricius came in person to fetch him. At the synod David is said to have spoken with such grace and eloquence as to silence his opponents completely, and he was thereupon unanimously elected primate of the Cambrian church, Dubricius having resigned in his favour. St David was obliged to accept, but he did so on condition that the episcopal seat should be transferred from Caerleon to Mynyw – now Saint David's – a quiet and solitary place.

An extraordinary story, fabricated presumably to demonstrate the imaginary metropolitan status of Saint David's, represents David as having made a pilgrimage to the Holy Land, where he was consecrated archbishop by the patriarch of Jerusalem. He is alleged to have called at Caerleon another council, known as the Synod of Victory, because it was said to mark the extirpation of Pelagianism in Britain. It ratified the decrees of Brefi and also a code of rules which had been drawn up for the regulation of the British church.

Of St David himself Giraldus tells us that he was the great ornament and example of his age and that he continued to rule his diocese until he was a very old man. At his death, which, according to Geoffrey of Monmouth, took place in his monastery at Mynyw, St Kentigern at Llanelwy saw his soul borne to Heaven by angels. His last words to his monks and neighbours are recorded as, 'Be joyful, brothers and sisters. Keep your faith, and do the little things that you have seen and heard with me.' His body was subsequently translated from the monastery church to Saint David's cathedral, where the empty tomb is still shown. It is said that the relics were removed to Glastonbury, but they were apparently at Saint David's in 1346.

DENIS, BISHOP OF PARIS, MARTYR (A.D. 258?)

A PATRON SAINT OF PARIS AND OF FRANCE; AND OF HEADACHES

9 OCTOBER

St Denis has popularly been regarded as a patron both of Paris and of France on the basis of the story of his mission and his martyrdom.

The medieval choice of St Denis as the saint to be invoked against headaches seems to have arisen from the story, recounted below, that his body walked from Montmartre carrying his head in its hands.

St Gregory of Tours, writing in the sixth century, tells us that St Denis, or St Dionysius, of Paris was born in Italy and sent in the year 250 with six other missionary bishops into Gaul, where he suffered martyrdom. The 'Martyrology of Jerome' mentions St Dionysius on 9 October, joining with him St Rusticus and St Eleutherius; later writers make of these the bishop's priest and deacon, who with him penetrated to Lutetia Parisiorum and established Christian worship on an island in the Seine. Their preaching was so effective that they were arrested and, after a long imprisonment, all three were beheaded. The bodies of the martyrs were thrown into the Seine, from which they were rescued and given honourable burial. A chapel was later built over their tomb, around which arose the great abbey of Saint-Denis.

This monastery was founded by King Dagobert I (*d.* 638), and it is possible that a century or so later the identification of St Dionysius with Dionysius the Areopagite began to gain currency, or at least the idea that he was sent by Pope Clement I in the first century. But it was not everywhere or even widely accepted until the time of Hilduin, abbot of Saint-Denis. In the year 827 the Emperor Michael II sent as a present to the emperor of the West, Louis the Pious, copies of the writings ascribed to St Dionysius the Areopagite. By an unfortunate coincidence they arrived in Paris and were taken to Saint-Denis on the eve of the feast of the patron of the abbey. Hilduin translated them into Latin, and when some years later Louis asked him for a life of St Dionysius of Paris, the abbot produced a work which persuaded Christendom for the next seven hundred years that Dionysius of Paris, Dionysius of Athens, and the author of the 'Dionysian' writings were one and the same person. In his 'Areopagitica' Abbot Hilduin made use of spurious and worthless materials, and it is difficult to believe in his complete good faith: the life is a tissue of fables. The Areopagite comes to Rome where Pope St Clement I receives him and sends him to evangelize the Parisii. They try in vain to put him to death by wild beasts, fire and crucifixion; then, together with Rusticus and Eleutherius, he is successfully beheaded on Montmatre. The dead body of St Dionysius rose on its feet and, led by an angel, walked the two miles from Montmarte to where the abbey church of Saint-Denis now stands, carrying its head in its hands and surrounded by singing angels, and so was there buried. Of which marvel the Roman Breviary makes mention.

DISMAS [THE GOOD THIEF] (A.D. 30)

PATRON SAINT OF THEFT AND THIEVES; OF CONDEMNED CRIMINALS; AND OF UNDERTAKERS

25 MARCH

The Good Thief – the name given him varies as the life indicates – was invoked against theft and thieves during the Middle Ages, presumably on the bàsis of the story that he preserved the Holy Family from being robbed on their journey into Egypt. For this reason, and because of his final repentance and the story, in the Gospel of St Luke, of the promise of heaven made to him by Christ on the cross, he was regarded as the patron of thieves and was commended as a patron to condemned criminals.

Sometimes too he is invoked as the patron of undertakers, not only because he is promised he will attain heaven, but because he then dies peacefully.

On the supposition that our Lord was crucified upon March 25 the Roman Martyrology for this day contains the following entry: 'At Jerusalem the commemoration of the holy thief who confessed Christ upon the cross and deserved to hear from Him the words: "This day shalt thou be with me in paradise."' We know no more of his history than is contained in the few sentences devoted to him by the evangelist St Luke, but, as in the case of most of the other personalities mentioned in the gospels, such as Pilate, Joseph of Arimathea, Lazarus, Martha, a story was soon fabricated which gave him a notable place in the apocryphal literature of the early centuries. In the Arabic 'Gospel of the Infancy' we are told how, in the course of the flight into Egypt, the Holy Family was waylaid by robbers. Of the two leaders, named Titus and Dumachus, the former, stirred by compassion, besought his companion to let them pass unmolested, and when Dumachus refused, Titus bribed him with forty drachmas, so that they were left in peace. Thereupon the Blessed Virgin said to her benefactor, 'The Lord God shall sustain thee with His right hand and give thee remission of sins'. And the Infant Jesus, intervening, spoke, 'After thirty years, mother, the Jews will crucify me in Jerusalem, and these two robbers will be lifted on the cross with me, Titus on my right hand Dumachus on my left, and after that day Titus shall go before me into paradise'. This story, with others, subsequently found popular acceptance in western Christendom, though the names there most commonly given to the thieves were Dismas and Gestas. But we also find Zoathan and Chammatha, and yet other variants. That genuine devotional feeling was sometimes evoked by the incident of the pardon of the good thief upon the cross seems to be shown by the vision of St Porphyrius (*c.* 400). We find the two thieves represented in pictures of the crucifixion at a quite early date, as, for example, in the Syriac manuscript illuminated by Rabulas in 586, which is preserved in the Laurentian Library at Florence. The words of the good thief, 'Lord, remember me when thou shalt come into thy kingdom', are adapted to very solemn usage in the Byzantine Mass, at the 'great entrance', and again at the communion of the ministers and people.

DOMINIC SAVIO (A.D. 1857)

PATRON SAINT OF PUERI CANTORES; CHOIRS AND CHOIRBOYS; BOYS AND JUVENILE DELINQUENTS

9 MARCH

St Dominic was declared the patron, to be precise, of the Pueri Cantores, *an organization of boys' choirs, rather than of choirboys, or choirs, in general. By extension, however, he seems to have been taken as such. Pius XII declared him patron of the* Pueri Cantores *in an Apostolic Letter of 8 June 1956 at the request, he said, of the president of twenty-six nation groups of* Pueri. *St Dominic seems to have been chosen for the fewness of his years, and because, as the Pope remarked in his letter, 'he sang the divine praises'. By further extension, he is often regarded as the patron of young boys in general, and also of juvenile delinquents.*

The Church has raised several child martyrs to her altars, but the case of Dominic Savio seems to be unique. He was canonized in 1954.

He was born in Riva in Piedmont in 1842, the son of a peasant, and grew up with the desire to be a priest. When St John Bosco began to make provision for training youths as clergy to help him in his work for neglected boys at Turin, Dominic's parish-priest recommended him. An interview took place, at which Don Bosco was most deeply impressed by the boy and in October 1854, when he was twelve, Dominic became a student at the Oratory of St Francis de Sales in Turin. His own personality apart, Dominic was best remembered at the oratory for the group he organized there. It was called the Company of the Immaculate Conception, and besides its devotional objects it helped Don Bosco in his work by undertaking various necessary jobs, from sweeping the floors to taking special care of boys who for one reason or another were misfits. When the time came, in 1859, for St John Bosco to form the kernel of his now world-wide Salesian congregation, among the twenty-two present were all the original members of the Company of the Immaculate Conception; all, that is, except Dominic Savio: he had been called to the congregation of Heaven two years before.

Early on at the oratory Dominic prevented a brutal fight with stones between two boys by characteristically direct action. Holding up a little crucifix between them, 'Before you fight,' he said, 'look at this, both of you, and say. "Jesus Christ was sinless, and He died forgiving His executioners; I am a sinner, and I am going to outrage Him by being deliberately revengeful". Then you can start – and throw your first stone at me.' The rascals slunk away. He was scrupulous in observing the discipline of the house, and some of the wilder spirits did not like it when he expected them to be equally scrupulous. They called him a sneak, and told him to 'run and tell Don Bosco' – thereby showing how little they knew about Don Bosco, who would not tolerate tale-bearing. Likely enough Dominic laughed it off; for he was a ready laugher, and sometimes it got him into trouble with the masters. But if he was no tale-bearer he was a good story-teller, and that endeared him to his companions, especially the younger ones.

It was a specially happy dispensation of Providence that brought Dominic Savio under the care of so moderate and wise a man as St John Bosco: otherwise he might have developed into a young fanatic and spoiled himself by excess. Don Bosco insisted on cheerfulness, on careful attention to daily duties, on joining in the games, so that Dominic would say, 'I can't do big things. But I want all I do, even the smallest thing, to be for the greater glory of God.' 'Religion must be about us like the air we breathe; but we must not weary the boys with too many devotions and observances and so forth,' Don Bosco used to say. And, true to that spirit, he forbade Dominic to inflict the least bodily mortification upon himself without express permission. 'For', he said, 'the penance God wants is obedience. There is plenty to put up with cheerfully – heat, cold, sickness, the tiresome ways of other people. There is quite enough mortification for boys in school life itself.' Nevertheless he found Dominic shivering in bed one cold night, with all the bed-clothes save one thin sheet thrown off. 'Don't be so crazy,' he said, 'You'll get pneumonia.' 'Why should I?' replied Dominic. 'Our Lord didn't get pneumonia in the stable at Bethlehem.'

The most important source for the details of Dominic Savio's short life is the account written by St John Bosco himself. In writing it he was careful not to set down anything that he could not vouch for, and he was most particularly careful when dealing with the spiritual experiences that were accorded to this boy: such things as supernatural knowledge – of people in need, of their spiritual state, of the future. Or the occasion when Dominic was missing all the morning till after dinner, Don Bosco found him eventually in the choir of the church, standing in a cramped position by the lectern, rapt in prayer. He had been there for about six hours, yet thought that early Mass was not yet over. Dominic called these times of intense prayer 'my distractions'. They would sometimes overtake him at play: 'It seems as though Heaven is opening just above me. I am afraid I may say or do something that will make the other boys laugh.'

St John Bosco tells us that the needs of England had an important part in this boy's prayers; and he records 'a strong distraction' in which Dominic saw a wide mist-shrouded plain, with a multitude of people groping about in it; to them came a pontifically-vested figure carrying a torch that lighted up the whole scene, and a voice seemed to say, 'This torch is the Catholic faith which shall bring light to the English people'. At Dominic's request Don Bosco told this to Pope Pius IX, who declared that it confirmed his resolution to give great care and attention to England.

Dominic's delicate health got worse and worse, and in February 1857 he was sent home to Mondonio for a change of air. His complaint was diagnosed as inflammation of the lungs, and according to the practice of the day he was bled, bled to excess. The treatment seems certainly to have hastened his end. He received the last sacraments, and on the evening of 9 March he asked his father to read the prayers for the dying. Towards the end of them he tried to sit up. 'Good-bye, Father,' he murmured, 'the priest told me something. . . . But I can't remember what. . . .' Suddenly his face lit up with a smile of intense joy, and he exclaimed, 'I am seeing most wonderful things!' He did not speak again.

DYMPNA, MARTYR (*c.* A.D. 650?)

15 MAY

Since mental illness was at one time regarded as a form of possession by the devil, so St Dympna, as patron of the mentally ill (for reasons which the following account makes clear), was also thought to help those diabolically possessed. Also, the practice of sleep-walking was looked upon in the Middle Ages as a form of possession by malign spirits, precisely as was mental illness. St Dympna came to be regarded therefore as someone who might be also invoked against sleep-walking.

In the town of Gheel, twenty-five miles from Antwerp, great honour is paid to St Dympna, whose body, and that of St Gerebernus, buried in two ancient marble sarcophagi, were there discovered, or re-discovered, in the thirteenth century. The body of St Dympna is preserved in a silver reliquary in the church which bears her name. Only the head of St Gerebernus now rests there, his other remains having been removed to Sonsbeck in the diocese of Münster.

The true history of these saints is probably lost, but popular belief, reaching back to the date of the finding of their relics, has attached to them a story which, with local variations, is to be found in the folk-lore of many European countries. Briefly summarized, it runs as follows. Dympna was the daughter of a pagan Irish, British or Armorican king and of a Christian princess who died when their child was very young, though not before she had been instructed in the Christian faith and baptized. As she grew up, her extraordinary resemblance to her dead mother whom he had idolized awakened an unlawful passion in her father. Consquently, by the advice of St Gerebernus, her confessor, she fled from home to avoid further danger. Accompanied by the priest and attended by the court jester and his wife, she embarked in a ship which conveyed them to Antwerp. From thence they made their way south-east, through a tract of wild forest country, until they reached a little oratory dedicated to St Martin and built on a site now covered by the town of Gheel. Here they settled, intending to live as solitaries. In the meantime, however, Dympna's father had started in pursuit and in due time arrived at Antwerp, from whence he sent out spies who discovered the refuge of the fugitives. The clue by which they were traced was the use of strange coins similar to those that the spies themselves proffered in payment. Coming upon them unawares, the king first tried by cajolery to persuade his daughter to return with him. She refused, and as she was supported by St Gerebernus, the tyrant ordered his attendants to kill them both. The men promptly despatched the priest, but hesitated to attack the princess. Thereupon the unnatural father struck off his daughter's head with his own sword. The bodies of the saints, which were left exposed on the ground, were afterwards buried by angelic or human hands in the place where they had perished.

Widespread interest was taken because the elevation of the relics of St Dympna was followed, it is alleged, by the restoration to normal health of a number of epileptics, lunatics and persons under malign influence who visited her shrine. Ever since then she has been regarded as the patroness of the mentally ill and the inhabitants of Gheel have been distinguished by the kindly provision they have made for those so afflicted. As early as the close of the thirteenth century an infirmary was built for their accommodation and at the present time the town possesses a first-class state sanatorium for the care and supervision of the mentally ill, the greater number of whom lead contented and useful lives in the homes of farmers or other local residents, whom they assist by their labour and whose family life they share.

ELIGIUS, or ELOI, BISHOP OF NOYON (A.D. 601)

PATRON SAINTS OF GOLDSMITHS, SILVERSMITHS, METALWORKERS, JEWELLERS
AND CRAFTSMEN AND CRAFTSWOMEN; OF COIN AND MEDAL COLLECTORS;
OF HORSES AND VETERINARIANS; OF BLACKSMITHS; OF GARAGE, OR GAS STATION
WORKERS

1 DECEMBER

*That St Eligius was himself a practising goldsmith, and his cult wide spread in
Europe, is sufficient explanation of the choice of him as patron of goldsmiths. From
goldsmiths the cult of the saint as patron extended to silversmiths and other kinds of
smiths and metalworkers, and also to jewellers and craftsmen and women of many
kinds.*

*There seems no special reason why St Eligius should be invoked by those who work
in garages, unless it be a combination of the saint's patronage of metal workers, and of
those concerned with horses and their care – garages, in a sense, being modern
versions of stables! St Eligius has also been associated with horses because of an
incident which allegedly happened shortly after his death. A horse that the saint had
been riding was inherited by a priest of the monastery at Noyon, but the bishop took a
liking to the animal, and, quite improperly, took it for himself. No sooner was the
animal in the bishop's stable, however, than it became ill, and resisted all the attempts
of the veterinarian to cure it. Meanwhile the priest of the monastery prayed at the
tomb of the saint that the horse be restored to him. The bishop, seeing the horse was no
use to him, did in fact give it back to the priest, and the animal promptly recovered –
which event was attributed to St Eligius. From then on St Eligius was invoked on
behalf of sick horses – horses are, in some places, blessed on the saint's feast day – and
by all who are involved with horses.*

*Because of his skill as a worker in precious metals, Eligius had long been regarded
as their patron by the Argentinian society dedicated to the collection and study of
coins and medals. They petitioned Rome that the saint's patronage be formally
recognized, and this was done by John Paul II in an Apostolic Letter of 11 July 1983.*

The name of Eligius, and those of his father, Eucherius, and his mother,
Terrigia, show him to have been of Roman Gaulish extraction. He was born
at Chaptelet, near Limoges, about the year 588, the son of an artisan. His
father, seeing in due course that the boy had a remarkable talent for
engraving and smithing, placed him with a goldsmith named Abbo, who
was master of the mint at Limoges. When the time of his apprenticeship
was finished Eligius went into France, that is, across the Loire, and became
known to Bobbo, treasurer to Clotaire II at Paris. This king gave Eligius an
order to make him a chair of state, adorned with gold and precious stones.
Out of the materials furnished he made two such thrones instead of one.
Clotaire admired the skill and honesty of the workman, and finding that he
was a man of parts and intelligence took him into his household and made

145

him master of the mint. His name is still to be seen on several gold coins struck at Paris and Marseilles in the reigns of Dagobert I and his son, Clovis II. His *vita* states that among other works the reliquaries of St Martin at Tours, of St Dionysius at Saint-Denis, of St Quintinus, SS. Crispin and Crispinian at Soissons, St Lucian, St Germanus of Paris, St Genevieve, and others, were made by Eligius. His skill as a workman, his official position and the friendship of the king soon made him a person of consideration. He did not let the corruption of a court infect his soul or impair his virtue, but he conformed to his state and was magnificently dressed, sometimes wearing nothing but silk (a rare material in France in those days), his clothes embroidered with gold and adorned with precious stones. But he also gave large sums in alms. When a stranger asked for his house he was told, 'Go to such a street, and it's where you see a crowd of poor people'.

A curious incident occurred when Clotaire tendered him the oath of allegiance. Eligius having a scruple lest this would be to swear without sufficient necessity, or fearing what he might be called upon to do or approve, excused himself with an obstinacy which for some time displeased the king. Still he persisted in his resolution and repeated his excuses as often as the king pressed him. Clotaire, at length perceiving that the motive of his reluctance was really a tenderness of conscience, assured him that his conscientious spirit was a more secure pledge of fidelity than the oaths of others. St Eligius ransomed a number of slaves, some of whom remained in his service and were his faithful assistants throughout his life. One of them, a Saxon named Tillo, is numbered among the saints and commemorated on January 7; he was first among the seven disciples of St Eligius who followed him from the workshop to the *évêché*. At the court he sought the company of such men as Sulpicius, Bertharius, Desiderius and his brother, Rusticus, and in particular Audoenus, all of whom became not only bishops but saints as well. Of these Audoenus (St Ouen) must have been a boy when St Eligius first knew him; to him was long attributed the authorship of the *Vita Eligii*, which is now commonly regarded as the work of a later monk of Noyon. By it St Eligius is described as having been at this time, 'tall, with a fresh complexion, his hair and beard curling without artifice; his hands were shapely and long-fingered, his face full of angelic kindness and its expression grave and unaffected'.

King Clotaire's regard for and trust in Eligius was shared by his son, Dagobert although, like many monarchs, he valued and took the advice of a holy man more willingly in public than in private affairs. He gave to the saint the estate of Solignac in his native Limousin for the foundation of a monastery, which in 632 was peopled with monks who followed the Rules of St Columban and St Benedict combined. These, under the eye of their founder, became noted for their good work in various arts. Dagobert also gave to St Eligius a house at Paris, which he converted into a nunnery and placed under the direction of St Aurea. Eligius asked for an additional piece of land to complete the buildings and it was granted him. But he found that he had somewhat exceeded the measure of the land which had been specified. Upon which he immediately went to the king and asked his pardon. Dagobert, surprised at his careful honesty, said to his courtiers, 'Some of my officers do not scruple to rob me of whole estates; whereas Eligius is afraid of having one inch of ground which is not his'. So trustworthy a man was valuable as an ambassador, and Dagobert is said to have sent him to treat with Judicaël, the prince of the turbulent Bretons.

St Eligius was chosen to be bishop of Noyon and Tournai, at the same time as his friend St Audoenus was made bishop of Rouen. They were consecrated together in the year 641. Eligius proved as good a bishop as he had been layman, and his pastoral solicitude, zeal and watchfulness were most admirable. Soon he turned his thoughts to the conversion of the infidels, who were a large majority in the Tournai part of his diocese, and a great part of Flanders was chiefly indebted to St Eligius for receiving the gospel. He preached in the territories of Antwerp, Ghent and Courtrai, and the inhabitants, who were as untamed as wild beasts, reviled him as a foreigner, 'a Roman'; yet he persevered. He took care of their sick, protected them from oppression, and employed every means that charity could suggest to overcome their obstinacy. The barbarians were gradually softened, and some were converted; every year at Easter he baptized those whom he had brought to the knowledge of God during the twelve preceding months. The author of the Life tells us that St Eligius preached to the people every Sunday and feast-day and instructed them with indefatigable zeal.

At Noyon St Eligius established a house of nuns, to govern which he fetched his *protégée*, St Godeberta, from Paris, and one of monks, outside the city on the road to Soissons. He was very active in promoting the *cultus* of local saints, and it was during his episcopate that several of the reliquaries mentioned above were made, either by himself or under his direction. He took a leading part in the ecclesiastical life of his day, and for a short time immediately before his death was a valued counsellor of the queen-regent, St Bathildis. His biographer gives several illustrations of the regard which she had for him, and they had in common not only political views but also a deep solicitude for slaves (she had been carried off from England and sold when a child). The effect of this is seen at the Council of Chalon (*c.* 647), which forbade their sale out of the kingdom and decreed that they must be free to rest on Sundays and holidays.

When he had governed his flock nineteen years Eligius was visited with a foresight of his death, and foretold it to his clergy. Falling ill of a fever, he on the sixth day called together his household and took leave of them. They all burst into tears and he was not able to refrain from weeping with them; he commended them to God, and died a few hours later, on 1 December 660. At the news of his sickness St Bathildis set out from Paris, but arrived only the morning after his death. She had preparations made for carrying the body to her monastery at Chelles. Others were anxious that it should be taken to Paris, but the people of Noyon so strenuously opposed it that the remains of their pastor were left with them. They were afterwards translated into the cathedral, where a great part of them remain.

ELIJAH, PROPHET (*c.* B.C. 900–850)

A PATRON SAINT OF FLYING

20 JULY (NOT IN THE ROMAN CALENDAR)

The choice of Elijah as one of the patrons of flying stems from the manner of his departing earthly existence as recounted in the Bible: he stepped into a fiery chariot and was carried heavenward in a whirlwind.

Elijah of Tishbe (perhaps Tosabe in Gilead) seems to have come from a family of herdsmen who were devoted to the strict worship of Yahweh, the God of Israel. He spent his life combatting the worship of Baal which had been introduced by the Tyrian Princess Jezebel, married to King Ahab. The famous contest between Elijah and the priests of Baal took place on Mount Carmel and ended with victory for the prophet. He called down fire from heaven to consume the sacrifice which had been prepared, while the priests of Baal failed to do likewise.

ELIZABETH OF HUNGARY, (A.D. 1231)

PATRON SAINT OF CATHOLIC CHARITIES

17 NOVEMBER

Her own charitable works are sufficient reason for the choice of Elizabeth as patron of all who work in Catholic charitable organizations. There is as yet, however, no official recognition by the Church of this patronage.

It is related by Dietrich of Apolda in his life of this saint that, on an evening in the summer of the year 1207, the minnesinger Klingsohr from Transylvania announced to the Landgrave Herman of Thuringia that that night a daughter had been born to the king of Hungary, who should be exalted in holiness and become the wife of Herman's son; and that in fact at that time the child Elizabeth was born, in Pressburg (Bratislava) or Saros-Patak, to Andrew II of Hungary and his wife, Gertrude of Andechs-Meran. Such an alliance had substantial political advantages to recommend it, and the baby Elizabeth was promised to Herman's eldest son. At about four years of age she was brought to the Thuringian court at the castle of the Wartburg, near Eisenach, there to be brought up with her future husband. In 1221, Louis being now twenty-one and landgrave in his father's place, and Elizabeth fourteen, their marriage was solemnized. They had three children, Herman, who was born in 1222 and died when he was nineteen, Sophia, who became Duchess of Brabant, and Bd Gertrude of Aldenburg. Louis, unlike some husbands of saints, put no obstacles in the way of his wife's charity, her simple and mortified life, and her long prayers.

The castle of the Wartburg was build on a steep rock, which the infirm and weak were not able to climb. St Elizabeth therefore built a hospital at the foot of the rock for their reception, where she often fed them with her own hands, made their beds, and attended them even in the heat of summer when the place seemed insupportable. Helpless children, especially orphans, were provided for at her expense. She was the foundress of another hospital in which twenty-eight persons were constantly relieved, and she fed nine hundred daily at her gate, besides numbers in different parts of the dominions, so that the revenue in her hands was truly the patrimony of the distressed.

At this time strenuous efforts were being made to launch another crusade, and Louis of Thuringia took the cross. On St John the Baptist's day he parted from St Elizabeth and went to join the Emperor Frederick II in Apulia; on September 11 following he was dead of the plague at Otranto. The news did not reach Germany until October, just after the birth of Elizabeth's second daughter.

What happened next is a matter of some uncertainty. According to the testimony of one of her ladies-in-waiting, Isentrude, St Elizabeth's brother-in-law, Henry, who was regent for her infant son, drove her and her children and two attendants from the Wartburg during that same winter that he might seize power himself; and there are shocking particulars of the hardship and contempt which she suffered until she was fetched away from Eisenach by her aunt, Matilda, Abbess of Kitzingen. It is alternatively claimed that she was dispossessed of her dower-house at Marburg, in Hesse, or even that she left the Wartburg of her own free will. From Kitzingen she visited her uncle, Eckembert, Bishop of Bamberg, who put his castle of Pottenstein at her disposal, whither she went with her son Herman and the baby, leaving the little Sophia with the nuns of Kitzingen. Eckembert had ambitious plans for another marriage for Elizabeth, but she refused to listen to them: before his departure on the crusade she and her husband had exchanged promises never to marry again. Early in 1228 the body of Louis was brought home and solemnly buried in the abbey church at Reinhardsbrunn; provision was made for Elizabeth by her relatives; and on Good Friday in the church of the Franciscan friars at Eisenach she formally renounced the world, later taking the unbleached gown and cord which was the habit of the third order of St Francis.

An influential part was played in all these developments by Master Conrad of Marburg, who henceforward was the determining influence in St

Elizabeth's life. This priest had played a considerable part therein for some time, having succeeded the Franciscan Father Rodinger as her confessor in 1225. From the Friars Minor St Elizabeth had acquired a love of poverty which she could put into action only to a limited extent all the time she was Landgravine of Thuringia. Now, the children having been provided for, she went to Marburg, but was forced to leave there and lived for a time in a cottage at Wehrda, by the side of the river Lahn. Then she built a small house just outside Marburg and attached to it a hospice for the relief of the sick, the aged and the poor, to whose service she entirely devoted herself.

In some respects Conrad acted as a prudent and necessary brake on her enthusiasm at this time: he would not allow her to beg from door to door or to divest herself definitely of all her goods or to give more than a certain amount at a time in alms or to risk infection from leprosy and other diseases. In such matters he acted with care and wisdom. But for her devoted waiting-women he substituted two who reported to him on her words and actions when these infringed his detailed commands in the smallest degree. He punished her with slaps in the face and blows with a 'long, thick rod' whose marks remained for three weeks.

Conrad's policy of breaking rather than directing the will was not completely successful. With reference to him and his disciplinary methods St Elizabeth compares herself to sedge in a stream during flood-time: the water bears it down flat, but when the rains have gone it springs up again, straight, strong and unhurt.

One day a Magyar noble arrived at Marburg and asked to be directed to the residence of his sovereign's daughter, of whose troubles he had been informed. Arrived at the hospital, he saw Elizabeth in her plain grey gown, sitting at her spinning-wheel. He would have taken her back to the court of Hungary, but Elizabeth would not go. Her children, her poor, the grave of her husband were all in Thuringia, and she would stay there for the rest of her life. It was not for long. St Elizabeth died in the evening of 17 November 1231, being then not yet twenty-four years old.

EMYGDIUS, MARTYR (A.D. 304)

PATRON SAINT OF EARTHQUAKES

9 AUGUST

Emygdius is patron of Ascoli in Italy, where there has been devotion to him from time immemorial. As protector against earthquakes, however, devotion to him has spread more widely, including to the United States, and is of relatively recent date. In the great earthquake of 1703 Ascoli escaped unharmed, and this blessing was attributed to the town's patron, who was promptly made patron of other towns in the hope that he might also protect them.

The saint's true history has long since been forgotten, but his legend is preserved in his so-called 'acts'. He is there described as a German who, after being converted to Christianity, left his native city of Trier and came to Rome during the pontificate of Pope Marcellus I. Full of zeal for the faith, Emygdius entered a heathen temple and dashed a statue of Aesculapius to the ground. The pagans of Rome were so incensed by this action that Pope Marcellus, in order to protect Emygdius from their vengeance, ordained him, consecrated him a bishop, and sent him to evangelize the territory of Ascoli Piceno. There he laboured with success, making many converts. He was beheaded during the persecution of Diocletian, together with three companions, SS. Eupolus, Germanus and Valentinus. Seeing that St Marcellus did not occupy the chair of St Peter until 308, he could scarcely have been the pope who ordained St Emygdius, but popular tradition is notoriously indifferent to chronology. On the other hand, it is possible that a careless scribe may have substituted the name of Marcellus for that of Marcellinus, who was his predecessor. The festival of St Emygdius is kept throughout Italy on August 9 and other days, in accordance with local use and tradition.

ERASMUS, or ELMO, BISHOP AND MARTYR (A.D. 303?)

PATRON SAINT OF SAILORS; SUFFERERS FROM STOMACH AND ABDOMINAL PAINS, INCLUDING WOMEN IN LABOUR

2 JUNE

It is difficult to determine precisely why Erasmus became patron of sailors, though his cult was very popular both in Gaeta and in nearby Naples, both sea-ports. It has been suggested that an incident from one of the legends surrounding him – he continued preaching even when a thunderbolt struck the ground beside him – encouraged the devotion of sailors who were in frequent danger from sudden storms or lightning. The electrical discharges at mast-heads of ships were taken to be a sign of his protection, and therefore became known as St Elmo's Fire.

A late legend developed that Erasmus was martyred by having his intestines drawn out and wound around a windlass – the windlass, it is suggested, originally being present in representations of Erasmus to symbolize his association with sailors. Because of this story he came to be patron of all who suffer from stomach or abdominal pains, ranging from colic to the pains of childbirth. He is therefore also the patron of women in labour.

St Erasmus, or St Elmo, formerly widely venerated as the patron of sailors and as one of the Fourteen Holy Helpers, is described as bishop of Formiae, in the Campagna, and we know from St Gregory the Great that his relics were preserved in the cathedral of that town in the sixth century. When Formiae was destroyed by the Saracens in 842, the body of St Erasmus was translated to Gaëta, of which city he still remains a principal patron. Nothing is actually known of his history, his so-called 'acts' being late compilations based on legends which confuse him with a namesake, a martyr bishop of Antioch.

ERIC, MARTYR (A.D. 1161)

A PATRON SAINT OF SWEDEN

18 MAY

The choice of Eric as one of the two patrons of Sweden needs no explanation. It was confirmed by a decree of the Sacred Congregation of Rites dated 10 March 1926, the same decree that confirmed St Birgitta, or Bridget, also as a patron of Sweden.

St Eric was acknowledged king in most parts of Sweden in 1150, and his line subsisted for a hundred years. He did much to establish Christianity in Upper Sweden and built or completed at Old Uppsala the first large church to be erected in his country. It is said that the ancient laws and constitutions of the kingdom were by his orders collected into one volume, which became known as King Eric's Law or the Code of Uppland. The king soon had to take up arms against the heathen Finns.

He vanquished them in battle, and at his desire St Henry, Bishop of Uppsala, an Englishman, who had accompanied him on the expedition, remained in Finland to evangelize the people.

The king's zeal for the faith was far from pleasing to some of his nobles, and we are told that they entered into a conspiracy with Magnus, the son of the king of Denmark. St Eric was hearing Mass on the day after the feast of the Ascension when news was brought that a Danish army, swollen with Swedish rebels, was marching against him and was close at hand. He answered calmly, 'Let us at least finish the sacrifice; the rest of the feast I shall keep elsewhere'. After Mass was over, he recommended his soul to God, and marched forth in advance of his guards. The conspirators rushed upon him, beat him down from his horse, and cut off his head. His death occurred on 18 May 1161.

The king's relics are preserved in the cathedral of Uppsala, and his effigy appears in the arms of Stockholm.

EUSTACE, MARTYR

PATRON SAINT OF HUNTSMEN; AND OF PEOPLE IN DIFFICULT SITUATIONS

20 SEPTEMBER (NO LONGER IN THE ROMAN CALENDAR)

The association of Eustace with hunting from time immemorial needs no explanation beyond that of his life and conversion, apart from the obvious comment that his story is identical with that of St Hubert. More difficult to explain is devotion to him by people in difficult situations, though this may simply arise from the wide popularity of his cult in the Middle Ages. The legends surrounding him certainly contain many difficult situations from which he extricated himself.

St Eustace (Eustachius, Eustathius) is among the most famous martyrs of the Church, venerated for many centuries in both East and West. He is one of the Fourteen Holy Helpers, and at least since the eighth century has given his name to the titular church of the cardinal-deacon at Rome. But there is nothing that can be said of him with any sort of certainty. His worthless legend relates that he was a Roman general under Trajan, by name Placidas, and while out hunting one day he saw coming towards him a stag, between whose antlers appeared a figure of Christ on the cross (which story appears also in the legend of St Hubert and other saints), and a voice issuing therefrom calling him by name. This is said to have occurred at Guadagnolo, between Tivoli and Palestrina. Placidas was at once converted by the vision and received baptism with his whole family. His own name he changed to Eustachius, that of his wife to Theopistis, and his sons' to Agapitus and Theopistus. Eustace soon after lost all his wealth, and in a series of misadventures was separated from the members of his family. Then he was recalled to command the army at a critical moment, and was romantically reunited with his wife and sons. But Eustace refused to sacrifice to the gods after his victory for the imperial arms, and he and his family were martyred by being confined in a brazen bull wherein they were roasted to death.

EXPEDITUS (DATE UNKNOWN)

PATRON SAINT OF URGENT CASES; AND AGAINST PROCRASTINATION

19 APRIL (NO LONGER IN THE ROMAN CALENDAR)

We have no adequate reason to think that any such saint was ever invoked in the early Christian centuries; in fact it is more than doubtful whether the saint ever existed. We may own that in the 'Hieronymianum' martyrology the name Expeditus occurs among a group of martyrs both on 18 and 19 April, being assigned in the one case to Rome, and in the other to Melitene in Armenia; but there is no vestige of any tradition which would corroborate either mention, whereas there is much to suggest that in both lists the introduction of the name is merely a copyist's blunder. Hundreds of similar blunders have been quite definitely proved to exist in the same document.

There is, however, a story which pretends to explain the origin of this 'devotion' by an incident of modern date. A packing-case, we are told, containing a *corpo santo* from the catacombs, was sent to a community of nuns in Paris. The date of its dispatch was indicated by the use of the word 'spedito', but the recipients mistook this for the name of the martyr and set to work with great energy to propagate his cult. From these simple beginnings, it is asserted, a devotion to St Expeditus spread rapidly through many Catholic countries. In answer to this is should be pointed out that though the recognition of St Expeditus as the patron of dispatch depends beyond doubt upon a *calembour* or play upon words – there are many similar examples in popular hagiology – still the particular story about the Paris nuns falls to pieces, because as far back as 1781 this supposed martyr, St Expeditus, was chosen patron of the town of Acireale in Sicily, and because pictures of him were in existence in Germany in the eighteenth century which plainly depicted him as a saint to be invoked against procrastination.

FERDINAND III OF CASTILE (A.D. 1252)

PATRON SAINT OF PERSONS IN AUTHORITY: RULERS, GOVERNORS, MAGISTRATES;
THE POOR; PRISONERS; ALSO OF THE ENGINEERS OF THE SPANISH ARMY

30 MAY

The life of St Ferdinand says of him that 'his wisdom showed itself particularly in the choice he made of governors, magistrates and generals', for which reason he came to be looked upon as the patron of all those in positions of authority in the state. But he was regarded as patron not only of the governors but also of those over whom they exercised their authority, the poor and the imprisoned in particular.

St Ferdinand has further been traditionally regarded by the Spanish army as the patron of their engineers, on account of his technical skills as a military commander. This devotion received official approval from the Sacred Congregation of Rites on 13 December 1961.

The father of Ferdinand III was Alfonso IX, king of Leon, and his mother was Berengaria, who was the elder daughter of Alfonso III, king of Castile: her mother was a daughter of Henry II of England, and her sister Blanche became the mother of St Louis of France. The death of her brother Henry in 1217 left Berengaria heiress to the throne of Castile, but she resigned her rights in favour of her eighteen-year-old son Ferdinand. Two years later he married Beatrice, daughter of King Philip of Swabia, and they had seven sons and three daughters.

Ferdinand was severe in the administration of justice, but readily forgave personal injuries. His wisdom showed itself particularly in the choice he made of governors, magistrates and generals; the archbishop of Toledo, Rodrigo Ximenes, was chancelleor of Castile and his principal adviser for marty years. In 1230, on the death of his father, Ferdinand became king also of Leon, but not without strife, for there were those who supported the claim of his two half-sisters.

King Ferdinand was the real founder of the great University of Salamanca; but it is as the tireless and successful campaigner against the Moors that he impressed himself on the minds and hearts of Spaniards. For twenty-seven years he was engaged in almost uninterrupted warfare with the oppressors. He drove them out of Ubeda in 1234, Cordova (1236), Murcia, Jaen, Cadiz and finally Seville itself (1249). It was at the battle of Xeres, when only ten Spanish lives were lost, that St James was said to have been seen leading the host on a white horse. In thanksgiving for his victories, Ferdinand rebuilt the cathedral of Burgos and turned the great mosque of Seville into a church. Unlike some warriors he was a forbearing ruler: it is remembered of him that he said that he 'feared the curse of one old woman more than a whole army of Moors'; and he fought primarily not to extend his territories but to rescue Christian people from the dominion of infidels.

On the death of Queen Beatrice, Ferdinand married Joan of Ponthieu, who bore him two sons and a daughter: that daughter was Eleanor, who became the wife of Edward I of England. He himself died on 30 May 1252, and was buried in the cathedral of Seville in the habit of the Friars Minor. Ferdinand was declared a saint by Pope Clement X in 1671.

FIACRE (A.D. 670?)

PATRON SAINT OF GARDENERS AND HORTICULTURISTS; OF SUFFERERS FROM
VENERAL DISEASE AND HAEMORRHOIDS; AND OF CAB OR TAXI-DRIVERS

1 SEPTEMBER

Devotion to St Fiacre as patron saint of gardeners and horticulturalists comes from the Middle Ages, and seems to have been based on the story of his ploughing the land with his staff, as recounted in his life, and then clearing the ground to create a garden.

It has been suggested that the traditional choice of Fiacre as patron of those who suffer from venereal disease may have arisen from his reputation, recounted in the legends of his life, as a misogynist. He is also regarded as the patron of haemorrhoid sufferers, a medieval devotion which seems to have developed from a play on French words 'fic [a small tumour] saint Fiacre'.

St Fiacre became the patron saint of taxi-drivers, however, by accident. The first place to offer coaches for hire was situated near the Hotel Saint-Fiacre in Paris, and such vehicles became known as fiacres.

St Fiacre (Fiachra) is not mentioned in the earlier Irish calendars, but it is said that he was born in Ireland and that he sailed over into France in quest of closer solitude, in which he might devote himself to God, unknown to the world. He arrived at Meaux, where St Faro, who was the bishop of that city, gave him a solitary dwelling in a forest which was his own patrimony, called Breuil, in the province of Brie. There is a legend that St Faro offered him as much land as he could turn up in a day, and that St Fiacre, instead of driving his furrow with a plough, turned the top of the soil with the point of his staff. The anchorite cleared the ground of trees and briars, made himself a cell with a garden, built an oratory in honour of the Blessed Virgin, and made a hospice for travellers which developed into the village of Saint-Fiacre in Seine-et-Marne. Many resorted to him for advice, and the poor for relief. His charity moved him to attend cheerfully those that came to consult him; and in his hospice he entertained all comers, serving them with his own hands, and he sometimes miraculously restored to health those that were sick. He never allowed any women to enter the enclosure of his hermitage, and St Fiacre extended the prohibition even to his chapel; several rather ill-natured legends profess to account for it.

The fame of St Fiacre's miracles of healing continued after his death and crowds visited his shrine for centuries. Mgr Seguier, Bishop of Meaux in 1649, and John de Châtillon, Count of Blois, gave testimony of their own relief. Anne of Austria attributed to the mediation of this saint the recovery of Louis XIII at Lyons, where he had been dangerously ill: in thanksgiving for which she made on foot a pilgrimage to the shrine in 1641. She also sent to his shrine a token in acknowledgement of his intervention in the birth of her son, Louis XIV. Before that king underwent a severe operation, Bossuet, Bishop of Meaux, began a novena of prayers at Saint-Fiacre to ask the divine blessing. His relics at Meaux are still resorted to and he is invoked against all sorts of physical ills, including venereal disease.

FLORIAN, MARTYR (A.D. 304)

PATRON SAINT OF THOSE IN DANGER FROM WATER AND FLOOD, AND OF DROWNING; ALSO A PATRON OF AUSTRIA AND POLAND

4 MAY

Because he was martyred by drowning, Florian has traditionally been invoked by those in danger from water by drowning or by flood. But he is also one of the patrons of Austria, confirmed as such along with St Coloman, by a decree of the Sacred Congregation of Rites dated 29 December 1913.

The Saint Florian commemorated in the Roman Martyrology on 4 May was an officer of the Roman army, who occupied a high administrative post in Noricum, now part of Austria, and who suffered death for the faith in the days of Diocletian. His legendary 'acts' state that he gave himself up at Lorch to the soldiers of Aquilinus, the governor, when they were rounding up the Christians, and that after making a bold confession he was twice scourged, half-flayed alive and finally thrown into the river Enns with a stone round his neck. His body, recovered and buried by a pious woman, was eventually removed to the Augustinian abbey of St Florian, near Linz. It is said to have been at a later date translated to Rome, and Pope Lucius III, in 1138, gave some of the saint's relics to King Casimir of Poland and to the Bishop of Cracow. In these translations there may have been some confusion with other reputed saints of the same name, but there has been great popular devotion to St Florian in many parts of central Europe, and the tradition as to his martyrdom not far from the spot where the Enns flows into the Danube is ancient and reliable.

THE FOUR CROWNED MARTYRS (A.D. 306)

PATRON SAINTS OF STONEMASONS, SCULPTORS, MASONS, AND MARBLE WORKERS

8 NOVEMBER

The choice of the Four Crowned Martyrs (or sometimes only the first named of them, Claudius) as patrons of medieval gilds of masons is a natural one, given the story below. A fifteenth-century manuscript in the British Library, setting out the articles of one of the stonemason's gilds, contains a poem, one section of which is headed Ars quatuor coronatorum *('The skill of the four crowned ones'), and it goes on to tell briefly the story 'of these martyres fowre, that in thys craft [i.e., stone-masonry] were of gret honoure'. Pius XII formally confirmed their status as patrons in his Apostolic Letter of 20 April 1954.*

Under the date of 8 November the Roman Martyrology has the following: 'At Rome, three miles from the City on the Via Lavicana, the passion of the holy martyrs Claudius, Nico-stratus, Symphorian, Castorius and Simplicius, who were first cast into prison, then terribly beaten with loaded whips, and finally, since they could not be turned from Christ's faith, thrown headlong into the river by order of Diocletian. Likewise on the Via Lavicana the birthday of the four holy crowned brothers, namely, Severus, Severian, Carpophorus and Victorinus, who, under the same emperor, were beaten to death with blows from leaden scourges. Since their names, which in after years were made known by divine revelation, could not be discovered it was appointed that their anniversary, together with that of the other five, should be kept under the name of the Four Holy Crowned Ones; and this has continued to be done in the Church even after their names were revealed.'

These two entries and the *passio* upon which they are founded provide a puzzle which has not yet been solved with complete certainty. Severus, Severian, Carpophorus and Victorinus, names which the Roman Martyrology and Breviary say were revealed as those of the Four Crowned Martyrs, were borrowed from the martyrology of the diocese of Albano, where their feast is kept on 8 August. On the other hand, the Four Crowned Martyrs were sometimes referred to as Claudius, Nicostratus, Symphorian and Castorius. These, with the addition of Simplicius, so far from being the names of Roman martyrs (as stated above), belonged to five martyrs under Diocletian in Pannonia.

The legend falls into two distinct parts, the conventional and vague 'Roman *passio*', preceded by the vivid and interesting 'Pannonian *passio*' wherein we have a striking picture of the imperial quarries and workshops at Sirmium (Mitrovica in Yugloslavia), and Diocletian appears not simply as a commonplace blood-stained monster but as the emperor of rather unstable temperament with a passion for building. His attention is drawn by the work of four specially skilled carvers, Claudius, Nicostratus, Simpronian and Castorius, all Christians, and a fifth, Simplicius, who also has become a Christian, because it seems to him that the skill of the others is due to their religion. Diocletian orders them to do a number of carvings, which are duly executed with the exception of a statue of Aesculapius, which they will not make because they are Christians (though their other commissions have already included a large statue of the Sun-god). 'If their religion enables them to do such good work, all the better,' says the emperor, and confides Aesculapius to some heathen workmen.

But public opinion was aroused against Claudius and his comrades, and they were jailed for refusing to sacrifice to the gods. Both Diocletian and his officer Lampadius treated them with moderation at first; but Lampadius dying suddenly, his relatives furiously blamed the five Christians, and the emperor was induced to order their death. Thereupon each was enclosed in a leaden box, and thrown into the river to drown. Three weeks later the bodies were retrieved by one Nicodemus.

A year later Diocletian was in Rome, where he built a temple to Aesculapius in the baths of Trajan, and ordered all his troops to sacrifice to the god. Four *cornicularii* refused: whereupon they were beaten to death with leaded scourges and their bodies cast into the common sewer. They were taken up and buried on the Via Lavicana by St Sebastian and Pope Miltiades, who later directed, their names having been forgotten, that they should be commemorated under the names of Claudius, Nicostratus, Symphorian and Castorius.

A basilica was built and dedicated in honour of the Four Crowned Ones on the Coelian hill at Rome, probably during the first half of the fifth century: it became, and its successor still is, one of the titular churches of the cardinal-priests of the City. There is evidence that those thus commemorated were four of the Pannonian martyrs (why Simplicius was omitted does not appear), and that their relics were later translated to Rome. Then, it has been suggested, their names and history became known, and there emerged the difficulty that they were five, not four; and accordingly a hagiographer produced the second story outlined above, showing that the *Quatuor Coronati* were four Romans, not five Pannonians, and soldiers, not stonemasons.

FRANCES OF ROME (A.D. 1440)

PATRON SAINT OF WIDOWS; AND OF MOTORISTS

9 MARCH

Frances of Rome is a traditional patron of widows, a natural choice given both the devotion of husband and wife before Lorenzo's death in 1435, and her work during the years that remained afterwards.

The choice of Frances as patron of motorists – specifically of motorists in Rome –

was made by Pius XI in 1925 and confirmed on 9 September 1951 by a decree of the Sacred Congregation of Rites. The reason for this choice is far from clear, although the one generally given is that for half her life she had a constant vision of her guardian angel, by the light of whose splendour she was able to see during the night hours.

Frances was born in the Trastevere district of Rome in 1384. Her parents, Paul Busso and Jacobella dei Roffredeschi, were of noble birth and ample means, and the child was brought up in the midst of luxury but in a pious household.

Frances was a precocious little girl, and when she was eleven she asked her parents to allow her to become a nun, only to be met by a point-blank refusal. Her parents had quite different plans for their attractive little daughter. Within a year they announced to her that they had arranged to betroth her to young Lorenzo Ponziano, whose position, character and wealth made him a suitable match. After a time Frances withdrew her objections, and the marriage was solemnized when she was barely thirteen. At first she found the new life very trying, although she did her best to please her husband as well as her parents-in-law, and Cannozza, the young wife of Lorenzo's brother Paluzzo, discovered her one day weeping bitterly. Frances told her of her frustrated hopes, and learnt to her surprise that this new sister of hers would also have preferred a life of retirement and prayer. This was the beginning of a close friendship which lasted till death, and the two young wives strove together henceforth to live a perfect life under a common rule. Plainly dressed they sallied out to visit the poor of Rome, ministering to their wants and relieving their distress, and their husbands, who were devoted to them, raised no objection to their charities and austerities. They went daily to the hospital of Santo Spirito in Sassia to nurse the patients, singling out more particularly those suffering from the most repellent diseases.

In 1400 a son was born to Frances, and for a time she modified her way of life to devote herself to the care of little John Baptist (Battista). The following year Donna Cecilia died, and Frances was bidden by her father-in-law take her place at the head of the household. In vain she pleaded that Vannozza was the wife of the elder brother: Don Andrew and Vannozza insisted that she was the more suitable, and she was obliged to consent. She proved herself worthy of this position, discharging her duties efficiently whilst treating her household not as servants but as younger brothers and sisters, and trying to induce them to labour for their own salvation. In all the forty years that she lived with her husband there was never the slightest dispute or misunderstanding between them. In addition to the eldest, two other children of Frances are known, a younger boy, Evangelist, and a girl, Agnes; and she allowed no one but herself to look after them during childhood.

In 1408 the troops of Ladislaus of Naples, the ally of the antipope, had entered Rome and a soldier of fortune, Count Troja, had been appointed governor. The Ponziani had always supported the legitimate pope, and in one of the frequent conflicts Lorenzo was stabbed and carried home to Frances, to whose devoted nursing he owed his restoration to health. Troja resolved to leave the city after having wreaked his vengeance on the principal papal supporters. Amongst these were the Ponziani, and he not only arrested Vannozza's husband Paluzzo, but also demanded as a hostage little Battista; but while his mother Frances was praying in the church of Ara Coeli the boy was released in circumstances that seemed to be miraculous. Then, in 1410 when the cardinals were assembled at Bologna for the election of a new pope, Ladislaus again seized Rome. Lorenzo Ponziano, who as one of the heads of the papal party went in danger of his life, managed to escape, but it was impossible for his wife and family to follow him. His palace was plundered and Battista was taken captive by the soldiers of Ladislaus, though he afterwards got away and was able to join his father. The family possessions in the Campagna were destroyed, farms being burnt or pillaged and flocks slaughtered, whilst many of the peasants were murdered.

Frances lived in a corner of her ruined home with Evangelist, Agnes and Vannozza, whose husband was still a prisoner, and the two women devoted themselves to the care of the children and to relieving as far as their means would allow the sufferings of their still poorer neighbours. During another pestilence three years later, Evangelist died. Frances then turned part of the house into a hospital, and God rewarded her labours and prayers by bestowing on her the gift of healing.

Twelve months after the death of Evangelist, as his mother was praying one day, a bright light suddenly shone into the room and Evangelist appeared accompanied by an archangel. After telling her of his happiness in Heaven he said that he had come to warn her of the impending death of Agnes. A consolation was, however, to be vouchsafed to the bereaved mother. The archangel who accompanied Evangelist was henceforth to be her guide for twenty-three years. He was to be succeeded in the last epoch of her life by an angel of still higher dignity. Very soon Agnes began to fail, and a year later she passed away at the age of sixteen.

After many delays Pope John XXIII summoned the Council of Constance which was to prepare the healing of the Great Schism, and in that same year 1414 the Ponziani regained their property after being recalled from banishment. Lorenzo was now a broken man and lived in retirement, being tended with the utmost devotion by his faithful wife. It was his great wish to see his son Battista married and settled before his death, and he chose for him a beautiful girl called Mobilia, who proved to have a violent and overbearing temper. She conceived a great contempt for Frances, of whom she complained to her husband and his father, and whom she ridiculed in public. In the midst of a bitter speech she was struck down by a sudden illness, through which she was nursed by the saint. Won by her kindness Mobilia found her contempt turned to love, and thenceforward she sought to imitate her saintly mother-in-law. By this time the fame of the virtues and miracles of St Frances had spread over Rome, and she was appealed to from all quarters, not only to cure the sick but also to settle disputes and heal feuds. Lorenzo, whose love and reverence for her only increased with age, offered to release her from all the obligations of married life provided only that she would continued to live under his roof.

She was now able to carry out a project which had been taking shape in her mind of forming a society of women living in the world and bound by no vows, but pledged to make a simple offering of themselves to God and to serve the poor. The plan was approved by her confessor Dom Antonio, who obtained the affiliation of the congregation to the Benedictines of Monte Oliveto, to which he himself belonged. Known at first as the Oblates of Mary, they were afterwards called the Oblates of Tor de' Specchi. The society had lasted seven yeras when it was thought desirable to take a house adapted for a community, and the old building known as Tor de' Specchi was acquired. Whatever time she could spare from her home duties St Frances spent with the oblates, sharing in their daily life and duties. She never allowed them to refer to her as the foundress, but insisted that all should be subject to Agnes de Lellis who was chosen superioress. Three years later Lorenzo died and was laid beside Evangelist and Agnes; and St Frances announced her intention of retiring to Tor de' Specchi. On the feast of St Benedict she entered her foundation as a humble supliant and was eagerly welcomed. Agnes de Lellis immediately insisted upon resigning office and Frances had to take her place in spite of her protestations.

One evening in the spring of 1440, though feeling very ill, she tried to get back home after visiting Battista and Mobilia. On the way she met her director, Dom John Matteotti, who, shocked at her appearance, ordered her to return at once to her son's house. It was soon evident that she was dying, but she lingered on for seven days. On the evening of 9 March her face was seen to shine with a strange light: 'The angel has finished his task: he beckons me to follow him' were her last words. Her body was removed to Santa Maria Nuova, and she was buried in the chapel of the church reserved for her oblates.

St Frances was canonized in 1608, and Santa Maria Nuova is now known as the church of Santa Francesca Romana.

FRANCES XAVIER CABRINI, VIRGIN (A.D. 1917)

FOUNDRESS OF THE MISSIONARIES OF THE SACRED HEART
PATRON SAINT OF EMIGRANTS AND MIGRANTS

13 NOVEMBER

In an Apostolic Letter of 8 September 1950, Pope Pius XII said that he was declaring St Frances the patron of emigrants at the request of the bishops of both the United States and Canada. She was already, he noted, 'rightly called the "Mother of Emigrants"', because of the work she had done, especially in the Americas.

Augustine Cabrini owned and farmed land around Sant' Angelo Lodigiano, between Pavia and Lodi; his wife, Stella Oldini was a Milanese; and they had thirteen children, of whom the youngest was born on 15 July 1850, and christened Maria Francesca (later she was to add Saverio to the second name, which is what Xavier becomes in Italian). Frances came particularly under the strict care of her sister Rosa, who had been a school-teacher and had not escaped all the dangers of that profession. But the child profited by Rosa's teaching, and family reading aloud from the 'Annals of the Propagation of the Faith' inspired her with an early determination to go to the foreign missions. Her parents however, had decided on Frances being a school-teacher, and when old enough she was sent to a convent boarding-school at Arluno. She duly passed her examinations when she was eighteen, but then in 1870 she lost both her parents.

During the two years that followed she lived on quietly with Rosa, her unassuming goodness making a deep impression on all who knew her. Then she sought admittance to the religious congregation at whose school she had been, and was refused on the ground of poor health; she tried another – with the same result. But the priest in whose school she was teaching at Vidardo had his eye on her. In 1874 this Don Serrati was appointed provost of the collegiate church at Codogno, and found in his new parish a small orphanage, called the House of Providence, whose state left much to be desired. It was managed, or rather mismanaged, by its eccentric foundress, Antonia Tondini, and two other women. The Bishop of Lodi and Mgr Serrati invited Frances Cabrini to help in this institution and to try to turn its staff into a religious community, and with considerable unwillingness she agreed.

Antonia Tondini had consented to her coming, but instead of cooperation gave her only obstruction and abuse. Frances stuck to it, however, obtained several recruits, and with seven of them in 1877 took her first vows. At the same time the bishop put her in charge as superioress. This made matters much worse. Sister Tondini's behaviour was such that it became an open scandal – indeed, she seems to have become somewhat insane. But for another three years Sister Cabrini and her faithful followers persevered in their efforts till the bishop himself gave up hope. He sent for Sister Cabrini and said to her, 'You want to be a missionary sister. Now is the time. I don't know any institute of missionary sisters, so found one yourself.'

There was an old, disused and forgotten Franciscan friary at Codogno. Into this Mother Cabrini and her seven faithful followers moved, and as soon as they were fairly settled in she set herself to draw up a rule for the community. Its work was to be principally the Christian education of girls, and its name The Missionary Sisters of the Sacred Heart. During the same year these constitutions were approved by the bishop of Lodi; within two years the first daughter house was opened, at Grumello, and soon there was another, at Milan. The general progress of the congregation and the trust of Mother Cabrini were such that in 1887 she went to Rome to ask the Holy See's approbation of her little congregation and permission to open a house in Rome. Influential efforts were made to dissuade her from this enterprise – seven years' trial was far too little: and the first interview with the cardinal vicar of the City, Parocchi, confirmed the prudence of her advisers. But only the first. The cardinal was won over; Mother Cabrini was asked to open not one but two houses in Rome, a free school and a children's home, and the decree of first approval of the Missionary Sisters of the Sacred Heart was issued within a few months.

The bishop of Piacenza, Mgr Scalabrini, who had established the Society of St Charles to work among Italian immigrants in America, suggested to Frances Cabrini that she should go out there to help the work of those priests. She would not entertain the idea. The archbishop of New York, Mgr Corrigan, sent her a formal invitation. She determined to consult the pope himself. And Leo XIII said, 'Not to the East, but to the West'. When a child Frances Cabrini once fell into a river, and ever afterwards she had a fear of water. She now, with six of her sisters, set out on the first of many voyages across the Atlantic; and on 31 March 1889, they landed in New York.

The sister's reception in New York was hardly encouraging. They had been asked to organize an orphanage for Italian children and to take charge of an elementary school: but on arrival, though warmly welcomed, they found no home ready for them, and had to spend the first night at least in lodgings that were filthy and verminous. And when Mother Cabrini met Archbishop Corrigan she learned that, owning to disagreements between himself and the benefactress concerned, the orphanage scheme had fallen through, and the school consisted of pupils but no habitable building. The archbishop wound up by telling her that he could see nothing for it but that the sisters should go back to Italy. To which St Frances replied with characteristic firmness and definiteness, 'No, Monsignor, not that. The pope sent me here, and here I must stay'. Within a few weeks she had made friends with the benefactress, Countess Cesnola, reconciled her with Mgr Corrigan, found a house for the sisters, and made a start with the orphanage on a modest scale. By July 1889 she was able to revisit Italy, taking with her the first two Italo-American recruits to her congregation.

Nine months later she returned to America with reinforcements to take over West Park, on the Hudson river, from the Society of Jesus. The growing orphanage was transferred to this house, which also became the mother house and novitiate of the congregation in the United States. Its work was prospering, both among immigrants in North America and among the people at home in Italy, and soon Mother Cabrini had to make a trying journey to Managua in Nicaragua where, in difficult and sometimes dangerous circumstances, she took over an orphanage and opened a boarding-school. On her way back she visited New Orleans at the request of its archbishop, the revered Francis Janssens. The upshot was that she was able to make a foundation in New Orleans.

That Frances Cabrini was an extraordinarily able woman needs no demonstration: her works speak for her. She was slow in learning English and never lost her accent; but this apparently was no handicap. In only one direction did her tact fail, and that was in relation to non-Catholic Christians. She met such in America for the first time in her life and it took her a long time to recognize their good faith and to appreciate their good lives. It is obvious that Mother Cabrini was a born ruler, and she was as strict as she was just. Sometimes she seems to have been too strict, and not to have seen where her inflexibility was leading. It is not clear, for instance, how she thought she was upholding sexual morality when she refused to take illegitimate children in her fee-paying schools: it would appear to be a gesture that penalized only the innocent. But love ruled all, and her strictness was no deterrent to the affection she gave and received.

The year 1892, fourth centenary of the discovery of the New World, was also marked by the birth of one of the best-known of St Frances's undertakings, the Columbus Hospital in New York. Then, after a visit to Italy, where she saw the start of a 'summer house' near Rome and a students' hostel at Genoa, she had to go to Costa Rica, Panama, Chile, across the Andes into Brazil, and so to Buenos Aires. In Buenos Aires she opened a high-school for girls. After another voyage to Italy, where she had to cope with a long lawsuit in the ecclesiastical courts and face riots in Milan, she went to France and made there her first European foundations outside Italy; and the autumn of 1898 saw her in England. Mgr (later Cardinal) Bourne, then Bishop of Southwark, had already met St Frances at Codogno and asked her to open a convent in his diocese, but no foundation was made at this time.

And so it went on for another dozen years. Her love for all the children of God took her back and forth over the western hemisphere from Rio to Rome, from Sydenham to Seattle; by the time the constitutions of the Missionary Sisters of the Sacred Heart were finally approved in 1907 the eight members of 1880 had increased to over a thousand, in eight countries; St Frances had made more than fifty foundations, responsible for free-schools and high-schools and hospitals and other establishments, no longer working in America for Italian immigrants alone – did not the prisoners in Sing-Sing send her an illuminated address at the congregation's jubilee? Of the later foundations only two can be named here: the great Columbus Hospital at Chicago and, in 1902, the school at Brockley, now at Honor Oak.

From 1911 Mother Cabrini's health was failing: she was then sixty-one and physically worn out. But it was not till six years later that she was seen be be failing alarmingly. And then the end came with extreme suddenness. No one was present when St Frances Xavier Cabrini died in the convent at Chicago on 22 December 1917. She was canonized in 1946, the first citizen of that country to be canonized.

FRANCIS BORGIA (A.D. 1572)

A PATRON SAINT OF PORTUGAL; AND OF EARTHQUAKES

10 OCTOBER

There would seem to be nothing specific in Francis Borgia's life to associate him with earthquakes, but he was certainly associated with Portugal and taken as patron of that country although the records do not seem to show a formal recognition of that role. It was after the great earthquake of 1756 in which Lisbon was almost totally destroyed, that Benedict XIV declared him to be patron of earthquakes in Portugal in a letter of 24 March 1756.

The family of Borja was one of the most noble of the kingdom of Aragon, but it was not till the fifteenth century that it became known outside Spain, when from 1455 to 1458 Alphonsus Borgia was pope under the name of Callistus III. At the end of that century there was another Borgia pope, Alexander VI, who at the time of his elevation to the papacy was the father of four children. As a provision for his son, Peter, he bought the dukedom of Gandia in Spain, and on Peter's death bestowed it upon another son, John. John was murdered soon after his marriage, and his son, the third duke of Gandia, married the daughter of a natural son of King Ferdinand V of Aragon. Of this union was born at Gandia in the year 1510 Francisco de Borja y Aragon, now known to us as St Francis Borgia, great-grandson of a pope and of a king and cousin of the Emperor Charles V. At the age of eighteen, his education completed, young Francis was received at the imperial court. At Alcalá de Henares Francis was impressed by the appearance of a man whom he saw being taken to the prison of the Inquisition. That man was Ignatius Loyola.

In the following year Francis Borgia, having been created marquis of Lombay, married Eleanor de Castro, and ten years later Charles V made him viceroy of Catalonia, whose capital was Barcelona. He devoted as much time to prayer as he could without prejudice to public affairs or the needs of his growing family, and the frequency of his sacramental communions caused comment, mostly unfavourable. In 1543 St Francis became duke of Gandia by the death of his father, whereupon he retired with his family to his estates, following on the refusal of King John of Portugal to recognize him as master of the household to Prince Philip of Spain, who was about to marry the king's daughter. This was a definite check to the public career of Francis Borgia and he proceeded to interest himself in more personal affairs. He fortified Gandia that it might not be exposed to the Moors and pirates from Barbary, built a convent for the Dominicans at Lombay, and repaired the hospital.

This happy and peaceful life at Gandia was bought suddenly to an end by the death in 1546 of Doña Eleanor. They had eight children, of whom the youngest was eight at his mother's death. Shortly afterwards Bd Peter Favre paid a brief visit to Gandia, and he left for Rome bearing a message to St Ignatius Loyola that Francis Borgia had resolved to ask to be received into the Society of Jesus – he had in fact made a vow to do so. St Ignatius advised the duke to defer the execution of his design till he had settled his children and finished the foundations he had begun, telling him in the meantime to study theology at Gandia in the university he had inaugurated there and to take the degree of doctor; he was, moreover, to take every precaution to prevent this astonishing piece of news from being prematuraly divulged. Francis obeyed but was troubled in the following year by being summoned to assist at the *cortes* of Aragon. He therefore wrote to St Ignatius and as a consequence was allowed to make his profession privately. Three years were enough to see his children properly established and on 31 August 1550, St Francis Borgia set out for Rome. He was forty years old.

After less than four months in Rome, Francis went back to Spain, and retired to a hermitage at Oñate, near Loyola. Here he received the emperor's permission to make over his titles and estates to his son Charles, whereupon he shaved his head and beard, assumed clerical dress, and was ordained priest in Whitsun week, 1551. 'A duke turned Jesuit' was the sensation of the day, and when Francis celebrated his first public Mass, for assistance at which the pope granted a plenary indulgence, the crowd at Vergara was so great that the altar had to be set up in the open air. Directly after his ordination he was allowed to preach throughout Guipùzcoa, and he went through the villages with a bell, calling the children to catechism, instructing and preaching. But within the house the superior treated Father Francis with such severity as he deemed the previous exalted position of his subject required.

St Francis's corporal mortifications after his 'conversion' became excessive: he was an exceedingly fat man, and his girth decreased very notably; his excesses were now curbed by religious obedience, but he was ingenious in the devising of physical discomforts. In after years he was of the opinion that he had been imprudent in his ways of mortifying his body, especially before he became a Jesuit. He left Oñate for several months to preach in other parts of Spain. Much success attended his labours and he was one of the first to recognize the greatness of the Carmelite nun of Avila, Teresa. After doing wonders in Castile and Andalusia, he seemed to surpass himself in Portugal, and in 1554 St Ignatius made him commissary general of the Society of Jesus in Spain, an office which he discharged at times with something of the autocracy of a distinguished nobleman.

During his years as commissary general St Francis Borgia was practically the founder of the Society in Spain, establishing in a short time houses and colleges at a score of places. But he did not neglect the immediate care of those whom he had left behind him in the world. He soothed and made sweet the last moments of the queen dowager, Joanna, who fifty years before had gone mad at the death of her husband and had shown a special aversion from the clergy. In the next year, soon after the death of St Ignatius, the Emperor Charles V abdicated, and sent for St Francis to visit him at Yuste. Charles had been prepossessed against the Society of Jesus and expressed his surprise that Francis should have preferred it to so many older orders. The saint removed his prejudices.

St Francis was no friend of the Inquisition, nor that body of him; and King Philip II listened to the calumnies which jealously was raising against Francis. He remained on the work of the Society in Portugal till 1561, and was then summoned to Rome by Pope Pius IV, at the instance of the Jesuit general, Father Laynez. St Francis was most warmly received in Rome and among these who regularly attended his sermons were Cardinal Charles Borromeo and Cardinal Ghislieri, afterwards St Pius V. Becoming acquainted with the work of the headquarters of the Jesuits, he filled high offices, and on the death of Father Laynez inn 1565 was elected father general. During seven years he promoted the work of the Society of Jesus in all parts of the world. St Francis's first care was to establish a properly regulated novitiate in Rome and to provide for the same in the provinces. When he first came to the city fifteen years before he had shown a strong interest in the project of a Roman college, and had given a large sum of money. He now concerned himself personally in the direction of the college and the arrangement of its curriculum. In effect he was the founder of this college, but he always refused the title, which is given to Pope Gregory XIII who re-established it as the Gregorian University. St Francis also built the church of Sant' Andrea on the Quirinal, with the adjoining residence, to house the novitiate, began the Gesù, and enlarged and improved the German college.

Pope St Pius V had confidence in the Society of Jesus and a great trust and admiration for its general, so that he could proceed freely with the projects he had at heart. St Francis provided for the extension of the Society of Jesus across the Alps, and established the province of Poland. He used his influence with the French court to obtain a more favourable reception for the Jesuits in France, where he was able to set up colleges. And he was engrossed by the foreign missions: those of the East Indies and the Far East were reformed and those of the Americas begun. St Francis published a new edition of the rules of the Society and drew up regulations and directions for those members who were engaged in special work of various kinds. Nor was St Francis so immersed in the responsibilities of his office that he had no time to spare for matters outside. This was shown when in 1566 a pestilence made great havoc in Rome, on which occasion he raised alms for the relief of the poor, and commissioned the fathers of his order, two and two, to attend the sick in all parts of the city, with imminent danger to their own lives.

In the year 1571 the pope sent Cardinal Bonelli on an embassy to Spain, Portugal and France, and St Francis accompanied him. Though politically not a great success, it was a personal triumph for the Jesuit. Everywhere crowds clamoured 'to see the saint' and to hear him preach, old animosities were forgotten, and King Philip received him as gladly as did his people. But the fatigues entailed were too much for St Francis. He had been for some time in bad health; his infirmities, inclination to retirement, and a deep sense of the weight of his post had worn him out, and at Ferrara on his return Duke Alfonso, who was his cousin, sent him from thence to Rome in a litter. He lived for two days only after his arrival. By his brother Thomas he sent his blessing to all his children and grandchildren, and as their names were rehearsed to him he prayed for each one. When he had lost his speech a painter was, with peculiar insensibility, introduced to his bedside. Francis saw him, expressed his displeasure with his dying hands and eyes, and turned away his face so that nothing could be done. He died at the midnight of 30 September–1 October 1572.

FRANCIS DE SALES, BISHOP OF GENEVA AND DOCTOR OF THE CHURCH (A.D. 1622)

CO-FOUNDER OF THE ORDER OF THE VISITATION
PATRON SAINT OF JOURNALISTS, EDITORS, AND WRITERS

24 JANUARY

Pope Pius XI, when declaring Francis de Sales patron of all those who 'make known Christian wisdom by writing in newspapers or in other journals meant for the general public', referred to the saint's example in The Controversies *of 'arguing forcefully, but with moderation and charity'. The solemn proclamation of the saint's patronage was contained in an Apostolic Letter of 26 January 1923.*

St Francis de Sales was born at the Château de Sales in Savoy on 21 August 1567, and on the following day was baptized in the parish church of Thorens under the name of Francis Bonaventure. His patron saint in after-life was the *Poverello* of Assisi, and the room in which he was born was known as 'St Francis's room', from a painting of the saint preaching to the birds and fishes. During his first years he was very frail and delicate, owing to his premature birth, but with care he gradually grew stronger, and, though never robust, he was singularly active and energetic throughout his career. His mother kept his early education in her own hands, aided by the Abbé Déage, who afterwards, as his tutor, accompanied Francis everywhere during his youth.

At the age of eight Francis went to the College of Annecy. There he made his first communion in the church of St Dominic (now known as St Maurice), there he also received confirmation, and a year later he received the tonsure. Francis had a great wish to consecrate himself to God, and regarded this as the first outward step. His father (who at this marriage had taken the name of de Boisy) seems to have attached little importance to it, and destined his eldest son for a secular career. In his fourteenth year Francis was sent to the University of Paris, which at that time, with its 54 colleges, was one of the great centres of learning. He was intended for the Collège de Navarre, as it was frequented by the sons of the noble families of Savoy, but Francis, fearing for his vocation in such surroundings, implored to be allowed to go to the Collège de Clermont, which was under Jesuit direction and renowned for piety as well as for learning. Having obtained his father's consent to this, and accompanied by the Abbé Déage, he took up his abode in the Hôtel de la Rose Blanche, Rue St Jacques, which was close to the Collège de Clermont.

Francis soon made his mark, especially in rhetoric and philosophy, and he ardently devoted himself to the study of theology. To satisfy his father he took lessons in riding, dancing and fencing, but cared for none of them. His heart was more and more set upon giving himself wholly to God.

He was twenty-four when he took his final degree, became a doctor of law at Padua, and rejoined his family at the Château de Thuille on the Lake of Annecy. Francis had so far only confided to his mother, to his cousin Canon Louis de Sales, and to a few intimate friends his earnest desire of devoting his life to the service of God. An explanation with his father, however, became inevitable. The death of the provost of the chapter of Geneva suggested to Canon Louis de Sales the possibility that Francis might be appointed to this post, and that in this way his father's opposition might relax. Francis put on ecclesiastical dress the very day his father gave his consent, and six months afterwards, on 18 December 1593, he was ordained priest. He took up his duties with an ardour which never abated.

At this time the religious condition of the people of the Chablais, on the south shore of the Lake of Geneva, was deplorable, and the Duke of Savoy applied to Bishop de Granier to send missioners who might win back his subjects to the Church. The bishop, summoning his chapter, put the whole matter before them, disguising none of the difficulties and dangers. The provost stood up and offered himself for the work. The bishop accepted at once, to Francis's great joy. But M. de Boisy took a different view of the matter and Francis had the disappointment of starting on his mission without his father's blessing. It was on September 14, 1594, Holy Cross day, that, travelling on foot and accompanied only by his cousin, Canon Louis de Sales, he set forth to win back the Chablais.

The missionaries worked and preached daily in Thonon, gradually extending their efforts to the villages of the surrounding country. One evening Francis was attacked by wolves, and only escaped by spending the night in a tree. Twice in January 1595 he was waylaid by assassins who had sworn to take his life, but on both these occasions, as also several times later, he was preserved seemingly by miracle. Time went by with little apparent result to reward the labours of the two missioners, and all the while M. de Boisy was sending letters to his son, alternately commanding and imploring him to give up so hopeless a task. Francis was constantly seeking new ways to reach the hearts and minds of the people, and he began writing leaflets setting forth the teaching of the Church. In every spare moment of his arduous day he wrote these little papers, which were copied many times by hand and distributed widely by all available means. These sheets, composed under such stress and difficulty, were later to form both the volume of 'Controversies', and the beginning of his activities as a writer.

In the summer of 1595, going up the mountain of Voiron to restore an oratory of our Lady which had been destroyed by the Bernese, he was attacked by a hostile crowd, who insulted and beat him. Soon afterwards his sermons at Thonon began to be more numerously attended. The tracts too had been silently doing their work, and his patient perseverance under every form of persecution and hardship had not been without its effect. Conversions became more and more frequent, and before very long there was a steady stream of lapsed Catholics seeking reconciliation with the Church. After three or four years, when Bishop de Granier came to visit the mission, the fruits of Francis's self-sacrificing work and untiring zeal were unmistakable. The bishop was made welcome, and was able to administer confirmation. He even presided at the 'Forty Hours', a possibility which had seemed unthinkable in Thonon.

Mgr de Granier, who had long been considering Francis in the light of a possible coadjutor and successor, felt that the moment had now come to give effect to this. When the proposal was made Francis was at first unwilling, but in the end he yielded to the persistence of the bishop, submitting to what he ultimately felt was a manifestation of the Divine Will. Soon he fell dangerously ill with a fever which kept him for a time hovering between life and death. When sufficiently recovered he proceeded to Rome, where Pope Clement VIII, having heard much in praise of the virtue and ability of the young provost, desired that he should be examined in his presence. The pope himself, Baronius, Bellarmine, Cardinal Frederick Borromeo (a cousin of St Charles) and others put no less than thirty-five abstruse questions of theology to Francis, all of which he answered with simplicity and modesty, but in a way which proved his learning. His appointment as coadjutor of Geneva was confirmed, and Francis returned to take up his work with fresh zeal and energy.

Francis succeeded to the see of Geneva on the death of Claud de Granier in the autumn of 1602, and took up his residence at Annecy, with a household organized on lines of the strictest economy. To the fulfilment of his episcopal duties he gave himself with unstinted generosity and devotion. He organized the teaching of the catechism throughout the diocese, and at Annecy gave the instructions himself, with such glowing interest and fervour that years after his death the 'Bishop's Catechisms' were still vividly remembered. Children loved him and followed him about. His unselfishness and charity, his humility and clemency, could not have been surpassed. In dealing with souls, though always gentle, he was never weak, and he could be very firm when kindness did not prevail.

A prominent place in this work of spiritual direction was held by St Jane Frances de Chantel, who first became known to him in 1604, when he was preaching Lenten sermons at Dijon. The foundation of the Order of the Visitation in 1610 was the result that evolved from this meeting of the two saints. His most famous book, the *Introduction to the Devout Life*, grew out of the casual notes of instruction and advice which he wrote to Mme de Chamoisy, a cousin by marriage, who had placed herself under his guidance. He was persuaded to publish them in a little volume which, with some additions, first appeared in 1608. The book was at once acclaimed a spiritual masterpiece, and soon translated into many languages.

In 1622, the Duke of Savoy, going to meet Louis XIII at Avignon, invited St Francis to join them there. Anxious to obtain from Louis certain privileges for the French part of his diocese, Francis readily consented, although he was in no state of health to risk the long winter journey. But he seems to have had a premonition that his end was not far off. Before quitting Annecy he put all his affairs in order, and took his leave as if he had no expectation of seeing people again. At Avignon he led as far as possible his usual austere life. But he was greatly sought after – crowds were eager to see him, and the different religious houses all wanted the saintly bishop to preach to them. On the return journey he stayed at Lyons, where he lodged in a gardener's cottage belonging to the convent of the Visitation. Here for a whole month, though sorely in need of rest, he spared himself no labour for souls. In bitterly cold weather, through Advent and over Christmas, he continued his preaching and ministrations, refusing no demand upon his strength and time. On St John's day he was taken seriously ill with some sort of paralytic seizure. He recovered speech and consciousness, and endured with touching patience the torturing remedies used in the hope of prolonging his life, but which only hastened the end. After receiving the last sacraments he lay murmuring words from the Bible expressive of his humble and serene trust in God's mercy. The last word he was heard to utter was the name of 'Jesus'. While those kneeling around his bed said the litany for the dying, and were invoking the Holy Innocents, whose feast it was, St Francis gently breathed his last, in the fifty-sixth year of his age.

The beatification of St Francis de Sales in 1662 was the first solemn beatification to take place in St Peter's at Rome, where he was canonized three years later. He was declared a doctor of the Church in 1877.

FRANCIS OF ASSISI, FOUNDER OF THE FRIARS MINOR (A.D. 1226)

PATRON SAINT OF ITALY; OF ITALIAN MERCHANTS; OF ECOLOGISTS AND ECOLOGY

4 OCTOBER

Pius XII declared St Francis to be a patron of Italy, alongside St Catherine of Siena, in an Apostolic Letter of 18 June 1939. He singled out Francis for the example he had given to the people of his turbulent age, and for teaching them the standards of Catholic behaviour. The Pope's declaration was confirmed by the Italian parliament on 25 February 1958. In practice, however, Francis had been hailed as a patron of Italy from shortly after his death.

Francis was proclaimed patron of Italian merchants at their request by Pius XII in an Apostolic Letter of 23 February 1952. As the Pope pointed out, before he 'rejected all the blandishments of this life', he had been a merchant himself.

Especially at the request of the 'Planning Environmental and Ecological Institute for Quality Life' [sic], John Paul II proclaimed Francis of Assisi patron of ecology and ecologists in an Apostolic Letter of 29 November 1979. He cited in particular Francis' famous Canticle of Creatures with its reference to Brother Sun and Sister Moon.

St Francis was born at Assisi in Umbria in 1181 or 1182. His father, Peter Bernadone, was a merchant, and his mother was called Pica. Much of Peter's trade was with France, and his son having been born while he was absent in that country, they called him *Francesco*, 'the Frenchman', though the name of John had been given him at his baptism. In his youth he was devoted to the ideas of romantic chivalry propagated by the troubadours; he had plenty of money and spent it lavishly, even ostentatiously. He was uninterested alike in his father's business and in formal learning.

When he was about twenty, strife broke out between the cities of Perugia and Assisi, and Francis was carried away prisoner by the Perugians. This he bore a whole year with cheerfulness and good temper. But as soon as he was released he was struck down by a long and dangerous sickness. On his recovery he determined to join the forces of Walter de Brienne, who was fighting in southern Italy. He bought himself expensive equipment and handsome outfit, but as he rode out one day in a new suit, meeting a gentleman reduced to poverty and very ill-clad, he was touched with compassion and changed clothes with him. At Spoleto he was taken ill again, and as he lay there a heavenly voice seemed to tell him to turn back, 'to serve the master rather than the man'. Francis obeyed. At first he returned to his old life, but more quietly and with less enjoyment. Then, riding one day in the plain of Assisi, he met a leper, whose sores were so loathsome that at the sight of them he was struck with horror. But he dismounted, and as the leper stretched out his hand to receive an alms, Francis, whilst he bestowed it, kissed the man.

Henceforward he often visited the hospitals and served the sick, and gave to the poor sometimes his clothes and sometimes money. One day as he was praying in the church of St Damian, outside the walls of Assisi, he seemed to hear a voice coming from the crucifix, which said to him three times, 'Francis, go and repair my house, which you see is falling down'. The saint, seeing that church was old and ready to fall, thought our Lord commanded him to repair that. He therefore went home, and in the simplicity of his heart took a horseload of cloth out of his father's warehouse and sold it, with the horse. The price he brought to the poor priest of St Damian's, asking to be allowed to stay with him. The priest consented, but would not take the money, which Francis therefore left on a window-sill. His father, hearing what had been done, came in great indignation to St Damian's, but Francis had hid himself. After some days spent in prayer and fasting, he appeared again, though so disfigured and ill-clad that people pelted him and called him mad. Bernardone, more annoyed than ever, carried him home, beat him unmercifully (Francis was about twenty-five), put fetters on his feet, and locked him up, till his mother set him at liberty while his father was out. Francis returned to St Damian's. His father, following him thither, hit him about the head and insisted that he should either return home or renounce all his share in his inheritance and return the purchase-price of the goods he had taken. Francis had no objection to being disinherited, but said that the other money now belonged to God and the poor. He was therefore summoned before Guido, Bishop of Assisi, who told him to return it and have trust in God. Francis did as he was told and, with his usual literalness, added, 'The clothes I wear are also his. I'll give them back.' He suited the action to the word, stripped himself of his clothes, and gave them to his father. The dress of a labourer, a servant of the bishop, was found, and Francis received this first alms with many thanks, made a cross on the garment with chalk, and put it on.

Francis went in search of shelter, singing the divine praises. He met a band of robbers, who asked him who he was. He answered, 'I am the herald of the great King'. They beat him and threw him into a ditch full of snow. He went on singing the praises of God. He passed by a monastery, and there received alms and a job of work as an unknown poor man. In the city of Gubbio, one who knew him took him into his house, and gave him a tunic, belt and shoes, such as pilgrims wore, which were decent though poor and shabby. These he wore two years, and he walked with staff in his hand like a hermit. He then returned to San Damiano at Assisi. For the repair of the church he gathered alms and begged in Assisi, where all had known him rich, bearing with joy the railleries and contempt with which he was treated by some. For the building he himself carried stones and served the masons and helped put the church in order. He next did the same for an old church which was dedicated in honour of St Peter. After this he went to a little chapel called Portiuncula, belonging to the abbey of Benedictine monks on Monte Subasio, who gave it that name probably because it was built on so small a piece of land. It stands in a plain two miles from Assisi, and was at that time forsaken and ruinous. The place appealed to St Francis, and he was delighted with the title which the chuch bore, it being dedicated in honour of our Lady of the Angels. He repaired it, and fixed his abode by it. Here, on the feast of St Matthias in the year 1209, his way of life was shown to St Francis. In those days the gospel of the Mass on this feast was Matt. x 7–19: 'And going, preach saying: The kingdom of Heaven is at hand . . . Freely have you received, freely give . . . Do not possess gold . . . nor two coats nor shoes nor a staff . . . Behold I send you as sheep in the midst of wolves. . . .' The words went straight to his heart and, applying them literally to himself, he gave away his shoes, staff and girdle, and left himself with one poor coat, which he girt about him with a cord. This was the dress which he gave to his friars the year following: the undyed woollen dress of the shepherds and peasants in those parts.

Many began to admire Francis, and some desired to be his companions and disciples. The first of these was Bernard da Quintavalle, a rich trades-man of Assisi. Bernard sold all his effects and divided the sum among the poor. Peter of Cattaneo, a canon of the cathedral of Assisi, desired to be admitted with him, and Francis 'gave his habit' to them both together on 16 April 1209. The third to join them was the famous Brother Giles, a person of great simplicity and spiritual wisdom. When his followers had increased to a dozen, Francis drew up a short informal rule consisting chiefly of the gospel counsels of perfection. This he took to Rome in 1210 for the pope's appro-bation. Innocent III afterwards told his nephew, from whom St Bonaventure heard it, that in a dream he saw a palm tree growing up at his feet, and in another he saw St Francis propping up the Lateran church, which seemed ready to fall. He therefore sent for St Francis, and approved his rule, but only by word of mouth, tonsuring him and his companions and giving them a general commission to preach repentance.

St Francis and his companions now lived together in a little cottage at Rivo Torto, outside the gates of Assisi, whence they sometimes went into the country to preach. After a time they had trouble with a peasant who wanted the cottage for the use of his donkey. Francis went off to see the abbot of Monte Subasio. The abbot, in 1212, handed over the Portiuncula chapel to St

Francis, upon condition that it should always continue the head church of his order. Round about the chapel the brothers built themselves huts of wood and clay. St Francis would not suffer any property to be vested in his order, or in any community or convent of it; he called the spirit of holy poverty the foundation of the order, and in his dress, in everything that he used, and in all his actions he showed the reality of his love for it. He never proceeded in holy orders beyond the diaconate, not daring to be ordained priest.

In the autumn of 1212 Francis, not content with all that he did and suffered for souls in Italy, resolved to go and preach to the Moslems. He embarked with one companion at Ancona for Syria, but they were driven straight on to the coast of Dalmatia and wrecked. The two friars could get no further and, having no money for their passage, travelled back to Ancona as stowaways. After preaching for a year in central Italy, during which the lord of Chiusi put at the disposal of the Franciscans as a place of retreat Mount Alvernia (La Verna) in the Tuscan Apennines, St Francis made another attempt to reach the Moslems; this time in Morocco by way of Spain. But again he was disappointed in his object, for somewhere in Spain he was taken ill, and when he recovered he returned into Italy, where again he laboured strenuously to advance the glory of God among all Christian people.

Out of humility St Francis gave to his order the name of Friars Minor, desiring that his brethren should really be below their fellows and seek the last and lowest places. Many cities were anxious to have the brothers in their midst, and small communities of them sprang up throughout Umbria, Tuscany, Lombardy and Ancona. In 1216 Francis is said to have begged from Pope Honorius III the Portiuncula indulgence, or pardon of Assisi; and in the following year he was in Rome, where he probably met his fellow friar St Dominic, who had been preaching faith and penance in southern France while Francis was still a 'young man about town' in Assisi. St Francis also wanted to preach in France, but was dissuaded by Cardinal Ugolino (afterwards Pope Gregory IX); so he sent instead Brother Pacifico and Brother Agnello, who was afterwards to bring the Franciscans to England. The development of the brotherhood was considerably influenced by the good and prudent Ugolino. The members were so numerous that some organization and systematic control was imperatively necessary. The order was therefore divided into provinces, each in charge of a minister to whom was committed 'the care of the souls of the brethren, and should anyone be lost through the minister's fault and bad example, that minister will have to give an account before our Lord Jesus Christ'. The friars now extended beyond the Alps, missions being sent to Spain, Germany and Hungary.

The first general chapter was held at the Portiuncula at Pentecost in 1217; and in 1219 was held the chapter called 'of Mats', because of the number of huts of wattles and matting hastily put up to shelter the brethren: there were said to be five thousand of them present. St Francis sent some of his friars from this chapter to Tunis and Morocco, reserving to himself the Saracens of Egypt and Syria. Innocent III's appeal at the Lateran Council in 1215 for a new crusade had resulted only in a desultory attempt to bolster up the Latin kingdom in the East: Francis would wield the sword of the word of God.

He set sail with twelve friars from Ancona in June 1219, and came to Damietta on the Nile delta, before which the crusaders were sitting in siege. Francis was profoundly shocked by the dissoluteness and self-seeking of the soldiers of the Cross. Burning with zeal for the conversion of the Saracens, he desired to pass to their camp, though he was warned that there was a price on the head of every Christian. Permission was given him by the papal legate and he went with Brother Illuminato crying out, 'Sultan! Sultan!' Being brought before Malek al-Kamil and asked his errand, he said boldly, 'I am sent not by men but by the most high God, to show you and your people the way of salvation by announcing to you the truths of the gospel'. Discussion followed, and other audiences. The sultan was somewhat moved and invited him to stay with him.

After some days Malek al-Kamil sent Francis back to the camp before Damietta. Disappointed that he could do so little either with the crusaders or their opponents, St Francis returned to Akka, whence he visited the Holy Place. Then summoned by an urgent message of distress, he returned to Italy.

Francis found that in his absence his two vicars, Matthew of Narni and Gregory of Naples, had introduced certain innovations whose tendency was to bring the Franciscans into line with the other religious orders and to confine their proper spirit within the more rigid framework of monastic observance and prescribed asceticism. With the sisters at San Damiano this had taken the form of regular constitutions, drawn up on the Benedictine model by Cardinal Ugolino. When St Francis arrived at Bologna he was amazed and grieved to find his brethren there housed in a fine convent: he refused to enter it, and lodged with the Friars Preachers, from whence he sent for the guardian of his brethren, upbraided him and ordered the friars to leave that house. St Francis saw these events as a betrayal: it was a crisis that might transform or destroy his followers. He went to the Holy See, and obtained from Honorius III the appointment of Cardinal Ugolino as official protector and adviser to the Franciscans, for he was a man who believed in St Francis and his ideas while being at the same time an experienced man of affairs. Then he set himself to revise the rule, and summoned another general chapter, which met at the Portiuncula in 1221. To this assembly he presented the revised rule, which abated nothing of the poverty, humbleness and evangelical freedom which characterized the life he had always set before them: it was Francis's challenge to the dissidents and legalists who now, beneath the surface, were definitely threatening the peaceful development of the Franciscans. Chief among them was Brother Elias of Cortona, who, as vicar of St Francis, who had resigned active direction of the order, was in effect minister general of the brethren; but he did not dare too openly to oppose himself to the founder whom he sincerely respected.

At the end of two years, throughout which he had to face the growing tendency to break away from his ideas and to expand in directions which seemed to him to compromise the Franciscan vocation, Francis once again revised his rule. This done, he handed it to Brother Elias for communication to the ministers. It was promptly lost, and St Francis had again to dictate it to Brother Leo, amid the protests of many of the brethren who maintained that the forbiddance of holding corporate property was impracticable. In the form in which it was eventually approved by Pope Honorius III in 1223, it represented substantially the spirit and manner of life for which St Francis had stood from the moment that he cast off his fine clothes in the bishop's court at Assisi. About two years earlier St Francis and Cardinal Ugolino may have drawn up a rule for the fraternity of lay people who associated themselves with the Friars Minor in the spirit of Francis's 'Letter to all Christians', written in the early years of the mission – the Franciscan tertiaries of today.

St Francis spent the Christmas of 1223 at Grecchio in the valley of Rieti where, he told his friend John da Vellita, 'I would make a memorial of that Child who was born in Bethlehem and in some sort behold with bodily eyes the hardships of His infant state, lying on hay in a manger with the ox and the ass standing by'. Accordingly a 'crib' was set up at the hermitage, and the peasants crowded to the midnight Mass, at which Francis served as deacon and preached on the Christmas mystery. The custom of making a crib was probably not unknown before this time, but this use of it by St Francis is said to have begun its subsequent popularity. He remained for some months at Grecchio in prayer and quietness, and the graces which he received from God in contemplation he was careful to conceal from men.

Towards the festival of the Assumption in 1224, St Francis retired to Mount Alvernia and there made a little cell. He kept Leo with him, but forbade any other person to come to him before the feast of St Michael. It was here on or about Holy Cross day 1224, that the miracle of the *stigmata* happened. Having been thus marked with the signs of our Lord's passion, Francis tried to conceal this favour of Heaven from the eyes of men, and for this purpose he ever after covered his hands with his habit, and wore shoes and stockings on his feet.

The two years that remained of his life were years of suffering and of happiness in God. His health was getting worse, the *stigmata* were a source of physical pain and weakness, and his sight was failing. He got so bad that in the summer of 1225 Cardinal Ugolino and the vicar Elias obliged him to put himself in the hands of the pope's physicians at Rieti. He complied with simplicity, and on his way thither paid his last visit to St Clare at San Damiano. Here, almost maddened with pain and discomfort, he made the 'Canticle of Brother Sun', which he set to a tune and taught the brethren to sing. He went to Monte Rainerio to undergo the agonizing treatment prescribed, and got but temporary relief. He was taken to Siena to see other physicians, but he was dying.

Then he went to Assisi and was lodged in the bishop's house. The doctors there, pressed to speak the truth, told him he could not live beyond a few weeks. 'Welcome, Sister Death!' he exclaimed, and asked to be taken to the Portiuncula. As they came on the way to a hill in sight of Assisi he asked for the stretcher to be put down, and turning his blind eyes towards the town called down the blessing of God upon it and upon his brethren. Then they carried him on to the Portiuncula. When he knew the end was close at hand, Francis asked that they would send to Rome for the Lady Giacoma di Settesoli, who had often befriended him, and ask her to come, bringing with her candles and a grey gown for his burial, and some of the cake that he liked so well. But the lady arrived before the messenger started.

He sent a last message to St Clare and her nuns, and bade his brethren sing the verse of the song he had made to the Sun which praises Death. Then he called for bread and broke it and to each one present gave a piece in token of mutual love and peace, saying, 'I have done my part; may Christ teach you to do yours'. He was laid on the ground and covered with an old habit, which the guardian lent him. He exhorted his brethren to the love of God, of poverty, and of the gospel 'before all other ordinances', and gave his blessing to all his disciples, the absent as well as those that were present. The passion of our Lord in the gospel of St John was read aloud, and in the evening of Saturday 3 October 1226, St Francis died.

He had asked to be buried in the criminals' cemetery on the Colle d'Inferno, but the next day his body was taken in solemn procession to the church of St George in Assisi. Here it remained until two years after his canonization when, in 1230, it was secretly removed to the great basilica built by Brother Elias.

FRANCIS OF PAOLA, (A.D. 1507)

FOUNDER OF THE MINIM FRIARS
PATRON SAINT OF SAILORS; OF NAVAL OFFICERS AND NAVIGATORS; OF ALL
PEOPLE ASSOCIATED WITH THE SEA

2 APRIL

Devotion to Francis of Paola is widespread in Italy, and particularly in southern Italy. He appears to have a special affinity for those associated with the sea, and this is usually traced to an event in 1464 when he had to cross the Straits of Messina to Sicily. He was refused use of a boat, so, laying his cloak on the sea, and tying one end to his staff to make a sail, he travelled across with his companions. Recalling the devotion to Francis of all Italians who lived by the sea, Pius XII declared him patron of naval officers and navigators in an Apostolic Letter of 27 March 1943.

St Francis was born about the year 1416 at Paola, a small town in Calabria. His parents were humble, industrious people who made it their chief aim to love and to serve God. As they were still childless after several years of married life, they prayed earnestly for a son, and when at last a boy was born to them, they named him after St Francis of Assisi, whose intercession they had specially sought. In his thirteenth year he was placed in the Franciscan friary at San Marco, where he learnt to read and where he laid the foundation of the austere life which he ever afterwards led.

After spending a year there he accompanied his parents on a pilgrimage which included Assisi and Rome. Upon his return to Paola, with their consent, he retired first to a place about half a mile from the town, and afterwards to a more remote seclusion by the sea, where he occupied a cave. He was scarcely fifteen years old. Before he was twenty, he was joined by two other men. The neighbours built them three cells and a chapel in which they sang the divine praises and in which Mass was offered for them by a priest from the nearest church.

This date, 1452, is reckoned as that of the foundation of his order. Nearly seventeen years later a church and a monastery were built for them in the same place, with the sanction of the archbishop of Cosenza. So greatly were they beloved by the people that the whole countryside joined in the work of construction. When the house was finished, the saint set himself to establish regular discipline in the community, whilst never mitigating anything of the austerity he practised. Though his bed was no longer a rock, it was a plank or the bare ground, with a log or a stone by way of a pillow. Only in extreme old age would he allow himself a mat. Penance, charity and humility formed the basis of his rule: charity was the motto he chose; but humility was the virtue which he inculcated continually on his followers. In addition to the three usual monastic obligations he imposed upon them a fourth, which bound them to observe a perpetual Lent, with abstinence not only from flesh but also from eggs and anything made with milk.

The new order received the sanction of the Holy See in 1474. At that time the community was composed of uneducated men, with only one priest. They were then called Hermits of St Francis of Assisi, and it was not until 1492 that their name was changed to that of 'Minims', at the desire of the founder, who wished his followers to be reckoned as the least (*minimi*) in the household of God.

In 1481 Louis XI, King of France, was slowly dying. Realizing that he was steadily growing worse, he sent into Calabria to beg St Francis to come and heal him, making many promises to assist him and his order. Then, as his request was not acceded to, he appealed to Pope Sixtus IV, who told Francis to go. He at once set out; and King Louis sent the dauphin to escort him to Plessi-les-Tours. Louis, falling on his knees, besought Francis to heal him. The saint replied that the lives of kings are in the hands of God and have their appointed limits; prayer should be addressed to Him. Many interviews followed between the sovereign and his guest. Although Francis was an unlearned man, Philip de Commines, who often heard him, wrote that his words were so full of wisdom that all present were convinced that the Holy Spirit spoke through his lips. By his prayers and example he wrought a change of heart in the king, who died in resignation in his arms. Charles VIII honoured Francis as his father had done, and would do nothing in the affairs of his conscience or even in state matters without his advice. He built for his friars a monastery in the park of Plessias and another at Amboise, at the spot where they had first met. Moreover, in Rome, he built for the Minims the monastery of Santa Trinità del Monte on the Pincian Hill, to which none but Frenchmen might be admitted.

St Francis passed twenty-five years in France, and died there. On Palm Sunday 1507 he fell ill, and on Maundy Thursday assembled his brethren and exhorted them to the love of God, to charity and to a strict observance of all the duties of their rule. Then he received viaticum barefoot with a rope round his neck, according to the custom of his order. He died on the following day, Good Friday, being then ninety-one years of age. His canonization took place in 1519.

FRANCIS XAVIER, (A.D. 1552)

PATRON SAINT OF MISSIONS; OF INDIA; OF PAKISTAN; OF OUTER MONGOLIA; OF SPANISH TOURISM; OF THE PELOTA PLAYERS OF ARGENTINA

3 DECEMBER

After the many and lengthy missionary journey which he undertook during his life, St Francis Xavier was a natural choice as patron saint of missions. He was declared such by Pope Pius X in an Apostolic Letter of 25 March 1904, and this was reaffirmed by Pius XI in an Apostolic Letter of 3 December 1922.

Because of the work he did on the Indian sub-continent, and the great devotion Indian Christians have shown to his memory, Francis Xavier has become a patron of India, formally recognized as such by a decree of the Sacred Congregation of Rites dated 27 June 1962; and of Pakistan, the decree for which is dated 10 January 1971. He had been recognized as patron of Outer Mongolia, however, much earlier – in a decree dated 28 September 1914.

Pope Pius XII proclaimed St Francis Xavier the patron of tourism in an Apostolic Letter dated 14 June 1952, citing as reasons for the choice of the Saint his travels to many parts of the world for the purpose of spreading religion.

In his Apostolic Letter of 14 February 1978 Paul VI wrote of the value of sport for physical and mental well-being, and he granted the request of Argentinian pelota players – and students of the sport – to have Francis Xavier as their patron. As the Pope remarked, pelota, a game played by throwing a ball by means of a wicker basket attached to the lower arm, is thought to be a Basque game in origin. Francis Xavier, himself a Basque, is reputed to have played it.

He was born in Spanish Navarre, at the castle of Xavier, near Pamplona, in 1506 (his mother-tongue was Basque), the youngest of a large family, and he went to the University of Paris in his eighteenth year. He entered the college of St Barbara and in 1528 gained the degree of licentiate. Here it was that he met Ignatius Loyola and, though he did not at once submit himself to his influence, he was one of the band of seven, the first Jesuits, who vowed themselves to the service of God at Montmartre in 1543. With them he received the priesthood at Venice three years later and in 1540 St Ignatius appointed him to join Father Simon Rodriguez on the first missionary expedition the Society sent out, to the East Indies.

They arrived at Lisbon about the end of June, and Francis went immediately to Father Rodriguez, who was lodged in a hospital in order to attend and instruct the sick. They made this place their ordinary dwelling, but catechized and instructed in the town, and were taken up all Sundays and holidays in hearing confessions at court, for the king, John III, had a high regard for these religious; so much so that eventually Rodriguez was retained by him at Lisbon. Before he at last sailed, on his thirty-fifth birthday, 7 April 1541, the king delivered to him briefs from the pope in which Francis Xavier was constituted apostolic nuncio in the East.

There were all sorts among the ship's company and passengers; Xavier had to compose quarrels, quell complaints, check swearing and gaming, and remedy other disorders. Scurvy broke out, and there was no one but the three Jesuits to nurse the sick. It took them five months to get round the Cape of Good Hope and arrive at Mozambique, where they wintered. They continued to hug the east coast of Africa and called at Malindia and Socotra, from whence it took them two months to reach Goa, where they arrived on 6 May 1542, after a voyage of thirteen months (twice the then usual time). St Francis took up his quarters at the hospital to await the arrival of his companions, who were following in another ship.

The scandalous behaviour of the Christians in Goa was like a challenge to Francis Xavier and he opened his mission with them, instructing them in the principles of religion and forming the young to the practice of virtue. Having spent the morning in assisting and comforting the distressed in the hospitals and prisons he walked through the streets ringing a bell to summon the children and slaves to catechism. He offered Mass with lepers every Sunday, preached in public and to the Indians, and visited private houses: the sweetness of his character and his charitable concern for his neighbours were irresistible to many. For the instruction of the very ignorant or simple he versified the truths of religion to fit popular tunes, and this was so successful that the practice spread till these songs were being sung every-where, in the streets and houses and fields and workshops.

After five months of this St Francis was told that on the Pearl Fishery coast, which extends from Cape Comorin to the isle of Manar, opposite Ceylon, there were people called Paravas, who to get the protection of the

Portuguese against the Arabs and others had been baptized, but for want of instruction still retained their superstitions and vices. Xavier went to the help of these people. Under every difficulty he set himself to learn the native language and to instruct and confirm those who had been already baptized, especially concentrating on teaching the rudiments of religion to the children. Then he preached to those Paravas to whom the name of Christ was till that time unknown. So great were the multitudes he baptized that sometimes by the bare fatigue of administering the sacrament he was scarcely able to move his arms, according to the account which he gave to his brethren in Europe. The Paravas were a low-caste people, and St Francis had a different reception and very little success among the Brahmans; at the end of twelve months he had converted only one. It seems certain that at this time God wrought a number of miracles of healing through him.

St Francis, as always, came before the people as one of themselves. His food was that of the poorest, rice and water; he slept on the ground in a hut. He was able to extend his activities to Travancore; here his achievements have been rather exaggerated by some writers, but village after village received him with joy, and after baptizing the inhabitants he wrote to Father Mansilhas telling him to come and organize the converts. His difficulties were increased by the misfortunes of the Christians of Comorin and Tuticorin, who were set upon by the Badagas from the north, who robbed, massacred and carried them into slavery. Xavier is said on one occasion to have held off the raiders by facing them alone, crucifix in hand. He was again handicapped by the Portuguese, their local commandant having his own secret dealings with the Badagas.

The ruler of Jaffna, in northern Ceylon, hearing of the progress of the faith in his island of Manar, slew six hundred Christians there. The governor, Martin de Sousa, ordered an expedition to punish this massacre and it was to fit out at Negapatam, whither St Francis went to join it; but the officers were diverted from their purpose and so Francis instead made a journey on foot to the shrine of St Thomas at Mylapore, where there was a small Portuguese settlement to be visited. Many incidents are related of him during these travels, especially of his conversion of notorious sinners among the Europeans by the gentle and courteous way in which he dealt with them; other miracles too were ascribed to him.

In the spring of 1545 St Francis set out for Malacca, on the Malay peninsula, where he spent four months. He was received with great reverence and cordiality, and his efforts at reform met with some success. For the next eighteen months his movements are difficult to follow, but they were a time of great activity and interest, for he was in a largely unknown world, visiting islands, which he refers to in general as the Moluccas, not all of which are now identifiable. He preached and ministered at Amboina, Ternate, Gilolo, and other places, in some of which there were Portuguese merchants and settlements. When he got back to Malacca he passed another four months there, ministering to a very unsatisfactory flock, and then departed for India again. But before he left he heard about Japan for the first time, from Portuguese merchants and from a fugitive Japanese named Anjiro. Xavier arrived back in India in January 1548.

The next fifteen months were spent in endless travelling between Goa, Ceylon and Cape Comorin, consolidating his work (notably the 'international college' of St Paul at Goa) and preparing for an attempt on that Japan into which no European had yet penetrated. In April 1549, St Francis set out, accompanied by a Jesuit priest and a lay-brother, by Anjiro – now Paul – and by two other Japanese converts. On the feast of the Assumption following they landed in Japan, at Kagoshima on Kyushu.

At Kagoshima they were not molested, and St Francis set himself to learn Japanese. A translation was made of a simple account of Christian teaching, and recited to all who would listen. The fruit of twelve months' labour was a hundred converts, and then the authorities began to get suspicious and forbade further preaching. So, leaving Paul in charge of the neophytes, Francis decided to push on further with his other companions and went by sea to Hirado, north of Nagasaki. Before leaving Kagoshima he visited the fortress of Ichiku, where the 'baron's' wife, her steward and others accepted Christianity. To the steward's care Xavier recommended the rest at departure; and twelve years later the Jesuit lay-brother and physician, Luis de Almeida, found these isolated converts still retaining their first fervour and faithfulness. At Hirado the missionaries were well received by the ruler (*daimyô*), and they had more success in a few weeks than they had had at Kagoshima in a year. These converts St Francis left to Father de Torres and went on with Brother Fernandez and a Japanese to Yamaguchi in Honshu. Francis preached here, in public and before the *daimyô*, but the missionaries made no impression and were treated with scorn.

Xavier's objective was Miyako (Kyoto), then the chief city of Japan, and having made a month's stay at Yamaguchi and gathered small fruit of his labours except affronts, he continued his journey with his two companions. It was towards the end of December, and they suffered much on the road from heavy rains, snow and the difficult country, and did not reach their destination till February. Here Francis found that he could not procure an audience of the mikado (who in any case was but a puppet) without paying a sum of money far beyond his resources; moreover, civil strife filled the city with such tumult that he saw it to be impossible to do any good there at that time and, after a fortnight's stay, they returned to Yamaguchi. Seeing that evangelical poverty did not have the appeal in Japan that it had in India, St Francis changed his methods. Decently dressed and with his companions as attendants he presented himself before the *daimyô* as the representative of Portugal, giving him the letters and presents (a musical-box, a clock and a pair of spectacles among them) which the authorities in India had provided for the mikado. The *daimyô* received the gifts with delight, gave Francis leave to teach, and provided an empty Buddhist monastery for a residence. When thus he obtained protection, Francis preached with such fruit that he baptized many in that city.

Hearing that a Portuguese ship had arrived at Funai (Oita) in Kyushu St Francis decided to make use of it to revisit his charge in India, from whence he now hoped to extend his mission to China. Francis found that good progress had been made in India, but there were also many difficulties and abuses, both among the missionaries and the Portuguese authorities, that urgently needed his attention. These matters he dealt with, lovingly and very firmly and thoroughly. At the end of four months, on 25 April 1552, with a Jesuit priest and a scholastic, an Indian servant and a young Chinese to interpret (but he had forgotten his own language), he sailed eastward again; he was awaited at Malacca by Diogo Pereira, whom the viceroy in India had appointed ambassador to the court of China.

At Malacca St Francis had to treat about this embassy with Don Alvaro da Ataide da Gama (a son of Vasco da Gama), the maritime authority there. This Alvaro had a personal grudge against Diogo Pereira, whom he flatly refused to let sail either as envoy or as private trader. At length Don Alvaro conceded that Xavier should go to China in Pereira's ship, but without its owner; and to this Pereira most nobly agreed. When the project of the embassy thus failed Francis sent his priest companion to Japan, and eventually was left with only the Chinese youth, Antony. With him he hoped to find means to land secretly in China, the country being closed to foreigners. In the last week of August 1552 the convoy reached the desolate island of Sancian (Shang-chwan), half-a-dozen miles off the coast and a hundred miles south-west of Hong Kong.

He had with great difficulty hired a Chinese merchant to land him by night in some part of Canton, for which Xavier had engaged to pay him, and bound himself by oath that nothing should ever bring him to confess the name of him who had set him on shore. Whilst waiting for his plans to mature, Xavier fell sick and, when the Portuguese vessels were all gone except one, was reduced to extreme want. The Chinese merchant did not turn up. A fever seized the saint on 21 November and he took shelter on the ship; but the motion of the sea was too much for him, so the day following he requested that he might be set on shore again, which was done. The vessel was manned chiefly by Don Alvaro's men who, fearing to offend their master by common kindness to Xavier, left him exposed on the sands to a piercing north wind, till a friendly Portuguese merchant led him into his hut, which afforded only a very poor shelter. He lay thus in a high fever, being bled with distressing results, praying ceaselessly between spasms of delirium. He got weaker and weaker till at last, in the early morning of 3 December which fell on a Saturday. 'I [Antony] could see that he was dying and put a lighted candle in his hand. Then, with the name of Jesus on his lips, he rendered his soul to his Creator and Lord with great repose and quietude'. St Francis was only forty-six years old, of which he had passed eleven in the East. His body was laid in the earth on the Sunday evening: four people were present, the Chinese Antony, a Portuguese and two slaves.

The coffin had been packed with lime around the body in case it should later be desired to move the remains. Ten weeks and more later the grave and coffin were opened. The lime being removed from the face, it was found quite incorrupt and fresh-coloured. The body was brought to Malacca, where it was received with great honour by all, except Don Alvaro. At the end of the year it was taken away to Goa, where its continued incorruption was verified by physicians; there it still lies enshrined in the church of the Good Jesus. St Francis Xavier was canonized in 1622, at the same time as Ignatius Loyola, Teresa of Avila, Philip Neri and Isidore the Husbandman.

GABRIEL THE ARCHANGEL

PATRON SAINT OF TELECOMMUNICATIONS, TELEVISION AND RADIO; OF THE
SIGNALS REGIMENTS OF ITALY, FRANCE AND COLOMBIA; OF THE DIPLOMATIC
SERVICES OF SPAIN AND ARGENTINA, AND SPECIFICALLY OF ARGENTINIAN
AMBASSADORS. PATRON ALSO OF THE POSTAL SERVICES, AND OF STAMP
COLLECTORS

29 SEPTEMBER

The association of the angel Gabriel with the bringing of messages is the reason why he is regarded as the patron of all those who work in any way with the telecommunications industry, especially telephonists, and radio and television workers. As Pius XII said in his Apostolic Letter of 12 January 1951, formally declaring Gabriel patron of telecommunications workers, they 'transmit words to people far away very quickly, allow people to speak to each other over long distances, send messages through the aethereal waves and bring before the eye images of things and events, making them present even though they occurred afar off'. Gabriel has also been formally declared the patron of the Signals regiment of Italy in an Apostolic Letter of Pius XII, dated 6 April 1956; of France in a decree of the Sacred Congregation of Rites dated 25 January 1952; and of Colombia by a decree of the Congregation for Divine Worship dated 31 January 1987. Because of his status as a messenger of God, Gabriel was also chosen to be patron of the diplomatic service of Spain in a decree of the Sacred Congregation of Rites of 25 March 1949, confirmed by an Apostolic Letter of Pius XII, dated 5 June of the same year, and of the diplomatic service of Argentina by a decree of the Sacred Congregation of Rites of 29 January 1962. Ten years later to the day John XXIII, in an Apostolic Letter, declared Gabriel to be the patron of Argentinian ambassadors. As postal services are similar, at least in purpose, to telecommunications, of which Gabriel was already the patron, said Paul VI in his Apostolic Letter of 9 December 1972, it is only appropriate that his patronage should be extended to the carrying of mail. By natural extension from this too, the Archangel is also the patron saint of stamp collectors and philatelists.

St Gabriel used to be honoured on 24 March and, as Alban Butler remarks, this was appropriate for 'God's ambassador' as this day immediately precedes the feast of the Annunciation of the Blessed Virgin. Now, however, all the archangels are honoured on the same day – 29 September.

According to Daniel (ix 21) it was Gabriel who announced to the prophet the time of the coming of the Messiah, that it was he again who appeared to Zachary 'standing on the right side of the altar of incense' (Luke i 10 and 19) to make known the future birth of the Precursor, and finally that it was he who as God's ambassador was sent to Mary at Nazareth (Luke i 26) to proclaim the mystery of the Incarnation.

There is abundant archaeological evidence that the *cultus* of St Gabriel is in no sense a novelty. An ancient chapel close beside the Appian Way, rescued from oblivion by Armellini, preserves the remains of the fresco in which the prominence given to the figure of the archangel, his name being written underneath, strongly suggests that he was at one time honoured in that chapel as principal patron. There are also many representations of Gabriel in the early Christian art both of east and West which make it plain that his connection with the sublime mystery of the Incarnation was remembered by the faithful in ages long anterior to the devotional revival of the thirteenth century.

GABRIEL POSSENTI (A.D. 1862)

PATRON SAINT OF STUDENTS, ESPECIALLY THOSE IN COLLEGES AND SEMINARIES; OF THE CLERGY; OF YOUNG PEOPLE INVOLVED IN CATHOLIC ACTION IN ITALY

A decree of the Sacred Congregation of Rites dated 13 April 1932 approving the liturgical celebrations for the saint, did so, it remarked, so that Gabriel might more clearly be held up as a patron of those in colleges and seminaries. That he was an appropriate model or patron follows naturally from his life, with his determination to enter a religious order, and his early death with a reputation for sanctity. For similar reasons he has been regarded as a patron for the clergy. Even earlier Cardinal Tardini, who was Cardinal Secretary of State and had a personal devotion to Gabriel, persuaded Pius XI to declare him patron of young people involved in Catholic Action in Italy.

This young saint was the son of a distinguished advocate who held a succession of official appointments under the government of the States of the Church. There were thirteen children in the family of Sante Possenti, of whom the future saint, born in 1838 and christened Francis, was the eleventh. Several died in infancy and their mother died in 1842, when Francis was only four years old. Signor Possenti had just then become 'grand assessor' (or registrar) of Spoleto, and in the Jesuit college there Francis received most of his education.

As a youth he read novels, he was fond of gaiety and of the theatre, though seemingly the plays he frequented were innocent enough, and on account of his cheerfulness and good looks he was a universal favourite. There must have been a certain relative frivolity in these years, and his friends, we are told, used in playful exaggeration to call him *il damerino*, 'the ladies' man'. As a consequence the call of God does not seem to have been at once attended to even when it was clearly heard. Before his very promising career as a student was completed he fell dangerously ill, and he promised if he recovered to enter religion; but when he was restored to health he took no immediate step to carry his purpose into effect. After the lapse of a year or two he was again brought to death's door by an attack of laryngitis, or possibly quinsy, and he renewed his promise, having recourse in this extremity to a relic of the Jesuit martyr St Andrew Bobola, just then beatified.

Once more he was cured, miraculously as he believed, and he made application to enter the Society of Jesus. But though he was accepted, he still delayed – after all, he was not yet even seventeen – possibly because he doubted whether God was not calling him to a more penitential life than that of the Society. Then his favourite sister died during an outbreak of cholera, and so, stricken with a sense of the precarious nature of all earthly ties, he at last, with the full approval of his Jesuit confessor, made choice of the Passionists. Thus in September 1856 he entered their noviceship at Morrovalle, where he was given the name in religion of Brother Gabriel-of-our-Lady-of-Sorrows.

After only four years spent in religion, in the course of which Brother Gabriel had given rise to the expectation of great and fruitful work for souls once the priesthood had been attained, symptoms of tuberculous disease manifested themselves so unmistakably that from henceforth he had to be exempted, very much against his will, from all the more arduous duties of community observance. Everyone was indescribably impressed by the example which he gave, but he himself shrank from any sort of favourable notice, and not long before his death, he succeeded in securing the destruction of all his private notes of the spiritual favours which God had bestowed upon him. He passed away in great peace in the early morning of 27 February 1862, at Isola di Gran Sasso in the Abruzzi. St Gabriel-of-our-Lady-of-Sorrows was canonized in 1920.

GALL (A.D. 635)

PATRON SAINT OF BIRDS

16 OCTOBER

It is not clear why Gall is taken to be the patron of birds. One possible reason is that it arises from a mistaken understanding of his name – 'Gallo' meaning 'cock' in Italian. Another possible origin is the legend of his exorcising a girl of an evil spirit after two bishops had failed in an attempt. When the saint succeeded, the demon left through the mouth of the girl in the form of a blackbird.

Among the eminent disciples which St Columban left to be imitators of his heroic life, none seems to have been more famous than this St Gall. He was born in Ireland and educated in the great monastery of Bangor under the direction of the holy abbot Comgall and of Columban. Studies, especially of sacred learning, flourished in his house, and St Gall was well versed in grammar, poetry and the Holy Scriptures, and was ordained priest there, according to some accounts. When St Columban left Ireland St Gall was one of those twelve who accompanied him into France, where they founded the monastery of Annegray and two years afterwards that of Luxeuil. St Gall lived here for twenty years, but the only incident recorded of that period is that, being sent to fish in one river, he went to another. On his return with an empty basket he was reproved for his disobedience, whereupon he went to the right river and made a big catch. When Columba was driven thence in 610 St Gall shared his exile and, after they had in vain tried to return to Ireland, they eventually found themselves in Austrasia, and preached around Tuggen, on Lake Zurich. The people did not receive their new teachers gladly, and they soon left 'that stiff-necked and thankless crowd', lest in trying to fertilize their sterile hearts they should waste efforts that might be beneficial to well-disposed minds', as St Gall's biographer says. Then one Willimar, priest of Arbon near the lake of Constance, afforded them a retreat. The servants of God built themselves cells near Bregenz, converted many idolaters, and at the end of one of his sermons Gall broke their brazen statues and threw them into the lake. The bold action made as many enemies as it did converts, but they stayed there for two years, made a garden and planted fruit, and St Gall, who was evidently a keen fisherman, occupied his spare time in knotting nets and fishing the lake. But the people who remained obstinate persecuted the monks and slew two of them; and on his opponent King Theoderic becoming master of Austrasia St Columban decided to retire into Italy, about 612. St Gall was unwilling to be separated from him, but was prevented from bearing him company by sickness. St Columban, however, says one legend, thought Gall was malingering, wherefore he imposed on him never again to celebrate Mass during his (Columban's) lifetime. This unjust sentence St Gall obeyed. After his master and brethren had departed, Gall packed up his nets and went off by boat to stay with Willimar at Arbon, where he soon recovered his health. Then, directed by the deacon Hiltibod, he selected a suitable spot by the river Steinach (that it had a good fishing-pool is expressly mentioned; also that they had trouble with water-sprites therein), and settled down there to be a hermit. He soon had disciples, who lived under his direction according to the Rule of St Columban, and the fame of Gall's holiness continued to grow year by year until his death, between 627 and 645, at Arbon, whither he had gone to preach.

GENESIUS THE COMEDIAN, MARTYR (DATE UNKNOWN)

PATRON SAINT OF ACTORS, AND OF THE THEATRICAL PROFESSION

25 AUGUST

The choice of Genesius as patron of actors, common from the Middle Ages, is an obvious one. He has also been invoked by a range of people associated in various ways with the theatrical profession. The story of St Genesius comes into the category of imaginative romances; it is even possible that Genesius never existed at all, but is a western version of St Gelasius of Heliopolis, of whom (and of others) a similar tale is told. The legend of Genesius is narrated by Alban Butler as follows.

The Emperor Diocletian coming to Rome, he was received with great rejoicings. Among other entertainments prepared for him, those of the stage were not neglected. In a comedy which was acted in his presence one of the players took it into his head to burlesque the ceremonies of Christian baptism, which could not fail to amuse the people, who held our religion and its mysteries in contempt and derision. This player therefore, whose name was Genesius and who had learned some things concerning Christian rites from friends who professed that religion, laid himself down on the stage, pretending to be ill, and said, 'Ah! my friends, there is a great weight upon me, and I would gladly be eased'. The others answered, 'what shall we do to give you ease? Would you like us to plane you and reduce the weight that way?' 'Idiots!' he exclaimed, 'I am resolved to die a Christian, that God may receive me on this day of my death as one who seeks His salvation by turning from idolatry and superstition.' Then a priest and exorcist were called, that is to say, two players who impersonated these characters. These, sitting down by his bedside, asked, 'Well, my child, why did you send for us?' But here Genesius was suddenly converted by a divine inspiration and replied, not in mockery but seriously, 'Because I desire to receive the grace of Jesus Christ and to be born again, that I may be delivered from my sins'.

The other players then went through the whole ceremony of baptism with him; but he in earnest answered the usual interrogatories, and on being baptized was clothed with a white garment. After this, other players, dressed like soldiers, to carry on the jest, seized him and presented him to the emperor, to be examined as the martyrs were wont to be. Genesius then declared himself openly and seriously, standing upon the stage, 'Hear! O emperor, and all you that are present, officers, philosophers, senators and people, hear what I am going to say. I never yet so much as heard the word Christian but I reviled it, and I detested my very relations because they professed that religion. I learned its rites and mysteries only that I might the better ridicule it, and inspire you with the utmost contempt for it; but when I was to be washed with the water and examined, I had no sooner answered sincerely that I believed, than I saw a company of angels over my head, who recited out of a book all the sins I had committed from my childhood; and having plunged the book into the water which had been poured upon me in your presence, they showed me the book whiter than snow. Wherefore I advise you, O great and mighty emperor, and all people here present who have mocked these mysteries, to believe with me that Jesus Christ is the true Lord; that He is the light and the truth; and that it is through Him you may obtain the forgiveness of your sins.'

Diocletian, enraged at these words, ordered him to be beaten, and afterward to be put into the hands of Plautian, the prefect of the praetorium, that he might compel him to sacrifice. Plautian put him upon the rack, where he was torn with iron hooks and then burnt with torches; but the martyr persisted in crying out, 'There is no other Lord beside Him whom I have seen. Him I worship and serve, and to Him I will cling, though I should suffer a thousand deaths. No torments shall remove Jesus Christ from my heart and my mouth. Bitterly do I regret that I once detested His holy name, and came so late to His service.' At length his head was struck off.

GENEVIEVE, OR GENOVEFA, VIRGIN (*c.* A.D. 500)

A PATRON SAINT OF PARIS; OF DISASTERS; OF DROUGHT, AND EXCESSIVE RAIN; OF FEVER; AND OF THE FRENCH SECURITY FORCES

3 JANUARY

The cult of St Genevieve as the patron of Paris is traditional and, in the light of her work for the city during the blockade by Childeric and when threatened by Attila, needs no explanation. So great was the devotion to her, however, that the people of Paris invoked her aid in a great number of different situations: in time of plague (her shrine was carried into the cathedral in 1129 during an outbreak of what appears to have been food poisoning), of drought, of excessive rain or of illness and fever; of disaster.

The saint's work for the safety of the city of Paris make her also the appropriate patron of the French security forces. This title was confirmed by Pope John XXIII in an Apostolic Letter dated 18 May 1962, at the request of Cardinal Feltin, the Archbishop of Paris and Bishop in charge of the French forces.

Genevieve's father's name was Severus, and her mother's Gerontia; she was born about the year 422 at Nanterre, a small village four miles from Paris, near Mont Valérien. When St Germanus, Bishop of Auxerre, went with St Lupus into Britain to oppose the Pelagian heresy, he spent a night at Nanterre on his way. The inhabitants flocked about them to receive their blessing, and St Germanus gave an address, during which he took particular notice of Genevieve, though she was only seven years of age. After his sermon he inquired for her parents, and foretold their daughter's future sanctity. He then asked Genevieve whether it was not her desire to serve God only and to be naught else but a spouse of Jesus Christ. She answered that this was what she desired, and begged that by this blessing she might be from that moment consecrated to God. The holy prelate went to the church, followed by the people, and during the long singing of psalms and prayers, says Constantius, 'he laid his hand upon the maiden's head'.

When she was about fifteen years of age, Genevieve was presented to the bishop of Paris to receive the religious veil, together with two other girls. From that time she frequently ate only twice in the week, on Sundays and Thursdays, and her food was barley bread with a few beans. After the death of her parents she left Nanterre, and settled with her godmother in Paris, but sometimes undertook journeys for motives of charity.

The Franks had at this time gained possession of the better part of Gaul, and Childeric, their king, took Paris. During the long blockade of that city, the citizens being reduced to extremities by famine, St Genevieve, as the author of her life relates, went out at the head of a company who were sent to procure provisions, and brought back from Arcis-sur-Aúbe and Troyes several boats laden with corn. Childeric, when he had made himself master of Paris, though always a pagan, respected St Genevieve, and upon her intercession spared the lives of many prisoners and did other generous acts. She also awakened the zeal of many persons to build a church in honour of St Denis of Paris, which King Dagobert I afterwards rebuilt with a monastery in 629. St Genevieve likewise undertook many pilgrimages, in company with other maidens, to the shrine of St Martin at Tours, and the reputation of her holiness is said to have been so great that her fame even reached St Simeon Stylites in Syria.

King Clovis, who embraced the faith in 496, often listened with deference to St Genevieve, and more than once granted liberty to captives at her request. Upon the report of the march of Attila with his army of Huns the Parisians were preparing to abandon their city, but St Genevieve encouraged them to avert the scourge by fasting and prayer. Many of her own sex passed whole days with her in prayer in the baptistery; from whence the particular devotion to St Genevieve, formerly practised at S.-Jean-le-Rond, the ancient public baptistery of the church of Paris, seems to have taken rise. She assured the people of the protection of Heaven, and though she was treated by many as an impostor, the event verified the prediction, for the barbarous invader suddenly changed the course of his march. Attributed to St Genevieve was the first suggestion of the church which Clovis began to build in honour of SS. Peter and Paul, in deference to the wishes to his wife, St Clotilda, in which church the body of St Genevieve herself was enshrined after her death about the year 500.

GENGULF, OR GENGOUL (A.D. 760)

PATRON SAINT OF UNHAPPY MARRIAGES

11 MAY

The life of St Gengulf and, if tradition is to be believed, the manner of his death, are enough to account for the long-standing devotion to him as patron of unhappy marriages.

St Gengulf was a Burgundian knight, so greatly beloved by Pepin the Short, at that time mayor of the palace, that he used to sleep in the great man's tent during his campaigns. Gengulf is said to have been married to a woman of rank in whom for a long time he trusted, but she proved scandalously unfaithful to him. Finding remonstrances and appeals useless, he quietly withdrew from her to a castle of his at Avallon (the birthplace of St Hugh of Lincoln, between Auxerre and Autun), after making suitable provision for her maintenance. There he spent his time in penitential exercises and his money in alms. He died – so the legend avers – from a wound inflicted by his wife's lover who, at her instigation, broke in upon him one night to murder him as he lay in bed. The fame of St Gengulf afterwards spread to Holland, Belgium and Savoy as the result of the distribution of his relics and the miracles with which he was credited.

GENTIAN, MARTYR (DATE UNKNOWN)

PATRON SAINT OF INNKEEPERS AND HOTELIERS

11 DECEMBER

From medieval times Gentian has been the patron of innkeepers, and hence hoteliers, on the basis of the legend recounted below. His feast is celebrated with that of his 'guests', Fuscian and Victoricus.

Legend tells us that Fuscian and Victoricus, Roman missionaries, came into Gaul at the same time as St Quintinus, and set themselves the task of evangelizing the Morini. Victoricus established his headquarters at Boulogne and Fuscian at Théorouanne, or rather nearby at the village of Helfaut, where he built a small church. Both of them met with opposition from the pagan Gauls and Romans, but made a number of conversions. After a time they went together to visit St Quintinus, but when they reached Amiens they found persecution raging against Christians; they therefore passed on to Sains, and there lodged with an old man named Gentian. He was a heathen, but well disposed towards Christianity, and in talking to him of the faith the two missionaries learned of the martyrdom of St Quintinus six weeks before. When he heard that two Christian priests were at Sains, the governor Rictiovarus arrived there with a troop of soldiers. He was met by Gentian with a drawn sword, threatening him because he was a persecutor and declaring that he was ready to die for the true God. Rictiovarus accordingly had him beheaded on the spot. Fuscian and Victoricus were then taken in chains to Amiens and, as they would not renounce their faith after divers tortures, they were beheaded at Saint-Fuscien-aux-Bois.

194

GEORGE, MARTYR (A.D. 303?)

PATRON SAINT OF ENGLAND; OF THE ORDER OF THE GARTER; OF ITALIAN
CAVALRY; OF ISTANBUL (CONSTANTINOPLE)

23 APRIL

*The account of how St George came to be the Patron Saint of England is given below,
quoted from* Butler's Lives of the Saints, *which also mentions his patronship of the
Order of the Garter.*

*Although modern cavalry employs armoured cars rather than horses, Pope Pius XI
remarked when proclaiming St George patron saint of Italian cavalry, the cavalry had
retained a devotion to the holy knight, and had asked, in 1937, that he be declared
their patron. This was conceded by a decree of the Sacred Congregation of Rites on 11
August 1937. Pius XII confirmed this on the saint's own feast day, 23 April, in 1956.
St George was made a patron of Istanbul by a decree of the Sacred Congregation of
Rites on 7 January 1914 along with St John Chrysostom and St Roch.*

We are told that St George was a Christian knight and that he was born in
Cappadocia. It chanced, however, that he was riding one day in the
province of Lybia, and there he came upon a city called Sylene, near which
was a marshy swamp. In this lived a dragon. The people had mustered
together to attack and kill it, but its breath was so terrible that all had fled. To
prevent its coming nearer they supplied it every day with two sheep, but
when the sheep grew scarce, a human victim had to be substituted. This
victim was selected by lot, and the lot just then had fallen on the king's own
daughter. No one was willing to take her place, and the maiden had gone
forth dressed as a bride to meet her doom. Then St George, coming upon the
scene, attacked the dragon and transfixed it with his lance. Further; he
borrowed the maiden's girdle, fastened it round the dragon's neck, and with
this aid she led the monster captive into the city. The people in mortal terror
were about to take to flight, but St George told them to have no fear. If only
they would believe in Jesus Christ and be baptized, he would slay the
dragon. The king and all his subjects gladly assented. The dragon was killed
and four ox-carts were needed to carry the carcass to a safe distance. The
story of the dragon, however, though given so much prominence, was a
later accretion, of which we have no sure traces before the twelfth century.

There is every reason to believe that St George was a real martyr who
suffered at Diospolis (*i.e.* Lydda) in Palestine, probably before the time of
Constantine. Beyond this there seems to be nothing which can be affirmed
with any confidence. The cult is certainly early.

It is not quite clear how St George came to be specially chosen as the patron
saint of England. His fame had certainly travelled to the British Isles long
before the Norman Conquest. The *Félire* of Oengus, under 23 April, speaks

of 'George, a sun of victories with thirty great thousands', while Abbot Aelfric tells the whole extravagant story in the metrical homily. William of Malmesbury states that Saints George and Demetrius, 'the martyr knights', were seen assisting the Franks at the battle of Antioch in 1098, and it seems likely that the crusaders, notably King Richard I, came back from the east with a great idea of the power of St George's intercession. At the national synod of Oxford in 1222 St George's day was included among the lesser holidays, and in 1415 the constitution of Archbishop Chichele made it one of the chief feasts of the year. In the interval King Edward III had founded the Order of the Garter, of which St George has always been the patron. During the seventeenth and eighteenth centuries (till 1778) his feast was a holiday of obligation for English Catholics, and Pope Benedict XIV recognized him as the Protector of the Kingdom.

GERARD MAJELLA (A.D. 1755)

PATRON SAINT OF MOTHERS

16 OCTOBER

This would appear to be an example of a popular modern devotion. It springs from no obvious story in the saints' life, although several aspects of it – in particular, perhaps, the way in which he supported his widowed mother – might be cited as partial explanations.

He was born in Muro, fifty miles south of Naples, the son of a tailor. His mother testified after his death: 'My child's only happiness was in church, on his knees before the Blessed Sacrament. He would stop there till he forgot it was dinner-time. In the house he prayed all day. He was born for Heaven.' At the age of ten he was allowed to receive holy communion every other day, which at a time when the influence of Jansenism was yet not purged away argues that his confessor was sensible of what manner of child Gerard was. When his father died he was taken away from school and apprenticed to a tailor, Martin Pannuto, a worthy man who understood and respected his apprentice. Not so his journeyman, a rough fellow who ill-treated young Gerard and was only exasperated by the boy's patience. When he had learned his trade, which he did very efficiently, he offered himself to the local Capuchins, of whom his uncle was a member, but they refused him as too young and delicate. He then became a servant in the household of the Bishop of Lacedogna. Humanly speaking this was an unfortunate experience, for this prelate was a man of ungovernable temper who treated Gerard with a great lack of consideration and kindness. Nevertheless he served him faithfully and uncomplainingly till the bishop died in 1745, when he returned home to Muro and set up as a tailor on his own. He lived with his mother and three sisters, and one-third of his earnings he handed over to her, another third was given in alms to the poor, and the rest in stipends for Masses for the souls in Purgatory. He had already begun to discipline himself with severity and several hours of the night were passed in prayer in the cathedral.

When Gerard was twenty-three a mission was given in Muro by some fathers of the newly founded Congregation of the Most Holy Redeemer. He offered himself to them as a lay-brother, but again his delicate appearance was against him and his mother and sisters were not at all anxious to let him go. But he persisted, and at length Father Cafaro sent him to the house of which he was rector at Deliceto, with the written message: 'I send you a useless brother'. When Father Cafaro returned thither he found he had been mistaken in his judgement, and at once admitted Gerard to the habit. Working first in the garden and then in the sacristy he was so industrious, punctual and self-effacing that it was said of him, 'Either he is a fool or a great saint'. St Alphonsus Liguori, founder of the Redemptorists, knew which he was and deliberately shortened his novitiate for him. Brother Gerard was professed in 1752, adding to the usual vows one always to do that which should seem the more pleasing to God. Father Tannoia, who wrote the lives both of St Gerard and of St Alphonsus and who was healed by Gerard's intercession after his death, tells us that when Gerard was a novice he one day saw him praying before the tabernacle. Suddenly he cried aloud, 'Lord, let me go, I pray thee! I have work that I *must* do'.

During his three years as a professed lay-brother Gerard was engaged as the community tailor and infirmarian, in begging for the house, and in accompanying the fathers on their missions and retreats because of his gift of reading souls. There are over twenty examples of his having brought secret sinners to repentance by revealing their own wickedness to themselves. This was the period, too, of the principal supernatural phenomena: ecstatic flight (he is said to have been carried through the air a distance of half a mile), 'bilocation', and power over inanimate nature and the lower animals are recorded of him, as well as prophecy and infused knowledge. In his ecstasies an appeal to his obedience was the only force that could recall him to his surroundings before the appointed time. At Naples he knew of the murder of the Archpriest of Muro at the time it happened fifty miles away, and on several occasions he was apprised of and correctly acted on the mental wishes of persons at a distance. He read the bad conscience of the secretary of the Archbishop of Conza with such accuracy that the man completely changed his life and was reconciled to his wife, so that all Rome was talking of it. But it is for the phenomenon called bilocation that St Gerard is most famous in this connection. He was alleged to have been with a sick man in a cottage at Caposele at the same time as he talked with a friend in the monastery at the same place. Father Tannoia states, among other examples, that he was seen at Muro on a day when he certainly did not leave Caposele.

Once the rector looked for him in his cell and he was apparently not there, so when he saw him in the church he asked where he had been. 'In my cell,' was the reply. 'What do you mean?' asked the rector, 'I have been there twice to look for you.' Pressed, Gerard explained that as he was in retreat he had asked God to make him invisible, lest he be disturbed. 'I forgive you this time,' said the rector. 'But don't make such prayers again.'

It is not, however, for these marvels that St Gerard Majella is canonized and revered; they were simply an effect of his surpassing holiness which God in His wisdom could have withheld, without abating thereby one jot of that goodness, charity and devotion which made him that model which Pius and Leo declared him to be. One of the most surprising results of his reputation was that he was allowed to be, in effect, the spiritual director of several communities of nuns – an activity not usually associated with lay-brothers. He interviewed individuals and gave community conferences at the *grille*, and wrote letters of advice to superiors, religious and priests. Some of these are extant. There is nothing remarkable in them: plain, straightforward statements of a Christian's duty in whatever state it has pleased God to call him; urging gentleness to a prioress, vigilance to a novice, tranquillity to a parish priest, conformity with the divine will to all. In 1753 the young divines at Deliceto went on an expedition to the shrine of St Michael at Monte Gargano. They had the equivalent of twelve shillings all told to cover their expenses, but they also had St Gerard with them, and he saw to it that they wanted nothing the whole time; their nine days' holiday was a succession of marvels. But just a year later he was brought under suspicion, and underwent a terrible trial. A young woman whom he had befriended, Neria Caggiano, who was of wanton conduct, accused Gerard of lechery and he was sent for by St Alphonsus at Nocera. Believing it to be in accordance with his vow to do the more perfect thing, he did not deny the charge, and thereby placed his superior in a quandary, for it was difficult to believe that Gerard was really guilty. So he was forbidden to receive holy communion or to have any dealings with the outside world. 'There is a God in Heaven. He will provide,' said Gerard. For some weeks suspicion rested on him, and then Neria and her accomplice voluntarily confessed that they had lied and trumped-up the charge. St Alphonsus asked St Gerard why he had not protested his innocence. 'Father,' he replied, 'Does not our rule forbid us to excuse ourselves?' A provision which, of course, was never intended to apply to circumstances such as these. Soon after this St Gerard was sent with Father Margotta to Naples, where his reputation and miracles caused the Redemptorist house to be beset day and night by people who wanted to see him; so at the end of four months he was removed to the house at Caposele and made porter there.

This was a job after his own heart, and 'our house at this time', wrote Father Tannoia, 'was besieged with beggars. Brother Gerard had the same concern for their good that a mother has for her children. He had the knack of always sending them away satisfied, and neither their unreasonableness nor cunning dodges ever made him lose patience'. During the hard winter of that year two hundred men, women and children came daily to the door and received food, clothes and firing; nobody but the porter knew where it all came from. In the spring he went again to Naples where, and at Calitri, Father Margotta's home, several miracles of healing were attributed to him. On returning to Caposele he was put in charge of the new buildings, and one Friday when there was not a penny in the house wherewith to pay the workmen his prayers brought an unexpected sum of money, sufficient for their immediate needs. He spent the summer searching for funds for these buildings, but the effort in the south Italian heat was too much for him, and in July and August his consumption made rapid advance. He was a week in bed at Oliveto, where he cured (or as he put it, 'gave effect to obedience') a lay-brother who had been sent to look after him and was himself taken ill, and then dragged himself back to Caposele. He was able to get up from bed again only for a few days in September, and his last weeks were a compound of physical suffering and spiritual ecstasy, in which his gifts of infused knowledge and prevision seemed more powerful than ever before. He died on the day and at the hour he had foretold, just before the midnight of 15–16 October in the year 1755. St Gerard Majella was canonized in 1904.

GILES (*c.* A.D. 710)

PATRON SAINT OF CRIPPLES AND OF THE LAME; OF BEGGARS; OF LEPERS; OF NURSING MOTHERS AND BREAST-FEEDING

1 SEPTEMBER

According to the legend recounted below, the arrow which wounded Giles crippled him for life – hence he became the patron saint of the lame and crippled. Because of the close association in medieval times between being crippled and begging for a living, Giles became the patron of beggars as well and, by extension, of lepers also.

In medieval times Giles was invoked by nursing mothers possibly, it has been suggested, because of the story of the saint giving refuge to a hind.

The legend of St Giles (Aegidius), one of the most famous of the Middle Ages, is derived from a biography written in the tenth century. According to this he was an Athenian by birth, and during his youth cured a sick beggar by giving him his own cloak, after the manner of St Martin. Giles dreaded temporal prosperity and the applause of men which, after the death of his parents, was showered on him because of the liberality of his alms and his miracles. He therefore took ship for the west, landed at Marseilles, and, after passing two years with St Caesarius at Arles, eventually made his hermitage in a wood near the mouth of the Rhône. In this solitude he was for some time nourished with the milk of a hind, which was eventually pursued by a certain king of the Goths, Flavius, who was hunting in the forest. The beast took refuge with St Giles in his cave, and the hounds gave up their chase; on the following day the hind was found again and the same thing happened; and again on the third day, when the king had brought with him a bishop to watch the peculiar behaviour of his hounds. This time one of the huntsmen shot an arrow at a venture into the bushes which screened the cave, and when they had forced their way through they found Giles, wounded by the arrow, sitting with the hind between his knees. Flavius and the bishop approached and asked the hermit to give an account of himself, and when they heard his story they begged his pardon and promised to send physicians to attend him. Giles begged them to leave him alone and refused all the gifts they pressed upon him.

King Flavius continued frequently to visit St Giles, who eventually asked him to devote his proffered alms to founding a monastery; this the king agreed to do provided Giles would become its first abbot. In due course the monastery was built near the cave, a community gathered round, and the reputation of the monks and of their abbot reached the ears of Charles, King of France (whom medieval romancers identified as Charlemagne). Giles was sent for to the court at Orleans, where the king consulted him on spiritual matters but was ashamed to name a grievous sin that was on his conscience. 'On the following Sunday, when the holy man was celebrating Mass according to custom and praying to God for the king during the canon, an angel of the Lord appeared to him and laid on the altar a scroll on which was written the sin which the king had committed, and which further said that he would be forgiven at Gile's intercession, provided he did penance and desisted from that sin in the future. . . . When Mass was ended Giles gave the scroll to the king to read, who fell at the saint's feet, begging him to intercede with the Lord for him. And so the man of the Lord commended him to God in prayer and gently admonished him to refrain from that sin in the future.' St Giles then returned to his monastery and afterwards went to Rome to commend his monks to the Holy See. The pope granted them many privileges and made a present of two carved doors of cedar-wood; to emphasize his trust in divine providence St Giles threw these doors into the Tiber, and they safely preceded him to France. After being warned of his approaching end in a dream, he died on a Sunday, 1 September, 'leaving the world sadder for his bodily absence but giving joy in Heaven by his happy arrival.'

GREGORY THE GREAT, POPE, DOCTOR OF THE CHURCH (A.D. 604)

A PATRON SAINT OF MUSIC; AND OF PROTECTION AGAINST PLAGUE

3 SEPTEMBER

The connection of Pope St Gregory with music is enshrined in the name 'Gregorian Chant', but he can have had little if any influence upon that type of singing. His association with Church music is difficult to establish. John the Deacon, in his life of the saint, attributes to him the founding of the 'Schola Cantorum' in Rome, but in this John, who was writing in the latter part of the ninth century, was certainly wrong. Nonetheless the tradition remained, and St Gregory was regarded as the patron of music during the Middle Ages until the sixteenth century when the Roman Academy of Music was put under the protection of St Cecilia.

As the life of the saint recounts, he was elected Bishop of Rome in the middle of a plague – from which his predecessor died – and was credited with bringing an end to the epidemic by ordering a procession through the streets of the city in penance.

Pope Gregory I, most justly called 'the Great', and the first pope who had been a monk, was elected to the apostolic chair when Italy was in a terrible condition after the struggle between the Ostrogoths and the Emperor Justinian, which ended with the defeat and death of Totila in 562. The state of Rome itself was deplorable: it had been sacked four times within a century and a half, and conquered four times in twenty years, but no one restored the damage done by pillage, fire and earthquake.

The saint's family, one of the few patrician families left in the city, was distinguished also for its piety, having given to the Church two popes, Agapitus I and Felix III, Gregory's great-great-grandfather. Little is known of Gordian, Gregory's father, except that he was a *regionarius* – whatever that might be – and that he owned large estates in Sicily as well as a house on the Coelian Hill; his wife Silvia is named as a saint in the Roman Martyrology. Gregory appears to have received the best education obtainable at that time in Rome, and to have taken up the career of a public official. At the age of about thirty we find him exercising the highest civil office in Rome – that of prefect of the city. Faithfully and honourably though Gregory fulfilled his duties, at length he resolved to retire from the world and to devote himself to the service of God alone. He was one of the richest men in Rome, but he gave up all, retiring into his own house on the Clivus Scauri, which he turned into a monastery and which he placed under the patronage of St Andrew and in the charge of a monk called Valentius.

It was not likely that a man of St Gregory's talents and prestige would be left long in obscurity at such a time, and we find him ordained seventh deacon of the Roman church, and then sent as papal *apocrisiarius* or ambassador at the Byzantine court. He had the great disadvantage of knowing no Greek, and more and more he lived a monastic life with several of the monks

201

of St Andrew's who had accompanied him. Most of the dates in St Gregory's life are uncertain but it was probably about the beginning of the year 586 that he was recalled to Rome by Pelagius II. He immediately settled down again, deacon of Rome though he was, in his monastery of St Andrew, of which he soon became abbot; and it seems that it is to this period we must refer the celebrated story told by the Venerable Bede on the strength of an old English tradition.

St Gregory, it appears, was one day walking through the market when he noticed three golden-haired, fair-complexioned boys exposed for sale and inquired their nationality. 'They are Angles or Angli', was the reply. 'They are well named,' said the saint, 'for they have angelic faces and it becomes such to be companions with the angels in heaven.' Learning that they were pagans, he asked what province they came from. 'Deira.' 'De ira!' exclaimed St Gregory. 'Yes, verily they shall be saved from God's ire and called to the mercy of Christ. What is the name of the king of that country?' 'Aella.' 'Then must Alleluia be sung in Aella's land.' So greatly was he impressed by their beauty and by pity for their ignorance of Christ that he resolved to preach the gospel himself in Britain, and started off with several of his monks. However, when the people of Rome heard of their departure they raised such an outcry that Pope Pelagius sent envoys to recall them to Rome.

A terrible inundation of the Tiber was followed by another and an exceptionally severe outbreak of the plague: Rome was again decimated, and in January 590 Pelagius died of the dread disease. The people unanimously chose Gregory as the new pope, and to obtain by penitence the cessation of the plague he ordered a great processional litany through the streets of Rome. From seven churches in the city proceeded seven columns of people, who met at St Mary Major.

A correspondence with John, Archbishop of Ravenna, who had modestly censured him for trying to avoid office, led to Gregory's writing the *Regula Pastoralis*, a book on the office of a bishop. In it he regards the bishop as first and foremost a physician of souls whose chief duties are preaching and the enforcement of discipline. The work met with immediate success, and the Emperor Maurice had it translated into Greek by Anastasius, Patriarch of Antioch. Later St Augustine took it to England, where 300 years later it was translated by King Alfred, and at the councils summoned by Charlemagne the study of the book was enjoined on bishops, who were to have a copy delivered to them at their consecration.

In his instructions to his vicar in Sicily and to the overseers of his patrimony generally, Gregory constantly urged liberal treatment of his vassals and farmers and ordered that money should be advanced to those in difficulties. Large sums were spent in ransoming captives from the Lombards, and we find him commending the bishop of Fano for breaking up and selling church plate for that object and advising another prelate to do the same. In view of a threatened corn shortage he filled the granaries of Rome, and a regular list was kept of the poor to whom grants were periodically made. St Gregory's sense of justice showed itself also in his enlightened treatment of the Jews, whom he would not allow to be oppressed or deprived of their synagogues. He declared that they must not be coerced but must be won by meekness and charity, and when the Jews of Cagliari in Sardinia complained that their synagogue had been seized by a converted Jew who had turned it into a church, he ordered the building to be restored to its former owners.

From the very outset of his pontificate the saint was called upon to face the aggressions of the Lombards, who from Pavia, Spoleto and Benevento made incursions into other parts of Italy. No help was obtained from Constantinople or from the exarch at Ravenna, and it fell upon Gregory, the one strong man, not only to organize the defences of Rome, but also to lend assistance to other cities. When in 593 Agilulf with a Lombard army appeared before the walls of Rome Gregory induced him to withdraw his army and leave the city in peace. For nine years he strove in vain to bring about a settlement between the Byzantine emperor and the Lombards; Gregory then proceeded on his own account to negotiate a treaty with King Agilulf, obtaining a special truce for Rome and the surrounding districts.

Of all his religious work in the West that which lay closest to Gregory's heart was the conversion of England, and the success which crowned his efforts in that direction was to him the greatest triumph of his life. The pope's first action was to order the purchase of some English slaves, boys of about seventeen or eighteen, in order to educate them in a monastery for the service of God. Still, it was not to them that he intended primarily to entrust the work of conversion. From his own monastery of St Andrew he selected a band of forty missionaries whom he sent forth under the leadership of Augustine.

During nearly the whole of his pontificate St Gregory was engaged in conflicts with Constantinople – sometimes with the emperor, sometimes with the patriarch, occasionally with both. He protested constantly against the exactions of Byzantine officials whose extortions reduced the Italian people to despair, and remonstrated with the emperor against an imperial edict which prohibited soldiers from becoming monks. With John the Faster, Patriarch of Constantinople, he had an acrimonious correspondence over the title of Oecumenical or Universal which that hierarch had assumed. It seemed to savour of arrogance, and Gregory resented it. For his own part, though one of the most strenuous upholders of the papal dignity, he preferred to call himself by the proudly humble title of *Servus servorum Dei* – Servant of the servants of God. Almost his last action was to send a warm winter cloak to a poor bishop who suffered from the cold. Gregory was buried in St Peter's, and as the epitaph on his tomb expresses it, 'after having confirmed all his actions to his doctrines, the great consul of God went to enjoy eternal triumphs'.

GREGORY THE WONDERWORKER, BISHOP OF NEOCAESAREA
(A.D. 268)

A PATRON SAINT OF THOSE IN DESPERATE SITUATIONS; OR UNDER THREAT FROM EARTHQUAKE OR FLOOD

17 NOVEMBER

It was St Gregory's fame as a miracle-worker that made him, in the Middle Ages, a natural choice as a patron of those in desperate situations.

It is reported that Gregory's body was eventually moved to a Byzantine monastery in Southern Italy, whence devotion to him spread into Sicily as well, and where he was invoked in a variety of situations of particular difficulty in the area, such as earthquakes. More importantly, however, he was invoked against flood, because of the story that he stopped the flooding of the River Lycus.

Theodore, afterwards called Gregory, and from his miracles surnamed Thaumaturgus or Worker of Wonders, was of Neocaesarea in Pontus, born of parents eminent in rank and pagan in religion. At fourteen years of age he lost his father, but continued his education, which was directed towards a career in the law. His sister going to join her husband, an official at Caesarea in Palestine, Gregory accompanied her with his brother Athenodorus, who was afterwards a bishop and suffered much for the faith of Jesus Christ. Origen had arrived at Caesarea a little before and opened a school there, and at the first meeting with Gregory and his brother discerned in them capacity for learning and dispositions to virtue which encouraged him to inspire them with a love of truth and an eager desire of attaining the sovereign good of man. Fascinated with his discourse, they entered his school and laid aside all thoughts of going to the law-school of Bairut, as they had originally intended. Gregory does justice to Origen by assuring us that he excited them to virtue no less by his example than by his words; and tells us that he inculcated that in all things the most valuable knowledge is that of the first cause, and thus he led them on to theology. He opened to their view all that the philosophers and poets had written concerning God, showing what was true and what was erroneous in the doctrines of each and demonstrating the incompetence of human reason alone for attaining to certain knowledge in the most important of all points that of religion. The conversion of the brothers to Christianity was complete and they continued their studies under their master for some years, going back home about the year 238. Before he took leave of Origen, Gregory thanked him publicly in an oration before a large audience, in which he extols the method and wisdom by which his great master conducted him through his studies, and gives interesting particulars of the way in which Origen taught. A letter also is extant from the master to the disciple: he calls Gregory his respected son and exhorts him to employ for the service of religion all the talents which he had received from God and to borrow from the heathen philosophy what might serve that purpose, as the Jews converted the spoils of the Egyptians to the building of the tabernacle of the true God.

On his return to Neocaesarea St Gregory intended to practise law, but within a short time, although there were only seventeen Christians in the town, he was appointed to be its bishop; but of his long episcopate few certain particulars have come down to us. St Gregory of Nyssa gives a good deal of information in his panegyric of the saint with regard to the deeds which earned him the title of Wonderworker, but there is little doubt that a good deal of it is legendary. However, it is known that Neocaesarea was rich and populous, deeply buried in vice and idolatry, that St Gregory, animated with zeal and charity, applied himself vigorously to the charge committed to him, and that God was pleased to confer upon him an extraordinary power of working miracles. St Basil tells us that 'through the co-operation of the Spirit, Gregory had a formidable power over evil spirits; he altered the course of rivers in the name of Christ; he dried up a lake that was a cause of dissension between two brothers; and his foretelling of the future made him equal with the other prophets. . . . Such were his signs and wonders that both friends and enemies of the truth looked on him as another Moses.'

When he first took possession of his see Gregory accepted the invitation of Musonius, a person of importance in the city, and lodged with him. That very day he began to preach and before night had converted a number sufficient to form a little church. Early next morning the doors were crowded with sick persons, whom he cured at the same time that he wrought the conversion of their souls. Christians soon became so numerous that the saint was enabled to build a church for their use, to which all contributed either money or labour.

The persecution of Decius breaking out in 250, St Gregory advised his flock rather to hide than to expose themselves to the danger of losing their faith; he himself withdrew into the desert, accompanied only by a pagan priest whom he had converted and who was then his deacon. The persecutors were informed that he was concealed upon a certain mountain and sent soldiers to apprehend him. They returned, saying they had seen nothing but two trees; upon which the informer went to the place and, finding the bishop and his deacon at their prayers, whom the soldiers had mistaken for two trees, judged their escape to have been miraculous and became a Christian. The persecution was followed by a plague, and the plague by an irruption of Goths into Asia Minor, so that it is not surprising to find that, with these added to the ordinary cares and duties of the episcopate, St Gregory was not a voluminous writer. What these cares and duties were he sets out in his 'Canonical Letter', occasioned by problems arising from the barbarian raids. It is stated that St Gregory organized secular amusements in connection with the annual commemorations of the martyrs, which attracted pagans as well as popularizing the religious gatherings among

Christians: doubtless, too, he had it in mind that the martyrs were honoured by happy recreation in addition to formally religious observances.

A little before his death St Gregory Thaumaturgus inquired how many infidels yet remained in the city, and being told there were seventeen he thankfully acknowledged as a great mercy that, having found but seventeen Christians at his coming thither, he left but seventeen idolaters. Having then prayed for their conversion, and the confirmation and sanctification of those that believed in the true God, he enjoined his friends not to procure him any special place of burial but that, as he lived as a pilgrim in the world claiming nothing for himself, so after death he might enjoy the common lot.

THE GUARDIAN ANGELS

PATRON SAINTS OF THE SPANISH ARMED POLICE

2 OCTOBER

The Sacred Congregation of Rites decree of 24 February 1926, confirmed on 13 December 1961, declared the Guardian Angels to be the patrons of the Spanish 'Policia Armada', or armed police.

From early times liturgical honour was paid to all angels in the office of the dedication of the church of St Michael the Archangel in *Via Salaria* on September 29, and in the oldest extant Roman sacramentary, called Leonine, the prayers for the feast make indirect reference to them as individual guardians. A votive Mass, *Missa ad suffragia angelorum postulanda*, has been in use at least from the time of Alcuin – he died in 804 – who refers to the subject twice in his letters. Whether the practice of celebrating such a Mass originated in England is not clear, but we find Alcuin's text in the Leofric Missal of the early tenth century. This votive Mass of the Angels was commonly allotted to the second day of the week (Monday), as for example in the Westminster Missal, written about the year 1375. In Spain it became customary to honour the Guardian Angels not only of persons, but of cities and provinces. An office of this sort was composed for Valencia in 1411. Outside of Spain, Francis of Estaint, Bishop of Rodex, obtained from Pope Leo X a bull in 1518 which approved a special office for an annual commemoration of the Guardian Angels on 1 March. In England also there seems to have been much devotion to them. Herbert Losinga, Bishop of Norwich, who died in 1119, speaks eloquently on the subject; and the well-known invocation beginning *Angele Dei qui custos es mei* is apparently traceable to the versewriter Reginald of Canterbury, at about the same period. Pope Paul V authorized a special Mass and Office and at the request of Ferdinand II of Austria granted the feast to the whole empire. Pope Clement X extended it to the Western church at large as of obligation in 1670 and fixed it for the present date, being the first free day after the feast of St Michael.

HENRY THE EMPEROR (A.D. 1024)

13 JULY

Henry's work for the Church in Eastern Europe led to his recognition as patron of Finland, formally confirmed by a decree of the Sacred Congregation of Rites dated 24 February 1961. Since he was always interested in monastic reform, he was declared patron of Benedictine oblates by Pope Pius X.

St Henry II was son of Henry, Duke of Bavaria, and Gisela of Burgundy, and was born in 972. He was educated by St Wolfgang, Bishop of Ratisbon, and in 995 succeeded his father in the duchy of Bavaria; in 1002, upon the death of his cousin Otto III, he was chosen emperor. He knew the end for which alone he was exalted by God to the highest temporal dignity, and worked his hardest to promote the peace and happiness of his realm. Nevertheless, Henry at times made use of the Church for political ends, in accordance with the imperial policy of his predecessor Otto the Great. He refused his support to ecclesiastical aggrandizement in temporal concerns, while maintaining the Church's proper authority; but some of his politics look equivocal when examined from the point of view of the welfare of Christendom.

He had to engage in numerous wars for the defence and consolidation of the empire, as for example in Italy, before he could receive that crown; Arduin of Ivrea had had himself crowned king at Milan, so the emperor crossed the Alps and drove him out. In 1014 he went in triumph to Rome, where he was crowned emperor by Pope Benedict VIII. Henry munificently repaired and restored the episcopal sees of Hildesheim, Magdeburg, Strasburg and Meersburg, and made benefactions to the churches of Aachen, Basle and others.

In 1006 Henry founded the see of Bamberg and built a great cathedral there, in order to solidify German power among the Wends. In this he was opposed by the bishops of Würzburg and Eichstätt, whose dioceses were thus dismembered, but Pope John XIX approved, and Benedict VIII consecrated the cathedral in 1020. Henry also built and endowed a monastery at Bamberg, and made foundations in several other places, that the divine honour and the relief of the poor might be provided for to the end of time. In 1021 the emperor again came to Italy, on an expedition against the Greeks in Apulia; on his way back he was taken ill at Monte Cassino, where he was said to have been miraculously cured at the intercession of St Benedict, but he contracted a lameness which never left him.

Henry identified himself in time with those ideas of ecclesiastical reform which radiated from the great monastery of Cluny, and in support of them he even opposed himself to his kinsman, friend, and former chaplain, Aribo, whom he had appointed archbishop of Mainz and who in synod had condemned appeals to Rome without episcopal permission. Accounts of his ascetic practices do not entirely accord with what is known of his character and life; Henry was one of the great rulers of the Holy Roman Empire, and triumphed precisely as a Christian statesman and soldier, whose ways were, in the nature of things, not those of the cloister.

What we know of him is mostly a matter of general history: he clearly promoted ecclesiastical reform, taking great care about episcopal appointments and supporting such great monks as St Odilo of Cluny and Richard of Saint-Vanne. St Henry was canonized by Eugenius III in 1146.

HIPPOLYTUS, MARTYR (c. A.D. 235)

PATRON SAINT OF PRISON OFFICERS; AND OF HORSES

13 AUGUST

Hippolytus has been patron of prison officers, for the reason that he himself was one, from the Middle Ages.

The story that this saint was martyred by being torn apart by horses seems an odd reason to take him as a patron saint of horses, but he has been so regarded.

The Roman Martyrology today mentions that Hippolytus the martyr who is mentioned in the *acta* of St Laurence. According to that very unreliable document Hippolytus was an officer in charge of Laurence when he was in prison, and was by him converted and baptized. He assisted at the burial of the martyr, and for so doing was summoned before the emperor, who rebuked him for disgracing the imperial uniform and commission and ordered him to be scourged. At the same time St Concordia, the nurse of Hippolytus, and nineteen others were beaten to death with leaded whips. St Hippolytus himself was sentenced to be torn apart by horses – a suspicious circumstance in the narrative when we remember the fate of Hippolytus, the son of Theseus who, flying from the anger of his father, met a monster the sight of which affrighted his horses, so that he fell from his chariot, and being entangled in the harness, was dragged along and torn to pieces. They took a pair of the most furious and unruly horses they could meet with, and tied a long rope between them to which they fastened the martyr's feet. The horses dragged him away furiously over ditches, briers and rocks; the ground, trees and stones were sprinkled with his blood, which the faithful that followed at a distance weeping dipped up with kerchiefs, and they gathered together all the mangled parts of his flesh and limbs which lay scattered about.

This story would appear to be a romance, and the martyr Hippolytus whose feast is kept by the Church on this day is probably a Roman priest who lived during the early part of the third century. He was a man of great learning and the most important theological writer (he wrote in Greek) in the early days of the Roman church. He may have been a disciple of St Irenaeus, and St Jerome called him a 'most holy and eloquent man'. Hippolytus censured Pope St Zephyrinus for being, in his opinion, not quick enough to detect and denounce heresy, and on the election of his successor, St Callistus I, he severed communion with the Roman church and permitted himself to be set up in opposition to the pope. With Pope St Pontian he was banished to Sardinia during the persecution of Maximinus in 235, and was reconciled to the Church. He died a martyr by his sufferings on that unhealthy island, and his body was afterwards translated to the cemetery on the Via Tiburtina.

Prudentius who, led astray by the inscription of Pope St Damasus over his grave, confuses his Hippolytus with another of that name, puts his martyrdom, by wild horses, at the mouth of the Tiber.

THE HOLY INNOCENTS

PATRON SAINTS OF BABIES

28 DECEMBER

There is no need to explain this patronage, which is self-evident from the account which follows.

Herod, called 'the Great', who governed Jewry under the Romans at the time of the birth of our Lord, was an Idumean; not a Jew of the house of David or of Aaron, but the descendant of people forcibly judaized by John Hyrcanus and himself exalted by the favour of imperial Rome. From the moment, therefore, that he heard that there was One 'born king of the Jews', and that already wise men came from the East to worship Him, Herod was troubled for his throne. He called together the chief priests and scribes, and asked them where it was that the expected Messias should be born; and they told him, 'In Bethlehem of Judea'. Then he sent for the Magi secretly, and cross-examined them about their movements and their expectations, and finally dismissed them to Bethlehem, saying, 'Go and find out all about this child. And when you know where he is, come and tell me – that I too may go and worship him.' but the Magi were warned in their sleep not to return to Herod, and they went back to their own country by another way. And God by an angel warned Joseph to take his wife Mary and her child Jesus and fly into Egypt, 'for it will come to pass that, Herod will seek the child to destroy him'.

'Then Herod, perceiving that he was deluded by the wise men, was exceeding angry. And sending killed all the men children that were in Bethlehem and in all the borders thereof, from two years old and under, according to the time which he had diligently inquired of the wise men.

Then was fulfilled that which was spoken by Jeremias the prophet, saying: A voice in Rama was heard, lamentation and great mourning; Rachel bewailing her children and would not be comforted, because they were not' (Matt, ii).

Josephus says of Herod that 'he was a man of great barbarity towards everybody', and narrates a number of his crimes, crimes so shocking that the slaughter of a few young Jewish babies becomes insignificant among them, and Josephus does not mention it. The number of Herod's victims is popularly supposed to have been great: the Byzantine liturgy speaks of 14,000, the Syrian menologies 64,000, and by an accommodation of Apocalypse xiv 1–5, it has even been put at 144,000. Of the lowest of these figures Alban Butler justly remarks that it 'exceeds all bounds, nor is it confirmed by any authority of weight'. Bethlehem was a small place, and even including the environs, could not at one time have had more than twenty-five boy-babies under two, at the very most; some inquirers would put the number so low as about half a dozen. There is an oft-repeated story told by Macrobius, a heathen writer of the fifth century, that the Emperor Augustus, when he heard that among the children under two which Herod had commanded to be slain his own son had been massacred, said, 'It is better to be Herod's hog (*hus*) than his son (*huios*)', alluding to the Jewish law of not eating, and consequently not killing, swine. But in fact the son referred to was an adult, Antipater, put to death by order of his dying father.

The feast of these Holy Innocents (who in the East are called simply the Holy Children) has been kept since the fifth century in the Church, which venerates them as martyrs, who died not only for Christ but actually instead of Christ: 'flores martyrum'; buds, as St Augustine says, killed by the frost of persecution the moment they showed themselves.

HOMOBONUS (A.D. 1197)

PATRON SAINT OF MERCHANTS, BUSINESS PEOPLE AND TRADESPEOPLE; OF TAILORS, CLOTHWORKERS, GARMENT WORKERS AND SHOEMAKERS

13 NOVEMBER

Because of his profession, Homobonus has been taken as patron by merchants, business and tradespeople, and in particular by tailors, and associated professions such as clothworkers, garment workers and shoemakers.

Homobonus was son of a merchant at Cremona in Lombardy, who gave him this name (which signifies 'good man') at baptism. Whilst he trained his son up to his own mercantile business without any school education, he inspired in him both by example and instruction a love of probity, integrity and virtue. The saint from his childhood abhorred the very shadow of untruth or injustice. To honesty Homobonus added economy, care and industry. His business he looked upon as an employment given him by God, and he pursued it with diligence and a proper regard to himself, his family and the commonwealth of which he was a member. If a tradesman's books are not well kept, if there is not order and regularity in the conduct of his business, if he does not give his mind seriously to it, he neglects an essential and Christian duty. Homobonus was a saint by acquitting himself diligently and uprightly for supernatural motives, of all the obligations of his profession.

In due course St Homobonus married, and his wife was a prudent and faithful assistant in the government of his household. Not content with giving his tenths to the distressed members of Christ, he seemed to set no bounds to his alms; he sought out the poor in their homes and, whilst he relieved their corporal necessities, he exhorted them to a good life. The author of his life assures us that God often recognized his charity by miracles in favour of those whom he relieved. It was his custom every night to go to the church of St Giles, for prayer accompanied all his actions and it was in its exercise that he gave up his soul to God. For, on 13 November 1197, during Mass, at the *Gloria in excelsis* he stretched out his arms in the figure of a cross and fell on his face to the ground, which those who saw him thought he had done out of devotion. When he did not stand up at the gospel they took more notice and, coming to him, found he was dead. Sicard, Bishop of Cremona, went himself to Rome to solicit his canonization, which Pope Innocent III decreed in 1199.

HONORATUS, BISHOP OF AMIENS (*c*. A.D. 600)

PATRON SAINT OF MILLERS, BAKERS AND CAKE MAKERS

16 MAY

There is no doubt about the devotion to Honoratus shown by French bakers, millers, cake makers and all who deal in flour in whatever way, and by an Apostolic Letter of 12 November 1980 John Paul II approved his patronage specifically of bakers and millers of Argentina. It is, however, difficult to find any obvious reason for this cult. One possible explanation may lie in an incident among the many miraculous things which happened to him. One day, while at mass, he was about to receive Holy Communion when the Lord's hand appeared over the chalice, took the bread, and gave the saint Communion.

The famous Faubourg and Rue Saint-Honoré in Paris derive their name from St Honoratus who was bishop of Amiens at the close of the sixty century. History has little to tell us about him except that he was born at Port-le-Grand in the diocese of Amiens where he also died, and that he elevated the relics of SS. Fuscianus, Victoricus and Gentianus, which a priest called Lupicinus had discovered after they had been forgotten for three hundred years. The *cultus* of St Honoratus received a great impetus and became widespread in France in consequence of a number of remarkable cures which followed the elevation of his own body in 1060, and which were attributed to his agency. In 1204 Reynold Cherez and his wife Sybil placed under his patronage the church they built in Paris. Nearly a hundred years later another bishop of Amiens, William of Mâcon, dedicated in honour of his saintly predecessor the charterhouse he was building at Abbeville.

HUBERT, BISHOP OF LIÈGE (A.D. 727)

A PATRON SAINT OF HUNTING AND HUNTSMEN; AND OF PROTECTION AGAINST RABIES OR HYDROPHOBIA

3 NOVEMBER

The devotion to St Hubert as a patron of hunting and hunting men comes from the Middle Ages, but no formal declaration appears to exist. His choice for this role can be easily understood from the account of his life.

His association with rabies is traditional, although there seems to be nothing specific in his life which could account for it. On the other hand as a huntsman he would have kept dogs, and therefore ran the risk of being bitten by them. According to legend he was once given by the Blessed Virgin a stole made of white silk and golden thread. From the twelfth century it appears to have become the custom to treat those suffering from rabies by making a small incision in the forehead and then applying to it a thread taken from the stole.

'God called St Hubert from a worldly life to his service in an extraordinary manner; though the circumstances of this event are so obscured by popular inconsistent relations that we have no authentic account of his actions before he was engaged in the service of the church under the discipline of St Lambert, Bishop of Maestricht'. The 'extraordinary manner' referred to in Alban Butler's commendably guarded statement is related to have been as follows: Hubert was very fond of hunting and one Good Friday went out after a stag when everybody else was going to church. In a clearing of the wood the beast turned, displaying a crucifix between its horns. Hubert stopped in astonishment, and a voice came from the stag, saying, 'Unless you turn to the Lord, Hubert, you shall fall into Hell'. He cast himself on his knees, asking what he should do, and the voice told him to seek out Lambert, the bishop of Maestricht, who would guide him. This, of course, is the same as the legend of the conversion of St Eustace.

However the retirement of Hubert from the world came about, he entered the service of St Lambert and was ordained priest. When the bishop was murdered at Liège about the year 705 Hubert was selected to govern the see in his place. Some years later he translated Lambert's bones from Maestricht to Liège, then only a village upon the banks of the Meuse, which from this grew into a flourishing city. St Hubert placed the relics of the martyr in a church which he built upon the spot where he had suffered and made it his cathedral, removing thither the episcopal see from Maestricht. Hence St Lambert is honoured at Liège as principal patron of the diocese and St Hubert as founder of the city and church and its first bishop.

In those days the forest of Ardenne stretched from the Meuse to the Rhine and in several parts the gospel of Christ had not yet taken root. St Hubert penetrated into the most remote places of this country and abolished the worship of idols. The author of his life relates as an eye-witness that on the rogation days the holy bishop went out of Maestricht in procession through the fields and villages, with his clergy and people according to custom, following the cross and the relics of the saints, and singing the litany. This procession was disturbed by a woman possessed by an evil spirit; but St Hubert silenced her and restored her to her health by signing her with the cross. Before his death he is said to have been warned of it in a vision and given as it were a sight of the place prepared for him in glory. Twelve months later he went into Brabant to consecrate a new church. He was taken ill immediately after at Tervueren, near Brussels. On the sixth day of his sickness he quietly died, on 30 May in 727. His body was conveyed to Liège and laid in the church of St Peter. It was translated in 825 to the abbey of Andain, since called Saint-Hubert, in Ardenne, on the frontiers of the duchy of Luxemburg. The 3 November, the date of St Hubert's feast, is probably the day of the enshrining of his relics at Liège sixteen years after his death.

HYACINTH (A.D. 1257)

A PATRON SAINT OF LITHUANIA

15 AUGUST

One of the several saints recognized by Rome as patrons of Lithuana, Hyacinth's patronage was confirmed by Innocent XI on 24 September 1686.

St Hyacinth (in Polish, Jacek, a form of John) was a Silesian, born in 1185, in the district called Oppeln, between Breslau and Cracow. He is venerated as an apostle of Poland, and was undoubtedly a great missionary; but the particulars of the achievements commonly attributed to him unfortunately depend on biographies that are of very little historical value.

He became a Dominican, perhaps in Rome, in 1217 or 1218, and came with other Dominicans to Cracow, where they were given the church of the Holy Trinity by the bishop, Ivo Odrowaz. Hyacinth is recorded as being at this priory again in 1228, and ten years later was preaching a crusade against the heathen Prussians. The field of his labours was doubtless extensive; but his biographers take him north-east into Lithuania, east to Kiev, south-east to the Black Sea, south to the Danube and north-west to Scandinavia, leaving Silesia, Pomerania and Bohemia to his fellow Dominican, Bd Ceslaus, who was said to be also his brother in the flesh. The miracles with which Hyacinth was credited are no less sensational, some of them being apparently suggested by what had been related of other holy ones in Poland and in his order. During his time the Friars Preachers did penetrate down the Vistula to Danzig and towards Russia and the Balkans, and a number of priories were founded; but much damage was done to their missions after the Mongols crossed the Volga in 1238, in the repairing of which no doubt St Hyacinth was active.

He died on the feast of the Assumption 1257, after exhorting his brethren to esteem poverty as men that had renounced all earthly things, 'For this is the testament, the sealed deed, by which we claim eternal life'. He was canonized in 1594.

IGNATIUS OF LOYOLA, (A.D. 1556)

FOUNDER OF THE SOCIETY OF JESUS
PATRON SAINT OF RETREATS AND SPIRITUAL EXERCISES; SCRUPLES

31 JULY

Citing the success of Ignatius' Spiritual Exercises as an aid to the giving of retreats, Pius XI declared him patron of retreats in an Apostolic Letter of 25 July 1922. Contained in the Spiritual Exercises are a number of 'rules' for the guidance of those who suffer from scruples. For that reason Ignatius has often been invoked also by those troubled by scruples.

St Ignatius was born, probably in 1491, in the castle of Loyola at Azpeitia, in Guipuzcoa, a part of Biscay that reaches to the Pyrenees. His father, Don Beltran, was lord of Oñaz and Loyola, head of one of the most ancient and noble families of that country, and his mother, Marina Saenz de Licona y Balda, was not less illustrious. They had three daughters and eight sons, and Ignatius (he was christened Inigo) was the youngest child.

His short military career came to an abrupt end on 20 May 1521 when, in the defence of Pamplona, a cannon ball broke his right shin and tore open the left calf. At his fall the Spanish garrison surrounded. The French then sent him in a litter to the castle of Loyola. His broken leg had been badly set, and the surgeons therefore thought it necessary to break it again, which he suffered without any apparent concern; but he limped for the rest of his life.

While he was confined to his bed, finding the time tedious, Ignatius called for some book of romances. None being found, a book of the life of our Saviour and another of legends of the saints were brought him. He read them first only to pass away the time, but afterward began to relish them and to spend whole days in reading them. Taking at last a firm resolution to imitate the saints at least in some respects, he began to treat his body with all the rigour it was able to bear, and spent his retired hours in weeping for his sins. He went on pilgrimage to the shrine of our Lady at Montserrat, and resolved thenceforward to lead a life of penance. Near Montserrat is the small town of Manresa, and here he stayed, sometimes with the Dominican friars, sometimes in a paupers' hospice; and there was a cave in a neighbouring hill whither he might retire for prayer and penance. So he lived for nearly a year. During this time he began to note down material for what was to become the book of his *Spiritual Exercises*.

In February 1523, Ignatius started on his journey to the Holy Land; begging his way, he took ship from Barcelona, spent Easter at Rome, sailed from Venice to Cyprus, and thence to Jaffa. He went by donkey from thence to Jerusalem, with the firm intention of staying there. But the Franciscan guardian of the Holy Places commanded him to leave Palestine, lest his attempts to convert Moslems should cause him to be kidnapped and held to ransom. He returned to Spain in 1524; and he now set himself to study.

He began at Barcelona with Latin grammar, being assisted by the charities of a pious lady of that city, called Isabel Roser: he was then thirty-three years old. After studying two years at Barcelona he went to the University of Alcala, where he attended lectures in logic, physics and divinity. He lodged at a hospice, lived by begging, and wore a coarse grey habit. He catechized children, held assemblies of devotion in the hospice, and by his mild reprehensions converted many loose livers. Those were the days of strange cults in Spain, and Ignatius was accused to the bishop's vicar general, who confined him to prison two-and-forty days. He declared him innocent of any fault at the end of it; but forbade him and his companions to wear any singular dress, or to give any instructions in religious matters for three years. So he migrated with his three fellows to Salamanca, where he was exposed again to suspicions of introducing dangerous doctrines, and the inquisitors imprisoned him; but after three weeks declared him innocent.

Recovering his liberty again, he resolved to leave Spain, and in the middle of winter travelled on foot to Paris, where he arrived in the beginning of February 1528. He spent two years improving himself in Latin; in vacation time he went into Flanders, and once into England, to procure help from the Spanish merchants settled there, from whom and from some friends at Barcelona he received support. He studied philosophy three years and a half in the college of St Barbara, where he induced many of his fellow-students to spend the Sundays and holy days in prayer, and to apply themselves more fervently to good works. In 1534 the middle-aged student – he was forty-three – graduated as master of arts of Paris.

At that time six students in divinity associated themselves with Ignatius in his spiritual exercises. They were Peter Favre, a Savoyard; Francis Xavier, a Basque like Ignatius; Laynez and Salmeron, both fine scholars; Simon Rodriguez, a Portuguese; and Nicholas Bobadilla. These made all together a vow to observe poverty and chastity and to go to preach the gospel in Palestine, or if they could not go thither to offer themselves to the pope to be employed in the service of God in what manner he should judge best. They pronounced this vow in a chapel on Montmartre, after they had all received holy communion from Peter Fayre, who had been lately ordained priest. This was on the feast of the Assumption, 1534. Ignatius returned home in spring 1535, and was joyfully received in Guipuzcoa, where, however, he refused to go to the castle of Loyola, taking up his quarters in the poor-house of Azpeitia.

Two years later they all met in Venice, but it was impossible to find a ship to sail to Palestine. Ignatius's companions (now numbering ten) therefore went to Rome, where Pope Paul III received them well, and granted them an indult that those who were not priests might receive holy orders from what bishop they pleased. They were accordingly ordained and then retired into a cottage near Vicenza to prepare themselves for the holy ministry of the altar.

There being no likelihood of their being able soon to go to the Holy Land, it was at length resolved that Ignatius, Favre and Laynez should go to Rome and offer the services of all to the pope, and they agreed that if anyone asked what their association was they might answer, 'the Company of Jesus', because they were united to fight against falsehood and vice under the standard of Christ. On his road to Rome, praying in a little chapel at La Storta, Ignatius saw our Lord loaded with a heavy cross, and he heard the words 'I will be favourable to you at Rome'. Paul III appointed Favre to teach in the Sapienza and Laynez to explain the Holy Scriptures; Ignatius laboured by means of his spiritual exercises and instructions to reform the manners of the people and the others were likewise employed in the city – that none of them yet spoke Italian properly did not deter them.

It was now proposed to form a religious order. It was resolved, first, besides the vows of poverty and chastity already made by them, to add a third of obedience, to appoint a superior general whom all should be bound to obey, subject entirely to the Holy See. They likewise determined to prescribe a fourth vow, of going wherever the pope should send them for the salvation of souls. It was agreed that the celebration of the Divine Office in choir (as distinct from the obligatory private recitation) should be no part of their duties. The cardinals appointed by the pope to examine this new order at first opposed it, but after a year changed their opinions, and Paul III approved it by a bull, dated 27 September 1540. Ignatius was chosen the first general superior, but only acquiesced in obedience to his confessor. He entered upon his office on Easterday, 1541, and the members all made their religious vows in the basilica of St Paul-outside-the-Walls a few days later.

For the rest of his life Ignatius lived in Rome, tied there by the immense work of directing the activities of the order which he ruled till his death. Among the establishments which he made there, he founded a house for the reception of converted Jews during the time of their instruction, and another for penitents from among women of disorderly life. St Francis Borgia in 1550 gave a considerable sum towards building the Roman College for the Jesuits; St Ignatius made this the model of all his other colleges and took care that it should be supplied with able masters and all possible helps for the advancement of learning. He also directed the foundation of the German College in Rome, originally intended for scholars from all countries seriously affected by Protestantism. Other universities, seminaries and colleges were established in other places; but the work of education for which the Jesuits are so famous was a development that only came by degrees, though well established before the founder's death. One of the most famous and fruitful works of St Ignatius was the book of his *Spiritual Exercises*, begun at Manresa and first published in Rome in 1548 with papal approval.

In the fifteen years that he directed his order St Ignatius saw it grow from ten members to one thousand, in nine countries and provinces of Europe, in

India and in Brazil. And in those fifteen years he had been ill fifteen times, so that the sixteenth time caused no unusual alarm. But it was the last. He died suddenly, so unexpectedly that he did not receive the last sacraments, early in the morning of 31 July 1556. He was canonized in 1622.

ISIDORE THE FARMER (A.D. 1130)

PATRON SAINT OF FARMERS AND FARM LABOURERS; NATIONAL CATHOLIC RURAL
CONFERENCE, USA; ALSO OF MADRID

15 MAY

Devotion to St Isidore as patron both of farmers (and farm labourers and all who work on the land), and of Madrid follows naturally from his life-story. In an Apostolic Letter of 16 December 1960, however, Pope John XXIII formally declared him patron of the farm labourers and of country dwellers of Spain. Decrees of the Sacred Congregation of Rites declared him patron of the same groups in Canada (16 March 1943) and Mexico (5 February 1962) and of the National Catholic Rural Conference of the United States (22 February 1947).

The patron of Madrid was born in the Spanish capital of poor parents, and was christened Isidore after the celebrated archbishop of Seville. As soon as he was old enough to work, Isidore entered the service of John de Vergas, a wealthy resident of Madrid, as a farm labourer on his estate outside the city, and with one employer he remained all his life. He married a girl as poor and as good as himself, but after the birth of one son, who died young, they agreed to serve God in perfect continence. Isidore's whole life was a model of Christian perfection lived in the world. He would rise early to go to church, and all day long, whilst his hand guided the plough, he would be communing with God, with his guardian angel or with the holy saints. Public holidays he would spent in visiting the churches of Madrid and the neighbouring districts. The saint's liberality to the poor was so great that he was wont to share his meals with them, often reserving for himself only the scraps they left over.

Amongst the numerous stories told of the holy man is one which illustrates his love for animals. On a snowy winter's day, as he was carrying a sack of corn to be ground, he saw a number of birds perched disconsolately on the bare branches, obviously unable to find anything to eat. Isidore opened the sack and, in spite of the jeers of a companion, poured out half its contents upon the ground. When, however, they reached their destination the sack proved to be still full and the corn, when ground, produced double the usual amount of flour.

St Isidore died on 15 May 1130. His wife survived him for several years and, like him, is honoured as a saint. Forty years after the death of St Isidore his body was transferred to a more honourable shrine, and a great impetus was given to his cult by the report of many miracles worked through his intercession. In 1211 he is said to have appeared in a vision to King Alphonsus of Castile, then fighting the Moors in the pass of Navas de Tolosa, and to have shown him an unknown path by means of which he was able to surprise and defeat the enemy.

The Spanish royal family had long desired to have St Isidore formally enrolled amongst the saints, and in March 1622 he was duly canonized.

IVO OF KERMARTIN (A.D. 1303)

PATRON SAINT OF LAWYERS, ADVOCATES, CANON LAWYERS, JUDGES AND
NOTARIES; OF ABANDONED CHILDREN AND ORPHANS; AND OF BRITTANY

19 MAY

Because of his profession before he became a priest, Ivo was taken as the patron of those engaged in the law including Canon law, in whatever capacity, whether as judges, notaries or advocates.

His particular concern for the needs of those who had lost both parents, as recounted in his life, was the reason for Ivo being taken as patron of orphans and abandoned children.

St Ivo has always been a particularly popular saint in his native region, and has long been regarded as Brittany's patron, although this was only formally recognized in 1924.

Ivo Hélory was born near Tréguier in Brittany at Kermartin, where his father was lord of the manor. At the age of fourteen he was sent to Paris, and before the end of a ten years' stay in its famous schools he had gained great distinction in philosophy, theology and canon law. He then passed on to Orleans to study civil law under the celebrated jurist Peter de la Chapelle. In his student days he began to practise austerities which he continued and increased throughout his life. He wore a hair shirt, abstained from meat and wine, fasted during Advent and Lent (as well as at other times) on bread and water, and took his rest – which was always short – lying on a straw mat with a book or a stone by way of a pillow. Upon his return to Brittany after the completion of his education, he was appointed by the archdeacon of Rennes diocesan 'official', in other words, judge of the cases that came before the ecclesiastical court. In this capacity he protected orphans, defended the poor and administered justice with an impartiality and kindliness which gained him the goodwill even of the losing side.

Before very long, however, his own diocesan claimed him, and he returned to his native district as official to Alan de Bruc, Bishop of Tréguier. Here his championship of the downtrodden won for him the name of 'the poor man's advocate'. Not content with dealing out justice to the helpless in his own court, he would personally plead for them in other courts, often paying their expenses, and visiting them when they were in prison. He would never accept the presents or bribes which had become so customary as to be regarded as a lawyer's perquisite. He always strove if possible to reconcile people who were at enmity, and to induce them to settle their quarrels out of court. In this manner he prevented many of those who came to him from embarking on costly and unnecessary lawsuits. St Ivo had received minor orders when he was made official at Rennes, and in 1284 he was ordained priest and given the living at Trédrez. Three years later he resigned his legal office and devoted the last fifteen years of his life to his parishioners – first at Trédrez, and afterwards in the larger parish of Lovannec.

St Ivo built a hospital in which he tended the sick with his own hands. He would often give the clothes off his back to beggars, and once, when he discovered that a tramp had passed the night on his doorstep, he made the man occupy his bed the following night, whilst he himself slept on the doorstep. He was as solicitous about the spiritual welfare of the people as about their temporal needs, losing no opportunity of instructing them. In great demand as a preacher, he would deliver sermons in other churches besides his own, giving his addresses sometimes in Latin, sometimes in French, and sometimes in Breton. All differences were referred to him, and his arbitration was nearly always accepted. He used to distribute his corn, or the value of it, to the poor directly after the harvest. When it was suggested that he should keep it for a time so as to obtain a better price for it, he replied, 'I cannot count upon being alive then to have the disposal of it'. From the beginning of Lent, 1303, his health failed visibly, but he would not abate his accustomed austerities. On Ascension eve he preached and celebrated Mass, although he was so weak that he had to be supported. He then lay down on his bed, which was a hurdle, and received the last sacraments. He died on 19 May 1303, in the fiftieth year of his age, and was canonized in 1347.

JAMES THE GREATER, APOSTLE (FIRST CENTURY)

PATRON SAINT OF SPAIN; OF GUATEMALA; AND OF NICARAGUA

25 JULY

James was honoured and invoked as patron of Spain from at least the ninth century, his authority increased by numerous stories of his appearing alongside the Christian soldiers in their battles with the Moslems. In the early seveneenth century there was an attempt to declare Teresa of Avila as patron, or co-patron. This had the support of the Spanish parliament, and even that of the Pope, Urban VIII, in a Brief of 21 July 1627. Three years later, however, the Pope was forced to cancel his earlier ruling, and James remained as the sole patron of the country, apart from Mary, B.V., the Immaculate Conception.

Both Guatemala and Nicaragua, former Spanish dominions, continued to share the same patron as their coloniser, formally recognized by decrees of the Sacred Congregation of Rites of 15 May 1914 for Nicaragua and 22 July of the same year for Guatemala.

St James, the brother of St John Evangelist, son of Zebedee, was called the Greater to distinguish him from the other apostle of the same name, surnamed the Less because he was the younger. St James the Greater was by birth a Galilean, and by trade a fisherman with his father and brother, living probably at Bethsaida, where St Peter also dwelt at that time. Jesus walking by the lake of Genesareth saw Peter and Andrew fishing, and He called them to come after Him, promising to make them fishers of men. Going a little farther on the shore, He saw two other brothers, James and John, in a ship, with Zebedee their father, mending their nets, and He also called them; they left their nets and their father and followed Him.

St James was present with his brother St John and St Peter at the cure of Peter's mother-in-law, and the raising of the daughter of Jairus from the dead, and in the same year Jesus formed the company of His apostles, into which He adopted James and John. He gave these two the surname of Boanerges, or 'Sons of Thunder', seemingly on account of an impetuous spirit and fiery temper. Those apostles who from time to time acted impetuously, and had to be rebuked, were the very ones whom our Lord turned to on special occasions. Peter, this James and John alone were admitted to be spectators of His glorious transfiguration, and they alone were taken to the innermost recesses of Gethsemani on the night of agony and bloody sweat at the beginning of His passion.

Where St James preached and spread the gospel after the Lord's ascension we have no account from the writers of the first ages of Christianity. According to the tradition of Spain, he made an evangelizing visit to that country, but the earliest known reference to this is only in the later part of the seventh century, and then in an oriental, not a Spanish source. St James was the first among the apostles who had the honour to follow his divine Master by martyrdom, which he suffered at Jerusalem under King Herod Agrippa I, who inaugurated a persecution of Christians in order to please the Jews.

He was buried at Jerusalem, but, again according to the tradition of Spain, dating from about 830, the body was translated first to Iria Flavia, now El Padron, in Galicia, and then to Compostela, where during the Middle Ages the shrine of Santiago became one of the greatest of all Christian shrines. The relics still rest in the cathedral and were referred to as authentic in a bull of Pope Leo XIII in 1884.

JAMES THE LESS, APOSTLE (A.D. 62?)

PATRON SAINT OF THE DYING

3 MAY

Nothing in what little is known of his life from the New Testament suggests a reason why James should be patron of the dying. Later stories of his own death, however, may provide a clue. According to some versions, James was thrown down from the pinnacle of the temple in Jerusalem, but survived this fall at least long enough to forgive his enemies. He is also credited with overseeing the burial of two New Testament figures, Zachary and Simeon.

The apostle St James – the Less, or the younger – is most commonly held to be the same individual who is variously designated 'James, the son of Alpheus' (*e.g.* Matt. x 3, and Acts i 13), and 'James, the brother of the Lord' (Matt. xiii 55; Gal. i 19). He may also possibly be identical with James, son of Mary and brother of Joseph (Mark xv 40). This, however, is not the place to discuss the rather intricate problem of the 'Brethren of our Lord' and the question connected with it. It may be assumed then, as Alban Butler infers, that the apostle James who became bishop of Jerusalem (Acts xv and xxi 18) was the son of Alpheus and 'brother' (*i.e.* first cousin) of Jesus Christ. Although no prominence is given to this James in the gospel narrative, we learn from St Paul that he was favoured with a special appearing of our Lord before the Ascension. Further, when St Paul, three years after his conversion, went up to Jerusalem and was still regarded with some suspicion by the apostles who remained there, James, with St. Peter, seems to have bid him a cordial welcome. Later we learn that Peter, after his escape from prison, sent a special intimation to James, apparently as to one whose pre-eminence was recognized among the Christians of the holy city. At what is called the Council of Jerusalem, where it was decided that the Gentiles who accepted Christian teaching need not be circumcised, it was St James who, after listening to St Peter's advice, voiced the conclusion of the assembly in the words, 'it hath seemed good to the Holy Ghost and to us' (Acts XV). He was, in fact, the bishop of Jerusalem, as Clement of Alexandria and Eusebius expressly state. Even Josephus, the Jewish historian, bears testimony to the repute in which James was held, and declares, so Eusebius asserts, that the terrible calamities which fell upon the people of that city were a retribution for their treatment of one 'who was the most righteous of men.'

Josephus also informs us that James was stoned to death, and assigns this to the year 62. This St James is commonly held to be the author of the epistle in the New Testament which bears his name.

JEROME, DOCTOR OF THE CHURCH (A.D. 420)

PATRON SAINT OF SCRIPTURE SCHOLARS AND EXEGETES

30 SEPTEMBER

Jerome was declared patron of all those who study the scriptures by Benedict XV in an encyclical letter dated 15 September 1920, published to mark the 1500th anniversary of his death.

Jerome (Eusebius Hieronymus Sophronius), the father of the Church most learned in the Sacred Scriptures, was born about the year 342 at Stridon, a small town upon the confines of Pannonia, Dalmatia and Italy, near Aquileia. His father took great care to have his son instructed in religion and in the first principles of letters at home and afterwards sent him to Rome. Jerome had there for tutor the famous pagan grammarian Donatus. He became master of the Latin and Greek tongues (his native language was Illyrian), read the best writers in both languages with great application, and made progress in oratory; but being left without a guide under the discipline of a heathen master he forgot some of the piety which had been instilled into him in his childhood. Jerome went out of this school free indeed from gross vices, but a stranger to a Christian spirit and enslaved to vanity and other weaknesses, as he afterward confessed and bitterly lamented. On the other hand he was baptized there. After some three years in Rome he determined to travel in order to improve his studies and, with his friend Bonosus, he went to Trier. Here it was that the religious spirit with which he was so deeply imbued was awakened, and his heart was entirely converted to God.

In 370 Jerome settled down for a time at Aquileia, where the bishop, St Valerian, had attracted so many good men that its clergy were famous all over the Western church. With many of these St Jerome became friendly, and their names appear in his writings.

Already he was beginning to provoke strong opposition, and after two or three years an unspecified conflict broke up the group. Jerome decided to withdraw into some distant country. Bonosus, who had been the companion of his studies and his travels from childhood, went to live on a desert island in the Adriatic. Jerome himself happened to meet a well-known priest of Antioch, Evagrius, at Aquileia, which turned his mind towards the East. With his friends Innocent, Heliodorus and Hylas (a freed slave of St Melania) he determined to go thither.

St Jerome arrived in Antioch in 374 and made some stay there. Innocent and Hylas were struck down by illness and died, and Jerome too sickened. In a letter to St Eustochium he relates that in the heat of fever he fell into a delirium in which he seemed to himself to be arraigned before the judgement-seat of Christ. Being asked who he was, he answered that he was a Christian. 'Thou liest', was the reply, 'Thou art a Ciceronian: for where thy treasure is, there is thy heart also.' This experience had a deep effect on him which was deepened by his meeting with St Malchus. As a result, St Jerome withdrew into the wilderness of Chalcis, a barren land to the south-east of Antioch, where he spent four years alone. He suffered much from ill health, and even more from strong temptations of the flesh.

The church of Antioch was at this time disturbed by doctrinal and disciplinary disputes. The monks of the desert of Chalcis vehemently took sides in these disputes and wanted St Jerome to do the same and to pronounce on the matters at issue. He preferred to stand aloof and be left to himself, but he wrote to Damasus, who had been raised to the papal chair in 366. However, not receiving a speedy answer he sent another letter on the same subject. The answer of Damasus is not extant: but it is certain that he and the West acknowledged Paulinus as bishop of Antioch, and St Jerome received from his hands the order of priesthood when he finally left the desert of Chalcis. Jerome had no wish to be ordained (he never celebrated the eucharist) and he only consented on the condition that he should not be obliged to serve that or any other church by his ministry: his vocation was to be a monk or recluse. Soon after he went to Constantinople to study the Scriptures under St Gregory Nazianzen. Upon St Gregory's leaving Constantinople in 382, St Jerome went to Rome with Paulinus of Antioch and St Epiphanius to attend a council which Damasus held about the schism at Antioch. When the council was over, Pope Damasus detained him and employed him as his secretary; Jerome, indeed, claimed that he spoke through the mouth of Damasus.

Side by side with this official activity he was engaged in fostering and directing the marvellous flowering of asceticism which was taking place among some of the noble ladies of Rome. But when St Damasus died in 384, and his protection was consquently withdrawn from his secretary, St Jerome found himself in a very difficult position. In the preceding two years, while impressing all Rome by his personal holiness, learning and honesty, he had also contrived to get himself widely disliked; on the one hand by pagans whom he had fiercely condemned and on the other by people who were offended by the saint's harsh outspokenness and sarcastic wit. It cannot be a matter of surprise that, however justified his indignation was, his manner of expressing it aroused resentment. His own reputation was attacked with similar vigour; even his simplicity, his walk and smile, the expression of his countenance were found fault with. Neither did the severe virtue of the ladies that were under his direction nor the reservedness of his own behaviour protect him from calumny: scandalous gossip was circulated about his relations with St Paula. He was properly indignant and decided to return to the East, there to seek a quiet retreat. He embarked at Porto in August 385.

At Antioch nine months later he was joined by Paula, Eustochium and the other Roman religious women who had resolved to exile themselves with him in the Holy Land. Soon after arriving at Jerusalem they went to Egypt, to consult with the monks of Nitria, as well as with Didymus, a famous blind teacher in the school of Alexandria. With the help of Paula's generosity a monastery for men was built near the basilica of the Nativity at Bethlehem, together with buildings for three communities of women. St Jerome himself lived and worked in a large rock-hewn cell near to our Saviour's birthplace, and opened a free school, as well as a hospice.

Here at last were some years of peace. But Jerome could not stand aside and be mute when Christian truth was threatened. At Rome he had composed his book against Helvidius on the perpetual virginity of the Blessed Virgin Mary, Helvidius having maintained that Mary had other children, by St Joseph, after the birth of Christ. This and certain associated errors were again put forward by one Jovinian. St Paula's son-in-law, St Pammachius, and other laymen were scandalized at his new doctrines, and sent his writings to St Jerome who in 393 wrote two books against Jovinian. In the first he shows the excellence of virginity embraced for the sake of virtue, which had been denied by Jovinian, and in the second confutes his other errors. This treatise was written in Jerome's characteristically strong style and certain expressions in it seemed to some persons in Rome harsh and derogatory from the honour due to matrimony; St Pammachius informed St Jerome of the offence which he and many others took at them. Thereupon Jerome wrote his Apology to Pammachius, sometimes called his third book against Jovinian, in a tone that can hardly have given his critics satisfaction. A few years later he had to turn his attention to Vigilantius – Dormantius, sleepy, he calls him – a Gallo-Roman priest who both decried celibacy and condemned the veneration of relics, calling those who paid it idolaters and worshippers of ashes.

From 395 to 400 St Jerome was engaged in a war against Origenism, which unhappily involved a breach of his twenty-five years friendship with Rufinus. Few writers made more use of Origen's works and no one seemed a greater admirer of his erudition than St Jerome; but finding in the East that some had been seduced into grievous errors by the authority of his name and some of his writings he joined St Epiphanius in warmly opposing the spreading evil. Rufinus, who then lived in a monastery at Jerusalem, had translated many of Origen's works into Latin and was an enthusiastic upholder of his authority.

St Augustine was distressed by the resulting quarrel, which, however, he the more easily understood because he himself became involved in a long controversy with St Jerome arising out of the exegesis of the second chapter of St Paul's epistle to the Galatians. By his first letters he had unintentionally provoked Jerome, and had to use considerable charitable tact to soothe his easily wounded susceptibilities.

Nothing has rendered the name of St Jerome so famous as his critical labours on the Holy Scriptures. While in Rome under Pope St Damasus he had revised the gospels and the psalms in the Old Latin version followed by the rest of the New Testament. His new translation from the Hebrew of most of the books of the Old Testament was the work of his years of retreat at Bethlehem, which he undertook at the earnest entreaties of many devout and illustrious friends, and in view of the preference of the original to any version however venerable. He did not translate the books in order, but began by the books of Kings, and took the rest in hand at different times. The psalms he revised again, with the aid of Origen's *Hexapla* and the Hebrew text.

In the year 404 a great blow fell on St Jerome in the death of St Paula and a few years later in the sacking of Rome by Alaric; many refugees fled into the East. Again towards the end of his life he was obliged to interrupt his studies by an incursion of barbarians, and some time after by the violence and persecution of the Pelagians who sent a troop of ruffians to Bethlehem to assault the monks and nuns who lived there under the direction of St Jerome, who had opposed them. Some were beaten, and a deacon was killed, and they set fire to the monasteries. In the following year St Eustochium died and Jerome himself soon followed her: worn out with penance and work his sight and voice failing, his body like a shadow, he died peacefully on 30 September 420. He was buried under the church of the Nativity close to Paula and Eustochium, but his body was removed long after and now lies somewhere in St Mary Major's at Rome.

JEROME EMILIANI (A.D. 1537)

FOUNDER OF THE SOMASCHI
PATRON SAINT OF ORPHANS AND ABANDONED CHILDREN

8 FEBRUARY

At the request of the Superior General of the Clerks Regular of Somascha, Pope Pius XI declared St Jerome the patron of orphans and abandoned children in a decree of the Sacred Congregation of Rites dated 14 March 1928.

Jerome was born at Venice in 1481, the son of Angelo Emiliani (*vulgo* Miani) and Eleanor Mauroceni, and served in the armies of the republic during the troubled times of the beginning of the sixteenth century. When the League of Cambrai was formed to resist the Venetians, he was appointed to the command of the fortress of Castelnuovo, in the mountains near Treviso; at the fall of the town he was taken prisoner and chained in a dungeon. Hitherto he had led a careless and irreligious life, but now he sanctified his sufferings by prayer and turning to God, and, in circumstances which appeared to be miraculous, he was enabled to make his escape. He made his way at once to a church in Treviso and, probably later, hung up his fetters as votive offerings before the altar of our Lady, to whom he had vowed himself; and was given the post of mayor in the town. But he shortly after returned to Venice to take charge of the education of his nephews and to pursue his own sacerdotal studies, and in 1518 he was ordained.

Famine and plague having reduced many to the greatest distress, St Jerome devoted himself to relieving all, but particularly abandoned orphans. These he gathered in a house which he hired; clothed and fed them at his own expense, and instructed them himself in Christian doctrine and virtue. After himself recovering from the plague, he resolved in 1531 to devote himself and his property solely to others, and founded orphanages at Brescia, Bergamo, and Como, a shelter for penitent prostitutes, and a hospital at Verona. About 1532 Jerome with two other priests established a congregation of men, and at Somascha, between Bergamo and Milan, he founded a house which he destined for the exercises of those whom he received into his congregation. From his house it took its name, the Clerks Regular of Somascha, and its principal work was the care of orphans. The instruction of youth and young clerics became also an object of his foundation, and continues still to be. It is claimed for St Jerome Emiliani that he was the first to introduce the practice of teaching Christian doctrine to children by means of a set catechism drawn up in the form of questions and answers. He was so unwearying in looking after the peasants around Somascha that they credited him with the gift of healing: he would work with them in the fields and talk of God and His goodness while he worked. While attending the sick in 1537 he caught an infectious disease of which he died on 8 February. He was canonized in 1767.

JOAN OF ARC (A.D. 1431)

A PATRON SAINT OF FRANCE; AND OF FRENCH SOLDIERS

30 MAY

It had been his predecessor's intention, said Pius XI in an Apostolic Letter of 2 March 1922, to declare Joan of Arc the secondary patron of France. Benedict XV had died before he was able to do so, so Pius now carries out his predecessor's wishes in the same letter in which, after recalling the devotion of the French to the Virgin Mary, he confirms the Feast of the Assumption of Our Lady to be the principal patronal feast of that country. This letter of Pius XI was reconfirmed by a decree of the Sacred Congregation of Rites dated 29 May 1962. An earlier decree of the same Congregation, dated 25 January 1952, had declared Joan to be patron of the French army.

In that same Apostolic Letter of 2 March 1922 Pius XI declared Joan of Arc to be the country's 'secondary' ('patronam minus principalem') patron because of the great admiration and veneration in which she was held as both a religious and a patriotic hero. The declaration was made very shortly after the canonization of Joan.

St Jeanne la Pucelle, or Joan of Arc as she has always been called in England, was born on the feast of the Epiphany 1412, at Domrémy, a little village of Champagne on the bank of the Meuse. Her father, Jacques d'Arc, was a peasant farmer of some local standing, a worthy man, frugal and rather morose; but his wife was a gentle affectionate mother to their five children.

Joan was very young when Henry V of England invaded France, overran Normandy and claimed the crown of the insane king, Charles VI. France, in the throes of civil war between the contending parties of the Duke of Burgundy and Orleans, was in no condition to put up an adequate resistance, and after the Duke of Burgundy had been treacherously murdered by the Dauphin's servants the Burgundians threw in their lot with the English, who supported their claims. The death of the rival kings in 1422 brought no relief to France.

St Joan was in her fourteenth year when she experienced the earliest of those supernatural manifestations which were to lead her through the path of patriotism to death at the stake. At first it was a single voice addressing her apparently from near by, and accompanied by a blaze of light: afterwards, as the voices increased in number, she was able to see her interlocutors whom she identified as St Michael, St Catherine, St Margaret and others. Only very gradually did they unfold her mission: but by May 1428 they had become insistent and explicit: she must present herself at once to Robert Baudricourt, who commanded the king's forces in the neighbouring town of Vaucouleurs. Joan succeeded in persuading an uncle who lived near Vaucouleurs to take her to him, but Baudricourt only laughed and dismissed her, saying that her father ought to give her a good hiding.

After Joan's return to Domrémy her Voices gave her no rest. When she protested that she was a poor girl who could neither ride nor fight, they replied: 'It is God who commands it'. Unable to resist such a call she secretly left home and went back to Vaucouleurs. Baudricourt's scepticism as to her mission was somewhat shaken when official confirmation reached him of a serious defeat of the French which Joan had previously announced to him. He now not only consented to send her to the king but gave her an escort of three men-at-arms. At her own request she travelled in male dress to protect herself. Although the little party reached Chinon, where the king was residing, on 6 March 1429, it was not till two days later that Joan was admitted to his presence. Charles had purposely disguised himself, but she identified him at once and, by a secret sign communicated to her by her Voices and imparted by her to him alone, she obliged him to believe in the supernatural nature of her mission. She then asked him for soldiers whom she might lead to the relief of Orleans. This request was opposed by La Trémouille, the king's favourite, and by a large section of the court, who regarded the girl as a crazy visionary or a scheming impostor. To settle the matter it was decided to send her to be examined by a learned body of theologians of Poitiers.

After a searching interrogatory extending over three weeks this council decided that they found nothing to disapprove of, and advised Charles to make prudent use of her services. Accordingly after her return to Chinon arrangements were pushed forward to equip her to lead an expeditionary force. A special standard was made for her bearing the words 'Jesus: Maria', together with a representation of the Eternal Father to whom two kneeling angels were presenting a fleur-de-lis. On 27 April the army left Blois with Joan at its head clad in white armour, and she entered Orleans on 29 April. Her presence in the city wrought marvels. By 8 May the English forts which surrounded Orleans had been captured and the siege raised, after she herself had been wounded in the breast by an arrow.

The Maid was allowed to undertake a short campaign on the Loire with the Duc d'Alençon, one of her best friends. It was completely successful and ended with a victory at Patay in which the English forces under Sir John Fastolf suffered a crushing defeat. Joan now pressed for the immediate coronation of the Dauphin. The road to Rheims had practically been cleared and the last obstacle was removed by the unexpected surrender of Troyes.

But the French leaders dallied, and only very reluctantly did they consent to follow her to Rheims where, on 17 July 1429, Charles VII was solemnly crowned, Joan standing at his side with her standard. That event, which completed the mission originally entrusted to her by her Voices, marked also the close of her military successes. A boldly planned attack on Paris failed, mainly for lack of Charles's promised support and presence. During the action Joan was wounded in the thigh by an arrow and had to be almost dragged into safety by Alençon. Then followed a truce which entailed a winter of inaction spent for the most part in the entourage of a worldly court, where Joan was regarded with thinly veiled suspicion. Upon the resumption of hostilities she hurried to the relief of Compiègne which was holding out against the Burgundians. She entered the city at sunrise on 23 May 1430, and that same day led an unsuccessful sortie. The drawbridge over which her company was retiring was raised too soon, leaving Joan and some of her men outside at the mercy of the enemy. She was dragged from her horse and led to the quarters of John of Luxembourg, one of whose soldiers had been her captor. From that time until the late autumn she remained the prisoner of the Duke of Burgundy. Never during that period or afterwards was the slightest effort made on her behalf by King Charles or any of his subjects.

But the English leaders desired to have her if the French did not: and on 21 November she was sold to them. Once in their hands her execution was a foregone conclusion. Though they could not condemn her to death for defeating them on open warfare, they could have her sentenced as a sorceress and a heretic. On 21 February 1431, she appeared for the first time before a tribunal presided over by Peter Cauchon, bishop of Beauvais, an unscrupulous man who hoped through English influence to become archbishop of Rouen. The judges were composed of dignitaries and doctors carefully selected by Cauchon, as well as of the ordinary officials of an ecclesiastical court. During the course of six public and nine private sessions the prisoner was examined and cross-examined as to her visions and 'voices', her assumption of male attire, her faith and her willingness to submit to the Church. At the conclusion of the sittings a grossly unfair summing-up of her statements was drawn up and submitted first to the judges, who on the strength of it declared her revelations to have been diabolical, and then to the University of Paris, which denounced her in violent terms.

In a final deliberation the tribunal decided that she must be handed over to the secular arm as a heretic if she refused to retract. This she declined to do, though threatened with torture. Only when she was brought into the cemetery of St Ouen before a huge crowd, to be finally admonished and sentenced, was she intimidated into making some sort of retractation. The actual terms of his retractation are uncertain and have been the occasion of much controversy. She was led back to prison but her respite was a short one. Either as the result of a trick played by those who thirsted for her blood or else deliberately of her own free-will, she resumed the male dress which she had consented to discard; and when Cauchon with some of his henchmen visited her in her cell to question her concerning what they chose to regard as a relapse, they found that she had recovered from her weakness. Once again she declared that God had truly sent her and that her voices came from God. On Tuesday 29 May 1431, the judges after hearing Cauchon's report condemned her as a relapsed heretic to be delivered over to the secular arm, and the following morning at eight o'clock Joan was led out into the market-place of Rouen to be burned at the stake.

She was not yet twenty years old. After her death her ashes were contemptuously cast into the Seine, but twenty-three years later Joan's mother and her two brothers appealed for a reopening of the case, and Pope Callistus III appointed a commission for the purpose. Its labours resulted, on 7 July 1456, in the quashing of the trial and verdict and the complete rehabilitation of the Maid. Over four hundred and fifty years later, on 16 May 1920, she was canonized.

JOHN, APOSTLE AND EVANGELIST (*c.* A.D. 100?)

PATRON SAINT OF PROTECTION AGAINST POISON; AND OF ASIATIC TURKEY

27 DECEMBER

The invocation of John against poisoning arises from the legend that, while at Ephesus, the high-priest of the goddess Diana challenged the saint to drink from a poisoned cup – which he did without incurring harm.

Much of the area which legend has associated with the latter years of the Apostle John now lies in Turkey, and a decree of the Sacred Congregation of Rites dated 26 October 1914 recognized the saint as that country's patron.

St John the Evangelist, distinguished as the 'disciple whom Jesus loved' and often called in England, as by the Greeks, 'the Divine' (*i.e.* the Theologian), was a Galilean, the son of Zebedee and brother of St James the Greater with whom he was brought up to the trade of fishing. He was called to be an apostle with his brother, as they were mending their nets on the sea of Galilee, soon after Jesus had called Peter and Andrew. Christ gave them the nick-name of Boanerges, 'sons of thunder', whether as commendation or on account of some violence of temperament (*cf.* Luke ix 54) is not clear. St John is said to have been the youngest of all the apostles, and outlived the others, being the only one of whom it is sure that he did not die a martyr. In the gospel which he wrote he refers to himself with a proud humility as 'the disciple whom Jesus loved', and it is clear he was one of those who had a privileged position. Our Lord would have him present with Peter and James at His transfiguration and at His agony in the garden; and He showed St John other instances of kindness and affection above the rest, so that it was not without human occasion that the wife of Zebedee asked the Lord that her two sons might sit the one on His right hand and the other on His left in His kingdom. John was chosen to go with Peter into the city to prepare the last supper, and at that supper he leaned on the breast of Jesus and elicited from Him, at St Peter's prompting, who it was should betray Him. It is generally believed that he was that 'other disciple' who was known to the high priest and went in with Jesus to the court of Caiaphas, leaving St Peter at the outer door. He alone of the apostles stood at the foot of the cross with Mary and the other faithful women, and received the sublime charge to care for the mother of his Redeemer: '"Woman, behold thy son." "Behold thy mother." And from that hour the disciple took her to his own.' Our Lord calls us all brethren, and He recommends us all as such to the loving care of His own mother: but amongst these adoptive sons St John is the first-born. To him alone was it given to be treated by her as if she had been his natural mother, and to treat her as such by honouring, serving and assisting her in person.

When Mary Magdalen brought word that Christ's sepulchre was open,

Peter and John ran there immediately, and John, who was younger and ran faster, arrived first. But he waited for St Peter to come up, and followed him in: 'and he saw and believed' that Christ was indeed risen. A few days later Jesus manifested Himself for the third time, by the sea of Galilee, and He walked along the shore questioning Peter about the sincerity of his love, gave him the charge of His Church, and foretold his martyrdom. St Peter, seeing St John walk behind and being solicitous for his friend, asked Jesus, 'Lord, what shall this man do?' And Jesus replied, 'If I will have him to remain till I come, what is it to thee? Follow thou me.' It is therefore not surprising that it was rumoured among the brethren that John should not die, a rumour which he himself disposes of by pointing out that our Lord did not say, 'He shall not die'. After Christ's ascension we find these two same apostles going up to the Temple and miraculously healing a cripple. They were imprisoned, but released again with an order no more to preach Christ, to which they answered, 'If it be just in the sight of God to hear you rather than God, judge ye. For we cannot but speak the things we have seen and heard.' Then they were sent by the other apostles to confirm the converts which the deacon Philip had made in Samaria. When St Paul went up to Jerusalem after his conversion he addressed himself to those who 'seemed to be pillars' of the Church, chiefly James, Peter and John, who confirmed his mission among the Gentiles, and about that time St John assisted at the council which the apostles held at Jerusalem. Perhaps it was soon after this that John left Palestine for Asia Minor. No doubt he was present at the passing of our Lady, whether that took place at Jerusalem or Ephesus; St Irenaeus says that he settled at the last-named city after the martyrdom of SS. Peter and Paul, but how soon after it is impossible to tell. There is a tradition that during the reign of Domitian he was taken to Rome, where an attempt to put him to death was miraculously frustrated; and that he was then banished to the island of Patmos, where he received those revelations from Heaven which he wrote down in his book called the Apocalypse.

After the death of Domitian in the year 96 St John could return to Ephesus, and many believe that he wrote his gospel at this time. His object in writing it he tells us himself: 'These things are written that you may believe that Jesus is the Christ, the Son of God; and that, believing, you may have life in His name'. It is entirely different in character from the other three gospels, and a work of such theological sublimity that, as Theodoret says, it 'is beyond human understanding ever fully to penetrate and comprehend'. His soaring thought is aptly represented by the eagle which is his symbol. St John also wrote three epistles. The first is called catholic, as addressed to all Christians, especially his converts, whom he urges to purity and holiness of life and cautions against the craft of seducers. The other two are short, and directed to particular persons: the one probably to a local church; the other to Gaius, a courteous entertainer of Christians. The same inimitable spirit of charity reigns throughout all his writings. This is not the place to refer to the objections that have been raised against St John's authorship of the Fourth Gospel.

The charity which he had so conspicuously himself he constantly and affectionately urged in others. St Jerome writes that when age and weakness grew upon him at Ephesus so that he was no longer able to preach to the people, he used to be carried to the assembly of the faithful, and every time said to his flock only these words: 'My little children, love one another.' When they asked him why he always repeated the same words, he replied, 'Because it is the word of the Lord, and if you keep it you do enough'. St John died in peace at Ephesus about the third year of Trajan, that is, the one hundredth of the Christian era, being then about ninety-four years old according to St Epiphanius.

JOHN THE BAPTIST

PATRON SAINT OF SPAS; AND OF MOTORWAYS

24 JUNE – THE FEAST OF HIS BIRTHDAY

The traditional association of John the Baptist with health-giving springs arose, presumably, out of John's practice of baptizing people in the health-giving (in a spiritual sense) waters of the Jordan, as recounted in the Gospel.

The modern – and as yet not officially recognized – patronage of motorways arises from the message the Gospel records John as preaching: 'Make straight the ways of the Lord'.

John's father, Zachary, was a priest of the Jewish law, and Elizabeth his wife was also descended from the house of Aaron; and the Holy Scriptures assure us that both of them were just, with a virtue which was sincere and perfect – 'and they walked in all commandments and justifications of the Lord without blame'. It fell to the lot of Zachary in the turn of his ministration to offer the daily morning and evening sacrifice of incense; and on a particular day while he did so, and the people were praying outside the sanctuary, he had a vision, the angel Gabriel appearing to him standing on the right side of the altar of incense. Zachary was troubled and stricken with fear, but the angel encouraged him, announcing that his prayer was heard, and that in consequence his wife, although she was called barren, should conceive and bear him a son. The angel told him: 'Thou shalt call his name John, and thou shalt have joy and gladness, and many shall rejoice in his birth, for he shall be great before the Lord'. The commendations of the Baptist are remarkable in this that they were inspired by God Himself. John was chosen to be the herald and harbinger of the world's Redeemer, the voice to proclaim to men the eternal Word, the morning star to usher in the sun of justice and the light of the world. Other saints are often distinguished by certain privileges belonging to their special character; but John eminently excelled in graces and was at once a teacher, a virgin and a martyr. He was, moreover, a prophet, and more than a prophet, it being his office to point out to the world Him whom the ancient prophets had foretold obscurely and at a distance.

The angel ordered that the child should be consecrated to the Lord from his very birth, and as an indication of the need to lead a mortified life if virtue is to be protected, no fermented liquor would ever pass his lips. The circumstance of the birth of John proclaimed it an evident miracle, for Elizabeth at that time was advanced in years and according to the course of nature past child-bearing. God had so ordained all things that the event might be seen to be the fruit of long and earnest prayer. Still, Zachary was amazed, and he begged that a sign might be given as an earnest of the realization of these great promises. The angel, to grant his request, and in a measure to rebuke the doubt which it implied, answered that he should continue dumb until such moment as the child was born. Elizabeth conceived; and in the sixth month of her pregnancy received a visit from the Mother of God, who greeted her kinswoman: 'and it came to pass that when Elizabeth heard the salutation of Mary, the infant leaped in her womb'.

Elizabeth, when the nine months of her pregnancy were accomplished, brought forth her son, and he was circumcised on the eighth day. Though the family and friends wished him to bear his father's name, Zachary, the mother urged that he should be called John. The father confirmed the desire by writing on a tablet 'John is his name'; and immediately recovering the use of speech, he broke into that great canticle of love and thanksgiving, the *Benedictus*, which the Church sings every day in her office and which she finds it not inappropriate to repeat over the grave of her faithful children when their remains are committed to the earth.

The Birthday of St John the Baptist was one of the earliest feasts to find a definite place in the Church's calendar, no other than where it stands now, 24 June. The *Hieronymianum* martyrology locates it there, the first edition stressing the point that this commemorates the *earthly* birthday of the Forerunner. The same day is indicated in the Carthaginian Calendar, and before that we have sermons of St Augustine delivered on this particular festival which sufficiently indicate the precise time of year by referring to those words of John reported in the Fourth Gospel: 'He must increase, but I must decrease'. St Augustine finds this appropriate, for he tells us that after the birthday of St John the days begin to get shorter, whereas after the birthday of our Lord the days begin to grow longer.

JOHN THE BAPTIST

PATRON SAINT OF JORDAN

29 AUGUST – THE FEAST OF HIS BEHEADING

John prepared for, and foretold, the coming of Jesus in the region which is now Jordan. It is understandable, therefore, that the Sacred Congregation of Rites confirmed him as the patron of that country.

John the Baptist, the preparation of whom for his unique office of forerunner of the Messiah has already been referred to on the feast of his birthday (24 June), began to fulfil it in the desert of Judaea, upon the banks of the Jordan, towards Jericho. Clothed in skins, he announced to all men the obligation of washing away their sins with the tears of sincere penitence, and proclaimed the Messiah, who was about to make his appearance among them. He exhorted all to charity and to a reformation of their lives, and those who came to him in these dispositions he baptized in the river. The Jews practised religious washings of the body as legal purifications, but no baptism before this of John had so great and mystical a signification. It chiefly represented the manner in which the souls of men must be cleansed from all sin to be made partakers of Christ's spiritual kingdom, and it was an emblem of the interior effects of sincere repentance; a type of that sacrament of baptism which was to come with our Lord. So noteworthy was this rite in St John's ministrations that it earned for him even in his own life the name of 'the Baptist', *i.e.* the baptizer. When he had already preached and baptized for some time our Redeemer went from Nazareth and presented Himself among the others to be baptized by him. The Baptist knew Him by a divine revelation and at first excused himself, but at length acquiesced out of obedience. The Saviour of sinners was pleased to be baptized among sinners, not to be cleansed himself but to sanctify the waters, says St Ambrose, that is, to give them the virtue to cleanse away the sins of men.

The solemn admonitions of the Baptist, added to his sanctity and the marks of his divine commission, gained for him veneration and authority among the Jews, and some began to look upon him as the Messiah himself. But he declared that he only baptized sinners with water to confirm them in repentance and a new life: that there was One ready to appear among them who would baptize them with the Holy Ghost, and who so far exceeded him in power and excellence that he was not worthy to untie His shoes. Nevertheless, so strong was the impression which the preaching and behaviour of John made upon the minds of the Jews that they sent priests and levites from Jerusalem to inquire of him if he were not the Christ. And St John 'confessed, and did not deny; and he confessed, I am not the Christ', neither Elias, nor a prophet. He was indeed Elias in spirit, being the herald of the Son of God, and excelled in dignity the ancient Elias, who was a type of

John. He was likewise a prophet, and more than a prophet, it being his office, not to foretell Christ at a distance, but to point Him out present among men. So, because he was not Elias in person, nor a prophet in the strict sense of the word, he answers 'No' to these questions and calls himself 'the voice of one crying in the wilderness'; he will not have men have the least regard for him, but turns their attention to the summons which God has sent them by his mouth. The Baptist proclaimed Jesus to be the Messiah at His baptism; and, the day after the Jews consulted him from Jerusalem, seeing Him come towards him, he called Him, 'the Lamb of God'. Like an angel of the Lord 'he was neither moved by blessing nor cursing', having only God and His will in view. He preached not himself, but Christ; and Christ declared John to be greater than all the saints of the old law, the greatest that had been born of woman.

Herod Antipas, Tetrarch of Galilee, had put away his wife and was living with Herodias, who was both his niece and the wife of his half-brother Philip. St John Baptist boldly reprehended the tetrarch and his accomplice for so scandalous a crime, and told him, 'It is not lawful for thee to have thy brother's wife'. Herod feared and reverenced John, knowing him to be a holy man, but he was highly offended at the liberty which the preacher took. Whilst he respected him as a saint he hated him as a censor, and felt a violent struggle between his veneration for the sanctity of the prophet and the reproach of his own conduct. His anger got the better of him and was nourished by the clamour and artifices of Herodias. Herod, to content her, and perhaps somewhat because he feared John's influence over the people, cast the saint into prison, in the fortress of Machaerus, near the Dead Sea; and our Lord during the time of his imprisonment spoke of him, saying, 'What went you out to see? A prophet? Yea, I tell you, and more than a prophet. This is he of whom it is written: Behold I send my angel before thy face, who shall prepare thy way before thee. Amen I say to you, amongst those that are born of women there is not a greater than John the Baptist'.

Herodias never ceased to endeavour to exasperate Herod against John and to seek an opportunity for his destruction. Her chance at length came when Herod on his birthday gave a feast to the chief men of Galilee. At this entertainment Salome, a daughter of Herodias by her lawful husband, pleased Herod by her dancing so much that he promised her with an oath to grant her whatever she asked though it amounted to half his dominions. Herodias thereupon told her daughter to demand the death of John the Baptist and, for fear the tyrant might relent if he had time to think it over, instructed the girl to add that the head of the prisoner should be forthwith brought to her in a dish. This strange request startled Herod; as Alban Butler says, 'The very mention of such a thing by a lady, in the midst of a feast and solemn rejoicing, was enough to shock even a man of uncommon barbarity'. But because of his oath, a double sin, rashly taken and criminally kept, as St Augustine says, he would not refuse the request. Without so much as the formality of a trial he sent a soldier to behead John in prison, with an order to bring his head in a dish and present it to Salome. This being done, the girl was not afraid to take that present into her hands, and deliver it to her mother. Thus died the great forerunner of our blessed Saviour, the greatest prophet 'amongst those that are born of women'. His disciples so soon as they heard of his death came and took his body and laid it in a tomb, and came and told Jesus. 'Which when Jesus had heard, He retired . . . into a desert place apart'. Josephus, in his *Jewish Antiquities*, gives remarkable testimony to the sanctity of John, and says, 'He was indeed a man endued with all virtue, who exhorted the Jews to the practice of justice towards men and piety towards God; and also to baptism, preaching that they would become acceptable to God if they renounced their sins and to the cleanness of their bodies added purity of soul'. He adds that the Jews ascribed to the murder of John the misfortunes into which Herod fell.

Although today's feast does not seem to have been adopted in Rome until a comparatively late period, we can trace it at an early date in other parts of the Western church. We find it mentioned not only in the 'Martyrology of Jerome' and in the Gelasian sacramentaries of both types, but it occurs in the *Liber comicus* of Toledo belonging to the middle of the seventh century. Moreover, either then or even sooner it had probably established itself firmly at Monte Cassino; and indeed we may assume that its observance was introduced into England from Naples as early as 668. As we find this special feast, as distinct from that of the Birthday of the Baptist, kept on the same day (29 August) in the synaxaries of Constantinople, it is quite likely that it was of Palestinian origin. In the *Hieronymianum* it is associated with a commemoration of the prophet Eliseus, the link being that both Eliseus and St John Baptist were believed in St Jerome's time to have been buried at Sebaste, a day's journey from Jerusalem.

JOHN BERCHMANS (A.D. 1621)

PATRON SAINT OF YOUNG PEOPLE, PARTICULARLY STUDENTS; AND OF ALTAR SERVERS

26 NOVEMBER

Given his devotion to, and his success at, his studies, John Berchmans was a natural choice as patron of 'studious youth', as he was declared by Pope Leo XIII in an Apostolic Letter of 25 March 1887. The wording of the letter, however, stressed that he was primarily patron of young people; and he has also been taken as a patron of altar servers.

John was the eldest son of a master-shoemaker, a burgess of the town of Diest in Brabant, and was born in 1599, at his father's shop at the sign of the

Big and Little Moon in Diest. He seems to have been a good and attractive child. He was most devoted to his mother, who suffered very bad health. His early education was in the hands first of a lay schoolmaster and then of Father Peter Emmerich, a Premonstratensian canon from the abbey of Tongerloo, who taught him Latin versification and took the boy with him when he visited the shrines or clergy of the neighbourhood. This rather encouraged John's tendency to prefer his own and his elders' company to that of other boys, but he entered wholeheartedly with them in their festival mystery-plays, and particularly distinguished himself in the part of Daniel defending Susanna. By the time he was thirteen his father's affairs had become straitened and there were growing brothers and sisters to be considered, so John was told that he must leave school and learn a trade. He protested that he wished to be a priest, and at length his father compromised by sending him as a servant in the household of one of the cathedral canons, John Froymont, at Malines, where he could also attend the classes at the archiepiscopal seminary.

The secular canon Froymont was a different sort of man from the regular canon Emmerich, and with him young John went duck-shooting rather than visiting shrines; he is said to have learned the difficult art of teaching a dog to retrieve, and his particular duty in the house was waiting at table. In 1615 the Jesuits opened a college at Malines and John Berchmans was one of the first to enter himself there. He studied with earnest application, continued to be an enthusiastic player of sacred dramas, and was sometimes found kneeling at the foot of his bed after midnight when asleep had overtaken him at his prayers. A year later, after some objection from his father, he joined the novitiate.

As was expected by those who knew him best, John Berchmans was an admirable novice, and throughout his ascetical notes and other writings of that time it appears that, like another holy young religious 350 years later, he kept before himself a way of perfection which he expressed in the phrase 'Set great store on little things'. His industry in writing down his reflections was remarkable, and it extended to making an analysis of Father Alphonsus Rodriguez's book on Christian perfection, which had been published less than ten years. Soon after his novitiate began his mother died (there is extant a touching letter from him to her during her last illness), and within eighteen months his father had been ordained priest and presented to a canonry in his native town. On 2 September 1618 Brother John wrote to Canon Berchmans announcing that he was about to take his first vows, and asking in a postscript, 'Please send me by his reverence the precentor, eleven ells of cloth, six ells of flannel, three ells of linen, and two calf-skins to make my clothes'. Canon Berchmans died the day before his son's profession, but John did not hear of this until he wrote to make an appointment to meet him at Malines before he set out for Rome where he was to begin his philosophy. Before leaving he wrote to his relatives expressing his astonishment and displeasure at their not having told him of his father's death, and another to his old master Canon Froymont asking him to keep an eye on his younger brothers, Charles and Bartholomew, 'whom perhaps I shall never see again'.

St John arrived in Rome on new year's eve 1618, after having walked with one companion from Antwerp in ten weeks, and began his studies at the Roman College under Father Cepari, who afterwards wrote his biography. A professor there, Father Piccolomini, testified that 'Berchmans had good talent, capable of taking in several different subjects at the same time, and in my opinion his enthusiasm and application to work have been rarely equalled and never surpassed. . . . He spared himself no labour or weariness thoroughly to master the various languages and branches of knowledge that go to make a learned and scholarly man'.

St John's success at his examination in May 1621, caused him to be selected to defend a thesis against all comers in a public debate. But the strain of prolonged study during the heat of a Roman summer had been too much for him, and he began rapidly to fail. On 6 August though feeling unwell, he took a prominent part in a public disputation at the Greek College, but the next afternoon he had to be sent off to the infirmary. He was cheerful as usual – Father Cepari records there was always a smile playing about his mouth. When he had drunk a peculiarly nasty dose of medicine he asked the attendant father to say the grace after meals, and he told the rector that he hoped the death of another Flemish Jesuit in Rome would not cause friction between the two provinces of the Society; when the doctor ordered his temples to be bathed with old wine he observed that it was lucky such an expensive illness would not last long. After four days Father Cornelius a Lapide, the great Biblical exegete, asked if aught were on his conscience. '*Nihil omnino*. Nothing at all', replied St John, and he received the last sacraments with great devotion. He lingered two more days (the doctors were at a loss to diagnose what it was that had brought him so low), and died peacefully on the morning of 13 August 1621.

There were extraordinary scenes at the funeral, numerous miracles were attributed to John's intercession, and the recognition of his holiness was spread so rapidly that within a few years Father Bauters, sj wrote from Flanders, 'Though he died in Rome, and but few of his countrymen knew him by sight, ten of our best engravers have already published his portrait and at least 24,000 copies have been struck off. This is not including the works of lesser artists and numbers of paintings'. Nevertheless, though his cause was begun in the very year of his death, the beatification of St John Berchmans did not take place till 1865, nor his canonization till 1888.

JOHN BOSCO (A.D. 1885)

FOUNDER OF THE SALESIANS OF DON BOSCO
PATRON SAINT OF EDITORS; OF YOUNG PEOPLE, YOUNG WORKERS, AND
APPRENTICES; OF YOUTH (MEXICAN)

31 JANUARY

Pius XII, in an Apostolic Letter of 24 May 1946 declared John Bosco to be patron of Catholic, and in particular of Italian Catholic, editors, citing his work not only as an author of highly popular religious books, but also his work in substituting acceptable Catholic statements for suspect passages in books written by non-Catholics.

To choose John Bosco as the patron saint of young people and of apprentices in particular arises from his work for poor children. He was formally declared patron of the apprentices of Italy in an Apostolic Letter of Pius XII of 17 January 1958, of apprentices in Colombia in an Apostolic Letter of John XXIII dated 16 October 1959, and of apprentices of Spain in an Apostolic Letter of the same pope on 22 April 1960.

He was specifically declared patron of Mexican youth by a decree of the Sacred Congregation of Rites of 26 June 1935.

Born in 1815, the youngest son of a peasant farmer in a Piedmontese village, John Melchior Bosco lost his father at the age of two and was brought up by his mother, a saintly and industrious woman who had a hard struggle to keep the home together. A dream which he had when he was nine showed him the vocation from which he never swerved. He seemed to be surrounded by a crowd of fighting and blaspheming children whom he strove in vain to pacify, at first by argument and then with his fists. Suddenly there appeared a mysterious lady who said to him: 'Softly, softly . . . if you wish to win them! Take your shepherd's staff and lead them to pasture'. As she spoke, the children were transformed into wild beasts and then into lambs. From that moment John recognized that his duty was to help poor boys, and he began with those of his own village, teaching them the catechism and bringing them to church. As an encouragement, he would often delight them with acrobatic and conjuring tricks, at which he became very proficient. One Sunday morning, when a perambulating juggler and gymnast was detaining the youngsters with his performances, the little lad challenged him to a competition, beat him at his own job, and triumphantly bore off his audience to Mass.

He was sixteen when he entered the seminary at Chieri and so poor that his maintenance money and his very clothes had to be provided by charity, the mayor contributing his hat, the parish priest his cloak, one parishioner his cassock, and another a pair of shoes. After his ordination to the diaconate he passed to the theological college of Turin and, during his residence there, he began, with the approbation of his superiors, to gather together on Sunday a number of the neglected apprentices and waifs of the city. St

Joseph Cafasso, then rector of a parish church and the annexed sacerdotal institute in Turin, persuaded Don Bosco that he was not cut out to be a missionary abroad: 'Go and unpack that trunk you've got ready, and carry on with your work for the boys. That, and nothing else, is God's will for you'. Don Cafasso introduced him, on the one hand, to those moneyed people of the city who were in time to come to be the generous benefactors of his work, and on the other hand to the prisons and slums whence were to come the beneficiaries of that work.

His first appointment was to the assistant chaplaincy of a refuge for girls founded by the Marchesa di Barola, the wealthy and philanthropic woman who had taken care of Silvio Pellico after his release. This post left him free on Sundays to look after his boys, to whom he devoted the whole day and for whom he devised a sort of combined Sunday-school and recreation centre which he called a 'festive oratory'. When the marchesa, who with all her generosity was somewhat of an autocrat, delivered an ultimatum offering him the alternative of giving up the boys or resigning his post at her refuge, he chose the latter.

In the midst of his anxiety, the holy man was prostrated by a severe attack of pneumonia with complications which nearly cost him his life. He had hardly recovered when he went to live in some miserable rooms adjoining his new oratory, and with his mother installed as his housekeeper he applied himself to consolidating and extending his work. A night-school started the previous year took permanent shape, and as the oratory was overcrowded, he opened two more centres in other quarters of Turin. It was about this time that he began to take in and house a few destitute children. In a short time some thirty or forty neglected boys, most of them apprentices in the city, were living with Don Bosco and his devoted mother, 'Mamma Margaret', in the Valdocco quarter, going out daily to work. He soon realized that any good he could do them was counterbalanced by outside influences, and he eventually determined to train the apprentices at home. He opened his first two workshops, for shoemakers and tailors, in 1853.

The next step was to construct for his flock a church, which he placed under the patronage of his favourite saint, Francis de Sales, and when that was finished he set to work to build a home for his increasing family. At first they attended classes outside, but, as more help became available, technical courses and grammar classes were started in the house and all were taught at home. By 1856 there were 150 resident boys, with four workshops including a printing-press, and also four Latin classes, with ten young priests, besides the oratories with their 500 children.

For years St John Bosco's great problem was that of help. Enthusiastic young priests would offer their services, but sooner or later would give up, because they could not master Don Bosco's methods or had not his patience with often vicious young ruffians or were put off by his scheme for schools and workshops when he had not a penny. Some even were disappointed because he would not turn the oratory into a political club in the interests of 'Young Italy'. By 1850 he had only one assistant left, and he resolved to train young men himself for the work. In any case something in the nature of a religious order had long been in his mind and, after several disappointments, the time came when he felt that he had at last the nucleus he desired. 'On the night of 26 January 1854, we were assembled in Don Bosco's room,' writes one of those present. 'Besides Don Bosco there were Cagliero, Rocchetti, Artiglia and Rua. It was suggested that with God's help we should enter upon a period of practical works of charity to help our neighbours. At the close of that period we might bind ourselves by a promise, which could subsequently be transformed into a vow. From that evening, the name of Salesian was given to all who embarked upon that form of apostolate.' The name, of course, came from the great Bishop of Geneva.

In December 1859, with twenty-two companions, he finally determined to proceed with the organization of a religious congregation, whose rules had received the general approval of Pope Pius IX; but it was not until fifteen years later that the constitutions received their final approbation, with leave to present candidates for holy orders. The new society grew apace: in 1863 there were 39 Salesians, at the founder's death 768, and today they are numbered in thousands, all over the world. Don Bosco lived to see twenty-six houses started in the New World and thirty-eight in the Old.

His next great work was the foundation of an order of women to do for poor girls what the Salesians were doing for boys. This was inaugurated in 1872 with the clothing of twenty-seven young women to whom he gave the name of Daughters of Our Lady, Help of Christians. This community increased almost as fast as the other, with elementary schools in Italy, Brazil and the Argentine, and other activities.

Any account of Don Bosco's life would be incomplete without some mention of his work as a church-builder. His first little church soon proving insufficient for its increasing congregation, the founder proceeded to the construction of a much larger one which was completed in 1868. This was followed by another spacious and much-needed basilica in a poor quarter of Turin, which he placed under the patronage of St John the Evangelist. The effort to raise the necessary money had been immense, and the holy man was out of health and very weary, but his labours were not yet over. During the last years of Pius IX, the project had been formed of building in Rome a church in honour of the Sacred Heart, and Pius had given the money to buy the site. His successor was equally anxious for the work to proceed, but it seemed impossible to obtain funds to raise it above the foundations. The task was proposed to Don Bosco and he undertook it.

When he could obtain no more funds from Italy he betook himself to France, the land where devotion to the Sacred Heart has always flourished pre-eminently. Everywhere he was acclaimed as a saint and a wonderworker, and the money came pouring in. The completion of the new church was assured, but, as the time for the consecration approached, Don Bosco was sometimes heard to say that if it were long delayed he would not be alive to witness it. It took place on 14 May 1887, and he offered Mass in the church once shortly after; but as the year drew on it became evident that his days were numbered. Two years earlier the doctors had declared that he had worn himself out and that complete rest was his only chance, but rest for him was out of the question. At the end of the year his strength gave way altogether, and he became gradually weaker until at last he passed away on 31 January 1888, so early in the morning that his death has been described, not quite correctly, as occurring on the morrow of the feast of St Francis de Sales. Forty thousand persons visited his body as it lay in the church, and his funeral resembled a triumph, for the whole city of Turin turned out to do him honour when his mortal remains were borne to their last resting-place. St John Bosco was canonized in 1934.

JOHN BAPTIST DE LA SALLE (A.D. 1719)

FOUNDER OF THE BROTHERS OF THE CHRISTIAN SCHOOLS
PATRON SAINT OF SCHOOLTEACHERS

7 APRIL

The choice of John Baptist de la Salle as patron of schoolteachers is a natural one, given his life story. It was, however, formalized by an Apostolic Letter of Pius XII, dated 15 May 1950.

The founder of the Institute of the Brothers of the Christian Schools was born at Rheims on 30 April 1651. His parents were both of noble family. From the instructions of a devout mother, the boy, John Baptist, early gave evidence of such piety that he was designated for the priesthood. He received the tonsure when he was only eleven, and became a member of the cathedral chapter of Rheims at the age of sixteen; in 1670 he entered the seminary of St Sulpice in Paris, being ordained priest in 1678. A young man of striking appearance, well connected, refined and scholarly, he seemed assured of a life of dignified ease or of high preferment in the Church.

But in 1679 he met a layman, Adrian Nyel, who had come to Rheims with the idea of opening a school for poor boys. Canon de la Salle gave him every encouragement, and, somewhat prematurely, two schools were started. Gradually the young canon became more and more drawn into the work and grew interested in the seven masters who taught in these schools. He rented a house for them, fed them from his own table, and tried to instil into them the high educational ideals which were gradually taking shape in his own mind. In 1681 he decided to invite them to live in his own home that he might have them under his constant supervision. The result must have been a great disappointment. Not only did two of his brothers indignantly leave his house but five of the schoolmasters soon took their departure, unable or unwilling to submit to a discipline for which they had never bargained. The reformer waited, and his patience was rewarded. Other men presented themselves, and these formed the nucleus of what was to prove a new congregation. To house them the saint gave up his paternal home, and moved with them to more suitable premises in the Rue Neuve. As the movement became known, requests began to come in from outside for schoolmasters trained in the new method, and de la Salle found his time fully engrosssed. Partly for that reason, and partly because he realized the contrast his disciples drew between his assured official income and their own uncertain position, he decided to give up his canonry.

Four schools were soon opened, but de la Salle's great problem at this stage was that of training teachers. Eventually he called a conference of twelve of his men, and it was decided to make provisional regulations, with a vow of obedience yearly renewable until vocations became certain. At the same time a name was decided upon for members of the community. They were to be called the Brothers of the Christian Schools.

Hitherto recruits had been full-grown men, but now applications began to be received from boys between the ages of fifteen and twenty. De la Salle, in 1685, accordingly decided to set up a junior novitiate. He lodged the youths in an adjoining house, gave them a simple rule of life, and entrusted their training to a wise brother, whilst retaining supervision of them himself. But soon there appeared another class of candidate who also, like the boys, could not well be refused and who likewise required to be dealt with apart. These were young men who were sent by their parish priests to the saint with a request that he would train them as schoolmasters, and send them back to teach in their own villages. He accepted them, found them a domicile, undertook their training, and thus founded the first training-college for teachers, at Rheims in 1687; others followed, at Paris (1699) and at Saint-Denis (1709).

All this time the work of teaching poor boys had been steadily going on, although hitherto it had been restricted to Rheims. In 1688 the saint, at the request of the curé of St Sulpice in Paris, took over a school in that parish. The brothers were so successful that a second school was opened in the same district. The control of these Paris foundations was entrusted to Brother L'Heureux, a gifted and capable man whom de la Salle designed to be his successor, and whom he was about to present for ordination. It had been his intention to have priests in his institution to take charge of each house, but Brother L'Heureux's unexpected death made him doubt whether his design had been according to God's will. After much prayer it was borne in upon him that if his order was to confine itself strictly to the work of teaching, for which it had been founded, and to remain free from 'caste' distinctions the brothers must continue to be laymen. He therefore laid down the statute that no Brother of the Christian Schools should ever be a priest, and that no priest should ever become a member of the order.

About 1695, de la Salle drew up the first draft of the mature rule, with provision for the taking of life vows. He also wrote his manual of the *Conduct of Schools* which sets forth the system of education to be carried out – a system which revolutionized elementary education and is successfully pursued at the present day. It replaced the old method of individual instruction by class teaching and the 'simultaneous method', it insisted on silence while the lessons were being given, and it taught in French and through French – not through Latin.

As early as 1700 Brother Drolin had been sent to found a school in Rome, and in France schools were started at Avignon, at Calais, in Languedoc, in Provence, at Rouen, and at Dijon. In 1705 the novitiate was transferred to St Yon in Rouen. There a boarding-school was opened, and an establishment for troublesome boys, which afterwards developed into a reformatory-school. In 1717 the founder decided finally to resign; from that moment he would give no orders, and lived like the humblest of the brothers. He taught novices and boarders, for whom he wrote several books, including a method of mental prayer.

In Lent, 1719, St John Baptist suffered a good deal from asthma and rheumatism, but would give up none of his habitual austerities. Then he met with an accident, and gradually grew weaker. He passed away on Good Friday 7 April 1719, in the sixty-eighth year of his age. The Church has shown her appreciation of the character of this man, a thinker and initiator of the first importance in the history of education, by canonizing him in 1900.

JOHN CHRYSOSTOM, ARCHBISHOP OF CONSTANTINOPLE, AND DOCTOR OF THE CHURCH (A.D. 407)
PATRON SAINT OF PREACHING, AND SACRED ORATORY AND ELOQUENCE; AND OF ISTANBUL (CONSTANTINOPLE)

13 SEPTEMBER

As John's life relates, he earned the name Chrysostom or 'golden-mouthed' because of the eloquence of his preaching. He is therefore an obvious choice to be patron of preachers, and of sacred eloquence or oratory in general. This was confirmed in an Apostolic Letter of Leo XIII on 4 July 1884, and reconfirmed in a decree of the Sacred Congregation of Rites under Pius X on 8 July 1908.

The European capital of Turkey, Istanbul, the city which once was Constantinople, was the see of John Chrysostom. He is therefore an appropriate patron, and this was recognized by a decree of the Sacred Congregation of Rites dated 7 January 1914. The same decree also included as patrons St George and St Roch.

This incomparable teacher, on account of his eloquence, obtained after his death the surname of Chrysostom, or Golden Mouth. He was born about the year 347 at Antioch in Syria, the only son of Secundus, commander of the imperial troops. His mother, Anthusa, left a widow at twenty, divided her time between the care of her family and her exercises of devotion. She provided for her son the ablest masters which the empire at that time afforded. Eloquence was esteemed the highest accomplishment, and John studied that art under Libanius, the most famous orator of the age.

According to a common custom of those days young John was not baptized till he was over twenty years old, being at the time a law student. Soon after, together with his friends Basil, Theodore (afterwards bishop of Mopsuestia) and others, he attended a sort of school for monks, where they studied under Diodorus of Tarsus; and in 374 he joined one of the loosely-knit communities of hermits among the mountains south of Antioch. He afterwards wrote a vivid account of their austerities and trials. He passed four years under the direction of a veteran Syrian monk, and afterwards two years in a cave as a solitary. The dampness of this abode brought on a dangerous illness, and for the recovery of his health he was obliged to return into the city in 381. He was ordained deacon by St Meletius that very year, and received the priesthood from Bishop Flavian in 386, who at the same time constituted him his preacher, John being then about forty. He discharged the duties of the office for twelve years, supporting during that time a heavy load of responsibility as the aged bishop's deputy.

Nectarius, Archbishop of Constantinople, dying in 397, the Emperor Arcadius, at the suggestion of Eutropius, his chamberlain, resolved to procure the election of John to the see of that city. He therefore despatched an order to the count of the East, enjoining him to send John to Constantinople, but to do so without making the news public, lest his intended removal should case a sedition. Theophilus, Archbishop of Alexandria, a man of proud and turbulent spirit, had come to Constantinople to recommend a nominee of his own for the vacancy; but he had to desist from his intrigues, and John was consecrated by him on 26 February in 398.

When regulating his domestic concerns, the saint cut down the expenses which his predecessors had considered necessary to maintain their dignity, and these sums he applied to the relief of the poor and supported many hospitals. The next thing he took in hand was the reformation of his clergy. This he forwarded by zealous exhortations and by disciplinary enactments, which, while very necessary, seem in their severity to have been lacking in tact. But to give these his endeavours their due force, he lived himself as an exact model of what he inculcated on others. The immodesty of women in their dress aroused him to indignation, and he showed how false and absurd was their excuse in saying that they meant no harm. By his zeal and eloquence St John tamed many sinners, converting, moreover many idolaters and heretics.

Not all Chrysostom's opponents were blameworthy men: there were undoubtedly good and earnest Christians amongst those who disagreed with him – he who became St Cyril of Alexandria among them. His principal ecclesiastical adversary was Archbishop Theophilus of Alexandria, already mentioned, who had several grievances against his brother of Constantin-ople. A no less dangerous enemy was the empress Eudoxia. John was accused of referring to her as 'Jezebel', and when he had preached a sermon against the profligacy and vanity of so many women it was represented by some as an attack levelled at the empress. Knowing the sense of grievance entertained by Theophilus, Eudoxia, to be revenged for the supposed affront to herself, conspired with him to bring about Chrysostom's depos-ition. Theophilus landed at Constantinople in June 403, with several Egyp-tian bishops; he refused to see or lodge with John; and got together a cabal of thirty-six bishops in a house at Chalcedon called The Oak. They proceeded to a sentence of deposition against him, which they sent to the Emperor Arcadius, accusing him at the same time of treason, apparently in having called the empress 'Jezebel'. Thereupon the emperor issued an order for his banishment.

For three days Constantinople was in an uproar, and Chrysostom delivered a vigorous manifesto from his pulpit. Then he surrendered himself, unknown to the people, and an official conducted him to Praene-tum in Bithynia. But his first exile was short. The city was slightly shaken by an earthquake. This terrified the superstitious Eudoxia, and she implored Arcadius to recall John; she got leave to send a letter the same day, asking him to return and protesting her own innocence of his banishment. All the city went out to meet him, and the Bosphorus blazed with torches. Theophi-lus and his party fled by night.

But the fair weather did not last long. A silver statue of the empress having been erected before the great church of the Holy Wisdom, the dedication of it was celebrated with public games which, besides disturbing the liturgy, were an occasion of disorder, impropriety and superstition. Chrysostom fearing lest his silence should be construed as an approbation of the abuse, spoke loudly against it with his usual freedom and courage. The vanity of the Empress Eudoxia made her take the affront to herself, and his enemies were invited back. Theophilus sent three deputies. This second cabal appealed to certain canons of an Arian council of Antioch, made to exclude St Athanasius, by which it was ordained that no bishop who had been deposed by a synod should return to his see till he was restored by another synod. Arcadius sent John an order to withdraw.

Chrysostom was suffered to remain at Constantinople two months after Easter. On the Thursday after Pentecost the emperor sent an order for his banishment. The holy man bade adieu to the faithful bishops, and took his leave of St Olympias and the other deaconesses, who were overwhelmed with grief. He then left the church by stealth to prevent a sedition, and was conducted into Bithynia, arriving at Nicaea on 20 June 404. The Emperor Arcadius chose Cucusus, a little place in the Taurus mountains of Armenia, for St John's exile. He set out from Nicaea in July, and suffered very great hardships from the heat, fatigue and the brutality of his guards. After a seventy days' journey he arrived at Cucusus where the good bishop of the place vied with his people in showing him every mark of kindness and respect.

Meanwhile Pope Innocent and the Emperor Honorius sent five bishops to Constantinople to arrange for a council, requiring that in the meantime Chrysostom should be restored to his see. But the deputies were cast into prison in Thrace, for the party of Theophilus (Eudoxia had died in childbirth in October) saw that if a council were held they would inevitably be condemned. They also got an order from Arcadius that John should be taken farther away, to Pityus at the eastern end of the Black Sea, and two officers were sent to convey him thither. They had often to travel in scorching heat, from which the now aged Chrysostom suffered intensely; and in the wettest weather they forced him out of doors and on his way. When they reached Comana in Cappadocia he was very ill, yet he was hurried a further five or six miles to the chapel of St Basiliscus.

The next day, exhausted and ill, John begged that he might stay there a little longer. No attention was paid; but when they had gone four miles, seeing that he seemed to be dying, they brought him back to the chapel. There the clergy changed his clothes, putting white garments on him and he received the Holy Mysteries. A few hours later St John Chrysostom uttered his last words, 'Glory be to God for all things', and gave up his soul to God. It was Holy Cross day, 14 September 407.

JOHN DE BRITTO, MARTYR (A.D. 1693)

PATRON SAINT OF PORTUGUESE MISSIONS

4 FEBRUARY

John de Britto, an obvious choice as patron of the missions in (former) Portuguese territories as his life indicates, was declared such by a decree of the Sacred Congregation of Rites of 11 July 1947.

It is stated that when John de Britto as a child fell grievously ill, his mother, a lady of noble family connected with the court of Lisbon, invoked the aid of St Francis Xavier and dedicated her son to him. Be this as it may, John, though he was the favourite companion of the Infante Don Pedro, who eventually succeeded to the throne of Portugal, aspired only to wear the habit of the great missionary and to devote his life to the conversion of the infidel. Born in March 1647, he made application at the age of fifteen to be received into the Society of Jesus, and in spite of much opposition he accomplished his purpose. His success in his studies was so remarkable that great efforts were made after his ordination to keep him in Portugal, but grace triumphed, and in 1673 he set sail for Goa with sixteen of his fellow Jesuits; the rest of his life, except for a brief interval, was spent amid incredible hardships and hindrances of all kinds in evangelizing southern India. He was made superior of the Madura mission and travelled most painfully on foot through all that vast region, only ten degrees north of the equator. Those who worked with him in their letters to Europe speak in glowing terms of his courage and devotion, of the extraordinary austerity of his life, and of the rich harvest of conversions which were the fruit of his labours.

From the beginning Father de Britto realized the wisdom of the method previously adopted by the missionary Father de Nobili, *viz.* of living a life identical with that of the natives of the country, adopting their dress, abstaining from animal food, and respecting in all things lawful the ineradicable prejudices of caste. To describe in detail the terrible odds against which de Britto had to contend would be impossible here, not the least handicap being the delicacy of his constitution which, in the fevers to which he was subject, repeatedly brought him face to face with death.

Many times Father de Britto and his Indian catechists were subjected to brutal violence. On one occasion in 1686, after preaching in the Marava country, he and a handful of devoted Indians were seized, and upon their refusal to pay honour to the god Siva, were subjected for several days in succession to excruciating tortures. They were hung up by chains from trees, and at another time by means of a rope attached to an arm or foot and passing over a pulley, were dipped repeatedly in stagnant water, with other indescribable outrages.

Father de Britto's recovery was deemed miraculous, and not long after he was set at liberty he was summoned back to Lisbon. Great efforts were made by King Pedro II and by the papal nuncio to induce him to remain in Europe, but he pleaded so strongly that duty called him back to Madura that he was allowed to have his way. For three years more he returned to his mission to lead the same life of heroic self-sacrifice; he was arrested and eventually put to death at Oriur, near Ramaud, by order of the Rajah Raghunatha. Father de Britto sent two letters from his prison the day before his execution. 'I await death', he writes to the father superior, 'and I await it with impatience. It has always been the object of my prayers. It forms today the most precious reward of my labours and my sufferings.' The next morning, 4 February 1693, a large crowd gathered to see the end of this teacher (*guru*) who was sentenced to die because he had taught things subversive of the worship of the gods of the country. After a long delay, for the local prince was nervous about the whole business, St John's head was struck from his body. When the news reached Lisbon, King Pedro ordered a solemn service of thanksgiving; and the martyr's mother was there, dressed not in mourning but in a festal gown. St John de Britto was canonized in 1947.

JOHN FRANCIS REGIS (A.D. 1640)

PATRON SAINT OF MARRIAGE; OF ILLEGITIMATE CHILDREN; AND OF SOCIAL
WORKERS, ESPECIALLY MEDICAL SOCIAL WORKERS

16 JUNE

*In recognition of his work among prostitutes St John Francis Regis has traditionally
been invoked to promote the sacrament of marriage among those who, in the eyes of the
Church, are in illicit relationships. For similar reasons he has traditionally been
invoked also on behalf of illegitimate children, especially with reference to their
education.*

*Because of St John's concern for the poor, the needy, those sick in hospital as well as
for prostitutes he has come to be thought of as patron of all engaged in social work, but
in particular of medical social workers.*

St John Francis Regis was born in 1597 at Fontcouverte, in the diocese of
Narbonne, of a family that had recently emerged from the *bourgeoisie* into the
ranks of the small landed gentry. He was educated at the Jesuit college of
Béziers, and in 1615 sought admittance into the Society of Jesus. His conduct
from the time he was allowed to begin his noviciate was exemplary. The first
year of noviciate ended, he passed on to follow courses of rhetoric and
philosophy at Cahors and Tournon. Whilst at Tournon, every Sunday and
holiday, he accompanied the father who served the little town of Andance,
and through the catechetical instructions he gave when the priest was
hearing confessions he gained a wonderful influence not only over the
children but also over their elders. He was then only twenty-two years of age.

In 1628 he was sent to Toulouse to begin his theology course. A companion who shared his room at this time informed the superior that Regis
spent the greater part of the night at prayer in the chapel. In 1631 he was
ordained, and on Trinity Sunday, 15 June, he celebrated his first Mass. His
superiors had already destined him for the missionary work that was to
occupy the last ten years of his life: beginning in Languedoc, it was to extend
throughout the Vivarais, and to end in the Velay, of which Le Puy was the
capital. The summers were spent in the towns, but the winter months were
to be devoted to the villages and the countryside. He may be said to have
initiated his campaign in the autumn of that same year, 1631, by a mission
which he conducted in the Jesuit church at Montpellier. Unlike the formal
rhetorical sermons of the day, his discourses were plain – even homely – but
so eloquently expressive of the fervour that burnt within him that they
attracted enormous congregations, drawn from all classes. He addressed
himself particularly to the poor: the rich, he was wont to say, never lack confessors. He would himself convey to his humble protégés any comforts he
could procure for them, and when warned that he was making himself
ridiculous he retorted, 'So much the better: we are doubly blest if we can

relieve a poor brother at the expense of our dignity'. His mornings were spent in the confessional, at the altar and in the pulpit: the afternoons he devoted to prisons and hospitals. Very often he was so busy that he forgot to take his meals. Before he left Montpellier he had converted several Huguenots and many lax Catholics, he had formed a committee of ladies to look after prisoners, and had reclaimed a number of women from a life of sin. After Montpellier he made his temporary headquarters at Sommières, from whence he penetrated into the most out-of-the-way places, winning the confidence of the people by talking to them and instructing them in their own patois.

His success at Montpellier and Sommières prompted Mgr de la Baume, bishop of Viviers, to apply for the services of Father Regis and of another Jesuit to help him in his diocese. No part of France had suffered more as the result of prolonged civil and religious strife than the wild, mountainous regions of south-eastern France known as the Vivarais and the Velay. Law and order seemed to have disappeared, the poverty-stricken peasantry were lapsing into savagery, and the nobles were often no better than brigands. Absentee prelates and negligent priests had allowed the churches to fall into ruin, whole parishes having been deprived of the sacraments for twenty years or more. A considerable proportion of the inhabitants, indeed, were traditionally Calvinist, but their Protestantism in many cases was a mere party badge, and in laxity of morals and indifference to religion there was little to choose between Catholics and Protestants. With the help of his Jesuit assistants Bishop de la Baume undertook a thorough visitation of his diocese, and Father Regis went everywhere a day or two in advance of him, conducting a kind of mission. It proved the beginning of a three-years' ministry, during the course of which he succeeded in effectively bringing back religious observance, as well as in converting a great number of Protestants.

That such a vigorous campaign should remain unopposed was scarcely to be expected, and in fact there was actually a moment when those who resented his activities were on the point of obtaining his recall. He himself never said a word in his own defence: but the bishop's eyes were opened in time to the baselessness of the charges that had been made against him. About this time Father Regis made the first of several unsuccessful applications to be sent on the Canadian mission to the North American Indians. His superiors were no doubt satisfied with the work he was doing in France, but he always regarded it as a punishment for his sins that he was not allowed the chance of winning the crown of martyrdom. So instead he extended his missions to the wildest and most desolate part of all that highland district, a region where no man went unarmed, and where the winters were rigorous in the extreme. On one occasion he was held up by a snow-drift for three weeks, with only a little bread to eat and with the bare ground for a bed.

The four last years of the saint's life were spent in Velay. All through the summer he worked in Le Puy, where the Jesuit church proved too small for congregations which often numbered four or five thousand. His influence reached all classes and brought about a very real and lasting spiritual revival. He established and organized a complete social service with prison visitors, sick-nurses and guardians of the poor drawn from his women penitents. With the help of money freely given to him by the well-to-do he set up a granary for the poor, and a refuge for women and girls who had been leading sinful lives. This last enterprise involved him in many difficulties. Evil men, robbed of their victims, assaulted him and blackened his character, whilst some of his own brethren questioned his prudence. For a short time his activities were checked by an over-timorous superior, and Father Regis made no attempt to justify himself; but God, who exalts the humble, was pleased to set the seal of His approval upon His servant by granting him the gift of miracles. Numerous cures were wrought by him, including the restoration of sight to a boy, and to a middle-aged man who had been blind for eight years. In a time of dearth, when many demands upon his granary had to be satisfied, the store of corn was three times miraculously renewed – to the utter bewilderment of the good woman who had been left in charge.

The work went on until the autumn of 1640, when St John Francis seems to have realized that his days were numbered. He had to give a mission at La Louvesc towards the end of Advent. Before doing so he made a three-days' retreat at the college of Le Puy and settled a few small debts. On the eve of his departure he was invited to stay on until the semi-annual renewal of vows, but replied: 'The Master does not wish it. He wishes me to leave to-morrow,' adding, 'I shall not be back for the renewal of vows: my companion will.' They set out in appalling weather, lost their way, and were overtaken by night in the woods. They were obliged to rest in a ruined house open to the piercing wind, and Father Regis, already completely exhausted, contracted pleurisy. Nevertheless, the next morning he managed to crawl to La Louvesc, where he opened his mission. He preached three times on Christmas day, three times on St Stephen's day, and spent the rest of those days in the tribunal of penance. At the close of the last address when he again entered the confessional he fainted twice. He was carried to the curé's house and was found to be dying. On 31 December, during the whole day, he kept his eyes on the crucifix: in the evening he suddenly exclaimed, 'Brother! I see our Lord and His Mother opening Heaven for me!' Then with the words: 'Into Thy hands I commend my spirit', he passed to his eternal reward. He was forty-three years of age. His body remains to this day at La Louvesc, where he died, and his tomb is visited by pilgrims from every part of France. It was such a pilgrimage to La Louvesc that St John Vianney, the Curé d'Ars, made in 1806: he ascribed to St Francis Regis the realization of his vocation to the priesthood.

JOHN GUALBERT, ABBOT, (A.D. 1073)

FOUNDER OF THE VALLAMBROSIAN BENEDICTINES
PATRON SAINT OF FORESTERS; AND OF PARK-KEEPERS

12 JULY

*The region in which St John founded the monastery of Vallambrosa was wild and
desolate. It was reclaimed by the monks of the monastery who turned the surrounding
countryside into parkland by planting it with fir and pine trees. It was from this that
St John came to be regarded, from medieval times, as the patron of foresters, and more
recently of park-keepers. On 12 January 1951, Pope Pius XII formally declared him
the patron of Italian foresters in an Apostolic Letter and of their Brazilian equivalents
in an Apostolic Letter of 24 April 1957.*

St John Gualbert was born at Florence towards the end of the tenth century,
the son of a nobleman. Hugh, his elder and only brother, was murdered by a
man reputed to be his friend, and John conceived it to be his duty to avenge
his brother. One day he came upon the murderer in so narrow a passage that
it was impossible for either to avoid the other. John drew his sword and
advanced upon the defenceless man, who fell upon his knees, his arms
crossed on his breast. The remembrance of Christ, who prayed for His
murderers on the cross seized the heart of the young man; he put up his
sword, embraced his enemy, and they parted in peace.

John went on his way till he came to the monastery of San Miniato, where
going into the church, he offered up his prayers before a crucifix. And as he
continued his prayer the crucifix miraculously bowed its head, as it were to
give a token how acceptable were the sacrifice of his revenge and his sincere
repentance. Divine grace so took possession of his heart that he went to the
abbot and asked to be admitted to the religious habit. The abbot was
apprehensive of his father's displeased; but after a few days John cut off his
hair himself, and put on a habit which he borrowed. John devoted himself to
his new state in the dispositions of a true penitent, so that he became entirely
a new man.

When the abbot of San Miniato died John, apparently on account of a
scandal concerning the abbatial succession, left the house with one companion in quest of a closer solitude. He paid a visit to the hermitage of
Camoldoli, and while there decided to make a new foundation of his own.
This he did in a pleasant place near Fiesole, called Vallis Umbrosa, where
with his companions he built a small monastery of timber and mud walls
and formed a little community serving God according to the primitive
austere rule and spirit of St Benedict. The abbess of Sant' Ellero gave them
ground on which to build. The saint added to the original Rule of St Benedict
certain constitutions, one of which was the provision of *conversi*, laybro-
thers, and the abolition of manual work for choir-monks. Vallombrosa was

perhaps the first monastery in which the institution of *conversi* appeared. The life of this congregation was one of great austerity, and for some time it flourished and established other houses.

St John Gualbert feared no less the danger of too great lenience and forebearance than of harshness, and was a true imitator of both the mildness and zeal of Moses, whom the Holy Ghost calls 'a man exceeding meek above all men that dwelt upon earth'. His humbleness would not allow him to receive even minor orders; he was zealous for poverty, and would not allow any of his monasteries to be built on a costly or imposing scale, thinking such edifices not agreeable to a spirit of poverty. His kindness to the poor was not less active than his love for poverty. He would have no poor person sent from his door without an alms, and often emptied the stores of his monasteries in relieving them. Pope St Leo IX went to Passignano on purpose to converse with him and Stephen X had the greatest esteem for him. Pope Alexander II testified that the whole country where he lived owed to his zeal the extinction of simony, for John's enthusiasm for the purely contemplative life did not prevent him and his monks from taking an active part in putting down that disorder, which was rife at the time.

St John Gualbert died on 12 July 1073, the only certain date in his history, being eighty or more years old. Pope Celestine III enrolled him among the saints in 1193.

JOHN NEPOMUCEN, MARTYR (A.D. 1393)

A PATRON SAINT OF CZECHOSLOVAKIA AND BOHEMIA; OF CONFESSORS;
OF BRIDGES; AND AGAINST SLANDER OR DETRACTION

16 MAY

St John was born and spent his life in Bohemia and is a natural choice as a patron of that region, now part of Czechoslovakia.

St John Nepomucen has traditionally been invoked as the patron both of confessors, and of those desirous of making a good confession. This devotion stems from the story, now recognized to be without historical validity, that he died to safeguard the secrecy of the confessional. The manner of his death – he was thrown from a bridge into the river – is the basis of much of the devotion to him.

Popular tradition held that St John had died because of the lies told about him. He is therefore a natural choice of saint to be invoked against slander or detraction.

St John Nepomucen was born in Bohemia, probably between the years of 1340 and 1350. The appellation by which he is distinguished is derived from his native town of Nepomuk, or Pomuk, but his family name was actually Wölflein or Welflin. He studied at the University of Prague which had recently been founded by the Emperor Charles IV, king of Bohemia. Later on we find him occupying various ecclesiastical posts, and eventually he was appointed vicar general to the archbishop of Prague, John of Genzenstein (Jenstein).

The Emperor Charles IV had died at Prague in 1378, and had been succeeded by his son Wenceslaus IV, a vicious young man who gave way unrestrainedly to fits of rage or caprice in which he would perpetrate acts of savage cruelty. It is said that John of Pomuk received from Wenceslaus the offer of the bishopric of Litomerice, which he refused. There seems no evidence for this, or for the statement that he was appointed almoner and confessor to the king's wife. Shamelessly unfaithful himself, Wenceslaus was intensely jealous, and harboured suspicions of his young wife, whose conduct was irreproachable. A tradition, widely credited in Bohemia to this day, attributes the martyrdom of St John Nepomucen to the resentment aroused in the king by the holy man's uncompromising refusal to reveal to him the substance of the queen's confessions. On the other hand, no mention of his appears in the contemporary documents, or indeed for forty years after John's violent death. Thereafter, history and legend became so entangled that a theory (now abandoned) was evolved whereby there were two canons of Prague, both named John, who at ten years' interval both suffered death in the same way, in consequence of differing circumstances.

The only contemporary evidence about the circumstances of St John's murder comes from a report sent to Rome by Archbishop John of Genzenstein relating to his own difficulties with his sovereign, King Wenceslaus. It is an *ex parte* statement, but even so it appears that these grave difficulties arose principally from matters of material interests about which the archbishop was willing to concede but little. It appears further that St John Nepomucen's cruel death was no more than an incident in this rather disedifying series of quarrels. He was obedient in his ecclesiastical superior, and fell a victim to the king's anger in consequence.

In 1393 Wenceslaus resolved to found a new diocese at Kladrau, in order to give a bishopric to one of his favourites. To furnish a cathedral and endowment he proposed to confiscate the church and revenues of the ancient Benedictine abbey of Kladrau as soon as the abbot, who was very old, should die. This proposal was strenuously opposed by Archbishop John of Genzenstein and by St John Nepomucen as his vicar general. Acting under instructions from them, the monks, immediately after the abbot's death, proceeded to the election of a new superior. The archbishop and his two vicars general ratified the appointment so promptly that the king was informed at the same moment of the death of the one abbot and the institution of the new. Wenceslaus sent envoys to the archbishop, who came to an agreement with them, but then, for reasons unknown, the king had one of his tempests of rage. He confronted the two vicars general and other dignitaries of the chapter and, after striking the aged dean, Boheslaus, on the head with the hilt of his sword, ordered them to be tortured: it is likely that he suspected some conspiracy against himself and wanted to get information about it. He with his own hand wreaked his fury on St John and his coadjutor Nicholas Puchnik, by applying a burning torch to their sides.

Then king Wenceslaus came to himself, and he released his victims on condition they should say nothing of his mishandling of them. But John Nepomucen was already dying of the injuries he had received, and so, to get rid of the evidence, he was made away with. His body was trussed up, 'like a wheel', his heels tied to his head; lest he should cry out a gag was forced into his mouth, and he was then borne secretly through the streets to the Karlsbrücke and cast into the river Moldau. This was on 20 March 1393. In the morning the body was washed ashore, and it was immediately recognized. It was later buried in the cathedral of St Vitus, where it still is. On the old bridge the place from which he was thrown is marked by a metal plate adorned with seven stars, in reference to the story that on the night of his murder seven stars hovered over the water.

BD JOHN OF AVILA (A.D. 1569)

PATRON SAINT OF DIOCESAN, OR SECULAR, PRIESTS (SPANISH)

10 MAY

Blessed John's most important work was possibly that of reforming the clergy of Spain of his generation. He became the central figure in a group of priests who dedicated their lives to preaching and acting as chaplains in the schools he had founded. After his beatification by Pope Leo XIII on 13 April 1894 devotion to him grew considerably. In his brief, Dilectus Filius *of 1946, Pius XII declared him principal patron of the Spanish secular clergy.*

Amongst the great religious leaders of sixteenth-century Spain, one of the most influential and most eloquent was Bd John of Avila, the friend of St Ignatius Loyola and the spiritual adviser of St Teresa, St John of God, St Francis Borgia, St Peter of Alcantara and of Louis of Granada, who became his biographer. He was born in New Castile at Almodovar-del-Campo of wealthy parents, who sent him at the age of fourteen to Salamanca University to prepare to take up law. This career, however, had no attraction for the boy and he returned home, where for three years he gave himself up to devotional exercises and austerities. Then, at the suggestion of a Franciscan who was greatly impressed by his piety, he went to Alcalá to study philosophy and theology. There he had as his master the celebrated Dominic Soto; there also he laid the foundation of a life-long friendship with Peter Guerrero, afterwards archbishop of Granada. His parents died while he was still at Alcalá, leaving him their sole heir, but no sooner had he been ordained priest than he distributed the proceeds of his inheritance to the poor. From the moment he began to preach it was clear that he possessed extraordinary oratorical powers, and when he expressed a desire to go as a missionary to Mexico, the archbishop of Seville bade him remain in Spain and evangelize his fellow countrymen. Appointed missioner for Andalusia, he laboured indefatigably for nine years in this great province. Rich and poor, young and old, learned and unlearned, saints and sinners – all flocked to hear him. Countless souls were brought by him to penance and amendment of life, whilst many were led into the path of perfection under his direction. When he preached, he spoke like one inspired and, indeed, the only preparation he ever made for his sermons was his daily meditation of four hours. To a young priest who asked him how to become a good preacher, he replied that the only way he knew was to love God very much.

By his fearless denunciation of vice in high places, he made for himself some bitter enemies who actually succeeded in obtaining his imprisonment by the Inquisition at Seville on a charge of preaching rigorism and the exclusion of the rich from the kingdom of Heaven. The accusation could not be substantiated, and his first public appearance after his release was made the occasion for an extraordinary popular ovation. When his time in Andalusia was completed, Bd John devoted himself to giving what were practically missions, in all parts of Spain but especially in the cities. Moreover, he kept up a vast correspondence with his spiritual children and other persons who desired his advice. For the last seventeen years of his life he was in constant pain which he bore with unflinching patience. Of his writings the most celebrated are a collection of his letters and a treatise entitled *Audi Filia*, which he drew up for Doña Sancha Carillo, a rich and beautiful young woman who under his direction had given up great worldly prospects at court to lead a life of prayer and solitude under her father's roof.

JOHN OF CAPISTRANO (A.D. 1456)

PATRON SAINT OF MILITARY CHAPLAINS

23 OCTOBER

The exploits of John of Capistrano outlined in the last paragraph below provide sufficient reason for his election as patron of military chaplains everywhere. This was confirmed by an Apostolic Letter of John Paul II on 10 February 1984.

John was born in 1386. From early youth the boy's talents made him conspicuous. He studied law at Perugia with such success that in 1412 he was appointed governor of that city and married the daughter of one of the principal inhabitants. During hostilities between Perugia and the Malatestas he was imprisoned, and this was the occasion of his resolution to change his way of life and become a religious. How he got over the difficulty of his marriage is not altogether clear. But it is said that he rode through Perugia on a donkey with his face to the tail and with a huge paper hat on his head upon which all his worst sins were plainly written. He was pelted by the children and covered with filth, and in this guise presented himself to ask admission into the noviceship of the Friars Minor. At that date, 1416, he was thirty years old.

In 1420 John was raised to the priesthood. Meanwhile he made extraordinary progress in his theological studies, leading at the same time a life of extreme austerity, in which he tramped the roads barefoot without sandals, gave only three or four hours to sleep and wore a hair shirt continually. In his studies he had St James of the Marches as a fellow learner, and for a master St Bernardino of Siena, for whom he conceived the deepest veneration and affection. Very soon John's exceptional gifts of oratory made themselves perceptible.

But the work of preaching and the conversion of souls by no means absorbed all the saint's attention. There is no occasion to make reference here in any detail to the domestic embarrassments which had beset the Order of St Francis since the death of their Seraphic Founder. But all these difficulties required adjustment, and Capistran, working in harmony with St Bernardino of Siena, was called upon to bear a large share in this burden. Further, he was keenly interested in that reform of the Franciscan nuns which owed its chief inspiration to St Colette, and in the tertiaries of the order.

When the Emperor Frederick III, finding that the religious faith of the countries under his suzerainty was suffering grievously from the activities of heretical sectaries, appealed to Pope Nicholas V for help, St John Capistran was sent as commissary and inquisitor general, and he set out for Vienna in 1451 with twelve of his Franciscan brethren to assist him. John's work as inquisitor and his dealings with the Hussites and other Bohemian heretics have been severely criticized. His zeal was of the kind that scars and consumes, though he was merciful to the submissive and repentant, and he was before his time in his attitude to witchcraft and the use of torture.

It was the capture of Constantinople by the Turks which brought this spiritual campaign to an end. Capistran was called upon to rally the defenders of the West and to preach a crusade. His earlier efforts in Bavaria, and even in Austria, met with little response, and early in 1456 the situation became desperate. St John wore himself out in preaching and exhorting the Hungarian people in order to raise an army which could meet the threatened danger, and himself led to Belgrade the troops he had been able to recruit. Very soon the Turks were in position and the siege began. Animated by the prayers and the heroic example in the field of Capistran the garrison in the end gained an overwhelming victory. The siege was abandoned, and western Europe for the time was saved. But the infection bred by thousands of corpses which lay unburied round the city cost the life a month or two later of Capistran. He died most peacefully at Villach on 23 October 1456, and was canonized in 1724.

JOHN OF GOD (A.D. 1550)

FOUNDER OF THE BROTHERS HOSPITALLER

PATRON SAINT OF HOSPITALS AND THE SICK; OF NURSES; AND OF BOOKSELLERS, BOOKBINDERS AND THE BOOK TRADE IN GENERAL

8 MARCH

The choice of St John as patron of hospitals and of the sick is an obvious one. It was confirmed by Pope Leo XIII in an Apostolic Letter of 22 June 1886.

In conjunction with St Camillus de Lellis, John of God was declared patron of nurses, and of any pious associations of nurses, by Pius XI in an Apostolic Letter of 28 August 1930.

In his early life, John earned a living by peddling books, and for that reason has come to be invoked by those engaged in the book trade, including bookbinders.

This St John was born at Monte Mor il Nuovo in Portugal and spent part of his youth in the service of the bailiff of the count of Oroprusa in Castile. In 1522 he enlisted in a company of soldiers raised by the count, and served in the wars between the French and the Spaniards and afterwards in Hungary against the Turks. The troop having been disbanded, he went to Andalusia, where he entered the service of a woman near Seville as a shepherd. At the age of about forty, stung with remorse for his past misconduct, he resolved to amend his life, and began to consider how he could best dedicate the rest of his life to God's service.

In Gibraltar the idea suggested itself that by turning pedlar and selling sacred pictures and books he might find opportunities of doing good to his customers. He succeeded well in his business, and in 1538, when he was forty-three, he was able to open a shop in Granada. On St Sebastian's day, which is kept as a great festival in that city, it happened that they had invited as special preacher the famous John of Avila. Amongst those who flocked to hear him was this other John, who was so affected by his sermon that he filled the church with his cries, beating his breast and imploring mercy. Then, as though demented, he ran about the streets, tearing his hair and behaving so wildly that he was pelted with sticks and stones and returned home a pitiable object. There he gave away his stock and began roaming the streets distractedly as before, until some kindly persons took him to Bd John of Avila. The holy man spoke to him in private, gave him advice and promised him help. John was quieted for a time, but soon returned to his extravagances and was carried off to a lunatic asylum, where, according to the practice of the times, the most brutal methods were employed to bring him to his senses. When John of Avila was informed of what had befallen, he came to visit his penitent and told him that he had practised his singular method of penance long enough, and advised him to occupy himself for the future in something more conducive to his own spiritual profit and that of his neighbour. This exhortation had the effect of instantly calming John – much to the astonishment of his keepers – but he remained in the hospital, waiting upon the sick, until St Ursula's day 1539, when he finally left it.

His mind was now set upon doing something to relieve the poor, and he began selling wood in the market-place to earn money for feeding the destitute. Soon afterwards he hired a house in which to harbour the sick poor, whom he served and catered for with such wisdom, zeal and economy as to astonish the whole city: this was the foundation of the order of Brothers of St John of God. John never thought of founding a religious order. The rules which bear his name were only drawn up six years after his death, and religious vows were not introduced among his brethren before 1570.

Worn out at last by ten years' hard service, St John fell ill. The immediate cause was over-fatigue through his efforts to save his wood and other things for the poor in a flood, and to rescue a drowning man. At first he concealed his symptoms that he might not be compelled to diminish his work, but he carefully went over the inventories of the hospital and inspected the accounts. He also revised the rules of administration, the time-tables, and the devotional exercises to be observed. As his disease gained greater hold it became impossible to conceal it, and the news quickly spread.

He named Antony Martin superior over his helpers, and before leaving he visited the Blessed Sacrament, remaining there so long that the masterful Lady Anne Ossorio caused him to be lifted forcibly into her coach, in which she conveyed him to her own home. He complained that whilst our Saviour in His agony drank gall, he, a miserable sinner, was served with good food. The magistrates begged him to give his benediction to his fellow townsfolk. This he was loath to do, saying that his sins made him the scandal and reproach of the place, but that he recommended to them his brethren, the poor and those who had served him. At last, at the wish of the archbishop, he gave the city his dying blessing. St John passed away, on his knees before the altar, on 8 March 1550, being exactly fifty-five years old. He was buried by the archbishop, and the whole of Granada followed in procession. He was canonized in 1690.

JOHN VIANNEY (LE CURÉ D'ARS), (A.D. 1859)

PATRON SAINT OF PRIESTS AND PAROCHIAL CLERGY

4 AUGUST

Although St John Vianney tried for much of his life to leave his parish with its cure of souls, for which he believed himself unsuitable, he was made patron saint of the parochial clergy of France by decree of the Sacred Congregation of Rites of 12 April 1905, even before he had been canonized. He was declared patron of parochial clergy throughout the world, and of all who have the cure of souls, by an Apostolic Letter of Pius XI, on 23 April 1929.

The world into which John Mary Vianney was born, at Dardilly, near Lyons, on 8 May 1786, was a disturbed one. When he was three the French Revolution began and two years later Dardilly found itself saddled with a 'constitutional priest', so the little John and his parents had to assist in secret at the Mass of any fugitive loyal priest who came to the neighbourhood. While the Terror was going on, no less at Lyons than at Paris and elsewhere, he was learning to be a herd-boy, shepherding the cattle and sheep of Matthew Vianney's farm in the meadows on either side of the little river Planches. He made his first communion, in secret, when he was thirteen, and very shortly after Mass could be offered again in public at Dardilly. Five years later he broached to his father his project of becoming a priest. But it was not until he was twenty that John Mary could get permission to leave home for the neighbouring village of Ecully, where the Abbé Balley had established a 'presbytery-school'.

His studies were a source of great trouble to him; he had little natural aptitude and his only schooling had been a brief period at the village school opened at Dardilly when he was nine. Through his name not having been entered on the roll of exempt ecclesiastical students, John Mary Vianney was conscripted for the army; he had to report at the depot in Lyons on 26 October 1809. Two days later he was taken ill and sent to hospital, and his draft for the army in Spain left without him. On 5 January, being barely convalescent, he was ordered to report to Roanne for another draft on the morrow, and, having gone into a church to pray, arrived only after it had gone. However, he set out to catch up the draft at Renaison, having still no military acoutrements but his knapsack.

While he was resting at the approach to the mountains of Le Forez a stranger suddenly appeared, picked up the knapsack, and peremptorily ordered him to follow; he presently found himself in a hut near the remote mountain village of Les Noës. He now learned that the stranger was a deserter from the army, and that many more such were hiding in the woods and hills around. John saw at once that his situation was compromising, and reported himself to the mayor of the commune. M. Fayot was an humane official and a sensible man; he pointed out to John that he was already technically a deserter, and that of two evils the lesser was to remain in refuge where he was; and found him a lodging in the house of his own cousin. His hiding-place was in a stable under a hay-loft. For fourteen months John Mary was at Les Noës. Several times he was nearly taken by gendarmes, once feeling the point of a sword between his ribs as it was thrust about in the hay of the loft. In March 1810 the emperor, on the occasion of his marriage with the Archduchess Marie-Louise, had proclaimed an amnesty for all defaulters, and early in the following year, on his brother volunteering to join up before his time as a substitute, John Mary was able to return home, a free man.

In 1811 he received the tonsure and at the end of the following year was sent for a year's philosophy to the *petit séminaire* at Verrières. He plodded on humbly and doggedly, and in the autumn of 1813 went to the *grand séminaire* at Lyons. Here John Mary made no headway at all. At the end of the first term he left the seminary to be coached privately by M. Balley at Ecully, and after three months presented himself for examination. On 2 July 1814, John Mary Vianney received the minor orders and subdiaconate. He returned to Ecully to continue his studies with M. Balley, and in June 1815 he received the diaconate (five days after the battle of Waterloo), and on 12 August the priesthood. He offered his first Mass the following day, and was appointed curate to M. Balley, to whose clear-sightedness and perseverance is due, under God, the fact that St John Mary Vianney ever attained to the priesthood.

In 1817, to the infinite sorrow of his pupil, M. Balley died, and early in the following year the Abbé Vianney was made parish-priest of Ars-en-Dombes, a remote and neglected place of 230 souls. When he had personally visited every household under his care and provided a regular catechism-class for the children, he set to work in earnest to make a real conversion of Ars, by the confessional, and by laboriously and carefully prepared sermons which he delivered naturally, but not quietly. He waged relentless war against blasphemy, profanity and obscenity, and was not afraid to utter from the pulpit the words and expressions that offended God, so there should be no mistake as to what he was talking about. For eight years and more he struggled for a proper observance of Sunday: not merely to get everybody to Mass and Vespers, but to abolish work which at times was done on Sunday without a shadow of necessity. Above all he set his face against dancing, maintaining that it was of necessity an occasion of sin to those who took part, and even to those who only looked on; to those who took part in it, whether publicly or privately, he was merciless: they must give it up entirely and keep to their resolution, or absolution was refused them. M. le Curé waged this battle, and the associated engagement of modesty in clothes, for twenty-five years; but he won in the end.

In 1824 there was opened at Ars by the enterprise of the curé a free school for girls, run by Catherine Lassagne and Benedicta Lardet, two young women of the village whom he had sent away to a convent to be trained. From this school sprang, some three years later, the famous institution of *La Providence*, a shelter for orphans and other homeless or deserted children, neither babies on the one hand nor adolescent girls on the other being turned away. Another of the astonishing circumstances of the abbé Vianney's incumbency of Ars was its becoming a place of pilgrimage even during his lifetime: and that not to the shrine of 'his dear little St Philomena', which he had set up, but to himself. People from afar began to consult him so early as 1827; from 1830 to 1845 the daily visitors averaged over three hundred; at Lyons at special booking-office was opened for Ars, and 8-day return tickets issued – one could hardly hope to get a word with the *curé* in less. For him this meant not less than eleven or twelve hours every day in the confessional in winter, and anything up to sixteen in summer; nor was he content with that: for the last fifteen years of his life he gave an instruction every day in the church at eleven o'clock.

It is not surprising that as time went on M. Vianney longed more and more for solitude and quiet. But there is more to it than that: every one of his forty-one years at Ars was spent there against his own will; all the time he had to fight his personal predilection for the life of a Carthusian or Cistercian. He left the village three times, 'ran away' in fact, and in 1843, after a grave illness, it needed the diplomacy of the bishop to get him to return.

In 1852 Mgr Chalandon, Bishop of Belley, made M. Vianney an honorary canon of the chapter; he was invested almost by force and never again put on his *mozzetta*, which indeed he sold for fifty francs which he required for some charitable purpose. Three years later he was made a knight of the Imperial Order of the Legion of Honour. But with this he positively refused to be invested, and no persuasion could induce him to have the imperial cross pinned to his cassock, even for a moment. In 1853 M. Vianney made his last attempt at flight from Ars. It is a moving story, of the old and worn-out priest cajoled back to his presbytery on behalf of the numerous poor sinners who were unable to do without him.

It is not impossible that Bishop Chalandon should have been mistaken in not allowing him to resign his cure. But such a possibility was not one which M. Vianney would entertain; he devoted himself to his ministry more assiduously than ever. In the year 1858–9 over 100,000 pilgrims visited Ars; the *curé* was now a very old man of seventy-three, and the strain was too much. On 18 July he knew the end was at hand, and on July 29 he lay down on his bed for the last time. On 3 August the Bishop of Belley arrived in haste, and at two o'clock in the morning of 4 August amid a storm of thunder and lightning, the earthly life of the Curé of Ars came to a gentle end.

St John Mary Baptist Vianney was canonized by Pius XI in 1925.

JOSEPH, HUSBAND OF OUR LADY ST MARY (FIRST CENTURY)

PATRON SAINT OF THE UNIVERSAL CHURCH; OF OPPOSITION TO COMMUNISM; OF WORKERS; OF CARPENTERS; OF DOUBTERS; OF TRAVELLERS; OF HOUSE HUNTING; OF HAPPY DEATH; ALSO OF AUSTRIA; BOHEMIA; CANADA; MEXICO; BELGIUM; PERU; RUSSIA; (SOUTH) VIETNAM; AND OF MISSIONS TO THE CHINESE

19 MARCH

Universal Church. *Pius IX declared Joseph to be patron in a decree of the Sacred Congregation of Rites dated 8 December 1870, and confirmed this in an Apostolic Letter of 7 July 1871. On 15 August 1889 Pope Leo XIII reaffirmed this patronage in an encyclical letter. The basis of this role as patron is the notion that Joseph, as the husband of Mary, was head of the Holy Family.*

Opposition to Communism.   *Joseph was invoked as patron of those who combat atheistic Communism by Pius XI in his encyclical* Divini Redemptoris *of 19 March 1937. This was basically on the grounds that he was already patron of the Universal Church, that he took care of the infant Jesus, and that he was a worker.*

Workers.   *In a discourse of 1 May (May Day and the traditional workers' 'festival') 1955 Pope Pius XII declared Joseph a model for workers, and instituted the feast of St Joseph the Worker – since somewhat reduced in liturgical status. Specifically he declared him patron of the Italian trade union ACLI (Association of Italian Catholic Workers).*

Carpenters.   *The traditional choice of Joseph as patron of carpenters follows naturally from his own profession as it is recorded in the Gospel. He is, of course, also invoked by those in similar occupations to carpenters – joiners, cabinet makers etc.*

Doubters.   *It is because Joseph doubted whether or not to take Mary as his wife, according to the Gospel narrative, that he has been invoked by those who doubt or hesitate.*

Travellers.   *Joseph has been invoked by travellers presumably on the basis of the flight into Egypt, recounted in the Gospel.*

House hunting.   *It fell to Joseph to find somewhere to stay in Bethlehem, according to the Gospel account. Presumably this is why he has been invoked by those looking for accommodation.*

Happy death.   *The traditional choice of Joseph as patron of a happy death is believed to spring from the pious belief that he died long before his son (he is not mentioned again in the Gospel after the Finding in the Temple when Jesus was twelve years old), and, dying with Mary and Jesus beside him, he must himself have had a happy death.*

Austria.   *At the instigation of Leopold I, Pope Clement X in 1675 declared Joseph to be patron of Austria, or what then constituted Austria.*

Bohemia.   *In 1665 Ferdinand III had Joseph declared special patron of Bohemia.*

Canada.   *Canada was consecrated to St Joseph in 1624.*

Mexico (and Belgium).   *Joseph was declared patron of 'New Spain', Mexico and the Philippines, in the first synod of New Spain, held in 1555. In an Apostolic Letter of 19 April 1679 Pope Innocent XI confirmed the decision of Charles II of Spain that Joseph should be patron of all the king's dominions. As far as Spain itself was concerned, James was shortly afterwards preferred to Joseph, but Joseph remained the patron of a number of the crown's possessions in the New World, and also of Belgium.*

Peru.   *Pope Pius XII granted the petition, formulated by the conference of Peruvian bishops held in January 1957, that Joseph be declared principal patron of that country in an Apostolic Letter of 19 March 1957. The Pope gives no special reasons for the choice, although he points out that the Peruvian government had previously decreed Joseph to be the country's patron in 1928.*

Russia.   *In a letter dated 2 February 1930 to his Vicar for Rome, Cardinal Pamphilj, in which he listed the outrages committed against the Church by the Soviet government, Pius XI included Joseph among the special protectors of Russia.*

Vietnam.   *The decree of the Sacred Congregation of Rites dated 11 January 1952 declaring Joseph to be patron of Vietnam refers only to the (then independent) South of that country.*

Missions to the Chinese.   *From the sixteenth to eighteenth centuries there was a particularly wide-spread devotion to Joseph, and St Vincent de Paul, for example, wished him to be patron of his Congregation of the Mission. These priests, known sometimes as 'Lazarists', entered upon the Chinese mission. Pope (St) Innocent XI declared Joseph patron of the missions to the Chinese in a decree of 17 August 1678.*

According to the Roman Martyrology 19 March is 'the [heavenly] birthday of St Joseph, husband of the most Blessed Virgin Mary and confessor, whom the Supreme Pontiff Pius IX, assenting the desires and prayers of the whole Catholic world, had proclaimed patron of the Universal Church'.

What is told in the gospels is familiar: he was of royal descent and his genealogy has been set out for us both by St Matthew and by St Luke. He was the protector of our Lady's good name, and in that character of necessity the confidant of Heaven's secrets, and he was the foster-father of Jesus, charged with the guidance and support of the holy family, and responsible for the education of Him who, though divine, loved to call Himself 'the son of man'. It was Joseph's trade that Jesus learnt, it was his manner of speech that the boy will have imitated, it was he whom our Lady herself seemed to invest with full parental rights when she said without qualification, 'Thy father and I have sought thee sorrowing'.

None the less our positive knowledge concerning St Joseph's life is very restricted, and the 'tradition' enshrined in the apocryphal gospels must be pronounced to be quite worthless. We may assume that he was betrothed to Mary his bride with the formalities prescribed by Jewish ritual, but the nature of his ceremonial is not clearly known, especially in the case of the poor; and that Joseph and Mary were poor is proved by the offering of only a pair of turtle-doves at Mary's purification in the Temple. By this same poverty the story of the competition of twelve suitors for Mary's hand, of the rods deposited by them in the care of the High Priest and of the portents which distinguished the rod of Joseph from the rest, is shown to be quite improbable.

We must be content to know the simple facts that when Mary's pregnancy had saddened her husband his fears were set at rest by an angelic vision, that he was again warned by angels – first to seek refuge in Egypt, and afterwards to return to Palestine – that he was present at Bethlehem when our Lord was laid in the manager and the shepherds came to worship Him, that he was present also when the Infant was placed in the arms of Holy Simeon, and finally that he shared his wife's sorrow at the loss of her Son and her joy when they found Him debating with the doctors in the Temple. St Joseph's merit is summed up in the phrase that 'he was a just man', that is to say, a godly man. This was the eulogy of Holy Writ itself.

JOSEPH CAFASSO (A.D. 1860)

PATRON SAINT OF PRISONERS; AND OF SPIRITUAL DIRECTORS OF CLERGY

23 JUNE

The choice of Joseph of Cafasso as a patron of prisoners is a natural one, given the fame he won through his concern for those in the gaols of Turin. It was confirmed by a decree of the Sacred Congregation of Rites of 9 April 1948.

Pius XII described Joseph as a 'model of all spiritual directors of priests' in an exhortation addressed to the Italian clergy, and he became patron of the Union of Secular Priests to the Sacred Heart by decree of the Sacred Congregation of Rites of 10 January 1948.

His birthplace was that of St John Bosco and of several other remarkable ecclesiastics, the small country town of Castelnuovo d'Asti in the Piedmont, where he was born in 1811. His parents, John Cafasso and Ursula Beltramo, were peasants in good circumstances, and he was the third of four children, of whom the last born, Mary Anne, was to be the mother of Canon Joseph Allamano, founder of the missionary priests of the Consolata of Turin. As a boy Joseph Cafasso made his mark at the local school, and he was always willing to help others with their lessons. His father sent him at the age of thirteen to the school at Chieri, from whence he proceeded to the seminary newly opened in the same place by the archbishop of Turin. He was the best student of his time, became prefect of the establishment during his last year, and was ordained priest in 1833, by dispensation on account of his youth.

After his ordination, together with his friend and fellow student John Allamano, Joseph Cafasso took very modest lodgings in Turin in order to pursue further theological studies. He soon became dissatisfied with the metropolitan seminary and with the university, and found his true spiritual home at the institute (*convitto*) attached to the church of St Francis of Assisi, founded for young priests some years before by its rector, the theologian Luigi Guala. After three years of study here Don Cafasso passed the diocesan examination with great distinction, and was straightway engaged as a lecturer at the institute by Don Guala.

When Guala asked his assistant whom to have as lecturer, the reply had been, 'Take the little one', meaning Cafasso. And that he was undersized and somewhat deformed by a twist of the spine was what was first noticed about his appearance. But his features were fine and regular, his eyes dark and clear, his hair thick and black, and from his mouth, generally lit up by a half smile, came a voice of unusual sonorousness and quality. In spite of his littleness and stoop, Don Cafasso's appearance was striking, almost majestic. His contemporaries frequently refer to St Philip Neri and St Francis de Sales when speaking of him, and they indeed seem to have been his examplars; a serene gaiety and kindness distinguished him, and St John Bosco among others remarks on his 'undisturbed tranquillity'. And so it soon became talked about that the Institute of St Francis at Turin had a new lecturer who was little in body but very big in soul. His subject was moral theology, and he was not content to instruct without educating: he aimed not only to 'teach things', but by enlightening and directing the understanding to enlighten and direct the heart, to present knowledge not as an abstraction but as a living flame to give life to the spirit.

Don Cafasso was also soon well known as a preacher. He was no rhetorician, for all that words came easily to him: 'Jesus Christ, the Infinite Wisdom', he said to Don Bosco, 'used the words and idioms that were in use among those whom He addressed. Do you the same'. And there were not wanting tendencies and teachings to be fought in colloquial words to the multitude as well as in more technical terms to the young clergy. Don Cafasso was outstanding among those who destroyed the remnants of Jansenism in northern Italy, encouraging hope and humble confidence in the love and mercy of God, and fighting a morality that looked on the slightest fault as a grave sin. And he had a big part in bringing up a generation of clergy who should at all points combat and refuse to compromise with civil authorities whose idea of the church-state relationship was one of domination and interference.

In 1848 Don Guala died, and Don Cafasso was appointed to succeed him as rector of St Francis's church and the annexed institute. He proved no less a good superior than subordinate; and the position was not an easy one, for there were some sixty young priests, from several dioceses, of varied education and culture, and, what was important at that time and place, of differing political views. Don Cafasso made of them a single body, with one heart and mind, and if a strong hand and rigid discipline played its part in this achievement, the holiness of the new rector and his high standards did more. His love and care for young priests and inexperienced curates, and his insistence that their worst enemy was a spirit of worldliness, had a marked influence on the clergy of Piedmont, nor was his care confined to them: nuns and sisters and lay people, especially the young, all shared in his interest and solicitude. He had a remarkable intuition in dealing with penitents, and people of all kinds, high and lowly, clerical and lay, flocked to his confessional; the archdeacon of Ivrea, Mgr Francis Favero, was among those who gave personal testimony to the power of healing the broken spirit that Don Cafasso exercised.

His activities, whether in preaching and ministering to all and sundry, or in guiding and educating the young clergy, were not confined to St Francis's and the institute, and foremost among the places where he was well known was the sanctuary of St Ignatius away in the hills at Lanzo. At the suppression of the Society of Jesus, this sanctuary came into the hands of the archdiocese of Turin, and in due course Don Luigi Guala was appointed its administrator, to be succeeded at his death by Don Cafasso. He continued his predecessor's work there of preaching to pilgrims and conducting retreats for both clergy and laity, enlarging the accommodation and finishing the highway to it that Guala had begun. But of all the activities of Don Cafasso none struck the imagination of the general public more than his work for prisoners and convicts. The prisons of Turin in those days were horrible institutions, whose inmates were herded together in barbarous conditions likely still more to degrade those who suffered them. This was a challenge to Don Cafasso, and one which he accepted with both hands. The best known of his converts in these unpromising circumstances was Peter Mottino, a deserter from the army who had become the leader of a particularly notorious band of brigands. Executions took place in public, and Don Cafasso accompanied over sixty men to the scaffold in various places, no one of whom died impenitent: he called them this 'hanged saints', and asked them to pray for him.

John Bosco and Joseph Cafasso first met on a Sunday in the fall of 1827, when the first was still a lively boy and the second already tonsured. Fourteen years later Don Bosco celebrated his first Mass at the church of St Francis in Turin, and afterwards joined the institute, studying under Cafasso and sharing many of his undertakings, especially the religious instruction of boys. It was Don Cafasso who persuaded him that work for boys was his vocation.

Inspiration and encouragement, help and direction, were also found in St Joseph Cafasso by the Marchioness Juliet Falletti di Barolo, who founded a dozen charitable institutions, by Don John Cocchi, who devoted his life to establishing a college for artisans and other good works in Turin, by the priests Dominic Sartoris, who began the Daughters of St Clare, and Peter Merla, who cared for delinquent children, by the founders of the Sisters of the Nativity and the Daughters of St Joseph, Francis Bono and Clement Marchisio respectively, by Laurence Prinotti, who set up an institute for necessitous deaf-mutes, and by Caspar Saccarelli, who organized an establishment for the education of poor girls. All these also may be said to have contributed to the glory of St Joseph Cafasso.

In the spring of 1860 Don Cafasso foretold that death would take him during the year. He drew up a spiritual testament, enlarging on the means of preparation for a good death that he had so often expounded to retreatants at St Ignatius's, namely, a godly and upright life, detachment from the world, and love for Christ crucified. And he made a will disposing of his property, the residuary legatee of which was the rector of the Little House of Divine Providence at Turin, the foundation of St Joseph Cottolengo. Among the other legatees was St John Bosco, who received a sum of money and some land and buildings adjoining the Salesian oratory at Turin. Don Bosco was at this time having difficulties with the civil governor of Piedmont, which was a cause of worry to Don Cafasso and adversely affected his health. After hearing confessions on 11 June he retired to bed, worn out and ill. Pneumonia developed, and he died on Saturday, 23 June 1860, at the hour of the morning angelus.

Enormous crowds attended the funeral, at St Francis's and the parish church of the Holy Martyrs, where, as was fitting, St John Bosco preached. Thirty-five years later the cause of Don Cafasso was introduced in the diocesan court of Turin; and in 1947 he was canonized.

JOSEPH CALASANCTIUS (A.D. 1648)

FOUNDER OF THE CLERKS REGULAR OF THE RELIGIOUS SCHOOLS
PATRON SAINT OF ALL CHRISTIAN SCHOOLS

25 AUGUST

In a lengthy Apostolic Letter of 12 August 1948, in which he recapitulated the saint's work for education and the difficulties he had to endure in the course of it, Pope Pius XII declared him patron of all Christian schools.

Joseph Calasanctius was the youngest of five children borne by Maria Gaston to her husband Pedro Calasanz. He was born in his father's castle near Peralta de la Sal in Aragon in the year 1556, and in due course was sent to study the humanities at Estadilla, where his virtue and religious observances were regarded with considerable disrespect by his fellow students. His father wanted him to be a soldier, but Joseph had other ideas and induced Don Petro instead to send him to the University of Lerida, where he took his doctorate in law before going on to Valencia.

He continued his theology at Alcalá, and in 1583 he was ordained priest, being already twenty-eight years old. Soon the fame of Joseph's wisdom, learning and goodness was spread abroad, and after varied experience he was appointed by the bishop of Urgel vicar-general of the district of Trempe. He was so successful here that he was sent to deal with the Pyrenean part of the diocese, which comprises the valleys of Andorra of which the bishop of Urgel was joint sovereign prince (he still holds the title) as well as ordinary. This lonely and inaccessible region was in a terrible state of religious and moral disorder, and St Joseph conducted a long and arduous visitation of which the first task was to bring the clergy to a sense of their responsibilities and obligations; on its completion he returned to Trempe and remained there until he was made vicar general of the whole diocese. But for some time Joseph had been listening to an interior call to undertake a quite different sort of work; at length he resigned his office and benefices, divided his patrimony between his sisters and the poor, reserving a sufficient income for himself, endowed several charitable institutions, and in 1592 left Spain for Rome.

Here Joseph met an old friend of Alcalá, Ascanio Colonna, already a cardinal, and for five years he was under the direct patronage of the Colonnas. During the plague of 1595 he distinguished himself by his devotion and fearlessness, and entered into a holy rivalry with his friend St Camillus of Lellis as to who should expend himself the more freely in the service of the sick and dying. But during these years St Joseph never lost sight of the work which had drawn him to Rome, namely, the instruction of young children, of whom there were so many, neglected or homeless, in the most urgent need of interest and care. He had become a member of the Confraternity of Christian Doctrine, whose business it was to teach both children and adults on Sundays and feast-days, and in so doing was brought home vividly to St Joseph the stage in which so many of the children of the poor lived. He was soon convinced that periodiocal instruction was utterly inadequate to cope with the situation, and that free day-schools for both religious and secular education was required. He therefore first of all invited the official parish-schoolmasters to admit poor pupils to their schools without payment, but they would not undertake the extra work without a rise in salary, and this the Roman senate refused to grant. He approached the Jesuits and the Dominicans, but neither order could see a way to extending its activities, for their members were already fully engaged. St Joseph then came to the conclusion that it was God's will that he should begin the work himself, single-handed if necessary. Don Antonio Brendani, parish-priest of Santa Dorotea, offered him the use of two rooms and his own services, two more priests joined them, and in November 1597 a public free school was opened.

At the end of a week the school had a hundred pupils and before long many more, and the founder had to engage paid teachers from among the unbeneficed clergy of the city. In 1599 it was moved into new quarters and St Joseph obtained permission from Cardinal Ascanio to leave the Colonna household and take up his residence on the school premises with the other masters; they lived a quasi community life and the founder acted as superior. During the following couple of years the pupils increased to seven hundred, and in 1602 another move was made to a large house adjoining the church of Sant' Andrea della Valle. While hanging a bell in the courtyard St Joseph fell from a ladder and broke his leg, an accident the effects of which were a source of lameness and pain for the rest of his life. Pope Clement VIII having made a grant towards the rent, and people of consequence having begun to send their children to the school, the parish-schoolmasters and others began to criticize it with some vehemence; complaints of its disorders were made to the pope and he directed Cardinals Antoniani and Baronius to pay it a surprise visit of inspection. This was done and as a result of their report Clement took the institution under his immediate protection. In similar circumstances the same course was taken and the grant doubled in 1606 by Paul V. But these difficulties were the beginning of trials and persecutions which beset St Joseph until the end of his life. Nevertheless during the succeeding five years the work prospered and grew in spite of all opposition, and in 1611 a *palazzo* was purchased to house it near the church of San Pantaleone; there were about a thousand pupils, including a number of Jews whom the founder himself invited to attend and encouraged by his kindness. Other schools were opened, and in 1621 the teachers were recognized as a religious order, of which St Joseph was named superior general. He did not let the cares of the generalate diminish either his religious observances or his care for the needy, the sick, and any to whom he could be of service. For ten years the congregation continued to prosper and extend, and spread from Italy into the Empire.

In 1630 was admitted to the institute at Naples one Mario Sozzi, a middle-aged priest, who in due course was professed. For several years his forward and perverse behaviour made him a great nuisance to his brethren but, having by a show of zeal gained the good will and influence of the Holy Office, he contrived to get himself, in 1639, made provincial of the Clerks Regular of the Religious Schools in Tuscany, with extraordinary powers and independence of the superior general. He proceeded to administer the province in most capricious and damaging way, harmed as much as he could the reputation of St Joseph with the Roman authorities, and at length denounced him to the Holy Office. Cardinal Cesarini, as protector of the new institute and in order to vindicate Joseph, ordered Father Mario's papers and letters to be seized; these included some documents of the Holy Office and that congregation, spurred on by Sozzi, straightway had St Joseph arrested and carried through the streets like a felon. He was brought before the assessors and only saved from imprisonment by the intervention of Cardinal Cesarini. But Father Mario was unpunished, and continued to plot for control of the whole institute, representing St Joseph to be too old and doddering for the responsibility; he managed by deceit to get him suspended from the generalate and contrived that a visitor apostolic be appointed who was favourable to himself. This visitor and Father Mario became in effect in supreme command, and St Joseph was subjected by them to the most humiliating, insulting and unjust treatment, while the order was reduced to such confusion and impotence that the loyal members were unable to persuade the superior authorities of the true state of affairs.

Towards the end of 1643 Mario Sozzi died and was succeeded by Father

271

Cherubini, who pursued the same policy. St Joseph bore these trials with marvellous patience, urging the order to obey his persecutors for they were *de facto* in authority, and on one occasion sheltering Cherubini from the violent opposition of some of the younger fathers who were indignant at his treachery. The Holy See had some time previously set up a commission of cardinals to look into the whole matter, and at length in 1645 it ordered the reinstatement of St Joseph as superior general; this announcement was received with great joy but led at once to renewed efforts on the part of the malcontents, who had the support of an aggrieved female relative of the pope. They were successful, and in 1646 Pope Innocent X published a brief of which the effect was to make the Clerks Regular of the Religious Schools simply a society of priests subject to their respective bishops. Thus in his ninetieth year St Joseph saw the apparent overturning of all his work by the authority to which he was so greatly devoted and the indirect disgrace of himself before the world; when the news was brought to him he simply murmured, 'The Lord gave and the Lord hath taken away. Blessed be the name of the Lord'.

The business of drawing up new constitutions and regulations for the shattered institute of Religious Schools was entrusted to Father Cherubini, but within a few months he was convicted by the auditors of the Rota of the maladministration of the Nazarene College, of which he was rector. He retired from Rome in disgrace, but returned in the following year to die, repentant of the part he had played and reconciled to St Joseph, who consoled him on his death-bed. A few months later, on 25 August, 1648, St Joseph himself died, and was buried in the church of San Pantaleone; he was ninety-two years old.

The failure of St Joseph's foundation was only apparent. Its suppression was strongly objected to in several places, and it was reconstituted with simple vows in 1656 and restored as a religious order in 1669. Today the Clerks Regular of the Religious Schools (commonly called Piarists or Scolopi) flourish in various parts of the world.

JOSEPH OF ARIMATHEA (FIRST CENTURY)

PATRON SAINT OF GRAVE-DIGGERS, COFFIN-BEARERS, PALLBEARERS AND CEMETERY KEEPERS OR CARETAKERS; ALSO OF TIN MINERS

17 MARCH

In the light of Joseph's involvement with the burial of Christ, it is understandable that he should have been taken as patron by all those concerned with the care of the dead, especially grave diggers, coffin-bearers and cemetery keepers and caretakers.

Joseph was, according to one legend current in England, a tin merchant and uncle of Jesus. On one of his visits to the tin mines of south-west Britain, the story goes on, he brought Jesus with him – and planted the bush at Glastonbury which is reputed to flower on Christmas Day.

We know nothing authentically of St Joseph of Arimathea beyond what is recorded in the Gospels. He is mentioned by all four evangelists and we learn from them that he was a disciple of our Lord, but 'secretly, for fear of the Jews'. He was 'a counsellor, a good and just man'. He had not taken any part in the vote of the Sanhedrin against Jesus and 'was himself looking for the kingdom of God'. The scenes beside the cross would seem to have given him courage, so 'he went in boldly to Pilate and begged for the body of Jesus'. Having obtained his request, he bought fine linen, and wrapping the body therein he laid Him in a sepulchre which was hewed out of the rock and in which 'never yet any man had been laid'. History has no more to tell us about Joseph, but the apocryphal gospels, and in particular that fuller redaction of the 'Gospel of Nicodemus', which was originally known as the 'Acts of Pilate', contain further references, but of a legendary kind.

But the most astonishing of the legends associated with the name of Joseph of Arimathea is of much later date. It was at one time supposed that William of Malmesbury in his *De Antiqitate Glastoniensis Ecclesiae* (*c.* 1130) was already familiar with the story of the coming of this Joseph to Glastonbury. This, however, has been shown to be an error. It was not until more than a century later that a chapter by another hand, embodying this fiction, was prefixed to William's book. Here at last we are told how, when St Philip the Apostle was preaching the gospel in Gaul, he was accompanied by Joseph of Arimathea, who was his devoted disciple. St Philip sent over to England twelve of the clerics in his company and placed them all under Joseph's direction. The king in Britain to whom they addressed themselves would not accept their Christian teaching, but he gave them an island, Yniswitrin, afterwards known as Glastonbury, in the midst of the swamps, and there at the bidding of the archangel Gabriel they built a church of wattles in honour of our Blessed Lady, thirty-one years after the passion of Jesus Christ and fifteen after the assumption of the Blessed Virgin. This tale, before the end of the fourteenth century, is found very much developed in John of Glastonbury's history of the abbey. John informs us that besides St Philip's twelve disciples, no less than one hundred and fifty other persons, men and women, came from France to Britain to spread the gospel and that at our Lord's command all of them crossed the sea borne upon the shirt of Josephes, the son of Joseph of Arimathea, on the night of our Saviour's resurrection, and reached land in the morning. They were afterwards imprisoned by the 'king of North Wales', but, on being released, St Joseph, Josephes and ten others were permitted to occupy the isle of Yniswitrin, which is here identified not only with Glastonbury but also with Avalon. Here, as previously stated, the chapel of wattles was built, and in due course St Joseph of Arimathea was buried there.

Neither in Bede, Gildas, Nennius, Geoffrey of Monmouth, the authentic William of Malmesbury nor any other chronicler for eleven hundred years do we find any trace of the supposed coming of Joseph of Arimathea to Glastonbury. Not even in the legend as presented by John of Glastonbury about the year 1400 is mention made of the Holy Grail, though this is so conspicuously associated with Joseph and his son Josephes in the Grail romances. On the other hand, much is made by the later Glastonbury writers of two silver cruets which Joseph is supposed to have brought with him, one containing the blood and the other the sweat of our Saviour. But when this legend did obtain currency towards the close of the fourteenth century, it was enthusiastically adopted as a sort of national credential, and at the Councils of Constance (1417) and of Basle (1434) the English representatives claimed precedence on the ground that Britain had accepted the teaching of Christianity before any other country of the West.

JOSEPH OF CUPERTINO (A.D. 1663)

PATRON SAINT OF STUDENTS, AND EXAMINATION OR DEGREE CANDIDATES; ALSO OF FLYING AND AVIATION; AND OF ASTRONAUTS

18 SEPTEMBER

The saint's remarkable reputation for levitation, mentioned in his life, is the reason why he has popularly been regarded as the patron of all those engaged in aviation, and hence astronauts.

St Joseph's own very considerable problems with his studies on the way to his ordination is the reason why he has traditionally been taken as a patron saint of students, and especially of candidates for examinations.

Joseph Desa was born 17 June 1603, at Cupertino, a small village between Brindisi and Otranto. His parents were so poor that Joseph himself was born in a shed at the back of the house: his father, a carpenter, was unable to pay his debts and the home was being sold up. His childhood was unhappy. His widowed mother looked on him as a nuisance and a burden, and treated him with great severity, and he developed an extreme absentmindedness and inertia. He would forget his meals, and when reminded of them say simply, 'I forgot', and wander open-mouthed in an aimless way about the village so that he earned the nick-name of 'Boccaperta', the gaper. He had a hot temper, which made him more unpopular, but was exemplary and even precocious in his religious duties. When the time came for him to try and earn his own living, Joseph was bound apprentice to a shoemaker, which trade he applied himself to for some time, but without any success. When he was seventeen he presented himself to be received amongst the Conventual Franciscans, but they refused to have him. Then he went to the Capuchins, and they took him as a lay brother; but after eight months he was dismissed as unequal to the duties of the order.

Joseph then turned for help to a wealthy uncle, who curtly refused to aid an obvious good-for-nothing, and the young man returned home in despair and misery. His mother was not at all pleased to see him on her hands again and used her influence with her brother, a Conventual Franciscan, to have him accepted by the friars of his order at Grottella as a servant. He was given a tertiary habit and put to work in the stables. A change then seems to have come over Joseph; he was more successful in his duties, and his humility, his sweetness, his love of mortification and penance gained him so much regard that in 1625 it was resolved he should be admitted amongst the religious of the choir, that he might qualify himself for holy orders. Joseph therefore began his novitiate, and his virtues rendered him an object of admiration; but his lack of progress in studies was also remarked.

After having received the priesthood in 1628 he passed five years without tasting bread or wine, and the herbs he ate on Fridays were so distasteful that only himself could use them. His fast in Lent was so rigorous that he took no nourishment except on Thursdays and Sundays, and he spent the hours devoted to manual work in those simple household and routine duties which he knew were, humanly speaking, all he was fitted to undertake. From the time of his ordination St Joseph's life was one long succession of ecstasies, miracles of healing and supernatural happenings on a scale not paralleled in the reasonably authenticated life of any other saint.

During the seventeen years he remained at Grottella over seventy occasions are recorded of his levitation, the most marvellous being when the friars were building a calvary. The middle cross of the group was thirty-six feet high and correspondingly heavy, defying the efforts of ten men to lift it. St Joseph is said to have 'flown' seventy yards from the door of the house to the cross, picked it up in his arms 'as if it were a straw', and deposited it in its place. This staggering feat is not attested by an eye-witness, and, in common with most of his earlier marvels, was recorded only after his death, when plenty of time had elapsed in which events could be exaggerated and legends arise. But, whatever their exact nature and extent, the daily life of St Joseph was surrounded by such disturbing phenomena that for thirty-five years he was not allowed to celebrate Mass in public, to keep choir, to take his meals with his brethren, or to attend processions and other public functions.

There were not wanting persons to whom these manifestations were an offence, and when St Joseph attracted crowds about him as he travelled in the province of Bari, he was denounced. The vicar general carried the complaint to the inquisitors of Naples, and Joseph was ordered to appear. The heads of his accusation being examined, the inquisitors could find nothing worthy of censure, but did not discharge him; instead they sent him to Rome to his minister general, who received him at first with harshness, but he became impressed by St Joseph's innocent and humble bearing and he took him to see the pope, Urban VIII. The saint went into ecstasy at the sight of the vicar of Christ, and Urban declared that if Joseph should die before himself he would give evidence of the miracle to which he had been a witness. It was decided to send Joseph to Assisi, where again he was treated by his superiors with considerable severity, they at least pretending to regard him as a hypocrite. He arrived at Assisi in 1639, and remained there thirteen years. At first he suffered many trials, both interior and exterior. God seemed to have abandoned him; his religious exercises were accompanied with a spiritual dryness that afflicted him exceedingly and terrible temptations cast him into so deep a melancholy that he scarce dare lift up his eyes. The minister general, being informed, called him to Rome, and having kept him there three weeks he sent him back to Assisi. The saint on his way to Rome experienced a return of those heavenly consolations which had been withdrawn from him.

In 1653, for reasons which are not known, the Inquisition of Perugia was instructed to remove St Joseph from the care of his own order and put him in charge of Capuchins at at lonely friary among the hills of Pietrarossa, where he was to live in the strictest seclusion. In effect, he had gone to prison. He was not allowed to leave the convent enclosure, to speak to anyone but the friars, to write or to receive letters; he was completely cut off from the world. But soon his whereabouts were discovered and pilgrims flocked to the place; whereupon he was spirited away to lead the same sort of life with the Capuchins of Fossombrone. The rest of his life was spent like this. When in 1655 the chapter general of the Conventual Franciscans asked for the return of their saint to Assisi, Pope Alexander VII replied that one St Francis at Assisi was enough, but in 1657 he was allowed to go to the Conventual house at Osimo. Here the seclusion was, however, even more strict, and only selected religious were allowed to visit him in his cell. But all this time, and till the end, supernatural manifestations were his daily portion: he was in effect deserted by man but God was ever more clearly with him. He fell sick on 10 August 1663, and knew that his end was at hand; five weeks later he died, at the age of sixty. He was canonized in 1767.

JOSEPH OF LEONESSA (A.D. 1612)

PATRON SAINT OF CAPUCHIN MISSIONS TO TURKEY

4 FEBURARY

The choice of Joseph of Leonessa as patron of the Capuchin missions to Turkey follows naturally from the story of his life, but it was confirmed by Pius XII in an Apostolic Letter of 12 January 1952.

This saint was born in 1556 at Leonessa in Umbria, and at the age of eighteen made his profession as a Capuchin friar in his native town, taking the name of Joseph, whereas he had previously been called Eufranio. He was humble, obedient and mortified to a heroic degree, and three days of the week he took no other sustenance but bread and water. He generally preached with a crucifix in his hand, and the fire of his words kindled a flame in the hearts of his hearers. In 1587 he was sent to Turkey as a missioner among the Christians in Pera, a suburb of Constantinople. There he encouraged and served the Christian galley-slaves with wonderful devotion, especially during a virulent pestilence in which he himself caught the infection, though he afterwards recovered.

Joseph was twice imprisoned, and the second time he was condemned to a cruel death. He was hung on a gibbet by one hand which was pierced with a sharp hook at the end of a chain, and was suspended by one foot in the same way. However, after he had been thus tortured for many hours, he was released and his sentence commuted to banishment. He landed in Venice and, after an absence of two years, arrived back at Leonessa, where he resumed his labours with extraordinary zeal. Towards the end of his life he suffered greatly from cancer, for the removal of which he underwent two operations without the least groan or complaint, holding all the while a crucifix on which he kept his eyes fixed. When it was suggested before the operation that he should be bound, he pointed to the crucifix saying, 'This is the strongest bond; this will hold me better than any cords could do'. The operation proving unsuccessful, St Joseph, died happily on 4 February 1612, at the age of fifty-eight. He was canonized in 1745.

JUDE, APOSTLE (FIRST CENTURY)

A PATRON SAINT OF THOSE IN DESPERATE, OR HOPELESS, SITUATIONS

28 OCTOBER

Prayer to Jude, as a patron of those in desperate, or hopeless, situations is a very common practice, but it is not easily explained. One possible reason is the similarity of Jude's name with that of Judas, the disciple who betrayed Jesus. As a consequence of the similarity no one invoked him for anything – except when all else failed!

The apostle Jude (Judas), also called Thaddeus (or Lebbeus), 'the brother of James', is usually regarded as the brother of St James the Less. It is not known when and by what means he became a disciple of Christ, nothing having been said of him in the gospels before we find him enumerated among the apostles. After the Last Supper, when Christ promised to manifest Himself to His hearers, St Jude asked Him why He did not manifest Himself to the rest of the world; and Christ answered that He and the Father would visit all those who love Him, 'we will come to him, and will make our abode with him' (John xiv 22–23). The history of St Jude after our Lord's ascension and the descent of the Holy Spirit is as unknown as that of St Simon. Jude's name is borne by one of the canonical epistles, which has much in common with the second epistle of St Peter. It is not addressed to any particular church or person, and in it he urges the faithful to 'contend earnestly for the faith once delivered to the saints. For certain men are secretly entered in . . . ungodly men, turning the grace of our Lord God into riotousness, and denying the only sovereign ruler and our Lord Jesus Christ'.

St Jude Thaddeus has often been confounded with the St Thaddeus of the Abgar legend, and made to die in peace at Bairut or Edesa. According to a Western tradition he was martyred with St Simon in Persia. Eusebius quotes a story that two grandsons of St Jude, Zoker and James, were brought before the Emperor Domitian, who had been alarmed by the report that they were of the royal house of David. But when he saw they were poor, hard-working peasants, and heard that the kingdom for which they looked was not of this world, he dismissed them with contempt.

JUSTIN, MARTYR (*c*. A.D. 165)

PATRON SAINT OF PHILOSOPHERS AND PHILOSOPHY; OF APOLOGISTS

1 JUNE

The choice of Justin as patron of philosophers is a traditional one, and follows directly from the story of his life.

Pre-eminent amongst those who suffered death for the faith in the reign of Marcus Aurelius stands the layman who has become famous as St Justin Martyr, the first great Christian apologist known to us by works of any considerable length. His own writings give us interesting particulars of his early life, including the circumstances which led to his conversion. He tells us that he was in one sense a Samaritan, being a native of Flavia Neapolis (Nablus, near the ancient Sichem), but he knew no Hebrew and his parents, who were pagans, seem to have been of Greek origin. They were able to give their son a liberal education, of which he took full advantage, devoting himself specially to rhetoric and to reading poetry and history. Afterwards a thirst for knowledge induced him to apply himself to philosophy. For some time he studied the system of the Stoics, but abandoned it when he found that it could teach him nothing about God. A peripatetic master to whom he next addressed himself disgusted him at the outset by his eager demand for fees. In the school of Pythagoras he was told that a preliminary knowledge of music, geometry and astronomy would be required, but an eminent Platonist undertook to lead him to the science of God. One day, as he was walking in a field near the sea-shore – perhaps at Ephesus – pondering one of Plato's maxims, he turned round and saw, following in his wake, a venerable-looking old man with whom he soon found himself discussing the problem uppermost in his mind. The stranger aroused his interest by telling him of a philosophy nobler and more satisfying than any he had hitherto studied. It was one which had been revealed by God to the Hebrew prophets of old and had reached its consummation in Jesus Christ. He concluded by urging the young man to pray fervently that the doors of light might be opened to allow him to obtain the knowledge which God alone can give. The old man's words inspired Justin with a desire to study the Scriptures and to know more about the Christians. He seems to have been about thirty when he actually embraced the Christian faith, but we know neither the date nor the scene of his baptism. Probably it was at Ephesus or at Alexandria, which he is known to have visited.

Up to this period, although there had been a few Christian apologists, very little was known to the outside world about the beliefs and practices of the followers of our Lord. The early Christians, many of whom were simple and unlearned, were satisfied to bear misrepresentation in order to protect their sacred mysteries from profanation. Justin, on the other hand, was convinced from his own experience that there were many who would gladly accept Christianity if it were properly expounded to them. Moreover, to quote his own words, 'It is our duty to make known our doctrine, lest we incur the guilt and the punishment of those who have sinned through ignorance'. Consequently, in his oral teaching as well as in his writings, he set forth the faith of the Christians and described what took place at their meetings. Still wearing the cloak of a philosopher, he appears to have travelled in various lands where he held disputations with pagans, heretics and Jews, but eventually he came to Rome. Here he argued in public with a Cynic called Crescens whom he convicted of ignorance as well as of wilful misrepresentation. It is thought that it was mainly through the efforts of Crescens, of whose enmity he was well aware, that Justin was apprenhended during a second visit to Rome. After a bold confession followed by refusal to sacrifice to the gods, he was condemned to be beheaded. With him perished six other Christians, five men and one woman. The exact date of their execution is not recorded, but St Justin is commemorated in the Roman martyrology on 14 April, the day following the feast of St Carpus, whose name immediately precedes his in the Chronicle of Eusebius.

LEBUIN, OR LIAFWINE (c. A.D. 773)

PATRON SAINT OF THE DYING

12 NOVEMBER

Many saints wre invoked by those on the point of death in medieval times. Lebuin was one of them, but there seems to be no particular reason for this choice.

This saint was by birth an Englishman, called in his own tongue Liafwine, and became a monk in the monastery of Ripon where he was promoted to priest's orders. That he might employ his talent for the salvation of souls, he went over into lower Germany sometime after 754, where several English missionaries were planting the gospel, and he addressed himself to St Gregory, vicar at Utrecht for that diocese. This holy man received him with joy, and sent him with St Marchelm (Marculf) to carry the gospel into the country now called Overyssel. St Lebuin was joyfully received by a lady named Abachilda and, many being converted, they built a chapel on the west bank of the river near Deventer; later a church and residence were built on the other bank, at Deventer itself. But many shut their ears to the truth, from whom the saint had much to suffer; he seemed to gather greater courage from persecutions and continued his work until his enemies allied themselves with the Westphalian Saxons, burned down his church, and scattered his Frisian converts.

These Saxons used to hold a yearly assembly at Marklo, upon the river Weser, to deliberate on the affairs of their nation, and St Lebuin determined to brave them thereat. Clothed in his priestly vestments, he entered the assembly, holding a cross and a gospel-book. And he cried to them with a loud voice, saying, 'Hear me, all of you! Listen to God who speaks to you by my mouth. Know that the Lord, the Maker of the heavens, the earth and all things, is the only true God'. They stopped to listen, and he went on, affirming that their gods were powerless dead things and that he had been sent by the Lord of Heaven to promise them His peace and His salvation if they would acknowledge Him and receive baptism. But if they refused he threatened (perhaps a little tactlessly) that they should be speedily destroyed by a prince whom God in His wrath would raise up against them. Whereupon many of the Saxons ran to the hedges and plucked up sharp stakes to murder him. But one in authority cried out that they had often received with respect ambassadors from men; much more ought they to honour an ambassador from a god who was so powerful that his messenger had escaped from their hands, as Lebuin had done. This impressed the barbarians and it was agreed that he should be permitted to travel and preach where he pleased. St Lebuin after this heroic venture returned to Deventer and continued his work till he died.

LEONARD OF NOBLAC (SIXTH CENTURY?)

PATRON SAINT OF CHILDBIRTH; OF PRISONERS; AND OF THOSE IN DANGER FROM BRIGANDS, ROBBERS AND THIEVES

6 NOVEMBER

The choice of Leonard as patron of women about to give birth follows from the story of Clovis's wife which is narrated below.

According to legend, Clovis promised to free every captive whom Leonard could visit. Perhaps in memory of that, in 1103 Bohemund, Prince of Antioch, came on pilgrimage to Noblac after his release from Moslem capitivity. The invocation of Leonard by those in danger from brigands may stem from the fact that, because he was able to free them from captivity, he was responsible for their being a danger to the public!

Although he was one of the most 'popular' saints of western Europe in the later Middle Ages, nothing is heard of this St Leonard before the eleventh century, when a life of him was written, upon which, however, no reliance can be put. According to it he was a Frankish nobleman who was converted to the faith by St Remigius. Clovis I was his godfather, and offered St Leonard a bishopric, which he refused. He went into the country of Orleans, to the monastery of Micy, where he took the religious habit and lived until, aspiring after a closer solitude, he chose for his retirement a forest not far from Limoges. Here he built himself a cell, lived on vegetables and fruit, and had for some time no witness of his penance and virtues but God alone. One day Clovis came hunting in that forest and his queen was there brought to bed by a difficult labour. By the prayers of St Leonard she was safely delivered, and the king in gratitude gave him as much land as he could ride round in a night on his donkey. Leonard formed a community, which in succeeding times became a flourishing monastery, first called the abbey of Noblac and now identified as the town of Saint-Léonard. From it the saint evangelized the surrounding neighbourhood, and died there, it is said, about the middle of the sixth century, revered for his holiness and miracles.

LEONARD OF PORT MAURICE (A.D. 1751)

PATRON SAINT OF MISSIONERS IN CATHOLIC LANDS

26 NOVEMBER

The account of his life is indication enough why St Leonard should be chosen as patron of those who attempt to revive devotion among Catholics. He was formally proclaimed patron of those who give missions in Catholic areas by Pius XI in an Apostolic Letter of 17 March 1923.

281

Doubtless while Alban Butler was writing his *Lives of the Saints* the fame often reached his ears of the Franciscan Father Leonard Casanova, whose missionary labours in Italy were at their height in the second quarter of the eighteenth century and who died five years before the publication of Butler's work. The name by which that friar is now known is taken from his native town, Porto Maurizio on the Italian Riviera, where he was born in 1676, and baptized Paul Jerome. His father, Dominic Casanova, was a master-mariner and a good Christian man, and when his eldest son was thirteen he entrusted him to the care of his wealthy uncle Augustine at Rome, who sent the boy to the Roman College of the Jesuits. Paul soon realized that he had a religious vocation and his own inclination was towards the Friars Minor. His uncle, who wanted him to be a physician, objected and eventually turned him out of his house; but Paul found shelter with another relative, Leonard Ponzetti, with whom he stayed until he received his father's ready permission to become a friar. He was clothed, when he was twenty-one, at the Franciscan novitiate at Ponticelli, taking the name of Leonard in gratitude for the kindness of Ponzetti, and completed his studies at St Bonaventure's on the Palatine, where he was ordained in 1703. This friary was the principal house of an off-shoot of the strict *Riformati* branch of the Franciscans, called *Riformella*, and throughout his life St Leonard, both for himself and for others, combined active missionary work with a severely ascetic monastic observance and much solitude: the first that he might live *for* God and the last he might live *in* God, as he himself expressed it.

In 1709 St Leonard was sent with other friars, under Father Pius, to take over the monastery of San Francesco del Monte at Florence, which the Grand Duke Cosimo III de' Medici had presented to the *Riformella*. These friars lived according to the austerest principles of St Francis, refusing to accept endowments from Cosimo, or Mass and preaching stipends from the clergy and people, depending solely for material support on what they could beg as required. The community flourished and increased in numbers, and became a great religious centre whence Leonard and his companions preached with great fruit throughout Tuscany. The saint himself was appointed guardian of del Monte, and he established the hermitage of St Mary at Incontro in the neighbouring mountains, where individual religious might retire for a space twice in every year. The regulations which he drew up for this retreat-house provided for strict enclosure, almost perpetual silence, fasting on bread, vegetables and fruit, and a daily discipline, with nine hours of the day devoted to the Divine Office and other spiritual exercises, and the rest to manual work.

For many years St Leonard laboured in Tuscany, but after a time he was frequently called to preach further afield, and at his first preaching visit to Rome his services were so long in request that Duke Cosimo sent a ship to the Tiber to fetch him back. For six years he was conducting missions around Rome, and in 1736, when he was sixty years old, he had to take up the office of guardian at St Bonaventure's there. From thence he preached for three weeks at Civita Vecchia, particularly to the soldiers and sailors, convicts and galley-slaves.

After a year he was released from office, and preached in Umbria, Genoa and the Marches, where such crowds assembled that he had often to leave the churches, and speak in the open air. To command the attention of those who were too hard-hearted and stiff-necked to take any notice of him otherwise, St Leonard would sometimes discipline himself in public, but the 'devotion' which he principally used was the Way of the Cross, and it is to him that its popularity today is largely due. He often gave it as a penance and preached it continually, and the setting up of the stations became a part in every mission he undertook. It is said that he set them up in 571 places in Italy. He also encouraged the exposition of the Blessed Sacrament and devotion to the Sacred Heart and to our Lady as conceived free from original sin, all of which were very far less widespared than they are today. In particular he made zealous efforts to get the Immaculate Conception defined as a dogma of faith and he was the first to suggest, what was done a century later, that the mind of the Church should be sounded on the matter without summoning a general council.

St Leonard was for a time the spiritual director of Clementina Sobieska of Poland, the wife of him who was recognized in Italy as King James III of England. All his letters to her were destroyed, but there are extant one written by James to St Leonard a month after the queen's death in 1735, thanking him for his prayers and asking to see him, and several of direction written by the saint to one of the queen's ladies. Pope Benedict XIV had a great regard for Leonard and his capabilities and in 1744, in concert with the Genoese Republic, the sovereign of the island, he sent him to Corsica to try and bring the people there to peace and order. He was not well received, being regarded as an agent of the doge disguished as a missioner. Admittedly there was a political aspect to his mission, for the troubles in Corsica were mainly due to discontent with the domination of Genoa. What with the political situation, the turbulent temperament of the Corsicans (they came to his sermons with weapons in their hands), and the mountainousness of the country, this was the most arduous of all St Leonard's missionary tasks.

But the fatigue, the intrigues, the strain of constant vigilance were too much for St Leonard, who was now sixty-eight, and at the end of six months he was so ill that a ship was sent from Genoa to bring him back. He had gauged the state of Corsican affairs correctly, for the pope wrote to him soon after, 'The Corsicans have got worse than ever since the mission, and so it is not thought advisable that you should go back there'. Side by side with his public missions St Leonard gave retreats to nuns and lay-people, especially at Rome in preparation for the year of Jubile 1750. That year saw one of his ambitions realized, when Benedict XIV permitted him to set up the stations of the cross in the Colosseum, Leonard preaching to a large and fervent crowd a sermon which is still preserved. 'I am getting old,' he wrote. 'My voice carried as it did two years ago, but I felt worn out. However, it is a consolation to see this Colosseum no longer a common resort but a real sanctuary. . . .

In the spring of the following year, when St Leonard went off to give missions at Lucca and elsewhere, the pope told him to give up travelling on foot and to go by carriage. He had been a missioner of the most powerful energy for forty-three years, and was beginning to fail. Owing to this and to the hostility and indifference of certain places, some of these last missions were relatively unsuccessful. At length, at the beginning of November, he turned south, and he knew his work was done. His carriage broke down and he had to walk part of the way through rain to Spoleto, where the friars tried in vain to detain him. On the evening of 26 November he arrived in Rome and was carried to bed at St Bonaventure's, and while they prepared to give him the last sacraments he sent a message to Pope Benedict that he had kept his promise – to come to Rome to die. At nine o'clock Mgr Belmonte arrived from the Vatican with an affectionate message from the pope. Before midnight St Leonard was dead.

In spite of his amazing activity St Leonard found time during the intervals of solitude and contemplation which he prized so much to write many letters, sermons and devotional treatises. His *Resolutions*, for the better attainment of Christian perfection, is a work valuable both in itself and for what it tells us about its author. The cause of his beatification in 1796 was furthered by Cardinal Henry of York, son of that Queen Clementina whose director St Leonard had been sixty years before. He was canonized in 1867.

LEOPOLD (A.D. 1136)

A PATRON SAINT OF AUSTRIA

15 NOVEMBER

Leopold, sometimes known as Leopold of Austria, was confirmed as a patron of that country on 17 December 1913.

This prince, known as 'the Good', was canonized 350 years after his death by Pope Innocent VIII, but only a few reliable particulars of his life have survived. He was born at Melk in 1073, brought up under the influence of the reforming bishop St Altman of Passau, and succeeded his father when he was twenty-three years old. In 1106 he married Agnes, daughter of the Emperor Henry IV and a widow. She had had two sons by her first husband, and she now gave eighteen children to Leopold. Of the eleven who survived childhood, one was the historian, Otto of Freising, and it was at the request of this Otto, then Cistercian abbot of Morimond in Burgundy, that St Leopold founded the still existing abbey of Heiligenkreuz in the Wiener-wald. Another great foundation of his was Klosterneuburg, near Vienna, for Augustinian canons. This abbey is also still in being, and is a most influential centre of the 'liturgical movement' among German-speaking peoples. The Benedictine monastery of Mariazell, in Styria, whose church is now a popular place of pilgrimage, was also founded by St Leopold. By these benefactions he forwarded the cause of true religion in his country, setting before the people examples of charity, self-abnegation and devotion to the worship of God.

In the tortuous and difficult politics, ecclesiastical and secular, of his time Leopold IV played an inconspicuous part, but no doubt an important one, for when his brother-in-law Henry V died in 1125 the Bavarians wished the imperial crown to be offered to him. But in any case Leopold refused to be nominated. After a reign of forty years St Leopold died in 1136, and was buried at Klosterneuburg amid the lamentations of his people.

LOUIS OF FRANCE (LOUIS IX) (A.D. 1270)

PATRON SAINT OF THE FRENCH MONARCHY; OF FRENCH SOLDIERS;
OF STONEMASONS, SCULPTORS, MASONS AND WORKERS IN MARBLE; OF BUTTON
MAKERS; OF FRANCISCAN TERTIARIES

25 AUGUST

St Louis became patron of the French monarchy from the time of the Bourbons onwards. Also, in the light of his military exploits, Louis is an obvious choice as patron of French troops, and this was confirmed by the Sacred Congregation of Rites in a decree of 25 January 1952.

As his life indicates, Louis was responsible for a good deal of ecclesiastical building which provided work for stonemasons, and for those with related skills, in particular for the Sainte Chapelle, a model of which he is often depicted as carrying. On the other hand there does not seem to be any special reason to associate Louis with button makers, but he has traditionally served as their patron.

Louis was son of Louis VIII and was eight years old when the death of his grandfather, Philip II Augustus, put his father in possession of the crown of France. He was born at Poissy on 25 April 1214. His mother was Blanche, daughter of Alfonso of Castile and Eleanor of England, and to her care and attention in the education of St Louis we are indebted, under God, for the great example of his virtues.

King Louis VIII died on 7 November 1226, and Queen Blanche was declared regent for her son, who was then only twelve years old. The whole time of the king's minority was disturbed by ambitious barons, but Blanche by several alliances and by her courage and diligence overcame them in the field and forced their submission. Louis was merciful even to rebels, and by his readiness to receive any proposals of agreement gave the proof that he neither sought revenge nor conquests. Never had any man a greater love for the Church, or a greater veneration for its ministers. Yet this was not blind; for he opposed the injustices of bishops.

When he was nineteen Louis IX married Margaret, the eldest daughter of Raymund Berenger, Count of Provence, whose second daughter, Eleanor, was married to Henry III, King of England; his third, Sanchia, to his brother Richard of Cornwall; and Beatrice; the youngest, to Charles, brother to St Louis. The marriage was blessed with a happy union of hearts and eleven children, five sons, six daughters. In 1235, having come of age, St Louis took the government of his kingdom into his own hands. But he continued to show deference to his mother, and to profit by her counsel, though Blanche was inclined to be jealous of and unkind to her daughter-in-law.

The first of many religious foundations for which Louis was responsible was the abbey of Royaumont. In 1239 Baldwin II, the Latin emperor at Constantinople, made St Louis (in gratitude for his largesse to the Christians in Palestine and other parts of the East) a present of the Crown of Thorns, which was then in the hands of the Venetians as a pledge for a loan of money to Baldwin, which Louis had to discharge. He sent two Dominican friars to bring this treasure to France, and met it himself beyond Sens, attended by his whole court. To house it he pulled down his chapel of St Nicholas and built the *Sainte Chapelle*, which is now empty of its relic. He brought the Carthusians to Paris and endowed them with the palace of Vauvert, and helped his mother in the foundation of the convent of Maubuisson.

Several ordinances of this prince show us how much he applied himself to see justice well administered. In succeeding reigns, whenever complaints were raised among the people, the cry of those dissatisfied was to demand that abuses should be reformed and justice impartially administered as was done in the reign of St Louis. In 1230 he forbad all manner of usury, and restrained the Jews in particular from practising it. He published a law commanding all who should be guilty of blasphemy to be branded, and thus punished a rich and important citizen of Paris; to some who murmured at this severity he said that he would undergo that punishment himself if thus he might put a stop to the crime. He protected vassals from oppressive lords, and when a Flemish count had hanged three children for hunting rabbits in his woods, had him imprisoned and tried, not by his peers as he demanded, but by the ordinary judges, who condemned him to death. He afterwards spared his life, but subjected him to a fine which deprived him of the greater part of his estates. This money the king ordered to be expended on religious and charitable works.

Hugh of Lusignan, Count of La Marche, made trouble soon after the king's majority. Hugh's wife, Isabel, was the widow of King John and mother of Henry III of England, who came over to support his stepfather. St Louis defeated King Henry III (who was never born to be a soldier) at Taillebourg in 1242. Henry fled to Bordeaux and the next year returned to England, having made a truce with the French. Seventeen years later Louis concluded another treaty with Henry III. By it he yielded to England the Limousin and Périgord, King Henry renouncing on his side all pretensions to Normandy, Anjou, Maine, Touraine and Poitou.

After an illness in 1244 Louis determined to undertaken a crusade in the East. At the thirteenth general council at Lyons in 1245 all benefices were taxed a twentieth of their income for three years for the relief of the Holy Land (the English representatives strongly protested against this), and this gave encouragement to the crusaders. In 1248 Louis sailed for Cyprus, where he was joined by William Longsword, Earl of Salisbury, and two hundred English knights. The objective was Egypt. Damietta, in the delta of the Nile, was easily taken and St Louis made a solemn entry into the city, not with the pomp of a conqueror but with the humility of a truly Christian prince, walking barefoot with the queen, the princes his brothers and other great lords, preceded by the papal legate.

The crusaders could not follow up their advantage, and it was not till six months had passed that they advanced to attack the Saracens, who were on the other side of the river. Then followed another six months of desultory fighting, in which the crusaders lost many by battle and sickness, until in April 1250 St Louis himself was taken prisoner, and his army routed with frightful slaughter. During his captivity the king recited the Divine Office every day with two chaplains just as if he had been in perfect health in his own palace, and to the insults that were sometimes offered him he opposed an air of majesty and authority which kept his guards in awe. The sultan at that time was overthrown by the Mamluk emirs, and these eventually released the king and the other prisoners.

St Louis then sailed to Palestine with the remainder of the his army. There he remained until 1254, visiting all the holy places he could, encouraging the Christians, and strengthening the defences of the Latin Kingdom. Then, news being brought to him of the death of his mother, who was regent in his absence, he returned to France. He had been away almost six years, but he was oppressed by the memory of the distresses of the Christians in the East and he continued to wear the cross on his clothes to show that he intended to return to their assistance. People were not surprised when in 1267 he announced another crusade: nor were they pleased.

The king embarked with his army at Aigues-Mortes on 1 July 1270; when the fleet was over against Cagliari in Sardinia it was resolved to proceed to Tunis, where soon after landing the king himself and his eldest son Philip both sickened with typhus. It was soon seen that Louis was dying. He gave his last instructions to his sons and to his daughter, the queen of Navarre, and composed himself for death. On 24 August, which was Sunday, he received the last sacraments, and called for the Greek ambassadors, whom he strongly urged to reunion with the Roman Church. He lost his speech the next day from nine till twelve o'clock; then, recovering it, he repeated aloud the words of the psalmist, 'Lord, I will enter into thine house; I will worship in thy holy temple, and will give glory to thy name'. He spoke again at three in the afternoon, 'Into thy hands I commend my soul', and immediately after breathed his last. His bones and heart were taken back to France and enshrined in the abbey-church of St Denis, whence they were scattered at the Revolution; he was canonized in 1297.

LOUIS BERTRAND (A.D. 1581)

PATRON SAINT OF COLOMBIA

9 OCTOBER

A decree of the Sacred Congregation of Rites dated 20 July 1962 declared Louis Bertrand a secondary patron of Colombia, alongside Peter Claver.

Luis Bertrán was born at Valencia in Spain in 1526. He was related through his father to St Vincent Ferrer and was baptized at the same font as that saint had been 175 years before. The celebrated Father John Mico, who had been bought up a shepherd in the mountains, gave the Dominican habit to young Betrand when he was eighteen. Sacerdotal ordination was given to him by the archbishop of Valencia, St Thomas of Villanova, in 1547. Louis was made master of novices five years after profession, and discharged that office for periods which totalled thirty years. He was very severe and strict, but both by his example and words taught them sincerely and perfectly to renounce the world and to unite their souls to God.

In 1557 a pestilence raged in Valencia and the saint knew no danger and spared no pains in comforting and assisting the sick. He about this time made the acquaintance of St Teresa, who wrote and asked his advice about her projected convent of reformed Carmelites.

In 1562 St Louis left Spain to preach the gospel to the Indians in America, and landed at Cartagena in New Granada (Columbia). He spoke only Spanish and had to use an interpreter, but the gifts of tongues, of prophecy and of miracles were conferred by Heaven on this apostle, the bull of his canonization tell us. In the isthmus of Panama and the province of Cartagena, in the space of three years, he converted to Christ many thousand souls. The baptismal registers of Tubera, in St Louis's own hand-writing, show that all the inhabitants of that place were converted, and he had a like success at Cipacoa. The people of Paluato were more difficult, but in his next mission, among the inhabitants of the mountains of Santa Marta, he is said to have baptized about fifteen thousand persons; and also a tribe of fifteen hundred Indians who, having changed their minds, had followed him thither from Paluato. He visited the Caribs of the Leeward Islands, San Thomé in the Virgin Islands, and San Vincente in the Windwards, and then returned to Columbia. He was pierced to the quick to see the avarice and cruelty of the Spanish adventurers in the Indies and not to be able to find any means of putting a stop to those evils. He was desirous to seek redress in Spain, and about that time he was recalled thither, thus ending a marvellous mission of six years.

St Louis arrived at Seville in 1569, whence he returned to Valencia. He trained up many excellent preachers, who succeeded him in the ministry of the word. The first lesson he gave them was that humble and fervent prayer must always be the principal preparation of the preacher: for words without works never have power to touch or change hearts.

The two last years of his life was afflicted with painful illness; in 1580 he went to preach in the cathedral at Valencia, where he was carried from the pulpit to his bed, from which he never rose again, dying eighteen months later on 9 October 1581, being fifty-five years old. St Louis Bertrand was canonized in 1671.

LOUISE DE MARILLAC (A.D. 1660)

CO-FOUNDER OF THE VINCENTIAN SISTERS OF CHARITY
PATRON SAINT OF SOCIAL WORKERS

15 MARCH

Pope John XXIII, in an Apostolic Letter dated 10 February 1960, cited St Louise's care for the poor as the reason for proclaiming her patron of all those to dedicate themselves to social work.

Louise, born in 1591, lost her mother when still a child, but had a good upbringing and education, thanks partly to the nuns of Poissy, and partly to the personal instruction of her own father, who, however, died when she was little more than fifteen.

She married Antony Le Gras, a man who seemed destined for a distinguished career. A son was born to them, and her twelve years of married life were happy except that before very long her husband fell ill of a lingering sickness in which she nursed him most devotedly.

Not long before the death of her husband, Louise made a vow not to marry again but to devote herself wholly to the service of God. He died in 1625, but before this she had already made the acquaintance of 'M. Vincent', as the holy priest known to us as St Vincent de Paul was then called, and he, though showing reluctance at first, consented eventually to act as her confessor. Only after some five years personal association with Mlle Le Gras did M. Vincent, who was ever patient to abide God's own good time, send this devoted soul in May 1629 to make what we might call a visitation to the 'Charity' of Montmirail he had founded. This was the precursor of many similar missions, and in spite of much bad health, of which St Vincent himself was by no means inconsiderate, his deputy, with all her reckless self-sacrifice did not succumb. Quietly, however, and very gradually, as activities multiplied, in the by-ways of Paris as well as in the country, the need of robust helpers made itself felt.

Hence it came about that in 1633 a sort of training centre or noviceship was established in what was then known as the Rue des Fossé-Saint-Victor. This was the unfashionable dwelling Mlle Le Gras had rented for herself after her husband's death, and she now gave hospitality to the first candidates who were accepted for the service of the sick and poor.

These, with Louise as their directress, formed the grain of mustard seed which has grown into the world-wide organization known as the Sisters of Charity of St Vincent de Paul. Soon it became evident that some rule of life and some guarantee of stability was desirable. Louise had long wanted to bind herself to this service by vow, but St Vincent, always prudent and content to wait for a clear manifestation of the will of God, had restrained her ardour. But in 1634 her desire was gratified; St Vincent had now complete confidence in his spiritual daughter, and it was she who drafted something in the nature of a rule of life to be followed by the members of their association. The substance of this document forms the kernel of the religious observance of the Sisters of Charity down to the present day. But although this was a great step forward, the recognition of the Sister of Charity as an institute of nuns was still far distant. St Vincent himself insisted that he had never dreamed of founding a religious order. It was not until 1642 that he allowed four of the company to take annual vows of poverty, chastity and obedience, and it was not until 1655 that Cardinal de Retz, Archbishop of Paris, despatched from Rome the formal approbation of the company and placed them definitely under the direction of St Vincent's own congregation of priests.

Meanwhile the good works of the Daughters of Charity had multiplied apace. The patients of the great Paris hospital of the Hôtel-Dieu had passed in large measure under their care, the brutal treatment of an abandoned child had led St Vincent of organize a home for foundings, and despite the illiteracy of many of their own recruits the associates had found themselves compelled to undertake the teaching of children. In all these developments Madame Le Gras had borne the heaviest part of the burden.

As we may learn from her letters to St Vincent and others, two things only troubled her; the one was the respect and veneration with which she found her visits welcomed, the other was her anxiety for the spiritual welfare of her son Michael. With all her occupations she never forgot him.

He came with his wife and child to visit his mother on her deathbed and she blessed them tenderly.

St Louise de Marillac died on 15 March 1660, and St Vincent followed her only six months later. She was canonized in 1934.

LUCY, MARTYR (A.D. 304)

PATRON SAINT OF SUFFERERS FROM EYE DISEASES; OF GLAZIERS; OF SUFFERERS FROM HAEMORRHAGE, AND THROAT INFECTIONS; AND OF CUTLERS

13 DECEMBER

Possibly on account of her name, which is suggestive of light or lucidity, Lucy was invoked during the Middle Ages by those who suffered eye trouble, and as patron by glaziers. Legends then seem to have grown up about her to explain the association with eyes in a more straightforward fashion. In one version of these legends she herself tore out her eyes to discourage a suitor, but they were then miraculously restored to her, more beautiful than before.

According to the life of St Lucy, her mother was, by Lucy's prayers, healed of a haemorrhage.

Lucy herself was killed, according to the legend, by a sword being thrust through her throat. Possibly because she died in this fashion, after other attempts to kill her had failed, she was also taken by cutlers as their patron.

The English bishop St Aldhelm of Sherborne at the end of the seventh century celebrated St Lucy both in prose and verse, but unfortunately the 'acts' on which he relied are a worthless compilation. They relate that Lucy was a Sicilian, born of noble and wealthy parents in the city of Syracuse, and brought up in the faith of Christ. She lost her father in infancy, and she was yet young when she offered her virginity to God. This vow, however, she kept a secret, and her mother, Eutychia, pressed her to marry a young man who was a pagan. Eutychia was persuaded by her daughter to go to Catania and offer up prayers to God at the tomb of St Agatha for relief of a haemorrhage from which she suffered. St Lucy accompanied her, and their prayers were answered. Then the saint disclosed her desire of devoting herself to God and bestowing her fortune on the poor, and Eutychia in gratitude left her at liberty to pursue her inclinations. Her suitor was very indignant, and in his anger accused her before the governor as a Christian, the persecution of Diocletian then being at its height. When Lucy remained resolute the judge commanded her to be exposed to prostitution in a brothel; but God rendered her immovable, so that the guards were not able to carry her thither. Then attempt was made to burn her, but this also was unsuccessful. At length a sword was thrust into her throat.

Though the *acta* of St Lucy, preserved in various recensions both Latin and

Greek, are quite unhistorical, her connection with Syracuse and her early *cultus* admit of no question. She was honoured at Rome in the sixth century amongst the most illustrious virgin martyrs whose triumphs the Church celebrates, and her name was inserted in the canon of the Mass both at Rome and Milan.

LUDMILA, MARTYR (A.D. 921)

A PATRON SAINT OF CZECHOSLOVAKIA

16 SEPTEMBER

One of the several saints adopted by the people of what is now Czechoslovakia as their patrons, Ludmila was confirmed in that role by decrees of the Sacred Congregation of Rites dated 4 May 1914 and 11 December 1935.

Ludmila was born about the year 860, the daughter of a Slav prince in the country between the confluence of the Elbe and the Moldau. She married Borivoy, Duke of Bohemia, and when her husband was baptized by St Methodius she followed him into the Church. They built the first Christian church in Bohemia, at Levy Hradec to the north of Prague. The princely neophytes had a very difficult time, for most of the leading families were utterly opposed to the new religion. In accordance with the all-too-common practice of those days Borivoy tried to force Christianity on his people, which led to much discontent and increased his difficulties. After his death he was succeeded by his sons Spytihinev and Ratislav. The latter had married a Slav 'princess', Drahomira, who was only nominally Christian, and when a son, Wenceslaus, was born to them, Ludmila was entrusted with his upbringing. She was now about fifty years of age, a woman of virtue and learning, and it was to her unfailing care and interest that Wenceslaus in a large measure owed his own sanctity.

The premature death of Ratislav and the consequent regency of Draho-mira removed Wenceslaus from Ludmila's immediate charge. The regent was in the hands of the anti-Christian party in Bohemia, and was, moreover, not unnaturally, jealous of the responsibility which had been confided to Ludmila and of the influence she exercised over her grandson. St Ludmila's gentleness and charity had made her greatly beloved among the people, and probably she hoped that, if young Wenceslaus could be persuaded to seize the government before his time, they would rally to him, and Christianity in Bohemia, now threatened, be saved. The opposing party saw this possibility clearly, and every effort was made to keep Wenceslaus and Ludmila apart. The more desperate characters decided to take no risks; on 16 September 921, two of them came to the castle of Tetin, near Podybrad, and there strangled Ludmila. That this crime was instigated by Drahomira is often asserted, but it is not certain, nor is she surely known to have been privy to it. St Ludmila was acclaimed as a martyr, and her body was translated, perhaps by St Wenceslaus himself, to St George's church at Prague.

LUKE (FIRST CENTURY)

A PATRON SAINT OF THE MEDICAL PROFESSION, DOCTORS AND PHYSICIANS;
OF ARTISTS, PAINTERS, SCULPTORS AND CRAFTWORKERS; OF LACEMAKERS;
OF NOTARIES; AND OF BUTCHERS

18 OCTOBER

That Luke was himself a doctor St Paul testifies – see the biography that follows – and therefore he is a natural patron for the medical profession in general. Pius XII declared him in particular patron of the Madrid Medical Association in an Apostolic Letter of 11 November 1954.

There is a tradition, though it does not seem to go back beyond the sixth century, that St Luke painted a portrait of the Virgin Mary. As a painter, he became in time the patron of a variety of artists and craftworkers, including lacemakers.

Because the Gospel which bears his name was believed to be an accurate account of the life of Christ, and especially of Christ's birth, Luke was taken as one of the patrons of notaries.

As one of the four evangelists, Luke's symbol is an ox. This may account for his being taken as patron of butchers.

We learn from St Paul that St Luke was a gentile, for he is not named among those of his helpers whom Paul mentions as Jews (Col. iv 10–11) that he was a fellow worker with the apostle, 'Mark, Aristarchus, Demas and Luke, who share my labours'; and that he was a medical man, 'Luke, the beloved physician' (or 'the beloved Luke, the physician'), who doubtless had the care of Paul's much-tried health.

The first time in the history of the mission of St Paul that Luke speaks in his own name in the first person is when the apostle sailed from Troas into Macedonia (Acts xvi 10). Before this he had doubtless been for some time a disciple of St Paul, and from this time seems never to have left him, unless by his order for the service of the church he had planted; he was certainly with him not only during the first but also during the second imprisonment in Rome. According to Eusebius, Luke's home was at Antioch, and he was almost certainly a Greek; and his journeyings and tribulations with St Paul are, of course, set out by Luke himself in the Acts of the Apostles.

Luke was with St Paul in his last days: after writing those famous words to Timothy, 'The time of my dissolution is at hand. I have fought a good fight: I have finished my course: I have kept the faith . . .', the apostle goes on to say, 'Only Luke is with me'. Of what happened to St Luke after St Paul's martyrdom we have no certain knowledge: the later statements about him are impossible to reconcile. But according to a fairly early and widespread tradition he was unmarried, wrote his gospel in Greece, and died at the age of 84 in Boeotia.

MAGNUS OF FUSSEN (A.D. 772)

PATRON SAINT OF THE PROTECTION OF CROPS FROM VERMIN AND OTHER FORMS
OF DAMAGE; AND AGAINST LIGHTNING

6 SEPTEMBER

*St Magnus is credited with having blessed the fields with a staff inherited, legend
has it, from St Columbanus, and thereby to have driven out all vermin harmful to the
crops. From this, at least in Bavaria, he came to be invoked against all forms of
damage to the crops, including by storms, and the peasants extended the patronage to
include themselves, invoking Magnus for protection against being struck by
lightning, and ringing bells dedicated to him for the same purpose.*

When stories that he was a disciple of St Columbanus have been discounted,
St Magnus first emerges as a monk of the monastery of St Gall which he left
with Theodore and a priest named Tozzo to work as missionaries in the
region between Germany and Switzerland. Bishop Witkerp of Epfach –
whom Tozzo succeeded as bishop in 771 – sent him to Fussen, and eventually ordained him priest. Not only did he found a settlement at Fussen, he
erected a monastery there under the rule of St Benedict. It was at Fussen that
he seems to have died, aged seventy-six, on 6 September 772 after well over
twenty years dedicated to missionary work and to the service of the poor. He
became known as the Apostle of the Allgau and devotion to him, always
strong in Bavaria, spread to Swabia, the Tyrol and Switzerland and, eventually, to the whole of Germany.

MAGNUS OF ORKNEY, MARTYR (A.D. 1116)

A PATRON SAINT OF NORWAY

16 APRIL

*One of the two formally acknowledged patrons of Norway, Magnus was confirmed as
such, alongside St Olaf, by a decree of the Sacred Congregation of Rites dated 7 March
1941.*

In the second half of the eleventh century the Orkney Islands were governed
by two brothers, Paul and Erling, who, like their subjects, were Christians,
at any rate nominally. Erling had two sons, Magnus, our saint, and Erlend,
whilst Paul had one son, Haakon, a young man of such an ambitious and
quarrelsome disposition that his father sent him to the Norwegian court to
put an end to his intrigues against his kinsmen. Time and distance only
increased Haakon's animosity, and he found King Magnus Barefoot eager to
adopt his suggestion of equipping a force to subdue, or at least harry, the
isles and coasts of Scotland. King Magnus, with his young guest on board,

set sail for the Orkneys, which he subdued; and he made Magnus Erlingsson and his brother Erlend accompany the fleet on a piratical cruise to the Hebrides and then along the western coast of Scotland and the north of England.

Opposite Anglesey the earls of Chester and Shrewsbury with a large body of Welshmen came out to give battle. In the fight which ensued St Magnus refused to take part, saying that he would not injure those who had never injured him. Thereupon the king, scornfully dubbing him a coward, dismissed him to the hold, where he sat reading his psalter during the engagement. Soon afterwards he managed to escape from his captors by jumping into the sea and swimming to land. He found his way to the court of King Malcolm III of Scotland, by whom he was kindly received. Either there or in the house of a bishop where he lived for some time, Magnus was led to repent of the excesses of his youth, and to enter upon a course of penitence and prayer which he pursued until his death.

After King Magnus Barefoot had been killed in battle against the Irish, his son Sigurd allowed Haakon to return to the Orkneys, of which he wished to be the sole ruler. But Magnus, whose brother Erlend had also been slain, gathered a body of men and proceeded to his native country, where he vindicated his right to share in the government of the islands. Although the two cousins could unite against a common foe, disputes often arose between them. At last Haakon, whose overbearing spirit could no longer brook a rival, invited Magnus to meet him with a few followers on the island of Egilsay, under pretext of cementing a lasting peace. Magnus unsuspectingly complied, but was overpowered by a large band of men brought by Haakon and was treacherously slain, refusing to resist. The cathedral of Kirkwall, where he was buried (and where what seem to have been his bones were found in 1919), and many other churches have been dedicated in honour of St Magnus, who was regarded as a martyr, in spite of the fact that he was murdered on political rather than on religious grounds.

MARGARET, OR MARINA, MARTYR (NO DATE)

A PATRON SAINT OF PREGNANT WOMEN, CHILDBIRTH; AND OF DEATH

20 JULY (NO LONGER IN THE ROMAN CALENDAR)

It seems likely that Margaret was invoked as the patron of safe childbirth because of the legend of the dragon's belly opening to allow her to emerge unscathed. According to some versions of her story, however, she promised before her death that pregnant women who called upon her would have safe deliveries.

Among the promises St Marina is reputed to have made before her death was also one that whoever invoked her, when they were themselves dying, would escape the clutches of the devil.

Her *cultus*, under the name of 'the very great martyr Marina', began in the East; as Margaret she appears in the martyrology of Rabanus Maurus in the ninth century, and in the Bosworth Psalter, and soon her fame spread in England, France and Germany, and continued throughout the middle ages; she is one of the Fourteen Holy Helpers, and hers was one of the 'voices' that spoke to St Joan of Arc. Her alleged relics were stolen from Antioch in 908 and brought to San Pietro della Valle on the lake of Bolsena, and in 1145 were translated to Montefiascone; part of them were further translated, to Venice, in 1213, an event noted in the Roman Martyrology on 17 July, which is the saint's feast-day among the Greeks. Many other relics of her are shown throughout Europe. Her acts are a pure forgery, written by a man who called himself Theotimus and represented himself to be her attendant who had been the spectator of all he related. They belong to the same family of legends as those of St Pelagia of Antioch (*alias* Margaret, *alias* Marina; 8 October) and her congeners.

The story they tell is briefly this. Margaret was the daughter of a pagan priest of Antioch in Pisidia, who was put out to nurse with a Christian woman. Margaret herself became a Christian, and on being driven away in consequence from her father's house she went to live with her old nurse and made a living as a shepherdess. While thus employed she was seen by the prefect Olybrius, who marvelled at her beauty and grace and would have had her as his wife were she free, as his mistress were she a slave. But she would not have him either way, and in revenge he ordered her to be brought before his tribunal and charged as a Christian; and after she had been tortured she was cast into prison. There she underwent a terrible ordeal with the Devil, who appeared to her in the form of a dragon and eventually swallowed her: but the cross which she had in her hand (or the sign of the cross) was an irritation to the dragon's stomach, which opened and emitted her in safety (even the *Golden Legend* says that 'this swallowing and breaking of the belly of the dragon is said to be apocryphal'). Then she had conflict with another demon, whom she overcame, and they talked together, and he told her how he had been with others like him enclosed in a brazen vessel by Solomon, and how the vessel had been found in Babylon and broken open by people who thought it to contain treasure, so that the demons were released to plague the world – the affinities of which tale are not hard to see. The next day an attempt was made to slay her in various ways both by fire and by water; but the only result was to convert thousands of the spectators, who were all put to the sword. At length she was killed by beheading, the executioner immediately after falling dead also: not, it appears, as a retribution but as a reward whereby he would join her in Heaven, for he had been unwilling to fulfil his office. And this is stated to have taken place during the persecution of Diocletian. The faithful Theotimus took up Margaret's body and it was buried by a noble widow of the city.

MARIA GORETTI, MARTYR (A.D. 1902)

PATRON SAINT OF THE CHILDREN OF MARY; OF TEENAGERS, ESPECIALLY GIRLS

6 JULY

Citing the manner of her death, Pius XII formally granted the pious association known as The Children of Mary the martyr St Maria Goretti as their patron in an Apostolic Letter of 25 November 1950. Because of the age at which she died, she has also been taken by teenage girls as a patron.

Maria Goretti was born in 1890 at Corinaldo, a village some thirty miles from Ancona, the daughter of a farm-labourer, Luigi Goretti, and his wife Assunta Carlini. They had five other children, and in 1896 the family moved to Colle Gianturco, near Galiano, and later to Ferriere di Conca, not far from Nettuno in the Roman Campagna. Almost at once after settling down here, Luigi Goretti was stricken with malaria and died. His widow had to take up his work as best she could, but it was a hard struggle and every small coin and bit of food had to be looked at twice. Of all the children none was more cheerful and encouraging to her mother than Maria, commonly called Marietta.

On a hot afternoon in July 1902 Maria was sitting at the top of the stairs in the cottage, mending a shirt: she was not yet quite twelve years old. A cart stopped outside, and a neighbour, a young man of eighteen named Alexander, ran up the stairs. He beckoned Maria into an adjoining bedroom: she refused to go. Alexander seized hold of her, pulled her in, and shut the door. Maria struggled and tried to call for help, but she was being half-strangled and could only protest hoarsely, gasping that she would be killed rather than submit. Whereupon Alexander half pulled her dress from her body and began striking at her blindly with a long dagger. She sank to the floor, crying out that she was being killed: Alexander plunged the dagger into her back, and ran away.

An ambulance fetched Maria to hospital, where it was seen at once that she could not possibly live. Her last hours were most touching – her concern for where her mother was going to sleep, her forgiveness of her murderer (she disclosed that she had been going in fear of him, but did not like to say anything lest she cause trouble with his family), her childlike welcoming of the holy viaticum. Some twenty-four hours after the assault, Maria Goretti died. Her mother, the parish priest of Nettuno, a Spanish noblewoman and two nuns, had watched by her bed all night.

Alexander was sentenced to thirty years' penal servitude. He was unrepentant. Then one night he had a dream in which Maria Goretti appeared gathering flowers and offering them to him. From then on he was a changed man. At the end of twenty-seven years he was released: his first act when free was to visit Maria's mother to beg her forgiveness.

Meanwhile the memory of his victim had become more and more revered. On 27 April 1947, Maria Goretti was declared blessed by Pope Pius XII. When he afterwards appeared on the balcony of St Peter's he was accompanied by Maria's mother, Assunta Goretti, then eighty-two years old, together with two of Maria's sisters and a brother. Three years later the same pope canonized Maria Goretti in the piazza of St Peter's, before the biggest crowd ever assembled for a canonization. Her murderer was still alive.

BD MARIA TERESA LEDOCHOWSKA (A.D. 1922)

PATRON SAINT OF POLISH MISSIONS

6 JULY

Despite the many difficulties under which it has to labour, the Church in Poland has continued to produce many priests who have dedicated their lives to missionary work outside the confines of their country. Of these missionary activities Maria Teresa makes a particularly suitable patron, and was declared such by an Apostolic Letter of Paul VI dated 20 January 1976.

Maria came from a family remarkable for their zeal for the Church. Not only did she have an uncle who was a Cardinal, her brother Vladimir became General of the Society of Jesus, and a sister, Orsola, founded a congregation of nuns. Maria herself was born on 29 April 1863 at Loosdorf in Austria, though her father was a Polish count, and her mother a Swiss countess. Her early years she spent in Austria, attending a school run by the 'English Ladies', the Sacred Heart nuns, before moving to Lipnica Murowana near Cracow where her father had acquired an estate. After her father's death she went to Salzburg, to the court of the Grand Duchess of Tuscany. In 1886, however, she met some sisters of the Franciscan Missionaries of Mary. Inspired by their example and encouraged by her uncle the Cardinal she determined to give herself to the service of God in some manner. Just how was decided by a meeting with Cardinal Lavigerie in 1889. She now began to produce articles, and edit a periodical about missionary work in Africa and especially about the evils of the slave-trade. She was still combining these tasks with her duties as a courtier, but decided to resign from these in order to dedicate herself more fully to her work for the missions.

For a time she lived with the Sisters of Charity at Solnogrod, but in 1893 she drew up the statutes of her own association which she called the Sodality (now the Institute) of St Peter Claver. These were approved by Rome and in September 1895 she took her vows as the first member of her own congregation. From then on she was a tireless worker for the missions and against slavery – she organized a major anti-slavery congress at Vienna in 1900. She died in Rome, where she had established the mother-house of her Insitute, on 6 July 1922, and was beatified by Pope Paul VI.

MARK (FIRST CENTURY)

PATRON SAINT OF CATTLE BREEDERS (OF SPAIN); OF EGYPT; OF VENICE; AND OF NOTARIES

25 MAY

Pius XII formally declared St Mark to be patron of Spanish cattle breeders in an Apostolic Letter of 4 October 1951. There does not appear to be any obvious connection between the saint and the rearing of cattle, but in the Letter the Pope cites long devotion to Mark among the cattle breeders of Spain.

As his life indicates, Mark is traditionally believed to have been Bishop of Alexandria, and for this reason is regarded as patron saint of Egypt. He is also, as the life below explains, honoured as the principal patron of Venice.

Since, according to tradition, the gospel which bears Mark's name is an accurate record of St Peter's memories of Christ, St Mark has been regarded by notaries and writers as their patron too.

It is generally believed that he must be identical with the 'John surnamed Mark' of Acts xii 12 and 25, and that the Mary whose house in Jerusalem was a kind of rendezvous for the apostles was consequently his mother. From Col. iv 10 we learn that Mark was a kinsman of St Barnabas who, as stated in Acts iv 36, was a Levite and a Cypriot, and from this it is not unlikely that St Mark was of a levitical family himself. When Paul and Barnabas returned to Antioch, after leaving in Jerusalem the alms they had brought, they took John surnamed Mark with them, and in their apostolic mission at Salamis in Cyprus, Mark helped them in their ministry (Acts xiii 5), but when they were at Perga in Pamphylia he left and returned to Jerusalem (Acts xiii 13), St Paul seems consequently to have suspected Mark of a certain instability, and later, when preparing for a visitation of the churches in Cilicia and the rest of Asia Minor, he refused to include John Mark, though Barnabas desired his company. The difference of opinion ended in Barnabas separating from St Paul and going with Mark again to Cyprus. None the less when Paul was undergoing his first captivity in Rome, Mark was with him and a help to him (Col. iv 10). Also in his second Roman captivity, shortly before his martyrdom, St Paul writes to Timothy, then at Ephesus, enjoining him to 'take Mark and bring him with thee, for he is profitable to me for the ministry'.

On the other hand tradition testifies strongly in the sense that the author of the second gospel was intimately associated with St Peter. Clement of Alexandria (as reported by Eusebius), Irenaeus and Papias speak of St Mark as the interpreter or mouthpiece of St Peter, though Papias declares that Mark had not heard the Lord and had not been His disciple. In spite of this last utterance, many commentators incline to the view that the young man (Mark xiv 51) who followed our Lord after His arrest was Mark himself. What is certain is that St Peter, writing from Rome (1 Peter v 13), speaks of 'my son Mark' who apparently was there with him. We can hardly doubt that this was the evangelist, and there is at any rate nothing which conclusively shows that this young man is a different person from the 'John surnamed Mark' of the Acts.

That St Mark lived for some years in Alexandria and became bishop of that see is an ancient tradition, though his connection with their native city is not mentioned either by Clement of Alexandria or by Origen.

The city of Venice claims to possess the body of St Mark which is supposed to have been brought there from Alexandria early in the ninth century. The authenticity of the remains preserved for so many hundred years has not passed unquestioned. It is certain, however, that St Mark has been honoured from time immemorial as principal patron of the city.

MARTHA (FIRST CENTURY)

PATRON SAINT OF HOUSEWIVES, AND SERVANTS; ALSO OF HOTELIERS (ITALIAN), AND WAITERS AND WAITRESSES

29 JULY

Because she seems to have had charge of the house, and because she waited upon Jesus, St Martha has traditionally been regarded as the patron both of housewives and of servants. A decree of the Sacred Congregation of Rites dated 1 July 1963 declared her to be the patron also of Italian hoteliers, their staff, waiters and waitresses. An Apostolic Letter of Paul VI, dated 1 July 1973, written at the request of the Italian Federation of Hotels and Tourism, confirmed the decision of the Congregation. The Church is concerned, said the Pope, that guests should be 'kindly and humanely received' – and he drew attention the rule of hospitality among some 'ethnic peoples'. Martha, he went on, was an example of this when she received Jesus into her house.

Martha was sister to Mary and Lazarus, and lived with them at Bethany, a small town two miles distant from Jerusalem, a little beyond Mount Olivet. Our blessed Redeemer had made His residence usually in Galilee, till in the third year of His public ministry He preached frequently in Judaea, during which interval He frequented the house of these three disciples, who perhaps had removed from Galilee to be nearer Him. St John particularly tells us that 'Jesus loved Martha and her sister Mary and Lazarus'. Martha seems to have been the eldest, and to have had the chief care and direction of the household, for, when Jesus visited them, St Luke tells us that Martha showed great solicitude to entertain and serve Him, to be herself busy in preparing everything for their guest. Mary sat all the while at our Saviour's feet, feeding her soul with heavenly doctrine.

With so great love did Martha wait on our Redeemer that, as we cannot doubt, she thought that if the whole world were occupied in attending to so great a guest, all would be too little. She wished that all men would employ their hands, feet and hearts, all their faculties and senses, with their whole strength, in serving their Creator who was made for us our brother. Therefore she asked Him to bid her sister Mary help her. Our Lord was indeed well pleased with the affection and devotion wherewith Martha waited on Him; yet He commended more the quiet repose with which Mary attended only to that which is of the greatest importance, the attendance of the soul on God. 'Martha, Martha,' said He, 'thou art careful and troubled about many things; but one thing is necessary. Mary hath chosen the best part. . . .'

MARTIN, BISHOP OF TOURS (A.D. 397)

PATRON SAINT OF SOLDIERS, INFANTRY AND CAVALRY; OF HORSES AND HORSE-RIDERS; OF BEGGARS; ALSO OF GEESE; AND OF WINEGROWERS

11 NOVEMBER

It was St Martin's early life as a soldier that inspired the Italian infantry to seek his formal appointment as their patron. This was granted by Pius XII in an Apostolic Letter of 21 May 1951. Shortly afterwards, on 25 January 1952, a decree of the Sacred Congregation of Rites declared him to be the patron also of the French infantry.

St Martin is said to have been riding by, and is certainly generally depicted on a horse, when he divided his cloak with a beggar. Hence he came to be regarded too as the patron of the cavalry, and of horses and horse-riders in general. His kindness to the beggar in this instance makes him a natural choice too as the patron of beggars.

The traditional invocation of St Martin on behalf of geese is thought to stem from the fact that his feast falls at about the time geese migrate. The association of St Martin with wine, and particularly with harvesting the grapes and therefore more particularly with winegrowers, is also believed to arise not only from the general popularity of his cult in France, but especially the date of his feast, which falls just after the vendange.

The great St Martin was a native of Sabaria, a town of Pannonia. From thence his parents, who were pagans, had to remove to Pavia in Italy, for his father was an officer in the army, who had risen from the ranks. At the age of fifteen he was, as the son of a veteran, forced into the army against his will and for some years, though not yet formally a Christian, he lived more like a monk than a soldier. It was while stationed at Amiens that is said to have occurred the incident which tradition and image have made famous. One day in a very hard winter, during a severe frost, he met at the gate of the city a poor man, almost naked, trembling and shaking with cold, and begging alms of those that passed by. Martin, seeing those that went before take no notice, cut his cloak into two pieces, gave one to the beggar and wrapped himself in the other half. That night Martin in his sleep saw Jesus Christ, dressed in that half of the garment which he had given away, and heard

Jesus say, 'Martin, yet a catechuman, has covered me with this garment'. His disciple and biographer Sulpicius Severus states that he had become a catechuman on his own initiative at the age of ten, and that as a consequence of this vision he 'flew to be baptized'. Martin did not at once leave the army, and when he was about twenty there was a barbarian invasion of Gaul. With his comrades he appeared before Julian Caesar to receive a war-bounty, and Martin refused to accept it. 'Hitherto', he said to Julian, 'I have served you as a soldier; let me now serve Christ. Give the bounty to these others who are going to fight, but I am a soldier of Christ and it is now lawful for me to fight.' Julian stormed and accused Martin of cowardice, who retorted that he was prepared to stand in the battle-line unarmed the next day and to advance alone against the enemy in the name of Christ. He was thrust into prison, but the conclusion of an armistice stopped further developments and Martin was soon after discharged. He went to Poitiers, where St Hilary was bishop, and this doctor of the Church gladly received the young 'conscientious objector' among his disciples.

Martin had in a dream a call to visit his home. He went into Pannonia, and converted his mother and others; but his father remained in his infidelity. In Illyricum he opposed the Arians with so much zeal that he was publicly scourged and had to leave the country. In Italy he heard that the church of Gaul also was oppressed by those heretics and St Hilary banished, so he remained at Milan. But Auxentius, the Arian bishop, soon drove him away. He then retired with a priest to the island of Gallinaria in the gulf of Genoa, and remained there till St Hilary was allowed to return to Poitiers in 360. It being Martin's earnest desire to pursue his vocation in solitude, St Hilary gave him a piece of land, now called Ligugé, where he was soon joined by a number of other hermits. This community – traditionally the first monastic community founded in Gaul – grew into a great monastery which continued till the year 1607, and was revived by the Solesmes Benedictines in 1852. St Martin lived here for ten years, directing his disciples and preaching throughout the countryside, where many miracles were attributed to him. About 371 the people of Tours demanded Martin for their bishop. He was unwilling to accept the office, so a stratagem was made use of to call him to the city to visit a sick person, where he was conveyed to the church. Some of the neighbouring bishops, called to assist at the election, urged that the meanness of his appearance and his unkempt air showed him to be unfit for such a dignity. But such objections were overcome by the acclamations of the local clergy and people.

St Martin continued the same manner of life. He lived at first in a cell near the church, but not being able to endure the interruptions of the many visitors he retired from the city to where was soon the famous abbey at Marmoutier. The place was then a desert, enclosed by a steep cliff on one side and by a tributary of the river Loire on the other; but he had here in a short time eighty monks, with many persons of rank amongst them. A very great decrease of paganism in the district of Tours and all that part of Gaul was the fruit of the piety, miracles and zealous instruction of St Martin. Every year St Martin visited each of his outlying 'parishes', travelling on foot, on a donkey, or by boat. According to his biographer he extended his apostolate from Touraine to Chartres, Paris, Autun, Sens and Vienne, where he cured St Paulinus of Nola of an eye trouble.

Whilst St Martin was spreading the kingdom of Jesus Christ, the churches in Spain and Gaul were disturbed by the Priscillianists, a gnostic-manichean sect named after their leader. Priscillian appealed to the Emperor Maximus from a synod held at Bordeaux in 384, but Ithacius, Bishop of Ossanova, attacked him furiously and urged the emperor to put him to death. Neither St Ambrose at Milan nor St Martin would countenance Ithacius or those who supported him, because they wanted to put heretics to death and allowed the emperor's jurisdiction in an ecclesiastical matter. Martin begged Maximus not to spill the blood of the guilty, saying it was sufficient that they be declared heretics and excommunicated by the bishops. Ithacius, far from listening to his advice, presumed to accuse him of the heresy involved, as he generally did those whose lives were too ascetic for his taste, says Sulpicius Severus. Maximus, out of regard to St Martin's remonstrances, promised that the blood of the accused should not be spilt. But after the saint had left Trier, the emperor was prevailed upon, and committed the case of the Priscillianists to the prefect Evodius. He found Priscillian and others guilty of certain charges, and they were beheaded. St Martin came back to Trier to intercede both for the Spanish Priscillianists, who were threatened with a bloody persecution, and for two adherents of the late emperor, Gratian; he found himself in a very difficult position, in which he seemed to be justified in maintaining communion with the party of Ithacius, which he did: but he was afterwards greatly troubled in conscience as to whether he had been too complaisant in this matter.

He was at a remote part of his diocese when his last sickness came on him. He died on 8 November 397. 11 November was the day of his burial at Tours, where his successor St Britius built a chapel over his grave, which was later replaced by a magnificent basilica.

MARTIN DE PORRES (A.D. 1639)

PATRON SAINT OF SOCIAL JUSTICE; OF PUBLIC EDUCATION, AND TELEVISION, IN PERU; OF TRADE UNIONISTS (SPANISH); OF PERU'S PUBLIC HEALTH SERVICE; OF PEOPLE OF MIXED RACE; OF ITALIAN BARBERS AND HAIRDRESSERS

3 NOVEMBER

St Martin was declared patron of all work for justice, specifically in Peru, by Pius XII in an Apostolic Letter of 10 January 1935. The choice, made at the request of the Peruvian hierarchy, was a natural one as the life of the saint indicates. Thirty years

later the bishops of Peru asked that St Martin be declared the patron of public education in their country because of the concern for the needy which he displayed during his life. The type of education the Peruvian hierarchy had in mind was intended to reach as many as possible by means of television. When Paul VI formally approved him therefore as patron of public education, in an Apostolic Letter of 29 April 1965, he also included the patronage of television in Peru.

Those who struggle against the unjust situation in which they find themselves, says Paul VI in his Apostolic Letter of 25 April 1973, need the help of heaven, so they seek the support of the saints. The 'Spanish national syndicate for various trades' – or general workers' union – had chosen Martin as their particular patron, a choice which was confirmed by the Episcopal Conference of Spain on 10 March 1973. In his Apostolic Letter mentioned above, Pope Paul is confirming the choice.

There is no doubt, said John Paul II in an Apostolic Letter of 6 April 1982, of Martin's devotion to the sick of his own country. He was therefore conceding the request that Martin be recognized as patron of the public health service of Peru.

St Martin, as his life indicates, was of mixed race, with a European father and an indigenous American mother. For that reason, and because of his own colour, he has been taken as the patron of people of mixed race. St Martin had been apprenticed as a barber-surgeon. Paul VI declared him patron of all Italian hairdressers and barbers in an Apostolic Letter of 20 July 1966 at the request of that country's Society of Hairdressers.

He was born in Lima in Peru in 1579, the natural child of John de Porres (Porras), a Spanish knight, and a coloured freed-woman from Panama, Anna by baptism. Young Martin inherited the features and dark complexion of his mother, which was a matter of vexation to the noble Porres, who nevertheless acknowledged the boy and his sister as his children, but eventually left Martin to the care of his mother. When he was twelve she apprenticed him to a barber-surgeon; but three years later, having received the habit of the third order of St Dominic, he was admitted to the Rosary convent of the Friars Preachers at Lima, eventually becoming a professed lay-brother.

Martin extended his care of the sick to those of the city, and was instrumental in establishing an orphanage and foundling-hospital, with other charitable institutions attached; he was given the office of distributing the convent's daily alms of food to the poor (which he is said sometimes to have increased miraculously); and he took upon himself to care for the slaves who were brought to Peru from Africa.

Brother Martin's charity embraced the lower animals (which seems to have surprised the Spaniards) and even vermin, excusing the depredations of rats and mice on the ground that the poor little things were insufficiently fed, and he kept a 'cats' and dogs' home' at his sister's house.

St Martin's protégé, Juan Vasquez Parra, shows the lay-brother as eminently practical in his charities, using carefully and methodically the money and goods he collected, raising a dowry for his niece in three days (at the same time getting as much and more for the poor), putting up the banns, showing Parra how to sow camomile in the well-manured hoof-prints of cattle, buying a negro slave to work in the laundry, looking after those who needed blankets, shirts, candles, sweets, miracles or prayers – the procurator apparently both of the priory and the public.

St Martin was a close friend of St Rose of Lima as well as of Bd John Massias, who was a lay-brother at the Dominican priory of St Mary Magdalen in the same town. Martin was at the Rosary priory, and he died there on 3 November 1639: he was carried to his grave by prelates and noblemen. He was beatified in 1837, after long delays, and canonized on 6 May 1962.

THE MARTYRS OF NORTH AMERICA

PATRON SAINTS OF CANADA

19 OCTOBER

This natural choice was confirmed by a decree of the Sacred Congregation of Rites of 16 October 1940.

By the wish of the French King Henry IV, in 1608 two Jesuits, Peter Biard and Ennemond Massé, sailed from Europe, and on their arrival in Acadia (Nova Scotia) began work among the Souriquois Indians at Port Royal (now Annapolis). Their first task was to learn the language. Massé went into the woods to live with these nomad tribes and to pick up what he could of their speech, while Biard stayed at the settlement and bribed with food and sweets the few Indians who remained, in order to induce them to teach him the words he required. After a year they were able to draw up a catechism and to begin to teach.

By the time the missionaries were joined by fresh colonists and by two more Jesuit priests, as well as by a lay-brother, the work of evangelization seemed well inaugurated. But in 1613 a raid was made from the sea by the piratical English captain of a merchant vessel, who descended with his crew on the unfortunate inhabitants, pillaged the settlement, and set adrift fifteen of the colony, including Massé. He then sailed back to Virginia with Biard and Quentin on board. Eventually the missionaries found their way back to France, but their work of preaching the gospel was brought to a standstill.

In the meantime Samuel Champlain, governor of New France, was continually imploring that good religious should be sent out, and in 1615 several Franciscans arrived at Tadroussac. They laboured heroically, but finding that they could not obtain enough men or enough money to convert the Indians, they invited the Jesuits to come to their assistance. In 1625 three priests of the Society of Jesus landed in Quebec in time to meet the Indian traders who had just murdered the friar Vial and his catechist and had thrown them into that part of the rapids which is still known as Sault-au-Récollet. Of the three newcomers one was Massé, returning to his former labours, but the two others, Brébeuf and Charles Lalemant, were new to the work.

As Brébeuf was unable to trust himself at once to the Hurons he wintered with the Algonquins, learning their speech and their customs under conditions of appalling discomfort and occasionally of hunger. The following year he went with a Franciscan and a fellow Jesuit to the Huron country. The Jesuits settled at Tod's Point, but Brébeuf's companions were soon recalled and Brébeuf was left alone with the Hurons, whose habit of living, less migratory than that of other tribes, gave the missionaries a better prospect of evangelizing them. During that period however, he failed to make a single convert among them, but his stay was cut short. The colony was in distress: the English closed the St Lawrence to all relief from France and obliged Champlain to surrender. Colonists and missionaries were forced to return to their own country, and Canada became, for the first time and for a short period, a British colony. Before long the indefatigable Champlain brought the matter to the law courts in London, and was able to prove so conclusively that the seizure of the colony was unjust that in 1632 Canada reverted to France.

The Franciscans were immediately invited to return, but they had not enough men, and the Jesuits took up the work of evangelization once more. Father Le Jeune, who was placed in charge of the mission, came to New France in 1632, Antony Daniel soon followed, and in 1633 Brébeuf and Massé arrived with Champlain, the governor. Le Jeune conceived the plan of keeping the entire nation informed of the actual conditions in Canada by a series of graphic descriptions, beginning with his own personal experiences on the voyage and his first impressions of the Indians. The earliest reports were written and despatched to France within two months and were published at the end of the year. These missives, known as 'The Jesuit Relations', continued to pass from New to Old France almost without interruption, and often embodied the letters of other Jesuits, such as Brébeuf and Perrault. They awakened interest not only in France but in all Europe.

When the Hurons came to Quebec for their annual market they were delighted to meet Brébeuf and to be addressed by him in their own language. They wished him to go back with them, and he was eager to do so, but they were frightened at the last moment by an Ottawa chieftain, and for the time refused. The following year, however, when they came again, they agreed to take Brébeuf, Daniel and another priest named Darost, and after a most uncomfortable journey in which they were robbed and abandoned by their guides, the three Jesuits reached their destination, where the Hurons built a hut for them. Brébeuf gave his companions lessons in Huron, and

Daniel, who proved himself an apt pupil, could soon lead the children in chanting the Lord's Prayer when Brébeuf held assemblies in his cabin.

It was resolved to establish a seminary at Quebec for Indians, and Daniel started back with two or three children to found the new institution which became the centre of the missionaries' hopes. For a short time Brébeuf was again alone among the Hurons and he then wrote for those who were to come to the Huron mission an instruction which afterwards became famous.

In 1636 arrived five more Jesuits, two of them were destined to be numbered among the martyrs – Jogues, who was to become the apostle of a new Indian nation, the Garnier. Isaac Jogues had been born at Orléans, and after entering the Jesuit novitiate at Rouen at the age of seventeen had studied at the royal college of La Flèche, which Descartes considered one of the first schools of Europe. After his ordination he was appointed to Canada and sailed with the governor of New France, Huault de Montmagny. Charles Garnier was a Parisian, educated at the Clermont college. At nineteen he became a Jesuit, and after his ordination in 1635 he volunteered for the Canadian mission. He sailed with Jogues in 1636. Garnier was then thirty years of age, Jogues was twenty-nine.

While Brébeuf was alone with the Hurons he had gone through the excitement of a threatened invasion by their bitter enemies the Iriquois, and had to witness the horrible sight of an Iroquois tortured to death. He could do nothing to avert this; but, as he had baptized the captive shortly before, he was determined to stand by to encourage him.

Five of the newcomers went almost at once to join Father de Brébeuf, and Jogues, who had not been intended at first for the Huron mission, followed a few months later. A second mission was established at Teanaustaye, and Lalement was appointed in charge of both stations, whilst Brébeuf at his own wish undertook the care of a new location, called Sainte-Marie, at some distance from the Indian villages. This settlement acted as a central bureau for missions and as a headquarters for priests and their attendants, as well as for the Frenchmen who served as labourers or soldiers. A hospital and a fort were erected and a cemetery established, and for five years the pioneers worked perseveringly, often undertaking long and perilous expeditions to other tribes – to the Petun or Tobacco Indians, the Ojibways, and to the Neuters north of Lake Erie – by whom they were more often than not very badly received. The first adult to be baptized (in 1637) was followed by over eighty, two years later, and by sixty in 1641. It did not seem much, but it proved that genuine conversion was possible.

In 1642 the Huron country was in great distress: harvests were poor, sickness abounded, and clothing was scarce. Quebec was the only source of supplies, and Jogues was chosen to lead an expedition. It reached its objective safely and started back well supplied with goods for the mission, but the Iroquois, the bitter enemies of the Hurons, and the fiercest of all Indian tribes, were on the war-path and ambushed the returning expedition. The story of the ill-treatment and torture of the captives cannot here be told. Suffice it to say that Jogues and his assistant René Goupil, besides being beaten to the ground and assailed several times with knotted sticks and fists, had their hair, beards and nails torn off and their forefingers bitten through.

The first of all the martyrs to suffer death was Goupil, who was tomahawked on 29 September 1642, for having made the sign of the cross on the brow of some children. This René Goupil was a remarkable man. He had tried hard to be a Jesuit and had even entered the novitiate, but his health forced him to give up the attempt. He then studied surgery and found his way to Canada, where he offered his services to the missionaries, whose fortitude he emulated.

Jogues remained a slave among the Mohawks, one of the Iroquois tribes, who, however, had decided to kill him. He owed his escape to the Dutch, who, ever since they had heard of the sufferings he and his friends were enduring, had been trying to obtain his release. Through the efforts of the governor of Fort Orange and of the governor of New Netherlands he was taken on board a vessel and, by way of England, got back to France, where his arrival roused the keenest interest. But early in 1644 Jogues was again at sea on his way back to New France. Arriving at Montreal, then recently founded, he began to work among the Indians of that neighbourhood, pending the time when he could return to the Hurons, a journey which was becoming yearly more perilous because Iroquois Indians were everywhere along the route. Unexpectedly the Iroquois sent an embassy to Three Rivers to sue for peace: Jogues, who was present at the conference, noticed that no representative came from the chief village, Ossernenon. Moreover, it was clear to him that the Iroquois only desired peace with the French – not with the Hurons. However, it was considered desirable to send a deputation from New France to meet the Iroquois chiefs at Ossernenon, and Jogues was selected as ambassador, together with John Bourdon, who represented the government of the colony.

They went by the route of Lake Champlain and Lake George, and after spending a week in confirming the pact they returned to Quebec, Jogues leaving behind a box of religious articles because he was resolved later to return to the Mohawks as a missionary, and was glad to be relieved of one of his packages. This box proved the immediate cause of his martyrdom. The Mohawks had had a bad crop, and soon after Jogues's departure an epidemic broke out which they attributed to a devil concealed in the box. So when they heard that Jogues was paying a third visit to their villages, they waylaid, stripped and ill-treated him and his companion Lalande. Some of them treacherously invited Jogues to a meal on the evening of 18 October and tomahawked him as he was entering the cabin. His head they cut off and placed on a pole facing the route by which he had come. The following day his companion Lalande and the Huron guide were likewise tomahawked and beheaded, their bodies being afterwards thrown into the river. John Lalande was, like René Goupil, a *donné* or oblate of the mission. The martyrdom of Jogues sealed the fate of the Hurons, who were gradually becoming Christian, and with a period of peace the whole tribe would have been converted. But the Iroquois were unremitting in their hostilities. They began to attack and pillage the Huron villages, sparing no one, and on 4 July 1648, they appeared at Teanaustaye, just as Daniel had finished celebrating Mass. He went forth alone to meet the enemy. They surrounded him on all sides, covering him with arrows till he fell dead. They stripped him and threw his body into the church, which they set on fire.

Within a year, on 16 March 1649, the Iroquois attacked the village at which Brébeuf and Lalemant were stationed. The torture of these two missionaries was as atrocious as anything recorded in history. At the height of the torments Father Lalemant raised his eyes to Heaven and invoked God's aid, whilst Father de Brébeuf set his face like a rock as though insensible to the pain. Then, like one recovering consciousness, he preached to his persecutors and to the Christian captives until the savages gagged his mouth, cut off his nose, tore off his lips, and then, in derision of baptism, deluged him and his companion martyrs with boiling water. Finally, large pieces of flesh were cut out of the bodies of both the priests and roasted by the Indians, who tore out their hearts before their death by means of an opening above the breast, feasting on them and on their blood, which they drank while it was warm.

Before the end of the year 1649 the Iroquois had penetrated as far as the Tobacco nation, where Father Garnier had founded a mission in 1641 and where the Jesuits now had two stations. The inhabitants of the village of Saint-Jean, hearing that the enemy was approaching, sent out their men to meet the attackers, who, however, took a roundabout way and arrived at the gates unexpectedly. An orgy of incredible cruelty followed, in the midst of which Garnier, the only priest in the mission, hastened from place to place giving absolution to the Christians and baptizing the children and catechumens, totally unmindful of his own fate. While thus employed he was shot down by the musket of an Iroquois. He strove to reach a dying man whom he thought he could help, but after three attempts he collapsed, and subsequently received his death-blow from a hatchet.

Father Noel Chabanel, the missionary companion of Garnier, was immediately recalled. He had started on his way back with some Christian Hurons when they heard the cries of the Iroquois returning from Saint-Jean. The father urged his followers to escape, but was too much exhausted to keep up with them. His fate was long uncertain, but a Huron apostate eventually admitted having killed the holy man out of hatred of the Christian faith.

These martyrs of North America, *viz.* SS. John de Brébeuf, Isaac Jogues, Antony Daniel, Gabrial Lalemand, Charles Garnier, Noel Chabanel, René Goupil and John Lalande, were canonized in 1930.

MARY, THE BLESSED VIRGIN

(FIRST CENTURY)

Mary was a Jewish maiden of the house of David and the tribe of Judah, whose parents are commonly referred to as St Joachim and St Anne. At her conception, that is, when God infused a soul into her embryonic body, she was preserved by Him from all taint of original sin (the Immaculate Conception, 8 December); her birth, which the Church celebrates on 8 September, may have taken place at Sepphoris or Nazareth, but a general tradition favours Jerusalem, at a spot adjoining the Pool of Bethesda, close to a gate still called by Mohammedans (but not, curiously enough, by Christians), *Bab Sitti Maryam*, the Gate of the Lady Mary. She is believed to have been a child of promise to her long childless parents, and on 21 November the Church keeps a feast of her presentation in the Temple, though upon what occasion is not certain. According to apocryphal writings she remained within the Temple precincts in order to be brought up with other Jewish children, and at the age of fourteen was betrothed to a carpenter, Joseph, her husband being indicated to the high priest by a miracle. While still only betrothed she was visited by the Archangel Gabriel (the Annunciation, 25 March) and the Second Person of the Blessed Trinity became incarnate by the power of the Holy Ghost in her womb. This was at Nazareth, and she journeyed into Judaea to see her cousin St Elizabeth, who also was with child, St John the Baptist (the Visitation, 2 July). The marriage with St Joseph was duly ratified, and in due course, going up with him to Jerusalem for the enrolment ordered by Caesar Augustus, Mary gave birth in a rock-hewn stable at Bethlehem to Jesus Christ, the God-man (Christmas day, 25 December). Forty days later, in accordance with the Jewish law, she presented herself and her Child in the Temple for her ritual purification (2 February), an observance abrogated by the law of Christ which sees nought but honour in sanctified child-bearing. Warned by an angel, St Joseph fled with his wife and the holy Child into Egypt, to avoid the jealous rage of King Herod; it is not known how long they lived there, but when Herod was dead they returned to their old home at Nazareth.

For the thirty years before the public ministry of Jesus began Mary lived the outward life of any other Jewish woman of the common people. There are some who, concentrating their hearts and minds on our Lady in her glorified state as queen of Heaven, or as participating in the chief mysteries of the life of her Son, lose all memory of her day by day life as a woman in this world. The sonorous and beautiful titles given to her in the litany of Loreto; representations of her in art, from the graceful delicate ladies of Botticelli to

311

the prosperous *bourgeoises* of Raphael; the efforts of writers and preachers who feel that ordinary language is inadequate to describe her perfections; these and many other influences help to glorify the Mother of God – but somewhat tend to make us forget the wife of Joseph the carpenter. The Lily of Israel, the Daughter of the princes of Judah, the Mother of all Living, was also a peasant-woman, a Jewish peasant-woman, the wife of a working-man. Her hands were scored with labour, her bare feet dusty, not with the perfumed powder of romance but with the hard stinging grit of Nazareth, of the tracks which led to the well, to the olive-gardens, to the synagogue, to the cliff whence they would have cast Him. And then, after those thirty years, those feet were still tired and dusty, but now with following her divine Son from afar in His public life, from the rejoicings of the wedding-feast at Cana to His dereliction and her desolation on Mount Calvary, when the sword spoken of by Simeon at the purification pierced her heart. The dying Jesus confided her to the care of St John, 'and from that hour the disciple took her to his own'. On the day of Pentecost the Holy Ghost descended on our Lady when He came upon the Apostles and other disciples gathered together in the upper room at Jerusalem: that is the last reference to her in the Sacred Scriptures. The rest of her earthly life was probably passed at Jerusalem, with short sojourns at Ephesus and other places in company with St John and during the times of Jewish persecution.

Mary is the mother of Jesus, Jesus is God, therefore she is the Mother of God; the denial of this was condemned by the third general council at Ephesus in 431. Both before and after her miraculous child-bearing she was a virgin and so remained all her days, according to the unanimous and perpetual tradition and teaching of the Church. That she remained for her whole life absolutely sinless is affirmed by the Council of Trent. As the 'second Eve' Mary is the spiritual mother of all living, and veneration is due to her with an honour above that accorded to all other saints; but to give divine worship to her would be idolatry, for Mary is a creature, like the rest of human-kind, and all her dignity comes from God.

It has been for ages the explicit belief of the Church that the body of the Blessed Virgin was preserved from corruption and taken into Heaven and re-united to her soul, by an unique anticipation of the general resurrection. This preservation from corruption and assumption to glory was a privilege which seems due to that body which was never defiled by sin, which was ever the most holy and pure temple of God, preserved from all contagion of Adam and the common curse of mankind: that body from which the eternal Word received His own flesh, by whose hands He was nourished and clothed on earth, and whom He vouchsafed to obey and honour as His mother. Whether or not our Lady died is not certain; but it is generally held that she did in fact die before her glorious assumption, some conjecture at Ephesus but others think rather at Jerusalem. But did this feast commemorate only the assumption of her soul, and not of her body as well, its object would still be the same. For, as we honour the departure of other saints out of this world, so we have great reason to rejoice and praise God on this day when the Mother of Christ entered into the possession of those joys which He had prepared for her.

The Blessed Virgin Mary, the Feast of her Assumption into Heaven

PATRON SAINT OF FRANCE; OF AIRCREW (FRENCH); OF SOLDIERS (PARAGUAY); OF PARAGUAY; OF JAMAICA; OF SOUTH AFRICA; AND OF NEW CALEDONIA

15 AUGUST

Having recounted the sedulous devotion of the French to the Virgin Mary, Pius XI declared her the principal patron of the country in an Apostolic Letter of 2 March 1922, at the same time as he declared Joan of Arc to be the 'secondary' (or more accurately 'not quite so principal') patron of the country.

The feast of the Assumption, as it is usually depicted in art, has the Virgin flying through clouds. This would appear to make the feast a suitable patronal feast for those involved in flying. It was so declared for French pilots and aircrew in a decree of the Sacred Congregation of Rites of 25 January 1952.

In his Apostolic Letter of 13 July 1951, confirming the Assumption of the Virgin as the patronal festival of Paraguay and particularly of the Paraguayan army, Pius XII pointed out that the town of Asunción, named after the feast, was the centre of the conquest of the area, and in 1547 had become the first episcopal see. This Pius understood as evidence of Paraguayan devotion to the Virgin.

The Assumption was declared the patronal feast of Jamaica by a decree of the Sacred Congregation of Rites of 4 October 1951; and, on the occasion of a Marian Congress being held in Durban, also patron of South Africa, in an Apostolic Letter of Pope Pius XII of 15 March 1952.

The feast of the Assumption was also declared the patronal feast of New Caledonia by a decree of the Sacred Congregation of Rites dated 18 April 1963.

At the time that Alban Butler wrote, belief in our Lady's bodily assumption to Heaven was still, in the words of Pope Benedict XIV, a probable opinion the denial of which would be impious and blasphemous; and so it remained for another two hundred years. Then, in 1950, after taking counsel with the whole Church through her bishops, Pope Pius XII solemnly declared this doctrine to be divinely revealed and an article of faith. In the bull *'Munificentissimus Deus'* he declared that:

The remarkable unanimity of the Catholic episcopacy and faithful in the matter of the definibility of our Lady's bodily assumption into Heaven as a dogma of faith showed us that the ordinary teaching authority of the Church and the belief of the faithful which it sustains and directs were in accord, and thereby proved with infallible certainty that that privilege is a truth revealed by God and is contained in the divine deposit which Christ entrusted to His bride the Church, to be guarded faithfully and declared with infallible certainty.

And on 1 November, the feast of All Saints, the pope promulgated the bull publicly in the square before St Peter's basilica at Rome, defining the doctrine in the following terms:

Having repeatedly raised prayers of urgent supplication to God and having called upon the light of the Spirit of Truth – to the glory of Almighty God, who has bestowed His signal favours on Mary; in honour of His Son, deathless King of all ages and conqueror of sin and death; to the increase of the glory of the same exalted Mother: and to the joy and exultation of the whole Church: By the authority of our Lord Jesus Christ, by that of the blessed apostles Peter and Paul, and by our own authority, We pronounce, declare and define to be divinely revealed the dogma that the immaculate Mother of God, the Ever-virgin Mary, was on the completion of her earthly life assumed body and soul into the glory of Heaven.

The assumption of the Virgin Mary is 'St Mary's day' *par excellence*, the greatest of all the festivals which the Church celebrates in her honour, and it is the titular feast of all churches dedicated under her name without any special invocation. It is the consummation of all the other great mysteries by which her life was made wonderful; it is the birthday of her greatness and glory, and the crowning of all the virtues of her whole life, which we admire singly in her other festivals. It is for all these gifts conferred on her that we praise and thank Him who is the author of them, but especially for that glory with which He has crowned her. Nevertheless, whilst we contemplate the glory to which Mary is raised on this day, we ought to consider how she arrived at this honour and happiness, that we may walk in her steps. That she should be the mother of her Creator was the most wonderful miracle and the highest dignity; yet it was not properly this that God crowned in her. It was her virtue that He considered: her charity, her humility, her purity, her patience, her meekness, her paying to God the most perfect homage of worship, love, praise and thanksgiving.

To discuss in brief space the introduction and development of our Lady's Assumption feast is not easy. Three points, however, seem clear. First that the building of churches in veneration of Mary, the *Theotokos*, Mother of

God, inevitably brought in its train the celebration of some sort of dedication feast. That such churches dedicated to our Lady existed both in Ephesus and at Rome in the first half of the fifth century is certain, and some scholars think it probable that 'a commemoration of the ever-virgin Mary, Mother of God' was known at Antioch as early as A.D. 370. Secondly, in such a commemoration or annual feast of the Blessed Virgin no stress was at first laid upon the manner of her departure from this world. In her case, as in the case of the martyrs and other saints, it was simply the heavenly 'birthday' (*natalis*) which was originally honoured, and the festival was spoken of indifferently either as the 'birthday', or the 'falling-asleep' (*dormitio*), the 'passing away' (*transitus*), the 'deposition', or the 'assumption'. Thirdly, according to an apocryphal but ancient belief, the Blessed Virgin actually died on the anniversary of her Son's birth, *i.e.* on Christmas day. As this day was consecrated to the veneration of the Son, any distinctive commemoration of the Mother had to be postponed. In some parts of the world this separate feast was assigned to the winter season. Thus we know from St Gregory of Tours (*c.* 580) that a great feast in Mary's honour was then kept in Gaul in the middle of January. But it is equally certain that in Syria there was a summer feast on the fifth day of the month Ab, roughly August. This, with some fluctuations, was also adopted in the West, and in England St Aldhelm (*c.* 690) speaks plainly of our Lady's 'birthday' being kept in the middle of August.

The Birthday of the Blessed Virgin Mary of Charity

PATRON SAINT OF CUBA

8 SEPTEMBER

The feast of the birthday (or Nativity) of the Blessed Virgin Mary is one of the older celebrations of the Virgin in the Roman calendar dating, it is thought, from *c.* 790 and in the East probably earlier. In Cuba, however, it is associated with a particular statue of the Virgin which, it is said, was in the possession of one of the *conquistadores* and was left behind by him in an Indian village in 1508, as a thank-offering for the help he had received. In time this village, a few miles west of Santiago de Cuba, became a very popular shrine.

After the war of independence from Spain, at the end of the nineteenth century, the Cuban troops petitioned the Holy See that this feast of the Blessed Virgin Mary should be acknowledged as the country's patron. This was formally conceded by a decree of the Sacred Congregation of Rites dated 16 August 1917.

The Blessed Virgin Mary Immaculate

PATRON SAINT OF PORTUGAL; AND OF THE PHILIPPINES

11 FEBRUARY

According to the visionary at Lourdes in 1858, the Blessed Virgin proclaimed herself 'The Immaculate Conception'. The popularity of St Bernadette's visions led to there being instituted in the diocese of Tarbes, in which Lourdes is situated, a special feast of Mary Immaculate. That was in 1890. In 1907 Pius X extended the feast to the whole Church.

In an Apostolic Letter of 25 March 1936 Pius XI, who less than two years before had declared Antony of Padua principal patron of Portugal alongside Francis Borgia, recalled that the parliament and clergy of Portugal in 1646 had chosen Mary the Immaculate as the patronal feast of their country. This had been confirmed by Pope Clement X in a letter of 8 May 1671. Pius XI therefore added his voice to that of his predecessor and confirmed it again.

In his Apostolic Letter of 12 September 1942 Pius XII remarks that the Blessed Virgin Mary, under the title of Immaculate, had long been an object of devotion in the Philippines, and had been declared patron of the islands at the first (episcopal) Council of Manila, held in 1907. The Pope also recalls, however, that Pudentiana had been chosen as patron in the sixteenth, and Rose of Lima in the seventeenth century. These two saints the Pope now confirmed as secondary patrons, with Mary Immaculate as principal patron.

The Blessed Virgin Mary Immaculate, 'Aparecida'

PATRON SAINT OF BRAZIL

11 MAY

An Apostolic Letter of Pius XI, dated 30 July 1930, declared Our Lady Aparecida to be the principal patron of Brazil, at which time Brazil was consecrated to her in the presence of the President, ministers and other statesman, as well as clergy and faithful. The consecration was renewed in 1946.

In 1717 a group of fishermen found cast up upon the shore of the river Parahyba in Brazil a small statue of the Virgin Mary carved out of black wood. It rapidly became an object of devotion, and to it were attributed many miracles. Eventually a splendid church was built, not far from Sao Paulo, to house the statue and, on the fifteenth anniversary of the proclamation of the dogma of the Immaculate Conception, the Archbishop of Sao Paulo solemnly crowned Our Lady 'Aparecida' ('she who has appeared').

Comforter of the Afflicted

PATRON SAINT OF LUXEMBOURG

This title is a variation on Our Lady of Consolation. From the early seventeenth century a medieval statue of the Comforter of the Afflicted has been venerated in Luxembourg. Devotion was fostered by the Jesuits and it became a centre of pilgrimage. In 1666 the Virgin Mary under this title was proclaimed patron of the city of Luxembourg, and in 1678 of the whole duchy. The statue was originally in a special votive chapel outside the city walls, but in 1773 it was moved to the former Jesuit church, and in 1870 to the cathedral. The patronage of the Virgin was formally recognized by a decree of the Sacred Congregation of Rites dated 19 May 1914.

Faithful Virgin

PATRON SAINT OF THE ITALIAN POLICE

21 NOVEMBER

The title 'Virgo fidelis' is one of the seven beginning with 'Virgo' to be found in the Litany of Loreto. In an Apostolic Letter of 9 November 1949 Pius XII declared the Virgin Mary under this title to be the patron of the Carabinieri. He also fixed the day on which the feast was to be celebrated.

Great Queen of Hungary

PATRON OF HUNGARY

8 OCTOBER

In 1896, to celebrate Hungary's thousand years of history, Leo XIII approved a feast of the Blessed Virgin Mary under that title, thereby formally recognizing her as the country's patron.

Fervent devotion to the Virgin Mary in Hungary goes back at least to the time of King (Saint) Stephen at the beginning of the eleventh century. The symbols of the kingdom, in particular the crown sent by Pope Sylvester II but including also the national flag, were regarded as belonging to Mary. Legend has it that when Stephen died in 1038 he bequeathed his realm to Mary, who from then on was taken as its patron and its sovereign, under the title of *Magna Hungariae Domina*.

Health of the Sick

PATRON OF THE SICK PEOPLE OF POLAND

13 NOVEMBER

The 'Pious Union of the Apostolate of the Sick' in Poland chose the Blessed Virgin Mary under this title to be their patron. Paul VI confirmed their choice in an Apostolic Letter of 27 January 1968, and extended the patronage to all sick people of Poland.

This title of the Virgin Mary occurs in the Litany of Loreto, though there its meaning would seem to extend beyond physical sickness because the *salus* of *salus infirmorum* can mean salvation as well as health.

The Immaculate Conception of the Blessed Virgin Mary

PATRON SAINT OF THE UNITED STATES OF AMERICA, AND OF AMERICAN CATHOLIC SOLDIERS; OF SPAIN, THE SPANISH INFANTRY AND HIGH COMMAND, AND OF SPANISH ARMY CHAPLAINS; OF PHILIPPINE ARMY CHAPLAINS; OF INNER MONGOLIA; OF TANZANIA; OF ZAIRE; AND OF EQUATORIAL GUINEA

8 DECEMBER

In 1846 the bishops attending the sixth provincial council of Baltimore requested the Pope that he declare the Blessed Virgin Mary patron of the United States under the title of the Immaculate Conception. This request was granted by Rome on 7 February 1847, and confirmed again by a decree of the Sacred Congregation of Rites of 26 March 1914. In an Apostolic Letter of 8 May 1942, Pius XII declared the Immaculate Conception to be the special patron of American Catholic soldiers.

The Virgin Mary, under the title of the Immaculate Conception, was formally recognized as patron of Spain by a decree of the Sacred Congregation of Rites dated 6 July 1962. A further decree, dated 13 December 1961, declared her to be patron of the corps of military chaplains in Spain, and of the country's infantry and of its high command.

Since the Virgin Mary, under the title of Immaculate, is patron of the Philippines, it is appropriate that this title should also be the title of the patron of the military vicariate, as approved by Pius XII in an Apostolic Letter of 16 July 1958.

A decree of the Sacred Congregation of Rites dated 25 November 1914 formally recognized the Virgin, under the title of the Immaculate Conception, to be patron of Inner Mongolia.

The Virgin Mary under this title was declared patron of Tanzania in an Apostolic Letter of 8 November 1984. At the request of the bishops of the country, however, it was agreed by John Paul II that the feast should be celebrated to coincide with Independence Day, and not on the feast according to the Roman Calendar.

In his Apostolic Letter of 21 July 1891 Leo XIII recalled the devotion of Belgian

missionaries who were evangelizing the Congo, as it then was, to the Immaculate Conception of the Virgin. It was at their request, and to aid their efforts to bring the people of that territory to the knowledge of Christ, that the Pope was declaring Mary, under the title of the Immaculate Conception, to be the patron of Zaire.

The Immaculate Conception was confirmed as the title under which the Blessed Virgin was declared patron of Equatorial Guinea, formerly Spanish Guinea in West Africa, in a decree of the Sacred Congregation for Divine Worship on 26 May 1986.

By the bull *Ineffabilis Deus* of 8 December 1854, Pope Pius IX, by an exercise of his supreme pontifical power of infallible teaching, pronounced and defined it to be 'a doctrine revealed by God and therefore to be believed firmly and constantly by all the faithful that the Blessed Virgin Mary in the first instant of her conception was, by an unique grace and privilege of Almighty God in view of the merits of Jesus Christ the Saviour of the human race, preserved exempt from all stain of original sin'. That is to say that her soul at the first moment of its creation and infusion into her body was clothed in sanctifying grace, which to every other child of Adam is only given in the first instance after birth and, since Christ, at baptism (though it is generally held that Jeremias and St John Baptist received it before birth, but not at conception); the stain of original sin was not removed but excluded from her soul. For two hundred and fifty years before this solemn definition the doctrine of the Immaculate Conception had been universally believed in the Church and public teaching to the contrary was forbidden; but it was not 'of faith' (it had somewhat the same position as the doctrine of the Assumption of our Lady held until 1950).

A liturgical feast commemorating the conception of our Lady by the power of her father in the womb of her mother (without any reference to Mary's sinlessness) seems to have been originally celebrated in Palestine; and there is much reason to believe that the idea of this conception feast for our Lady was suggested by the earlier existence of a conception feast for St John Baptist, which is found at the beginning of the seventh century. For a long time the expression Conception of Mary was taken to mean the conception of our incarnate Lord within her womb by the power of the Holy Ghost (which we celebrate on the feast of the Annunciation), and consequently the new feast too was called the Conception of (or by) St Anne. In the ninth century it was imported to southern Italy and Sicily from Constantinople, still called the Conception of St Anne and with no idea of the *immaculate* conception. The first clear evidences of a feast of the Conception of our Lady, and under that name, in the West came from England, at Winchester, Canterbury and Exeter just before the Norman Conquest. This was identified with 8 December; and when we remember that in Jerusalem and Constantinople, and also in Naples, 9 December was the day assigned for this observance it seems probable that the determining influence came from the East.

In England, again as in the East, the observance began in the monasteries, and its first two mentions are found in calendars of the abbey called the New Minster, at Winchester. It met with opposition as an innovation. But a disciple of St Anselm, the monk Eadmer, wrote an important treatise on our Lady's conception, and the archbishop's nephew, another Anselm, introduced the feast of the Conception into his own abbey at Bury St Edmunds. It was soon taken up by Saint Albans, Reading, Gloucester and others. Some monks of Westminster, where the prior, Osbert of Clare, favoured the feast, challenged its lawfulness, but it was approved by a synod in London in 1129. At the same time the feast began to spread in Normandy, though whether it was first brought there from England or from southern Italy, then in Norman occupation, is not clear.

The adoption of the feast in the cathedral church of Lyons, about the year 1140, was the occasion of a protest by St Bernard which precipitated a theological controversy that was to last for three hundred years, the point at issue being the moment at which the sanctification of Mary took place. But however the controversy fluctuated from one to another of its several sides, the observance of the feast of the Conception of our Lady steadily progressed. In 1263 it was adopted by the whole Order of Friars Minor, who became the great defenders of the Immaculate Conception, whereas the Dominican theologians generally opposed it. But in spite of its popularity in England, Canterbury did not adopt the feast until 1328, and it was not till 1476 that the Franciscan pope, Sixtus IV, officially adopted it for the Roman church. The feast was still of the Conception of the Immaculate One rather than of the Immaculate Conception as we understand it, though, as Alban Butler pertinently notes, the sanctification of our Lady rather than her bare conception is the object of the Church's devotion. But in 1661 Pope Alexander VII declared that the feast celebrated the immunity of our Lady from original sin in the first moment of the creation of her soul and its infusion into her body, *i.e.* the moment of 'passive conception' in the sense of the Catholic doctrine. In 1708 Pope Clement XI imposed the festival on the whole Western church as a feast of precept.

Madonna of Castellazzo, or Our Lady of Grace and of Crete

PATRON SAINT OF MOTORCYCLISTS

The title of 'Our Lady of Grace', or 'Mother of Grace', is an old one, dating back at least to medieval times, though the feast, where it was kept at all, was celebrated on a variety of different dates. That the particular shrine of Our Lady of Grace at Castellazzo should have become the focus of devotion for motorcyclists seems to have been a matter of chance. In his Apostolic Letter of 11 February 1947, Pius XII outlines in unusually picturesque Latin the behaviour of the motorcyclists of Italy, France and Switzerland who would visit the shrine for the feast, receive a blessing, affix an image of the Virgin venerated at Castellazzo to their machines, and then tear off, with considerable noise, along the very ancient Roman roads. The Pope therefore declared the shrine of Our Lady of Grace at Catellazzo to be the patronal shrine of motorcyclists.

Mediatrix of All Graces

PATRON SAINT OF ARMY CHAPLAINS OF BELGIUM

31 MAY

The feast of Mediatrix of All Graces was introduced in Belgium in 1921, and afterwards spread to other parts of the world. It was confirmed as the patronal feast of the military vicariate of Belgium in a decree of the Sacred Congregation of Rites dated 16 February 1962.

Although it is the belief of the Catholic Church that Jesus Christ can be the only true mediator between God and humankind, it has also been the belief of the Church that saints intercede with their prayers. Among those who intercede, chief place is taken by Mary, for it was her cooperation with God the Father that brought Jesus, the source of all grace, into the world. There was at one time a movement to have the doctrine that the Virgin Mary was the Mediatrix of all graces defined as a dogma of the Roman Catholic faith. That this was the teaching of many theologians, and the belief of very many Catholics, there can be no doubt, but in recent years the proposal to have it declared an article of faith has been dropped.

The Most Pure of Heart of Mary

PATRON SAINT OF CENTRAL AFRICA; OF ANGOLA; AND OF ECUADOR

22 AUGUST

Early (that is, seventeenth-century) missionaries introduced devotion to Mary Most Pure into Central Africa, and the second wave of missionary activity, in the nineteenth century, discovered that some of it had survived. Our Lady, under this title, was formally declared patron of the region in a decree of the Sacred Congregation of Rites dated 30 April 1915.

The Blessed Virgin Mary, under the title of the 'Immaculate Heart', was declared patron of Angola in an Apostolic Letter of 21 November 1984. John Paul II, in his letter, recalled the devotion to the Immaculate Heart in that part of Africa, and said that he was formally recognizing this as the patronal feast of the country at the request of the country's bishops.

There has always been a strong devotion to the Blessed Virgin Mary in Ecuador as throughout Latin America. President Garcia Moreno officially consecrated the

Republic both to the Sacred Heart of Jesus, and to the Most Pure Heart of Mary in a solemn act on 25 March 1875, and the patronage of Mary under that title was formally recognized by a decree of the Sacred Congregation of Rites dated 24 July 1914.

The first liturgical celebrations of the Heart of Mary were devised by St John Eudes, and used by him privately in 1648. Shortly afterwards the Mass and office were approved for France, but formal approbation by the Holy See did not come until 1805. Exactly half a century later the feast itself was allowed to enter the calendar and in 1944 it was extended to the whole Church by Pius XII, who allotted to it the octave day of the Feast of the Assumption.

Mother of Good Counsel

PATRON SAINT OF ALBANIA

26 APRIL

It is part of the legend of the icon of Our Lady of Good Counsel that before its appearance at Gennazzano (see below) it had been venerated at Skodra in Albania. The Sacred Congregation of Rites in a decree dated 15 May 1915 therefore declared the Virgin Mary to be patron of that country, under the title of Mother of Good Counsel.

The picture of Our Lady, venerated under the title of Our Lady of Good Counsel, is to be found at Gennazzano, to the south-east of Rome. It rests on a narrow ledge, apparently miraculously held in place. A bomb which exploded nearby during the Second World War failed to dislodge, or even to damage it in any way, though it is painted on to very thin plaster. Its presence in the church is reported first in 1467, and it rapidly became an object of devotion as stories of miracles grew in number. The church was under the charge of Augustinian friars who, from 1779, were allowed to celebrate the feast of the Blessed Virgin Mary under this title. From them it spread to the whole Church.

Our Lady Help of Christians

PATRON SAINT OF AUSTRALIA; OF NEW ZEALAND; OF ARMY CHAPLAINS OF AUSTRALIA; AND OF SECURITY FORCES OF ANDORRA

24 MAY

Early missionaries in Australia, and in New Zealand, were priests of the Society of Mary, or Marists. They actively encouraged devotion to the Blessed Virgin Mary and, in 1844, the First Provincial Synod, held in Sydney, chose the Virgin Mary under the title of Help of Christians as principal patron of both countries. This choice was confirmed by the Sacred Congregation of Rites in a decree of 17 July 1916.

The patronage of Our Lady Help of Christians, was extended to the military chaplains of Australia by an Apostolic Letter of 16 July 1970.

It was a decree from the Sacred Congregation for Divine Worship, dated 14 May 1986, which declared the Virgin Mary, under the title of Help of Christians, to be patron of the police and security services of the Principality of Andorra.

From at least the middle of the sixteenth century the title 'Help of Christians' entered the prayer in honour of the Blessed Virgin Mary known as the Litany of Loreto. There was a liturgical celebration of this title only from 1815, however, when Pius VII ordered its observance in the newly-restored Papal States in thanksgiving for their deliverance from Napoleon. The celebration has since spread, but it is not a feast of the universal Church.

Our Lady of Agua Santa de Baños

PATRON SAINT OF INDIAN MISSIONS IN ECUADOR

This shrine was declared patron of missions to the native Indian population of Ecuador, especially that in the east of the country, in an Apostolic Letter of Pius XII, dated 3 March 1957.

This image of the Virgin has been an object of devotion in Ecuador since the early seventeenth century. As the name indicates, it is to be found at a place which is famous for its curative waters.

Our Lady of the Angels

PATRON SAINT OF COSTA RICA

2 AUGUST

After Costa Rica gained independence, the Constituent Assembly declared the image of the Blessed Virgin Mary described below to be the country's patron, and this was confirmed by a decree of the Sacred Congregation of Rites dated 14 November 1914.

A tiny chapel of St Mary of the Angels was associated with Francis of Assisi, and is now contained within the basilica at Assisi which honours the saint. The Franciscans celebrate the feast of Our Lady of the Angels on 2 August, and it was on 2 August 1636, so the story goes, near the city of Cartago in Costa Rica that an old Indian found a stone statue of the Virgin, holding the Child Jesus in her arms. The tradition goes on that every time the Indian tried to move the statue from where he had found it, it moved back again. At last the people built a church on the spot. It was titled Our Lady of the Angels because of the day on which it had been found.

Our Lady of Arabia

PATRON SAINT OF ARABIA

In 1948, on the Feast of the Immaculate Conception, 8 December, a church was dedicated in the town of Ahmadi to 'Our Lady of Arabia'. Two years later a statue of the Virgin was blessed by the Pope in the Vatican, and taken 'through the regions of desert' to be placed in the church which was much frequented, Pope Pius remarks in his Apostolic Letter of 25 January 1957, by devout oil men of many nations who were working in the area. A Marian sodality flourished, and a group came to Rome on pilgrimage in 1954, taking back with them, this time to Kuwait, another small statue of the Virgin, also blessed by the Pope. The Vicar Apostolic of Kuwait had asked the the Pope that 'Our Lady of Arabia' be declared patron of the whole region, and this Pius XII conceded in the Apostolic Letter quoted above.

Our Lady of Bethlehem on her Flight into Egypt

PATRON SAINT OF SPANISH ARCHITECTS

Spanish architects chose the Virgin under this title with the addition of the words 'on her Flight into Egypt' as their patron, presumably because both in Bethlehem and during the journey into Egypt, Mary was homeless. The choice was approved by a decree of the Sacred Congregation of Rites on 28 January 1949.

A number of religious orders, none of which is still in existence, took the name of Bethlehem as part of their title, and were responsible for the propagation of a devotion to Our Lady of Bethlehem. There are several shrines to the Virgin under this invocation in Spain, and in Spanish-speaking lands in general, although there is no widely accepted date for the feast day.

Our Lady of Chevremont

PATRON SAINT OF SPORTSMEN AND SPORTSWOMEN OF BELGIUM

9 JULY

In an Apostolic Letter of 27 March 1953 Pope Pius XII declared Our Lady of Chevremont to be patron of all those in the area around Liège who took exercise, the 'Sportifs Wallons'. He recalled that the club had a particular devotion to this shrine, and because sport, and exercise in general, was good for bodily health, he thought it appropriate that a patron should be appointed.

In 1688 the English Jesuits from their college at Liège in Belgium restored a ruined chapel on a hill, called Chevremont, which was near to their holiday house. They put there a small statue of the Virgin Mary, and an inscription saying 'Holy Mary pray for England'. The English Jesuit college returned to England at the end of the eighteenth century, but the chapel which had been restored remained a place of devotion for people in the locality.

Our Lady of Chiquinquira

PATRON SAINT OF COLOMBIA; AND OF THE VENEZUELAN NATIONAL GUARD

18 NOVEMBER

During the wars against Spain in the early nineteenth century, the Colombian armies of independence were consecrated to Our Lady of Chiquinquira, and the last of the presidents who ruled the country before its recapture by Spain ordered prayers to be said to her, and the captured spoils laid at her feet. In 1919, during the country's first Marian congress, the picture (see below) was crowned and Our Lady of Chiquinquira was proclaimed Queen of Colombia. This was confirmed by a decree of the Sacred Congregation of Rites dated 20 July 1962.

Veneration for the Virgin of Chiquinquira was, and is, far wider than the boundaries of Colombia. The Venezuelan National Guard chose her as patron, and this was confirmed by Apostolic Letter of 30 July 1980.

A picture of Our Lady of the Rosary had been taken from public view because it was in tatters. It was installed in the private oratory of Antonio de Santana at Chiquinquira, high up in the Andes to the North of the Bogota. There, on 26 December 1586, while a cousin of Santana's, Maria Ramos, was praying before the picture, there was a bright light, and a new image of Our Lady was left on the canvas. Naturally the picture attracted much attention, and before long miracles were reported and a shrine constructed. Devotion to the Blessed Virgin Mary under this title, strong in Colombia, is also to be found in Venezuela and Ecuador.

Our Lady of Consolation

PATRON SAINT OF PENSIONERS, OLD PEOPLE, AND SENIOR CITIZENS

20 JUNE (AND OTHER DATES)

In his Apostolic Letter of 26 May 1961 John XXIII declared the Virgin Mary under this title to be the patron of the old and of pensioners because the nuns in charge of two societies recently set up to look after old people in Italy were themselves Sisters of the Most Holy Mary of Consolation.

There is in Turin a Byzantine icon of the Virgin Mary, venerated from at least the eleventh century, which has the title of the Consolata – Our Lady of

Consolation or of Solace. The picture resides in a church especially built for it in 1682, and it was crowned in 1829. This title of the Virgin is identical with Comforter of the Afflicted.

Our Lady of Copacabana

PATRON SAINT OF THE BOLIVIAN NAVY

5 AUGUST

At the request of the military vicar, and of all the Bolivian hierarchy, the Blessed Virgin Mary under this title was declared the patron of the Bolivian fleet by Paul VI in an Apostolic Letter in 1969.

Copacabana is a stretch of land, almost an island and surrounded by islands, on Lake Titicaca in Bolivia. The Indian population of the lake and the area around it were converted to Christianity early in the sixteenth century, and one of their leaders wished to demonstrate his devotion by carving a statue of the Blessed Virgin Mary as an Inca princess. This he did, despite rebuffs from the ecclesiastical authorities in the first instance, and the church in which this statue remains has become the centre of Marian devotion in Bolivia. The statue was crowned as Queen of the country on 2 August 1925.

Our Lady of Coromoto

PATRON SAINT OF VENEZUELA

11 SEPTEMBER

The bishops of Venezuela declared Our Lady of Coromoto patron of Venezuela in 1942, and sought confirmation from the Holy See. This was given by Pius XII in an Apostolic Letter of 7 October 1944.

Near the town of Guanare in Venezuela there was a tribe of Indians who, it is claimed, converted to Christianity at the insistence of the Virgin Mary who appeared several times to their chieftain in the years 1651 and 1652. The tribe, the Cospes, set off to find a mission station and settled near one in a village they created for themselves, called Coromoto. The chieftain, however, put off the date of his baptism and reverted to his old ways. One night the Virgin appeared to him in his hut – she was seen also by three others – and rebuked him to such an extent that the chieftain lost his temper and attacked her. He had his hands about her neck in an attempt to strangle her when the vision disappeared, and he found himself holding a statue of the Blessed Virgin Mary. This was moved to the parish church at Guarane which rapidly became a national centre of devotion and pilgrimage.

Our Lady of Divine Providence

PATRON SAINT OF PUERTO RICO

Because of the great devotion to Our Lady of Divine Providence shown by the people of Puerto Rico, said Paul VI in his Apostolic Letter of 19 November 1969, he was confirming the Blessed Virgin under that title to be patron of the country.

Our Lady of Graces

PATRON SAINT OF SKIERS (ITALIAN)

9 JUNE

In his Apostolic Letter of 7 January 1955 Pius XII refers to the custom among skiers in Italy of paying particular devotion to an image of Our Lady of Graces in the church of the town of Folgaria, in the diocese of Triento. For that reason he declared her patron of Italian skiers.

The feast of Our Lady of Grace, of Graces, or Mother of Grace has been celebrated from medieval times, but has never become a feast of the universal Church. There are many shrines around the world with this title, a good number of which are in Italy.

Our Lady of Guadalupe

PATRON SAINT OF MEXICO; OF CENTRAL AND SOUTH AMERICA; AND OF STUDENTS OF PERU

12 DECEMBER

For the people of Mexico the shrine of Our Lady of Guadalupe has become not only a place of pilgrimage but a national symbol. Banners of the Virgin led rebels into battle during the struggle for independence from Spain in the early nineteenth century. They were again used as symbols of revolt by Emiliano Zapata in the first quarter of the twentieth century. The patronage of Our Lady of Guadalupe was formally confirmed by a decree of the Sacred Congregation of Rites dated 5 February 1962.

Devotion to the Virgin Mary under this title spread to all countries of Central and South America, and as patron of this area, the devotion was formally confirmed by a decree of the Sacred Congregation of Rites dated 12 December 1962.

Young people engaged in studies, said Paul VI in his Apostolic Letter of 20 September 1965, are accustomed to turn to the Virgin under the title of 'Help of Christians', or 'Seat of Wisdom'. In Peru, however, they approach her, went on the Pope, under the title of Our Lady of Guadalupe, and under that title he was now confirming her patronage.

Guadalupe is in Estremadura, a Spanish province to the south-west of Madrid. There, in the fourteenth century, the Virgin Mary appeared to a shepherd on a hillside, and led him to where a statue of herself lay hidden. This image rapidly became the most venerated image of the Virgin in the country after that of the Virgin of the Pillar, although in the splendour of its shrine it probably outshines the latter. The Mexican national shrine shares the same name, and its history is somewhat similar, though the first appearance of Mary on the hill called Tepeyac, just to the north of what is now known as Mexico City, can be dated precisely. It was the early morning of 9 December 1531. A Christian Indian, hurrying to Mass, heard singing on the hill and went to investigate. There a young girl of some fourteen years identified herself as the Virgin Mary, and told the Indian, whose name was Juan Diego, to instruct the local bishop that a shrine should be built to her on the hill-top. Twice the bishop rejected the request, disbelieving Juan Diego's story. But the third time the Virgin told Juan to pick some roses, growing miraculously on the hill, bundle them up in his cloak, and to give them to the bishop. When he let fall his cloak and the roses tumbled to the floor, there on the Indian's cloak was an image of the Virgin. The shrine was therefore built, and the cloak may still be seen there, an object of considerable veneration not only by the people of Mexico but of many from other adjacent countries.

Our Lady of Lanka

PATRON SAINT OF SRI LANKA

Our Lady of Lanka was declared patron of Sri Lanka – it was then called Ceylon – in an Apostolic Letter of Pius XII dated 11 June 1948.

Devotion to the Virgin Mary in the Christian areas of Sri Lanka was fostered in particular by the missionary congregation of Oblates of Mary Immaculate, and the whole ecclesiastical province based upon Colombo was dedicated to Mary Immaculate at the request of the Archbishop. Devotion to the Virgin Mary increased among Catholics after the war, for many of the devout attributed escaping invasion by the Japanese to her intercession. The Archbishop of Colombo dedicated the island to 'Our Lady of Lanka' on 15 February 1947.

Our Lady of Lapurdo

PATRON SAINT OF SHEPHERDS

In his Apostolic Letter of 11 July 1958 Pius XII remarks that shepherds, removed from people's company and the noise of the city, find it easier to turn their minds to spiritual and heavenly things. They have, he says, joined in great numbers the pious association set up for them. This particular association has a devotion to the shrine of the Virgin at Lapurdo in Italy, and the Pope declares the Virgin Mary under this title to be their patron.

Our Lady of Loreto

PATRON SAINT OF AVIATION, AIRCREW OR FLIGHT CREW; AND OF ALL INVOLVED IN FLYING

10 DECEMBER

Because of the legend that the Holy House flew through the air, carried by angels, from Galilee to Italy by way of what is now Yugoslavia, the feast of Our Lady of Loreto has seemed a suitable one to declare to be patron of all those involved in flying. A decree of the Sacred Congregation of Rites of 24 March 1920 gave official approval. The wording of this decree seems to be very general. However, the Sacred Congregation of Rites has made specific decrees for pilots of Belgium (16 February 1962) and of Spain (13 December 1961). The decree in favour of the Argentinians, on the other hand, refers more explicitly to the Air Force (16 May 1958).

Loreto is a town on Italy's Adriatic coast, south of Ancona. It seems to have been a shrine of the Virgin Mary from the twelfth century, and it was alleged that the image of the Virgin to be found there had been brought by angels. Towards the end of the fifteenth century, however, the shrine at Loreto contained the Holy House in which Mary had been born, and in which the Annunciation had taken place. It was this which had been brought to Italy by angelic hands in, an early sixteenth-century document insisted, the year 1294, after a brief stay across the Adriatic in Dalmatia. Many miracles have been attributed to the shrine, a small rectangular building now encased in marble and situated within a domed basilica. The building is made of materials not to be found in the vicinity of Loreto, and has no foundations, but despite these peculiarities few writers, even the most devout, accept the story attached to the shrine. This does not impair its importance as a place of devotion to the Virgin. A local feast was permitted in 1632, and is now observed throughout Italy as well as in some other areas of the world and by some religious orders. A fire in 1921 destroyed the original statue of the Virgin, but another was swiftly produced, crowned by Pope Pius XI in 1924 and replaced in the shrine.

Our Lady of Lujan

PATRON SAINT OF ARGENTINA; OF URUGUAY; OF PARAGUAY; OF ARGENTINA'S
MILITARY CHAPLAINS

SATURDAY BEFORE THE FOURTH SUNDAY AFTER EASTER

*In an Apostolic Letter dated 8 September 1930, Pius XI declared Our Lady of Lujan to
be patron not only of Argentina but of Uruguay and Paraguay as well. A decree of the
Sacred Congregation of Rites dated 16 May 1958 declared her patron of the Argentinian military vicariate, i.e. of chaplains to the armed forces.*

In 1630 a Portuguese landowner living at Cordoba in Argentina asked a
friend in Buenos Aires to send him a statue of the Virgin for a small
sanctuary he wished to construct in honour of the Immaculate Conception.
It seems that two statues were in fact sent, one of which reached its destination. The second, however, did not. After an overnight halt the oxen
refused on the third morning to restart the journey until one of the crates
containing a statue had been unloaded. This was near the small town of
Lujan, about forty miles west of Buenos Aires, and a local landowner, Don
Rosendo Oramas, built an altar for the small, terracotta figure with blue eyes
in his own ranch house. It was looked after by a young African slave, who
had belonged to the man in charge of taking the statue to Cordoba. The first
proper church was completed by 1685. In 1754 a rich Spaniard began the
construction of the second church, as a thank-offering for a miraculous cure.

The present basilica, said to be one of the finest in the Western hemisphere, was begun in 1887 and on 8 May that year the statue was solemnly
crowned with a crown which had been blessed by Pope Leo XIII. The basilica
was finally completed to mark the three hundredth anniversary of the shrine
in 1930.

Our Lady of Mercy

PATRON SAINT OF THE DOMINICAN REPUBLIC; OF THE ARGENTINIAN ARMY, AND
THE ECUADORIAN ARMY

24 SEPTEMBER

*Not perhaps the most favoured of the Marian cults in the Dominican Republic, the
feast of Our Lady of Mercy (or of Mercies) is nonetheless the devotion of the country's
capital city which has had a bishop since 1511. This devotion was formally recognized
as that of the country's patron by a decree of the Sacred Congregation of Rites dated 16
February 1914.*

*A decree of the Sacred Congregation of Rites dated 16 May 1958 declared Our Lady
of Mercy to be patron of the Argentinian army.*

In Ecuador, said Paul VI in his Apostolic Letter of 21 February 1964, the army has chosen the Virgin Mary under this title to be its patron, and his letter is simply confirming the choice.

There seem to be two quite separate origins for this devotion. One is proper to Savona in Italy where in 1536 a vision of the Virgin Mary promised 'mercy not justice' to the people of the town, if they should repent of their sins. From there the devotion spread over Italy and elsewhere. The other is associated with the Mercedarians, a religious order founded about the year 1220 to look after the sick and rescue Christians who had been taken as slaves by the Moors. The full name of the order was 'Of Our Lady of Mercy', and members kept a feast under that title which was, in 1680, extended to the whole of Spain and to the whole Church in 1696. The image with which this title is associated, namely a picture of the Virgin stretching out a cloak to cover those who seek her help, is somewhat older than the shrine at Savona, and seems to have come from a thirteenth-century Cistercian source.

Our Lady of Mount Carmel

PATRON SAINT OF CHILE; OF BOLIVIA; OF THE SPANISH NAVY

16 JULY

Devotion to Our Lady of Mount Carmel in Chile can be traced back at least to the middle of the seventeenth century, and it was a particular devotion of Bernardo O'Higgins, the country's liberator. He dedicated his army to her in January 1817 before marching on the Spaniards. Although he was victorious, the victory was not complete, and the military high command made a vow, in the cathedral of Santiago, to dedicate the country to her, should they win decisively – which they did at Maipu, in the suburbs of Santiago. The promise of a sanctuary was promptly fulfilled, and, a century later, in December 1926, the statue of Our Lady of Mount Carmel was solemnly crowned Queen of Chile. The original sanctuary proved too small, and a new one has been built, which remains a centre of pilgrimage, at the site of the battle of Maipu. Formal recognition of Our Lady of Mount Carmel as the patron of Chile was given in decrees of the Sacred Congregation of Rites dated 24 October 1923 and 27 August 1957.

Bolivia was formally committed to the patronage of Our Lady of Mount Carmel by a decree of the Sacred Congregation of Rites dated 3 October 1914.

The patronage of Our Lady of Mount Carmel for the Spanish navy was confirmed by a decree of the Sacred Congregation of Rites dated 13 December 1961.

The Order of Mount Carmel was founded in Palestine in the middle of the twelfth century, taking its name from a hill on the Palestinian coast. The church of the Order which stands on the hill contains a statue of the Virgin Mary, representing a vision, reputedly on 16 July 1251, to St Simon Stock,

331

the Englishman who reorganized the Order. Towards the end of the fourteenth century the custom arose of celebrating the vision, first among the Carmelites themselves for whom it became the patronal feast in 1600. In 1674 permission to celebrate Our Lady of Mount Carmel was granted to Spain and its dominions. In 1726 it became a feast of the whole Church.

Our Lady of Peace

PATRON SAINT OF EL SALVADOR

21 NOVEMBER

Pope Paul VI declared the Blessed Virgin Mary under this title patron of El Salvador in an Apostolic Letter of 10 October 1966.

In the parish church of St Michael, in the city of San Salvador, there is an ancient statue of the Virgin Mary holding an olive branch which, according to some accounts, was brought there from a shipwreck. In September 1787 the inhabitants of the city attributed to the statue their safety when threatened by a volcanic eruption. The Virgin was also held up as a model of peace among warring factions in the country at the time of the war of independence. The statue was solemnly crowned in November 1921, in the presence of the country's president.

Our Lady of Perpetual Succour

PATRON SAINT OF HAITI

27 JUNE

Veneration of the Virgin Mary under this title is an ancient practice of Haiti, said Paul VI in his Apostolic Letter of 30 April 1966, especially in times of trouble, and the Haitians dedicated their country to Our Lady of Perpetual Succour in 1942. In January 1966 the country's bishops asked the Pope to confirm this choice of patron, which he was doing in his letter.

This title of the Virgin Mary – meaning Our Lady of Constant Help – derives from a fourteenth-century icon, probably painted in Crete. It was venerated from the end of the fifteenth century to the late eighteenth century in the church of St Matthew in Rome, when the church was destroyed. It was later replaced by a church in the charge of Redemptorists, and dedicated to St Alphonsus. The celebration of a feast of the Virgin under this title was approved by Pius IX.

Our Lady of the Pillar

PATRON SAINT OF THE SPANISH POLICE

12 OCTOBER

Our Lady of the Pillar was formally declared patron of the police in Spain – specifically of the Guardia Civil – by a decree of the Sacred Congregation of Rites dated 13 December 1961.

According to legend, St James the Elder was preaching near Zaragoza in Spain when there appeared to him a vision of the Virgin Mary carrying the Infant Christ. Behind her there came angels carrying a pillar. Mary asked that a church be built there in her honour, and the pillar placed within it as a sign of the constancy of the Spanish people's faith. Whatever the truth of the story, and there is no sure evidence for the Marian shrine before the twelfth century, the devotion of the Spanish to Our Lady of the Pillar is not in doubt.

Our Lady of the Rosary, 'La Naval'

PATRON SAINT OF THE PHILIPPINE NAVY

7 OCTOBER (FEAST OF OUR LADY OF THE ROSARY)

In the seventeenth century, Paul VI said in his Apostolic Letter of 19 May 1978, the navy of the Philippines had driven off five attacks against all the odds. The sailors attributed these victories to the Virgin Mary under the title of Our Lady of the Rosary. So great was her aid to the fleet that they gave Mary the particular title of 'La Naval'. In his Letter, the Pope formally confirmed this title, at the request of the military vicar, and of the entire episcopal conference of the Philippines.

As the Roman Martyrology today reminds us, Pope St Pius V in 1572 ordered an annual commemoration of our Lady of Victory to be made to implore God's mercy on His Church and all the faithful, and to thank Him for his protection and numberless benefits, particularly for His having delivered Christendom from the arms of the infidel Turks by the sea victory of Lepanto in the previous year, a victory which seemed a direct answer to the prayers and processions of the rosary confraternities at Rome made while the battle was actually being fought. A year later Gregory XIII changed the name of the observance to that of the Rosary, fixing it for the first Sunday in October (the day of Lepanto). On 5 August the feast of the dedication of St Mary Major, in the year 1716, again while Marian processions were taking place, the Turks were again signally defeated, by Prince Eugene at Peterwardein in Hungary. In thanksgiving therefore, Pope Clement XI decreed that the feast of the Holy Rosary should be observed throughout the Western church. The feast is now kept on the date of the battle of Lepanto, 7

October (except by the Dominicans, who observe the original first Sunday of the month).

According to the tradition of the Order of Preachers, recognized by many popes and accepted in the Roman Breviary, the rosary, just as we know it, was devised by St Dominic himself, and used by him in his missionary work among the Albigensians, in consquence of a vision in which our Lady revealed it to him. No tradition of the kind has been more passionately supported and few have been more devastatingly attacked. Its truth was first questioned some two hundred years ago, and the resulting controversy has been carried on at intervals ever since. It is well known that the use of beads or similar objects as a device for aiding the memory and keeping count is not only pre-Dominican but pre-Christian; and the monks of the Eastern church use a rosary of ancient origin, having 100 or more beads, on a different plan from and entirely independent of the Western devotion. Nor is it now disputed that the custom of saying a number of *Paters* or *Aves* (often 150, corresponding to the number of the psalms), and keeping count of them by means of a string of beads, etc., was widespread in the West before the thirteenth century. The famous Lady Godiva of Coventry, who died about 1075, left by will to a certain statue of our Lady 'the circlet of precious stones which she had threaded on a cord in order that by fingering them one after another she might count her prayers exactly' (William of Malmesbury). Moreover there seems to be no doubt that such strings of beads were used for long only for the counting of *Paters*. In the thirteenth century and throughout the Middle Ages such articles were called 'paternosters'; their makers were 'paternosterers'; and in London they worked in the street we still call Paternoster Row. A learned Dominican bishop, Thomas Esser, maintained that meditation while reciting numerous *Aves* was first practised by certain Carthusians in the fourteenth century. None of the stories about the origin of the rosary current before the fifteenth century mention St Dominic, and for another hundred years there was no uniformity in the way it was said, even among the Friars Preachers themselves. None of the early accounts of St Dominic make any mention of the rosary, either in referring to his methods of prayer or to anything else; the early constitutions of his order are quite silent about it; and there is little trace of a rosary in early Dominican iconography, from Fra Angelico's paintings down to St Dominic's sumptuous tomb at Bologna (finished in 1532).

Our Lady of Suyapa

PATRON SAINT OF HONDURAS

3 FEBRUARY

So great was the devotion of the indigenous inhabitants of Honduras to Our Lady of Suyapa that, in 1925, the Archbishop of Tegucigalpa had the statue (see below) declared the country's patron, and this was confirmed by a decree of the Sacred Congregation of Rites dated 25 June 1953.

In February 1747 a group of Indians coming back from work was forced to spend the night beside the road. As they lay down to sleep their leader's hand touched something hard on the ground, which, the following morning, he discovered to be a small statue of the Virgin Mary. He took it back to his village where the statue rapidly became an object of veneration, and renowned for miracles.

Our Lady of the Thirty-Three

PATRON SAINT OF URUGUAY

In 1825, when Uruguay was still occupied by Brazil, thirty-three Uruguayan exiles returned to their country determined to free it from foreign domination. On 25 May their leader set up his headquarters in the city of Florida, where there existed a shrine to Our Lady of Lujan. On 14 June the Uruguayan freedom flags were laid before the Virgin Mary, and in the parochial office the declaration of independence was signed on 25 August. Because this rising against Brazil proved successful, the 'Virgin of the Thirty-Three' became honoured as patron of the country, and this was confirmed by a decree of the Sacred Congregation of Rites on 21 November 1962.

Our Lady of the Thorns

PATRON SAINT OF BLOOD DONORS

Our Lady of the Thorns is the title of an image of the Virgin Mary venerated at Sissa in the diocese of Parma. According to the Apostolic Letter of 18 September 1981, this image has been an object of veneration by blood donors in the Province of Parma. The letter formally recognized the Virgin under this title as patron of blood donors in the region.

Our Lady of Valle

PATRON SAINT OF THE VENEZUELAN NAVY

Our Lady of Valle is the name of an image of the Virgin Mary in the parish church of the Holy Spirit on the island of Margarita in Venezuela. According to the Apostolic Letter of 16 March 1981, this image of the Virgin is much venerated by sailors of the Venezuelan navy, and the chaplain-in-chief of that country's armed forces, together with the rest of the bishops, asked that this shrine should be recognized as patron of the navy. The Apostolic letter confirmed this.

'Patron of India'

PATRON SAINT OF INDIA

At a meeting in Bangalore in January 1950 the bishops in India unanimously pronounced the Blessed Virgin Mary as 'Patron of India', and asked the Pope to confirm this title, which Pius XII did in an Apostolic Letter of 26 January 1951.

'Queen of China'

PATRON SAINT OF CHINA

At the suggestion of the papal delegate, Mgr Constantini, the bishops of China, gathered at Shanghai for a conference in 1924, determined to consecrate China to Mary. This they did in a solemn ceremony that same year, on 12 June. Mary's patronage was officially recognized by the Holy See in a decree of the Sacred Congregation of Rites dated 5 February 1941.

From the time that Christianity began to spread in China, there was considerable devotion to the Virgin Mary. It was affected by the culture of the people, and centred upon the idea of Mary as Queen of Heaven.

'Queen of Nigeria'

PATRON SAINT OF NIGERIA

A gathering of the bishops of Eastern Nigeria at Enugu on 11 April 1961 unanimously agreed that Mary, under the title of 'Queen of Nigeria', should be principal patron of the country, and St Patrick secondary patron. John XXIII confirmed these choices in an Apostolic Letter of 24 June of the same year. The selection of Patrick no doubt owed much to the fact that Eastern Nigeria in particular had been evangelized by Irish clergy, particularly the Holy Ghost fathers, or 'Spiritans'.

'Queen of Palestine'

PATRON SAINT OF PALESTINE

This title of the Blessed Virgin Mary was formally recognized in two decrees of the Sacred Congregation of Rites, dated 16 August 1933 and 1 March 1940.

'Queen of Peace'

PATRON SAINT OF CIVILIAN WAR VICTIMS

9 JULY (AND OTHER DATES)

Reflecting on the way in which war has so developed that it is no longer the army or the other fighting services which only bear the casualties, John XXIII welcomed the formation in Italy of an association of civilian war victims, and approved as patron the Virgin Mary under this title.

An image of the Virgin Mary in Toledo was given this title because, shortly after it had been erected in 1085, peace was negotiated with the Moors. A less localized feast was granted in 1658, which was associated with a miraculous statue in Paris, and the devotion was spread by several religious orders. It was after the First World War, however, that the title became widely known, and was included in the Litany of Loreto.

'Queen of Poland'

PATRON SAINT OF POLAND

3 MAY

Pius X approved this title in the course of an address to Polish pilgrims in Rome, on 5 May 1904. It was confirmed again by a decree of the Sacred Congregation of Rites dated 31 August 1962.

The origin of the use of this title for the Virgin Mary is lost in history. In the middle of the seventeenth century, however, during the war with the Swedes, the Polish people attributed the successful defence of the shrine of Czestochowa to Mary. On 1 April 1656 the King, John Casimir swore to liberate his people from all the injustices which afflicted them, and called upon the aid of Mary as Queen and Sovereign to help him.

'Star of the Sea'

PATRON SAINT OF THE ARGENTINIAN NAVY

The Virgin Mary as Star of the Sea was declared patron of the Argentinian navy in a decree of the Sacred Congregation of Rites of 16 May 1958.

The title 'Star of the Sea', as used of Mary, is very old. It is thought to date back to the very beginning of the fifth century when St Jerome interpreted the Hebrew name Miryam, the original name of Mary, as meaning Star of the Sea. It quickly became, and has remained to this day enshrined in hymns both Latin and English, a popular invocation of the Virgin Mary. It is naturally much used in a maritime context.

MATTHEW

PATRON SAINT OF ACCOUNTANTS; OF TAX COLLECTORS, AND CUSTOMS OFFICERS; AND OF SECURITY GUARDS

21 SEPTEMBER

Given his profession as a publican, or tax collector, for the Roman administration, it is appropriate that St Matthew should have been regarded as patron of accountants – or their earlier equivalents – from medieval times. Pius XII, however, formally declared him patron of Italian accountants in an Apostolic Letter of 6 August 1954.

It is also wholly understandable that St Matthew should be, in the light of his profession, the patron of tax collectors; but it was confirmed by a decree of the Sacred Congregation of Rites of 7 October 1957. The decree also included customs officers as being under his patronage. An Apostolic Letter of Paul VI extended Matthew's patronage further to those involved in collecting Italy's consumer, or purchase, tax.

In an Apostolic Letter of 10 April 1934 Pius XI declared St Matthew to be patron of those soldiers who, in the Italy of that time, were charged with what the pope recognized to be the particularly dangerous task of keeping guard over financial institutions such as banks. In an Apostolic Letter of 25 March 1964 Paul VI included under Matthew's patronage the 'Guarda Fiscal' of Portugal.

St Matthew is called by two evangelists Levi, and by St Mark 'the son of Alpheus'; it is probable that Levi was his original name and that he took, or was given, that of Matthew ('the gift of Yahveh') when he became a follower of our Lord. But Alpheus his father was not he of the same name who was father of St James the Less. He seems to have been a Galilaean by birth, and was by profession a publican, or gatherer of taxes for the Romans, a profession which was infamous to the Jews, especially those of the Pharisees' party; they were in general so grasping and extortionate that they were no more popular among the Gentiles. The Jews abhorred them to the extent of refusing to marry into a family which had a publican among its members, banished them from communion in religious worship, and shunned them in all affairs of civil society and commerce. But it is certain that St Matthew was a Jew, as well as a publican.

The story of Matthew's call is told in his own gospel. Jesus had just confounded some of the Scribes by curing a man who was sick of the palsy, and passing on saw the despised publican in his custom-house. 'And He saith to him, "Follow me". And he arose up and followed him.' Matthew left all his interests and relations to become our Lord's disciple and to embrace a spiritual commerce. We cannot suppose that he was before wholly unacquainted with our Saviour's person or doctrine, especially as his office was at Capharnaum, where Christ had resided for some time and had preached and wrought many miracles, by which no doubt Matthew was in some measure prepared to receive the impressions which the call made upon him. St Jerome says that a certain shiningness and air of majesty which appeared in the countenance of our divine Redeemer pierced his soul and strongly attacked him. But the great cause of his conversion was, as St Bede remarks, that 'He who called him outwardly by His word at the same time moved him inwardly by the invisible instinct of His grace'.

The calling of St Matthew happened in the second year of the public ministry of Christ, who adopted him into that holy family of the apostles, the spiritual leaders of His Church.

It is said that St Matthew, after having made a harvest of souls in Judea, went to preach Christ to the nations of the East, but of this nothing is known for certain. He is venerated by the Church as a martyr, though the time, place and circumstances of his end are unknown.

MAURICE, MARTYR (A.D. 287?)

PATRON SAINT OF SOLDIERS, ARMIES, AND OF ALPINE TROOPS; OF AUSTRIA, PIEDMONT, SAVOY AND SARDINIA; OF DYERS AND WEAVERS

22 SEPTEMBER

Although there is little or no historical evidence of his existence, the cult of St Maurice, and the Theban Legion of which he was said to be a member, was extremely popular, in particular spreading into Austria, Piedmont, Savoy and Sardinia, of which countries or regions he became the patron. His choice as patron of soldiers needs no explanation, but for Alpine troops of Italy his patronage was formally recognized by a decree of the Sacred Congregation of Rites of 2 July 1941, of their French counterparts on 25 January 1952, and of the Belgian equivalents on 16 February 1962.

St Maurice has long been regarded as a patron saint of dyers and weavers, but in neither case is there any direct evidence why.

A number of the Gauls, called Bagaudae, having risen in revolt, the *Augustus* Maximian Herculius marched against them with an army, of which one unit was the Theban Legion. This had been recruited in Upper Egypt and was composed entirely of Christians. When he arrived at Octodurum (Martigny), on the Rhône above the lake of Geneva, Maximian issued an order that the whole army should join in offering sacrifice to the gods for the success of their expedition. The Theban Legion hereupon withdrew itself, encamped near Agaunum (now called St Maurice-en-Valais), and refused to take any part in these rites. Maximian repeatedly commanded them to obey orders, and upon their constant and unanimous refusal sentenced them to be decimated. Thus every tenth man was put to death, according as the lot fell. After the first decimation, a second was commanded, unless the soldiers obeyed the orders given; but they cried out that they would rather suffer all penalties than to do anything contrary to their religion. They were principally encouraged by three of their officers, Maurice, Exuperius and Candidus, referred to respectively as the *primicerius*, the *compiductor* and the *senator militum*. Maximian warned the remainder that it was of no use for them to trust to their numbers, for if they persisted in their disobedience not a man among them should escape death. The legion answered him by a respectful remonstrance: 'We are your soldiers, but are also servants of the true God. We owe you military service and obedience; but we cannot renounce Him who is our Creator and Master, and also yours even though you reject Him. In all things which are not against His law we most willingly obey you, as we have done hitherto. We readily oppose all your enemies, whoever they are; but we cannot dip our hands into the blood of innocent persons. We have taken an oath to God before we took one to you: you can place no confidence in our second oath if we violate the first. You command us to punish the Christians; behold, we are such. We confess God the Father, author of all things, and His Son, Jesus Christ. We have seen our companions slain without lamenting them, and we rejoice at their honour. Neither this nor any other provocation has tempted us to revolt. We have arms in our hands, but we do not resist because we would rather die innocent than live by any sin.'

This legion consisted of about 6600 men, and Maximian, having no hopes of overcoming their constancy, commanded the rest of his army to surround them and cut them to pieces. They made no resistance but suffered themselves to be butchered like sheep, so that the ground was covered with their dead bodies, and streams of blood flowed on every side. Maximian gave the spoils of the slain to his soldiers for their booty, and they were sharing it out when a veteran named Victor refused to join in. At this the soldiers inquired if he was also a Christian. He answered that he was, upon which they fell upon him and slew him. Ursus and another Victor, two straggling soldiers of this legion, were found at Solothurn and there killed, and according to local legends many others elsewhere, such as St Alexander at Bergomo, SS. Octavius, Adventor and Solutor at Turin, and St Gereon at Cologne.

St Maurice and his companions have been the subject of much discussion. That a whole legion was put to death is highly improbable; Roman imperial generals were not incapable of such a wholesale slaughter, but the circumstances of the time and the lack of early evidence of an entirely satisfactory sort are all against it. Alban Butler notes with pain that 'the truth of this history is attacked by some Protestant historians', but it has been questioned by Catholic scholars as well, and some have even gone so far as to reject the whole of it as fabrication. But it seems clear that the martyrdom at Agaunum of St Maurice and his companions is an historical fact; what was the number of men involved is another matter; in the course of time a squad could easily be exaggerated into a legion.

MAXIMUS, BISHOP OF RIEZ (*c.* A.D. 460)

PATRON SATIN OF THE DYING; AND OF BABIES

27 NOVEMBER

Maximus was famed, in accounts of his life, for healing those who were on their death-beds. Hence he became the patron of the dying – and of all those in life-threatening situations, which included the period of infancy. He was also, therefore, taken to be patron of babies.

St Maximus was born in Provence, near Digne. His Christian parents brought him up in the love of virtue, and no one was surprised when as a young man he retired to the monastery of Lérins, where he was received by St Honoratus, its founder. When the last named was made bishop of Arles in 426, Maximus was chosen the second abbot of Lérins. St Sidonius assures us that the monastery seemed to acquire a new lustre by his prudent example; and the gift of miracles and the reputation of his sanctity drew crowds to his monastery from the mainland. At one time he felt obliged to quit the house and conceal himself in a forest and we are assured that the reason why he thus lay hid, in a very rainy season, was that the clergy and people of Fréjus had demanded him for bishop. However, not long after, the see of Riez in Provence became vacant and he was compelled to fill it, although he tried to get away in a boat. His parents were originally of that city so the saint was looked upon as already a citizen and on account of his holiness received with great joy. As a bishop he continued to observe the monastic rule so far as was compatible with his duties; he retained the same love of poverty, the same spirit of penance and prayer, the same indifference to the world, and the same humility for which he had been so conspicuous in the cloister.

MICHAEL THE ARCHANGEL

PATRON SAINT OF BATTLE, SECURITY FORCES AND PARATROOPS; OF BRUSSELS; OF
BANKING; OF RADIOLOGISTS AND RADIOTHERAPISTS; OF DEATH; OF ENGLAND,
GERMANY, PAPUA NEW GUINEA AND THE SOLOMON ISLANDS; OF THE SICK AND
THOSE POSSESSED BY THE DEVIL

29 SEPTEMBER (DEDICATION OF THE BASILICA OF ST MICHAEL THE ARCHANGEL,
COMMONLY CALLED MICHAELMAS DAY)

*Michael's soldierly exploits in heaven against Lucifer made him a natural choice as a
saint to be invoked in battle.*

Pope Pius XII declared Michael to be patron of the security forces of Italy in an
Apostolic Letter of 29 September 1949; and he gave as his reason Michael's battle for
good and against 'the powers of darkness'. John XXIII made him patron equally of the
security forces of Brazil, in an Apostolic Letter of 31 October 1959. Pope John cited
the benefits which had flowed from Michael's patronage of the Italian forces. Similarly, Michael was declared patron of French paratroops in a decree of the Sacred
Congregation of Rites of 25 January 1952, and of Italian ones in a similar decree of 17
June 1955.

From medieval times Michael has been regarded as the protector of the city of
Brussels.

Pius XII also declared Michael to be patron of those engaged in banking in an
Apostolic Letter of 3 September 1957. Although he cited the dangers which beset those
who deal in money, he gave no reasons why Michael, rather than another saint,
should be the patron of banking beyond the fact that, seemingly, some bankers were
already devoted to him.

As the 'life' indicates, Michael has been invoked by the sick from the earliest times.
In a decree of the Sacred Congregation of Rites of 15 January 1941, however, he is
made especial patron of radiologists and radiotherapists. Cardinal Salotti, Prefect of
the Congregation, remarked that radium treatment is not without its dangers to the
doctors themselves, to safeguard against which it is proper to call upon the intercession of the angels and saints – hence the choice of Michael as patron.

Michael's association with death is already to be found in some of the early
apocryphal writings quoted in Michael's 'life'. It is referred to explicitly in the
offertory chant of the Roman mass for the dead, and the Archangel was often depicted
in medieval times as holding a balance and weighing the souls of those who had just
died.

In England there was a considerable early devotion to Michael. In Germany he was
taken as the protector of Germany in medieval times, and was frequently depicted
upon banners and flags. It is recorded that early missionaries substituted sanctuaries
of the Archangel for those of the Germanic war-gods.

In an Apostolic Letter John Paul II pointed to the role of a patron in commending *the individual to God, seeking pardon for his or her sins, being a refuge against the enemies of faith and morals. The Episcopal Conference of Papua New Guinea and the Solomon Islands had therefore declared Michael the Archangel to be their patron, a decision already confirmed by the Congregation for the Evangelization of Peoples, and now ratified in this Letter dated 31 May 1979.*

It cannot be disputed that in the apocryphal literature, which, both before and after the coming of Christ, was so prevalent in Palestine and among the Jewish communities of the Diaspora, the archangel Michael (Michael = who is like to God?) played a great part. A starting-point may be found in the authentic scriptures, for the tenth and twelfth chapters of the Book of Daniel speak of Michael as 'one of the chief princes', the special protector of Israel, and describe how at that time shall Michael rise up, 'the great prince who standeth for the children of thy people' (Dan. xii i). In the *Book of Henoch*, which is regarded as the most important and influential of all the Old Testament apocrypha, Michael comes before us repeatedly as 'the great captain', 'the chief captain', he 'is set over the best part of mankind', *i.e.* over the chosen race who are the inheritors of the promises. He is merciful, and it is he who will explain the mystery which underlies the dread judgements of the Almighty. Michael is depicted as ushering Henoch himself into the divine presence, but he is also associated with the other great archangels, Gabriel, Raphael and Phanuel, in binding the wicked potentates of earth and casting them into a furnace of fire. The merciful concept of the leader's office is, however, especially emphasized in the *Testaments of the Twelve Patriarchs* and in the *Ascension of Isaias* (*c.* A.D. 90?) in which last we read of 'the great angel Michael always interceding for the human race', but in this same work he is further presented as the scribe who records the deeds of all men in the heavenly books.

In New Testament times it is written in the Apocalypse of St John (xii 7-9) that 'there was a great battle in Heaven. Michael and his angels fought with the dragon, and the dragon fought and his angels; and they prevailed not, neither was their place found any more in Heaven. And that great dragon was cast out, that old serpent who is called the Devil and Satan, who seduceth the whole world: and he was cast unto the earth, and his angels were thrown down with him.' Still more significant of the close association of a cult of St Michael with Jewish traditions or folk-lore is the mention of his name in the Epistle of St Jude (v 9): 'When Michael the archangel, disputing with the Devil, contended about the body of Moses, he durst not bring against him the judgement of railing speech, but said: "The Lord rebuke thee."' Whether this is a direct quotation from the apocryphal writing known as *The Assumption of Moses* may be disputed, because we do not possess the text of the latter part of that work; but Origen expressly states that it is a quotation and names this book. The story there recounted seems to have been that when Moses died, 'Samsel' (*i.e.* Satan) claimed the body on the ground that Moses, having killed the Egyptian, was a murderer. This blasphemy kindled the wrath of Michael, but he restrained himself, saying only: 'The Lord rebuke thee, thou slanderer (*diabole*)'. What seems certain is that *The Assumption of Moses* did give prominence to the part played by St Michael in the burial of Moses, and also that this same book was cited by certain fathers at the Council of Nicaea in A.D. 325. It was probably of pre-Christian origin, but we find in the *Shepherd of Hermas*, dating from the early part of the second century A.D., an illustration of the veneration in which St Michael was held by those who were undoubtedly Christians. In the eighth 'similitude' we have the allegory of the twigs cut from the great willow tree, some of which sprout into vigorous life when planted and watered, while others droop of wither away. An angel of majestic aspect presides over the awards when these twigs are brought back for inspection and judgement is passed upon them. This, we are told, is 'the great and glorious angel Michael who has authority over this people and governs them; for this is he who gave them the law and implanted it in the hearts of believers; he accordingly superintends them to whom he gave it to see if they have kept the same'.

The *Shepherd of Hermas* was treated by some of the early fathers as if it formed part of the canon of scripture, but it hardly seems to have been so widely popular as a very extravagant apocryphal writing of Jewish origin known as the *Testament of Abraham*, which is probably not very much later in date. In this the archangel Michael throughout plays almost the leading part. His difficult task is to reconcile Abraham to the necessity of death. Michael is presented to the reader as God's commander-in-chief, the organizer of all the divine relations with earth, one whose intervention is so powerful with God that at his word souls can be rescued even from Hell itself. These apocryphal writings were very widely circulated and we find echoes of them even in a canonical epistle like that of St Jude and still more in several of the early Greek fathers. The liturgy itself was imperceptibly coloured by them. A most conspicuous example is the still existing offertory chant in Masses for the dead.

This festival of Michaelmas Day has been kept with great solemnity at the end of September ever since the sixth century at least. The Roman Martyrology implies that the dedication of the famous church of St Michael on Mount Gargano gave occasion to the institution of this feast in the West, but it would appear that it really celebrates the dedication of a basilica in honour of St Michael on the Salarian Way six miles north of Rome. In the East, where Michael was regarded as having care of the sick (rather than, as today, captain of the heavenly host and protector of soldiers), veneration of this archangel began yet earlier and certain healing waters were named after him, as at Khariotopa and Colossae. Sozomen tells us that Constantine the Great built a church in his honour, called the Michaelion, at Sosthenion, some way from Constantinople, and that in it the sick were often cured and other wonders wrought. Many churches in honour of St Michael stood in the city of Constantinople itself, including a famous one at the Baths of Arcadius, whose dedication gave the Byzantines their feast of 8 November.

Though only St Michael is mentioned in the title of this festival, it appears from the prayers of the Mass that all the good angels are its object, together with this glorious tutelary angel of the Church.

MONICA (A.D. 387)

PATRON SAINT OF MOTHERS

27 AUGUST

Monica's feast is celebrated the day before that of her son St Augustine (of Hippo). It is for her devotion to Augustine, for never losing faith in him and praying for his salvation – as Augustine himself recalls – that she has come to be regarded as the patron of mothers.

She was born in North Africa – probably at Tagaste, sixty miles from Carthage – of Christian parents, in the year 332. Her early training was entrusted to a faithful retainer who treated her young charges wisely, if somewhat strictly. Amongst the regulations she inculcated was that of never drinking between meals. 'It is water you want now,' she would say, 'but when you become mistresses of the cellar you will want wine – not water – and the habit will remain with you.' But when Monica grew old enough to be charged with the duty of drawing wine for the household, she disregarded the excellent maxim, and from taking occasional secret sips in the cellar, she soon came to drinking whole cupfuls with relish. One day, however, a slave who had watched her and with whom she was having an altercation, called her a wine-bibber. The shaft struck home: Monica was overwhelmed with shame and never again gave way to the temptation. Indeed, from the day of her baptism, which took place soon afterwards, she seems to have lived a life exemplary in every particular.

As soon as she had reached a marriageable age, her parents gave her as wife to a citizen of Tagaste, Patricius by name, a pagan not without generous qualities, but violent-tempered and dissolute. Monica had much to put up with from him, but she bore all with the patience of a strong, well-disciplined character. He, on his part, though inclined to criticize her piety and liberality to the poor, always regarded her with respect and never laid a hand upon her, even in his worst fits of rage. When other matrons came to complain of their husbands and to show the marks of blows they had received, she did not hesitate to tell them they very often brought this treatment upon themselves by their tongues. In the long run, Monica's prayers and example resulted in winning over to Christianity not only her husband, but also her cantankerous mother-in-law, whose presence as a permanent inmate of the house had added considerably to the younger woman's difficulties. Patricius died a holy death in 371, the year after his baptism. Of their children, at least three survived, two sons and a daughter, and it was in the elder son, Augustine, that the parents' ambitions centred, for he was brilliantly clever, and they were resolved to give him the best possible education. Nevertheless, his waywardness, his love of pleasure and his fits of idleness caused his mother great anxiety. He had been admitted a catechumen in early youth and once, when he was thought to be dying, arrangements were made for his baptism, but his sudden recovery caused it to be deferred indefinitely. At the date of his father's death he was seventeen and a student in Carthage, devoting himself especially to rhetoric. Two years later Monica was cut to the heart at the news that Augustine was leading a wicked life, and had as well embraced the Manichean heresy. For a time after his return to Tagaste she went so far as to refuse to let him live in her house or eat at her table that she might not have to listen to his blasphemies. But she relented as the result of a consoling vision which was vouchsafed to her. She seemed to be standing on a wooden beam bemoaning her son's downfall when she was accosted by a radiant being who questioned her as to the cause of her grief. He then bade her dry her eyes and added, 'Your son is with you'. Casting her eyes towards the spot he indicated, she beheld Augustine standing on the beam beside her. Afterwards, when she told the dream to Augustine he flippantly remarked that they might easily be together if Monica would give up her faith, but she promptly replied, 'He did not say that I was with you: he said that you were with me'.

Her ready retort made a great impression upon her son, who in later days regarded it as an inspiration. This happened about the end of 377, almost nine years before Augustine's conversion. During all that time Monica never ceased her efforts on his behalf. She stormed heaven by her prayers and tears: she fasted: she watched: she importuned the clergy to argue with him, even though they assured her that it was useless in his actual state of mind. 'The heart of the young man is at present too stubborn, but God's time will come,' was the reply of a wise bishop who had formerly been a Manichean himself. Then, as she persisted, he said in words which have become famous: 'Go now, I beg of you: it is not possible that the son of so many tears should perish'. This reply and the assurance she had received in the vision gave her the encouragement she was sorely needing, for there was as yet in her elder son no indication of any change of heart.

Augustine was twenty-nine years old when he resolved to go to Rome to teach rhetoric. Monica, though opposed to the plan because she feared it would delay his conversion, was determined to accompany him if he persisted in going, and followed him to the port of embarkation. Augustine, on the other hand, had made up his mind to go without her. He accordingly resorted to an unworthy stratagem. He pretended he was only going to speed a parting friend, and whilst Monica was spending the night in prayer in the church of St Cyprian, he set sail alone. 'I deceived her with a lie,' he wrote afterwards in his *Confessions*, 'while she was weeping and praying for me.' Deeply grieved as Monica was when she discovered how she had been tricked, she was still resolved to follow him, but she reached Rome only to find that the bird had flown. Augustine had gone on to Milan. There he came under the influence of the great bishop St Ambrose. When Monica at last tracked her son down, it was to learn from his lips, to her unspeakable joy, that he was no longer a Manichean. Though he declared that he was not yet a Catholic Christian, she replied with equanimity that he would certainly be one before she died.

To St Ambrose she turned with heartfelt gratitude and found in him a true father in God. She deferred to him in all things, abandoning at his wish practices which had become dear to her. For instance, she had been in the habit of carrying wine, bread and vegetables to the tombs of the martyrs in Africa and had begun to do the same in Milan, when she was told that St Ambrose had forbidden the practice as tending to intemperance and as approximating too much to the heathen *parentalia*. She desisted at once, though Augustine doubted whether she would have given in so promptly to anyone else. At Tagaste she had always kept the Saturday fast, which was customary there as well as in Rome. Perceiving that it was not observed in Milan, she induced Augustine to question St Ambrose as to what she herself ought to do. The reply she received has been incorporated into canon law: 'When I am here, I do not fast on Saturday, but I fast when I am in Rome; do the same, and always follow the custom and discipline of the Church as it is observed in the particular locality in which you find yourself'. St Ambrose, on his part, had the highest opinion of St Monica and was never tired of singing her praises to her son. In Milan as in Tagaste, she was foremost among the devout women, and when the Arian queen mother, Justina, was persecuting St Ambrose, Monica was one of those who undertook long vigils on his behalf, prepared to die with him or for him.

At last, in August 386, there came the long-desired moment when Augustine announced his complete acceptance of the Catholic faith. For some time previously Monica had been trying to arrange for him a suitable marriage, but he now declared that he would from henceforth live a celibate life. Then, when the schools rose for the season of the vintage, he retired with his mother and some of his friends to the villa of one of the party named Verecundius at Cassiciacum. There the time of preparation before Augustine's baptism was spent in religious and philosophical conversations, some of which are recorded in the *Confessions*. In all these talks Monica took part, displaying remarkable penetration and judgement and showing herself to be exceptionally well versed in the Holy Scriptures. At Easter, 387, St Ambrose baptized St Augustine, together with several of his friends, and soon afterwards the party set out to return to Africa. They made their way to Ostia, there to await a ship, but Monica's life was drawing to an end, though no one but herself suspected it. In a conversation with Augustine shortly before her last illness she said, 'Son, nothing in this world now affords me delight. I do not know what there is now left for me to do or why I am still here, all my hopes in this world being fulfilled. All I wished to live for was that I might see you a Catholic and a child of Heaven. God has granted me more than this in making you despise earthly felicity and consecrate yourself to His service.'

Monica had often expressed a desire to be buried beside Patricius, and therefore one day, as she was expatiating on the happiness of death, she was asked if she would not be afraid to die and be buried in a place so far from home. 'Nothing is far from God,' she replied, 'neither am I afraid that God will not find my body to raise it with the rest.' Five days later she was taken ill, and she suffered acutely until the ninth day, when she passed to her eternal reward. She was fifty-five years of age. Augustine, who closed her eyes, restrained his own tears and those of his son Adeodatus, deeming a display of grief out of place at the funeral of one who had died so holy a death. But afterwards, when he was alone and began to think of all her love and care for her children, he broke down altogether for a short time. He writes: 'If any one thinks it wrong that I thus wept for my mother some small part of an hour – a mother who for many years had wept for me that I might live to thee, O Lord – let him not deride me. But if his charity is great, let him weep also for my sins before thee.'

NICHOLAS, CALLED 'OF BARI', BISHOP OF MYRA (FOURTH CENTURY)

PATRON SAINT OF CHILDREN; OF BRIDES, AND UNMARRIED WOMEN; OF
PAWNBROKERS; OF PERFUMERS OR PERFUMIERS; OF RUSSIA; OF TRAVELLERS,
PILGRIMS AND SAFE JOURNEYS; AND OF SAILORS AND MARITIME PILOTS

6 DECEMBER

It is the legend of the three children, narrated below, that turned St Nicholas into the patron of children, which in time became associated with the giving of presents at Christmastide. Further, the story of his kindness in supplying the dowries is the origin of the choice of Nicholas as patron of brides and unmarried women. Further too, the three bags of gold given as dowries is believed by some authorities to be the origin of the pawnbrokers' sign of three hanging golden balls.

From St Nicholas' shrine at Bari there was said to come a fragrant 'myrrh'. For this reason, it seems, he was taken by makers of perfumes as their patron.

St Nicholas has always been one of the most universal of saints, such was his popularity in the Middle Ages. His cult became especially strong in Russia where he came to be venerated as a national patron. He also came to be regarded as a patron of travellers and of pilgrims, for it is claimed that, in his early life, he travelled to the Holy Land and to Egypt. In addition the legend of St Nicholas has him appearing to storm-tossed sailors off the coast of Lycia, and then bringing them safely to port.

He is said to have been born at Patara in Lycia, a province of Asia Minor. Myra, the capital, not far from the sea, was an episcopal see, and this church falling vacant, the holy Nicholas was chosen bishop, and in that station became famous by his extraordinary piety and zeal and many astonishing miracles. The Greek histories of his life agree that he suffered imprisonment for the faith and made a glorious confession in the latter part of the persecution raised by Diocletian, and that he was present at the Council of Nicaea and there condemned Arianism. He died at Myra, and was buried in his cathedral.

This summary account tells us all that is known about the life of the famous St Nicholas, and even a little more: for his episcopate at Myra during the fourth century is really all that seems indubitably authentic. Nevertheless, the universal popularity of the saint for so many centuries requires that some account of the legends should be given here.

His parents died when he was a young man, leaving him well off, and he determined to devote his inheritance to works of charity. An opportunity soon arose. A citizen of Patara had lost all his money, and had moreover to support three daughters who could not find husbands because of their poverty; he was going to give them over to prostitution. This came to the ears of Nicholas, who thereupon took a bag of gold and, under cover of darkness, threw it in at the open window of the man's house. Here was a dowry for the eldest girl, and she was soon duly married. At intervals

Nicholas did the same for the second and third; at the last time the father was on the watch, recognized his benefactor, and overwhelmed him with his gratitude. It would appear that the three purses, represented in pictures, came to be mistaken for the heads of three children, and so they gave rise to the absurd story of the children, resuscitated by the saint, who had been killed by an innkeeper and pickled in a brine-tub.

St Methodius asserts that 'thanks to the teaching of St Nicholas the metropolis of Myra alone was untouched by the filth of the Arian heresy, which it firmly rejected as death-dealing poison', but says nothing of his presence at the Council of Nicaea in 325. According to other traditions he was not only there but so far forgot himself as to give the heresiarch Arius a slap in the face. Whereupon the conciliar fathers deprived him of his episcopal insignia and committed him to prison: but our Lord and His Mother appeared there and restored to him both his liberty and his office.

The accounts are unanimous that St Nicholas died and was buried in his episcopal city of Myra, and by the time of Justinian there was a basilica built in his honour at Constantinople. When Myra and its great shrine finally passed into the hands of the Saracens, several Italian cities saw this as an opportunity to acquire the relics of St Nicholas for themselves. There was great competition for them between Venice and Bari. The last-named won, the relics were carried off under the noses of the lawful Greek custodians and their Muslim masters, and on 9 May 1087 were safely landed at Bari, a not inappropriate home seeing that Apulia in those days still had large Greek colonies. A new church was built to shelter them and Pope Urban II was present at their enshrining. Devotion to St Nicholas was known in the West long before his relics were brought to Italy, but this happening naturally greatly increased his veneration among the people, and miracles were as freely attributed to his intercession in Europe as they had been in Asia.

NICHOLAS OF TOLENTINO

PATRON SAINT OF THE DYING; OF SOULS IN PURGATORY; OF FIRES; OF SICKNESS IN ANIMALS; OF BABIES AND MOTHERS

10 SEPTEMBER

The cult of Nicholas was very popular in Italy, and in Spain and its former territories. As his 'life' relates, Nicholas went about comforting, and sometimes miraculously healing, the dying. Moreover, according to some legends, he heard angelic choirs for a number of months before his own death, assuring him of his salvation.

According to one account of his life, Nicholas had on several occasions visions of his prayers freeing souls from purgatory and even, in one instance, of rescuing from damnation the soul of someone killed while in a state of sin.

Nicholas is said to have healed people by giving them pieces of bread over which he

had invoked the blessing of the Blessed Virgin Mary. The use of 'St Nicholas' bread' became very popular in some parts of Europe, and numerous apparent miracles were claimed for it, including the extinguishing of fires (one in the Doge's Palace in Venice, for example), and the healing of sickness in animals.

The life of Nicholas demonstrates his concern for children, but the particular devotion to him as protector of mothers and babies derives more especially from intercession to him in life-threatening situations.

This saint received his surname from the town which was his residence for the most considerable part of his life, and in which he died. He was a native of Sant' Angelo, a town near Fermo in the March of Ancona, and was born in the year 1245. His father lived many years in happiness with his wife, but when both had reached middle age they were still childless. Nicholas was the fruit of their prayers and pilgrimage to the shrine of St Nicholas at Bari, in which his mother especially had earnestly begged of God a son who should faithfully serve Him. At his baptism he received the name of his patron.

While still a boy he received minor orders, and was presented to a canonry in the collegiate church of St Saviour at Sant' Angelo; and there were not wanting those who were willing to use their influence for his promotion within the ranks of the secular clergy. Nicholas, however, aspired to a state which would allow him to consecrate his whole time and thoughts directly to God, and it happened that he one day went into the Augustinian church and heard a friar preaching on the text: 'Love not the world, nor the things which are in the world. . . . The world passeth away. . . .' This sermon finally determined him absolutely to join the order of that preacher. This he did so soon as his age would allow, and he was accepted by the Augustinian friars at Sant' Angelo. He went through his novitiate under the direction of the preacher himself, Father Reginald, and made his profession before he had completed his eighteenth year.

Friar Nicholas was sent to San Ginesio for his theology, and he was entrusted with the daily distribution of food to the poor at the monastery gate. He made so free with the resources of the house that the procurator complained and reported him to the prior. About 1270 he was ordained priest at Cingoli, and in that place he became famous among the people, particularly on account of his healing of a blind woman. But he did not stay there long, for during four years he was continually moving from one to another of the friaries and missions of his order. For a short time he was novice-master at Sant' Elpidio, where there was a large community which included two friars who are venerated as *beati* among the Augustinians today, Angelo of Furcio and Angelo of Foligno. While visiting a relative who was prior of a monastery near Fermo, Nicholas was tempted by an invitation to make a long stay in the monastery, but while praying in the church he seemed to hear a voice directing him: 'To Tolentino, to Tolentino. Persevere there.' Shortly after to Tolentino he was sent, and stopped there for the remaining thirty years of his life.

This town had suffered much in the strife of Guelf and Ghibelline, and civil discord had had its usual effects of wild fanaticism, schism and reckless wickedness. A campaign of street-preaching was necessary, and to this new work St Nicholas was put. He was an immediate success. He went about the slums of Tolentino, comforting the dying, waiting on (and sometimes mira-culously curing) the sick and bed-ridden, watching over the children, appealing to the criminals, composing quarrels and estrangements: one woman gave evidence in the cause of his canonization that he had entirely won over and reformed her husband who for long had treated her with shameful cruelty.

The final illness of St Nicholas lasted nearly a year, and in the last months he got up from bed only once, to absolve a penitent who he knew intended to conceal a grievous sin from any priest but himself. The end came quietly on 10 September 1305.

NICHOLAS VON FLUE (A.D. 1487)

PATRON SAINT OF SWITZERLAND

22 MARCH

Nicholas, or 'Bruder Klaus' as he is often called, became, and remained, a much revered figure in the history of Switzerland both for the manner of his life and for his devotion to his homeland. Pius XII spelled out this devotion in the Apostolic Letter of 2 June 1947 in which he declared this 'patrem patriae', or 'father of his fatherland', principal patron of Switzerland.

The holy man, who was born near Sachseln in Unterwalden in 1417, belonged to a much respected family of small farmers, owners of the Kluster Alp or pasture in the Melchthal and of the estate of Flüeli on the Sachster-berg, from which they derived their surname. His father Henry also held a civil post in the cantonal service, whilst his mother, Emma Robert, was a native of Wolfenschiessen. She was a deeply religious woman who brought up her two sons. Nicholas and Peter, to belong as she did to the brotherhood of the Friends of God (*Gottesfreunde*). The members of this society were scattered over Germany, Switzerland and the Netherlands, and were drawn from both sexes and all classes. Adhering loyally to the Catholic Church, they sought by strictness of life as well as by constant meditation on the passion of our Lord and similar devotions, to enter, as their name implied, into specially close relationship with God. Some of them lived in their own families, others formed small communities, and a few retired from the world altogether to lead an eremitic life. Nicholas was specially responsive to the training he received, and was remarkable from childhood for his piety, his love of peace and his sound judgement.

At the age of twenty-two, and in spite of his peace-loving disposition, Nicholas fought in the ranks in the war with Zürich. Fourteen years later, on the occasion of the occupation of the Thurgau, he again took up arms, but this time he was captain of a company. The high esteem in which he was held caused him to be appointed magistrate and judge and to be sent on various occasions as deputy for Obwalden to councils and meetings, where his clear-sighted wisdom carried great weight. He was repeatedly offered the highest post of all, that of *landamman*, or governor, but he could never be induced to accept it. He had married a religious-minded girl called Dorothea Wissling, and their union had been a happy one. Of their ten children, John, the eldest son, became *landamman* during his father's lifetime, and the youngest studied at the University of Basle, and was afterwards for many years parish-priest of Sachseln. Throughout the years of his married life, Nicholas had continued the devout practices of his youth. To quote the testimony of his eldest son: 'My father always retired to rest at the same time as his children and servants; but every night I saw him get up again, and heard him praying in his room until morning. Often too he would go in the silence of the night to the old church of St Nicholas or to other holy places.' In obedience to what seemed to him a supernatural call to contemplation, for he had many visions and revelations, he used at times to withdraw into solitude in the valley of the Melch, but when he was about fifty he felt irresistibly drawn to abandon the world altogether and to spend the rest of his days far from home as a hermit. His wife did not oppose him, for the Friends of God recognized such vocations as sent from on high. Nicholas resigned his offices, took leave of his wife, his father and his children in the early autumn of 1467 and set forth barefoot and bareheaded, clad in a grey-brown habit and carrying his rosary and his staff.

His destination appears to have been Strasbourg, in the neighbourhood of which was a settlement of the brethren, Alsace having been their headquarters. Before crossing the frontier, however, he received hospitality from a peasant whom he discovered to be also a Friend of God, and in the course of conversation his host sought to deter him from leaving the country, assuring him that the Swiss were unpopular in Alsace and elsewhere abroad on account of their rough manners, and that he might fail to find the peaceful retreat he sought. That night there was a terrific thunderstorm, and as Nicholas looked at the little town of Liechstall beyond the frontier, the flashes of lightning made it appear to be in flames. He took this to be a sign which confirmed the advice he had received, and immediately retraced his steps. One evening during the homeward journey, as he lay under a tree, he was seized with such violent gastric spasms that he thought his last hour had come: the pain passed off, but from that time he lost all desire for ordinary food or drink, and became in fact incapable of taking either. Later that autumn, hunters who had been looking for game in the Melchthal brought home news that they had come across Nicholas on his pasture land of the Klüster, where he had made himself a shelter of boughs under a larch tree. His brother Peter and other friends went to beseech him not to remain there to die of exposure, and he was persuaded to move to Ranft, another part of the valley, where the people of Obwalden soon built him a little cell with a chapel attached.

In this spot, which was situated above a narrow gorge, the loneliness of which was emphasized by the roar of the mountain torrent in the valley below, St Nicholas spent nineteen peaceful years. The hours from midnight to midday were passed in prayer and contemplation, but in the afternoon he would interview those who found their way to his hermitage to seek his advice on spiritual or even on temporal matters. God had given him the spirit of counsel, as he once admitted to his friend Henry Imgrund, and he continued to exercise it as he had done in the past. Strangers also were attracted by the fame of this remarkable man, who was reported to live without eating and drinking. Never very talkative, he was particularly sparing of his words to those who came out of mere curiosity. So also, when questioned as to his abstention from food, he would only reply, 'God knows'. That no one brought him provisions the cantonal magistrates proved by having all approaches to his cell watched for a month, and unprejudiced foreigners, such as Archduke Sigismund's physician and envoys from the Emperor Frederick III, satisfied themselves of the truth of the report and were profoundly impressed by the hermit's sincerity. Once a year Nicholas took part in the great Musegger procession in Lucerne, but otherwise he only left his retreat to attend divine service and occasionally to visit Einsiedeln. The gifts of the faithful enabled him in his later years to found a chantry for a priest in connection with his own little chapel, and he was thus able to assist at Mass daily and to communicate often.

At this epoch the Swiss Confederation had just passed through the most glorious phase in its history. Within six years, in the three battles of Grandson, Morat and Nancy, the sturdy mountain folk had vindicated their independence and had routed the hitherto unconquered Charles the Bold, master of the two Burgundies and nearly the whole of Belgium: their reputation was so great that every prince in Europe sought their alliance. The hour of their most signal triumph proved nevertheless to be the hour of their greatest danger, for internal dissensions threatened to undo the success which their arms had won. Quarrels arose over the division of booty and between the country party and the towns. Another source of contention was the proposal to include Fribourg and Soleure (or Solothurn) in the confederation. At length agreement was reached on most points and was embodied in a document known as the Edict of Stans. On the subject of the inclusion of Fribourg and Soleure, however, no accommodation could be reached, and feeling ran so high that it seemed that the question would have to be settled by arms. This meeting was breaking up in disorder when the parish priest of Stans suggested seeking a final opinion from Nicholas von Flüe. The deputies gave their consent and he set out to seek the hermit. His suggestion was no casual or sudden inspiration. As we know from the protocols of the Council of Lucerne, that city, which occupied an ambiguous position between the two parties, had, at an early stage of the strife, sent delegates to Brother Nicholas to obtain his advice, and it is quite possible that other districts had done the same. It has been even suggested that the Edict of Stans, a most statesmanlike charter, may have been drafted in the hermit's cell. In any case, it is greatly to the credit of the deputies that, in the heat of their quarrel, they should have been willing to refer the matter to him. The chronicler Diebold Schilling, who represented his father at the council, tells us that the priest Imgrund arrived back in Stans streaming with perspiration, and that, seeking out the deputies in their lodgings, he besought them with tears to reassemble to hear the message which he must impart to them alone. Schilling does not record the words of that message, but he informs us that within an hour the council had arrived at a unanimous agreement. Fribourg and Soleure were to be admitted into the Swiss Confederation, but upon certain conditions, which were accepted for them by Hans von Stall, the delegate of Soleure. The date was 22 December 1481.

That Christmas was a specially joyful one throughout Switzerland, and the Stans Council expressed in laudatory terms its gratitude to Nicholas for his services. Letters of thanks from Berne and Soleure to the holy man are still extant, as well as a letter written on his behalf by his son John, thanking Berne for a gift which would be expanded upon the Church. (He himself could neither read nor write, but used a special seal by way of a signature.) Several of the hermit's visitors have left accounts of their interviews with him, and that written by Albert von Bonstetten, dean of the monastery of Einsiedeln, is particularly interesting. He describes the recluse as tall, brown and wrinkled, with thin grizzled locks and a short beard. His eyes were bright, his teeth white and well preserved, and his nose shapely. He adds, 'He praises and recommends obedience and peace. As he exhorted the Confederates to maintain peace, so does he exhort all who come to him to do the same'. The dean held him in great veneration, but with regard to the prophetical gifts ascribed to Nicholas in some quarters, he says cautiously that he had received no evidence of them from trustworthy sources. Six years after the Council of Stans, Nicholas was seized with his last illness, which lasted only eight days, but caused him intense suffering. He bore it with perfect resignation and died peacefully in his cell, on his birthday, having attained the age of seventy. Immediately his death became known he was honoured in all Switzerland both as patriot and as a saint, though it was only in 1669 that his *cultus* was sanctioned: he was canonized in 1947.

OLAF, MARTYR (A.D. 1030)

A PATRON SAINT OF NORWAY

29 JULY

For reasons which his life makes clear, Olaf was regarded as patron of Norway long before official confirmation by a decree of the Sacred Congregation of Rites dated 7 March 1941 – at the same time that St Magnus was confirmed as patron.

Olaf was the son of Harold Grenske, a lord in Norway, and after eight years of piracy and fighting succeeded to his father in 1015 at the age of twenty, at a time when most of Norway was in the hands of the Danes and Swedes. These parts he conquered and then set about the subjection of the realm to Christ, for he himself had already been baptized at Rouen by Archbishop Robert; the work had been begun, but had not made much real progress, by Haakon the Good and by Olaf Tryggvason, whose methods of evangelization seem to have been preposterous and wicked. In 1013 Olaf Haraldsson had sailed to England and assisted King Ethelred against the Danes, and he now turned to that country for help in his more peaceable task. He brought over from England a number of priests and monks, one of whom, Grimkel, was chosen bishop of Nidaros, his capital. Olaf relied much on the advice of this prelate, and by his counsel published many good enactments and abolished ancient laws and customs contrary to the gospel. Unfortunately, like St Vladimir of Russia and other princes he used force without compunction. To his enemies he was merciless, added to which some of his legislation and political objects were not everywhere approved. Therefore many rose in arms, and, with the assistance of Canute, King of England and Denmark, defeated and expelled him. St Olaf fled, but returned with a few Swedish troops to recover his kingdom; he was slain by his rebellious and infidel subjects in a battle fought at Stiklestad, on 29 July 1030.

The king's body was buried in a steep sandbank by the river Nid, where he had fallen; here a spring gushed out whose waters became credited with healing power and the bishop, Grimkel, in the following year ordered that he was to be there venerated as a marytr and a chapel built over the place. In 1075 the chapel was replaced by a bishop's church, dedicated to Christ and St Olaf, which in time became the metropolitan cathedral of Nidaros (Trondhjem).

OLIVER PLUNKET, ARCHBISHOP OF ARMAGH, MARTYR (A.D. 1681)

PATRON SAINT OF THE URBAN UNIVERSITY ROME

3 DECEMBER

The Urban University in Rome is the direct descendant of the college belonging to the Congregation for the Propagation of the Faith for the training of priests for missionary work, at which Oliver taught for twelve years. Paul VI recalled this fact in his Apostolic Letter of 10 August 1977 in which he declares him to be the secondary patron of the University. He also appointed 3 December for Oliver's feast, though he is more widely celebrated on 1 July.

The last Catholic to die for his faith at Tyburn and the first of the Irish martyrs to be beatified was born in 1629 at Loughcrew, in county Meath; through his father he was connected with the earl of Fingall and the barons of Dunsany and Locriff, and his mother was a Dillon and near kin to the earl of Roscommon. He was given his name after that young Oliver Plunket who had been done to death when the Spanish prisoners were massacred at Smerwick in Kerry in 1580. His youth was spent in the turmoil and confusion of parties consequent on the rebellion against King Charles I in England, the Plunkets naturally being among those Catholics nobles and gentry who were for the king's prerogative and freedom for the Irish; but Oliver himself was already destined for the priesthood and studied under his kinsman Patrick Plunket, Benedictine abbot of St Mary's in Dublin.

In 1645, when he was sixteen, he went to Rome with four other young men who had been chosen to be educated at his own expense for the priesthood by Father Pierfrancesco Scarampi, the Oratorian who had been sent in 1643 by Pope Urban VIII to assist at the supreme council of the Irish Confederate party. He did brilliantly under the Jesuits at the then lately established Irish College, followed the course of civil and canon law at the *Sapienza*, and was ordained in 1654. The state of affairs in Ireland made it impossible for him at once to go on the mission there, so by the good offices of Father Scarampi he was appointed to the chair of theology in the College *de Propaganda Fide*. He lodged with the Oratorians, and was appointed a consultor of the Sacred Congregation of the Index and procurator for the Irish bishops to the Holy See. He thus lived a busy and devoted life in Rome for twelve years.

In March 1669 Edmund O'Reilly, Archbishop of Armagh and Primate of All Ireland died in exile in France. Pope Clement IX chose to succeed him Dr Oliver Plunket, and in November of that year he was consecrated at Ghent. He then went on to London, where he was weather-bound and was secretly lodged in his own apartments by Father Philip Howard, O.P. (afterwards cardinal), almoner of Charles II's queen, Catherine of Braganza. He reached Dublin in March 1670, where he was received by his noble relatives, including his former tutor, Dom Patrick Plunket, now bishop of Meath. He was one of the two bishops in Ireland, the aged and worn-out bishop of Kilmore being the other; there were only three others, and they were in exile: Oliver's predecessor, O'Reilly, had been able to pass only two of his twelve years of episcopate in the country. The new archbishop within three months held a provincial synod, two ordinations, and confirmed ten thousand persons of all ages – and still there were fifty thousand unconfirmed in his province. The first two years of his rule were peaceful, owing to the fairness and moderation of the viceroy, Lord Berkeley of Stratton; he was tolerant to Catholics and personally friendly towards Oliver. Unhappily this peace was marred by a dispute among Catholics, in this case between the Archbishop of Armagh and his cousin the Archbishop of Dublin, Peter Talbot, as to the extent and implications of Armagh's primacy, a matter of considerable canonical importance to the Church of Ireland. Oliver interpreted his primacy as being not merely titular but carrying with it primatial jurisdiction over the other metropolitans; Dr Talbot saw in it only a precedence of rank.

These two years were not otherwise uneventful, but a period of tremendously hard and difficult work, of clearing the ground for an improvement of the spiritual state of the people which the new primate was not to see. The Synod of Clones legislated rigorously against abuses among both clergy and laity. He established the Jesuits in Drogheda, where they ran a school for boys and a college for ecclesiastical students; he even aspired to extend his ministry to the Gaelic-speaking Catholics of the highlands and isles of Scotland, but the difficulties were too great; he laboured to maintain discipline among his clergy, to put into force the decrees of the Council of Trent, and to forestall Jansenist infiltration through those who had been trained in France and Flanders, to enforce better observance among the friars, and to adjust the strained relationships both between seculars and regulars and between the orders themselves, whose differences were deliberately aggravated by the civil authorities for political ends. All this, the day-to-day care of his flock, and much more, had to be done with one eye all the time on the likelihood of incurring the penalties of *praemunire* for acknowledging the Pope's jurisdiction and resorting to the Holy See; moreover, it had to be done under conditions of 'astounding poverty', which Oliver shared with all his brother bishops and clergy. He was on friendly terms with the Protestant bishops and gentry of Ulster, who had great regard for him and for his sake were disposed not to oppress Catholics.

In 1673 the tortuous politics of King Charles II provoked a fresh outbreak of persecution. Archbishop Talbot was banished and the Archbishop of Tuam fled to Spain; at first Oliver was not interfered with, but he went into hiding with Dr Brennan of Waterford, who was in 1676 advanced to the see of Cashel. These two were in continual danger of arrest and lived under circumstances of grinding physical handicap and penury, carrying on their pastoral work to the best of their ability. It was made even more difficult for

Oliver by the enmity of a section of schismatic or quasi-schismatic Catholics.

In 1678 the Oates Plot was launched. The panic which it caused in England had its repercussions in Ireland, where an order of expulsion was made against all Catholic bishops and regular priests, and people were officially encouraged by proclamation to 'make any further discovery of the horrid popish plot, Lord Shaftesbury's agent, Hetherington, MacMoyer, an expelled Franciscan, and Murphy, an excommunicated secular priest, informed against Oliver in London, and the lord-lieutenant was ordered to arrest him. On 6 December 1679, he was shut up in Dublin Castle: here he was able to help his old opponent, Dr Talbot, on his death-bed, for the archbishop of Dublin had been allowed to return to Ireland, but was arrested for complicity in the 'popish plot', although a dying man. Oliver Plunket was put on trial at Dundalk for conspiring against the state by plotting to bring 20,000 French soldiers into the country and levying a tax on his clergy to support 70,000 armed men for rebellion. For two days no witnesses turned up for the prosecution, and on the third day only MacMoyer, who was drunk, and asked for a remand until the other witnesses could be procured. It was obvious to Shaftesbury that the archbishop would never be convicted on so absurd an indictment in Ireland; he was therefore removed to Newgate prison in London.

At the first trial the grand jury found no true bill; he was not released, but it was adjourned till June 1681. There is a doubt if the court had jurisdiction over the Irishman, and the second trial was conducted with only a semblance of justice, so that Lord Campbell, writing of the judge, Sir Francis Pemberton, calls it 'a disgrace to himself and country': the jury found the accused guilty of high treason; and judgement was reserved. It was pronounced a week later, and the Primate of All Ireland was condemned to be hanged, disembowelled and quartered.

The execution took place on Friday 1 July (o.s.), 1681; there was a huge crowd at Tyburn to whom the martyr protested his innocence of treason and his loyalty to the king, praying for him and for his own enemies. He was dead before he was cut down from the scaffold. The mutilated body was buried in the churchyard of St Giles-in-the-Fields, whence it was taken to the English Benedictine abbey of Lamspring in Westphalia in 1684; two hundred years later the relics were translated to Downside Abbey, where they are now enshrined; the martyr's head is preserved in St Peter's church at Drogheda. Oliver Plunket was beatified in 1920 and canonized in 1975.

ONUPHRIUS (*c.* A.D. 400?)

PATRON SAINT OF WEAVERS

12 JUNE

There seems to be little to connect Onuphrius with weavers except that, when Paphnutius met him, he was wearing no clothes at all and was dressed only in his beard.

Amongst the many hermits in the Egyptian desert during the fourth and fifth centuries was a holy man called Onuphrius. The little that is known of him is derived from an account attributed to a certain Abbot Paphnutius of a series of visits paid by him to some of the hermits of the Thebaïd. This account seems to have been committed to writing by one or more of the monks to whom it was related, and several versions of it became current. Obviously the story has lost nothing in telling.

Paphnutius undertook the pilgrimage in order to study the eremitic life and to discover whether he himself was called to lead it. For sixteen days after leaving his monastery he wandered in the desert, meeting with one or two strange and edifying adventures, but on the seventh day he was startled at the sight of what appeared to be an aged man with hair and beard falling to the ground, but covered with fur like an animal and wearing a loincloth of foliage. So alarming was the apparition that he began to run away. The figure, however, called after him, inviting him to return and assuring him that he also was a man and a servant of God. They entered into conversation and Paphnutius learned that the stranger's name was Onuphrius, that he had once been a monk in a monastery of many brethren, but that he had felt a vocation for the solitary life which he had now led for seventy years. In reply to further questions he admitted that he had suffered severely from hunger and thirst, from extremes of temperature, and from violent temptations. Nevertheless God had given him consolation and had nourished him with the dates that grew on a palm-tree beside his cell. He then conducted Paphnutius to his cave, where they spent the rest of the day discoursing of heavenly things. At sunset some bread and water suddenly appeared before them and they were wonderfully refreshed after partaking of this food. All that night they prayed together.

In the morning Paphnutius was distressed to see that a great change had come over his host, who was evidently at the point of death. But Onuphrius said, 'Fear not, brother Paphnutius, for the Lord of His infinite mercy has sent you here to bury me'. To a suggestion made by Paphnutius that he should remain on in the cell after his host's death, the aged hermit replied that God willed it otherwise. He then asked to be commended to the prayers and oblations of the faithful for whom he promised to intercede, and after having blessed Paphnutius he prostrated himself to the ground and gave up the ghost. His visitor made a shroud for him with half his tunic which he rent asunder. He then buried the old man in a cleft of the rock which he covered with stones. No sooner was this done than the cave crumbled and the date palm faded away, thus clearly indicating to Paphnutius that he was not intended to linger in that place.

PANTALEON, OR PANTELEIMON, MARTYR (C. A.D. 305?)

PATRON SAINT OF DOCTORS, AND OF THE MEDICAL PROFESSION

27 JULY

The choice of Pantaleon as patron of doctors, and of the medical profession in general, dates from the middle ages, and is explained by his chosen profession.

That there was a martyr of this name (Παντελεήμων: the all-compassionate) there can be little doubt, but the legends which have come down to us are without any value. According to them he was the son of a pagan father, Eustorgius of Nicomedia, brought up in the faith by his Christian mother, Eubula. He became learned in medicine and was physician to the Emperor Galerius Maximian at Nicomedia. For a time he failed under a temptation which is sometimes more dangerous than the severest trials or fierce torments, bad example, which, if not shunned, insensibly weakens and at length destroys the strongest virtue. Pantaleon, being perpetually obsessed by it in a wicked and idolatrous court, and deceived by often hearing the false wisdom of the world applauded, fell into apostasy. But a zealous Christian, called Hermolaos, by his prudent admonitions awakened his conscience to a sense of his guilt, and brought him again into the Church. When Diocletian's persecution broke out at Nicomedia in 303, he distributed all his possessions among the poor Christians, and was shortly after denounced to the authorities by some jealous fellow-physicians; he was arrested together with Hermolaos and two others. The emperor wished to save him and urged him to apostatize, but Pantaleon refused, and miraculously cured a paralytic as a sign of the truth of the faith. After suffering many torments they were all condemned to lose their heads, but St Pantaleon suffered the day after the rest. He was subjected to six different attempts to kill him, by burning, liquid lead, drowning, wild beasts, the wheel, and the sword; all of these, with the help of the Lord under the appearance of Hermolaos, he frustrated, till at length he permitted himself to be beheaded: there poured from his severed veins milk instead of blood, and the olive tree to which he was bound sprang into fruit.

St Pantaleon is one of the Fourteen Holy Helpers and is honoured in the East, as the 'Great Martyr and Wonder-worker' and one of the Holy Moneyless Ones (ἀνάργυροι), who treated the sick without payment. In the past he has been almost as famous in the West. Alleged relics of his blood are preserved at Constantinople, Madrid and Ravello, and these are said to liquefy on his feast-day exactly as does that of St Januarius at Naples.

PASCHAL BAYLON (A.D. 1592)

PATRON SAINT OF SHEPHERDS; PATRON OF THE EUCHARIST, AND OF
EUCHARISTIC GUILDS, SOCIETIES AND CONGRESSES; AND OF ITALIAN WOMEN

17 MAY

*Paschal Baylon as patron of shepherds follows naturally from the manner of his life
from seven to twenty-four years of age.*

*As his 'life' narrates, Paschal Baylon is best remembered as the saint of the
eucharist, and was declared patron of eucharistic guilds, societies and congresses in
an Apostolic Letter of Leo XIII, dated 28 November 1897. He has also won the
devotion of Italian women as their protector for no obvious reason except that, it has
been suggested, his name ('Baylonna' in Italian) rhymes readily with 'donna'!*

Thanks mainly to his fellow religious, superior and biographer, Father
Ximenes, we are well informed regarding Paschal's early days. He first saw
the light at Torre Hermosa, on the borders of Castile and Aragon, on a
Whitsunday, and to that accident he seems to have owed his Christian
name, for in Spain, as well as in Italy, the term *Pascua* is given to other great
feasts of the year besides Easter. So the little son born to Martin Baylon and
his wife Elizabeth Jubera was called Pascual.

From his seventh to his twenty-fourth year Paschal, first as the deputy of
his own father, and then serving other employers, led the life of a shepherd.
When Paschal, seemingly about the age of eighteen or nineteen, first
sought admission among the barefooted Friars Minor, St Peter of Alacan-
tara, the author of the reform, was still living. Probably the friars of the
Loreto convent, knowing nothing of the young shepherd who came from a
district two hundred miles away, doubted his fortitude. At any rate, they
put him off, but when they admitted him some few years later, they soon
realized that God had committed a treasure to their keeping. The community lived at the level of the first fervour of the reform, but Brother
Paschal even in this ascetical atmosphere was recognized as being eminent
in every religious virtue.

It is, however, as the saint of the Eucharist that St Paschal is best remembered outside his own country. The long hours which he spent before the
tabernacle, kneeling without support, his clasped hands held up in front of,
or higher than, his face, had left a deep impression upon his brethren. He
was on one occasion sent into France as the bearer of an important communication to Father Christopher de Cheffontaines, the very learned Breton
scholar who at that time was minister general of the Observants. For a friar
wearing the habit of his order the journey across France at that time, when
the wars of religion had reached their most acute phase, was extremely
dangerous. He succeeded in his mission, but was very roughly handled; on
several occasions barely escaping with his life. At one town in particular,

where he was stoned by a party of Huguenots, he seems to have sustained an injury to his shoulder which was a cause of suffering for the rest of his days.

St Paschal died, as he was born, on a Whitsunday, in the friary at Villareal. He was fifty-two years old. It was held to be significant of his life-long devotion to the Blessed Sacrament that, with the holy name of Jesus on his lips, he passed away just as the bell was tolling to announce the consecration at the high Mass. St Paschal's canonization took place in 1690.

PATRICK, ARCHBISHOP OF ARMAGH, APOSTLE OF IRELAND (A.D. 461?)

PATRON SAINT OF IRELAND; AND OF NIGERIA

17 MARCH

Possibly one of the best-known of the patron saints of countries, the traditional patronage of Patrick was confirmed by a decree of the Sacred Congregation of Rites on 3 December 1962. He was also appointed secondary patron of Nigeria at the same time as the Virgin Mary was proclaimed principal patron as 'Queen of Nigeria' (see page 336) on 11 April 1961.

Whether Patrick's birthplace was near Dumbarton on the Clyde, or in Cumberland to the south of Hadrian's Wall, or at the mouth of the Severn or elsewhere is of no great moment. We may infer from what he says of himself that he was of Romano-British origin. His father Calpurnius was a deacon and a municipal official, his grandfather a priest, for in those days no strict law of celibacy had yet been imposed on the Western clergy. We cannot be far wrong in supposing that he was born about 389, and that about 406 he with many others was carried off by raiders to become a slave among the still pagan inhabitants of Ireland. There amid the bodily hardships of this bondage his soul grew marvellously in holiness.

After six years he heard a voice in his sleep warning him to be ready for a brave effort which would bring him back to freedom in the land of his birth. Accordingly he ran away from his master and travelled 200 miles to the ship of whose approaching departure he had had some strange intimation. His request for free passage was refused at first, but, in answer to his silent prayer to God, the sailors called him back, and with them he made an adventurous journey. They were three days at sea, and when they reached land it was only to travel in company for a month through some uninhabited tract of country.

At length they reached human habitations – probably in Gaul – but the fugitive was safe, and thus eventually Patrick, at the age of twenty-two or twenty-three, was restored to his kinsfolk. They welcomed him warmly and besought him not to depart from them again, but after a while, in the watches of the night, fresh visions came to him, and he heard 'the voices of those who dwelt beside the wood of Foclut which is nigh to the western sea, and thus they cried, as if with one mouth, "We beseech thee, holy youth, to come and walk among us once more".' 'Thanks be to God', he adds 'that after many years the Lord granted to them according to their cry.'

With regard to the order of events which followed there is no certainty, and to trace in detail the course of the saint's heroic labours in the land of his former captivity is impossible, left as we are to the confused, legendary and sometimes contradictory data supplied by his later biographers.

When Patrick had gathered many disciples round him, such, for example, as Benignus, who was destined to be his successor, the work of evangelization was well under way. He maintained his contacts abroad, and it has been suggested that the 'approval' of which we read was a formal communication from Pope St Leo the Great. In 444, according to the Annals of Ulster, the cathedral church of Armagh, the primatial see of Ireland, was founded, and no long time probably elapsed before it became a centre of education as well as administration.

It seems possible that Patrick died and was buried, in or about the year 461, at Saul on Strangford Lough, where he had built his first church.

PAUL, APOSTLE (FIRST CENTURY)

PATRON SAINT OF THE LAY APOSTOLATE, THE 'CURSILLO' MOVEMENT AND CATHOLIC ACTION; ALSO OF MALTA AND GREECE

29 JUNE

The 'Cursillo' movement, which originated in Spain, is a form of intense spiritual formation with the purpose of preparing lay people for the apostolate. It chose Paul as its patron. In 1973, the year in which Spain celebrated the 1900th anniversary of Paul's supposed visit to that country, Paul VI formally declared Paul the Apostle to be the patron of the 'Cursillo' movement and, implicitly, of Catholic Action in general. He did this in an Apostolic Letter of 14 December.

As the Acts of the Apostles relates, Paul was shipwrecked upon Malta, and devotion to him has always been strong in the island. The feast 'The Arrival of St Paul' was formally recognized as the patronal one of Malta in a decree of the Sacred Congregation of Rites dated 27 July 1962. But long before he reached Malta, Paul had visited Greece, as both the Acts and his own writings testify. A feast of the same name, the Arrival of St Paul, is also the patronal feast of Greece, approved by decree of the Sacred Congregation of Rites on 16 July 1914.

The Apostle of the Gentiles was a Jew of the tribe of Benjamin. At his circumcision on the eighth day after his birth he received the name of Saul, and being born in Tarsus in Cilicia he was by privilege a Roman citizen. His parents sent him when young to Jerusalem, and there he was instructed in the law of Moses by Gamaliel, a learned and noble Pharisee. Thus Saul became a scrupulous observer of the law, and he appeals even to his enemies to bear witness how conformable to it his life had always been. He too embraced the party of the Pharisees, which was of all others the most severe, even while it was, in some of its members, the most opposed to the humility of the gospel. It is probable that Saul learned in his youth the trade which he practised even after his apostleship – namely, that of making tents. Later on Saul, surpassing his fellows in zeal for the Jewish law and traditions, which he thought the cause of God, became a persecutor and enemy of Christ: he took part in the murder of St Stephen. In the fury of his zeal he applied to the high priest for a commission to arrest all Jews at Damascus who confessed Jesus Christ, and bring them bound to Jerusalem.

Saul was almost at the end of his journey to Damascus when, about noon, he and his company were on a sudden surrounded by a great light from Heaven. They all saw this light, and being struck with amazement fell to the ground. Then Saul heard a voice which to him was articulate and distinct, though not understood by the rest: 'Saul, Saul, why dost thou persecute me?' Saul answered, 'Who art thou, Lord?' Christ said, 'Jesus of Nazareth, whom thou persecutest. It is hard for thee to kick against the goad.' Christ told him to arise and proceed on his journey to his destination, where he would learn what was expected of him. When he got up from the ground Saul found that though his eyes were open he could see nothing.

There was a Christian in Damascus much respected for his life and virtue, whose name was Ananias. Christ appeared to this disciple and commanded him to go to Saul, who was then in the house of Judas at prayer. Ananias trembled at the name of Saul, being no stranger to the mischief he had done in Jerusalem, or to the errand on which he had travelled to Damascus. But he went to Saul, and laying his hands upon him said, 'Brother Saul, the Lord Jesus, who appeared to thee on thy journey, hath sent me that thou mayest receive thy sight, and be filled with the Holy Ghost'. Immediately something like scales fell from his eyes, and he recovered his sight.

Saul arose, was baptized, and ate. He stayed some days with the disciples at Damascus, and began immediately to preach in the synagogues that Jesus was the Son of God, to the great astonishment of all that heard him, who said, 'Is not this he who at Jerusalem persecuted those who called on the name of Jesus, and who is come hither to carry them away prisoners?' Thus a blasphemer and a persecutor was made an apostle, and chosen to be one of the principal instruments of God in the conversion of the world.

After recovering from his temporary blindness, Paul spent three years of seclusion in 'Arabia'. Then, returning to Damascus, he began to preach the gospel with fervour. But fury against his teaching was such that he had to make his escape, being let down the city wall in a basket. He directed his steps to Jerusalem, and there, perhaps not unnaturally, he was at first regarded by the Apostles and their converts with considerable suspicion, until the generous support of Barnabas allayed their fears. In Jerusalem, however, he could not stay – the resentment of the Jews against him was too strong – and being warned by a vision which came to him in the temple, Saul went back for a time to his native city of Tarsus. Barnabas went to seek him, and yielding to his persuasion Saul accompanied him to Antioch in Syria, where the two preached with such success that a great community of believers was founded who, in that city for the first time, began to be known as 'Christians'.

After a twelve-months' stay Saul, in 44, paid his second visit to Jerusalem, coming with his companion to bring contributions to the brethen who were suffering from famine. By this time all doubts concerning Saul's stability had been laid at rest. By the direction of the Holy Spirit he and Barnabas, after their return to Antioch, were ordained, and set out on a missionary journey, first to Cyprus and then to Asia Minor. In Cyprus they converted the proconsul, Sergius Paulus, and exposed the false prophet Elymas, by whom he had been duped. Crossing to Perga, they made their way through the Taurus mountains to Antioch of Pisidia, and went on to preach in Iconium and then in Lystra, where, healing a cripple, they were at first taken for gods – Barnabas was Jupiter and Paul Mercury, 'because he was the chief speaker'; but enemies among the Jews provoked a revulsion of feeling, Paul, as he now begins to be called by his Gentile name, was stoned and left for dead. They escaped, however, and fled secretly to Derbe, whence in time they pursued their journey to the more peaceful atmosphere of the Syrian Antioch. Two or three years had probably been spent in this first missionary expedition, and it seems to have been in the summer of 49 that Paul came to Jerusalem for the third time, and was present at the meeting in which the question of the attitude of the Christian Church towards Gentile converts was finally decided. The incident in which Paul, as recorded in the second chapter of the Epistle to the Galatians, remonstrated with St Peter at Antioch over his too conservative Judaism, had perhaps occurred in the preceding winter.

Then the years from 49 to 52 were spent by St Paul in his second great missionary journey. Taking Silas with him, he travelled through Derbe to Lystra, regardless of what had previously befallen him in that place, but he was rewarded by the faithful discipleship of Timothy, whose parents dwelt there, Paul, on his part, being seemingly more careful to avoid giving unnecessary offence to the Jews; for he had Timothy circumcised, as his mother was a Jewess, though his father was a Greek. Accompanied by both Timothy and Silas, St Paul went through Phrygia and Galatia preaching and founding churches. He was, however, prevented from proceeding farther in a northerly direction by a vision which summoned him to Macedonia. Accordingly he crossed over from Troas; the beloved physician, St Luke, the author of a Gospel and the Acts, being now apparently of the party. At

Philippi we have the very interesting episode of the girl with the divining spirit who called after them 'These men are the servants of the most high God'. But though this might have seemed to help the cause, Paul commanded the spirit to go out of her. This put an end to the girl's powers of divining, and her masters, deprived of a source of profit, raised a clamour and brought Paul and Silas before the magistrates. The two missionaries were beaten and thrown into prison, but were miraculously set at liberty. We need not trace the further stages of his journey. The missionaries made their way through Macedonia, Beroea and Athens to Corinth. At Athens we have an account of the address delivered by St Paul on the Areopagus, in which he took occasion to comment upon their altar dedicated 'to the unknown god'. In Corinth his preaching made a deeper impression and we are told that he settled there for a year and six months. In the year 52 St Paul seems to have left Corinth to come to Jerusalem – his fourth visit – possibly to be present there for Pentecost, but he remained for only a short time and went on to Antioch.

The third missionary journey is thought to have covered the years 52 to 56. St Paul traversed Galatia, the Roman province of 'Asia', Macedonia, Achaia, crossed back to Macedonia, and made a return by sea which allowed him to pay his fifth visit to Jerusalem. During this period he probably spent three winters at Ephesus, and it was at Ephesus that occurred the great disturbance raised by Demetrius the silversmith, when Paul's preaching interfered with the profitable trade which many of the townspeople carried on in making and selling images of Diana. Then at Jerusalem we have the story told in detail of the apostle's reception by the elders and of the intense popular commotion excited by his visit to the Temple. He was arrested, roughly handled, and bound with chains, but before the tribune he defended himself with vigour. The official inquiry ended by his being conveyed to Caesarea. There he was kept in captivity for two years, under the proconsuls Felix and Festus, while the uncertain trial dragged on, for the governors, though all evidence of any real offence was lacking, were unwilling to face the unpopularity and the danger of an outbreak which might occur if they delivered a verdict in his favour. Paul meanwhile 'appealed to Caesar'; in other words, demanded, as a Roman citizen, that the cause should be heard by the emperor himself. In charge of a centurion, Julius, the prisoner was sent to Myra and then conveyed in an Alexandrian wheat-ship to Crete. The vessel, however, was caught in a hurricane and suffered shipwreck at Malta. St Paul, after some delay, was transferred to another ship, brought to Puteoli, and thence by land to Rome. There the book of the Acts of the Apostles leaves him, awaiting his trial before Nero.

The later movements and history of the great apostle are very uncertain. It seems probable that he was tried and acquitted in Rome after a lengthy imprisonment. We have evidence of yet another, a fourth, missionary journey. It is held by some that he visited Spain, but we can affirm with great confidence that he found his way to Macedonia once more and probably spent the winter of 65–66 at Nicopolis. Returning to Rome he was again arrested and imprisoned. Whether he was condemned in company with St Peter is not certain, but as a Roman citizen his punishment was different. There is a strong and seemingly reliable tradition that he was beheaded on the Ostian Way, at a place called Aquae Salviae (now Tre Fontane), near where the basilica of St Paul Outside the Walls stands today; and in that church his burial-place is venerated.

Shortly before, he had written to St Timothy those famous words: 'I am even now ready to be sacrificed, and the time of my dissolution is at hand. I have fought a good fight; I have finished my course; I have kept the faith. As for the rest, there is laid up for me a crown of justice which the Lord, the just judge, will render to me in that day: and not only to me, but to them also that love His coming.'

PEREGRINE LAZIOSI (A.D. 1345)

PATRON SAINT OF CANCER SUFFERERS

1 MAY

The choice of Peregrine as patron by those who suffer from cancer has not been formally confirmed by the Church, but it follows naturally from his life, and his remarkable cure.

The only son of well-to-do parents, St Peregrine Laziosi was born in 1260 at Forlì, in the Romagna. As a young man he took an active part in the politics of his native city, which belonged to the anti-papal party. On the occasion of a popular rising, St Philip Benizi, who had been sent by the pope to act as a mediator, was severely mishandled by the popular leaders, and Peregrine himself struck him on the face with his fist. The holy Servite's only reply was to offer the other cheek – an action which brought his assailant to immediate repentance, and from that time Peregrine was a reformed character. Turning away from his worldly companions, he spent hours upon his knees in the chapel of our Lady in the cathedral. One day the Blessed Virgin herself appeared to him in that place, and addressed him, saying, 'Go to Siena: there you will find the devout men who call themselves my servants: attach yourself to them'. Peregrine instantly obeyed. Having received the Servite habit, he set about following with zeal the path of perfection. It became his guiding principle that one must never rest in the way of virtue, but must press on to the appointed goal. It is said that for thirty years he never sat down, and as far as he could he observed silence and solitude.

After he had spent some years in Siena, his superiors sent him to Forlì to found a new house for the order. By this time he had been ordained and had proved himself to be an ideal priest – fervent in the celebration of the holy mysteries, eloquent in preaching, untiring in reconciling sinners. A great affliction now befell him in the form of cancer of the foot, which, besides being excruciatingly painful, made him an object of repulsion to his neighbours. He bore this trial without a murmur. At last the surgeons decided that the only thing to do was to cut off the foot. St Peregrine spent the night before the operation in trustful prayer; he then sank into a light slumber, from which he awoke completely cured – to the amazement of the doctors, who testified that they could no longer detect any trace of the disease. This miracle greatly enhanced the reputation which the holy man had already acquired by his exemplary life. He lived to the age of eighty, and was canonized in 1726.

PETER, PRINCE OF THE APOSTLES (A.D. 64?)

PATRON SAINT OF FISHERMEN

29 JUNE

Peter is the obvious choice as patron of those involved in fishing, and it needs no explanation. But it ought perhaps to be said that so popular was Peter in the Middle Ages that he came to be regarded as patron of a whole variety of occupations or situations which have no clear connection with his life-story.

The story of St Peter as recounted in the gospels is so familiar that there can be no need to retrace it here in detail. We know that he was a Galilean, that his original home was at Bethsaida, that he was married, a fisherman, and that he was brother to the apostle St Andrew. His name was Simon, but our Lord, on first meeting him told him that he should be called Kephas, the Aramaic equivalent of the Greek word whose English form is Peter (*i.e.* rock). No one who reads the New Testament can be blind to the predominant role which is everywhere accorded to him among the immediate followers of Jesus. It was he who, as spokesman of the rest, made the sublime profession of faith: 'Thou art the Christ, the Son of the living God'.

Not less familiar is the story of Peter's triple denial of his Master in spite of the warning he had previously received. The very fact that his fall is recorded by all four evangelists with a fullness of detail which seems out of proportion to its relative insignificance amid the incidents of our Saviour's passion, is itself a tribute to the position which St Peter occupied among his fellows. After the Ascension we still find St Peter everywhere taking a leading part. Almost all that we know for certain about the later life of St Peter is derived from the Acts of the Apostles and from slight allusions in his own epistles and those of St Paul. Of special importance is the account of the conversion of the centurion Cornelius; for this raised the question of the continuance of the rites of circumcision and the maintenance of the prescriptions of Jewish law in such matters as food and intercourse with Gentiles.

The passion of St Peter took place in Rome during the reign of Nero (A.D. 54–68), but no written account of it (if there was such a thing) has survived. According to an old but unverifiable tradition he was confined in the Mamertine prison, where the church of San Pietro in Carcere now stands. Tertullian (d. *c.* 225) says that the apostle was crucified; and Eusebius adds, on the authority of Origen (d. 253), that by his own desire he suffered head downwards. The place has always been believed to be the gardens of Nero, which saw so many scenes of terror and glory at this time. The, at one time, generally accepted tradition that St Peter's pontificate lasted twenty-five years is probably no more than a deduction based upon inconsistent chronological data.

The joint feast of SS. Peter and Paul seems always to have been kept at Rome on 29 June, and the practice is believed to go back at least to the time of Constantine; but the celebration in the East was at first commonly assigned to 28 December.

PETER CLAVER (A.D. 1654)

PATRON SAINT OF MISSIONS TO THE NEGRO SLAVES; AND OF COLOMBIA

9 SEPTEMBER

Peter as a secondary patron of Colombia, in which republic he spent much of his life, was confirmed on 20 July 1962 in the same decree of the Sacred Congregation of Rites that made Our Lady of the Rosary of Chiquinquira principal patron of Colombia, and Louis Bertrand another secondary patron. His patronage of missions to negro slaves is explained by his life.

He was born at Verdu, in Catalonia, about 1581, and as he showed fine qualities of mind and spirit was destined for the Church and sent to study at the University of Barcelona. Here he graduated with distinction and, after receiving minor orders, determined to offer himself to the Society of Jesus. He was received into the novitiate of Tarragona at the age of twenty, and was sent to the college of Montesione at Palma, in Majorca. Here he met St Alphonsus Rodriguez, who was porter in the college, though with a reputation far above his humble office.

In after years St Peter Claver said that St Alphonsus had actually foretold to him that he would go and the very place wherein he would work. Moved by the fervour of these exhortations Peter Claver approached his provincial, offering himself for the West Indies, and was told that his vocation would be decided in due course by his superiors. He was sent to Barcelona for his theology and after two years was, at his further request, chosen to represent the province of Aragon on the mission of Spanish Jesuits being sent to New Granada. He left Spain for ever in April 1610, and after a wearisome voyage landed with his companions at Cartagena, in what is now the republic of Colombia. He went to the Jesuit house of Santa Fé to complete his theological studies, and was employed as well as sacristan, porter, infirmarian and cook, and was sent for his tertianship to the new house of the Society at Tunja. He returned to Cartagena in 1615 and was there ordained priest.

By this time the slave trade had been established in the Americas for nearly a hundred years, and the port of Cartagena was one of its principal centres, being conveniently situated as a clearing-house. The trade had recently been given a considerable impetus, for the local Indians were not physically fitted to work in the gold and silver mines, and there was a big demand for negro slaves from Angola and the Congo.

At the time of Father Claver's ordination the leader of the work among the Negroes was Father Alfonso de Sandoval, a great Jesuit missionary who spent forty years in the service of the slaves, and after working under him Peter Claver declared himself 'the slave of the Negroes for ever'. Although by nature shy and without self-confidence he threw himself into the work with method and organization. He enlisted bands of assistants, whether by money, goods or services, and as soon as a slave-ship entered the port he went to wait on its living freight. The slaves were disembarked and shut up in the yards. Into these yards or sheds St Peter Claver plunged, with medicines and food, bread, brandy, lemons, tobacco to distribute among the Negroes, some of whom were too frightened, others too ill, to accept them. 'We must speak to them with our hands, before we try to speak to them with our lips', Claver would say. When he came upon any who were dying he baptized them, and then sought out all babies born on the voyage that he might baptize them. He had a band of seven interpreters, one of whom spoke four Negro dialects, and with their help he taught the slaves and prepared them for baptism, not only in groups but individually; for they were too backward and slow and the language difficulty too great for him to make himself understood otherwise. He made use of pictures, showing our Lord suffering on the cross for them, above all he tried to instil in them some degree of self-respect, to give them at least some idea that as redeemed human beings they had dignity and worth, even if as slaves they were outcast and despised.

It is estimated that in forty years St Peter Claver instructed and baptized over 300,000 slaves. When there was time and opportunity he took the same trouble to teach them how properly to use the sacrament of penance, and in one year is said to have heard the confessions of more than five thousand. Every spring after Easter Peter would make a tour of those plantations near Cartagena in order to see how the Negroes were getting on. He was not always well received. The masters complained that he wasted the slaves' time with his preaching, praying and hymn-singing; their wives complained that after the Negroes had been to Mass it was impossible to enter the church; and when they misbehaved Father Claver was blamed. But he was not deterred, not even when the ecclesiastical authorities lent too willing an ear to the complaints of his critics.

Many of the stories both of the heroism and of the miraculous powers of St Peter Claver concern his nursing of sick and diseased slaves, in circumstances often that no one else, black or white, could face, but he found time to care for other sufferers besides slaves. There were two hospitals in Cartagena, one for general cases, served by the Brothers of St John-of-God; this was St Sebastian's; and another, of Lazarus, for lepers and those suffering from the complaint called 'St Antony's Fire'. Both these he visited every week, waiting on the patients in their material needs and bringing hardened sinners to penitence. He also exercised on apostolate among the Protestant traders, sailors and others whom he found therein, and brought about the conversion of an Anglican dignitary, represented to be an archdeacon of London, whom he met when visiting prisoners-of-war on a ship in the harbour.

His country missions in the spring, during which he refused as much as possible the hospitality of the planters and owners and lodged in the quarters of the slaves, were succeeded in the autumn by a mission among the traders and seamen, who landed at Cartagena in great numbers at that season and further increased the vice and disorder of the port. Sometimes St Peter would spend almost the whole day in the great square of the city, where the four principal streets met, preaching to all who would stop to listen. He became the apostle of Cartagena as well as of the Negroes, and in so huge a work was aided by God with those gifts that particularly pertain to apostles, of miracles, or prophecy, and of reading hearts.

In the year 1650 St Peter Claver went to preach the jubilee among the negroes along the coast, but sickness attacked his emaciated and weakened body, and he was recalled to the residence at Cartagena. But here a virulent epidemic had begun to show itself, and one of the first to be attacked among the Jesuits was the debilitated missionary, so that his death seemed at hand. After receiving the last sacraments he recovered, but he was a broken man. For the rest of his life pain hardly left him, and a trembling in his limbs made it impossible for him to celebrate Mass. He perforce became almost entirely inactive, but would sometimes hear confessions, especially of his dear friend Doña Isabella de Urbina, who had always generously supported his work with her money. Otherwise he remained in his cell, not only inactive but even forgotten and neglected; the numbers in the house were much reduced, and those who remained were fully occupied in coping with the confusion and duties imposed by the spreading plague, but even so their indifference to the saint is surprising. Doña Isabella and her sister remained faithful to him; doubtless his old helper, Brother Nicholas Gonzalez, visited him when he could.

In the summer of 1654 Father Diego Ramirez Fariña arrived in Cartagena from Spain with a commission from the king to work among the Negroes. St Peter Claver was overjoyed and dragged himself from his bed to greet his successor. He shortly afterward heard the confession of Doña Isabella, and told her it was for the last time, and on September 6, after assisting at Mass and receiving communion, he said to Nicholas Gonzalez, 'I am going to die'. That same evening he was taken very ill and became comatose. The rumour of his approaching end spread round the city, everyone suddenly remembered the saint again, and numbers came to kiss his hands before it was too late; his cell was stripped of everything that could be carried off as a relic. St Peter Claver never fully recovered consciousness, and died two days later on the birthday of our Lady, 8 September 1654. The civil authorities who had looked askance at his solicitude for mere Negro slaves, and the clergy, who had called his zeal indiscreet and his energy wasted, now vied with one another to honour his memory.

St Peter Claver was never again forgotten and his fame spread throughout the world: he was canonized at the same time as his friend St Alphonsus Rodriguez in 1888, and he was declared by Pope Leo XIII patron of all missionary enterprises among Negroes.

PETER MARY CHANEL, MARTYR (A.D. 1841)

PATRON SAINT OF OCEANIA

28 APRIL

As first martyr of Oceania in the Pacific, and an apostle of that region, Peter Mary Chanel was a natural choice as its patron, confirmed on 24 January 1947 by a decree of the Sacred Congregation of Rites.

The first martyr of Oceania and of the Society of Mary, Peter Louis Mary Chanel, was born in 1803 in the diocese of Belley. Set to mind his father's sheep from the age of seven, he was one day noticed by the Abbé Trompier, parish priest of Cras, who was struck by his intelligence and piety, and obtained leave from the boy's parents to educate him in the little Latin school which he had started. Both as a student at Cras and in the seminary Peter won the affectionate esteem of masters and pupils alike.

A year after his ordination he was appointed to the parish of Crozet – a district which bore a bad reputation. In the three years he remained there he brought about a great revival of religion, his devotion to the sick opening to him many doors which would otherwise have remained closed. But his heart had long been set on missionary work, and in 1831 he joined the Marists, who had recently formed themselves into a society for evangelistic work at home and abroad. His aspirations were not at once realized, for he was given professional work for five years in the seminary of Belley.

However, in 1836, Pope Gregory XVI gave canonical approval to the new congregation, and St Peter was one of a small band of missionaries commissioned to carry the faith to the islands of the Pacific. Peter with one companion went to the island of Futuna in the New Hebrides. They were well received by the people, whose confidence they gained by healing the sick. But after the missionaries had acquired the language and had begun to teach, the chieftain's jealousy was aroused. Suspicion turned to hatred when his own son expressed a desire for baptism, and on 28 April 1841, he sent a band of warriors, one of whom felled St Peter with his club and the rest cut up the martyr's body with their hatchets. The missionary's death swiftly completed the work he had begun, and within a few months the whole island was Christian. Peter was canonized in 1954.

PHILIP AND JAMES, APOSTLES (FIRST CENTURY)

JOINT PATRON SAINTS OF URUGUAY

3 MAY

As secondary patrons of Uruguay, Rome has recognized both these apostles in a common feast.

St Philip the apostle came from Bethsaida in Galilee, and seems to have belonged to a little group of earnest men who had already fallen under the influence of St John the Baptist. In the synoptic gospels there is no mention of Philip except in the list of apostles which occurs in each. But St John's gospel introduces his name several times, recording in particular that the call of Philip came the day after that given to St Peter and St Andrew. Jesus, we are told, 'found Philip' and said to him, 'Follow me.'

From the account given by the evangelist, we should naturally infer that Philip responded without hesitation to the call he had received. He goes at once to find his friend Nathanael and tells him, 'We have found him of whom Moses, in the law and the prophets did write'. At the same time Philip gives proof of a sober discretion in his missionary zeal. He does not attempt to force his discovery upon unwilling ears. When Bathanael objects, 'Can anything good come from Nazareth?' his answer is not indignant declamation, but an appeal for personal inquiry – 'Come and see.' In the description of the feeding of the five thousand Philip figures again. 'When Jesus,' we are told, 'had lifted up His eyes and seen that a very great multitude cometh to Him, He said to Philip, "Whence shall we buy bread that these may eat?" And this He said to try him; for He Himself knew what He would do.' Once more we get an impression of the sober literalness of St Philip's mental outlook when he replies: 'Two hundred pennyworth of bread is not sufficient for them that every one may take a little'. It is in accord with the same amiable type of character which hesitates before responsibilities that, when certain Gentiles among the crowds who thronged to Jerusalem for the pasch came to Philip saying, 'Sir, we would see Jesus', we find him reluctant to deal with the request without taking counsel. 'Philip cometh and telleth Andrew. Again Andrew and Philip told Jesus.' Finally another glimpse is afforded us of the apostle's earnestness and devotion conjoined with defective spiritual insight, when on the evening before the Passion our Lord announced, 'No man cometh to the Father but by me. If you had known me, you would without doubt have known my Father also: and from henceforth you shall know Him, and you have seen Him'. Philip saith to Him: 'Lord, show us the Father, and it is enough for us.' Jesus saith to him: 'Have I been so long a time with you; and have you not known me? Philip, he that seeth me seeth the Father also. How sayest thou: Show us the Father?' (John xiv 6–9).

Apart from the fact that St Philip is named with the other apostles who spent ten days in the upper room awaiting the coming of the Holy Ghost at Pentecost, this is all we know about him with any degree of certainty.

For St James (the Greater), see page 221.

PHILIP OF ZELL (EIGHTH CENTURY)

PATRON SAINT OF BABIES AND SMALL CHILDREN

3 MAY

Philip was honoured as a saint soon after his death, and came to be regarded as the protector of small children, though nothing in his life (or in his subsequent miracles), suggests a reason.

During the reign of Charlemagne's father, King Pepin, there was living in the Rhenish palatinate, not far from the present city of Worms, a hermit named Philip who had an extraordinary reputation for sanctity and miracles. An Englishman by birth, he had settled in the Nahegau after he had made a pilgrimage to Rome, where he was ordained priest. Amongst those who sought out the recluse was King Pepin himself who, according to the legend, often visited him and conversed familiarly with him about holy things. The historian of St Philip, who wrote a century after his death, states that through his intercourse with the hermit, Pepin 'began to fear as well as to love God and to place all his hope in Him'.

As is so often the case with solitaries, Philip exercised a great attraction over the wild creatures of the forest: birds perched on his shoulder and ate from his hands, whilst hares frisked about him and licked his feet. He was joined in his solitude by another priest, Horskolf by name, who served God with him in prayer and helped to cultivate the land. One evening, thieves stole the two oxen which the hermits kept to aid them in their labours. All night long the miscreants wandered about the woods, unable to find their way out, and in the morning they discovered that they were back again in front of the hermitage. In dismay they threw themselves at St Philip's feet, begging forgiveness. The holy man reassured them, entertained them as guests and sped them on their way. Gradually disciples gathered round the two hermits and a church was built.

A story is told that Horskolf, on his return from a journey, found Philip dead and lying in his coffin. With tears the disciple besought his master to give him the usual blessing which, for some reason, had been omitted when they had last parted. In reply the corpse sat up and said, 'Go forth in peace, and may God prosper you abundantly in all things. Take care of this place as long as you live. Safe and sound you shall go forth; safe and sound shall you return'. Then, having given the desired blessing, he sank back into death. Horskolf continued to reside in the hermitage until, at the age of 100, he passed away to rejoin his master. On the site of the cells was built a monastery, and then a collegiate church, in the midst of what became the parish of Zell, *i.e.* cell, named after St Philip's hermitage.

PIRMINUS, BISHOP (A.D. 753)

PATRON SAINT AGAINST POISON AND SNAKE-BITE

3 NOVEMBER

Pirminus, according to one of the legends surrounding his life, escaped unharmed from a poisonous snake-bite, for which he has been invoked both against poisons in general, and against snake-bites in particular.

The early evangelization of what was formerly the grand-duchy of Baden was principally the work of several monasteries, and St Pirminus was a prominent figure among their founders. He probably came from southern Gaul or Spain, a refugee from the Moors, and he rebuilt the abbey of Dissentis in the Grisons, it having been destroyed by the Avars. But he is best known as the first abbot of Reichenau, on an island in Lake Constance, which he founded – the oldest Benedictine house on German soil, it is said – in 724; Reichenau for a time was a rival of Saint Gall in influence. But for political reasons the founder was subsequently exiled and went to Alsace, where he founded the monastery of Murbach, between Trier and Metz. He also founded the Benedictine house at Amorbach in Lower Franconia, and to him is attributed a summary manual of popular instruction, known as the *Dicta Pirmini* or *Scarapsus*, which was very widely circulated in Carolingian times. St Pirminus was a regionary bishop, but never bishop of Meaux, as stated in the Roman Martyrology. He died in 753.

PIUS X, POPE (A.D. 1914)

PATRON SAINT FOR SICK PILGRIMS

21 AUGUST

In 1910 Pius X approved the establishment of, and gave his blessing to, the Unio Nationalis Italicae Traiciendis Aegrotis Lapurdum et ad Sanctuaria Internationalia or UNITALSI, a society dedicated to taking sick people to the Italian shrine of Lapurdo, and to shrines in other countries. UNITALSI petitioned that Pius X should be recognized as its patron, and this John Paul II agreed in his Apostolic Letter of 8 February 1983.

He was born in 1835, son of the municipal messenger and postman of the big village of Riese in Venetia, and was then known as Giuseppe Sarto (*i.e.* Joseph Taylor); he was the second of ten children, and the circumstances of the family were very poor. Young Joseph went to the local elementary school, from thence, through the encouragement of his parish priest, to the 'grammar school' at Castelfranco, walking five miles there and back every day, and then by bursary to the seminary at Padua. He was ordained priest by dispensation at the age of twenty-three, and for seventeen years gave himself wholeheartedly to the pastoral ministry; then he became a canon of Treviso, where his hard work and generous charities were very marked, and in 1884 bishop of Mantua, a diocese then in a very low state, with a negligent clergy and two towns in schism. So brilliantly successful was he in handling this charge that in 1892 Pope Leo XIII appointed Mgr Sarto cardinal-priest of St Bernard-at-the-Baths and promoted him to the metropolitan see of Venice, which carries with it the honorary title of patriarch. Here he became a veritable apostle of Venetia, his simplicity and forthrightness standing out in a see that rather prided itself on its pomp and magnificence.

On the death of Leo XIII in 1903 it was generally believed that Cardinal Rampolla del Tindaro would succeed him, and the first three ballots of the conclave so far bore this out that Cardinal Puzyna, Archbishop of Cracow, communicated to the electors the formal veto against Rampolla of the Emperor Francis Joseph of Austria. There was a profound sensation, and the cardinals solemnly protested against the interference: but Rampolla withdrew his candidature with great dignity, and after four more ballots Cardinal Sarto was elected. Thus there came to the chair of Peter a man of obscure birth, of no outstanding intellectual attainments, and with no experience of ecclesiastical diplomacy, but one who, if ever man did, radiated goodness: 'a man of God who knew the unhappiness of the world and the hardships of life, and in the greatness of his heart wanted to comfort everybody'.

One of the new pope's earliest acts, by the constitution 'Commission nobis', was to put an end once and for all to any supposed right of any civil power to interfere in a papal election, by veto or in any other way; and later he took a cautious but definite step towards reconciliation between church and state in Italy by relaxing in practice the 'Non expedit'. His way of dealing with the most critical situation that soon arose in France was more direct and assuredly not less effective than ordinary diplomatic methods would have been. After a number of incidents the French government in 1905 denounced the concordat of 1801, decreed the separation of church and state, and entered on an aggressive campaign against the Church. For dealing with ecclesiastical property it proposed an organization called *associations cultuelles*, to which many prominent French Catholics wanted to give a trial; but, after consultation with the French episcopate, Pope Pius in two strong and dignified pronouncements condemned the law of separation and forbade the *associations* as uncanonical. Of those who complained that he had sacrificed all the possessions of the Church in France he said, 'They are too concerned about material goods, and not enough about spiritual'. A good aspect of the separation was that the Holy See could now appoint French bishops direct, without nomination by the civil power. 'Pius X', declared the bishop of Nevers, Mgr Gauthey, 'at the cost of sacrificing our property emancipated us from slavery. May he be blessed for ever for not shrinking from imposing that sacrifice on us.' The pope's strong action caused the French government such difficulties that twenty years later it agreed to another and canonical arrangement for the administration of church property.

The name of Pius X is commonly and rightly associated with the purging of the Church of that 'synthesis of all heresies', somewhat unhappily called Modernism. A decree of the Holy Office in 1907 condemned certain writers and propositions, and it was soon followed by the encyclical letter 'Pascendi dominici gregis', wherein the far-reaching dangerous tendencies were set out and examined, and manifestations of Modernism in every field were pointed out and condemned. Strong disciplinary measures were also taken and, though there was some fierce opposition, Modernism was practically killed in the Church at one blow. It had made considerable headway among Catholics, but there were not wanting those even among the orthodox who thought the pope's condemnation was excessive to the verge of an obscurantist narrowness. How far he could be from that was seen when in 1910 his encyclical on St Charles Borromeo had been misunderstood and given offence to Protestants in Germany. Pius had his official explanation of the misunderstood passages published in the *Osservatore Romano*, and recommended the German bishops not to give the encyclical any further publication in pulpit or press.

In his first encyclical letter Pius X had announced his aim to be to 'renew all things in Christ', and nothing was better calculated to do that than his decrees concerning the sacrament of the Eucharist. These formally recommended daily communion when possible, directed that children should be allowed to approach the altar upon attaining the use of reason, and facilitated the communion of the sick. But there is a ministry of the word as well as of the altar, and he also strongly urged daily reading of the Bible – but here the pope's words did not receive so much heed. With the object of increasing the worthiness of divine worship he in 1903 issued on his own initiative (*motu proprio*) an instruction on church music which struck at current abuses and aimed at the restoration of congregational singing of the Roman plainchant. He encouraged the work of the commission for the codifying of canon law, and was responsible for a thorough reorganization of the tribunals, offices and congregations of the Holy See. Pius also set up a commission for the revision and correction of the Vulgate text of the Bible (this work was entrusted to the monks of St Benedict), and in 1909 founded the Biblical Institute for scriptural studies in charge of the Society of Jesus.

Pius X was ever actively concerned for the weak and oppressed. He strongly denounced the foul ill-treatment of the Indians on the rubber-plantations of Peru, and greatly encouraged the Indian missions in that country. He sent a commission of relief after the earthquake at Messina, and sheltered refugees at his own expense in the hospice of Santa Marta by St Peter's, while his general charities, in Rome and throughout the world, were so great that people wondered where all the money came from. The quiet simplicity of his personal habits and the impressive holiness of his character were both exemplified in his custom of preaching publicly on the day's gospel in one of the Vatican courtyards every Sunday. Pius was embarrassed – perhaps a little shocked – by the ceremoniousness and some of the observances of the papal court. At Venice he had refused to let anyone but his sisters cook for him, and now he declined to observe the custom of conferring titles of nobility on his relatives. 'The Lord has made them sisters of the pope,' he said, 'that should suffice'. 'Look how they have dressed me up,' he exclaimed to an old friend, and burst into tears. And to another he said, 'It is indeed a penance to be forced to accept all these practices. They lead me about surrounded by soldiers like Jesus when he was seized in Gethsemane'.

Those are not merely entertaining anecdotes. They go right to the heart of Pius's single-minded goodness. To an English convert who wished to be a monk but had made few studies, he said, 'To praise God well it is not necessary to be learned'. At Mantua infamous charges were made against him in print. He refused to take any action; and when the writer went bankrupt, the bishop privately sent him money: 'So unfortunate a man needs prayers more than punishment'.

On 24 June 1914, the Holy See signed a concordat with Serbia; four days later the Archduke Francis of Austria and his wife were assassinated at Sarajevo; by the midnight of 4 August, Germany, France, Austria, Russia, Great Britain, Serbia, Belgium were at war: it was the eleventh anniversary of the pope's election. Pius X had not merely foreseen this European war –

many people had done that – he had foretold it definitely for the summer of 1914, but its outbreak was nevertheless a blow that killed him: 'This is the last affliction that the Lord will visit on me. I would gladly give my life to save my poor children from this ghastly scourge'. After a few days' illness he developed bronchitis on 19 August: next day he was dead – the first great victim of a war called great. 'I was born poor, I have lived poor and I wish to die poor,' he said in his will: and its contents bore out the truth of his words, so that even the anti-clerical press was moved to admiration.

After the funeral in St Peter's Mgr Cascioli wrote, 'I have no doubt whatever that this corner of the crypt will before long become a shrine and place of pilgrimage. . . . God will glorify to the world this pope whose triple crown was poverty, humility and gentleness'. And so indeed it came about. The pontificate of Pius X had not been a quiet one, and the pope had been resolute in his policies. If he had no enemies – for it takes two to make an enemy – he had many critics, inside the Church as well as outside. But now the voice was unanimous: from all quarters, from high and low, came a call for the recognition of the sanctity of Pius X, once Joseph Sarto, the postman's little boy. In 1923 the cardinals in curia decreed that his cause be introduced, Cardinal Aidan Gasquet representing England among the twenty-eight signatories; and in 1954 Pope Pius XII solemnly canonized his predecessor before a vast multitude in St Peter's Square at Rome – the first canonized pope since Pius V in 1672.

PROCESSUS AND MARTINIAN, MARTYRS (DATE UNKNOWN)

PATRON SAINTS OF PRISON OFFICERS

2 JULY

That these two martyrs existed at all is not beyond dispute: that they were the gaolers of Peter and Paul is pure legend – but the legend is the reason for their choice as patrons of prison officers.

These martyrs were publicly venerated in Rome from at least the fourth century, but of their history and passion nothing is known. No credence can be given to the legend in their sixth-century *acta*, adopted by the Roman Martyrology and Breviary. According to this, while SS. Peter and Paul were confined in the Mamertine prison, their warders, Processus and Martinian, and forty others, were converted by the miracles and teaching of the apostles, to whom they offered their liberty. A flow of water miraculously sprang from the rock to enable St Peter to baptize them. The officer in charge, Paulinus, tried to persuade Processus and Martinian from their new faith, and afterwards subjected them to cruel tortures when they would not offer incense on the altar of Jupiter; their sufferings only wrung from them the words, 'Blessed be the name of the Lord'. So they were slain with the sword. Whoever these two martyrs may actually have been, they were buried, it is said, by a woman called Lucina on her own property, near the second milestone on the Via Aurelia, and in the fourth century a basilica was built over their tomb, wherein St Gregory the Great preached his thirty-second homily on their feast-day, in the course of which he said that at that place the sick were healed, the possessed were freed, and the forsworn were tormented. In the beginning of the ninth century Pope St Paschal I translated their relics to St Peter's, where they still rest under the altar dedicated in their honour in the south transept.

PUDENTIANA (*c.* 160)

A PATRON SAINT OF THE PHILIPPINES

19 MAY (NO LONGER PART OF THE ROMAN CALENDAR)

When confirming the Blessed Virgin Mary under the title of the Immaculate Conception as principal patron of the Philippines, Pope Pius XII, in his Apostolic Letter of 12 September 1942, recalled that Pudentiana had been chosen as patron in the sixteenth century, and Rose of Lima in the seventeenth. He was now confirming both these saints as secondary patrons of the Philippines.

In the Roman Martyrology for 19 May we used to read: 'At Rome (the commemoration) of St Pudentiana, virgin, who after innumerable contests, after caring reverently for the burial of many of the martyrs, and distributing all her goods to the poor, at length passed from earth to heaven. In the same city of St Pudens, a senator, father of the aforesaid maiden, who was by the Apostles adorned for Christ in baptism, and guarded his vesture unspotted unto a crown of life'. Opinions are divided as to whether this Pudens is to be identified with the Pudens mentioned in 2 Tim. iv 21. But there can be no reasonable doubt that at an early date there was a Christian so named in Rome who gave a plot of ground with which was subsequently connected a church and 'title'. It was first known as the *ecclesia Pudentiana* or *titulus Pudentis*; but by a later confusion people came to speak of the *ecclesia Sanctae Pudentianae*, and this supposed patroness was honoured as a martyr and a daughter of Pudens. Owing to a slurred pronunciation the name was also often written Potentiana. After the close of the eighth century a story was fabricated purporting to be the Acts of SS.Pudentiana and Praxedes, in which the two maidens were described as sisters (Pudentiana being only sixteen years old) and the daughters of Pudens. They were probably associated in the story because Praxedes and Pudentiana stand together first in the list of the virgins whose bodies were transferred from the catacombs to the church of Praxedes by Pope Paschal I (817–824).

RAPHAEL THE ARCHANGEL

PATRON SAINT OF TRAVELLERS AND SAFE JOURNEYS; OF YOUNG PEOPLE LEAVING
HOME; OF PHARMACISTS; OF BLIND PEOPLE, AND AGAINST EYE DISEASES; AND OF
HEALTH INSPECTORS

29 SEPTEMBER

*Because of the care he showed for Tobias, Raphael has long been invoked by travellers
for a safe journey. Raphael not only accompanied young Tobias on the road, but took
care of his safety. In the Middle Ages, at least in some parts of Italy, Raphael was therefore taken to be the patron of young people leaving home for the first time.*

*According to the Book of Tobit, Raphael gave the young Tobias the ointment to cure
old Tobias' blindness. The Archangel has been invoked therefore against eye diseases,
and is also taken as their patron by pharmacists.*

*In an Apostolic Letter of 7 March 1964 Paul VI declared Raphael to be the 'patron of
the inspectors of the Annonae', strictly speaking inspectors of the food supply in Rome
though those being described are, according to the Letter, concerned with the 'bodily
welfare of the citizens'. And that, as Paul VI pointed out, was the role that Raphael
fulfilled for Tobias.*

Of the seven archangels, who in both Jewish and Christian tradition are
venerated as pre-eminently standing before the throne of God, three only
are mentioned by name in the Bible, Michael, Gabriel and Raphael. These
have been venerated in the Church from early times, especially in the East,
but it was not till the pontificate of Pope Benedict XV that the liturgical feasts
of the two last were made obligatory throughout the Western church.

It is recorded in the sacred book of the history of Tobias that St Raphael
was sent by God to minister to the old Tobias, who was blind and greatly
afflicted, and to Sara, daughter of Raguel, whose seven bridegrooms had
each perished on the night of their wedding. And when the young Tobias
was sent into Media to collect money owing to his father, it was Raphael
who, in the form of a man and under the name of Azarias, accompanied him
on the journey, helped him in his difficulties, and taught him how safely to
enter into wedlock with Sara. 'He conducted me,' says Tobias, 'and brought
me safe again. He received the money of Gabalus. He caused me to have my
wife, and he chased from her the evil spirit. He gave joy to her parents.
Myself he delivered from being devoured by the fish; thee also he hath made
to see the light of Heaven; and we are filled with all good things through
him.' The offices of healing performed by the angel in this story and the fact
that his name signifies 'God has healed' has caused Raphael to be identified
with the angel who moved the waters of the healing sheep-pool (John v 1–4);
this identity is recognized in the liturgy by the reading of that passage of the
gospel in the Mass of St Raphael's feast. In Tobias xii 12 and 15, the archangel
directly speaks of himself as 'one of the seven who stand before the Lord',
and says that he continually offered the prayers of young Tobias up to God.

RAYMUND NONNATUS (A.D. 1240)

CARDINAL OF THE HOLY ROMAN CHURCH
PATRON SAINT OF MIDWIVES; OF CHILDBIRTH, CHILDREN AND PREGNANT
WOMEN; AND OF INNOCENT PEOPLE, FALSELY ACCUSED

31 AUGUST

From the Middle Ages Raymund Nonnatus has been regarded as the patron of midwives and of all those who have to do with childbirth, because of the circumstances of his own birth.

No doubt because of the sufferings he had to endure while in North Africa, Raymund has traditionally been regarded as the patron of innocent people, and of all who are falsely accused.

The true story of the career of this saint is wrapped in impenetrable mystery for lack of reliable materials, and no confidence can be put in the accuracy of the details furnished by Alban Butler's account, summarized below.

St Raymund was brought into the world at Portello in Catalonia in the year 1204, and was called *non natus*, 'not born', because he was taken out of the body of his mother after her death in labour. When he grew up he got his father's leave to enter the newly founded Mercedarian Order, and was admitted to profession therein at Barcelona by St Peter Nolasco.

So swift was the progress he made that within two or three years after his profession he was judged qualified to discharge the office of ransomer, in which he succeeded St Peter. Being sent into Barbary with a considerable sum of money he purchased at Algiers the liberty of a number of slaves. When all other resources were exhausted, he voluntarily gave himself up as hostage for the ransom of others, whose situation was desperate and whose faith was exposed to imminent danger. The sacrifice which the saint made of his liberty served only to exasperate the Algerians, who treated him with barbarity till, fearing lest if he died in their hands they would lose the ransom stipulated for the slaves for whom he remained a hostage, the magistrate gave orders that he should be treated with more humanity. He was permitted to go about the streets and he made use of this liberty to comfort and encourage the Christians, and he converted and baptized some Moslems. When the governor heard of this he condemned him to be impaled. However, the persons who were interested in the ransom of the captives prevailed that his life should be spared lest they should be losers; and, by a commutation of his punishment, he was made to run the gauntlet. This did not daunt his courage. So long as he saw souls in danger, he thought he had yet done nothing; nor could he let slip any opportunity to ministering to them.

St Raymund had, on one side, no more money to employ in releasing poor captives; on the other, to speak to a Moslem upon the subject of religion was by the Islamic law to court death. He could, however, still exert his endeavours with hope of some success or of dying a martyr of charity. He therefore did so. The governor was enraged, and commanded the servant of Christ to be whipped at the corners of all the streets in the city, his lips to be bored with a red-hot iron, and his mouth shut up with a padlock, the key of which he kept himself and only gave to the gaoler when the prisoner was to eat. In this condition he was kept in a dungeon, where he lay full eight months, till his ransom was brought by some of his order, who were sent with it by Nolasco. Raymund was unwilling to leave the country for he wanted to remain to assist the slaves; but he acquiesced in obedience, begging God to accept his tears, seeing he was not worthy to shed his blood for the souls of his neighbours.

Upon his return to Spain in 1239 he was nominated cardinal by Pope Gregory IX. But so little was he affected by the unlooked-for honour that he neither changed his dress, nor his poor cell in the convent at Barcelona, nor his manner of living. The pope called him to Rome. St Raymund obeyed, but could not be persuaded to travel otherwise than as a poor religious. He got no farther than Cardona (Cerdagne), which is only six miles from Barcelona; he was seized with a violent fever and died there, being only about thirty-six years old. He was buried in the chapel of St Nicholas at Portello, and his name was inscribed in the Roman Martyrology in 1657.

RAYMUND OF PEÑAFORT (A.D. 1275)

PATRON SAINT OF LAWYERS, INCLUDING CANON LAWYERS; SCHOOLS AND
FACULTIES OF LAW

7 JANUARY

Raymund of Peñafort has been regarded as patron of lawyers, and in particular of canon lawyers, from the Middle Ages onwards, for his collection of cases of conscience and his five books of Decretals. The State faculties of law in Spain also recognize him.

The family of Peñafort claimed descent from the courts of Barcelona, and was allied to the kings of Aragon. Raymund was born in 1175, at Peñafort in Catalonia, and made such rapid progress in his studies that at the age of twenty he taught philosophy at Barcelona. This he did gratis, and with great reputation. When he was about thirty he went to Bologna to perfect himself in canon and civil law. He took the degree of doctor, and taught with the same disinterestedness and charity as he had done in his own country. In 1219 Berengarius, Bishop of Barcelona, made Raymund his archdeacon and 'official'. He was a perfect model to the clergy by his zeal, devotion and boundless liberalities to the poor. In 1222 he assumed the habit of St Dominic at Barcelona, eight months after the death of the holy founder, and in the forty-seventh year of his age. He begged his superiors that they would enjoin some severe penance to expiate the complacency which he said he had sometimes taken in his teaching. They, indeed, imposed on him a penance, but not quite such as he expected: it was to write a collection of cases of conscience for the convenience of confessors and moralists. This led to the compilation of the *Summa de casibus poenitentialibus*, the first work of its kind.

Pope Gregory IX, having called St Raymund to Rome in 1230, nominated him to various offices and took him for his confessor, in which capacity Raymund enjoined the pope, for a penance, to receive, hear and expedite immediately all petitions presented by the poor. Gregory also ordered the saint to gather into one body all the scattered decrees of popes and councils since the collection made by Gratian in 1150. In three years Raymund completed his task; and the five books of the 'Decretals' were confirmed by the same Pope Gregory in 1234.

For his health St Raymund returned to his native country, and was received with as much joy as if the safety of the kingdom depended on his presence. Being restored again to his dear solitude at Barcelona he continued his former contemplation, preaching and work in the confessional. He was frequently employed in important commissions, both by the Holy See and by the king. In 1238, however, he was thunderstruck by the arrival of deputies from the general chapter of his order at Bologna with the news that he had been chosen third master general, Bd Jordan of Saxony having lately died. He wept and entreated, but at length acquiesced in obedience. He made the visitation of his order on foot without discontinuing any of his austerities or religious exercises. He instilled into his spiritual children a love of regularity, solitude, studies and the work of the ministry, and reduced the constitutions of his order into a clearer method, with notes on the doubtful passages. The code which he drew up was approved in three general chapters. In one held at Paris in 1239 he procured that the voluntary resignation of a superior, founded upon just reasons, should be accepted: the year following he resigned the generalship which he had held only two years. He grounded his action on the fact that he was now sixty-five years old.

But St Raymund still had thirty-four years to live, and he spent them in the main opposing heresy and working for the conversion of the Moors in Spain. With this end in view, he engaged St Thomas to write his work *Against the Gentiles*; he contrived to have Arabic and Hebrew taught in several convents of his order; and he established friaries, one at Tunis, and another at Murcia, among the Moors. In 1256 he wrote to his general that ten thousand Saracens had received baptism. He was active in getting the Inquisition established in Catalonia; and once he was accused – not without some reason – of compromising a Jewish rabbi by a trick.

During the saint's last illness, Alphonsus, King of Castile, and James of Aragon visited him, and received his final blessing. St Raymund gave up his soul to God on 6 January in the year 1275, the hundredth of his age.

RITA OF CASCIA (A.D. 1457)

PATRON OF THOSE IN DESPERATE SITUATIONS; OF PARENTHOOD, AND AGAINST INFERTILITY

22 MAY

Rita's own life was full of what might be described as 'desperate or almost impossible situations', which she overcame. But this devotion to her as a patron of those in particularly difficult situations, which dates from medieval times, probably stems, like that to St Gregory, more from her reputation as a miracle-worker.

Traditionally Rita has been invoked by those who wanted children, and against infertility. She was herself the daughter of parents who might have been regarded as beyond the age of child bearing.

Rita was born in 1381 in Roccaborena in the central Apennines. She showed from her earliest years extraordinary piety and love of prayer. She had set her heart upon dedicating herself to God in the Augustinian convent at Cascia, but when her father and mother decreed that she should marry, she sorrowfully submitted, deeming that in obeying them she was fulfilling God's will. Her parents' choice was an unfortunate one. Her husband proved to be brutal, dissolute and so violent that his temper was the terror of the neighbourhood. For eighteen years with unflinching patience and gentleness Rita bore with his insults and infidelities. As with a breaking heart she watched her two sons fall more and more under their father's evil influence, she shed many tears in secret and prayed for them without ceasing. Eventually there came a day when her husband's conscience was touched, so that he begged her forgiveness for all the suffering he had caused her: but shortly afterwards he was carried home dead covered with wounds.

Her sons vowed to avenge their father's death, and in an agony of sorrow she prayed that they might die rather than commit murder. Her prayer was answered. Before they had carried out their purpose they contracted an illness which proved fatal. Their mother nursed them tenderly and succeeded in bringing them to a better mind, so that they died forgiving and forgiven. Left alone in the world, Rita's longing for the religious life returned, and she tried to enter the convent at Cascia. She was informed, however, to her dismay that the constitutions forbade the reception of any but virgins. Three times she made application, and three times the prioress reluctantly refused her. But her persistence triumphed: the rules were relaxed in her favour and she received the habit in 1413.

In the convent St Rita displayed the same submission to authority which she had shown as a daughter and wife. No fault could be found with her observance of the rule. On the other hand, where latitude was allowed by the rule – as in the matter of extra austerities – she was pitiless to herself. Her charity to her neighbour expressed itself in her care for her fellow religious during illness and for the conversion of negligent Christians. From childhood she had had a special devotion to the sufferings of our Lord, and when in 1441 she heard an eloquent sermon on the crown of thorns from St James della Marca, a strange physical reaction seems to have followed. While she knelt, absorbed in prayer, she became acutely conscious of pain – as of a thorn which had detached itself from the crucifix and embedded itself in her forehead. It developed into an open wound which suppurated and became so offensive that she had to be secluded from the rest. The wound was healed for a season to enable her to accompany her sisters on a pilgrimage to Rome during the year of the jubilee, 1450, but it was renewed after her return and remained with her until her death, obliging her to live practically as a recluse.

She died on 22 May 1457, and her body has remained incorrupt until modern times.

ROBERT BELLARMINE, DOCTOR OF THE CHURCH (A.D. 1621)

ARCHBISHOP OF CAPUA, AND CARDINAL
PATRON SAINT OF CATECHISTS AND CATECHUMENS

17 SEPTEMBER

Robert Bellarmine not only composed two catechisms, but himself taught catechism to children when he was Archbishop of Capua. He is therefore an appropriate choice to be patron of catechists. He was named for this role by Pius XI in his Apostolic Letter of 26 April 1932, together with St Charles Borromeo.

Born in 1542 at Montepulciano in Tuscany, of a noble but impoverished family, he was the son of Vincent Bellarmino and Cynthia Cervini, half-sister to Pope Marcellus II. Even as a boy Robert showed great promise. He knew Virgil by heart, he wrote good Latin verses, he played the violin, and he could hold his own in public disputations, to the great admiration of his fellow-citizens. Moreover, he was so deeply devout that in 1559, when Robert was seventeen, the rector of the Jesuit college at Montepulciano described him in a letter as 'the best of our school, and not far from the Kingdom of Heaven'. It was his ambition to enter the Society of Jesus, but he had to encounter strong opposition from his father, who had formed other plans for his son. Robert's mother, however, was on his side, and eventually he obtained the permission he desired. In 1560 he went to Rome to present himself to the father general of the order, by whom his noviciate was curtailed to enable him to pass almost immediately into the Roman College to enter upon the customary studies.

Ill-health dogged his steps from the cradle to the grave, and his delicacy became so pronounced that, at the close of his three years of philosophy, his superiors sent him to Florence to recruit his strength in his native Tuscan air, whilst at the same time teaching boys and giving lectures on rhetoric and on the Latin poets. Twelve months afterwards he was transferred to Mondovi in Piedmont. There he discovered that he was expected to instruct his pupils in Cicero and Demosthenes. He knew no Greek except the letters of the alphabet, but with characteristic obedience and energy he set to work to study at night the grammar lesson he was expected to give the next day. Father Bellarmine strongly objected to the flogging of boys, and himself never did so. In addition to teaching he preached sermons which attracted crowds. Amongst the congregation on one occasion was his provincial superior, Father Adorno, who promptly transferred him to Padua that he might prepare himself in that famous university town to receive ordination. Again he studied and preached, but before the completion of his course he was bidden by the father general, St Francis Borgia, to proceed at once to Louvain in Belgium to finish his studies there and to preach to the under-graduates, with a view to counteracting the dangerous doctrines which were being propagated by Dr Michael Baius, the chancellor, and others. It is interesting to note that on his journey he had as companion for part of the way the Englishman William Allen, afterwards to become like himself a cardinal. From the time of his arrival at Louvain until his departure seven years later, Robert's sermons were extraordinarily popular, although they were delivered in Latin, and although the preacher had no physical advan-tages to commend him, for he was small of stature and had to stand on a stool in the pulpit to make himself properly seen and heard. But men declared that his face shone with a strange light as he spoke and that his words seemed like those of one inspired.

After his ordination at Ghent in 1570, he was given a professorship in the University of Louvain – the first Jesuit to hold such a post – and began a course of lectures on the *Summa* of St Thomas Aquinas, which were at the same time brilliant expositions of doctrine and a vehicle through which he could, and did, controvert the teachings of Baius on such matters as grace, free will and papal authority. In contrast to the controversial brutality of the time he never made personal attacks on his enemies or mentioned them by name. Not content with the great labour entailed on him by his sermons and lectures, St Robert during his stay at Louvain taught himself Hebrew and embarked upon a thorough study of the Holy Scriptures and of the Fathers. To assist the studies of others he also made time to write a Hebrew grammar, which became extremely popular.

A serious breakdown in health, however, necessitated his recall to Italy and there, in spite of the efforts of St Charles Borromeo to secure his services for Milan, he was appointed to the recently established chair of controversial theology at the Roman College. For eleven years, from 1576, he laboured untiringly, giving lectures and preparing the four great volumes of his

Disputations on the Controversies of the Christian faith which, even three hundred years later, the great ecclesiastical historian Hefele described as 'the most complete defence of Catholic teaching yet published'. It showed such profound acquaintance with the Bible, the Fathers, and the heretical writers, that many of his opponents could never bring themselves to believe that it was the work of one man. They even suggested that his name was an anagram covering a syndicate of learned and wily Jesuits. The work was one urgently needed at that particular moment, because the leading Reformers had recently published a series of volumes purporting to show, by an appeal to history, that Protestantism truly represented the Church of the Apostles. As these were published at Magdeburg, and as each volume covered a century, the series became known as the 'Centuries of Magdeburg'. The answer which Baronius set out to furnish in the field of history, St Robert Bellarmine supplied in the field of dogmatics. The success of his *Controversies* was instantaneous: laymen and clergy, Catholics and Protestants, read the volumes with avidity, and even in Elizabethan England, where the work was prohibited, a London bookseller declared, 'I have made more money out of this Jesuit than out of all the other divines put together'.

In 1589 he was separated for a while from his books to be sent with Cardinal Cajetanus on a diplomatic embassy to France, then in the throes of war between Henry of Navarre and the League. No tangible results came of the mission, but the party had the experience of being in Paris for eight months during the siege, when, to quote St Robert's own words, they 'did practically nothing though they suffered a very great deal'. As opposed to Cardinal Cajetanus, who had Spanish sympathies, St Robert was openly in favour of trying to make terms with the king of Navarre if he would become a Catholic, but within a very short time of the raising of the siege the members of the mission were recalled to Rome by the death of Pope Sixtus V. Soon afterwards we find St Robert taking the leading part on a papal commission appointed by Pope Clement VIII to edit and make ready for publication the new revision of the Vulgate Bible, which had been called for by the Council of Trent. An edition had indeed already been completed during the reign of Sixtus V and under that pope's immediate supervision, but it contained many errors due to defective scholarship and to a fear of making important alterations in the current text. Moreover, it was never in general circulation. The revised version, as produced by the commission and issued with the *imprimatur* of Clement VIII, is the Latin Bible as we have it today, with a preface composed by St Robert himself. He was then living at the Roman College, where, as official spiritual director to the house, he had been brought into close contact with St Aloysius Gonzaga, whose death-bed he attended and to whom he was so deeply attached that in his will he asked to be buried at the feet of the youthful saint.

Recognition of Bellarmine's great qualities followed quickly. In 1592 he was made rector of the Roman College; in 1594 he was made provincial of

Naples; and three years later he returned to Rome in the capacity of theologian to Clement VIII, at whose express desire he wrote his two celebrated catechisms, one of which is still in general use throughout Italy. These catechisms are said to have been translated more frequently than any other literary work except the Bible and the *Imitation of Christ*. In 1598, to his great dismay, he was nominated a cardinal by Clement VIII on the ground that 'he had not his equal for learning'. Though obliged to occupy apartments in the Vatican and to keep up some sort of an establishment, he relaxed none of his former austerities. Moreover, he limited his household and expenses to what was barely essential: he lived on bread and garlic – the food of the poor; and he denied himself a fire even in the depth of winter. Once he ransomed a soldier who had deserted from the army; and he used the hangings of his rooms to clothe poor people, remarking, 'The walls won't catch cold'.

In 1602 he was, somewhat unexpectedly, appointed archbishop of Capua, and within four days of his consecration he left Rome to take up his new charge. Admirable as the holy man appears in every relation of life, it is perhaps as shepherd of his immense flock that he makes the greatest appeal to our sympathy. Laying aside his books, the great scholar, who had no pastoral experience, set about evangelizing his people with all the zeal of a young missionary, whilst initiating the reforms decreed by the Council of Trent. He preached constantly, he made visitations, he exhorted the clergy, he catechized the children, he sought out the necessitous, whose wants he supplied, and he won the love of all classes. He was not destined, however, to remain long away from Rome. Paul V, who was elected pope three years later, at once insisted upon retaining Cardinal Bellarmine by his side, and the archbishop accordingly resigned his see. From that time onwards, as head of the Vatican Library and as a member of almost every congregation, he took a prominent part in all the affairs of the Holy See. When Venice ventured arbitrarily to abrogate the rights of the Church, and was placed under an interdict, St Robert became the pope's great champion in a pamphlet contest with the Republic's theologian, the famous Servite, Fra Paolo Sarpi. A still more important adversary was James I of England. Cardinal Bellarmine had remonstrated with his friend, the Archpriest Blackell, for taking the oath of allegiance to James – an oath purposely so worded as to deny to the pope all jurisdiction over temporals. King James, who fancied himself as a controversialist, rushed into the fray with two books in defence of the oath, both of which were answered by Cardinal Bellarmine. In the earlier rejoinder, St Robert, writing in the somewhat lighter vein that so became him, made humorous references to the monarch's bad Latin; but his second treatise was a serious and crushing retort, covering every point in the controversy. Standing out consistently and uncompromisingly as a champion of papal supremacy in all things spiritual, Bellarmine nevertheless held views on temporal authority which were displeasing to extremists of both parties. Because he maintained that the pope's jurisdiction over foreign rulers was indirect, he lost favour with Sixtus V, and because, in opposition to the Scots jurist, Barclay, he denied the divine right of kings, his book, *De potestate papae*, was publicly burnt by the *parlement* of Paris.

The saint was on friendly terms with Galileo Galilei, who dedicated to him one of his books. He was called upon, indeed, to admonish the great astronomer in the year 1616, but his admonition, which was accepted with a good grace, amounted to a caution against putting forward, otherwise than as a hypothesis, theories not yet fully proved.

It would be impossible in limited space even to enumerate the various activities of St Robert during these later years. He continued to write, but his works were no longer controversial. He completed a commentary on the Psalms and wrote five spiritual books, all of which, including the last, on the *Art of Dying*, were soon translated into English. When it became clear that his days were drawing to a close, he was allowed to retire to the Jesuit novitiate of St Andrew. There he died, at the age of seventy-nine, on 17 September 1621 – on the day which, at his special request, had been set aside as the feast of the Stigmata of St Francis of Assisi. St Robert Bellarmine was canonized in 1930, and declared a doctor of the Church in 1931.

ROCH (c. A.D. 1378)

PATRON SAINT OF CONTAGIOUS DISEASES, INCLUDING PLAGUE AND CHOLERA; OF PHYSICIANS AND SURGEONS; OF CATTLE; OF PRISONERS; OF ISTANBUL

17 AUGUST

The invocation of Roch against the plague, against cholera, or contagious diseases in general, is a traditional one, and stems from the stories of his life. Because of his association with care of the sick he has also been taken as the patron of physicians and surgeons; and because he not only cured people but healed their sick cattle as well, his name is also invoked on behalf of these animals. As his life narrates, Roch was himself imprisoned for a time, and hence has traditionally been taken as a patron of prisoners. Along with St John Chrysostom and St George, he was decreed to be a patron of Istanbul (Constantinople) by the Sacred Congregation of Rites on 7 January 1914.

We find this servant of God venerated in France and Italy during the early fifteenth century, not very long after his death, but we have no authentic history of his life. No doubt he was born in Montpellier and nursed the sick during a plague in Italy but that is almost all that can be affirmed about him. His 'lives' are chiefly made up of popular legends, which may have a basis in fact but cannot now be checked. According to the one written by a Venetian, Francis Diedo, in 1478, Roch was son of the governor of Montpellier, and upon being left an orphan at the age of twenty he went on a pilgrimage of Rome. Finding Italy plague-stricken he visited numerous centres of population, Acquapendente, Cesena, Rome, Rimini, Novara, where he not only devoted himself to care of the sick but cured large numbers simply by making the sign of the cross on them. At Piacenza he was infected himself, and not wishing to be a burden on any hospital he dragged himself out into the woods to die. Here he was miraculously fed by a dog, whose master soon found Roch and looked after him; when he was convalescent he returned to Piacenze and miraculously cured many more folk, as well as their sick cattle. At length he got back to Montpellier, where his surviving uncle failed to recognize him; he was there imprisoned, and so he remained five years, till he died. When they came to examine his body it was recognized who he really was, the son of their former governor, by a cross-shaped birth-mark on his breast. He was therefore given a public funeral, and he performed as many miracles when dead as he had done when alive. Another biography, shorter, simpler and perhaps older, says that St Roch was arrested as a spy and died in captivity at Angera in Lombardy.

ROSE OF LIMA (A.D. 1617)

PATRON SAINT OF PERU; OF CENTRAL AND SOUTHERN AMERICA; THE
PHILIPPINES; INDIA; OF THE SECURITY FORCES AND THE NURSES OF PERU; AND OF
FLORISTS AND GARDENERS

23 AUGUST

So great was the devotion of the people of Peru to Rose that Clement X – who had a considerable devotion to her himself – proclaimed her patron of that country in 1670, two years before she was canonized; and he extended that patronage to the whole of Central and South America, to the Philippines where she is a secondary patron along with St Pudentiana, and to India.

Devotion to Rose remains strong in Peru in general, and in Lima in particular, and in 1965 Paul VI was requested to declare her the patron of the security forces of that country, specifically the Guardia Civil, which he did.

Rose has been described as 'operating the first free clinic on the Continent', and it is therefore not surprising she should have been declared patron of Peruvian nurses by a decree of the Sacred Congregation of Rites of 5 September 1958.

Rose, whose name is that of a flower, lived in, and loved, her parents' garden. She has been known as the 'Flower of Lima' from a poem written to celebrate her canonization, and has appropriately, if unofficially, become a patron of both gardeners and florists.

She was of Spanish extraction, born at Lima, the capital of Peru, in 1586, her parents, Caspar de Flores and Maria del Oliva, being decent folk of moderate means. She was christened Isabel but was commonly called Rose, and she was confirmed by St Toribio, Archbishop of Lima, in that name only. When she was grown up, she seems to have taken St Catherine of Siena for her model, in spite of the objections and ridicule of her parents and friends. Hearing others frequently commend her beauty, and fearing lest it should be an occasion of temptation to anyone, she used to rub her face with pepper, in order to disfigure her skin with blotches. A woman happening one day to admire the fineness of the skin of her hands and her shapely fingers, she rubbed them with lime, and in consequence was unable to dress herself for a month. By these and other even more surprising austerities she armed herself against external dangers and against the insurgence of her own senses.

Her parents having been reduced to straitened circumstances by an unsuccessful mining venture, Rose by working all day in the garden and late at night with her needle relieved their necessities. These employments were agreeable to her, and she probably would never have entertained any thoughts of a different life if her parents had not tried to induce her to marry. She had to struggle with them over this for ten years, and to strengthen herself in her resolution she took a vow of virginity. Then, having joined the third order of St Dominic, she chose for her dwelling a little hut in the garden, where she became practically a recluse. She wore upon her head a thin circlet of silver, studded on the inside with little sharp prickles, like a crown of thorns.

God favoured St Rose with many great graces, but she also suffered during fifteen years persecution from her friends and others, and the even more severe trial of interior desolation and anguish in her soul. The last three years of her life were spent under the roof of Don Gonzalo de Massa, a government official, and his wife, who was fond of Rose. In their house she was stricken by her last illness, and under long and painful sickness it was her prayer, 'Lord, increase my sufferings, and with them increase thy love in my heart'. She died on 24 August 1617, thirty-one years old. The chapter, senate, and other honourable corporations of the city carried her body by turns to the grave. She was canonized by Pope Clement X in 1672, being the first canonized saint of the New World.

ROSE OF VITERBO (A.D. 1252?)

PATRON SAINT OF FLORISTS AND FLOWER GROWERS (CENTRAL ITALY)

4 SEPTEMBER

No doubt in part because of her name, and in part because of the name of the convent which refused her admission, she has become the patron of florists and of flower growers in central Italy. In his Apostolic Letter of 8 February 1983 John Paul II recognized that he was only confirming what the people had already decided.

When Frederick II was excommunicated for the second time by Pope Gregory IX the emperor set out to conquer the papal states, and in 1240 he occupied Viterbo in the Romagna. A few years previously there had been born in this city, to parents of lowly station, a girl child, who was christened Rose.

During an illness when she was eight years old Rose is said to have had a vision or dream of our Lady, who told her that she was to be clothed in the habit of St Francis, but that she was to continue to live at home and to set a good example to her neighbours by both word and work. Rose soon recovered her health, received the dress of lay penitent in due course, and began when she was about twelve years old to preach up and down the streets, upbraiding the people for their supineness in submitting to Frederick. Crowds would gather outside her house to get a glimpse of her, till her father became frightened, and forbade her to show herself in public; if she disobeyed she would be beaten. At the instance of their parish priest her father withdrew his prohibition and for about two years the pope's cause continued to be preached in public by this young girl. Then the partisans of the emperor became alarmed and clamoured that Rose should be put to death as a danger to the state. The *podestà* of the city would not hear of this: he was a just man, and moreover he feared the people; but instead he passed a sentence of banishment against St Rose and her parents. They took refuge at Soriano, and here, in the beginning of December 1250, St Rose is said to have announced the approaching death of the Emperor Frederick II. He in fact died in Apulia on the 13 December; the papal party thereupon got the upper hand in Viterbo, and St Rose returned.

She now went to the convent of St Mary of the Roses at Viterbo and asked to be received as a postulant. The abbess refused, for want of a dowry. Her parish priest, however, took it upon himself to open a chapel close by the convent, with a house attached wherein St Rose and a few companions might lead a religious life; but the nuns got an order from Pope Innocent IV for it to be closed, on the ground that they had the privilege of having no other community of women within a given distance of their own. St Rose therefore returned to her parents' house, where she died on March 6 1252, about the age of seventeen. She was buried in the church of Santa Maria in Podio, but her body was on 4 September in 1258 translated to the church of the convent of St Mary of the Roses, as she had foretold.

Immediately after her death Pope Innocent IV ordered an inquiry into her virtues but St Rose's canonization was not achieved until 1457.

SEBASTIAN, MARTYR (A.D. 288?)

PATRON SAINT OF MUNICIPAL, OR LOCAL, POLICE AND NEIGHBOURHOOD WATCH SCHEMES; OF ARCHERS AND SOLDIERS; OF CONTAGIOUS DISEASES, ESPECIALLY PLAGUE; AND OF PHYSICIANS

20 JANUARY

There are, wrote Pius XII in his Apostolic Letter of 3 May 1957, many associations both civil and military, which venerate Sebastian because of his example of Christian virtue. One of these, he said, was that force which policed the towns of Italy, the 'vigili urbani'. This can be interpreted as 'municipal' or 'local' police, but it seems also to suggest vigilantes and people engaged in 'neighbourhood watch' type schemes.

Because Sebastian was regarded in the Middle Ages as the patron of archers, he was seen also as the patron of all soldiers. There was a considerable following of Sebastian as someone who would protect people against the plague, and hence too a protector of physicians generally. It has been suggested that this goes back to a particular incident when invocation of the saint was successful in halting the spread of disease – an outbreak of the plague in Rome in 680 being proposed as the occasion in question. Another possible explanation is that the arrows were likened metaphorically to the chastisement of God, and therefore to the plague (v. Psalms 7:13).

According to the 'acts', assigned without any adequate reason to the authorship of St Ambrose, St Sebastian was born at Narbonne in Gaul, though his parents had come from Milan, and he was brought up in that city. He was a fervent servant of Christ, and though his natural inclinations were averse from a military life, yet to be better able to assist the confessors and martyrs in their sufferings without arousing suspicion, he went to Rome and entered the army under the Emperor Carinus about the year 283. It happened that the martyrs, Marcus and Marcellian, under sentence of death, appeared in danger of faltering in their resolution owing to the tears of their friends; Sebastian, seeing this, intervened and made them a long exhortation in constancy, which he delivered with an ardour that strongly affected his hearers. Zoë, the wife of Nicostratus, who had for six years lost the use of speech, fell at his feet, and when the saint made the sign of the cross on her mouth, she spoke again distinctly. Thus Zoë, with her husband, Nicostratus, who was master of the rolls (*priminscrinius*), the parents of Marcus and Marcellian, the gaoler Claudius, and sixteen other prisoners were converted; and Nicostratus, who had charge of the prisoners, took them to his own house, where Polycarp, a priest, instructed and baptized them. Chromatius, governor of Rome, being informed of this, and that Tranquillinus, the father of Marcus and Marcellian, had been cured of the gout by receiving baptism, desired to follow their example, since he himself was grievously afflicted with the same malady. Accordingly, having sent for Sebastian, he was cured by him, and baptized with his son Tiburtius. He then released the converted prisoners, made his slaves free, and resigned his prefectship.

Not long after Carinus was defeated and slain in Illyricum by Diocletian, who the year following made Maximian his colleague in the empire. The persecution was still carried on by the magistrates in the same manner as under Carinus, without any new edicts. Diocletian, admiring the courage and character of St Sebastian, was anxious to keep him near his person; and being ignorant of his religious beliefs he created him captain of a company of the pretorian guards, which was a considerable dignity. When Diocletian went into the East, Maximian, who remained in the West, honoured Sebastian with the same distinction and respect. Chromatius retired into the country in Campania, taking many new converts along with him. Then followed a contest of zeal between St Sebastian and the priest Polycarp as to which of them should accompany this troop to complete their instruction, and which should remain at the post of danger in the city to encourage and assist the martyrs. Pope Caius, who was appealed to, judged that Sebastian should stay in Rome. In the year 286, the persecution growing fiercer, the pope and others concealed themselves in the imperial palace, as the place of greatest safety, in the apartments of one Castulus, a Christian officer of the court. Zoë was first apprehended, when praying at St Peter's tomb on the feast of the apostles. She was stifled with smoke, being hung by the heels over a fire. Tranquillinus, ashamed to show less courage than a woman, went to pray at the tomb of St Paul, and there was seized and stoned to death. Nicostratus, Claudius, Castorius and Victorinus were taken, and after being thrice tortured, were thrown into the sea. Tiburtius, betrayed by a false brother, was beheaded. Castulus, accused by the same wretch, was twice stretched upon the rack, and afterwards buried alive. Marcus and Marcellian were nailed by the feet to a post, and having remained in that torment twenty-four hours were shot to death with arrows.

St Sebastian, having sent so many martyrs to Heaven before him, was himself impeached before Diocletian; who, after bitterly reproaching him with his ingratitude, delivered him over to certain archers of Mauritania, to be shot to death. His body was pierced through with arrows, and he was left for dead. Irene, the widow of St Castulus, going to bury him, found him still alive and took him to her lodgings, where he recovered from his wounds, but refused to take to flight. On the contrary, he deliberately took up his station one day on a staircase where the emperor was to pass, and there accosting him, he denounced the abominable cruelties perpetrated against the Christians. This freedom of language, coming from a person whom he supposed to be dead, for a moment kept the emperor speechless; but recovering from his surprise, he gave orders for him to be seized and beaten to death with cudgels, and his body thrown into the common sewer. A lady called Lucina, admonished by the martyr in a vision, had his body secretly buried in the place called *ad catacumbas*, where now stands the basilica of St Sebastian.

STANISLAUS, BISHOP OF CRACOW, MARTYR (A.D. 1079)

PATRON SAINT OF POLAND

11 APRIL

Stanislaus was confirmed as one of Poland's several patrons by a decree of the Sacred Congregation of Rites dated 31 August 1962.

Stanislaus Szczepanowski was born on 26 July 1030, at Szczepanow. He came of noble parents, who had been childless for many years until this son was vouchsafed to them in answer to prayer. They devoted him from his birth to the service of God, and encouraged in every way the piety which he evinced from early childhood. He was educated at Gnesen and afterwards he was ordained priest by Lampert Zula, bishop of Cracow, who gave him a canonry in the cathedral and subsequently appointed him his preacher and archdeacon. The eloquence of the young priest and his saintly example brought about a great reformation of morals amongst his penitents – clergy as well as laity flocking to him from all quarters for spiritual advice. Bishop Lampert wished to resign the episcopal office in his favour, but Stanislaus refused to consider the suggestion. However, upon Lampert's death, he could not resist the will of the people seconded by an order from Pope Alexander II, and he was consecrated bishop in 1072.

Poland at that epoch was ruled by Boleslaus II, a prince whose finer qualities were completely eclipsed by his unbridled lust and savage cruelty. Stanislaus alone ventured to beard the tyrant and to remonstrate with him at the scandal his conduct was causing. At first the king endeavoured to vindicate his behaviour, but when pressed more closely he made some show of repentance. The good effects of the admonition, however, soon wore off: Boleslaus relapsed into his evils ways. There were acts of rapacity and political injustice which brought him into conflict with the bishop and at length he perpetrated an outrage which caused general indignation. A certain nobleman had a wife who was very beautiful. Upon this lady Boleslaus cast lustful eyes, and when she repelled his advances he caused her to be carried off by force and lodged in his palace. The Polish nobles called upon the archbishop of Gnesen and the court prelates to expostulate with the monarch. Fear of offending the king closed their lips, and the people openly accused them of conniving at the crime. St Stanislaus, when appealed to, had no such hesitation, he went again to Boleslaus and rebuked him for his sin. He closed his exhortation by reminding the prince that if he persisted in his evil courses he would bring upon himself the censure of the Church.

Finding all remonstrance useless, Stanislaus launched against him a formal sentence of excommunication. The tyrant professed to disregard the ban, but when he entered the cathedral of Cracow he found that the services were at once suspended by order of the bishop. Furious with rage, he pursued the saint to the little chapel of St Michael outside the city, where he was celebrating Mass, and ordered some of his guards to enter and slay him. The men, however, returned, saying that they could not kill the saint as he was surrounded by a heavenly light. Upbraiding them for cowardice, the king himself entered the building and dispatched the bishop with his own hand. The guards then cut the body into pieces and scattered them abroad to be devoured by beasts of prey: the sacred relics were rescued three days later by the cathedral canons and privately buried at the door of the chapel in which Stanislaus had been slain.

There seems no doubt that there were some political considerations behind the murder of St Stanislaus, though the whole business is very uncertain and obscure. It is not true that the action of Boleslaus led to an immediate rising of the people which drove him from Poland; but it certainly hastened his fall from power. Pope St Gregory VII laid the country under an interdict, and nearly two centuries later, in 1253, St Stanislaus was canonized by Pope Innocent IV.

STANISLAUS KOSTKA (A.D. 1568)

PATRON SAINT OF YOUNG PEOPLE; AND OF POLAND

13 NOVEMBER

Stanislaus Kostka is venerated as the patron of youth because of his own comparative youth at the time of his death. The Apostolic Letter of Pius XI dated 13 June 1926 declaring him as such links his name with that of the other young Jesuit saint, Aloysius Gonzaga.

Stanislaus' links with Poland are clear enough from his life story, and he has long been venerated there as one of the secondary patrons of that country – a devotion recognized in a decree of the Sacred Congregation of Rites dated 31 August 1962.

He was the second son of John Kostka, senator of Poland, and Margaret Kryska, and was born in the castle of Rostkovo in 1550. The first elements of letters he learned at home under a private tutor, Dr John Bilinsky, who attended him and his elder brother, Paul, to the college of the Jesuits at Vienna when the saint was fourteen years old.

When he arrived at Vienna and was lodged among the pupils of the Jesuits, everyone was struck by the recollection and devotion with which he lived and prayed. Eight months after their arrival the Emperor Maximilian II took from the Jesuits the house which Ferdinand I had lent them for their students. Paul Kostka, two years older than his brother, was a high-spirited youth, fond of amusement, and he prevailed on Bilinsky to take lodgings in a Lutheran's house in the city. This did not at all please Stanislaus, but Paul treated his brother's devotion and reserve with contemptuous amusement.

After nearly two years of this Stanislaus was taken ill and wished to receive viaticum; but the Lutheran landlord would not allow the Blessed Sacrament to be brought to his house. The boy in extreme affliction recommended himself to the intercession of St Barbara (to whose confraternity he belonged), and he seemed in a vision to be communicated by two angels. The Blessed Virgin is said to have appeared to him in another vision, told him that the hour of his death was not yet come, and bade him devote himself to God in the Society of Jesus. He had already entertained such a thought, and after his recovery petitioned to be admitted. At Vienna the provincial, Father Maggi, dared not receive him, for fear of incurring the anger of his father. Stanislaus therefore determined to walk if necessary to Rome itself to ask the father general of the Society in person. He stole away on foot to Augsburg and thence to Dillingen, to make the same request first to St Peter Canisius, provincial of Upper Germany. He set out on his 350-mile walk, dressed in coarse clothes, and immediately his flight was discovered Paul Kostka and Bilinsky rode off in pursuit. Various reasons are given to account for their failure to overtake or recognize him. St Peter Canisius received him encouragingly and set him to wait on the students of the college at table and clean out their rooms, which he did with such respect and humility that the students were astonished, though he was utterly unknown to them. Canisius, after having kept him three weeks, sent him with two companions to Rome, where he went to St Francis Borgia, then general of the Society, and earnestly renewed his petition. St Francis granted it, and Stanislaus was admitted in 1567, when he was seventeen years old. He had received from his father a most angry letter, threatening that he would procure the banishment of the Jesuits out of Poland and abusing Stanislaus for putting on 'contemptible dress and following a profession unworthy of his birth'. Stanislaus answered it in the most dutiful manner, but expressed a firm purpose of serving God according to his vocation. Without disturbance or trouble or mind he applied himself to his duties, recommending all things to God.

It was the saint's utmost endeavour, declared his novice-master, Father Fazio, to sanctify in the most perfect manner all his ordinary actions, and he set no bounds to his mortifications except what obedience to his director prescribed. His faults he exaggerated with unfeigned simplicity, and the whole life of this novice seemed a continual prayer. The love which he had for Jesus Christ in the Holy Sacrament was so ardent that his face appeared on fire as soon as he entered the church, and he was often seen in a kind of ecstasy at Mass and after receiving communion. But his model novitiate was not destined to last more than nine months. The summer heat of Rome was too much for St Stanislaus, he had frequent fainting-fits, and he knew that he had not long to live. On the feast of the dedication of St Mary Major, talking with Father Emmanuel de Sa about the Assumption of our Lady, he said: 'How happy a day for all the saints was that on which the Blessed

Virgin was received into Heaven! Perhaps the blessed celebrate it with special joy, as we do on earth. I hope myself to be there for the next feast they will keep of it.' No particular significance was attached to this remark at the time, but ten days later it was remembered. On St Laurence's day he found himself ill and two days later, when taken to a better bedroom, he made the sign of the cross upon his bed, saying he should never more rise from it. Father Fazio jokingly rallied him on his physical weakness. 'O man of little heart!' he said. 'Do you give up for so slight a thing?' 'I am a man of little heart', replied Stanislaus, 'but it is not so slight a matter, for I shall die of it.' Early in the morning of the Assumption he whispered to Father Ruiz that he saw the Blessed Virgin accompanied with many angels, and quietly died a little after three o'clock in the morning. A month later Paul Kostka arrived in Rome with instructions from his father to bring back Stanislaus to Poland at all costs. The shock of finding him dead made Paul carefully consider his own behaviour with regard to his brother, and during the process of beatification he was one of the principal witnesses. Dr Bilinsky was another. He said among other things that, 'The blessed boy never had a good word from Paul. And we both knew all the time the holiness and devotion of all that he did.' Paul was bitterly remorseful all his life, and at the age of sixty asked for admission to the Society of Jesus. St Stanislaus was canonized in 1726.

STEPHEN, THE FIRST MARTYR (*c.* A.D. 34)

PATRON SAINT OF BRICKLAYERS AND THOSE IN BUILDING TRADES; AND OF DEACONS

26 DECEMBER

Because of the manner of his death – by stoning – from medieval times Stephen has been regarded as their patron by all those engaged in the building trades such as stonecutters and stonemasons. Stephen was also, of course, the leader of the first seven deacons, as narrated below.

That St Stephen was a Jew is unquestionable, and he probably was a Hellenist of the Dispersion, who spoke Greek. The name Stephen is Greek, Stephanos, and signifies 'crown'. The circumstances of his conversion to Christianity are not known. We are told of him in the book of the Acts of the Apostles when, there being numerous converts, the Hellenists murmured against the Hebrews, complaining that their widows were neglected in the daily ministration. The Apostles assembled the faithful and told them that they could not relinquish the duties of preaching and prayer to attend to the care of tables; and recommended them to choose seven men of good character, full of the Holy Ghost and wisdom, who might superintend that business. The suggestion was approved, and the people chose Stephen, 'a man full of faith and of the Holy Ghost', and Philip, Prochorus, Nicanor,

Timon, Parmenas and Nicholas a proselyte of Antioch. These seven were presented to the Apostles, who praying, imposed hands upon them, and so ordained them the first deacons.

Stephen spoke with such wisdom and spirit that his hearers were unable to resist him, and a plot was laid by the elders of certain synagogues in Jerusalem. At first they undertook to dispute with Stephen: but finding themselves unequal to the task they suborned false witnesses to charge him with blasphemy against Moses and against God. The indictment was laid in the Sanhedrin, and he was dragged thither. The main point urged against him was that he affirmed that the temple would be destroyed, that the Mosaic traditions were but shadows and types no longer acceptable to God, Jesus of Nazareth having put an end to them. Leave was given him to speak, and in a long defence, set out in Acts vii 2–53, he showed that Abraham, the father and founder of their nation, was justified and received the greatest favours of God in a foreign land; that Moses was commanded to set up a tabernacle, but foretold a new law and the Messias; that Solomon built the Temple, but it was not to be imagined that God was confined in houses made by hands: the temple and the Mosaic law were temporary, and were to give place when God introduced more excellent institutions by sending the Messias himself. He ended with a stinging rebuke: 'You stiff-necked and uncircumcised in hearts and ears, you always resist the Holy Spirit; as your fathers did, so do you also. Which of the prophets have not your fathers persecuted? And they have slain them who foretold of the coming of the Just One, of whom you have been now the betrayers and murderers: who have received the law by the disposition of angels, and have not kept it.'

The whole assembly raged at Stephen, but he, being full of the Holy Spirit and looking up steadfastly to the heavens, saw them opened and beheld the glory of God and the Saviour standing at the right hand of the Father. And he said, 'Behold, I see the heavens opened, and the Son of man standing on the right hand of God'. 'And they, crying out with a loud voice, stopped their ears and with one accord ran violently upon him. And, casting him forth without the city, they stoned him; and the witnesses laid down their garments at the feet of a young man whose name was Saul. And they stoned Stephen, invoking and saying, "Lord Jesus, receive my spirit". And falling on his knees, he cried with a loud voice, saying, "Lord, lay not this sin to their charge". And when he had said this he fell asleep in the Lord.'

STEPHEN OF HUNGARY (A.D. 1038)

PATRON SAINT OF HUNGARY

16 AUGUST

No explanation is needed to account for devotion to Stephen in Hungary, and he has formally been recognized by a decree of the Sacred Congregation of Rites as patron of that country. See also page 317 – the Blessed Virgin Mary, under the title of Great Queen of Hungary.

Geza, duke of the Magyars, saw the political necessity of Christianity to Hungary and (encouraged by St Adalbert of Prague) he was baptized and a number of his nobles followed his example. But it was largely a conversion of expediency, and the Christianity of the converts was largely nominal. An exception to this was Geza's son Vaik, who had been baptized at the same time as his father and been given the name of Stephen (Istvan); he was then only about ten. In the year 995, when he was twenty, he married Gisela, sister of Henry, Duke of Bavaria, better known as the Emperor St Henry II, and two years later he succeeded his father as governor of the Magyars.

Stephen was soon engaged in wars with rival tribal leaders and others; and when he had consolidated his position he sent St Astrik, whom he designed to be the first archbishop, to Rome to obtain Pope Silvester II's approval for a proper ecclesiastical organization for his country; and at the same time to ask his Holiness to confer upon him the title of king. Silvester was disposed to grant his request, and prepared a royal crown to send him with his blessing, acting no doubt in concert with political representations from the Emperor Otto III who was then in Rome. At the same time the pope confirmed the religious foundations which the prince had made and the elections of bishops. St Stephen went to meet his ambassador upon his return and listened, standing with great respect, to the pope's bulls whilst they were read. The same prelate who had brought the crown from Rome crowned him king with great solemnity in the year 1001.

King Stephen established episcopal sees only gradually, as Magyar clergy became available; Vesprem is the first of which there is reliable record, but within some years Esztergom was founded and became the primatial see. At Szekesfehervar he build a church in honour of the Mother of God, in which the kings of Hungary were afterwards both crowned and buried; this city St Stephen made his usual residence. He also completed the foundation of the great monastery of St Martin, begun by his father.

For the support of the churches and their pastors and the relief of the poor throughout his dominions he commanded tithes to be paid. Every tenth town had to build a church and support a priest; the king himself furnished the churches. He abolished customs derived from the former religion and repressed blasphemy, murder, theft, adultery and other public crimes. He commanded all persons to marry except religious and churchmen, and forbade all marriages of Christians with idolators.

The example of his virtue was a most powerful sermon to those who came under his influence, and it was exemplified in his son, Bd Emeric, to whom St Stephen's code of laws was inscribed. These laws he caused to be promulgated throughout his dominions, and they were well suited to a fierce and rough people newly converted to Christianity. He abolished tribal divisions and divided the land into 'counties', with a system of governors and magistrates. Thus, and by means of a limited application of feudal ideas, making the nobles vassals of the crown, he welded the Magyars into a unity; and by retaining direct control over the common people he prevented undue accumulation of power into the hands of the lords. St Stephen was indeed the founder and architect of the independent realm of Hungary.

As the years passed, Stephen wanted to entrust a greater part in the government to his only son, but in 1031 Emeric was killed while hunting. The death of Emeric left him without an heir and the last years of his life were embittered by family disputes about the succession, with which he had to cope while suffering continually from painful illness. He eventually died, aged sixty-three, on the feast of the Assumption 1038, and was buried beside Bd Emeric at Szekesfehervar.

TERESA OF AVILA (A.D. 1582)

FOUNDRESS OF THE DISCALCED CARMELITES

PATRON SAINT OF SPANISH CATHOLIC WRITERS; AND OF THE SPANISH ARMY
COMMISSARIAT

15 OCTOBER

Paul VI, expressing regret at the obnoxious deluge of books and newspapers which do nothing but harm to the soul, commended Teresa, whose several books, he remarked, were full of admirable wisdom, as patron of those upon whom falls the responsibility for producing modern books and journals. The patronage of Teresa had been sought, he said in an Apostolic Letter of 18 September 1965, by many in Spain from all walks of life.

Teresa was declared patron of the Spanish Military Commissariat by a decree of the Sacred Congregation of Rites of 13 December 1961.

St Teresa was born at or near Avila in Castile on 28 March 1515, and when only seven took great pleasure in the lives of the saints, in which she spent much time with a brother called Rodrigo, who was near the same age. The martyrs seemed to them to have bought Heaven very cheaply by their torments, and they resolved to go into the country of the Moors, in hopes of dying for their faith. They set out secretly, praying as they went that they might lay down their lives for Christ. But when they had got as far as Adaja they were met by an uncle, and brought back to their frightened mother, who reprimanded them; whereupon Rodrigo laid all the blame on his sister.

Teresa and the same little brother then wanted to become hermits at home, and built themselves hermitages with piles of stones in the garden, but could never finish them. Teresa sought to be much alone, and had in her room a picture of our Saviour discoursing with the Samaritan woman at the well, before which she often repeated the words, 'Lord, give me of that water that I may not thirst'. Her mother died when she was fourteen, and the change in Teresa was sufficiently noticeable to disturb the mind of her father. He placed his daughter, who was then fifteen, with a convent of Augustinian nuns in Avila where many young women of her rank were educated.

After a year and a half spent in this convent Teresa fell sick, and her father took her home, where she began to deliberate seriously about undertaking the religious life. She told her father that she wished to become a nun, but he would not give his consent; after his death she might dispose of herself as she pleased. Fearing she might relapse, though she felt a severe interior conflict in leaving her father, she went secretly to the convent of the Incarnation of the Carmelite nuns outside Avila, where her great friend, Sister Jane Suarez, lived. She was then twenty years old and, the step being taken, Don Alonso ceased to oppose it. A year later she was professed. An illness, which seized her before her profession, increased very much after it, and her father got her removed out of her convent. Sister Jane Suarez bore her company, and she remained in the hands of physicians. Their treatment only made her worse (she seems to have been suffering from malignant malaria), and she could take no rest day or night. The doctors gave her up, and she got worse and worse. Under these afflictions she was helped by the prayer which she had then begun to use. Her devout uncle Peter had put into her hands a little book of Father Francis de Osuna, called the *Third Spiritual Alphabet*. Taking this book for her guide she applied herself to mental prayer, but for want of an experienced instructor she made little solid progress. But after three years' suffering Teresa was restored to bodily health.

By an irregular custom of her convent quite common in those days, visitors of all kinds were freely received and mixed with, and Teresa spent much time conversing in the parlour of the monastery. She began to neglect mental prayer, and persuaded herself that this was a part of humility, as her unrecollected life rendered her unworthy to converse so much or so familiarly with God. She also said to herself that there could be no danger or sin in what so many others, more virtuous than she, did; and for her neglect of meditation she alleged the infirmities to which she was subject.

When her father died his confessor, a Dominican friar, pointed out to Teresa the dangerous state she was in. At his insistence she returned to the practice of private prayer and never again abandoned it. But she had not yet the courage to follow God perfectly, or entirely to renounce dissipating her time and gifts. Becoming more and more convinced of her own unworthiness, she had recourse to the two great penitents, St Mary Magdalen and St Augustine, and with them were associated two events decisive in fixing her will upon the pursuit of religious perfection. One was the reading of St Augustine's *Confessions*: the other was a movement to penitence before a picture of our suffering Lord, in which 'I felt St Mary Magdalen come to my assistance . . . from that day I have gone on improving much ever since in my spiritual life'.

After she had finally withdrawn herself from the pleasures of social intercourse and other occasions of dissipation and faults St Teresa was very frequently favoured by God with the prayer of quiet, and also with that of union, which latter sometimes continued a long time with great increase of joy and love, and God began to visit her with intellectual visions and interior communications. The warning of certain women who had been miserably duped by imagination and the Devil much impressed her and, though she was persuaded her graces were from God, she was perplexed, and consulted so many persons that, though binding them to secrecy, the affair was divulged abroad, to her mortification and confusion. One to whom she spoke was Francis de Salsedo, a married man who was an example of virtue to the whole town. He introduced to her Dr Daza, a learned and virtuous priest, who judged her to be deluded by the Devil, saying that such divine favours were not consistent with a life so full of imperfections as she claimed hers to be. Teresa was alarmed and not satisfied, and Don Francis (to whom the saint says she owed her salvation and her comfort) bade her not to be discouraged. He recommended that she should consult one of the fathers of the newly-formed Society of Jesus, to whom she made a general confession in which, with her sins, she gave him an account of her manner of prayer and her extraordinary favours. The father assured her these were divine graces, but told her she had neglected to lay the true foundation of an interior life. On his advice, though he judged her experiences in prayer to be from God, she endeavoured for two months to resist and reject them. But her resistance was in vain.

Another Jesuit, Father Balthasar Alvarez, told her she would do well to beg of God that He would direct her to do what was most pleasing to Him, and for that purpose to recite every day the *Veni Creator Spiritus*. She did so, and one day whilst she was saying that hymn she was seized with a rapture, in which she heard these words spoken to her within her soul, 'I will not have you hold conversation with men, but with angels'. The saint afterwards had frequent experience of such interior speeches and explains how they are even more distinct and clear than those which men hear with their bodily ears, and how they are also operative, producing in the soul the strongest impressions and sentiments of virtue, and filling her with an assurance of their truth, with joy and with peace. Whilst Father Alvarez was her director she suffered grievous persecutions for three years.

In 1557 St Peter of Alcantara came to Avila, and of course visited the now famous, or notorious, Carmelite. He declared that nothing appeared to him more evident than that her soul was conducted by the Spirit of God; but he foretold that she was not come to an end of her persecutions and sufferings. If the various proofs by which it pleased God to try Teresa served to purify her virtue, the heavenly communications with which she was favoured served to humble and fortify her soul, to give her a strong disrelish of the things of this life, and to fire her with the desire of possessing God. In raptures she was sometimes lifted in the air, of which she gives a careful description, and adds that God 'seems not content with drawing the soul to Himself, but He must needs draw up the very body too, even whilst it is mortal and compounded of so unclean a clay as we have made it by our sins'.

During this time took place such extraordinary manifestations as spiritual espousals, mystical marriage, and the piercing (*transverberatio*) of the saint's heart. Her response to this remarkable happening was in the following year (1560) to make a vow that she would in everything do always that which seemed to be the most perfect and best pleasing to God.

The necessity of the spirit of prayer, and way it is practised, and the nature of its fruits are set out incomparably in her writings. Those works were written during the years in which she was actively engaged in the most difficult business of founding convents of reformed Carmelite nuns and thus, quite apart from their nature and contents, are significant of St Teresa's vigour, industry and power of recollection. She wrote the *Way of Perfection* for the direction of her nuns, and the book of *Foundations* for their edification and encouragement, but the *Interior Castle* may be said to have been written for the instruction of the Church.

The Carmelite nuns, and indeed those of other orders as well, were very much relaxed from their early austerity and enthusiasm in sixteenth-century Spain. We have seen how the parlour at Avila was a sort of social centre for the ladies and gentlemen of the town, and that the nuns went out of their enclosure on the slightest pretext: those who wanted an easy and sheltered life without responsibilities could find it in a convent. The size of the communities was both a cause and an effect of this mitigation: there were 140 nuns in the convent at Avila. This state of things was so taken for granted that when a Carmelite of the Incarnation house at Avila, her niece, began to talk of the possibility of the foundation of a small community bound to a more perfect way of life, the idea struck St Teresa not as a very natural one but as an inspiration from Heaven. She had been a nun for twenty-five years: she now determined to undertake the establishment of such a reformed convent, and received a promise of immediate help from a wealthy widow, Doña Guiomar de Ulloa. The project was approved by St Peter of Alcantara, St Louis Bertrand, and the Bishop of Avila, and Teresa procured the licence and approbation of Father Gregory Fernandez, prior provincial of the Carmelites; but no sooner had the project taken shape than he was obliged by the objections which were raised to recall his licence. A storm fell upon Teresa through the violent opposition which was made by her fellow nuns, the nobility, the magistrates and the people. Father Ibañez, a Dominican, secretly encouraged her, and assisted Doña Guiomar to pursue the enterprise, together with Doña Juana de Ahumada, a married sister of the saint, who began with her husband to build a new convent at Avila in 1561, but in such a manner that the world took it for a house intended for herself and her family.

Eventually a brief arrived from Rome authorizing the establishment of the new convent. St Peter of Alcantara, Don Francis de Salsedo and Dr Daza had persuaded the bishop to concur, the new monastery of St Joseph was set up by his authority, and on St Bartholomew's day in 1562 was made subject to him, Mass being celebrated in the chapel and the saint's niece and three other novices taking the habit. Hereupon great excitement broke out in the town. The people of Avila looked on the new foundation as uncalled for, were nervous of suspicious novelities, and feared that an unendowed convent would be too heavy a burden on the town. The mayor and magistrates would have had the new monastery demolished, had not Father Bañez, also a Dominican, dissuaded them from so hasty a resolution. Amidst slanders and persecution the saint remained calm, recommending to God His own work, and was comforted by our Lord in a vision. In the meantime Francis de Salsedo and other friends of the new establishment deputed a priest to go before the royal council to plead for the convent, the two Dominicans, Ibañez and Bañez, reasoned with the bishop and the provincial, the public clamour abated, and at the end of four months Father Angel sent Teresa to the new convent, whither she was followed by four other nuns from the old house.

Strict enclosure was established with almost perpetual silence, and the most austere poverty, at first without any settled revenues; the nuns wore habits of coarse serge, sandals instead of shoes (whence they are called 'discalced'), and were bound to perpetual abstinence. At first St Teresa would not admit more than thirteen nuns to a community, but in those which should be founded with revenues, and not to subsist solely on alms, she afterwards allowed twenty-one. The prior general of the Carmelites, John Baptist Rubeo (Rossi), came to Avila in 1567, and was charmed with the foundress and the wise regulations of the house. He gave St Teresa full authority to found other convents upon the same plan, in spite of the fact that St Joseph's had been established without his knowledge or leave, and she even received from him a licence for the foundation of two houses of reformed friars ('Contemplative Carmelites') in Castile. St Teresa passed five years in her convent of St Joseph with thirteen nuns.

In August 1567 she went to Medina del Campo and, having conquered many difficulties, founded there a second convent. The Countess de la Cerda earnestly desired to found a convent of this order at her town of Malagon, and Teresa went to see her about it, incidentally paying a visit to Madrid which she describes as 'boring'. When this convent was safely launched she went to Valladolid and there founded another. St Teresa made her next foundation at Toledo. At Medina del Campo she had met with two Carmelite friars who were desirous to embrace her reform, Antony-of-Jesus (de Heredia), then prior there, and John Yepes (afterwards John-of-the-Cross). As soon, therefore, as an opportunity offered itself she founded a convent for men at a village called Duruelo in 1568, and in 1569 a second at Pastrana, both in extreme poverty and austerity. After these two foundations St Teresa left to St John-of-the-Cross the care of all other foundations that should be made for men. At Pastrana she also established a nunnery. When Don Ruy Gomez de Silva, who had founded these houses at Pastrana, died, his widow wished to make her religious profession there, but claimed many exemptions and would still maintain the dignity of princess. Teresa, finding she could not be brought to the humility of her profession, ordered the nuns, lest relaxations should be introduced, to leave that house to her and retire to a new one in Segovia. In 1570 St Teresa founded a convent at Salamanca.

At this time Pope St Pius V appointed visitors apostolic to inquire into relaxations in religious orders with a view to reform, and he named a

well-known Dominican, Peter Fernandez, to be visitor to the Carmelites of
Castile. At Avila he not surprisingly found great fault with the convent of
the Incarnation, and to remedy its abuses he sent for St Teresa and told her
she was to take charge of it as prioress. It was doubly distasteful to her to be
separated from her own daughters and to be put from outside at the head of
a house which opposed her activities with jealousy and warmth. The nuns at
first refused to obey her; some of them went into hysterics at the very idea.
She told them that she came not to coerce or instruct but to serve, and to
learn from the least among them.

The prior general, Father Rubeo, who had hitherto favoured St Teresa,
now sided with the objectors and upheld a general chapter at Plasencia
which passed several decrees gravely restricting the reform. The new nuncio apostolic, Philip de Sega, dismissed Father Gracián from his office of
visitor to the Discalced Carmelites, and St John-of-the-Cross was
imprisoned in a monastery; St Teresa herself was told to choose one of her
convents to which to retire and to abstain from further foundations. While
recommending her undertaking to God, she did not disdain to avail herself
of the help of her friends in the world. These interested the king, Philip II, on
her behalf, and he warmly espoused her cause. The nuncio was called before
him and sternly rebuked for his activities against the discalced friars and
nuns, and in 1580 an order was obtained at Rome to exempt the Reformed
from the jurisdiction of the mitigated Carmelites, so that each should have
their own provincial. Father Garcián was elected for the Reformed.

St Teresa was certainly endowed with great natural talents. The sweetness of her temperament, the affectionate tenderness of her heart, and the
liveliness of her wit and imagination, poised by an uncommon maturity of
judgement and what we should now call psychological insight, gained the
respect of all and the love of most. The quality of St Teresa is seen very
clearly in her selection of novices for the new foundations. Her first requirement, even before any promise of a considerable degree of piety, was
intelligence. A person can train herself to piety, but more hardly to intelligence, by which quality she meant neither cleverness nor imagination, but a
power of good judgement.

By the time of the separation between the two observances of the Carmelite Order in 1580 St Teresa was sixty-five years old and quite broken in
health. During her last two years she saw her final foundations, making
seventeen in all. The last foundation, at Burgos, was made under difficulties, and when it was achieved in July 1582 St Teresa wished to return to
Avila, but was induced to set out for Alba de Tormes, where the Duchess
Maria Henriquez was expecting her. Bd Anne-of-St-Bartholomew describes
the journey, not properly prepared for and the foundress so ill that she
fainted on the road; one night they could get no food but a few figs, and
when they arrived at Alba St Teresa went straight to bed. Three days later
she said to Bd Anne, 'At last, my daughter, the hour of death has come'. St

Teresa-of-Jesus died in the arms of Bd Anne at nine in the evening of 4 October 1582.

The very next day the Gregorian reform of the kalendar came into force and ten days were dropped, so that it was accounted 15 October the date on which her feast was ultimately fixed. Her body was buried at Alba de Tormes, and there it remains. She was canonized in 1622, and declared a Doctor of the Church in 1970.

TERESA OF JESUS JORNET E IBARS (A.D. 1897)

CO-FOUNDER OF THE LITTLE SISTERS OF THE AGED POOR
PATRON SAINT OF OLD PEOPLE, OLD AGE PENSIONERS, AND SENIOR CITIZENS

26 AUGUST

The Spanish title of St Teresa's order is 'The Little Sisters of the Abandoned Old', so it is not surprising that she has been chosen as patron of the old in several countries of Latin America. This was confirmed for Colombia by John Paul II in an Apostolic Letter of 27 June 1980, for Brazil by a similar Letter of 28 May 1984, and for Ecuador, also by an Apostolic Letter of 7 December 1984.

Teresa was born at Aytona, near Lerida, in Spain on 9 January 1843. She was a devout girl and, after a brief period as a teacher, determined to enter religious life, trying first, in 1862, a congregation founded by her uncle and six years later the Poor Clares at Burgos: the latter she had to leave because of ill-health. In 1872, however, she was the first person to join a new congregation founded in Barbastro, in Spain, by a priest of that town, Saturnino Lopez Novoa. He had been much moved by the elderly poor, especially those who had no one at all to care for them, and had opened his own house to them before buying a special property. The new congregation grew swiftly – Teresa's sister was the first novice mistress, while she herself was Mother General. Two years after the foundation the mother house moved to Valencia, and Fr Lopez Novoa was unable to play as large a part in the development of his congregation, leaving it more to Mother Teresa, though he still found time to draw up the constitutions. These received papal approval only a few days before Teresa's death on 26 August 1897. By that time the congregation had spread to many of the major cities of Spain, and across the Atlantic to Cuba, Puerto Rico and Colombia. Teresa was canonized in 1974 by Pope Paul VI.

THÉRÈSE OF LISIEUX, VIRGIN (A.D. 1897)

PATRON SAINT OF MISSIONS; OF FLORISTS AND FLOWER GROWERS; AND OF FRANCE

1 OCTOBER

On 14 December 1927, a little over two years after she was canonized, St Thérèse was proclaimed patron of the missions. As her life indicates, she had considered the possibility of going to Hanoi but, even though that was not to be, she continuously prayed for the work of missionaries, and corresponded with a number of them.

Contemplating her own death, Thérèse wrote that after it 'I will let fall a shower of roses' – meaning favours or miracles through her intercession. Because of the remark, however, she has been taken as patron by those associated with flowers, especially florists and, indeed, is commonly known as 'the Little Flower'.

Pius XII proclaimed St Thérèse a joint 'secondary patron' of France alongside St Joan of Arc (the Mother of God is the principal patron) in an Apostolic Letter dated 3 May 1944, both because of the devotion shown to the saint by the people of France, and because France had become itself a missionary country and St Thérèse was already a patron of the missions.

The parents of the saint-to-be were Louis Martin, a watchmaker of Alençon, son of an officer in the armies of Napoleon I, and Azélie-Marie Guérin, a maker of point d'Alençon in the same town, whose father had been a gendarme at Saint-Denis near Séez. Five of the children born to them survived to maturity, of whom Thérèse was the youngest. She was born on 2 January 1873, and baptized Marie-Françoise-Thérèse. Her childhood was happy and ordinary. She had a quick intelligence and an open and impressionable mind. In 1877 Mme Martin died, and M. Martin sold his business at Alençon and went to live at Lisieux (Calvados), where his children might be under the eye of their aunt, Mme Guérin. M. Martin had a particular affection for Thérèse, but it was an older sister, Marie, who ran the household and the eldest, Pauline, who made herself responsible for the religious upbringing of her sisters.

When Thérèse was nine, this Pauline entered the Carmel at Lisieux and Thérèse began to be drawn in the same direction. When Thérèse was nearly fourteen her sister Marie joined Pauline in the Carmel and on Christmas eve of the same year Thérèse underwent an experience which she ever after referred to as her conversion. Characteristically, the occasion of this sudden accession of strength was a remark of her father about her child-like addiction to Christmas observances, not intended for her ears at all.

During the next year Thérèse told her father of her wish to become a Carmelite, and M. Martin agreed; but both the Carmelite authorities and the bishop of Bayeux refused to hear of it on account of her lack of age. A few months later she was in Rome with her father and a French pilgrimage on the occasion of the sacerdotal jubilee of Pope Leo XIII. At the public audience, when her turn came to kneel for the pope's blessing, Thérèse boldly broke the rule of silence on such occasions and asked him, 'In honour of your jubilee, allow me to enter Carmel at fifteen'. Leo was clearly impressed by her appearance and manner, but he upheld the decision of the immediate superiors.

At the end of the year the bishop, Mgr Hugonin, gave his permission, and on 9 April 1888, Thérèse Martin entered the Carmel at Lisieux whither her two sisters had preceded her. In 1889 the three sisters in blood and in Carmel sustained a sad blow when their beloved father's mind gave way following two paralytic attacks and he had to be removed to a private asylum, where he remained for three years. But 'the three years of my father's martyrdom', wrote St Thérèse, 'seem to me the dearest and most fruitful of our life. I would not exchange them for the most sublime ecstasies.' She was professed on 8 September 1890.

One of the principal duties of a Carmelite nun is to pray for priests, a duty which St Thérèse discharged with great fervour at all times; and she never ceased in particular to pray for the good estate of the celebrated ex-Carmelite Hyacinth Loyson, who had apostatized from the faith. Although she was delicate she carried out all the practices of the austere Carmelite rule from the first, except that she was not allowed to fast. The autobiography which St Thérèse wrote at the command of her prioress, *L'histoire d'une âme*, is a unique and engaging document, written with a delightful clarity and freshness, full of surprising turns of phrase, bits of unexpected knowledge and unconscious self-revelation, and, above all, of deep spiritual wisdom and beauty.

In 1893 Sister Thérèse was appointed to assist the novice mistress and was in fact mistress in all but name. In 1894 M. Martin died and soon after Céline, who had been looking after him, made the fourth Martin sister in the Lisieux Carmel. Eighteen months later, during the night between Maundy Thursday and Good Friday, St Thérèse heard, 'as it were, a far-off murmur announcing the coming of the Bridegroom': it was a haemorrhage at the mouth. At the time she was inclined to respond to the appeal of the Carmelites at Hanoi in Indo-China, who wished to have her, but her disease took a turn for the worse and the last eighteen months of her life was a time of bodily suffering and spiritual trials. In June 1897 she was removed to the infirmary of the convent and never left it again; from 16 August on she could no longer receive holy communion because of frequent sickness. On 30 September with words of divine love on her lips, Sister Thérèse of Lisieux died. She was beatified by Pope Pius XI in 1923, and in 1925 the same pope declared Thérèse-of-the-Child-Jesus to have been a saint.

THOMAS, APOSTLE (FIRST CENTURY)

PATRON SAINT OF BUILDERS, BUILDING CRAFTSMEN AND CONSTRUCTION
WORKERS; OF ARCHITECTS AND SURVEYORS; OF BLIND PEOPLE; OF INDIA AND
PAKISTAN

3 JULY

Because of the legend that Thomas built a palace for the Indian king he has been taken as patron by a whole range of occupations concerned with construction, such as builders themselves, masons, architects, carpenters, and joiners. The Sacred Congregation of Rites, in a decree dated 18 November 1955, confirmed him as patron of the Italian society of quantity surveyors.

St Thomas has been invoked by blind people because of his own spiritual blindness in failing to accept the word of the other apostles that they had seen the risen Christ.

Though not formally a patron of India, Thomas has long been the object of considerable devotion among Christians there because of the story that he it was who first brought the faith to that part of the world.

St Thomas was a Jew and probably a Galilean of humble birth, but we are not told that he was a fisherman or the circumstances in which our Lord made him an apostle. His name is Syriac, and means the 'twin'; Didymus, as we know he was also called, is the Greek equivalent. This apostle is especially remembered for his incredulity after our Lord had suffered, risen from the dead, and on the same day appeared to His disciples to convince them of the truth of His resurrection. Thomas was not then with them and refused to believe their report that He was truly risen: 'Except I shall see in His hands the print of the nails, and put my finger in the place of the nails, and put my hand into His side, I will not believe.' Eight days later, when they were all together and the doors shut, the risen Christ was suddenly in the midst of them, greeting them: 'Peace be to you.' Then He turned to Thomas and said, 'Put in thy finger hither, and see my hands; and bring hither thy hand and put it into my side. And be not faithless, but believing.' And Thomas fell at His feet, exclaiming, 'My Lord and my God!' Jesus answered, 'Because thou hast seen me, Thomas, thou hast believed. Blessed are they that have not seen, and have believed.'

As with the other apostles, there are traditions, of great unreliability, about his missionary activities after the descent of the Holy Ghost at Pentecost. Eusebius states that he sent St Thaddeus (Addai; 5 August) to Edessa to baptize King Abgar, and the field of his own ministry is assigned to Parthia and 'the Medes, Persians, Carmanians, Hyrcanians, Bactrians and other nations in those parts'. But the most persistent tradition is that which says that he preached the gospel in India. This is supported from several seemingly independent sources, of which the chief is the *Acta Thomae*, a document dating apparently from the first quarter of the third century. The story told by these *acta* is as follows: When the Apostles at Jerusalem divided the countries of the world for their labours, India fell to the lot of Judas Thomas (so he is often called in Syriac legends). He was unwilling to go, pleading lack of strength and that a Hebrew could not teach Indians, and even a vision of our Lord could not alter his resolution. Thereupon Christ appeared to a merchant named Abban, the representative of Gundafor, a Parthian king who ruled over part of India, and sold Thomas to him as a slave for his master. When he understood what had taken place, Thomas said, 'As thou wilt, Lord, so be it', and embarked with Abban, having only his purchase price, twenty pieces of silver, which Christ had given to him.

Abban and Thomas came to Gundafor's court in India and when the king asked the apostle's trade he replied, 'I am a carpenter and builder. I can make yokes and ploughs and ox-goads, oars for boats and masts for ships; and I can build in stone, tombs and monuments and palaces for kings.' So Gundafor ordered him to build a palace. Gundafor went on a journey, and in his absence Thomas did no building but spent all the money given him for the work on the poor. And he went about the land preaching and healing and driving out evil spirits. On his return Gundafor asked to be shown his new palace. 'You cannot see it now, but only when you have left this world', replied Thomas. Whereupon the king cast him into prison and purposed to flay him alive. But just then Gundafor's brother died, and being shown in Heaven the palace that Thomas's good works had prepared for Gundafor, he was allowed to come back to earth and offer to buy it from the king for himself. Gundafor declined to sell, and in admiration released Thomas and received baptism together with his brother and many of his subjects.

It is agreed that there is no truth behind the story just outlined, though there was undoubtedly a king named Gondophernes or Guduphara, whose dominions about the year a.d. 46 included the territory of Peshawar. Unfortunately, speculation about St Thomas cannot be left there. At the other end of India from the Punjab, along what is known as the Malabar Coast, particularly in the states of Cochin and Travancore, there is a large population of native Christians who call themselves 'the Christians of St Thomas'. Their history is known in detail since the sixteenth century, but their origin has not yet been indisputably determined. There have certainly been Christians there since very early times, and in their liturgy they use forms and a language (Syriac) that undoubtedly were derived from Mesopotamia and Persia. They claim, as their name indicates, to have been originally evangelized by St Thomas in person. They have an ancient oral tradition that he landed at Cranganore on the west coast and established seven churches in Malabar; then passed eastward to the Coromandel Coast, where he was martyred, by spearing, on the 'Big Hill', eight miles from Madras; and was buried at Mylapore, now a suburb of that city. There are several medieval references to the tomb of St Thomas in India, some of which name Mylapore; and in 1522 the Portuguese discovered the alleged tomb there, with certain small relics now preserved in the cathedral of St Thomas at Mylapore. But the bulk of his reputed relics were certainly at Edessa in the fourth century, and the *Acta Thomae* relate that they were taken from India to Mesopotamia. They were later translated from Edessa to the island of Khios in the Aegean, and from thence to Ortona in the Abruzzi, where they are still venerated.

THOMAS AQUINAS, DOCTOR OF THE CHURCH (A.D. 1274)

PATRON SAINT OF ROMAN CATHOLIC SCHOOLS, COLLEGES, ACADEMIES AND UNIVERSITIES; OF SCHOLARS AND STUDENTS; OF APOLOGISTS, PHILOSOPHERS AND THEOLOGIANS; AND OF BOOKSELLERS

28 JANUARY

In an Apostolic Letter of 4 August 1880 Leo XIII, the pope who promoted within the Catholic Church the study of the teaching of Thomas Aquinas, declared him formally the patron of Catholic schools, colleges or universities, and of their teachers and students; and a patron too of those who pursue learning – apologists, philosophers, theologians and scholars in general.

Because Thomas Aquinas has been proclaimed by Leo XIII as patron of education in general, by association he has also been taken, quite informally, as patron by booksellers.

The family of the counts of Aquino was of noble lineage, tracing its descent back for several centuries to the Lombards. St Thomas's father was a knight, Landulf, and his mother Theodora was of Norman descent. There seems something more northern than southern about Thomas's physique, his imposing stature, massive build and fresh complexion. The precise year of his birth is uncertain, but it was about 1225 and took place in the castle of Rocca Secca, the ruins of which are still to be seen on a mountain crag dominating the fertile plain of Campagna Felice and the little town of Aquino.

A few miles to the south of Rocca Secca, on a high plateau, stands the abbey of Monte Cassino, whose abbot at this time was a kinsman of the Aquino family, Landulf Sinibaldo. As a child of five Thomas was taken here as an oblate and he remained till he was about thirteen, living in the monastery and getting his schooling there. He was taken away probably because of the disturbed state of the times, and about 1239 was sent to the University of Naples, where for five years he studied the arts and sciences. He became attracted by the Order of Preachers, whose church he loved to frequent and with some of whose members he soon became intimate. At the age of about nineteen, he was received and clothed in the habit of the order.

News of this was soon carried to Rocca Secca, where it aroused great indignation – not because he had joined a religious community, for his mother was quite content that he should become a Benedictine, and indeed probably saw in him the destined abbot of Monte Cassino, but because he had entered a mendicant order. Theodora herself set out for Naples to persuade her son to return home. The friars, however, hurried him off to their convent of Santa Sabina in Rome, and when the angry lady followed in pursuit, the young man was no longer to be found there. The master general of the Dominicans, who was on his way to Bologna, had decided to take Thomas with him, and the little party of friars had already set out on foot together. Theodora, not to be baulked, sent word to the saint's elder brothers, who were serving with the emperor's army in Tuscany, desiring them to waylay and capture the fugitive. As Thomas was resting by the roadside at Aquapendente near Siena, he was overtaken by his brothers at the head of a troop of soldiers, and after a vain attempt to take his habit from him by force, was brought back, first to Rocca Secca and then to the castle of Monte San Giovanni, two miles distant, where he was kept in close confinement, only his worldly-minded sister Marotto being allowed to visit him. During his captivity Thomas studied the *Sentences* of Peter Lombard, learned by heart a great part of the Bible, and is said to have written a treatise on the fallacies of Aristotle.

This captivity lasted two years before Thomas's family gave up and in 1245 permitted him to return to his order. It was now determined to send him to complete his studies under St Albert the Great, and he set out in company with the master general, John the Teutonic, who was on his way to Paris; from thence Thomas went on to Cologne. The schools there were full of young clerics from various parts of Europe eager to learn and equally eager to discuss, and the humble reserved newcomer was not immediately appreciated either by his fellow students or by his professors. His silence at disputations as well as his bulky figure led to his receiving the nickname of 'the dumb Sicilian ox'.

There are chronological difficulties about these years of St Thomas's life, but certainly in 1252, at the instance of St Albert and Cardinal Hugh of Saint-Cher, he was ordered to Paris to teach as a bachelor in the university. Academical degrees were then very different from what they are now, and were conferred only in view of the actual work of teaching. In Paris Thomas expounded the Holy Scriptures and the *Libert sententiarum* of Peter Lombard; he also wrote a commentary on these same Sentences, and others on Isaias and St Matthew's Gospel. Four years later he delivered his inaugural lecture as master and received his doctor's chair, his duties being to lecture, to discuss and to preach; and towards the end of the time he began the *Summa contra Gentiles*. From 1259 to 1268 he was in Italy. Here he was made a preacher general, and was called upon to teach in the school of selected scholars attached to the papal court, and, as it followed the pope in his movement, St Thomas lectured and preached in many of the Italian towns. About 1266 he began the most famous of all his written works, the *Summa Theologiae*.

In 1269 he was back again in Paris. St Louis IX held him in such esteem that he constantly consulted him on important matters of state, but perhaps a greater testimony to his reputation was the resolution of the university to refer to his decision a question upon which they were divided, *viz.* whether in the Blessed Sacrament of the altar the accidents remained really or only in appearance. St Thomas, after fervent prayer, wrote his answer in the form of a treatise which is still extant, and laid it on the altar before making it public. His decision was accepted by the university first and afterwards by the whole Church.

In 1272 there was a sort of 'general strike' among the faculties, in the midst of which St Thomas was recalled to Italy and appointed regent of the study-house at Naples. It was to prove the last scene of his labours. On the feast of St Nicholas the following year he was celebrating Mass when he received a revelation which so affected him that he wrote and dictated no more, leaving his great work, the *Summa Theologiae*, unfinished. To Brother Reginald's expostulations he replied, 'The end of my labours is come. All that I have written appears to be as so much straw after the things that have been revealed to me'.

He was ill when he was bidden by Pope Gregory X to attend the general council at Lyons for the reunion of the Greek and Latin churches and to bring with him his treatise 'Against the Errors of the Greeks'. He became so much worse on the journey that he was taken to the Cistercian abbey of Fossa Nuova near Terracina, where he was lodged in the abbot's room and waited on by the monks. In compliance with their entreaties he began to expound to them the Canticle of Canticles, but he did not live to finish his exposition. His soul passed to God in the early hours of 7 March 1274, when he was only about fifty years of age.

St Thomas was canonized in 1323, but it was not until 1368 that the Dominicans succeeded in obtaining possession of his body, which was translated with great pomp to Toulouse, where it still lies in the cathedral of Saint-Sernin. St Pius V conferred upon him the title of doctor of the Church.

THORLAC, BISHOP OF SKALHOLT (A.D. 1193)

PATRON SAINT OF ICELAND

23 DECEMBER

Although, as is remarked in the 'life', the cultus of Thorlac has not been confirmed by the Holy See, it has certainly been implicitly recognized in the formal declaration of Thorlac as patron of Iceland by an Apostolic Letter of John Paul II dated 12 January 1984, in which the Pope comments upon the devotion which has long been shown him.

Christianity was planted in Iceland at the end of the tenth and the beginning of the eleventh century, and made such progress that the island was soon divided into two dioceses, Skalholt and Holar, which in 1152 were made suffragans of Nidaros (Trondhjem): Iceland had been colonized and evangelized from Norway. During the twelfth century two bishops, one from each see, were venerated as saints locally and in Norway, namely, John of Holar and Thorlac of Skalholt. The life of the last-named is narrated in the *Thorlakssaga* by a cleric of Skalholt. We are told that Thorlac Thorhallsson was a deacon when he was fifteen and a priest three years later, and then, being a promising young man, was sent abroad to study: he is said to have visited Lincoln. After ten years, in 1161, Thorlac returned to Iceland full of reforming zeal. He was joyfully received by his mother and sisters, who expected him to settle down to the semi-secular life led by most of the clergy there in those days, but instead he devoted himself to study and the ministry. His biographer gives an account of Thorlac's daily rule of life, which began with the singing of the *Credo, Pater noster*, and a hymn directly he awoke; he recited a third of the psalter every day, and had an especial devotion to the titular saints of the churches in which he ministered. Some years later an heirless farmer died, leaving his land and house to the Church with instructions that Thorlac should establish a monastery there, and he accordingly formed a community of canons regular, of which he was abbot. We are told that Thorlac's mother went with him to Thykkviboer to be cook and housekeeper for the new community. In 1178 he became bishop of Skalholt, and was consecrated by Archbishop St Eystein in Nidaros.

The way was now clear for Thorlac to introduce and promote the higher spiritual standards and improved ecclesiastical discipline which he knew that the good of souls required and the Church demanded. On the side of discipline this resolved itself chiefly into endeavours to impose the observance of clerical celibacy and to abolish lay patronage and impropriation, with their associated abuse of simony, and his episcopal career is a record of his efforts in these directions and the successes, difficulties and checks with which he met. He received far more opposition than encouragement, often from men of goodwill or from those to whom he could reasonably look for support, but to the end he did not withdraw from the struggle or modify his policy. He had the encouragement of his metropolitan, the forceful St Eystein, who was fighting a similar battle in Norway, and with his approval used the weapon of excommunication for the first time in Iceland. In his sixtieth year Thorlac determined to resign his see and retire to the abbey of Thykkviboer, but death overtook him before he could put this resolution into effect, on 23 December 1193. Five years later he was canonized by the *althing* (assembly) of Iceland. This proceeding of course had no valid ecclesiastical effect, but it encouraged the popular and liturgical *cultus* that was undoubtedly accorded to Thorlac until the change of religion. This *cultus* has not been confirmed by the Holy See. Two books of the miracles of Thorlac Thorhallsson were written down within a few years of his death.

TURIBIUS, ARCHBISHOP OF LIMA (A.D. 1606)

PATRON SAINT OF THE BISHOPS OF LATIN AMERICA

23 MARCH

Turibius' zeal for the spiritual welfare of the people of Latin America is abundantly evident from his life. The bishops who make up CELAM – the Conference of Latin American Bishops – asked that he be recognized as their patron, and this was granted by John Paul II in an Apostolic Letter of 10 May 1983.

St Turibius is, equally with St Rose of Lima, the first known saint of the New World. It is true that he was not born on the American continent, and not canonized until fifty-five years after her; but they lived in the same place at the same time, Turibius died first, and it was he who conferred the sacrament of confirmation on Rose. His memory is held in great veneration throughout Peru, for although he did not plant Christianity in that land he greatly promoted it, and cleansed the Church there from grave abuses which were sapping its vitality and bringing discredit upon its name; his feast is, more-over, observed throughout South America.

Turibius, Toribio Alfonso de Mogrobejo, was born in 1538 at Mayorga in Spain. His childhood and youth were notably religious, but he had no intention of becoming a priest and was, in fact, educated for the law. He was so brilliant a scholar that he became professor of law in the University of Salamanca, and while there he attracted the notice of King Philip II (widower of Mary I of England), who eventually made him chief judge of the ecclesiastical court of the Inquisition at Granada. This was a surprising position for a layman to hold, and it was not a pleasant or easy post for anyone, lay or cleric. But it led to an even more surprising development. After some years the archbishopric of Lima in the Spanish colony of Peru became vacant. Turibius had carried out his judge's duties so well, and displayed such a fine missionary spirit, that it was decided to send him to Peru as archbishop: he seemed to be the one person who had force of character sufficient to remedy the serious scandals which stood in the way of the conversion of the Peruvians.

Turibius himself was shocked by the decision, and he wrote forthwith to the royal council, pleading his incapacity and appealing to the canons which forbade the promotion of laymen to ecclesiastical dignities. His objections were overruled; he received all the orders and episcopal consecration, and immediately afterwards sailed for Peru. Arriving in Lima in 1581, it did not take him long to realize the arduous nature of the charge which had been laid upon him. His diocese stretched for some 400 miles along the coast, and inland amongst the spurs of the Andes, a most difficult country to traverse. Far more serious, however, than the physical difficulties were those created by the attitude of the Spanish conquerors towards the native population.

With few exceptions the officials and colonists had come there to make their fortunes, and they made the Indians serve that purpose by every sort of extortion and tyranny. Communications with the central authority at home were incredibly slow. The most flagrant abuses might continue for years without the possibility of redress and, the Spaniards quarrelling continually among themselves and sending home contradictory reports, it was often impossible for the supreme Council of the Indies to know whom to believe. Worse than all, the sense of religion seemed to be completely lost, and the example given to the natives was one of almost universal rapacity and self-indulgence.

The clergy themselves were often among the most notorious offenders, and it was the first care of Turibius to restore ecclesiastical discipline. He at once undertook a visitation of his diocese, and was inflexible in regard to scandals amongst the clergy. Without respect of persons, he reproved injustice and vice, using his authority always to protect the poor from oppression. He naturally suffered persecution from those in power, who often thwarted him in the discharge of his duties, but by resolution and patience he overcame their opposition in the end. To those who tried to twist God's law to make it accord with their evil practice he would oppose the words of Tertullian: 'Christ said, "I am the truth". He did not say, "I am the custom".' The archbishop succeeded in eradicating some of the worst abuses, and he founded numerous churches, religious houses and hospitals; in 1591 he established at Lima the first ecclesiastical seminary in the New World.

Right on into old age St Turibius continued to study the Indian dialects so that he could address the people in their own speech and not through an interpreter. Thus he succeeded in making many conversions. In order to teach his flock he would sometimes stay two or three days in a place where he had neither bed nor sufficient food. Every part of his vast diocese was visited, and when danger threatened from marauders or physical obstacles he would say that Christ came from Heaven to save man and that we ought not to fear danger for His glory. The archbishop offered Mass daily, even when on a journey, and always with intense fervour, and every morning he made his confession to his chaplain. Among those St Turibius confirmed, as well as St Rose, are said to have been St Martin de Porres and Bd John Massias. From 1590 he had the help of another great missionary, the Franciscan St Francis Solano, whose denunciations of the wickedness of Lima so alarmed the people that the viceroy had to call on the archbishop to calm them. The charities of St Turibius were large, and he had feeling for the sensitive pride of the Spaniards in his flock. He knew that many were shy of making their poverty or other needs known, that they did not like to accept public charity or help from those they knew: so he did all he could to assist them privately, without their knowing from whom their benefactions came.

St Turibius was in his sixty-eighth year when he fell ill at Pacasmayo, far to the north of Lima. Working to the last, he struggled as far as Santa, where he realized the end was at hand. He made his will, giving his personal belongings to his servants and all the rest of his property for the benefit of the poor. He asked to be carried into the church to receive viaticum, and was then brought back to bed and anointed. While those about him sang the psalm, 'I was glad when they said unto me, We will go into the house of the Lord', St Turibius died on 23 March 1606. In 1726 he was canonized.

UBALD, BISHOP OF GUBBIO (A.D. 1160)

PATRON SAINT FOR PROTECTION FROM DOG BITES, RABIES, OR HYDROPHOBIA

16 MAY

Apparently through Ubald's intercession both during his lifetime and after his death people were cured of what was then interpreted as demonic possession. It is perhaps for this reason that he was associated with invocation against rabies, or hydrophobia.

We are fortunate in possessing an excellent and reliable biography of Ubald Baldassini, bishop of Gubbio, compiled by Theobald, his immediate successor. The saint, descended from a noble family in Gubbio, became an orphan at an early age and was educated by his uncle, also bishop of the same see, in the cathedral school. Having completed his studies, he was ordained priest and appointed dean of the cathedral, young though he was, that he might reform the canons amongst whom grave irregularities were rampant. The task was no easy one, but he succeeded before long in persuading three of the canons to join him in a common life. Then, that he might obtain experience in the management of a well-conducted household, he resided for three months with a community of regular canons which had been established by Peter de Honestis in the territory of Ravenna. The rule which they followed he brought back to Gubbio, and within a short time it was accepted by the whole chapter. A few years later, after their house and cloisters had been burnt down, Ubald thought it a favourable moment to retire from his post into some solitude. With this object in view he made his way to Fonte Avellano where he communicated his intention to Peter of Rimini. That great servant of God, however, regarded the plan as a dangerous temptation and exhorted him to return to the post in which God had placed him for the benefit of others. The saint accordingly returned to Gubbio, and rendered his chapter more flourishing than it had ever been before. In 1126 St Ubald was chosen bishop of Perugia; but he hid himself so that the deputies from that city could not find him; then he went to Rome, threw himself at the feet of Pope Honorius II and begged that he might be excused. His request was granted; but when, two years later, the see of Gubbio fell vacant, the pope himself directed that the clergy should elect Ubald.

In his new office the saint displayed all the virtues of a true successor to the apostles, but perhaps his most distinguishing characteristic was a mildness and patience which made him appear insensible to injuries and affronts. On one occasion workmen repairing the city wall encroached upon his vineyard and were injuring his vines. He gently drew their attention to this. Thereupon the foreman, who probably did not recognize him, became abusive and pushed him so roughly that he fell into a pool of liquid mortar. He rose up, splashed all over with lime and dirt, and without a word of expostulation returned to his house. Eye-witnesses, however, reported the incident and the citizens clamoured loudly that the foreman should be punished. So great was the popular indignation that a severe sentence seemed a foregone conclusion, when St Ubald appeared in court and claimed that, since the offence had been committed against an ecclesiastic, it came under his jurisdiction as bishop. Then, turning to the culprit, he bade him give him the kiss of peace in token of reconciliation, and, after a prayer that God would forgive him that and all his other trespasses, he directed that the man should be set at liberty.

The saint often defended his people in public dangers. The Emperor Frederick Barbarossa during his wars in Italy had sacked the city of Spoleto and threatened to subject Gubbio to a similar fate. Ubald met the emperor on the road and diverted the tyrant from his purpose. During the last two years of his life, the holy bishop suffered from a complication of painful diseases which he bore with heroic patience. On Easter day 1160, although very ill, he rose to celebrate Mass, and, that he might not disappoint his people, preached and gave them his blessing. He was carried back to bed, from which he never rose again. At Pentecost, as he lay dying, the whole population of Gubbio filed past his couch, anxious to take a last farewell of one whom each individual regarded as his dear father in God. Ubald died on 16 May 1160, and the people who flocked to his funeral from far and wide were eye-witnesses of the many miracles God performed at his tomb.

VALENTINE, MARTYR (*c.* A.D. 269)

PATRON SAINT OF LOVERS

14 FEBRUARY

The association of Valentine with love and romance is always traced back as far as Chaucer, who suggested that birds pair on that day. According to another version, St Valentine's Day was a means of Christianizing the Roman Lupercalia. It has recently been argued, however, that Chaucer's poetic association of the saint with lovers refers not to the Valentine of 14 February but to another Valentine, Bishop of Genoa, whose feast day was 2 May. On 3 May 1381 Richard II was betrothed to Anne of Bohemia: Chaucer's remarks in his poems may stem from this. According to this theory, the identification of the patron saint of lovers with the Roman Valentine occurred by accident sometime after Chaucer's death.

The Roman martyrology records the death on this day of two Roman martyrs with the name Valentine, one of them a Roman priest who died in 269 or thereabouts, the other the Bishop of Terni – though it is said he died in Rome – who was martyred in 273. The existence of neither is certain, but there is no good reason for doubting it apart from the coincidence of names. The priest Valentine is usually the one associated with lovers. He seems to have been buried on the Flaminian Way, and a basilica was erected to him less than a century after his death and his relics were later taken to the church of St Praxedes. Otherwise nothing is known of him.

VENANTIUS, MARTYR (A.D. 257?)

PATRON SAINT AGAINST DANGER FROM FALLING, OR JUMPING AND LEAPING

18 MAY

The invocation of Venantius against the danger of falling and hence jumping, is traditional, and follows from one story of his martyrdom, according to which the prefect had him thrown from the city walls, from which attempt at execution he picked himself up, praising God.

There is but the slenderest evidence of any *cultus* of this martyr. The fact that the name of Venantius appears in church dedications, or was attached to relics, proves little, because there was an authentic St Venantius who was the first bishop of Salona in Dalmatia, on the shore of the Adriatic. The apocryphal 'acts' of the martyr of Camerino narrate that this youth came before the judge to profess himself a Christian, that he was scourged, seared with torches, suspended head downward over fire and smoke, had his teeth knocked out and his jaw broken, was thrown to the lions who only licked his feet, was precipitated without suffering any injury from a high cliff, and finally had his head cut off, with a number of other martyrs who had declared themselves Christians after witnessing the spectacle of his constancy. All this was attended with supernatural apparitions, with the death of two judges who successively presided over the tribunal before which he appeared, and finally with earthquakes and a portentous storm of thunder and lightning.

VENERIUS, HERMIT (6TH-7TH CENTURY)

PATRON SAINT OF LIGHTHOUSE KEEPERS

13 SEPTEMBER

There is no direct connection between Venerius and lighthouse keepers although, as John XXIII remarked in an Apostolic Letter of 10 March 1961, on the isle of Tino the radiance of his life shone out. He became patron of lighthouse keepers because of the devotion to him in and around the Gulf of La Spezia, and a formal confirmation of him as patron of this profession in Italy was solicited from, and conceded by, Pope John in that same Letter of 10 March 1961.

Tradition is sufficiently firm to indicate that, about the year 600, a holy recluse called Venerius lived either on the island of Palmaria in the Gulf of Spezia, or on the isle of Tino. Very little else, however, is known about him. Such records as exist are the commonplace accounts of all those who are revered for their holiness: that he was born of good family, entered a monastery but was dissatisfied and sought ever greater austerity in the eremitical life. What is more certain is that, very soon after his death, a cult began and Venerius was recognized as a saint, and that his body was transported from place to place until, as recently as 1960, a relic of Venerius was returned, with great solemnity, to the isle of Tino.

VINCENT PALLOTTI (A.D. 1850)

FOUNDER OF THE SOCIETY OF CATHOLIC APOSTOLATE
PATRON SAINT OF MISSIONARY PRIESTS

22 JANUARY

The appropriateness of the choice of Vincent Pallotti as patron of missionary clergy is clear from his life, especially if 'missionary' is understood in its wider sense. John XXIII declared him patron of the Pontifical Missionary Union of Clergy in an Apostolic Letter of 6 April 1963.

Vincent Pallotti was born in Rome, son of a well-to-do grocer, in 1795, and his vocation to the priesthood was foreshadowed at an early age. His beginnings at school were disappointing: 'He's a little saint', said his master, Don Ferri, 'but a bit thick-headed'. However, he soon picked up, and was ordained priest when he was only twenty-three. He took his doctorate in theology soon after, and became an assistant professor at the University of Rome. Pallotti's close friendship with St Caspar del Bufalo increased his apostolic zeal, and he eventually resigned his post to devote himself to active pastoral work.

Don Pallotti was in very great repute as a confessor, and filled this office at several Roman colleges, including the Scots, the Irish and the English, where he became a friend of the rector, Nicholas Wiseman. But he was not appreciated everywhere. When he was appointed to the Neapolitan church in Rome he endured persecution from the other clergy there of which the particulars pass belief. Equally astonishing is it that this went on for ten years before the authorities took official notice and brought the scandal to an end. Vincent's most implacable tormentor, the vice-rector of the church, lived to give evidence for him at the informative process of his beatification. 'Don Pallotti never gave the least ground for the ill-treatment to which he was subjected', he declared. 'He always treated me with the greatest respect; he bared his head when he spoke to me, he even several times tried to kiss my hand.'

St Vincent began his organized work for conversion and social justice with a group of clergy and lay people, from whom the Society of Catholic Apostolate developed in 1835. He wrote to a young professor: 'You are not cut out for the silence and austerities of Trappists and hermits. Be holy in the world, in your social relationships, in your work and your leisure, in your teaching duties and your contacts with publicans and sinners. Holiness is simply to do God's will, always and everywhere'. Pallotti himself organized schools for shoemakers, tailors, coachmen, joiners and market-gardeners, to improve their general education and pride in their trade; he started evening classes for young workers, and an institute to teach better methods to young agriculturalists. But he never lost sight of the wider aspects of his mission. In 1836 he inaugurated the observance of the Epiphany octave by the celebration of the Mysteries each day with a different rite, in special supplication for the reunion of Eastern dissidents: this was settled at the church of Sant Andrea delle Valle in 1847, and has continued there annually ever since.

It was well said that in Don Pallotti Rome had a second Philip Neri. How many times he came home half naked because he had given his clothes away; how many sinners did he reconcile, on one occasion dressing up as an old woman to get to the bedside of a man who threatened – and meant it – to shoot the first priest who came near him; he was in demand as an exorcist, he had knowledge beyond this world's means, he healed the sick with an encouragement or a blessing. St Vincent foresaw all Catholic Action, even its name, said Pius XI; and Cardinal Pellegrinetti added, 'He did all that he could; as for what he couldn't do – well, he did that too'. St Vincent Pallotti died when he was only fifty-five, on 22 January 1850.

He was beatified one hundred years later to the day, and canonized in 1963 during the Second Vatican Council.

VINCENT DE PAUL (A.D. 1660)

FOUNDER OF THE CONGREGATION OF THE MISSION THE SISTERS OF CHARITY
PATRON SAINT OF CHARITIES; OF MADAGASCAR; AND OF HOSPITALS AND
PRISONERS

27 SEPTEMBER

From the story of his life, it is clear why Vincent is a suitable patron of charities. He was declared patron of those in France in an Apostolic Letter of 22 June 1883, and of all those throughout the world in another Apostolic Letter of 12 May 1885, both by Leo XIII. He has also, and for equally obvious reasons, been regarded as a patron of hospitals and of prisoners, though without formal acknowledgement by the Church.

One of the first places to which Vincent sent his missionaries was to Madagascar. He has therefore been recognized as patron of that country by decrees of the Sacred Congregation of Rites dated 9 November 1949 and 25 October 1961.

St Vincent de Paul was a native of Pouy, a village near Dax, in Gascony. His parents occupied a very small farm, upon the produce of which they brought up a family of four sons and two daughters, Vincent being their third child. His father placed him under the care of the Cordeliers (Franciscan Recollects) at Dax. Vincent finished his studies at the university of Toulouse, and in 1600 was ordained priest at the age of twenty. His ambition was to be comfortably off. He was already one of the chaplains of Queen Margaret of Valois and, according to the custom of the age, he was receiving the income of a small abbey. He went to lodge with a friend in Paris. And there it was that we first hear of a change in him. His friend was robbed of four hundred crowns. He charged Vincent with the theft, thinking it could be nobody else; Vincent calmly denied the fact. He bore this slander for six months, when the true thief confessed.

At Paris Vincent became acquainted with the holy priest Peter de Bérulle, afterwards cardinal. Bérulle conceived a great esteem for Vincent and prevailed with him to become tutor to the children of Philip de Gondi, Count of Joigny. Mme de Gondi was attracted by Vincent, and chose him for her spiritual director and confessor.

In the year 1617, whilst they were at a country seat at Folleville, Monsieur Vincent was sent for to hear the confession of a peasant who lay dangerously ill. He discovered that all the former confessions of the penitent had been sacrilegious, and the man declared before many persons and the Countess of Joigny herself, that he would have been eternally lost if he had not spoken to Monsieur Vincent. The good lady was struck with horror to hear of such past sacrileges. To Vincent himself also appears to have come at that moment an enlightening as to the terrible spiritual state of the peasantry of France. Mme de Gondi had no difficulty in persuading him to preach in the church of Folleville, and fully to instruct the people in the duty of repentance and confession of sins. He did so; and such crowds flocked to him to make general confessions that he was obliged to call the Jesuits of Amiens to his assistance.

With the help of Father de Bérulle, St Vincent left the house of the countess in 1617 to become pastor of Châtillon-les-Dombes. He there converted the notorious Count de Rougemont and many others from their scandalous lives. But he soon returned to Paris, and began work among the galley-slaves who were confined in the Conciergerie. He was officially appointed chaplain to the galleys (of which Philip de Gondi was general), and in 1622 gave a mission for the convicts in them at Bordeaux.

Mme de Gondi now offered him an endowment to found a perpetual mission among the common people in the place and manner he should think fit, but nothing at first came of it, for Vincent was too humble to regard himself as fit to undertake the work. She induced her husband to concur with her in establishing a company of missionaries to assist their tenants, and the people of the countryside in general. This project they proposed to their brother, who was archbishop of Paris, and he gave the Collège des Bons Enfants for the reception of the new community. Its members were to renounce ecclesiastical preferment, to devote themselves to the smaller towns and villages, and to live from a common fund. St Vincent took possession of this house in April 1625.

Vincent attended the countess till her death, which happened only two months later; he then joined his new congregation. In 1633 the priory of the canons regular of St Victor gave to this institute the prior of Saint-Lazare, which was made the chief house of the congregation, and from it the Fathers of the Mission are often called Lazarists, but sometimes Vincentians, after their founder. They are a congregation of secular priests, who make four simple vows of poverty, chastity, obedience and stability. They are employed in missions, especially among country people, and undertake the direction of diocesan and other seminaries; they now have colleges and missions in all parts of the world. St Vincent lived to see twenty-five houses founded in France, Piedmont, Poland and other places, including Madagascar. For this purpose he also established confraternities of charity (the first had been at Châtillon) to attend poor sick persons in each parish, and from them, with the help of St Louise de Marillac, sprang the institute of Sisters of Charity. He invoked the assistance of the wealthy women of Paris and banded them together as the Ladies of Charity to collect funds for and assist in his good works. He procured and directed the foundation of several hospitals for the sick, foundlings, and the aged, and at Marseilles the hospital for the galley-slaves, which, however, was never finished. All these establishments he settled under excellent regulations, and found for them large sums of money.

During the wars in Lorraine, being informed of the miseries to which those provinces were reduced, St Vincent collected alms in Paris, which were sent there to the amount of thousands of pounds. He sent his missionaries to the poor and suffering in Poland, Ireland, Scotland, the Hebrides, and during his own life over 1200 Christian slaves were ransomed in North Africa, and many others succoured. He was sent for by King Louis XIII as he lay dying, and was in high favour with the queen regent, Anne of Austria, who consulted him in ecclesiastical affairs and in the collation of benefices; during the affair of the Fronde he in vain tried to persuade her to give up her minister Mazarin in the interests of her people. It was largely due to Monsieur Vincent that English Benedictine nuns from Ghent were allowed to open a house at Boulogne in 1652.

Towards the end of his life he suffered much from serious ill-health. In the autumn of 1660 he died calmly in his chair, on 27 September being fourscore years old. Monsieur Vincent, the peasant priest, was canonized by Pope Clement XII, in 1737.

VINCENT OF SARAGOSSA, MARTYR (A.D. 304)

PATRON SAINT OF WINE-GROWERS; AND VINEGAR-MAKERS

22 JANUARY

No clear reason associates Vincent with wine-growers (or vinegar-makers, of which group he is also patron). It has been suggested that the similarity of the name Vincent with the French word for wine is the basis for this patronage!

The glorious martyr St Vincent was instructed in the sacred sciences and Christian piety by St Valerius, Bishop of Saragossa, who ordained him his deacon, and appointed him, though very young, to preach and instruct the people. Dacian, a cruel persecutor, was then governor of Spain. The Emperors Diocletian and Maximian published their second and third edicts against the Christian clergy in the year 303, which in the following year were put in force against the laity. It seems to have been before these last that Dacian put to death eighteen martyrs at Saragossa, who are mentioned by Prudentius and in the Roman Martyrology for 16 January, and that he apprehended Valerius and Vincent. They were soon after transferred to Valencia, where the governor let them lie long in prison, suffering extreme famine and other miseries. The proconsul hoped that this lingering torture would shake their constancy, but when they were at last brought before him he was surprised

to see them still intrepid in mind and vigorous in body, so that he reprimanded his officers for not having treated the prisoners according to his
orders. Then he employed alternately threats and promises to induce the
prisoners to sacrifice. Valerius, who had an impediment in his speech,
making no answer, Vincent said to him, 'Father, if you order me, I will
speak'. 'Son,' said Valerius, 'as I committed to you and the dispensation of
the word of God, so I now charge you to answer in vindication of the faith
which we defend.' The deacon then informed the judge that they were
ready to suffer everything for the true God, and that in such a cause they
could pay no need either to threats or promises. Dacian contented himself
with banishing Valerius. As for St Vincent, he was determined to assail his
resolution by every torture which his cruel temper could suggest. St
Augustine assures us that he suffered torments beyond what any man could
have endured unless supported by a supernatural strength; and that in the
midst of them he preserved such peace and tranquillity as astonished his
very persecutors. The rage and chagrin felt by the proconsul were manifest
in the twitching of his limbs, the angry glint in his eyes and the unsteadiness
of his voice.

The martyr was first stretched on the rack by his hands and feet, whilst he
hung his flesh was torn with iron hooks. Vincent, smiling, called the executioners weak and faint-hearted. Dacian thought they spared him, and
caused them to be beaten, which afforded Vincent an interval of rest; but
they soon returned to him, resolved fully to satisfy the cruelty of their
master. But the more his body was mangled the more did the divine
presence cherish and comfort his soul; and the judge seeing the blood which
flowed from his body and the frightful condition to which it was reduced,
was obliged to confess that the courage of this young cleric had vanquished
him. He ordered a cessation of the torments, telling Vincent that if he could
not be prevailed upon to offer sacrifice to the gods, he could at least give up
the sacred books to be burnt, according to the edicts. The martyr answered
that he feared torments less than false compassion. Dacian, more incensed
than ever, condemned him to the most cruel of tortures – that of fire upon a
kind of gridiron, called by the acts *quaestio legitima*, 'the legal torture'.
Vincent mounted cheerfully the iron bed, in which the bars were full of
spokes made red-hot by the fire underneath. On this dreadful gridiron the
martyr was stretched at full length, and his wounds were rubbed with salt,
which the activity of the fire forced the deeper into his flesh. The flames,
instead of tormenting, seemed, as St Augustine says, to give the martyr new
vigour and courage, for the more he suffered, the greater seemed to be the
inward joy and consolation of his soul. The rage and confusion of the tyrant
exceeded all bounds: he completely lost his self-command, and was continually inquiring what Vincent did and said, but was always answered that
he seemed every moment to acquire new strength and resolution.

At last he was thrown into a dungeon, and his wounded body laid on the floor strewed with potsherds, which opened afresh his ghastly wounds. His legs were set in wooden stocks, stretched very wide, and orders were given that he should be left without food and that no one should be admitted to see him. But God sent His angels to comfort him. The gaoler, observing through the chinks the prison filled with light, and Vincent walking and praising god, was converted upon the spot to the Christian faith. At this news Dacian even wept with rage, but he ordered that the prisoner should be allowed some repose. The faithful were then permitted to see him, and coming they dressed his wounds, and dipped cloths in his blood, which they kept for themselves and their posterity. A bed was prepared for him, on which he was no sooner laid than his soul was taken to God. Dacian commanded his body to be thrown out upon a marshy field, but a raven defended it from beasts and birds of prey. The 'acts' and a sermon attributed to St Leo add that it was then cast into the sea in a sack, but was carried to the shore and revealed to two Christians.

VITUS (A.D. 300?)

PATRON SAINT OF EPILEPSY AND NERVOUS DISEASES; OF DANCERS, ACTORS AND COMEDIANS; OF SICILY; OF PROTECTION AGAINST LIGHTNING AND STORMS; AND AGAINST DANGER FROM ANIMALS, INCLUDING SNAKE-BITE

15 JUNE

Little or, more probably, nothing is known of Vitus and his companions, but this did not prevent a considerable cult building up in the Middle Ages. Likewise it is not clear why the saint's name should have become associated with Sydenham's Chorea (St Vitus' Dance); but from his patronage of that complaint a number of others, including nervous diseases in general and epilepsy, even rabies, appear to stem. From the name 'St Vitus' Dance' there has also developed his patronage of dancers in general, actors, and comedians.

Vitus and his mythical companions are said to have come from Sicily, and in that island they have been regarded as patrons. According to legend, they were unharmed when a great storm destroyed many pagans. For that reason Vitus has been taken, together with Modestus and Crescentia, as a patron against storms.

Because the legends recount that Vitus was untouched by a lion which had been set upon him, his name came to be invoked by those in danger from animals, and also by victims of snake-bite.

The story told in the popular legend may be summarized as follows: Vitus was the only son of a senator of Sicily named Hylas. The boy was converted to Christianity at the age of seven or twelve, and was baptized without the knowledge of his parents. The numerous miracles and conversions he effected, however, attracted the notice of Valerian, the administrator of

Sicily, who joined with Hylas in trying to detach him from the faith. But neither promises nor threats nor even torture could shake the boy's constancy. Moved by divine inspiration, Vitus escaped from Sicily with his tutor Modestus, and his attendant, Crescentia. An angel guided their boat safely to Lucania, where they remained for a time preaching the gospel to the people and sustained by food brought them by an eagle. They then went to Rome, and St Vitus cured the son of the Emperor Diocletian by expelling the evil spirit which possessed him; but because he would not sacrifice to the gods his powers were attributed to sorcery. He was cast into a cauldron filled with molten lead, pitch and resin, from which he emerged as from a refreshing bath; a lion to which he was exposed crouched before him and licked his feet. Then Modestus, Crescentia and he were racked on the iron horse until their limbs were dislocated. At this juncture a great storm arose which destroyed many temples, killing a multitude of pagans. An angel now descended from Heaven, set the martyrs free, and led them back to Lucania, where they peacefully expired, worn out by their sufferings.

WENCESLAUS OF BOHEMIA, MARTYR (A.D. 929)

PATRON SAINT OF CZECHOSLOVAKIA; BOHEMIA AND MORAVIA;
AND OF BREWERS

28 SEPTEMBER

Wenceslaus is patron of Bohemia (and of Moravia) for reasons clear enough from the story of his life. This patronage was confirmed by the Sacred Congregation of Rites in decrees dated 5 May 1914, 11 December 1935 and 25 March 1936.

Czechoslovakia is famous for its beer, and it was natural that the country's most famous saint should become associated with brewing. Wenceslaus's own interests, however, were more with wine, which he produced from his own vineyards for use at Mass. According to the story of his life, he had an intuition that he was to be murdered and on the eve of the assassination he toasted, in wine, St Michael the Archangel, the guide of souls after death.

The baptism of the ruler of Bohemia, Borivoy, and his wife St Ludmila was not followed by the conversion of all their subjects, and many of the powerful Czech families were strongly opposed to the new religion. From the year 915 Duke Borivoy's son Ratislav governed the whole country. He married a nominally Christian woman, Drahomira, daughter of the chief of the Veletians, a Slav tribe from the north, and they had two sons, Wenceslaus (Vaclav), born in 907 near Prague, and Boleslaus. St Ludmila, who was still living, arranged that the upbringing of the elder might be entrusted to her, and she undertook with the utmost care to form his heart to the love of God. Ludmila joined with herself in this task a priest, her chaplain Paul, who had been a personal disciple of St Methodius and had baptized Wenceslaus. He was still young when his father was killed fighting against the Magyars, and his mother Drahomira assumed the government, pursuing an anti-Christian or 'secularist' policy.

St Ludmila, afflicted at the public disorders and full of concern for the interest of religion, which she and her consort had established with so much difficulty, showed Wenceslaus the necessity of taking the reins of government into his own hands. Fearing what might happen, two nobles went to Ludmila's castle at Tetin and there strangled her, so that, deprived of her support, Wenceslaus should not undertake the government of his people. But it turned out otherwise: other interests drove Drahomira out, and proclaimed Wenceslaus. He straightway announced that he would support God's law and His Church, punish murder severely, and endeavour to rule with justice and mercy. His mother had been banished to Budech, so he recalled her to the court, and there is no evidence that for the future she ever opposed Wenceslaus.

The political policy of St Wenceslaus was to cultivate friendly relations with Germany, and he preserved the unity of his country by acknowledging

King Henry I as his over-lord, about the year 926, seeing in him the legitimate successor of Charlemagne. This policy, and the severity with which he checked oppression and other disorders in the nobility, raised a party against him, especially among those who resented the influence of the clergy in the counsels of Wenceslaus. Then, when the young duke married and had a son, his jealous brother Boleslaus lost his chance of the succession, and he threw in his lot with the malcontents.

In September 929 Wenceslaus was invited by Boleslaus to go to Stara Boleslav to celebrate the feast of its patron saints Cosmas and Damian. On the evening of the festival Wenceslaus proposed a toast, said his prayers, and went to bed. Early the next morning, as Wenceslaus made his way to Mass, he met Boleslaus and stopped to thank him for his hospitality. 'Yesterday', was the reply, 'I did my best to serve you fittingly, but this must be my service to-day', and he struck him. The brothers closed and struggled; whereupon friends of Boleslaus ran up and killed Wenceslaus, who murmured as he fell at the chapel door, 'Brother, may God forgive you'.

At once the young prince was acclaimed by the people as a martyr.

WILLIBRORD, BISHOP OF UTRECHT (A.D. 739)

PATRON SAINT OF HOLLAND, THE NETHERLANDS; AND OF LUXEMBOURG

7 NOVEMBER

As his life makes clear, and as Pius XII's Apostolic Letter of 11 January 1940 recapitulates, Willibrord was the apostle of the area now known as Holland, as well as further afield, and therefore he makes a most suitable patron for that country. His links with Luxembourg were also strong. He was recognized as one of its patrons by a decree of the Sacred Congregtion of Rites dated 19 May 1914.

St Willibrord was born in Northumbria in the year 658, and placed before he was seven years old in the monastery of Ripon, which was at the time governed by St Wilfrid. In his twentieth year he went over to Ireland, where he joined St Egbert and St Wigbert who had gone thither to study in the monastic schools and lead a more perfect life among their monks. In their company he spent twelve years in the study of the sacred sciences. St Egbert was anxious to preach the gospel in northern Germany but was prevented, and his companion Wigbert came back to Ireland after spending two fruitless years on this mission. Thereupon Willibrord, who was then thirty-one, and had been ordained priest a year before, expressed a desire to be allowed to undertake this laborious and dangerous task, and was accordingly sent out with eleven other monks, Englishmen, among whom was St Swithbert.

They landed in 690 at the mouth of the Rhine, made their way to Utrecht, and then to the court of Pepin of Herstal, who encouraged them to preach in

Lower Friesland, between the Meuse and the sea, which he had conquered from the heathen Radbod. Willibrord set out for Rome and cast himself at the feet of Pope St Sergius I, begging his authority to preach the gospel to idolatrous nations. The pope granted him ample jurisdiction and gave him relics for the consecration of churches. He then returned and with his companions preached the gospel with success in that part of Friesland that had been conquered by the Franks. St Swithbert was consecrated as bishop by St Wilfrid in England, but perhaps Pepin did not approve of this, for Swithbert soon went off up the Rhine to preach to the Boructvari; and Pepin soon sent St Willibrord to Rome, with letters of recommendation that he might be ordained bishop. Pope Sergius received him with honour, changed his name to Clement and ordained him bishop of the Frisians in St Cecilia's basilica on her feast-day in the year 695. St Willibrord stayed only fourteen days in Rome and, coming back to Utrecht, built there the church of our Saviour, in which he fixed his see. Some years after his consecration, assisted by the liberality of Pepin and the abbess St Irmina, he founded the abbey of Echternach in Luxembourg, which soon became an important centre of his influence.

Willibrord extended his labours into Upper Friesland, which still obeyed Radbod, and penetrated into Denmark, but with no more success than to purchase thirty young Danish boys, whom he instructed, baptized and brought back with him. In his return, according to Alcuin, he was driven by stress of weather upon the island of Heligoland, revered as a holy place by the Danes and Frisians, where one of Willibrord's company was sacrificed to the superstition of the people and died a martyr for Jesus Christ. The saint, upon leaving Heligoland, went ashore on Walcheren and his charity and patience made considerable conquests to the Christian religion there. He overthrew and destroyed an idol, whereupon he was attacked by its out-raged priest who tried to kill the missionary, but he escaped and returned in safety to Utrecht. In 714 Charles Martel's son Pepin the Short, afterwards king of the Franks, was born, and baptized by St Willibrord.

In 715 Radbod regained the parts of Frisia he had lost, and undid much of Willibrord's work, destroying the churches, killing missionaries and induc-ing many apostasies. For a time Willibrord retired, but after the death of Radbod in 719 he was at full liberty to preach in every part of the country. He was joined in his apostolical labours by St Boniface who spent three years in Friesland before he went into Germany. By the prayers and labours of this apostle and his colleagues the faith was planted in many parts of Holland, Zeeland, and the Netherlands, whither St Amand and St Lebuin had never penetrated; and the Frisians, till then a rough and barbarous people, became more civilized and virtuous. He is commonly called the Apostle of the Frisians, a title to which he has every claim.

It had always been St Willibrord's habit to go from time to time to his monastery at Echternach for periods of retreat, and in his old age he made it his place of permanent retirement. There he died at the age of eighty-one on 7 November 739, and was buried in the abbey church, which has ever since been a place of pilgrimage.

ZITA, VIRGIN (A.D. 1278)

PATRON SAINT OF (WOMEN) SERVANTS

27 APRIL

Pope Pius XII declared St Zita to be heavenly protector of servants on 11 March 1955 acting, he said, at the request of the Archbishop and clergy and faithful of Lucca, of many cardinals, archbishops and bishops throughout the world, the heads of some women's religious congregations and a good many women who were employed as servants. The reasons why she was chosen are clear enough from St Zita's life: the Pope said he was appointing a patron for servants because of the extreme difficulty of the life they led. It should be noted that she is patron only of women servants.

Her parents were devout Christians, her elder sister afterwards became a Cistercian nun, and her uncle Graziano was a hermit who was locally regarded as a saint. As for Zita herself, it was enough for her mother to say 'This is pleasing to God' or 'That would displease God', to ensure her immediate obedience. At the age of twelve, she went to be a servant at Lucca, eight miles from her native village of Monte Sagrati, in the house of Pagano di Fatinelli, who carried on a wool and silk-weaving business. From the outset she formed the habit of rising during the night for prayer and of attending daily the first Mass at the church of San Frediano. The good food with which she was provided she would distribute to the poor, and more often than not she slept on the bare ground, her bed having been given up to a beggar. For some years she had much to bear from her fellow servants, who despised her way of living, regarded her industry as a silent reproach to themselves, and resented her open abhorrence of evil suggestions and foul language. They even succeeded for a time in prejudicing her employers against her. But she bore all her trials uncomplainingly.

Gradually Zita's patience overcame the hostility of the household, and her master and mistress came to realize what a treasure they possessed in her. Her work was part of her religion. The children of the family were committed to her care, and she was made housekeeper. One day the master suddenly expressed his intention of inspecting the stock of beans, for which he thought he could obtain a good sale. Every Christian family in that land and at that period gave food to the hungry, but Zita, as she acknowledged to her mistress had been led by pity to make considerable inroads on the beans, and Pagano had a violent temper. She could but tremble in her shoes and sent up an earnest prayer to Heaven. But no diminution could be detected in the store: that it had been miraculously replenished seemed the only possible explanation. On another occasion when she had unduly protracted her devotions, forgetting that it was baking day, she hurried home to find that she had been forestalled: a row of loaves had been prepared and lay ready to be placed in the oven.

In time Zita became the friend and adviser of the whole house, and the only person who could cope with the master in his rages; but the general veneration with which she was regarded embarrassed her far more than the slights she had had to bear in her earlier years. On the other hand, she found herself relieved of much of her domestic work and free to visit to her heart's content the sick, the poor and the prisoners. She had a special devotion to criminals under sentence of death, on whose behalf she would spend hours of prayer. In such works of mercy and in divine contemplation she spent the evening of her life. She died very peacefully, on 27 April 1278. She was sixty years of age and had served the same family for forty-eight years. The body of St Zita lies in the church of San Frediano at Lucca, which she had attended so regularly for the greater part of her life.

Index of Saints

Index of Saints

The index which follows is based upon that in the last complete edition of Butler's *Lives of the Saints*. The names of *beati*, other than the few who are regarded as patron saints, have been omitted; the other entries have been up-dated to take account both of recent canonizations and also of changes in the Roman calendar (see Editor's Introduction, p. ix).

Only those saints whose names are listed in bold type are described in the body of this book. (c) = date no longer in the Roman Calendar.

Aaron (with Julius)	3 *July*	Adelaide (empress)	16 *December*
Abachum	19 *January*	Adelaide of Bellich	5 *February*
Abbo. *See* Goericus		Adelard. *See* Adalhard	
Abbo of Fleury	13 *November*	Adelelmus (or Aleaume)	30 *January*
Abdon (and Sennen)	**30 *July***	Adeotus Aribert	14 *November*
Abercius	22 *October*	**Adjutor (or Ayoutre)**	**30 *April***
Abibus (with Gurias)	15 *November*	Adolf of Osnabrück	14 *February*
Abraham Kidunaia	16 *March*	**Adrian of Nicomedia**	**4 *March***
Abraham of Carrhae	14 *February*	Adrian (with Eubulus)	5 *March*
Abraham of Kratia	6 *December*	Adrian (with Natalia)	8 *September*
Abraham of Rostov	29 *October*	Adrian III	8 *July*
Abraham of Smolensk	21 *August*	Adrian of Canterbury	9 *January*
Abundius (with Abundantius)	16 *September*	Adulf	17 *June*
Acacius (or Achatius)	13 *March*	Aedesius. *See* Frumentius	
Acacius (or Agathus)	8 *May*	Aedh Mac Bricc	10 *November*
Acca	20 *October*	**Aegidius.** *See* **Giles**	
Achard. *See* Aichardus		Aelred (or Ailred)	3 *March*
Achatius. *See* Acacius		Aengus. *See* Oengus	
Achilleus (with Felix)	23 *April*	Aengus MacNisse. *See* Macanisius	
Achilleus (with Nereus)	12 *May*	Aemilius (with Castus)	22 *May*
Acisclus	17 *November*	Afan	16 *November*
Adalbald	2 *February*	Afra	5 *August*
Adalbert of Egmond	25 *June*	Agape (with Chionia)	3 *April*
Adalbert of Magdeburg	20 *June*	Agape of Terni	15 *February*
Adalbert of Prague	**23 *April***	Agapitus (martyr)	18 *August*
Adalhard (or Adelard)	2 *January*	Agapitus (with Sixtus)	7 *August*
Adam		Agapitus I	22 *April*
Adamnan of Coldingham	31 *January*	Agapius (with Timothy)	19 *August*
Adamnan (or Eunan) of Iona	23 *September*	**Agatha**	**5 *February***
Adauctus (with Felix)	30 *August*	Agathangelus (martyr)	23 *January*
Adaucus	7 *February*	Agatho (pope)	10 *January*
Addai	5 *August*	Agathonice	13 *April*
Adela	24 *December*	Agathopus	4 *April*

Euplus	12 *August*
Eupraxia. *See* Euphrasia	
Eurosia	25 *June*
Eusebia of Hamage	16 *March*
Eusebius (pope)	17 *August*
Eusebius (with Nestabus)	8 *September*
Eusebius of Cremona	5 *March*
Eusebius of Rome	14 *August*
Eusebius of Saint-Gall	31 *January*
Eusebius of Samosata	21 *June*
Eusebis (of Vercelli)	2 *August*
Eustace	**20 *September* (c)**
Eustace (with John)	14 *April*
Eustace White	10 *December*
Eustathius of Antioch	16 *July*
Eustathius of Carrhae. *See* Euthychius	
Eustochium of Bethlehem	28 *September*
Eustorgius of Milan	6 *June*
Eustratius of Sebastea	13 *December*
Euthymius the Enlightener	13 *May*
Euthymius the Great	20 *January*
Euthymius the Younger	15 *October*
Eutropius (with Tigrius)	12 *January*
Eutropius of Orange	27 *May*
Eutropius of Saintes	30 *April*
Eutychian (pope)	7 *December*
Eutychius (or Eustathius) of Carrhae	14 *March*
Eutychius of Constantinople	6 *April*
Eventius	3 *May*
Evergislus	24 *October*
Everild	9 *July*
Evermod	17 *February*
Evodius of Antioch	6 *May*
Evroult. *See* Ebrulf	
Ewalds, The Two	3 *October*
Expeditus	**19 *April* (c)**
Exsuperantius of Ravenna	30 *May*
Exsuperius (or Hesperus)	2 *May*
Exsuperius of Toulouse	28 *September*
Eystein	26 *January*

F

Fabian (pope)	20 *January*
Fabiola	27 *December*
Fachanan	14 *August*
Faith (with Hope)	1 *August*
Faith of Agen	6 *October*
Fanchea	21 *March*
Fantinus	30 *August*
Fare. *See* Burgundofara	
Faro	28 *October*
Faustinus (with Simplicius)	29 *July*
Faustus of Cordova	13 *October*
Faustus of Riez	28 *September*

Feargal. *See* Virgil of Salzburg	
Febronia	25 *June*
Fechin	20 *January*
Felician (with Primus)	9 *June*
Felician of Foligno	24 *January*
Felicissimus (with Sixtus)	7 *August*
Felicity (with Perpetua)	6 *March*
Felicity (with the Seven Brothers)	10 *July*
Felicula	13 *June*
Felim	9 *August*
Felix (with Achilleus)	23 *April*
Felix (with Adauctus)	30 *August*
Felix (with Cyprian)	12 *October*
Felix (with Fortunatus)	11 *June*
Felix (with Nabor)	12 *July*
Felix II (III)	1 *March*
Felix 'II'	29 *July*
Felix III (IV)	22 *September*
Felix of Bourges	1 *January*
Felix of Cantalice	18 *May*
Felix of Dunwich	8 *March*
Felix of Nantes	7 *July*
Felix of Nola	14 *January*
Felix of Thibiuca	24 *October*
Felix of Trier	26 *March*
Ferdinand III of Castile	**30 *May***
Fergus of Strathern	27 *November*
Ferreolus (with Ferrutio)	16 *June*
Ferreolus of Vienne	18 *September*
Ferrutio	16 *June*
Fiachra. *See* Fiacre	
Fiacre (or Fiachra)	**1 *September***
Fidelis of Como	28 *October*
Fidelis of Sigmaringen	24 *April*
Fillan (or Foelan)	19 *January*
Fina. *See* Seraphina	
Finan of Lindisfarne	17 *February*
Finbar (or Bairre)	25 *September*
Finnian Lobhar	16 *March*
Finnian of Clonard	12 *December*
Finnian of Moville	10 *September*
Fintan of Cloneenagh	17 *February*
Fintan of Rheinau	15 *November*
Fintan (or Munnu]) of Taghmon	21 *October*
Firminus of Amiens	25 *September*
First Martyrs of Church of Rome	30 *June*
Flannan	18 *December*
Flavian of Antioch	20 *July*
Flavian of Constantinople	18 *February*
Flora (with Mary)	24 *November*
Flora of Beaulieu	5 *October*
Florentius of Strasburg	7 *November*
Florian	**4 *May***
Floribert of Liège	27 *April*
Florus (with Laurus)	18 *August*
Foelan. *See* Fillan	
Foillan of Fosses	31 *October*
Forannan	30 *April*

Gleb (or David)	24 *July*	Gwenfrewi. *See* Winifred	
Glyceria of Heraclea	13 *May*	Gwladys	29 *March*
Goar	6 *July*		
Goban	20 *June*		
Godeberta	11 *April*		
Godehard	4 *May*	**H**	
Godeleva	6 *July*		
Godfrey (of Amiens)	8 *November*	Hallvard	15 *May*
Godric	21 *May*	Harvet (or Hervé)	17 *June*
Goericus (or Abbo)	19 *September*	Hedda. *See* Martyrs under the Danes	
Gohard	25 *June*	Hedda of Winchester	7 *July*
Gommaire. *See* Gummarus		Hedwig	16 *October*
Gonsalo Garcia. *See* Martyrs of Japan		Hegesippus	7 *April*
Gontran. *See* Guntramnus		Heimrad	28 *June*
Good Thief, The (Dismas)	**25 *March***	Heldrad	13 *March*
Gorazd. *See* Clement of Okhrida		Helen (empress)	18 *August*
Gordian	10 *May*	Helen of Skövde	31 *July*
Gorgonia	9 *December*	Helier	16 *July*
Gorgonius (martyr)	9 *September*	Heliodorus of Altino	3 *July*
Gorgonius (with Peter)	12 *March*	Helladius of Toledo	18 *February*
Gothard. *See* Godehard		Helpers, The XIV Holy	8 *August*
Gottschalk	7 *June*	Hemma. *See* Emma	
Gregory the Great (pope)	**3 *September***	**Henry the Emperor**	**13 *July***
Gregory II	11 *February*	Henry Morse	1 *February*
Gregory III	10 *December*	Henry Walpole	7 *April*
Gregory VII	25 *May*	Henry of Cocket	16 *January*
Gregory Barbarigo	18 *June*	Henry of Uppsala	19 *January*
Gregory Lopez	20 *July*	Herbert	20 *March*
Gregory Makar	16 *March*	Herculanus of Perugia	7 *November*
Gregory Nazianzen	2 *January*	Heribald	25 *April*
Gregory of Girgenti	23 *November*	Heribert	16 *March*
Gregory of Langres	4 *January*	Herluin	26 *August*
Gregory of Nyssa	9 *March*	Herman Joseph	7 *April*
Gregory of Spoleto	24 *December*	Hermenegild	13 *April*
Gregory of Tours	17 *November*	Hermenland	25 *March*
Gregory of Utrecht	25 *August*	Hermes of Rome	28 *August*
Gregory the Enlightener	30 *September*	Hermogenes (with Mennas)	10 *December*
Gregory the Wonderworker	**17 *November***	Hervé. *See* Harvey	
Grimbald	8 *July*	Hesperus. *See* Exsuperius	
Grimonia	7 *September*	Hesychius (abbot)	3 *October*
Gaulfardus. *See* Wolfhard		Hesychius of Durostorum	15 *June*
Guardian Angels, The	**2 *October***	Hidulf	11 *July*
Guarinus of Palestrina	6 *February*	Hilaria (with Claudius)	3 *December*
Guarinus (or Guérin) of Sion	6 *January*	Hilarion	21 *October*
Gudula	8 *January*	Hilarus	28 *February*
Gudwal (or Gurval)	6 *June*	Hilary of Arles	5 *May*
Guéolé. *See* Winwaloe		Hilary of Galeata	15 *May*
Guérin. *See* Guarinus of Sion		Hilary of Poitiers	13 *January*
Guibert	23 *May*	Hilda	17 *November*
Gummarus (or Gommaire)	11 *October*	Hildegard (abbess)	17 *September*
Gundisalvus. *See* Gonsalo		Hildegund (virgin)	20 *April*
Gundleus (or Woolo)	29 *March*	Hindegund (widow)	6 *February*
Guntramnus (or Gontran)	28 *March*	Hildelitha	3 *September*
Gurias	15 *November*	Himelin	10 *March*
Gurval. *See* Gudwal		**Hippolytus (of Rome)**	**13 *August***
Guthlac	11 *April*	**Holy Innocents, The**	**28 *December***
Guy of Anderlecht	12 *September*	Holy Name of Jesus, The	2 *January*
Guy of Pomposa	31 *March*	**Homobonus**	**13 *November***

John Eudes	19 *August*	**Joseph Calasanctius**	**25 *August***
John Fisher	22 *June*	Joseph Cottolengo	29 *April*
John Francis Regis	**16 *June***	Joseph Mary Tomasi	3 *January*
John Gualbert	**12 *July***	Joseph Mkasa	3 *June*
John Houghton	4 *May*	**Joseph of Arimathea**	**17 *March***
John Jones	12 *July*	**Joseph of Cupertino**	**18 *September***
John Joseph (-of-the-Cross)	5 *March*	**Joseph of Leonessa**	**4 *February***
John Kemble	22 *August*	Joseph of Palestine (*comes*)	22 *July*
John Lalande. *See* **Martyrs of**		Joseph Oriol	23 *March*
North America	**19 *October***	Joseph Pignatelli	28 *November*
John Lloyd	22 *July*	Josepha Rossello	7 *December*
John Massias	18 *September*	Josee. *See* Judoc	
John Nepomucen	**16 *May***	Judas Quiriacus. *See* Cyriacus	
John Nepomucene Neumann	5 *January*	**Jude (or Thaddeus) (apostle)**	**28 *October***
John Ogilvie	10 *March*	Judith	29 *June*
John Payne	2 *April*	Judoc (or Josse)	13 *December*
John Plesington	19 *July*	Julia Billiart	8 *April*
John de Ribera	6 *January*	Julia of Corsica	22 *May*
John Rigby	21 *June*	Julian (with Basilissa)	9 *January*
John Roberts	10 *December*	Julian (with Caesarius)	1 *November*
John Southworth	28 *June*	Julian (with Cronion)	27 *February*
John Stone	12 *May*	Julian (with Theodulus)	17 *February*
John Vianney	**4 *August***	Julian Sabas	17 *January*
John Wall	26 *August*	Julian of Antioch	16 *March*
John Zedazneli	4 *November*	Julian of Brioude	28 *August*
John of Avila, Bd	**10 *May***	Julian of Le Mans	27 *January*
John of Bergamo	11 *July*	Julian of Toledo	8 *March*
John of Beverley	7 *May*	Julian the Hospitaller	12 *February*
John of Bridlington	21 *October*	Juliana Falconieri	19 *June*
John of Capistrano	**23 *October***	Juliana of Cumae	16 *February*
John of Chinon	27 *June*	Julitta (with Cyricus)	16 *June*
John of Constantinople	28 *August*	Julitta of Caesarea	30 *July*
John of Egypt	27 *March*	Julius (with Aaron)	3 *July*
John of God	**8 *March***	Julius I (pope)	12 *April*
John of Gorze	27 *February*	Julius of Durostorum	27 *May*
John of the Goths	26 *June*	Justa (with Rufina)	19 *July*
John of Kanti	23 *December*	**Justin (martyr)**	**1 *June***
John of Matera (or of Pulsano)	20 *June*	Justin de Jacobis	31 *July*
John of Matha	8 *February*	Justina of Padua	7 *October*
John of Meda	26 *September*	Justua (with Pastor)	6 *August*
John of Nicomedia	7 *September*	Justus of Beauvais	18 *October*
John of Panaca	19 *March*	Justus of Canterbury	10 *November*
John of Sahagun	12 *June*	Justus of Lyons	14 *October*
John of the Cross	14 *December*	Justus of Urgel	28 *May*
John of Vilna	14 *June*	Jutta	5 *May*
John of Almsgiver	23 *January*	Juvenal of Narni	3 *May*
John the Dwarf	17 *October*	Juventinus	25 *January*
John the Good	10 *January*		
John 'of the Grating'	1 *February*	**K**	
John the Iberian	12 *July*		
John the Silent	13 *May*	Katherine. *See* Catherine	
Jonas (with Barachisius)	29 *March*	Kenelm	17 *July*
Josaphat (with Barlaam)	27 *November*	Kenneth. *See* Canice	
Josaphat (of Polotsk)	12 *November*	Kennoch. *See* Mochoemoc	
Joseph, Husband of Our Lady	**19 *March***	Kentigern (or Mungo)	14 *January*
the Worker	1 *May*	Kentigerna. *See* Fillan	
Joseph Barsabas	20 *July*	Kessog	10 *March*
Joseph Cafasso	**23 *June***	Kevin (or Coemgen)	3 *June*

Keyne	8 *October*	Lewis. *See* Louis	
Kieran of Clonmacnois	9 *September*	**Liafwine.** *See* **Lebuin**	
Kieran of Saighir (or of Ossory)	5 *March*	Liberata. *See* Wilgefortis	
Kilian (martyr)	8 *July*	Liberatus of Capua	17 *August*
		Libert. *See* Lietbertus	
L		Liborius	23 *July*
		Licinius (or Lésin)	13 *February*
Ladislaus of Hungary	27 *June*	Lietbertus (or Libert)	23 *June*
Laetus (with Donatian)	6 *September*	Lifard. *See* Liphardus	
Laisren. *See* Laserian		Limnaeus	22 *February*
Lambert of Lyons	14 *April*	Lioba	28 *September*
Lambert of Maestricht	17 *September*	Liphard. *See* Liudhard	
Lambert of Venice	26 *May*	Liphardus (or Lifard)	3 *June*
Landelinus (abbot)	15 *June*	Liudhard	7 *May*
Landericus (or Landry) of Paris	10 *June*	Livinus	12 *November*
Landoald	19 *March*	Loman	17 *February*
Landry. *See* Landericus		Longinus	15 *March*
Largus (with Cyriacus)	8 *August*	**Louis of France (Louis IX)**	**25 *August***
Laserian (or Molaisse)	18 *April*	**Louis Bertrand**	**9 *October***
Laurence (martyr)	10 *August*	Louis Grignion of Montfort	28 *April*
Laurence Giustiniani	5 *September*	Louis Versiglia	25 *February*
Laurence O'Toole	14 *November*	Louis of Anjou	19 *August*
Laurence of Brindisi	21 *July*	**Louise de Marillac**	**15 *March***
Laurence of Canterbury	3 *February*	Loup. *See* Lupus of Troyes	
Laurence of Spoleto	3 *February*	Luan. *See* Moloc	
Laurentinus (with Pergentinus)	3 *June*	Lubin. *See* Leobinus	
Laurus	18 *August*	Lucian (with Marcian)	26 *October*
Lazarus	17 *December*	Lucian of Antioch	7 *January*
Lazarus of Milan	11 *February*	Lucian of Beuvais	8 *January*
Leander of Seville	27 *February*	Lucillian	3 *June*
Lebuin (or Liafwine)	**12 *November***	Lucius ('king')	3 *December*
Leger (or Leodegarius)	2 *October*	Lucius (with Montanus)	24 *February*
Lelia	11 *August*	Lucius (with Ptolemaeus)	19 *October*
Leo (with Paragorius)	18 *February*	Lucius of Adrianople	11 *February*
Leo the Great	10 *November*	Lucretia (or Leocritia)	15 *March*
Leo II	3 *July*	**Lucy (martyr)**	**13 *December***
Leo III	12 *June*	Lucy Filippini	25 *March*
Leo IV	17 *July*	Ludan	12 *February*
Leo IX	19 *April*	Ludger	26 *March*
Leo (or Lyé) of Mantenay	25 *May*	**Ludmila**	**16 *September***
Leobinus (or Lubin)	14 *March*	Ludolf	30 *March*
Leocadia	9 *December*	Lufthildis	23 *January*
Leocritia. *See* Lucretia		Lughaidh. *See* Molua	
Leodegarius. *See* Leger		**Luke (evangelist)**	**18 *October***
Leonard Murialdo	30 *March*	Luke Kirby	30 *May*
Leonard of Noblac	**6 *November***	Luke the Younger	7 *February*
Leonard of Port Maurice	**26 *November***	Lull	16 *October*
Leonard of Vandoeuvre	15 *October*	Lupicinus	28 *February*
Leonides of Alexandria	22 *April*	Lupus (or Leu) of Sens	1 *September*
Leontius of Rostov	23 *May*	Lupus (or Loup) of Troyes	29 *July*
Leopold (of Austria)	**15 *November***	Lutgardis	16 *June*
Leopold Mandic	30 *July*	Luxorius	21 *August*
Lésin. *See* Licinius		Lyé. *See* Leo of Mantenay	
Lesmes. *See* Adelelmus			
Leu. *See* Lupus of Sens			
Leufroy. *See* Leutfridus		**M**	
Leutfridus (or Leufroy)	21 *June*		
Lewina	24 *July*	Macanisius	3 *September*

Matthias (apostle)	14 *May*
Matthias Murumba Lwanga.	
See **Charles Lwanga**	
Maturinus (or Mathurin)	1 *November*
Maturus. *See* Pothinus	
Maudez. *See* Mawes	
Maughold (or Maccul)	27 *April*
Maugille. *See* Madelgisilus	
Maura (with Brigid)	13 *July*
Maura (with Timothy)	3 *May*
Maura of Leucadia. *See* Anne (virgin)	
Maura of Troyes	21 *September*
Maurice (of Agaunum)	**22 September**
Maurice of Carnoët	13 *October*
Maurilius of Angers	13 *September*
Mauruntius	5 *May*
Mawes (or Maudez)	18 *November*
Maxellendis	13 *November*
Maxentia of Beauvais	20 *November*
Maxentius (abbot)	26 *June*
Maxima (with Martinian)	16 *October*
Maximian (with Bonosus)	21 *August*
Maximilian (martyr)	12 *March*
Maximilian Kolbe	14 *August*
Maximillian of Lorch	12 *October*
Maximinus (with Juventinus)	25 *January*
Maximinus of Aix	8 *June*
Maximinus of Trier	29 *May*
Maximus (with Tiburtius)	14 *April*
Maximus of Ephesus	30 *April*
Maximus of Riez	**27 November**
Maximus of Turin	25 *June*
Maximus the Confessor	13 *August*
May. *See* Marius	
Mayeul. *See* Majolus	
Mechtildis of Edelstetten	31 *May*
Mechtildis of Helfta	16 *November*
Medard	8 *June*
Medericus (or Merry)	29 *August*
Méen (or Mewan)	21 *June*
Meingold	8 *February*
Meinrad	21 *January*
Meinulf. *See* Magenulf	
Mel	6 *February*
Melaine	6 *November*
Melangel (or Monacella)	27 *May*
Melania the Younger	31 *December*
Melchiades. *See* Miltiades	
Melchu	6 *February*
Meletius	12 *February*
Meleusippus	17 *January*
Meliot	1 *April*
Mellitus of Canterbury	24 *April*
Mellon (or Mallonus)	22 *October*
Melorus. *See* Mylor	
Ménéhould. *See* Manechildis	
Mannas (with Hermogenes)	10 *December*
Mennas of Constantinople	25 *August*
Mannas of Egypt	11 *November*
Menodora	10 *September*
Mercurius of Caesarea	25 *November*
Meriadoc (or Meriasek)	7 *June*
Meriasek. *See* Meriadoc	
Merry. *See* Medericus	
Mesrop	19 *February*
Messalina. *See* Felician of Foligno	
Methodius (with Cyril)	**14 February**
Methodius (or Constantinople)	14 *June*
Methodius of Olympus	18 *September*
Metrodora	10 *September*
Metrophanes	4 *June*
Meuris. *See* Nemesius	
Mewan. *See* Méen	
Michael the Archangel	**29 September**
Michael Garicoïts	14 *May*
Michael de Sanctis	10 *April*
Michael of Chernigov	21 *September*
Milburga	23 *February*
Mildgytha. *See* Milburga	
Mildred	13 *July*
Miltiades (or Melchiades)	10 *December*
Mirin	15 *September*
Mochoemoc	13 *March*
Mochta	19 *August*
Mochuda. *See* Carthage	
Mochumma. *See* Machar	
Mocius. *See* Mucius	
Modan	4 *February*
Modestus. *See* Vitus	
Modoaldus	12 *May*
Modomnoc	13 *February*
Modwenna	6 *July*
Molaise. *See* Laserian	
Moling	17 *June*
Moloc (or Luan)	25 *June*
Molua (or Lughaidh)	4 *August*
Mommolinus	16 *October*
Monacella. *See* Melangell	
Monegundis	2 *July*
Monica	**27 August**
Monnine. *See* Modwenna	
Montanus (with Lucius)	24 *February*
Morand	3 *June*
Moses (bishop)	7 *February*
Moses (martyr)	25 *November*
Moses the Black	28 *August*
Mucius (or Mocius)	13 *May*
Munchin	2 *January*
Mungo. *See* Kentigern	
Munnu. *See* Fintan of Taghmon	
Muredach. *See* Murtagh	
Murtagh (or Muredach)	12 *August*
Mustiola	3 *July*
Mylor (or Melorus)	1 *October*

Index of Dates

Index of Dates

DATE		SAINT	PATRON SAINT OF
January	1	Clarus, Abbot	Short-sightedness
	2	Basil the Great	Russia
	3	Genevieve (Genofeva)	Paris; disasters; drought; rain (excessive); fever; security forces (French)
	7	Raymund of Peñafort	Lawyers, including canon lawyers; schools and faculties of law
	17	Antony the Abbot	Skin diseases; domestic animals; pets; basket makers; St Antony's Fire
	20	Sebastian	Municipal, or local, police; neighbourhood watch; archers; soldiers; contagious diseases; plague; physicians; surgeons
	22	Vincent Pallotti	Missionary priests
	22	Vincent of Saragossa	Wine-growers; vinegar makers
	24	Francis de Sales	Journalists; writers; editors
	28	Thomas Aquinas	Roman Catholic schools; colleges; academies and universities; scholars; students; apologists; philosophers; theologians; booksellers
	31	John Bosco	Editors; apprentices and young people; young people, Mexican
February	1	Brigid (Bride)	Ireland
	3	Anskar	Denmark; Germany; Iceland
	3	Blaise	Throat infections
	3	Mary, B.V., Our Lady of Suyapa	Honduras
	4	John de Britto	Missions, Portuguese
	4	Joseph of Leonessa	Capuchin missions to Turkey
	5	Agatha	Bell founders; volcanic eruptions; fire (danger from)
	6	Amand	Brewers; wine merchants and trade
	7	Apollonia	Dentists; toothache sufferers
	8	Jerome Emiliani	Orphans and abandoned children
	11	Mary, B.V., Immaculate	Philippines; Portugal
	14	Cyril and Methodius	Yugoslavia; Czechoslovakia; Bohemia; Moravia; Europe
	14	Valentine	Lovers
	27	Gabriel Possenti	Students; clergy; young people in Catholic Action in Italy
March	1	David (Dewi), bishop	Wales
	3	Cunegund	Luxembourg; Lithuania
	4	Adrian of Nicomedia	Arms dealers; butchers; prison guards
	4	Casimir of Poland	Lithuania; Russia; young people, Lithuanian

DATE		SAINT	PATRON SAINT OF
March	8	John of God	Hospitals; the sick; nurses; booksellers; bookbinders; book trade
	9	Dominic Savio	Pueri cantores; choirs and choirboys; boys, and juvenile delinquents
	9	Frances of Rome	Widows; motorists
	15	Louise de Marillac	Social workers
	17	Joseph of Arimathea	Gravediggers; coffin-bearers, pallbearers; cemetery keepers and caretakers; tin miners
	17	Patrick	Ireland; Nigeria
	18	(Bd) Fra Angelico	Painters; artists
	18	Venantius	Leaping
	19	Joseph, husband of Our Lady	The universal church; opposition to communism; workers; carpenters; joiners; cabinet makers; doubters; travellers; house hunting; death (happy); the dying; Austria; Belgium; Bohemia; Canada; Mexico; Peru; Russia; Vietnam (south); missions to the Chinese
	22	Nicolas von Flue	Switzerland
	23	Turibius	Bishops of Latin America
	24	Catherine of Sweden	Abortion
	25	Dismas	Theft, thieves; condemned criminals; undertakers
April	2	Francis of Paola	Sailors; naval officers; navigators; pilots, maritime
	7	John Baptist de la Salle	School teachers
	11	Stanislaus	Poland
	16	Magnus of Orkney	Norway
	19	Expeditus	Urgent cases; (against) procrastination
	23	Adalbert	Czechoslovakia (Bohemia); Poland; Prussia
	23	George	England; Order of the Garter; Cavalry, Italian
	26	Mary, B.V., Mother of Good Counsel	Albania
	27	Zita	Servants
	28	Peter Mary Chanel	Oceania
	29	Catherine of Siena	Italy; nurses, Italian
	30	Adjutor (Ayoutre)	Drowning (against death by); swimmers
May	1	Peregrine Laziosi	Cancer sufferers
	3	Mary, B.V., Queen of Poland	Poland
	3	James the Less, Apostle	The dying
	3	Philip and James, apostles	Uruguay
	3	Philip of Zell	Babies; small children
	4	Florian	Water, danger from, and flood; Austria; Poland
	10	(Bd) John of Avila	Clergy, diocesan or secular (Spanish)
	10	Cathal	Hernia sufferers
	11	Gengulf	Marriage (unhappy)
	11	Mary, B.V., Immaculate, 'Aparecida'	Brazil
	15	Dympna	Nervous diseases; mental illness; asylums (for mentally ill); nurses (of mentally ill); epilepsy; possession (by the Devil); sleepwalkers
	15	Isodore the Farmer	Farmers and farm labourers; Madrid
	16	Honoratus	Millers; bakers; cake makers
	16	John Nepomucen	Czechoslovakia; Bohemia; confessors; bridges; slander or detraction (against)

DATE		SAINT	PATRON SAINT OF
May	16	Ubald	Dog bites; rabies; hydrophobia
	17	Paschal Baylon	Shepherds; the eucharist; eucharistic guilds and congresses; Italian women
	18	Venantius	Falling; jumping; leaping
	19	Celestine V (pope)	Bookbinders
	19	Ivo of Kermartin	Lawyers, advocates; canon lawyers; judges and notaries; abandoned children; orphans; Brittany
	19	Pudentiana	Philippines
	20	Bernardino of Siena	Advertisers and advertising; hoarseness
	22	Rita of Cascia	Hopeless (or desperate) cases; parenthood; children, desire for; infertility
	24	Mary B.V., Our Lady Help of Christians	Australia; New Zealand; Chaplains, military, Australian; security forces, Andorran
	25	Mark	Cattle breeders, Spanish; Egypt; Venice; notaries
	28	Bernard of Montjoux	Mountaineers or mountain climbers; alpinists; travellers in, or inhabitants of, the Alps
	29	Bona	Air hostesses, air stewardesses, or flight attendants
	30	Ferdinand III of Castile	Rulers, persons in authority, governers, magistrates; the poor; prisoners; engineers, Spanish military
	30	Joan of Arc	France, and French soldiers
	31	Mary, B.V., Mediatrix of All Graces	Chaplains, military, Belgian
June	1	Justin Martyr	Philosophers and philosophy; apologists
	2	Erasmus (Elmo)	Sailors; stomach pains; abdominal pains; colic; childbirth; women in labour
	3	Charles Lwanga	African Catholic youth action; young people, African
	9	Columba, or Colmcille	Ireland
	9	Mary, B.V., Our Lady of Graces	Skiers
	11	Barnabas, Apostle	Cyprus
	12	Onuphrius	Weavers
	13	Antony of Padua	Lost articles; Portugal; the poor; harvests
	15	Vitus	Epilepsy; nervous diseases; dancers; actors; comedians; Sicily; lightning and storms, protection against; animals, danger from; snakebite
	16	John Francis Regis	Marriage; children, illegitimate or born out of wedlock; social workers
	20	Mary, B.V., Our Lady of Consolation	Pensioners and old people
	21	Aloysius	Young people, Christian; students in Jesuit colleges
	22	Vincent of Saragossa	Winegrowers
	23	Joseph Cafasso	Prisoners (Italian); spiritual directors of clergy
	24	John the Baptist (birthday)	Motorways; spas
	27	Mary, B.V., Our Lady of Perpetual Succour	Haiti
	28	Basilides	Prison officers (Italian)
	29	Paul, Apostle	Action, Catholic; lay apostolate; Cursillo movement; Greece; Malta

DATE		SAINT	PATRON SAINT OF
June	29	Peter, Prince of the Apostles	Fishermen
July	2	Processus and Martinian	Prison officers
	3	Thomas, Apostle	Builders, building craftsmen and construction workers; masons; architects; carpenters; joiners; quantity surveyors; *also* blind people; India and Pakistan
	6	Bd Maria Teresa Ledochowska	Missions, Polish
	6	Maria Goretti	Children of Mary; teenage girls
	9	Mary, B.V., Our Lady of Chevremont	Sportsmen and sportswomen (Belgian)
	9	Mary, B.V., Queen of Peace	Victims of war (civilian)
	11	Benedict, Abbot	Europe; Italian knights of labour; farm workers; Italian farmers; Engineers, Italian; speleologists (potholers or spelunkers); architects, Italian; poison; the dying
	12	John Gualbert	Foresters; park keepers
	13	Henry the Emperor	Finland
	14	Camillus de Lellis	Nurses, and nurses' associations
	16	Mary, B.V., Our Lady of Mount Carmel	Bolivia; Chile; Navy, Spanish
	20	Elijah, prophet	Flying
	20	Margaret (Marina)	Childbirth; pregnant women; death
	23	Bridget (Birgitte)	Sweden
	25	Christopher	Travellers; safe journeys; motorists; pilgrims
	25	James the Greater, Apostle	Spain; Guatemala; Nicaragua
	26	Anne	Miners; childless women
	27	Pantaleon	Doctors or physicians; the medical profession in general
	29	Martha	Housewives; servants; hoteliers (Italian); waiters and waitresses
	29	Olaf	Norway
	30	Abdon and Sennen	Barrel makers, or coopers
	31	Ignatius of Loyola	Retreats; spiritual exercises; scruples
August	1	Alphonsus de' Liguori	Confessors; moral theologians
	2	Mary, B.V., Our Lady of the Angels	Costa Rica
	4	John Vianney	Priests and parochial clergy
	8	Cyriacus	Possession (by the Devil)
	8	Mary, B.V., Great Queen of Hungary	Hungary
	9	Emygdius	Earthquakes
	11	Alexander the Charcoal-burner	Charcoal-burners
	11	Clare	Embroiderers; television
	13	Cassian of Imola	Shorthand writers and stenographers
	13	Hippolytus	Prison officers; horses
	15	Mary, B.V., on the Feast of her Assumption	France; aircrew (French); Paraguay; soldiers (Paraguayan); Southern Africa; New Caledonia; Jamaica
	16	Stephen of Hungary	Hungary

DATE		SAINT	PATRON SAINT OF
August	17	Roch	Contagious diseases; plague; cholera; physicians; surgeons; cattle; prisoners; Istanbul
	20	Bernard of Clairvaux	Gibraltar
	22	Mary, B.V., The Most Pure Heart of Mary	Africa, Central; Angola; Ecuador
	23	Rose of Lima	Peru; Central and South America; Philippines; India; security forces, Peruvian; nurses (Peruvian); florists and gardens
	25	Genesius the Comedian	Actors; theatrical profession
	25	Louis of France	French monarchy; French soldiers; sculptors; stonemasons; marble workers; button makers; Franciscan tertiaries
	26	Teresa of Jesus Jornet e Ibars	Old people, or senior citizens; old age pensioners
	27	Monica	Mothers
	29	John the Baptist ('Beheading')	Jordan
	31	Raymund Nonnatus	Midwives; children; childbirth; pregnant women; innocent people (falsely accused)
September	1	Fiacre	Gardeners; horticulturalists; sufferers from venereal disease; haemorrhoid sufferers; cab or taxi drivers
	1	Giles	Cripples and the lame; beggars; lepers; nursing mothers and breast feeding
	3	Basilissa	Nursing mothers; breast feeding; chilblains
	3	Gregory the Great, pope	Music; plague
	4	Rose of Viterbo	Florists and flower growers
	6	Magnus of Fussen	Protection of crops against vermin; and against hail, storms and lightning
	8	Mary, B.V., The Birthday of the Blessed Virgin of Charity	Cuba
	9	Peter Claver	Missions to the negro slaves; Colombia
	10	Nicholas of Tolentino	The dying; souls in purgatory; fires; sickness in animals; babies; mothers
	11	Mary, B.V., Our Lady of Coromoto	Venezuela
	13	John Chrysostom	Preaching; oratory (sacred); eloquence, (sacred); Constantinople
	13	Venerius	Lighthouse keepers
	15	Catherine of Genoa	Nurses, Italian
	16	Cyprian	Algeria; North Africa
	16	Ludmila	Czechoslovakia
	17	Robert Bellarmine	Catechists and catechumens
	18	Joseph of Cupertino	Students and examinees; flying and aviation; astronauts
	20	Eustace	Huntsmen; difficult or desperate situations
	21	Matthew	Accountants; tax collectors; customs officers; security guards
	22	Maurice	Soldiers; Alpine troops; Austria; Piedmont; Savoy; Sardinia; dyers; weavers
	24	Mary, B.V., Our Lady of Mercy	Dominican Republic; army, Argentinian; army, Ecuadorian
	25	Joseph Calasanctius	Schools, All Christian

DATE		SAINT	PATRON SAINT OF
September	26	Cosmas and Damian	Doctors; physicians; surgeons; pharmacists and chemists; druggists; apothecaries; barbers and hairdressers; blind people
	27	Vincent de Paul	Charities; Madagascar; hospitals; prisons
	28	(Bd) Bernardino of Feltre	Pawnbrokers; bankers
	28	Wenceslaus	Czechoslovakia; Bohemia and Moravia; brewers
	29	Gabriel the Archangel	Telecommunications; television and radio; signallers, military; diplomatic services; ambassadors, Argentina; postal services; stamp collectors and philatelists
	29	Michael the Archangel	Battle; security forces; paratroops; Brussels; banking; radiologists, radiotherapists; death; England; Germany; Gibraltar; Papua New Guinea; Solomon Islands; the sick; possession (by the Devil); Gibraltar
	29	Raphael the Archangel	Travellers and safe journeys; young people (leaving home); diseases of the eye; blind people; pharmacists; health inspectors
	30	Jerome	Scripture scholars and exegetes
October	1	Thérèse of Lisieux	Missions; florists and flower growers; France
	2	The Guardian Angels	Police, Spanish
	4	Francis of Assisi	Italy; merchants, Italian; ecologists and ecology
	7	Mary, B.V., Our Lady of the Rosary 'La Naval'	Navy, Philippine
	9	Andronicus (with Athanasia)	Silversmiths
	9	Denis, bishop of Paris	Paris; France; headaches
	9	Louis Bertrand	Colombia
	10	Francis Borgia	Portugal; earthquakes
	12	Mary, B.V., Our Lady of the Pillar	Police, Spanish
	13	Coloman	Austria
	15	Teresa of Avila	Writers (Spanish Catholic); Commissariat, Spanish military
	16	Gall	Birds
	16	Gerard Majella	Mothers
	18	Luke	The medical profession, doctors and physicians; artists, painters and sculptors; craft workers; lacemakers; notaries; butchers
	19	The martyrs of North America	Canada
	23	John of Capistrano	Chaplains, military, in general
	24	Anthony Claret	Weavers; savings banks
	25	Crispin and Crispinian	Shoemakers; cobblers; leatherworkers
	28	Jude	Hopeless or desperate cases or situations
November	3	Hubert	Hunting and huntsmen; (against) rabies or hydrophobia
	3	Martin de Porres	Social justice; education, public; television (Peru); trade unionists (Spanish); health service (Peru); people of mixed race; hairdressers and barbers (Italian)
	3	Pirminus	Poison; snake-bite

DATE	SAINT	PATRON SAINT OF
November 4	Charles Borromeo	Catechists and catechumens
6	Leonard of Noblac	Childbirth; prisoners; brigands, robbers and thieves (danger from)
7	Willibrord	Holland, or the Netherlands; Luxembourg
8	Four Crowned Martyrs	Stonemasons; sculptors; workers in marble
10	Andrew Avellino	Death, sudden; apoplexy; Naples; Sicily
11	Martin of Tours	Soldiers; infantry; cavalry; horses and horse riders; beggars; geese; winegrowers
12	Lebuin (Liafwine)	Dying
13	Frances Xavier Cabrini	Migrants and emigrants
13	Homobonus	Merchants; business people; tradespeople; tailors; clothworkers; shoemakers
13	Mary, B.V., The Health of the Sick	The sick of Poland
13	Stanislaus Kostka	Young people; Poland
15	Albert the Great	Scientists
15	Leopold	Austria
16	John Francis Regis	Social workers
17	Elizabeth of Hungary	Charities, Catholic
17	Gregory the Wonderworker	Desperate cases or situations; earthquake; flood
18	Mary, B.V., Our Lady of Chiquinquira	Colombia; National Guard, Venezuelan
21	Mary, B.V., Faithful Virgin	Police, Italian
22	Cecilia	Music
25	Catherine of Alexandria	Philosophers and philosophy; Christian apologists; learning; women students and young women; librarians, libraries; wheelwrights
26	John Berchmans	Young people, particularly students; altar servers
26	Leonard of Port Maurice	Missioners in Catholic lands
27	Maximus	Dying
December 1	Eligius (Eloi)	Goldsmiths; silversmiths; metalworkers; jewellers; craftsmen and women; coin and medal collectors; horses; veterinarians; blacksmiths; garage, or gas station, workers
3	Francis Xavier	Missions; India; Pakistan; Outer Mongolia; tourism (Spanish); pelota players of Argentina
3	Oliver Plunket	Urban University, Rome
4	Barbara	Gunners; artillery; marines, military engineers, and firemen (Italian); miners
6	Nicholas of Bari	Children; brides; unmarried women; pawnbrokers; perfumers or perfumiers; Russia; travellers and pilgrims; sailors; pilots, maritime
7	Ambrose	Commissariat, French military
8	Mary, B.V., The Immaculate Conception	Spain; United States of America; soldiers, American Catholic; Equatorial Guinea; Tanzania; Zaire; Inner Mongolia; chaplains, military, Spanish; chaplains, military, Philippine
10	Mary, B.V., Our Lady of Loreto	Aircrew and pilots; aircrew, Spanish; aircrew, Belgian; aviation; fliers; Air Force, Argentinian
11	Damasus	Archaeologists

DATE		SAINT	PATRON SAINT OF
December	11	Gentian	Innkeepers; hoteliers
	12	Mary, B.V., Our Lady of Guadalupe	Central and South America; Mexico; students of Peru
	13	Lucy	Sufferers from eye trouble; glaziers; sufferers from haemorrhage, and from throat infections
	23	Thorlac	Iceland
	26	Stephen	Bricklayers, stonemasons and workers in building trades; deacons
	27	John, Apostle and Evangelist	Poison, protection against; Turkey (Asiatic)
	28	The Holy Innocents	Babies
	30	Andrew, Apostle	Scotland; Russia; fishermen
		Mary, B.V., Our Lady of Lujan	Argentina; chaplains, military, Argentinian